D0315252

Hutchinson
POCKET
Encyclopedia

Hutchinson
London Melbourne Auckland Johannesburg

First published in 1987 by Century Hutchinson Ltd,
Brookmount House, 62-65 Chandos Place, London WC2N 4NW

Century Hutchinson Group (Australia) Pty Ltd
16-22 Church Street
Hawthorn
Melbourne
Victoria 3122

Century Hutchinson Group (NZ) Ltd
32-34 View Road
PO Box 40-086
Glenfield
Auckland 10

Century Hutchinson Group (SA) Pty Ltd
PO Box 337
Bergvlei 2012
South Africa

Set in Times and Univers by Saxon Printing Ltd, Derby

Printed and bound in Great Britain

Second edition 1989

Revised impression 1989
Reprinted 1989

ISBN 0-09-174224-2

How to Use This Book

Because the new Hutchinson Pocket Encyclopedia is so different from ordinary encyclopedias, please take a moment to read this page to be sure that you know how to get the most from this book.

The new Hutchinson Pocket Encyclopedia is more than a handy reference guide to people and places, dates, facts, and figures – it is also a compact, up-to-date, subject-by-subject guide to politics and world affairs, science and technology, art, music, literature, sport, and much more.

The Hutchinson Pocket Encyclopedia is arranged thematically, by subject area, rather than alphabetically. Within each subject area – Society, The Arts, Science and Technology – each individual section, such as Economics, Music, or Computing, is specially designed to provide an overview of a particular topic, prepared by an expert in that field. Each section contains the background to the subject – the important terms, ideas, and concepts, with concise definitions – as well as the essential names, dates, facts and figures. This means that within each section you will be able to see at a glance the context as well as the information. So, for example, all the computing terms and programming languages are grouped together, rather than scattered throughout the alphabet as in an ordinary encyclopedia. The final section is a Gazetteer, with concise information on all the countries of the world.

Because it can be used in two ways – both for an overview of a subject, and for quick reference like an ordinary A–Z encyclopedia – the Hutchinson Pocket Encyclopedia contains both a table of contents, arranged by subject, and an A–Z index listing every main entry.

The TABLE OF CONTENTS, at the beginning of the book, is the subject guide to all the major topics covered in the Pocket Encyclopedia.

The A–Z INDEX, at the end of the book, lists every entry in alphabetical order with the page number on which it appears, for quick reference when you want to look up a specific name or term.

Contents

Society

The study of society and human behaviour has a long history. All the great thinkers, in all the major civilizations, have asked questions about how and why people behave the way they do, as individuals and in groups. Western thought about society has been particularly influenced by the ideas and insights of such great theorists as Plato and Aristotle, Machiavelli, Rousseau, Hobbes, and Locke. The modern study of society, however, can be traced to the great intellectual period of the 18th century called the Enlightenment, and to the industrial and political revolutions of the 18th and 19th centuries, to the moral philosophy and political economy of such key figures as Adam Smith, David Hume, and David Ricardo. With the development of positive philosophy or positivism, the French thinker Auguste Comte (1798—1857), using the term social science, attempted to establish the study of society as a scientific discipline, capable of precision and prediction in the same way as natural science.

The modern academic social sciences are generally listed as sociology, economics, anthropology, political science, and psychology, but their area of study overlaps extensively with such subject areas as history, geography, law, philosophy, and even biology. And although some thinkers – such as Marx – have attempted to synthesise the study of society within one theory, none has yet achieved what Einstein has done for physics or Darwin for biology.

This part of the Pocket Encyclopedia focusses on various aspects of human society and the study of it, providing an overview of selected topics. It contains sections on History, Economics, Education, Language, Philosophy, Politics and Government, Psychology, Religion and Mythology, Resources, Sociology, Sport, and Women in Society.

History

The history of the world encompasses all the people who have ever lived, together with all the things they have ever done. As a result, any survey of world history, even one dealing only with powerful people and major events – monarchs and statesmen, wars and battles – has to be highly selective.

This section aims to provide a concise overview of some of the important people and events in world history by presenting them as a series of topics, from the ancient world to modern times, complemented by biographical entries. tables, and chronologies. It begins with a chronology of *The Ancient World*, followed by biographical notes on *Leaders of the Ancient World*. This is followed by a similar chronology and biographical notes for *The Medieval and Early Modern World*. *Wars and Battles* begins in the ancient world and continues to the present day, outlining the major conflicts, and indicating how they affected the course of world history. Next, *Revolutions* looks at the impact which certain rapid political and economic changes, key people, and institutions have had on the societies in which they occurred, and also on the world at large. Then there are outlines on the *Emergence of the Third World* and the *Search for Peace*, which highlight these two important, long-term processes in contemporary history. Finally, there are tables of rulers, monarchs, and heads of state, and biographical notes on *Leaders of the Modern World*, including leaders and statesmen from the last two centuries who have done most to influence the structure of the world as we know it today. The history of individual countries is covered in the separate Gazetteer section, and information on forms of government, along with a chronology of important political events, appears in the section on Politics and Government.

The Ancient World

14 million BC Africa, which is considered the 'cradle-continent', probably produced the first human-like creatures

3–5 million direct line of descent of modern humans established from E Africa

c. 60000 American Indians entered N America from Asia

15000 agriculture first practised in Egypt

10000–2000 the originally fertile Sahara became a barrier desert between northern and southern Africa

9000 Marmes man in N America, earliest human remains

5450–2500 era of Saharan rock and cave paintings, as in the Tassili

c. 3000 first dynasties of Mesopotamia: King Gilgamesh; Bronze Age civilizations: Minoan, Mycenaean

2800–2205 Sage kings in China, earliest Chinese dynasty; civilization spread to all of China

2500–1500 Indus valley civilization

1950 first Babylonian Empire established

625 birth of Buddha

550 birth of Confucius

246 Shi Huangdi, Emperor of China, succeeded to the throne of Qin. He had reunited the country as an empire by 221, and built the Great Wall of China

Egypt

5000 BC Egyptian culture already well established in the Nile Valley

3200 Menes united Lower Egypt (the Delta) with his own kingdom of Upper Egypt to form the Egyptian state

2800 Imhotep built step pyramid at Sakkara

c. 2600 Old Kingdom reached the height of its power and the kings of the 4th Dynasty built the pyramids at Giza

c. 2200–1800 Middle Kingdom, under which the unity lost towards the end of the Old Kingdom was restored

1730 invading Asiatic Hyksos established their kingdom in the Delta

c. 1580 New Kingdom established by the 18th Dynasty, following the eviction of the Hyksos, with its capital at Thebes; high point of Egyptian civilization

c. 1321 19th Dynasty

1191 Ramses III defeated the Indo-European 'Sea Peoples', but after him there was decline and eventual anarchy

8th–7th centuries brief interlude of rule by kings from Nubia

666 the Assyrians under Ashurbanipal occupied Thebes

525 after a brief resurgence of independence, Egypt became a Persian province following conquest by Cambyses

332 conquest by Alexander; on the division of his empire, Egypt went to Ptolemy, whose descendants ruled until Cleopatra's death in 30 BC

30 conquest by the Roman Emperor Augustus: Egypt a province of the Roman and Byzantine empires

641 AD conquest by the Arabs, so that the Christianity of later Roman rule was replaced by Islam

Greece

c. 1600–1200 BC Mycenean civilization

c. 1180 Siege of Troy

c. 1100 Dorian invasion, and the rise of the Greek city states, of which the greatest were Athens and Sparta

750–550 trading colonies founded round the Mediterranean, Black Sea, and elsewhere

5th century Persian Empire sought to establish its rule over the Greeks

490 Persians defeated at Marathon

480 The Spartans defended Thermopylae to the death against a fresh invasion by Xerxes, but the Persians were defeated at sea (Salamis 480) and on land (Plataea 479)

461–429 Pericles attempted to convert the alliance against the Persians into the basis of a Greek empire

431–404 Peloponnesian War prompted by Sparta's suspicion of Pericles's ambitions, with the resultant destruction of the political power of Athens

378–371 Sparta, successor to Athens in the leadership, overthrown by Thebes

358–336 Philip II of Macedon seized his opportunity to establish supremacy over Greece

334–331 Philip's son Alexander the Great defeated the decadent Persian Empire, and went on to found his own

3rd century Greek cities formed the Achaean and Aetolian Leagues to try and maintain their independence against Macedon, Egypt, and Rome

146 Greece annexed by Rome

330 AD capital of Roman Empire transferred to Constantinople

529 closure of the University of Athens by Justinian ended Greek cultural dominance

Persia

550 BC Cyrus II became king of the Medes and Persians, founding the Persian Empire, which at its height was to include Babylonia, Assyria, Asia Minor, Egypt, Thrace, and Macedonia

521 Darius I became king of Persia

499 revolt of the Ionian Greeks against Persian rule

490 Darius I defeated by the Greeks at Marathon

480 Xerxes I victorious at Thermopylae, which Leonidas, king of Sparta, and 1,000 men defended to the death against the Persians; Athens captured but Greek navy victorious at Salamis

479 Greeks under Spartan general Pausanias victorious at Plataea, driving the Persians from the country

334–326 conquest by Alexander the Great

Rome

753 BC traditional date for the foundation of Rome

510 the Etruscan dynasty of the Tarquins was expelled, and a republic was established, governed by two consuls, elected annually by the popular assembly, and a council of elders or senate. The concentration of power in the hands of the aristocracy aroused the opposition of the plebeian masses

390 Rome sacked by Gauls

367 the plebeians secured the right to elect tribunes, the codification of the laws, and the right to marry patricians; it was enacted that one consul must be a plebeian

338 the cities of Latium formed into a league under Roman control

343–290 the Etruscans to the north were subdued during the 5th and 4th centuries, and the Samnites to the south east

280–272 the Greek cities of the south were conquered

264–241 first Punic War, ending in a Roman victory and the annexation of Sicily

238 Sardinia seized from Carthage and became a Roman province

226–222 Roman conquest of Cisalpine Gaul (Lombardy); conflict with Carthage, which was attempting to conquer Sicily

218 Hannibal invaded Italy and won a brilliant series of victories

202 victory over Hannibal at Zama, followed by surrender of Carthage and relinquishing of its Spanish colonies

148 three wars with Macedon were followed by its conversion into a province

146 after a revolt Greece became in effect a Roman province. In the same year Carthage was annexed. On the death of the king of Pergamum, Rome succeeded to his kingdom in Asia Minor

133 Tiberius Gracchus put forward proposals for agrarian reforms and was murdered by the senatorial party

123 Tiberius's policy was taken up by his brother Gaius Gracchus, who was likewise murdered

109–106 the leadership of the democrats passed to Marius

91–88 Social War: a revolt of the Italian cities compelled Rome to grant citizenship to all Italians

87–84 while Sulla was repelling an invasion of Greece by Mithridates, Marius seized power

82 on his return Sulla established a dictatorship

and ruled by terror

70 Sulla's changes were reversed by Pompey and Crassus

66–62 defeat of Mithridates and annexation of Syria and the rest of Asia Minor

60 Pompey formed an alliance with the democratic leaders Crassus and Julius Caesar

51 Gaul conquered by Caesar as far as the Rhine

49 Caesar's return to Italy (crossing the Rubicon) led to civil war between Caesar and Pompey

48 defeat of Pompey at Pharsalus

44 Caesar's dictatorship ended by his assassination

32 the Empire divided between Caesar's nephew Octavian in the west, and Antony in the east; war between them

31 defeat of Antony at Actium

30 with the deaths of Antony and Cleopatra Egypt was annexed

27 Octavian took the name Augustus; he was by now absolute ruler, although in title only *Princeps* (first citizen)

43 AD Augustus made the Rhine and the Danube the frontiers of the Empire; Claudius added Britain

96–180 under the Flavian emperors Nerva, Trajan, Hadrian, Antoninus Pius, and Marcus Aurelius the Empire enjoyed a golden age

115 Trajan conquered Macedonia; peak of Roman territorial expansion

180 death of Marcus Aurelius. A century of war and disorder followed, during which a succession of generals were placed on the throne by their armies

284–305 Diocletian reorganized the Empire as a centralized autocracy

324–37 Constantine I realized the political value of Christianity and became a convert

330 Constantine removed the capital to Constantinople, and the Empire was divided

410 the Goths overran Greece and Italy, sacked Rome, and finally settled in Spain. The Vandals conquered Italy

451–2 the Huns raided Gaul and Italy

476 the last Western emperor was deposed

Leaders of the Ancient World

Alexander the Great 356–323 BC. King of Macedonia and conqueror of the Persian Empire. Son of Philip II of Macedon, he was tutored by Aristotle, and made his mark as a boy by taming the great horse Bucephalus. In 336 BC he succeeded to the throne on his father's assassination and immediately established his rule in Macedonia and Greece. In 334 BC he crossed the Dardanelles to what is now Asiatic Turkey, and began his assault on the Persian Empire, defeating Darius at Issus in 333 BC, and treating the Persian king's wife, mother, and children humanely. Making a detour to Syria and Egypt, he founded Alexandria, and then resumed his pursuit of Darius. In 331 BC he defeated Darius again at Arbela on the Tigris with 47,000 men against a Persian army of half a million (which included an 'armoured division' of scythed chariots and elephants). He continued his trail of conquest in a great arc into N India as far as the Sutlej, where he was only deterred from going on to the Ganges by the revolt of his weary soldiers. Turning back, he attempted to consolidate his empire by intermarriage between his followers and his new subjects, himself marrying one of Darius's daughters in addition to his wife Roxana (daughter of a chieftain in the Hindu Kush). He died in Babylon, his intended capital. He lives on in modern legend because of his powerful personality, strategic skill, intellectual stature (he always travelled with a copy of the *Iliad*, and sponsored exploration and scientific experiment), and his vision of a humanely civilized empire.

Amenhotep the name of four Egyptian pharaohs, including: *Amenhotep III c.*1400 BC, who built great monuments at Thebes, including the temples at Luxor. Two portrait statues at his tomb were known to the Greeks as the

Colossi of Memnon – one was cracked, and when the temperature changed at dawn gave out a weird sound, then thought supernatural. His son *Amenhotep IV* changed his name to Ikhnaton.

Augustus Gaius Julius Octavianus 63 BC–14 AD. First Roman emperor. He was the adopted son of his great-uncle, Julius Caesar, and, following the latter's murder, formed (with Mark Antony and Lepidus), the triumvirate which divided the Roman world among them, and proceeded to eliminate the opposition. On his return to Rome in 29 BC, he was in sole command (Antony a suicide and Lepidus in retirement); he restored the forms of the republic, but exercised a 'presidential rule' himself, backed by a 'kitchen cabinet' including Agrippa, Maecenas, and his second wife, Livia. Virgil and Horace were the 'poets laureate' and 'public relations' men of the new regime. Empire frontiers were established on defensible lines; a sound administration was created; and a professional army was formed with fixed pay and length of service, as well as a permanent fleet. Rome was given an adequate water supply, a fire brigade, a police force, and fine public buildings. The title Augustus 'venerable', was awarded to him by the populace in 27 BC. Having no male heir, he married his profligate daughter Julia to his unwilling stepson Tiberius, with disastrous results. In 6 BC a serious revolt in Pannonia (modern Yugoslavia) took his stepsons two years to subdue, and brought the threat of invasion to Rome itself. The three finest Roman legions were annihilated by Varus in 9 AD, so that Augustus died a broken man, saying: 'Varus, give me back my legions!'

Caesar Gaius Julius c. 102–44 BC. Roman statesman and general. A patrician, he allied himself with the popular party, and when elected Aedile in 65 BC nearly ruined himself with lavish amusements for the Roman populace. Although a free thinker, he was elected chief pontiff in 63 BC, and in 6l BC was appointed governor of Spain. Returning to Rome in 60 BC, he formed, with Pompey and Crassus, the first triumvirate, but as governor

of Gaul was engaged in its subjugation 58–50 BC, defeating the Germans under Ariovistus, and selling thousands of the Belgic tribes into slavery. In 55 BC he crossed into Britain, with a further campaigning visit in 54 BC. A revolt by the Gauls in 52 BC, under Vercingetorix, was crushed in 51 BC. His own Commentaries on the campaigns have a mastery worthy of fiction, as does his account of the ensuing Civil War. His governorship of Spain was to end in 49 BC, and, Crassus being dead, Pompey was now a rival. Declaring 'the die is cast', Caesar crossed the Rubicon (the small river separating Gaul from Italy) to meet the army raised against him. In the ensuing Civil War, he followed Pompey to Epirus in 48 BC, defeated him at Pharsalus, and chased him to Egypt, where he was murdered. Caesar stayed some months in Egypt, where he had a son (Caesarion) by Cleopatra, then executed a lightning campaign in 47 BC against King Pharnaces in Asia Minor, which he summarized: *Veni vidi vici* ('I came, I saw, I conquered'). By his final victory in Spain at Munda in 45 BC over the sons of Pompey, he established his position, having been awarded a ten-year dictatorship in 46 BC. On 15 Mar 44 BC, however, he was stabbed to death at the foot of Pompey's statue in the senate house. As statesman, general, author, Caesar was unparalleled but fell victim to the weakness of those whom he ruled and for whom he came to have contempt.

Cambyses reigned 529–522 BC. Emperor of Persia. He succeeded his father Cyrus the Great, assassinated his brother Smerdis and conquered Egypt in 525, outraging its religious customs. He died on his homeward journey in Syria, although it is unclear whether this was by suicide or accident.

Claudius 10 BC–54 AD. Nephew of Tiberius, made Roman emperor by his troops in 41, after the murder of Caligula, though more inclined to scholarly pursuits and the writing of histories. In 43 he took part in the invasion of Britain. He was long dominated by his third wife, Messalina, and is thought to have been poisoned by his fourth (Agrippina the Younger).

7

Cleopatra c. 68–30 BC; Queen of Egypt 51–48 BC and 47–30 BC. She succeeded her father jointly with her younger brother Ptolemy XIII, whom she married according to Pharaonic custom. When Julius Caesar arrived in Egypt in 49 BC, he restored her to the throne from which she had been ousted in favour of her brother. She became his mistress, returning with him to Rome until his assassination, and bore him a son, Caesarion. In 41 BC she met Mark Antony who, after returning to Rome in 40 BC to marry Octavia (sister of the future Augustus), settled with Cleopatra in Egypt, where she bore him three sons. In 32 BC open war broke out with Augustus, and after Actium in 31 BC, Antony and Cleopatra were besieged in Alexandria. Cleopatra killed herself with an asp after Antony's suicide. By descent she was Macedonian, not Egyptian. Caesarion was put to death by Augustus.

Constantine the Great c. 274–337 AD. First Christian emperor of Rome, and founder of Constantinople. Son of Emperor Constantius (ruler of the Western Empire 305–6), who died at York in 306, he was acclaimed by the troops there as his successor. He defeated his rival Maxentius in 312, and then, by defeating Licinius in 324, established his rule over the Eastern Empire. In 313 he recognized Christianity as one of the legal religions of the Empire by the Edict of Milan, summoned and presided over the first general council of the church at Nicaea 325, and with the aid of the church established a close-knit network of autocratic authority. He died on an expedition to defend the Euphrates frontier against the Persians.

Crassus Marcus Licinius c. 108–53 BC. Roman general who crushed the Spartacus rising in 71 BC. In 60 BC he joined with Caesar and Pompey in the first triumvirate and in 55 BC obtained command in the East. Invading Mesopotamia, he was defeated by the Parthians, captured, and put to death.

Cyrus the Great died 529 BC. Founder of the Persian Empire. King of Persia, originally as vassal to the Medes, whose empire he overthrew in 550 BC, he captured Croesus in 546 BC, and conquered all Asia Minor, adding Babylonia (including Syria and Palestine) to his empire in 539 BC. The exiled Jews were allowed to return to Jersualem. He died fighting in Afghanistan.

Darius I the Great c. 558–465 BC. King of Persia from 512 BC, he inscribed his conquests on a mountain rock-face at Behistun, but is chiefly remembered for his defeat by the Greeks at Marathon.

Diocletian (Gaius Valerius Diocletianus) 245–313 AD. Roman emperor 284–305, when he abdicated in favour of Galerius. He reorganized and sub-divided the Empire, with two joint and two subordinate emperors, and in 303 initiated severe persecution of the Christians.

Hadrian 76–138 AD. Roman emperor, adopted by his kinsman, the Emperor Trajan, whom he succeeded in 117. He abandoned Trajan's conquests in Mesopotamia, and adopted a defensive policy.

Hamilcar Barca c. 270–228 BC. Carthaginian general, father of Hannibal, who harassed the Romans in Italy 247–241, and died heading a battle expedition to Spain.

Hannibal 247–182 BC. Carthaginian general from 221, son of Hamilcar Barca. His siege of Saguntum (modern Sagunto, near Valencia) precipitated the second Punic War. Following a brilliant campaign in Italy (after crossing the Alps in 218 with 57 elephants), Hannibal was the victor at Trasimene in 217 and Cannae in 216, but failed to take Rome. In 203 he returned to Carthage to meet a Roman invasion, but was defeated at Zama in 202, and was exiled in 196 at Rome's insistence. He fled first to Syria, then to Bythinia (on the Black Sea). The Romans persistently sought his extradition until he took poison to prevent himself falling into their hands.

Hasdrubal died 207 BC. Carthaginian general, brother of Hannibal, who left him in command in Spain in 218, to fight against the Scipios. In 208 he marched to Italy to relieve Hannibal, and was defeated and killed to the north-west of Ancona.

Marcus Aurelius Antoninus 121–180 AD. Stoic philosopher (author of *Meditations*) and

Roman emperor from 161, when he succeeded his uncle Antoninus Pius. He persecuted the Christians (as politically divisive), and spent much of his reign combatting Germanic invasions. He died in Pannonia, where he had gone to fight off the Marcomanni.

Marius Gaius 155–86 BC. Roman general. Consul in 107 BC, he was appointed to defeat Jugurtha (who actually surrendered to Sulla), was again consul 104–100 BC, and defeated the Germanic tribes attacking Gaul and Italy in 102 and 101 BC. Incensed at the appointment of Sulla to the command against Mithridates, he had himself substituted by 'popular demand', until Sulla reversed the situation by marching on Rome. Marius fled, returned in 88 BC, after Sulla had gone east, attained a final consulship, and started a general massacre of his enemies, ended by his death.

Mark Antony (Marcus Antonius) 83–30 BC. Roman soldier-statesman, who served under Julius Caesar in the later campaign in Gaul, fought with him at Pharsalus, and as consul in 44 BC tried to secure for him the title of king. After Caesar's assassination, he formed a triumvirate with Octavius and Lepidus, and in 42 BC helped defeat Brutus and Cassius at Philippi. Touring the eastern provinces in 41 BC, Antony fell in love with Cleopatra, securing Egypt for his share when the triumvirs shared the Empire among them. By 37 BC Antony had left his wife Octavia (sister of Octavius) for Cleopatra, and by 33 BC relations between the two men had altogether broken down. The senate declared war on Cleopatra in 32 BC, and Antony committed suicide after being defeated by Octavius at Actium.

Menes traditionally the first king of the 1st Dynasty of ancient Egypt in c. 3400 BC, alleged founder of Memphis and of organized worship of the gods.

Nerva (Marcus Cocceius Nerva) c. 35–98 AD. Roman emperor. A senator, he was proclaimed emperor on Domitian's death in 96, and introduced state loans for farmers, family allowances, and allotments of land to poor citizens.

Pericles c. 490–429 BC. Athenian states-man, who dominated the city's politics from 461 BC (as leader of the democratic party), and under whom Greek culture reached its climax. He created a confederation of cities under the leadership of Athens, but the disasters of the Peloponnesian War led to his overthrow 430 BC. Although quickly reinstated, he died soon after.

Philip II of Macedon 382–336 BC. King of Macedonia from 359 BC. He seized the throne from his nephew, for whom he was regent, conquered the Greek city states and formed them into a league whose forces could be united against Persia. He was assassinated just as he was planning this expedition, and was succeeded by his son Alexander the Great. His tomb was discovered at Vergina, N Greece, in 1978 and, his skeleton having been identified by traces of an earlier eye injury from an arrow, his one-eyed head was reconstructed at Manchester University for exhibition in the city's museum in 1984.

Pompey the Great (Gnaeus Pompeius Magnus) 106–48 BC. Roman soldier-statesman. Originally a supporter of Sulla and the senatorial party, he joined the democrats when he became consul with Crassus in 70 BC. He defeated Mithridates of Pontus, and annexed Syria and Palestine. In 60 BC he formed the first triumvirate with Caesar (whose daughter Julia he married) and Crassus, and when it broke down after 53 BC he returned to the senatorial party. On the outbreak of civil war in 49 BC he withdrew to Greece, was defeated by Caesar at Pharsalia in 48 BC, and was murdered in Egypt.

Ptolemy name of dynasty of Macedonian kings who ruled Egypt over a period of 300 years; they included *Ptolemy I* (died 283 BC), king of Egypt from 304 BC, who was one of Alexander's generals, and possibly his half-brother. He established the library at Alexandria. *Ptolemy XIII* 63–47 BC was joint ruler of Egypt with his sister-wife Cleopatra; she put him to death.

Ramses name of 11 kings of ancient Egypt including: *Ramses II* reigned c. 1300–1225 BC. The son of Seti I, he campaigned successfully against the Hittites, and built two rock temples

9

at Abu Simbel in Upper Egypt (the larger commemorates himself and the other his wife Nefertari). Threatened with submersion when the Aswan High Dam was built in 1966, the temples were reconstructed above the water line. *Ramses III* reigned c. 1200–1168 BC. He won a naval victory over the Philistines and other barbarian peoples, and asserted his suzerainty over Palestine.

Solon c. 638–558 BC. Athenian statesman. As one of the chief magistrates c. 594 BC he carried out the revision of the constitution which laid the foundations of Athenian democracy.

Sulla Lucius Cornelius 138–78 BC. Roman soldier-statesman, a leader of the senatorial party. Forcibly suppressing the democrats in 88 BC, he departed for a successful campaign against Mithridates of Pontus. The democrats seized power in his absence, but on his return Sulla captured Rome and massacred all opponents. As dictator, his reforms, which strengthened the senate, were backward-looking and shortlived. He retired in 79 BC.

Thuthmose name of four Egyptian kings of the 18th Dynasty: *Thuthmose I* reigned c.1540–1501 BC and founded the Egyptian Empire in Syria. His grandson *Thutmose III* reigned c. 1500–1446 BC and extended the Empire to the Euphrates, and conquered Nubia.

Tiberius Claudius Nero 42 BC–37AD. Roman emperor, adopted son of Augustus and his successor from 14 AD. Under his conscientious rule the Empire prospered.

Trajan (Marcus Ulpius Trajanus) c. 52–117 AD. Roman emperor from 98, adopted heir of Nerva. Born in Seville, he was a just and conscientious ruler, corresponded with Pliny about the Christians, and conquered Dacia (approximately modern Romania) 101–107 and much of Parthia. Trajan's Column, Rome, commemorates his victories.

Tutankhamen king of Egypt of the 18th dynasty c. 1360–1350 BC. A son of Ikhnaton or of Amenhotep III, he was probably about 11 at his accession. In 1922 his tomb was discovered by Lord Carnarvon and Howard Carter in the Valley of the Kings at Luxor, almost

untouched by tomb robbers. The contents included many works of art and his solid gold coffin.

Xerxes c. 519–465 BC. King of Persia from 485 BC, when he succeeded his father Darius, and, after several years' preparation, continued the Persian invasion of Greece. In 480 BC at the head of an army of some 400,000 men, supported by a fleet of 800 ships, he crossed the Hellespont over a bridge of boats. He defeated the Greek fleet at Artemisium and, having stormed the pass of Thermopylae, captured and burnt Athens. But Themistocles annihilated the Persian fleet at Salamis and Xerxes was forced to retreat. He spent his later years on a grandiose extension of the capital Persepolis and was eventually murdered in a court intrigue.

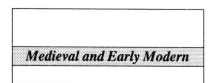

Medieval and Early Modern

300–1500 AD period of the great medieval states in Africa: Ghana, Mali, Songhai, Benin, Ife

320–550 Gupta dynasty in India

4th century Christianity became the established religion of the Roman Empire

4th–6th centuries Western Europe overrun by Anglo-Saxons, Franks, Goths, and Lombards

570 birth of Muhammad

7th–8th centuries Islamic expansion began in N, E, and Central Africa. Christendom threatened by Moorish invasions

800 Charlemagne given title of Emperor by the Pope

c. 1000 Leif Ericsson traditionally reached N America

1073 Gregory VII began 200 years of conflict between the Empire and the Papacy

1096–1291 the Crusades were undertaken to recover the Holy Land from the Muslims

1192 first Muslim kingdom of India established

12th century setting up of German, Flemish,

and Italian city states in Europe, which in the 14th and 15th centuries fostered the Renaissance

12th–14th centuries height of Moundbuilder and Pueblo cultures in N America

12th–15th centuries era of Arab travellers in Africa, such as Ibn Batuta, and of trade (for example Kilwa)

1280 Kublai Khan became emperor of China

1395 Tamerlane defeated the Golden Horde, the invading Mongol-Tartar army which had terrorized Europe from 1237

1398 Tamerlane captured Delhi

1453 Constantinople captured by the Turks

1488 Diaz rounded the Cape of Good Hope

1492, 12 Oct Columbus first sighted land in the Caribbean

16th century arrival of Europeans in S America, with the Spanish (Pizarro) and Portuguese conquest. American Indians were either killed, assimilated, or, where unsuitable as slave labour, replaced by imported slaves from Africa

1526 Babur established the Mogul Empire in India

1565 first Spanish settlements in N America

16th–17th centuries Europe dominated by rivalry of France and the Hapsburgs, the Protestant Reformation, and the Catholic Counter-Reformation

1607 first permanent English settlement in N America at Jamestown, Virginia

17th century beginnings of the British East India Company in India. Era of absolute monarchies in Europe (notably Louis XIV)

18th century War of Austrian Succession and Seven Years' War ended in loss of French colonial empire to Britain and the emergence of Prussia as a leading European power. Height of the Atlantic and Indian Ocean slave trade

1789–95 French Revolution and the overthrow of Louis XVI

Leaders

Babur title, meaning 'tiger', of Zahir ud-din Mohammed, 1483–1530. The first Great Mogul of India, he was a grandson of Tamerlane, and inherited Turkestan from his father when he was 12. By 1526 he had taken Delhi and established a dynasty which nominally lasted until 1858.

Borgia Cesare 1476–1507. Italian soldier, illegitimate son of Pope Alexander VI. Made a cardinal at 17 by his father, he resigned the honour to become captain-general of the papacy, campaigning successfully against the city republics of Italy. Ruthless and treacherous in war, he was an able ruler (the model of Machiavelli's *The Prince*) of conquered territory, but his power crumbled on the death of his father. He was a patron of artists, including Leonardo da Vinci.

Charlemagne or *Charles the Great* 742–814. King of the Franks 768–814 and Holy Roman Emperor 800–814, son of Pepin the Short. He campaigned against the Saxon tribes and the Lombards, and in N Spain, where the great warrior Roland was killed by the Basques at Roncesvalles. As ruler of Western Christendom, he introduced legal reforms; standardized coinage and weights and measures; organized and reformed the church; and initiated the Carolingian Renaissance by attracting the English scholar and poet Alcuin to his court at Aachen in 781. He had himself collected old heroic poetry, and after his death became the hero of a cycle of medieval romances.

Charles V 1500–58. Holy Roman Emperor 1519–56. Son of Philip of Burgundy and Joanna of Castile, he inherited the Netherlands from his father in 1506, then Spain, Naples, Sicily, Sardinia, and the Spanish dominions from his maternal grandfather (Ferdinand V) in 1516, and from his paternal grandfather (Maximilian) the Hapsburg dominions in 1519, when he was elected emperor. Such vast possessions led to rivalry from Francis I, whose alliance with the Turks brought Vienna under siege in 1529 and 1532. From 1517 the Empire was split by the rise of Lutheranism, Charles making unsuccessful attempts to reach a settlement at Augsburg in 1530, and being forced by the Treaty of Passau to give in to most of the Protestant demands. He abdicated in favour of his son, Philip II, in the Netherlands 1555 and Spain 1556, and yielded the imperial crown to his brother Ferdinand.

Columbus Christopher 1451–1506. Italian navigator. Sponsored by Ferdinand and Isabella of Spain to find a new route to the East, he set sail on 3 Aug 1492, and on 12 Oct sighted Watling Island (now San Salvador), later sighting Cuba and Haiti (site of his wrecked flagship, the *Santa Maria*, off Hispaniola, located in 1968). He made a second voyage 1493–96, discovering more West Indian islands, and a third in 1498, in which he discovered S America and the Orinoco. His colonists complained about him, however, and he was sent home in chains. Recovering favour, he made a fourth voyage 1502–4, still trying to find a passage to India. He died in poverty, and is buried in Seville Cathedral. The cost of his initial voyage was queried, until it was pointed out that it cost the same as one banquet for Isabella.

Elizabeth I 1533–1603. Queen of England. Daughter of Henry VIII and Anne Boleyn, she was born at Greenwich. Under Queen Mary her Protestant sympathies required that she live in retirement at Hatfield until she became queen in Nov 1558. Securing her throne by making a broad religious settlement, she refused to endanger her position by marriage or naming a successor, but she had several favourites (Leicester, Raleigh, Essex) and royal suitors. Mary Queen of Scots, who arrived in England in 1568 and whom Elizabeth imprisoned, was a focus of revolt and foreign intrigue, especially by Spain, until her execution in 1587. Open war with Spain and the despatch of the Armada followed, but neither this, nor growing Puritan discontent, nor grow-

ing assertiveness by Parliament, endangered Elizabeth's hold on the country. A rebellion by Essex in 1601 failed hopelessly.

Galileo Galilei 1564–1642. Italian mathematician, astronomer, and physicist, who revolutionized the scientific thinking of his time and ultimately changed the way people looked at their world. His observations and arguments were an unwelcome refutation of the ideas of Aristotle taught at the (church-run) universities, especially because they made plausible for the first time the heliocentric (sun-centred) theory of Copernicus. Galileo's persuasive *Dialogues on the Two Chief Systems of the World* 1632 was banned by the church authorities in Rome, while its author was made to recant by the Inquisition and put under house arrest for his last years.

Genghis Khan 1162–1227. Mongol conqueror (original name Temujin), who established his supremacy over all Mongol tribes by 1206, and assumed the name Genghis ('perfect warrior'). At his death he ruled an empire reaching from the Yellow Sea to the Black Sea.

Gustavus Adolphus 1594–1632. King of Sweden from 1611, he waged successful wars with Denmark, Russia, and Poland, and in the Thirty Years' War championed the Protestant cause. He was mortally wounded in the Battle of Lützen in 1632, when he defeated Wallenstein.

Hapsburg or *Habsburg* former imperial house of Austria-Hungary. The name comes from the family castle in Switzerland. The Hapsburgs held the title Holy Roman Emperor 1273–91, 1298–1308, 1438–1740, and 1745–1806. They ruled Austria from 1278, under the title of Emperor 1806–1918.

Innocent III 1161–1216. Pope from 1198, he asserted papal power over secular princes, especially over the succession of Holy Roman Emperors, and made King John of England his vassal. He promoted the fourth Crusade, and crusades against the pagan Livonians and Letts, and Albigensian heretics.

Kublai Khan 1216–94. Mongol emperor of China from 1259, grandson of Ghengis Khan. In 1281 he attempted to invade Japan, but his

4,400 ships were dispersed in battle.

Louis XIV 1638–1715. King of France (the 'Sun King') from 1643, though until 1661 the country was ruled by Mazarin. The policy of Louis as ruler was summed up in his saying 'L'Etat c'est moi' ('I am the State'). Greatest of his ministers was Colbert, whose work was undone by Louis' military adventures. Louis attempted 1667–8 to annex the Spanish Netherlands, but was frustrated by an alliance of Holland, England, and Sweden. Having detached England from the alliance, he invaded Holland in 1672, but the Dutch stood firm (led by William of Orange) and despite the European alliance formed against France, achieved territorial gains at the Peace of Nijmegen in 1678. When war was renewed 1688–97 between Louis and the Grand Alliance (including England), formed by William of Orange, the French were everywhere victorious on land, but the French fleet was almost destroyed at La Hogue in 1692. The acceptance by Louis of the Spanish throne in 1700 (for his grandson) precipitated the War of the Spanish Succession, however, and the Peace of Utrecht (1713) ended French supremacy in Europe. In 1660 Louis married the Infanta Maria Theresa of Spain, but his mistresses who included Louise de La Vallière, Mme de Montespan, and Mme de Maintenon, were also a significant influence on him.

Machiavelli Niccolò 1469–1527. Florentine politician, who was imprisoned and then exiled in 1513 by the Medici. His influential work *Il Principe/The Prince* 1513, a guide to the ruthless exercise of power for the future prince of a unified Italian state, gave rise to the term 'Machiavellian' (to mean cynical and manipulative), but reflects the actualities of contemporary statecraft.

Magellan Ferdinand c. 1480–1521. Portuguese navigator, sponsored by Spain to sail to the E Indies by the western route. Starting from Seville, he sailed through the Strait of Magellan, crossed the Pacific, which he named, and in 1521 reached the Philippines, where he was killed in battle. Other members of the expedition completed the return voyage under Del Cano, but Magellan and his Malay slave, Enrique de Malacca, were the first circumnavigators of the globe, since they had originally sailed from the Philippines to Europe.

Maria Theresa 1717–80. Austrian empress, daughter of Emperor Charles VI, whom she succeeded as archduchess of Austria and queen of Hungary and Bohemia in 1740. As a woman, her right to the crown was challenged by Charles of Bavaria (emperor from 1742), and Frederick of Prussia occupied Silesia. After the consequent War of the Austrian Succession, she retained most of her inheritance, though not regaining Silesia, and her husband (her cousin Francis of Lorraine, whom she had married in 1736) became emperor (1745–65). Intent on recovering Silesia, she allied with France and Russia against Prussia in the Seven Years' War (1756–63), which exhausted Europe and left the territorial position unchanged. Henceforward she concentrated on internal reforms. Though ruling despotically, she encouraged education, codified the law, and abolished torture. She was assisted by her son Joseph II (emperor from 1765), who succeeded her in the Hapsburg domains.

Mazarin Jules 1602–61. Italian-born French statesman, born at Piscina. He passed from the papal diplomatic service to that of Richelieu in 1639, was created cardinal in 1641, and succeeded Richelieu as chief minister in 1642. His attack on the power of the nobility led to the Fronde, a series of revolts against his administration, and his temporary exile, but his diplomacy achieved a successful conclusion to the Thirty Years' War, and, in alliance with Cromwell, he gained victory over Spain.

Medici family founded in Florence by Giovanni 1360–1429, businessman and banker, politically influential as a supporter of the popular party. His eldest son Cosimo 1389–1464, regarded as the embodiment of Macchiavelli's *Prince*, dominated the government from 1434, and was succeeded by his inept son Piero 1416–69, and grandson Lorenzo the Magnificent 1449–92, who was also a poet and, like his grandfather, a munificent patron of the arts. Lorenzo's son Giovanni 1475–1521, became pope in 1513 as Leo X.

Philip II of Spain 1527–98. Son of Emperor Charles V, on whose abdication (1556) he inherited Spain, the Netherlands (whose people he drove to revolt), and Spanish America; he annexed Portugal in 1580. In 1554 he married Queen Mary of England, and would have wished to marry Elizabeth I, but became involved in war with England instead and also with France from 1589. His reign marked the decline of Spanish power.

Richelieu Armand Jane du Plessis de 1585–1642. French cardinal from 1622 and chief minister (through the influence of Marie de' Medici) from 1624. He made the monarchy absolute by crushing the nobility and destroying Huguenot power (though leaving them religious freedom), and ensured French supremacy in Europe by backing Gustavus Adolphus and the German Protestant princes against Austria, and bringing France into the Thirty Years' War in 1635.

Saladin or *Sala-ud-din* 1138–93. Sultan of Egypt from 1175, in succession to the Atabeg of Mosul on whose behalf he had conquered it 1164–74. A Kurd, he conquered Syria 1174–87, and by his recovery of Jerusalem from the Christians in 1187, precipitated the third Crusade. Saladin, who was renowned for knightly courtesy, made peace with Richard I of England in 1192.

Savonarola Girolamo 1452–98. Italian reformer, a Dominican friar whose eloquent preaching won him popular influence. In 1494 he led a revolt in Florence which expelled the Medicis and established a democratic republic. However, his denunciations of Pope Alexander VI led to his excommunication in 1497, and in 1498 he was burned for heresy.

Tamerlane or *Timur i Leng* 1336–1405. Mongol ruler of Samarkand from 1369, who conquered Persia, Azerbaijan, Armenia, Georgia; defeated the Golden Horde 1395; sacked Delhi 1398; invaded Syria and Asia Minor, and captured the sultan at Ankara 1402. He died while invading China.

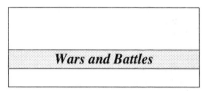

Wars and Battles

In the history of the world there have been many conflicts between peoples and between states. These have led to innumerable wars and battles in all parts of the globe. Represented here, in chronological order, are those conflicts which appear to have done most to shape the world as we know it today.

Peloponnesian War 431–404 BC. War between Athens and Sparta and their allies, originating in suspicions of 'empire-building' ambitions of Pericles. It ended in the destruction of the political power of Athens.

Punic Wars 264–146 BC. Series of wars between Rome and Carthage:

First 264–241 BC resulted in the cession of Sicily to Rome

Second 218–210 BC. Hannibal invaded Italy, defeating the Romans at *Cannae* but finally being defeated himself by Scipio at *Zama*

Third 149–146 BC ended in the destruction of Carthage, and her possessions becoming the Roman province of Africa

Actium Battle of 31 BC. Naval battle in which Octavian defeated the combined fleets of Antony and Cleopatra.

Rome Sack of 410 AD. The invasion and capture of the city of Rome by the Goths. Generally accepted as marking the effective end of the Roman Empire.

Crusades 1096–1291. A series of wars undertaken by various European rulers to recover the Holy Land from the Muslims. Motivated by religious zeal and the desire for more land – together with the trading ambitions of the major Italian cities – the Crusades were very varied in the effect they had and in the degree of success they achieved.

1st Crusade 1095–99 motivated by occupation of Asia Minor and Jerusalem by the Seljuk Turks. Crusade succeeded in recapturing Jerusalem and establishing a series of Latin kingdoms on the Syrian coast

2nd Crusade 1147–49 led by Louis VII of France and Emperor Conrad III – a complete failure

3rd Crusade 1189–92 led by Philip Augustus of France and Richard I of England. Failed to recapture Jerusalem seized by Saladin in 1187

4th Crusade 1202–4 directed against Egypt but diverted by the Venetians to sack and divide Constantinople

5th Crusade 1218–21 captured and then lost Damietta

6th Crusade 1228–29 led by Frederick II – recovered Jerusalem by negotiation with the Sultan of Egypt. City finally lost in 1244

7th and 8th Crusades 1249–54, 1270–72 both led by Louis IX of France. Acre, the last Christian fortress in Syria, was lost in 1291.

Hundred Years' War 1337-1453. The name given to the struggle between England and France that began with the claim of Edward III, through his mother, to the crown of France. At the outset the English were victorious at the naval battle of *Sluys* in 1340 and on land at *Crécy* in 1346 and *Poitiers* in 1356. After 1369 the tide turned in favour of the French, and when Edward III died in 1377 only Calais, Bordeaux, and Bayonne were in English hands. A state of half-war continued for many years until Henry V invaded France in 1415 and won a victory at *Agincourt*. After his death his brother Bedford was generally successful until Joan of Arc raised the siege of *Orléans* in 1429. Even after her capture and death the French continued their successful counter-offensive, and in 1453 only Calais was left in English hands.

Thirty Years' War 1618–48. A major war in central Europe, beginning as a conflict between Protestants and Catholics, it gradually became transformed into a struggle to determine whether the Hapsburgs would gain control of all Germany. After the defeat of a Bohemian revolt against Austrian rule 1618–20, some Protestant princes continued the struggle against Austria, with the aid of Denmark 1625–27. From 1630 Gustavus Adolphus of Sweden intervened on the Protestant side,

overrunning N Germany before his death in 1632. When the Swedes were defeated at *Nordlingen* 1634, Richelieu brought France into the war to inflict several defeats on Austria's Spanish allies. The **Treaty of Westphalia** 1648 gave France S Alsace, and Sweden certain Baltic provinces, the emperor's authority in Germany becoming only nominal. The mercenary armies of Wallenstein, Tilly, and Mansfeld devastated Germany.

Mohács Battle of 1687. An Austro-Hungarian defeat of the Turks which effectively marked the end of Turkish expansion into Europe. Also the site of an earlier Turkish victory in 1526.

Spanish Succession War of 1701–14. A war between Britain, Austria, the Netherlands, Portugal and Denmark (the Allies) and France, Spain, and Bavaria. Caused by Louis XIV's acceptance of the Spanish throne for his grandson, Philip – a violation of the *Partition Treaty* of 1700, by which the crown would have passed to Archduke Charles of Austria. The war produced a series of notable battles:

1704 French marched on Vienna to try and end the war but were defeated by John Churchill of Marlborough and Eugène of Savoy at *Blenheim*

1705 Allies invaded Spain, twice occupying Madrid but failing to hold it

1706 Marlborough victorious over French (under Villeroi) at *Ramillies* 23 May in Brabant, Belgium

1708 Marlborough and Eugène defeated French (under Duke of Burgundy and Vendôme) at *Oudenaarde* (near Ghent, Belgium) 30 Jun–11 Jul

1709 Marlborough and Eugène again defeated French (under Villars) at *Malplaquet* 11 Sept

The Treaties of *Utrecht* 1713 and *Rastatt* 1714 gave Philip recognition as king of Spain but Gibraltar, Minorca and Nova Scotia ceded to Britain, and Belgium, Milan and Naples to Austria.

Seven Years' War 1756–63. The war between Britain and Prussia on the one hand, and France, Austria, and Russia on the other. Its military interest centres on the successful struggle of Frederick II of Prussia against great odds. Britain's part in the war, under the direction of Chatham, was mainly confined to operations at sea, notably the victory of Quiberon Bay 1759, and in the N American and Indian colonies.

American Independence Wars of 1775–83. The revolt of the British N American colonies which resulted in the establishment of the USA. It was caused by colonial resentment at the contemporary attitude that commercial or industrial interests of any colony should be subordinate to those of the mother country, and the unwillingness of the colonists to pay for a standing army. It was preceded by:

1773 a government tax on tea which led citizens disguised as N American Indians to board the ships carrying the tea and throw it into the harbour (the *Boston Tea Party*).

1774–75 the *First Continental Congress* held in Philadelphia to call for civil disobedience in reply to British measures

1775 19 Apr hostilities began at Lexington and Concord, Massachusetts, the first shots being fired when British troops, sent to seize illegal military stores, were attacked by the local militia. The first battle was *Bunker Hill* Massachusetts, 17 Jun 1775, in which the colonists were defeated; George Washington was appointed colonial commander soon afterwards

1775–76 the *Second Continental Congress* on 4 Jul 1776 issued the *Declaration of Independence*

1776 27 Aug at *Long Island* Washington was defeated, forced to evacuate New York and retire to Pennsylvania, but re-crossed the Delaware to win successes at *Trenton* (26 Dec) and *Princeton* (3 Jan 1777)

1777 a British plan, for Sir William Howe (advancing from New York) and General Burgoyne (from Canada) to link up, miscarried. Burgoyne surrendered at *Saratoga* (17 October), but Howe invaded Pennsylvania, defeating Washington at *Brandywine* (11 Sept) and *Germantown* (4 Oct), and occupying Philadelphia; Washington wintered at Valley Forge 1777–78

1778 France and Spain entered the war on the American side

1780 12 May capture of *Charleston*, the most notable of a series of British victories in the American south, but they alienated support by attempting to enforce conscription

1781 19 Oct Cornwallis, besieged in *Yorktown* by Washington and the French fleet, surrendered

1782 peace negotiations opened

1783 3 Sept *Treaty of Paris* American independence recognized.

French Revolutionary Wars 1792-1862. A series of wars between France and the combined armies of England, Austria, Prussia, and others.

1791 Emperor Leopold II and Frederick William II of Prussia issued the *Declaration of Pillnitz* inviting the European powers to restore Louis XVI to power

1792 France declared war on Austria, who formed a coalition with Prussia, Sardinia, and (from 1793), Britain, Spain, and the Netherlands; victories for France at *Valmy* and *Jemappes*

1793 French reverses until the reorganization by Carnot

1795 Prussia, the Netherlands, and Spain made peace

1796 Sardinia forced to make peace by Napoleon's Italian campaign

1797 Austria compelled to peace under the *Treaty of Campo-Formio*

1798 Napoleon's fleet, after its capture of Malta, was defeated by Nelson in Egypt at the *Battle of the Nile* (Aboukir Bay), and he had to return to France without his army; William Pitt organized a new coalition with Russia, Austria, Naples, Portugal, and Turkey

1798–99 Coalition mounted its major campaign in Italy, but dissension led to the withdrawal of Russia

1799 Napoleon, on his return from Egypt, reorganized the French army

1800 14 Jun Austrians defeated by Napoleon at *Marengo* in NW Italy, and again on 3 Dec (by Moreau) at *Hohenlinden* near Munich

1801 Austria made peace under the *Treaty of Lunéville*; Sir Ralph Abercromby defeated the

French by land in Egypt at the **Battle of Alexandria**, but was himself killed

1802 Peace of Amiens truce between France and Britain, followed by the Napoleonic Wars.

Napoleonic Wars 1803–15. A series of wars which followed the Revolutionary Wars.

1803 British renewed the war, following an appeal from the Maltese against Napoleon's seizure of the island

1805 Napoleon's planned invasion of Britain from Boulogne ended by Nelson's victory at *Trafalgar*; coalition formed by Britain, Austria, Russia, Sweden. Austria defeated at *Ulm*; Austria and Russia at *Austerlitz*

1806 Prussia, latest member of the coalition, defeated at *Jena*; Napoleon instituted an attempted blockade, the *Continental System*, to isolate Britain from Europe

1807 Russia defeated at *Eylau* and *Friedland* and on making peace with Napoleon under the *Treaty of Tilsit* changed sides, agreeing to attack Sweden, and was forced to retreat

1808 Napoleon's invasion of Portugal, and habit of installing his relatives as puppet kings, led to his defeat in the Peninsular War

1809 revived Austrian opposition to Napoleon was ended by defeat at *Wagram*

1812 the Continental System finally collapsed on its rejection by Russia, and Napoleon made the fatal decision to invade; he reached Moscow but was defeated by the Russian resistance, and by the bitter winter as he retreated through a countryside laid waste by the retreating Russians (380,000 French soldiers died)

1813 Britain, Prussia, Russia, Austria, and Sweden formed a new coalition, defeated Napoleon at the *Battle of the Nations* and he abdicated and was exiled to Elba

1814 Louis XVIII became king of France, and the *Congress of Vienna* met to conclude peace

1815 Napoleon returned to Paris. 16 Jun Wellington defeated Ney at *Quatre Bras* (in Belgium, SE of Brussels), and after a hundred days Napoleon was finally defeated at *Waterloo* S of Brussels, 18 Jun. Wellington had 68,000 troops (24,000 British, the rest German, Dutch and Belgian) and Napoleon 72,000; in the last stage Wellington was supported by the Prussians under Blücher. The Congress resumed with Napoleon more securely incarcerated at St Helena.

Peninsular War 1808–14. War caused by Napoleon's invasion of Portugal and Spain. Portugal was occupied by the French in 1807, and in 1808 Napoleon placed his brother Joseph on the Spanish throne. Armed revolts followed all over Spain and Portugal. A British force under Sir Arthur Wellesley was sent to Portugal and defeated the French at *Vimeiro*; Wellesley was then superseded, and the French were allowed to withdraw. Sir John Moore took command and advanced into Spain, but was forced to retreat to Corunna, when his army was evacuated. Wellesley took a new army to Portugal in 1809, and advanced on Madrid, but after defeating the French at *Talavera* had to retreat. During 1810–11 Wellesley (now Viscount Wellington) stood on the defensive; in 1812 he won another victory at *Salamanca*, occupied Madrid, and forced the French to evacuate S Spain. The victory at *Vitoria* 1813 drove the French from Spain, and in 1814 Wellington invaded S France. The war was ended by Napoleon's abdication.

Mexican War 1846-48. War between the USA and Mexico, begun when General Zachary Taylor invaded New Mexico. Mexico City was taken in 1847, and under the *Treaty of Guadaloupe-Hidalgo*, Mexico lost Texas, New Mexico, and California (half its territory) to the USA for $15 million compensation.

Crimean War 1854-56. The war arose nominally from a disagreement over the custody of the Holy Places at Jerusalem, actually from British and French mistrust of Russia's ambitions in the Balkans. Hostilities began in 1853 with a Russian invasion of the Balkans (whence they were compelled to withdraw by Austrian intervention) and the sinking of the Turkish fleet at *Sinope*. Britain and France declared war on Russia in 1854, and were joined in 1855 by Sardinia. The main military operations were the invasion of the *Crimea*, the siege of *Sevastopol* (Sept 1854–Sept 1855), and the battles of the *Alma*, *Balaclava* (including the Charge of the Light Brigade), and *Inkerman*, fought in 1854. The French lost 62,500 men, the British 19,600 – 15,700 of them by disease, a scandalous state of affairs that led to the organization of proper military nursing services by Florence Nightingale. Conflict was settled by the *Treaty of Paris*, Feb 1856.

American Civil War 1861–65. War between the Southern or Confederate States (South Carolina, Mississippi, Florida, Alabama, Georgia, Louisiana, and Texas; joined later by Virginia, Arkansas, Tennessee, and North Carolina), and the northern or Federal States. The southerners wished to maintain their 'state rights', in particular the institution of slavery, and claimed the right to secede from the Union; the northerners fought to maintain the Union.

1861 seven southern states set up the Confederate States of America (president Jefferson Davis) on 8 Feb; Fort Sumter, Charleston, captured 12–14 Apr; Lee (Confederate) was victorious at the first *Battle of Bull Run* 21 Jul
1862 Battle of Shiloh 6–7 Apr was indecisive. Grant captured New Orleans in May, but the Confederates were again victorious at the second *Battle of Bull Run* 29–30 Aug. Lee's advance was then checked by McClellan at *Antietam* on 17 Sept
1863 the *Emancipation Proclamation* was issued by Lincoln on 1 Jan, freeing the slaves; *Battle of Gettysburg* (Union victory) on 1–4 Jul marked the turning point of the war; Lincoln delivered the *Gettysburg Address* at the dedication of the national cemetery on 19 Nov; Grant overran the Mississippi states, capturing *Vicksburg* on 4 Jul
1864 Battles of Cold Harbor near Richmond, Virginia; in the first, on 27 Jun 1862, Lee defeated McClellan, and by the second Grant was delayed in his advance on Richmond. Sherman marched through Georgia to the sea, taking *Atlanta* on 1 Sept and *Savannah* on 22 Dec
1865 Lee surrendered to Grant at Appomattox Court House on 9 Apr; Lincoln was assassinated on 14 Apr; last Confederate troops surrendered on 26 May. There were 359,528

Union dead and 258,000 Confederate dead. The war, and in particular its aftermath, when the South was occupied by Northern troops, left behind lasting bitterness. Industry prospered in the North while the economy of the South continued to decline.

Seven Weeks' War 1866. War between Austria and Prussia, engineered by Bismarck over the Schleswig–Holstein question. The *Battle of Sadowa* (Königgrätz) was the culmination of von Moltke's victories. By the *Treaty of Prague*, Prussia took both Holstein, previously seized by Austria, and Schleswig.

Franco-Prussian War 1870–71. War provoked by Franco-Prussian rivalry. Bismarck used the candidature of a German for the Spanish throne to provoke Napoleon III into a declaration of war. After trouncing him at Sedan, the Prussians successfully besieged Paris. The *Treaty of Frankfurt* in May 1871 brought Prussia Alsace and Lorraine, plus a large French indemnity, and established Prussia as Europe's leading power.

Pacific War 1879–83. War between an alliance of Bolivia and Peru against Chile. Chile (by seizing Antofagasta and the rest of the Bolivian Pacific coast) rendered Bolivia completely landlocked, and also annexed the Peruvian coastline (from Arica to the mouth of the Loa). Bolivia has since tried to regain Pacific access, either by a corridor across her former Antofagasta province or by a twin port with Arica at the end of the rail link from La Paz. Brazil supports the Bolivian claims which would facilitate her own transcontinental traffic.

Spanish-American War 1898. War by Cuban revolutionaries (with US backing) against Spanish rule. The *Treaty of Paris* ceded Cuba, the Philippines, Guam and Puerto Rico to the USA.

Russo-Japanese War 1904-5. War brought about by Russian penetration in Manchuria, culminating in the lease of Port Arthur in 1896, and the occupation of the Amur province in 1900. In 1904 diplomatic relations were broken off by the Japanese, who then without warning attacked the Russian fleet at Port Arthur. The outstanding events of the subsequent fighting were the siege and surrender of the Russian garrison in **Port Arthur** (May 1904–Jan 1905) and the destruction of the Russian Baltic fleet in the **Tsushima Straits** (May 1905). Peace was concluded at Portsmouth, USA, in 1905. Russian rights in Port Arthur passed to Japan, together with the Manchurian railway; Korea became a Japanese sphere of influence, and Sakhalin was divided between Russia and Japan.

World War I 1914-18. War between the Central European Powers (Germany, Austria-Hungary and allies), against the Triple Entente (Britain and the British Empire, France, and Russia), together with the USA, and their allies.

outbreak on 28 Jun 1914 the heir to the Austrian throne was assassinated at Sarajevo; on 28 Jul Austria declared war on Serbia; as Russia mobilized, Germany declared war on Russia and France, taking a short-cut in the west by invading Belgium; on 4 Aug Britain declared war on Germany

1914 Western Front the German advance reached within a few miles of Paris, but an Allied counter-attack at **Marne** drove them back to the River Aisne; the opposing lines then settled to trench warfare

Eastern Front Hindenburg halted the Russian advance at the **Battle of Tannenberg**

Africa on 16 Sept all Germany's African colonies were in Allied hands

Middle East on 1 Nov Turkey entered the war

1915 Western Front several offensives on both sides resulted in insignificant gains. Haig became British commander-in-chief

Eastern Front Mackensen and Hindenburg drove back the Russians and took Poland

Middle East British attacks against Turkey in **Mespotamia** (Iraq), the **Dardanelles**, and at **Gallipoli** were all unsuccessful

Italy declared war on Austria; Bulgaria joined the Central Powers

war at sea Germany declared all-out U-boat war, but the sinking of the liner *Lusitania* (with Americans among the 1,198 lost) led to demands in the USA to enter the war

1916 Western Front German attack on the Verdun salient, countered by the Allies on the **Somme** and at **Verdun**

Eastern Front Romania joined the Allies but was soon overrun by Germany

Middle East Kut was taken from the British by the Turks

war at sea the indecisive **Battle of Jutland**

1918 Eastern Front on 3 Mar Russia signed the **Treaty of Brest-Litovsk** with Germany

Western Front Germany began a final offensive. In Apr the Allies appointed Foch supreme commander, but by Jun (when the first US troops went into battle) the Allies had lost all gains since 1915, and the Germans were on the Marne. The battle at Amiens marked the launch of the victorious Allied offensive

Italy at **Vittorio Veneto** the British and Italians finally defeated the Austrians. German capitulation began with naval mutinies at Kiel, followed by uprisings in the major cities. Kaiser Wilhelm II abdicated, and on 11 Nov the armistice was signed

1919 18 Jun, *Peace Treaty of Versailles*.

Spanish Civil War 1936–39. War following attempted military revolt (pronouncement) by Spanish Army officers including Francisco Franco. His insurgents (Nationalists, who were supported by Fascist Italy and Nazi Germany) seized power in the S and NW, but were suppressed in Madrid, Barcelona, etc. by the workers' militia. The loyalists (Republicans) were aided by the USSR and the volunteers of the International Brigade, including George Orwell.

1937 Bilbao and the Basque country were bombed into submission by the Nationalists

1938 Catalonia was cut off from the main Republican territory

1939 Barcelona fell in Jan and Madrid in Apr, and Franco established a dictatorship.

World War II 1939-45. War between Germany, Italy, and Japan (the Axis powers), and Britain, the Commonwealth, France, the USA, USSR, and China.

1939 Sept German invasion of Poland; Britain and France declared war on Germany; USSR invaded Poland from the east; fall of Warsaw

(Poland divided between Germany and USSR) *Nov* USSR invaded Finland. On the Western front, the 'phoney war' with both sides entrenched behind defensive lines lasted until May 1940

1940 Mar Soviet peace treaty with Finland

Apr Germany invaded Denmark, Norway, Netherlands, Belgium, and Luxembourg. In Britain, a coalition government was formed under Churchill

May Germany outflanked the Maginot defensive line

May-Jun British evacuation of Dunkirk

Jun Italy declared war on Britain and France; Germans entered Paris; Petain signed the armistice with Germany

Jul-Oct Battle of Britain between British and German air forces

Sept Japanese invasion of French Indochina

Oct abortive Italian invasion of Greece

1941 Apr Germany overran Greece and Yugoslavia

Jun Germany invaded USSR; Finland declared war on USSR

Jul Germans entered Smolensk

Dec Germans within 40 km/25 mi of Moscow, with Leningrad under siege. First Soviet counter-offensive. Japan attacked Pearl Harbor, and declared war on USA and Britain. Germany and Italy declared war on USA

1942 Jan Japanese conquest of Philippines

Jun naval battle of Midway, the turning point of the Pacific War

Aug German attack on Stalingrad

Oct-Nov Battle of Alamein, first major victory for the Western Allies

Nov Soviet counter-offensive on Stalingrad

1943 Jan Casablanca conference; German surrender at Stalingrad

Mar Soviets drove Germans back to the River Donetz

May end of Axis resistance in N Africa

Aug beginning of campaign against Japanese in Burma

Sept Italy surrendered to Allies; Allied landings at Salerno; Soviets retook Smolensk

Oct Italy declared war on Germany

Nov-Dec Tehran conference

1944 Jan Allied landing at Anzio

Mar end of German U-boat campaign in the Atlantic

May fall of Monte Cassino

Jun D-Day: Allied landings in Normandy

Jul bomb plot against Hitler

Aug Romania joined Allies

Sept battle of Arnhem; Soviet armistice with Finland

Oct Tito and Soviets entered Belgrade

Dec German counter-offensive, Battle of the Bulge

1945 Feb Soviets reached German border; Yalta conference; Allied bombing campaign over Germany: Americans landed on Iwo Jima

Apr Hitler committed suicide

May German surrender to the Allies

Jul Potsdam conference

Aug atom bombs dropped on Hiroshima and Nagasak; Japan surrendered.

An estimated 55 million lives were lost, 20 million of them citizens of the USSR.

Arab-Israeli Wars wars between members of the Arab League and Israel, caused by conflict between Zionist aims in Palestine from 1913, furthered by the Balfour Declaration, and Arab opposition.

From 1920 there were anti-Zionist riots under Britain's League of Nations mandate in Palestine, and in 1936 an Arab revolt led to a British Royal Commission which recommended partition (approved by the United Nations in 1947, but rejected by the Arabs).

First Arab-Israeli War 14 October 1948–13 Jan/24 Mar 1949. This followed the British surrender of the mandate, when the Arabs attacked the new state, and resulted in the enlargement on all fronts of the original Israeli boundaries.

Second Arab-Israeli War 29 Oct–4 Nov 1956. Coincident with the Suez crisis, it resulted in the Israelis capturing Sinai and the Gaza Strip, from which they withdrew after the entry of a United Nations force.

Third Arab-Israeli War 5–10 Jun 1967, the 'Six Day War'. It resulted in the Israeli capture of the Golan Heights from Syria; Old Jerusalem and the West Bank from Jordan; and, in the south, occupation of the Gaza

Strip and Sinai Peninsula as far as the Suez Canal.

Fourth Arab-Israeli War 2–22/24 Oct 1973, the 'Oct War' or 'Yom Kippur War'. So-called because the Israeli forces were taken by surprise on the Day of Atonement. It started with the recrossing of the Suez Canal by Egyptian forces and initial gains, though there was some later loss of ground by the Syrians in the north. The Arab cause was adopted by the USSR and the Israeli by the USA; terrorist outrages by Arab extremist groups and retaliation by Israelis continued. In 1978 the Camp David Agreements brought Egypt–Israeli peace, but this was denounced by other Arab countries. Israel withdrew from Sinai 1979–82, but no final agreement on Jerusalem and the establishment of a Palestinian state on the W Bank was reached.

Fifth Arab-Israeli War from 1978 the presence of Palestinian guerrillas in Lebanon led to alternate Arab raids on Israel and Israeli retaliatory incursions, but on 6 Jun 1982 Israel launched a full-scale invasion. By 14 Jun Beirut was encircled, and PLO and Syrian forces were evacuated (mainly to Syria) 21–31 Aug, but in Feb 1985 there was a unilateral Israeli withdrawal from the country without any gain for losses incurred. This, however, has not prevented Israeli incursions making the withdrawal more nominal than actual.

Korean War 1950–53, between North Korea (supported by China) and South Korea, aided by the United Nations (including the UK, though the troops were mainly US). North Korean forces invaded the South 25 Jun 1950, and the Security Council of the United Nations, owing to a walk-out by the USSR, voted to oppose them. After a 'concertina' campaign up and down the peninsula, which ended in the restoration of the original boundary on the 38th parallel, an armistice was signed with the North, although South Korea did not participate.

Vietnam War 1954–75 between North Vietnam, then backed by China) and South Vietnam (backed by USA). Following the Tonkin Gulf incident, the USA intervened directly in the war, but by 1968 President Johnson offered to negotiate with North Vietnam (via Kissinger), and peace was concluded Jan 1973. The North overran the South Mar 1975, all US aid being withdrawn, and in 1976 Vietnam was reunited by the North. The war was the first military defeat for the USA; 2,500,000 US troops went to Vietnam, 58,000 were killed or reported missing, 200,000 wounded, and 100,000 are alleged to have committed suicide; Vietnamese casualties are unknown.

Afghan War 1979–89 between Soviet forces, Afghan government forces and Islamic fundamentalist guerrillas (mujaheddin) following the Soviet invasion of Afghanistan Dec 1979 to prop up the Afghan government. Soviet forces withdrew Feb 1989, leaving the government in Kabul to fight the guerrillas alone.

Iran-Iraq War or *Gulf War* 1980–88 between Iran and Iraq, claimed by the former to have begun with the Iraq offensive 21 Sept 1980, and by the latter with the Iranian shelling of border posts 4 Sept 1980. Occasioned by dispute over the Shatt al'Arab waterway, it fundamentally arose because of Iran's encouragement of the Shi'ite majority in Iraq to rise against their Sunni government. Among Arab states, Iran was supported by Syria and Libya, the remainder supporting Iraq. By 1985 stalemate had led to a willingness to compromise, notably in Iran's abandonment of a demand for the resignation of President Saddam Hussein of Iraq; but in 1987 fighting continued with Iranian advances into Iraqi territory and Iraqi bombing of Iranian cities. By 1988 the balance had shifted in Iraq's favour and a UN peace initiative was seized on by both sides, resulting in a ceasefire and, eventually, direct talks between the protagonists.

Falklands War 1982 between the UK and Argentina over the sovereignty of the Falkland Islands (Islas Malvinas), following their occupation by Argentina. The recovery of the islands precipitated the downfall of the military regime in Argentina.

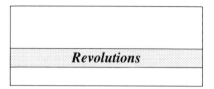

Revolutions

Revolution is a term that can be used to describe any rapid, far-reaching or violent change in the political, social or economic structure of society. It has usually been applied to different forms of political change: the American Revolution (War of Independence), where colonists broke free from their colonial ties and established a sovereign, independent state; the French Revolution, where an absolute monarchy was overthrown by opposition from inside the country and a popular rising; and the Russian Revolution, where a repressive monarchy was overthrown by those seeking to institute widespread social and economic changes in line with a socialist model. While political revolutions are often associated with violence, there are other types of change which often have just as much impact on society. Most notable is the Industrial Revolution, a process which has imposed massive changes on economies and societies since the mid-18th century. In the 1980s, a new 'silicon' revolution can be identified, involving the increasing use of computers to undertake tasks formerly done 'by hand'.

Industrial Revolution the sudden acceleration of technical development which occurred in Europe from the late 18th century, and which transferred the balance of political power from the landowner to the industrial capitalist, and created an organized industrial working class. The great achievement of the first phase (to 1830) was the invention of the steam engine in Britain, originally developed for draining mines, but rapidly put to use in factories and in the railways. In the second phase, from 1830 to the early 20th century, the Industrial Revolution enlarged its scope from Europe to the world, with some initial exploitation of 'colonial' possessions by European powers as a preliminary to their independent development. The internal combustion engine and electricity were developed, and in 1911 Rutherford split the atom at Manchester, opening up the prospect of nuclear power. Electronic devices were developed which made automation possible, with the eventual prospect of even managerial decision-making being in the hands of 'machines'.

French Revolution 1789-99. The forcible abolition of the *Ancien Régime* 'old order of things' (feudalism and absolute monarchy).

1789 5 May the *States General* (an assembly of the three 'estates', nobles, clergy, and commons) met at Versailles, bent on establishing a new constitution; 17 Jun *National Assembly* formed by the *Third Estate* (commons); 14 Jul Bastille was taken by the mob when Louis XVI attempted repressive moves

1791 20 Jun flight of the royal family to Varennes; 14 Sept Louis, brought back as a prisoner, accepted the new constitution

1792 20 Apr war declared on Austria, which threatened to suppress the revolution; 10 Aug royal palace stormed by the French mob; 21 Sept *First Republic* proclaimed

1793 21 Jan Louis XVI executed; 2 Jun overthrow of the moderate Girondists by the Jacobins; rule of the dictatorial *Committee of Public Safety*; 5 Sept the mass executions of the *Reign of Terror* began

1794 27 Jul (9 Thermidor under the Revolutionary calendar) fall of Robespierre and end of the Terror; the *Directory* (a body of five directors) established to hold a middle course between Royalism and Jacobinism. It ruled until Napoleon seized power in 1799.

Bastille a fortress prison in Paris, stormed by the mob at the beginning of the revolution on 14 Jul 1789, when it was found to contain only seven prisoners. The governor and most of the garrison were killed and the building razed.

Commune of Paris 1789–94. First body which took this name. It acted as the municipal government of Paris from the storming of the Bastille to the fall of Robespierre.

Jacobins extremist republican club founded at Versailles in 1789, which later used a former

Jacobin (Dominican) friary as its headquarters in Paris. It was led by Robespierre and closed after his execution in 1794.

Girondins right-wing republicans of the French Revolution whose leaders came from the Gironde departement of France.

Robespierre Maximilien. François Marie Isidere de 1758-94. French politician,'the Sea Green Incorruptible'. As Jacobin leader in the ***National Convention***, he supported the execution of Louis XVI and the overthrow of the Girondins, and as dominant member of the Committee of Public Safety instituted the Reign of Terror in 1793. His extremist zeal made him enemies on both left and right, resulting in his overthrow and death by guillotining in Jul 1794.

Danton Georges Jacques 1959-94. French lawyer and leading revolutionary. Influential in the early years of the revolution in Paris, he was instrumental in organizing the rising of 10 Aug 1792 which overthrew the monarchy. He also helped to instigate the revolutionary tribunal and the Committee of Public Safety in 1793. He led the Committee until Jul 1793 but was then superseded by Robespierre. An attempt to reassert his power failed and he was guillotined in 1794.

Marat Jean Paul 1743–93. French revolutionary leader and journalist. He was the idol of the Paris revolutionary crowds, and was elected in 1792 to the National Convention, where he carried on a long struggle with the Girondins, ending in their overthrow in May 1793. In Jul he was murdered by Charlotte Corday.

Revolutions of 1848 A series of revolts in various parts of Europe against monarchical rule. While some of the revolutionaries had republican ideas, many more were motivated by economic grievances. The revolution began in France and then spread to Italy, the Austrian Empire, and to Germany where the short-lived Frankfurt Parliament put forward ideas about German political unity. None of the revolutions enjoyed any lasting success, and most were violently suppressed within a few months.

Indian Mutiny 1857–58. The revolt of the Bengal Army against the British in India. The movement was confined to the North, from Bengal to the Punjab, and Central India. Most support came from the army and recently dethroned princes, but in some areas it developed into a peasant rising or general revolt. Outstanding episodes were the seizure of ***Delhi*** by the rebels, and its seige and recapture by the British, and the defence of ***Lucknow*** by a British garrison. The mutiny led to the end of rule by the East India Co. and its replacement by direct Crown administration.

Paris Commune 1871. The second body to bear this name. A provisional government of Socialist and left-wing Republicans, elected in Mar 1871 after an attempt by the right-wing National Assembly at Versailles to disarm the Paris National Guard, it held power until May, when the Versailles troops captured Paris and massacred at least 20,000 people. It is famous as the first Socialist government in history.

Chinese Revolution 1911-49. A series of major political upheavals which began in 1911 with a Nationalist revolt which overthrew the Manchu dynasty in 1922. Led by Sun Yat-sen (1923–25) and then by Chiang Kai-shek (1925–49), the Nationalists came under increasing pressure from the growing Communist movement. The 6,000-mile ***Long March*** of the Chinese Communists 1934–35 to escape from the Nationalist forces saw Mao Zedong emerge as leader. After World War II, the conflict expanded into open civil war 1946–49 with the Nationalists finally being defeated at ***Nanking***. This effectively established Communist rule in China under the leadership of Mao.

Sun Yat-sen or ***Sun Zhong Shan*** 1867–1925. Chinese revolutionary, founder of the Nationalist Guomindang, and moving spirit behind the revolution. He was briefly president 1912, but the reactionaries gained the ascendant, and he broke away to try to establish an independent republic in S China based on Canton. He lacked organizational ability, but his three 'people's principles' of nationalism, democracy, and social reform were influential.

Chiang Kai-shek or ***Jiang Jie Shi*** 1887-1975. Chinese statesman. He took part in

23

the revolution, and after the death of Sun Yat-sen was made commander-in-chief of the Guomindang armies in S China in 1925. The initial collaboration with the Communists, broken in 1927, was resumed following the Xi An incident, and he nominally headed the struggle against the Japanese invaders, receiving the Japanese surrender in 1945. Civil war then resumed between Communists and Nationalists, and ended in the defeat of Chiang in 1949, and the limitation of his rule to Taiwan.

Mao Zedong or *Mao Tse-Tung* 1893–1976. Chinese statesman, the 'Great Helmsman'. Born in Hunan, he became the leader of the Communists in 1927. After the rupture with the Nationalists, led by Chiang Kai-shek, Mao Zedong and his troops undertook the 6,000-mile 'Long March' 1934–35 from SE to NW China, the prelude to his ascent to power. Again in nominal alliance with Chiang against the Japanese 1937–45, he subsequently defeated him, and proclaimed the People's Republic of China in 1949. As Chairman of the Communist Party, he provided the pattern for the development of the country through the Great Leap Forward of 1959, and the Cultural Revolution of 1966 based on his thoughts contained in the 'Little Red Book'. His reputation plunged after his death, but was later somewhat restored.

Russian Revolution 1917. The name given to the two revolutions of Mar and Nov 1917 which began with the overthrow of the Romanov Imperial dynasty and ended with the the establishment of a state run by Lenin and the Bolsheviks. The revolution of Mar 1917 arose in part from the repressive nature of Tsarist government but primarily as a result of the mismanagement of the war after 1914. Riots in St Petersburg led to the abdication of Tsar Nicholas II and the formation of a provisional government under Kerensky. This ruled until Oct 1917 but found its power increasingly undermined by the soldiers' and workers' soviets in Petrograd (St Petersburg) and Moscow. During this period the Bolsheviks, under Lenin's guidance, had concentrated on gaining control of the soviets and advocating

an end to the war and land reform. Under the slogan 'All power to the soviets' they staged a coup on the night of 6–7 Nov which overthrew the government. The second All-Russian Congress of Soviets, which met the following day, proclaimed itself the new government of Russia. The Bolshevik seizure of power led to peace with Germany through the *Treaty of Brest-Litovsk*, but also to civil war as anti-Bolshevik elements within the army attempted to seize power. The war lasted until 1920, when the Red Army, organized by Trotsky, finally overcame 'white' opposition.

Lenin Pseudonym of Vladimir Ilich Ulyanov 1870–1924. He was converted to Marxism in 1889 and exiled to Siberia in 1895 as a result of subversive activity. After 1900, he spent most of his time in Western Europe, emerging as the leader of the more radical Bolshevik section of Russian Social Democracy. Returning to Russia in Apr 1917 with German help, Lenin assumed control of the Bolshevik movement and was instrumental in organizing the coup of 6–7 Nov. From then until his death in 1924, he effectively controlled Russia, establishing Bolshevik rule and the beginnings of Communism.

Trotsky Leon 1879–1940. Born 7 Nov at Yanovka. Communist theorist, agitator, and collaborator with Lenin after the two met in exile in London in 1902. Trotsky was a leading member of the Bolshevik movement in 1917 and helped overthrow the provisional government. He was instrumental in building up the Red Army so that it could win the civil war and acted as Commissioner for Foreign Affairs until 1924. He was ousted during the power struggle which followed Lenin's death, but remained active in opposing Stalin's rule until he was assassinated in Aug 1940.

Cuban Revolution 1959. Name given to the overthrow of the Batista regime in Jan 1959 by Castro and the 26 Jul Movement. Having led abortive coups in 1953 and 1956, Castro succeeded in overthrowing Batista with a force of only 5,000 men. Politically non-aligned, Castro was increasingly forced to seek Eastern Bloc help for government as a result of US opposition – opposition which culminated in the abortive *Bay of Pigs* invasion of 1961 sponsored by the CIA. The missile crisis of 1962 highlighted Russian involvement in Cuba. Between 1959 and 1974, Cuba, led by Castro, his brother Raúl and initially Che Guevara, adopted economic and social policies based on the principles of Marxism-Leninism and relied almost exclusively on Communist help. After 1974, in an attempt to stabilise the economy, Castro reintroduced incentives into society with the maxim that each 'should receive according to his work' rather than according to his need.

Castro Ruz Fidel 1927– . Cuban prime minister. Of wealthy parentage Castro was educated at Jesuit schools and, after studying law at the University of Havana, he gained a reputation through his work for poor clients. He strongly opposed the Batista dictatorship, and with his brother Raúl took part in an unsuccessful attack on the army barracks at Santiago de Cuba in 1953. After spending some time in exile in the US and Mexico, Castro attempted a secret landing in Cuba in 1956 in which all but 11 of his supporters were killed. He eventually gathered an army of over 5,000 which overthrew Batista in 1959 and became prime minister a few months later. He became president in 1976, and in 1979 also president of the Non-Aligned Movement. His brother Raúl was appointed Minister of Armed Forces in 1959.

Guevara Ernesto 'Che' 1928–67. Revolutionary. Born in Argentina, he was trained as a doctor, but in 1953 left the country because of his opposition to Peron. In effecting the Cuban revolution of 1959, he was second only to Castro and his brother, but in 1965 moved on to fight against white mercenaries in the Congo, and then to Bolivia, where he was killed in an unsuccessful attempt to lead a peasant rising.

Chilean Revolution 1970–73. Name given to the period of Salvador Allende's presidency, the world's first democratically elected Marxist head of state. Allende was brought to power in 1970 as the head of the Popular Unity alliance of Socialists, Communists, and radicals. He was committed to extensive social and economic reforms to be carried out within the existing political structure, but nationalization of key industries and increased contacts with Eastern Bloc countries strained Chile's traditional economic relations with the USA and the West. His failure to stabilize the economy created widespread opposition, culminating in a military coup in Sept 1973, when the Allende regime was overthrown and replaced by a four-man junta led by General Pinochet.

Allende Gossens Salvador 1908– . Born in Valparaiso, Chile, Allende became a Marxist activist in the 1930s and rose to prominence as a left-wing presidential candidate in 1952, 1958, and 1964. In each election he had the support of the Socialist and Communist movements but was defeated by the Christian Democrats and Nationalists. Eventually elected in 1970, Allende never succeeded in keeping the electoral alliance together in government, and the 1973 coup brought about his death and that of many of his supporters.

Nicaraguan Revolution 1978-79. The revolt led by the FSLN (Sandinist National Liberation Front named after Augusto Cesar Sandino, killed by the National Guard in 1934) against the dictatorship established by the father of the president Anastasio 'Tacho' Somoza. The dictatorship of the Somoza family had been underwritten by US support but this was of little help in 1978–79 when the Sandinistas mounted a full scale challenge to the regime and the hated National Guard. Somoza was forced into exile and assassinated in Paraguay in 1980. Since the revolution, the Sandinistas have taken political control of the country, introducing socialist policies and receiving help from Eastern Bloc countries as US aid dried up. The Sandinista government has had to contend with severe economic problems and also the activities of a counter-revolutionary movement, the Contras, operating in the north of the country with US monetary and technical support.

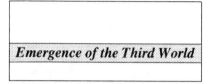

Emergence of the Third World

One of the major political changes to have taken place in recent years has been the break-up of the European overseas empires. Apart from the Spanish colonies in South and Central America which achieved their independence in the early 19th century, nearly all of this decolonization has taken place since the end of World War II, either by negotiation or by force. This has created many new, independent, sovereign states in South and Central America, Africa and Asia – all of whom share the experience of having been colonized as part of the Third World (where the USA and USSR form the First World, and the industrialized European states together with Canada and Japan the Second World). While the term Third World may indicate a colonial past, it also indicates the present economic situation of those countries; industrially less developed and dependent on the developed world for many essential products. This relationship between the industrialized nations and the Third World has created a severe debt crisis for many of the less developed nations where they are now having to raise loans internationally merely in order to pay off existing debts, rather than for industrial or agricultural development projects. There are well over one hundred Third World states and in recent years they have tried to exert some political influence in world affairs through the creation of the non-aligned movement within the United Nations; and economic influence through the creation of the 'Group of 77' (1964), an organization designed to bring pressure on the developed world to provide aid and monetary assistance. A series of selective tables over the following pages outlines the colonial origins of some of the more important Third World states and their recent political history. They are grouped according to the European country by which they were originally colonized and, within these groups, listed chronologically according to their date of independence.

BELGIUM

Current name	Colonial Names and History	Colonized/ Independent	Recent Events
Zaire	Belgian Congo	1885/1960	Republic of Congo 1960-71 under P Lumumba; J D Mobutu after coup 1965

FRANCE

Current name	Colonial Names and History	Colonized/ Independent	Recent Events
Kampuchea	Cambodia to 1970	1863/1953	Led by Prince Sihanouk except Khmer Republic 1970-75, Pol Pot regime 1976-78; invaded by Vietnam 1978
Laos	French Indo-China (protectorate)	1893/1954	Civil war until Vientiane Agreement divided country 1973; Communists in power from 1975
Vietnam	Tonkin, Annam, Cochin-China to 1954; N&S Vietnam 1954-76	1858/1954	Led by Ho Chi Minh to Vietnam War 1954-75; Socialist Republic from 1976

Current name	Colonial Names and History	Colonized/ Independent	Recent Events
Burkina Faso	Upper Volta to 1984	1896/1960	Military coups 1966, 1980, 1982, 1983; Captain Thomas Sankara president 1983-
Central African Republic	Ubangi-Shari	19th cent./ 1960	Republic 1960-76, 1979- ; Central African Empire 1976-79 led by Jean Bokassa
Chad	French Equatorial Africa	19th cent./ 1960	Continuing civil war with Libyan and French support
Côte d'Ivoire	Ivory Coast to 1986	1883/1960	Félix Houphouët-Boigny president of one-party state from 1960
Madagascar		1896/1960	Malagasy Republic 1960-75; Madagascar, under Didier Ratsiraka, 1975-
Mali	French Sudan	19th cent./ 1960	Moussa Traoré president from 1969; one-party state from 1974
Niger		1912/1960	Under Colonel Seyni Kountché since military coup 1974
Algeria	Colonized in 19th cent.; incorporated into France 1881	c.1840/1962	Led by Mohamed Ben Bella until overthrown by Huari Boumédienne 1965; Benjedid Chadli president of one-party state 1979-

GREAT BRITAIN

Current name	Colonial Names and History	Colonized/ Independent	Recent Events
India	British E India Co. 18th cent.-1858	18th cent./ 1947	Republic conceived by Mohandas K Gandhi, led by Pandit Nehru 1947-64, Indira Gandhi 1966-77, 1980-84, and Rajiv Gandhi 1984-
Pakistan	British E India Co. 18th cent.-1858	18th cent./ 1947	Republic established by Mohammad Ali Jinna, led by Zulfikar Ali Bhutto in 1970s, now under General Zia-ul-Haq since military coup 1977
Sri Lanka	Portuguese, Dutch 1602-1796; Ceylon 1802-1972	16th cent./ 1948	Led by Solomon Bandaranaike 1956-59, then his wife Sirimavo; republic from 1972, now under Junius Jayawardene
Ghana	Gold Coast	1618/1957	Several coups since Kwame Nkrumah deposed 1966; now under military rule

Current name	Colonial Names and History	Colonized/ Independent	Recent Events
Nigeria		1861/1960	Federal republic from 1963, led by Yakubu Gowon 1966-75; Biafran War 1967-70; now under military rule after several coups
Cyprus	Turkish to 1878, then British rule	1878/1960	Led by Archbishop Makarios 1960-77; divided into Greek and Turkish states from 1975
Sierra Leone	British protectorate	1788/1961	Made republic 1971; one-party state from 1978
Tanzania	German E Africa to 1921; British mandate from League of Nations/ UN as Tanganyika	19th cent./ 1961	Joined with Zanzibar 1964 to form Tanzania under Julius Nyerere 1962-85
Jamaica	Spanish to 1655	16th cent./ 1962	Led by Michael Manley 1972-80; in opposition to Edward Seaga from 1980
Trinidad & Tobago	Spanish 1532-1797; British 1797-1962	1532/1962	Republic under Ellis Clarke from 1976
Uganda	British protectorate	1894/1962	Led by Milton Obote 1962-71, 1980-85; Idi Amin 1971-79
Kenya	British colony from 1920	1895/1963	Led by Jomo Kenyatta 1963-78; Daniel Arap Moi 1978-
Malaysia	British interests from 1786; Federation of Malaya 1957-63	1874-1963	Federal republic led by Mahmud Iskander from 1984
Malawi	British protectorate of Nyasaland 1907-53; Federation of Rhodesia & Nyasaland 1953-64	1891/1964	One-party state under Hastings Banda from 1966
Malta	French 1798-1814	1798/1964	Led by Dom Mintoff to 1984; Mifsud Bonnici 1984-
Zambia	N Rhodesia – British protectorate; Federation of Rhodesia & Nyasaland 1953-64	1924/1964	Led by Kenneth Kaunda from 1964; one-party state from 1972
The Gambia		1888/1965	Led by Dawda K Jawara from 1965
Singapore	Federation of Malaya 1963-65	1858/1965	Led by Lee Kuan Yew from 1959
Guyana	Dutch to 1796; British Guiana 1796-1966	1620/1966	Led by Forbes Burnham to 1985; Desmond Hoyte 1985-
Botswana	Bechuanaland – British protectorate	1885/1966	Led by Seretse Khama to 1980; Quett Masire 1980-

Current name	Colonial Names and History	Colonized/ Independent	Recent Events
Lesotho	Basutoland	1868/1966	Monarchy under Moshoeshoe II from 1966
Bangladesh	British E India Co. 18th cent.-1858; British India 1858-1947; E Pakistan 1947-71	18th cent./ 1971	Led by Lt-General Ershad from 1982 after several coups; martial law ended 1986
Zimbabwe	S Rhodesia from 1923; UDI 1965-79 under Ian Smith	1895/1980	Led by Robert Mugabe from 1980

THE NETHERLANDS

Current name	Colonial Names and History	Colonized/ Independent	Recent Events
Indonesia	Netherlands Indies	17th cent./ 1949	Military rule of Dr Sukarno to 1966; General Suharto 1967- ; incorporated Dutch New Guinea 1963, E Timor 1976
Suriname	British colony 1650-67	1667/1975	Led by Lt-Col Desi Bouterse from 1982 after several coups

PORTUGAL

Current name	Colonial Names and History	Colonized/ Independent	Recent Events
Brazil		1532/1822	Military coup 1964; civilian rule from 1985
Uruguay	Province of Brazil	1533/1828	Military coup 1976; civilian rule from 1985
Mozambique		1505/1975	Led by Frelimo leader Samora Machel to 1986
Angola		1491/1975	Continuing civil war between dos Santos government and Jonas Savimbi

SPAIN

Current name	Colonial Names and History	Colonized/ Independent	Recent Events,
Paraguay	Viceroyalty of Buenos Aires	1537/1811	Military rule under Alfredo Stroessner from 1954

Current name	Colonial Names and History	Colonized/ Independent	Recent Events
Argentina	Viceroyalty of Buenos Aires	16th cent./ 1816	Military rule 1976-83; Raul Alfonsín president 1983-
Chile		1541/1818	Led by General Pinochet since military coup overthrew Allende 1974
Costa Rica		1563/1821	Led by Oscar Arias Sanchez 1986-
Mexico	Viceroyalty of New Spain	16th cent./ 1821	Federal republic under Miguel de la Madrid Hurtado 1982- and Institutional Revolutionary Party
Peru		1541/1824	Civilian rule since 1980 after several coups
Bolivia		16th cent./ 1825	Civilian rule under Dr Victor Paz Estenssoro 1985-
Ecuador	Greater Colombia 1822-30	16th cent./ 1830	Civilian rule from 1979; led by Febres Cordero 1984-
Venezuela	Captaincy-General of Caracas to 1822; Greater Colombia 1822-30	16th cent./ 1830	Led by Dr Jaime Lusinchi 1984-
Honduras	Federation of Central America 1821-38	1523/1838	Civilian rule under Roberto Suazo 1982-85, José Azcona del Hoyo 1985- , after long military rule
El Salvador	Federation of Central America 1821-39	16th cent./ 1839	Continuing conflict between guerrilla forces and government of José Duarte
Guatemala	Federation of Central America 1821-39	16th cent./ 1839	Civilian rule from 1985 after long military rule
Dominican Republic	Hispaniola to 1821; ruled by Haiti to 1844	16th cent./ 1844	Civilian rule from 1966, under Joaquin Balaguer 1986-
Cuba		1512/1898	Led by Castro from 1959; Bay of Pigs incident 1961
Colombia	Viceroyalty of New Granada to 1819; Greater Colombia to 1830	16th cent./ 1903	Led by Virgilio Barco Vargas 1986-
Panama	Part of Colombia to 1903	16th cent./ 1903	Panama-US treaty on canal 1977
Philippines	Spain 1565-1898; US 1898-1946	1565/1946	Led by Ferdinand Marcos 1963-86; Corazón Aquino 1986-

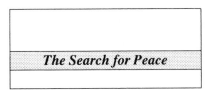

The Search for Peace

Europe in 1815 until the end of the 18th century, the idea of states making war against each other was regarded as an acceptable, and even a normal, way of settling international disputes. Following the catastrophic political and economic effects of the French Revolutionary and Napoleonic Wars, many leading statesman recognized the need, not only to reconstruct Europe politically, but also to develop some machinery for ensuring a lasting peace and the settlement of international disputes by negotiation. This change of attitude was reinforced by the belief that an equilibrium existed in which the aims and objectives of all European states could be made compatible. Towards the end of the war, the victorious powers, Russia, Prussia, Austria, and Britain arranged a peace conference in Vienna.

Congress of Vienna international congress held 1814–15 to discuss the reconstruction of continental Europe. National representatives included Prince Metternich (Austria), Alexander I (Russia), Castlereagh and Wellington (Britain). The settlement created the basis for the Quadruple Alliance of the Victorious Powers – transformed in 1818 into the Quintuple Alliance with the inclusion of France. The congress also produced other attempts at international co-operation.

Holy Alliance a 'Christian Union of Charity, Peace and Love' initiated by Alexander I of Russia in 1815 and signed by every crowned head in Europe. Although apparently an attempt to facilitate European co-operation through Christian principles, the alliance became associated with Russian attempts to preserve autocratic monarchies at any price and an excuse to meddle in the internal affairs of other states. The Idea of an international army acting in the name of the alliance were

rejected by Britain and Austria in 1818 and again in 1820.

Congress system developed from the Congress of Vienna. A series of international meetings at Aix-la-Chapelle 1818, Troppau 1820, and Verona 1822. British opposition to the repressive intentions of the congresses effectively ended them as a system of international arbitration, although congresses continued to meet into the 1830s.

International co-operation in the 19th century the period 1815–53 saw much internal political disruption in many European states but it was not until mid-century that a series of wars, most notably the Crimean, Seven Weeks', and Franco-Prussian, led to changes in the European order. New nation states were created in Italy and Germany, the Austrian empire was divided and France weakened. This also created a new impetus towards international co-operation.

Geneva Convention an international agreement regulating the treatment of the wounded in war, reached at a conference in 1864, and later extended to cover the treatment of the sick and prisoners, and protection of civilians in wartime. The rules were revised at conventions held in 1906, 1929, 1949, and 1977.

Red Cross international agency founded to assist the wounded and prisoners of war. Prompted by war horrors experienced by the Swiss Henri Dunant, the Geneva Convention laid down principles ensuring the safety of ambulances, hospitals and personnel distinguished by the emblem of the red cross. Red Cross societies were established in most western states and a parallel Red Crescent organization was created in Muslim countries.

Conference system a system of international conferences promoted principally by Bismarck to ease the integration of a new powerful German state into the 'Concept of Europe'. The conferences were intended to settle great power disputes, mainly related to the Balkans, the Middle East and the designation of colonies in Africa and Asia. Most important of these was the congress of Berlin 1878 which determined the boundaries of the

Balkan states after the Russo-Turkish War. The system fell into disuse with the retirement of Bismarck and the pressures of new European alliance blocks.

Alliance system and 'balance of power' the failure of both the congress and conference systems to produce any lasting machine led to an increasing reliance on individual alliances and the creation of hostile European blocks. The most important of these alliances were:

Three Emperors League (Dreikaiserbund) 1872 an informal alliance between the emperors of Russia, Germany and Austria. Effectively at an end by 1879.

Triple Alliance 1882 an alliance formed between Germany, Austria-Hungary and Italy which formed the basis of central power involvement in World War I (Italy remaining neutral and then joining allied powers).

Dual Entente 1893 an alliance between France and Russia which lasted until the Bolshevik Revolution of 1917.

Anglo-French Entente (Entente Cordiale) 1904 an alliance based on the need to settle colonial differences. Similar treaty with Russia in 1907 led to:

Triple Entente 1907–17 alliance of Britain, France and Russia. In 1911 this became a military alliance and formed the basis of the allied cause in World War I.

The failure of the alliance system to create a stable balance of power, coupled with universal horror of the carnage created by World War I, led to further attempts to create a new international order.

The League of Nations international organization suggested in President Woodrow Wilson's 'Fourteen Points' 1917 as part of the peace settlement for World War I. The league covenant was drawn up by the Paris Peace Conference in 1919 and incorporated into the Versailles and other peace treaties. Established in Geneva in 1920, the league included representatives from states throughout the world, but was severely weakened by the US decision not to become a member. The states which did become members undertook to preserve the territorial integrity of all, and to

submit international disputes to the league or to arbitration. The league enjoyed a good deal of success in the humanitarian field (international action against epidemics, drug traffic and the slave trade) and also established a number of important subsidiary organizations. Most notably:

International Labour Organization (*ILO*) based in Geneva and concerned primarily with working conditions and social welfare. Formed in 1919, the ILO continued to exist as an affiliated body of the United Nations.

High Commission for Refugees (Nansen Office) an organization created to assist refugees, primarily from Russia and eastern Europe. Built on the work of Norwegian explorer Fridtjof Nansen as first High Commissioner, the high commission declined in importance after his death and the entry of the USSR to the league. Formed the basis for post-1945 refugee work by the United Nations.

Permanent Court of Justice court created in The Hague in 1921, based on ideas for some form of international court put forward at The Hague Congress of 1907.

The league also achieved some success in organizing population exchanges after the Paris peace conferences had established new national boundaries, and in deferring arguments over disputed territories and former German colonies by mandating a league member to act as a caretaker administration for a specified period of time, or until a permanent solution could be found. Mandates were created for Palestine (Britain), SW Africa (S Africa), and Danzig. In the political and diplomatic field, the league was permanently hampered by internal rivalries and the necessity for unanimity in the decision-making process. No action was taken against Japan's aggression in Manchuria 1931; attempts to impose sanctions against Italy for the invasion of Ethiopia 1935–36 collapsed; no actions were taken when Germany annexed Austria and Czechoslovakia, nor when Poland was invaded. Japan (1932) and Germany (1933) simply withdrew from the league and the expulsion of Russia in 1939 had no effect on the Russo-Finnish War.

Long before the outbreak of World War II, diplomacy had abandoned international security and reverted to a system of direct negotiation and individual alliances.

Alliance, aggression and appeasement the period 1936–39 saw a series of alliances and treaties ostensibly to guarantee the security of individual states.

Rome-Berlin Axis the sometimes uneasy alliance of Nazi Germany and fascist Italy. The axis was formed in 1936 when Italy was threatened with 'sanctions' because of the invasion of Ethiopia, and became a full military and political alliance in May 1939. A ten-year alliance between Germany, Italy and Japan (Rome, Berlin, Tokyo Axis) was signed in Sept 1940 and was later joined by Hungary, Bulgaria, Romania, Slovakia and Croara. The axis collapsed with the fall of Mussolini in 1943.

Munich Agreement the agreement between Britain, France, Germany and Italy signed by Chamberlain, Daladier, Hitler and Mussolini at Munich on 29 Sept 1938. Its main provision was to cede Sudeten areas of Czechoslovakia to Germany. Although the signatories all guaranteed the new Czechoslovak frontiers, Hitler seized the rest of the country in Mar 1939. Britain and France did not respond immediately, leading Hitler to assume that they would not intervene anywhere in Eastern Europe. Nevertheless, Hitler's violation of the agreement did create a change in attitude and further guarantees to Poland.

Hitler-Stalin Pact agreement signed in August 1939 between Nazi Germany and the USSR by Ribbentrop and Molotov. The treaty provided for the partition of Poland between the two states.

International peace and security since 1945 at the end of World War II, an attempt was made to re-establish an organization for international security, as a successor to the discredited League of Nations.

United Nations (UN) an association of states pledged to maintain international peace and security, and to promote international co-operation. Its charter, which was drawn up by the San Francisco Conference in 1945, is based on proposals drafted at the Dumbarton Oaks Conference. Its six principal organs are:

General Assembly of representatives of all member states, which meets regularly once a year, and may discuss any matter within the scope of the charter, but may not make recommendations on anything already being dealt with by the Security Council. Decisions on important questions are made by a two-thirds majority of members voting, and on other questions by a simple majority, each member having one vote.

Security Council consisting of five permanent members (UK, USA, USSR, France, and Communist China), and six others elected for two years by the General Assembly. Its decisions must be supported by at least seven of its members, including all permanent members, who thus exercise the right of veto. Taking cognizance of disputes, it may undertake investigations into the circumstances and make recommendations to the parties concerned, and may call on all members to take economic or military measures to enforce its decisions.

Economic and Social Council consisting of representatives of 18 member states, elected for three years by the General Assembly, which initiates studies of international economic, social, cultural, educational, health and related matters, and may make recommendations to the General Assembly. It operates largely through specialized commissions of international experts on economics, transport and communications, human rights, status of women, etc. It also co-ordinates the activities of such specialized inter-governmental agencies as the United Nations Educational, Scientific and Cultural Organization (UNESCO 1946) to combat illiteracy, raise living standards through education, and so on; International Labour Organization; Food and Agriculture Organization (FAO 1945), to help the nations improve food and production and distribution, raise nutritional standards, and so on; International Atomic Agency (IAEA 1957), to develop the peaceful uses of atomic energy; World Health Organization (WHO 1946), to prevent the spread of, and eliminate, such diseases as malaria and tuberculosis; International Monetary Fund and International Bank for Reconstruction and Development, which promote international economic co-operation, and so on.

Trusteeship Councilconsisting of members administering Trust Territories, other permanent members of the Security Council, plus sufficient other elected members to balance the administering powers.

International Court of Justiceat the Hague which is the United Nation's principal judicial organ: the 15 judges are elected by the General Assembly and the Security Council, and the United Nation members are pledged by the charter to comply with the decisions of the court in cases to which they are a party.

Secretariatthe administrative body, consisting of the Secretary General, appointed by the General Assembly on the recommendation of the Security Council for five years, and an international staff. Members contribute according to their resources, an apportionment being made by the General Assembly, with the addition of voluntary contributions from some governments to the funds of the United Nations which finance the programme of assistance carried out by the United Nation, intergovernmental agencies, the United Nation Children's Fund (UNICEF), the United Nation refugee organizations, and the United Nation Special Fund for underdeveloped countries. There are six offical working languages: English, French, Russian, Spanish, Chinese, and Arabic. The preponderance of influence in the United Nations, originally with the Allied States of World War II, is now more widely spread. Although part of the value of the United Nations lies in recognition of member states as sovereign and equal, the rapid increase in membership of minor, in some cases minute, states was causing concern by 1980 (154 members) as lessening the weight of voting decisions. Taiwan (Nationalist China), formerly a permanent member of the Security Council, was expelled 1971 on the admission of Communist China. The United Nation also suffers from the lack of adequate and independent funds and forces, the latter having been employed with varying success, for example, in Korea, Cyprus, and Sinai, and the intrusion of the Cold War which divides members into adherents of the East or West and the uncommitted. In spite of its many successes, the United Nation and its subsidary organizations have failed to prevent the rebuilding of defensive alliances. Even before the end of World War II, relations between the USSR and the Western Powers became strained leading to the Cold War and the creation of the two huge defensive alliances – one based round the USSR and the other round the USA.

UN Peacekeeping InitiativesSince becoming UN Secretary-General in 1982, Javier Perez de Cuellar has been responsible for several successful peace initiatives, including the ending of the Iran–Iraq war and the withdrawal of South African and Cuban troops from Angola, paving the way for the independence of Namibia. He has also initiated talks between Greek and Turkish leaders in Cyprus.

North Atlantic Treaty Organization (NATO) defensive alliance created by the North Atlantic Treaty, signed in Washington DC on 4 Apr 1949 by Belgium, Canada, Denmark, France, Iceland, Italy, Luxembourg, the Netherlands, Norway, Portugal, the UK, and the USA. The signatories agreed that 'an armed attack against one or more of them in Europe or North America shall be considered an attack against them all'. Greece and Turkey acceded in 1952, and Germany in 1955. The chief body of the North Atlantic Treaty Organization is the Council of Foreign Ministers which holds periodic meetings and also functions in permanent session through the appointment of permanent representatives. The unified international secretariat has its headquarters at Brussels (until 1967 in Paris) as does a Military Committee consisting of chiefs of staff (until 1967 in Washington). The military headquarters are called the Supreme Headquarters Allied Powers, Europe (SHAPE) and moved from Rocquencourt, France, to Chièvres-Casteau, near Mons, Belgium, in 1967. The Supreme Allied Commanders, Europe and Atlantic, are Americans, but there is also an Allied

Commander, Channel – a British admiral. France withdrew from the organization, but not from the alliance, 1966, and Greece withdrew militarily, but not politically, in 1974 over the Cyprus issue, rejoining in 1981.

Warsaw Pact a pact signed on 14 May 1955 by Albania (excluded in 1962), Bulgaria, Czechoslovakia, East Germany, Hungary, Poland, Romania, and the USSR; extended in 1985 for a further 20 years. It established an alliance on NATO lines, the Warsaw Treaty Organization.

Cold War term used to describe the economic and political hostility that lasted for more than 20 years before the two superpowers began discussions on disarmament and other matters of mutual concern – beginning a process which has become known as détente.

Strategic Arms Limitation Talks (SALT) US–Soviet talks suggested by President Johnson in 1967 for the mutual limitation and eventual reduction of strategic nuclear weapons. They were delayed by the Soviet invasion of Czechoslovakia but began in 1969. SALT I operated from 1972 to 1977. SALT II was mainly negotiated before 1976, and signed by Brezhnev and Carter at Vienna in 1979, but the Soviet invasion of Afganistan prevented US ratification.

Strategic Arms Reduction Talks (START) a new phase in US–Soviet peace discussions, which began with talks in Geneva in 1983 leading to the signing of the Intermediate Nuclear Forces (INF) treaty in 1987. In 1989 proposals for reductions in conventional weapons were added to the agenda.

Intermediate Nuclear Forces (INF) treaty signed by the USA and the USSR in December 1987 to eliminate all ground-based intermediate nuclear weapons by 1989.

Helsinki Conference international conference in 1975 at which 35 countries, including the USSR and the USA, supposedly reached agreements on co-operation in security, economics, science, technology, and human rights. It is often regarded as marking the end of the Cold War. Further progress in relations between the two major powers has been hampered by Soviet actions in Afghanistan and US involvement in Central America. Arguments have centred on the supposed balance of forces (in Europe and elsewhere) being upset by the deployment of Pershing, Cruise, and Trident missiles by the USA and USSR SS20 missiles. More recently, the issue has been further complicated by President Reagan's adoption of the so-called Strategic Defence Initiative (SDI) or 'Star Wars'. The Soviet willingness to make concessions at the Rekjavik summit between Reagan and Gorbachev in 1986 suggest they are anxious to forestall this apparent extension of the arms race into space.

Peace Movement the collective opposition to war. The western peace movements of the 1980s can trace their origins back to the pacifists of the 19th century and conscientious objectors during World War I. Since World War II, the campaign has concentrated on opposing the spread, and even the existence of nuclear weapons. Thus it has attracted not only pacifists but also those opposed to all uses of nuclear power. Peace movements now exist in many western and non-aligned countries.

CHINESE DYNASTIES

Dynasty	Date	Major Events
Xia (Hsia)	c.2000-c1500 BC	agriculture, bronze, first writing
Shang (Yin)	c.1500-c.1066 BC	first major dynasty; first Chinese calendar
Zhou (Chou)	c.1066-c.221 BC	developed society using money, iron, written laws; age of Confucius
Qin (Ch'in)	221-206 BC	unification after period of Warring States, building of Great Wall began, roads built
Han	206 BC-220 AD	first centralized and effectively administered empire; introduction of Buddhism
San Kuo	220-280	division into three parts, prolonged fighting and eventual victory
(Three		of Wei over Chu and Wu; Confucianism superseded by Buddhism
Kingdoms)		and Taoism
Western Jin (Chin)	265-316	beginning of Hun invasions in the north
Eastern Jin (Chin)	317-439	
Southern and Northern	386-581	
Sui	581-618	reunification; barbarian invasions stopped; Great Wall refortified
Tang (T'ang)	618-907	centralised government; empire greatly extended; period of excellence in sculpture, painting and poetry
Wu Tai	907-960	economic depression and loss of territory in northern China,
(Five Dynasties		central Asia, and Korea; first use of paper money
Song (Sung)	960-1279	period of calm and creativity; printing developed (movable type); central government restored; northern and western frontiers neglected and Mongol incursions began
Yuan	1279-1368	beginning of Mongol rule in China, under Kublai Khan; Marco Polo visited China; dynasty brought to an end by widespread revolts, centred in Mongolia
Ming	1368-1644	Mongols driven out by native Chinese, Mongolia captured by 2nd Ming emperor; period of architectural development; Beijing flourished as new capital
Manchu	1644-1911	China once again under non-Chinese rule, conquered by nomads
or Qing (Ch'ing)		from Manchuria; initially, trade and culture flourished, but conservatism led to a decline, culminating in the dynasty's overthrow by revolutionaries led by Sun Yat-sen.

Pinyin spellings are given here, following official adoption of the *Pinyin* system in 1979, with the older romanized forms in brackets.

HOLY ROMAN EMPERORS

Carolingian Kings and Emperors

Charlemagne, Charles the Great	800-14
Louis I, the Pious	814-40
Lothair I	840-55
Louis II	855-75
Charles II, the Bald	875-77
Charles III, the Fat	881-87
Guido of Spoleto	891-94
Lambert of Spoleto (co-emperor)	892-98
Arnulf (rival)	896-901
Louis III of Provence	901-5
Berengar	905-24
Conrad I of Franconia (rival)	911-18

Saxon Kings and Emperors

Henry I, the Fowler	918-36
Otto I, the Great	936-73
Otto II	973-83
Otto III	983-1002
Henry II, the Saint	1002-24

Franconian (Salian) Emperors

Conrad II	1024-39
Henry III, the Black	1039-56
Henry IV	1056-1106
Rudolf of Swabia (rival)	1077-80
Hermann of Luxembourg (rival)	1081-93
Conrad of Franconia (rival)	1093-1101
Henry V	1106-25
Lothair II	1126-37

Hohenstaufen Kings and Emperors

Conrad III	1138-52
Frederick I Barbarossa	1152-90
Henry VI	1190-97
Otto IV	1198-1215
Philip of Swabia (rival)	1198-1208
Frederick II	1215-50
Henry Raspe of Thuringia (rival)	1246-47
William of Holland (rival)	1247-56
Conrad IV	1250-54
The Great Interrugnum	1254-73

Rulers from Various Noble Families

Richard of Cornwall (rival)	1257-72
Alfonso X of Castile (rival)	1257-73
Rudolf I, Hapsburg	1273-91
Adolf I of Nassau	1292-98
Albert I, Hapsburg	1298-1303
Henry VII, Luxembourg	1308-13
Louis IV of Bavaria	1314-47
Frederick of Hapsburg (co-regent)	1314-25
Charles IV, Luxembourg	1347-78
Wenceslas of Bohemia	1378-1400
Frederick III of Brunswick	1400
Rupert of the Palatinate	1400-10
Sigismund, Luxembourg	1411-37

Hapsburg Emperors

Albert II	1438-39
Frederick III	1440-93
Maximilian I	1493-1519
Charles V	1519-56
Ferdinand I	1556-64
Maximilian II	1564-76
Rudolf II	1576-1612
Matthais	1612-19
Ferdinand II	1619-37
Ferdinand III	1637-57
Leopold I	1658-1705
Joseph I	1705-11
Charles VI	1711-40
Charles VII of Bavaria	1742-45

Hapsburg-Lorraine Emperors

Francis I of Lorraine	1745-65
Joseph II	1765-90
Leopold II	1790-92
Francis II	1792-1806

ENGLISH SOVEREIGNS FROM 900

Dynasty	Name	Date	Title
West Saxon Kings	Edward the Elder	901	son of Alfred the Great
	Athelstan	925	son of Edward I
	Edmund	940	half-brother of Athelstan
	Edred	946	brother of Edmund
	Edwy	955	son of Edmund
	Edgar	959	brother of Edwy
	Edward the Martyr	975	son of Edgar
	Ethelred II	978	son of Edgar
	Edmund Ironside	1016	son of Ethelred
Danish Kings	Canute	1016	son of Sweyn
	Hardicanute	1040	son of Canute
	Harold I	1035	son of Canute
West Saxon Kings (restored)	Edward the Confessor	1042	son of Ethelred II
	Harold II	1066	son of Godwin
Norman Kings	William I	1066	
	William II	1087	son of William I
	Henry I	1100	son of William I
	Stephen	1135	son of Adela (daughter of William II)
House of Plantagenet	Henry II	1154	son of Matilda
	Richard I	1189	son of Henry II
	John	1199	son of Henry II
	Henry III	1216	son of John
	Edward I	1272	son of Henry III
	Edward II	1307	son of Edward I
	Edward III	1327	son of Edward II
	Richard II	1377	son of the Black Prince (son of Edward III)
House of Lancaster	Henry IV	1399	son of John of Gaunt
	Henry V	1413	son of Henry IV
	Henry VI	1422	son of Henry V
House of York	Edward IV	1461	son of Edward III
	Richard III	1483	brother of Edward IV
	Edward V	1483	son of Edward IV
House of Tudor	Henry VII	1485	son of Edward III
	Henry VIII	1509	son of Henry VII
	Edward VI	1547	son of Henry VIII
	Mary I	1553	daughter of Henry VIII
House of Stuart	Elizabeth I	1558	daughter of Henry VIII
	James I	1603	great-grandson of Margaret
The Commonwealth	Charles I	1625	son of James I
House of Stuart (restored)	Charles II	1660	son of Charles I
	James II	1685	son of Charles I

Dynasty	Name	Date	Title
	William III and Mary	1689	son of Mary (daughter of Charles I)/daughter of James II
	Anne	1702	daughter of James II
House of Hanover	George I	1714	son of Sophia (granddaughter of James I)
	George II	1727	son of George I
	George III	1760	son of Frederick (son of George II)
	George IV	1820	son of George III
	William IV	1830	son of George III
	Victoria	1837	daughter of Edward (son of George III)
House of Saxe-Coburg	Edward VII	1901	son of Victoria
House of Windsor	George V	1910	son of Edward VII
	Edward VIII	1936	son of George V
	George VI	1936	son of George V
	Elizabeth II	1952	daughter of George VI

FRANCE

Valois Kings

Philip VI	1328-50
John	1350-64
Charles V	1364-80
Charles VI	1380-1422
Charles VII	1422-61
Louis XI	1461-83
Charles VIII	1483-98
Louis XII	1498-1515
Francis I	1515-47
Henry II	1547-59
Francis II	1559-60
Charles IX	1560-74
Henry III	1574-89

Bourbon Kings

Henry IV	1589-1610
Louis XIII	1610-43
Louis XIV	1643-1715
Louis XV	1715-74
Louis XVI	1774-93

ITALY

Vittorio Emanuele II	1861-78
Umberto I	1878-1900
Vittorio Emanuele III	1900-46
Umberto II	1946
	(*abdicated*)

AUSTRIA

Emperors

Franz II and I	1804-35
Ferdinand I	1835-48

Emperors of Austria-Hungary from 1867

Franz Josef	1848-1916
Karl	1916-18
	(*abdicated*)

RUSSIAN TSARS/TSARINA (EMPERORS/ EMPRESSES) 1721-1917

Ivan IV ('the Terrible')	1547-84
Fyodor (Theodore) I	1584-98
(Regent: Boris Gudunov 1584-98)	
Irina (widow of Fyodor I)	1598
Boris Gudunov	1598-1605
Fyodor (Theodore) II	1605
Dmitri (Dimitri) III	1605-6
Vasily (Basil) IV	1606-10
Mikhail (Michael) Romanov	1613-45
Aleksei (Alexis)	1645-76
Fyodor (Theodore) III	1676-82
Pyotr I ('Peter the Great')/Ivan V (brothers)	
	1682-96
(Regent: Sophia Aleksevna 1682-89)	
Pyotr I ('Peter the Great'), Tsar	1689-1721,
Emperor	1721-25
Ekaterina (Catherine)I, (widow of Pyotr I)	
	1725-27
Pyotr (Peter) II	1727-30
Anna Ivanovna	1730-40
Ivan VI	1440-41
(Regents: Ernst Biron 1740; Anna Leopoldovna 1740-41)	
Elisaveta (Elizabeth)	1741-62
Pyotr (Peter) III	1762
Ekaterina II ('Catherine the Great'), (widow of Pyotr III)	1762-96
Pavel (Paul) I,	1796-1801
Aleksandr (Alexander) I	1801-25
Nikolai (Nicholas) I)	1825-55
Aleksandr (Alexander) II	1855-81
Aleksandr (Alexander) III	1881-94
Nikolai (Nicholas) II	1894-1917

BRITISH PRIME MINISTERS

Sir Robert Walpole	(Whig)	1721
Earl of Wilmington	(Whig)	1742
Henry Pelham	(Whig)	1743
Duke of Newcastle	(Whig)	1754
Duke of Devonshire	(Whig)	1756
Duke of Newcastle	(Whig)	1757
Earl of Bute	(Tory)	1762
George Grenville	(Whig)	1763
Marquess of Rockingham	(Whig)	1765
Duke of Grafton	(Whig)	1766
Lord North	(Tory)	1770
Marquess of Rockingham	(Whig)	1782
Earl of Shelburne	(Whig)	1782
Duke of Portland	(Coalition)	1783
William Pitt	(Tory)	1783
Henry Addington	(Tory)	1801
William Pitt	(Tory)	1804
Lord Grenville	(Whig)	1806
Duke of Portland	(Tory)	1807
Spencer Perceval	(Tory)	1809
Earl of Liverpool	(Tory)	1812
George Canning	(Tory)	1827
Viscount Goderich	(Tory)	1827
Duke of Wellington	(Tory)	1828
Earl Grey	(Whig)	1830
Viscount Melbourne	(Whig)	1834
Sir Robert Peel	(Conservative)	1834
Viscount Melbourne	(Whig)	1835
Sir Robert Peel	(Conservative)	1841
Lord J Russell	(Liberal)	1846
Earl of Derby	(Conservative)	1852
Lord Aberdeen	(Peelite)	1852
Viscount Palmerston	(Liberal)	1855
Earl of Derby	(Conservative)	1858
Viscount Palmerston	(Liberal)	1859
Lord J Russell	(Liberal)	1865
Earl of Derby	(Conservative)	1866
Benjamin Disraeli	(Conservative)	1868
W E Gladstone	(Liberal)	1886
Benjamin Disraeli	(Conservative)	1874
W E Gladstone	(Liberal)	1880
Marquess of Salisbury	(Conservative)	1885
W E Gladstone	(Liberal)	1886
Marquess of Salisbury	(Conservative)	1886
W E Gladstone	(Liberal)	1892
Earl of Rosebery	(Liberal)	1894
Marquess of Salisbury	(Conservative)	1895
A J Balfour	(Conservative)	1902
Sir H Campbell-Bannerman	(Liberal)	1905
H H Asquith	(Liberal)	1908
H H Asquith	(Coalition)	1915
D Lloyd George	(Coalition)	1916
A Bonar Law	(Conservative)	1922
Stanley Baldwin	(Conservative)	1923
Ramsay MacDonald	(Labour)	1924
Stanley Baldwin	(Conservative)	1924
Ramsay MacDonald	(Labour)	1929
Ramsay MacDonald	(National)	1931
Stanley Baldwin	(National)	1935
N Chamberlain	(National)	1937
Sir Winston Churchill	(Coalition)	1940
Clement Attlee	(Labour)	1945
Sir Winston Churchill	(Conservative)	1951
Sir Anthony Eden	(Conservative)	1955
Harold Macmillan	(Conservative)	1957
Sir Alec Douglas-Home	(Conservative)	1963
Harold Wilson	(Labour)	1964
Edward Heath	(Conservative)	1970
Harold Wilson	(Labour)	1974
James Callaghan	(Labour)	1976
Margaret Thatcher	(Conservative)	1979

PRESIDENTS OF THE UNITED STATES OF AMERICA

Name	Party	Took Office
1. George Washington	Federalist	1789
2. John Adams	Federalist	1797
3. Thomas Jefferson	Democratic Republican	1801
4. James Madison	Democratic Republican	1809
5. James Monroe	Democratic Republican	1817
6. John Quincy Adams	Democratic Republican	1825
7. Andrew Jackson	Democrat	1829
8. Martin Van Buren	Democrat	1837
9. William Henry Harrison	Whig	1841
10. John Tuler	Whig	1841
11. James Knox Polk	Democrat	1845
12. Zachary Taylor	Whig	1849
13. Millard Fillmore	Whig	1850
14. Franklin Pierce	Democrat	1853
15. James Buchanan	Democrat	1857
16. Abraham Lincoln	Republican	1861
17. Andrew Johnson	Democrat	1865
18. Ulysses Simpson Grant	Republican	1869
19. Rutherford Birchard Hayes	Republican	1877
20. James Abram Garfield	Republican	1881
21. Chester Alan Arthur	Republican	1881
22. Grover Cleveland	Democrat	1885
23. Benjamin Harison	Republican	1889
24. Grover Cleveland	Republican	1893
25. William McKinley	Republican	1897
26. Theodore Roosevelt	Republican	1901
27. William Howard Taft	Republican	1909
28. Woodrow Wilson	Democrat	1913
29. Warren Gamaliel Harding	Republican	1921
30. Calvin Coolidge	Republican	1923
31. Herbert C Hoover	Republican	1929
32. Franklin Delano Roosevelt	Democrat	1933
33. Harry S Truman	Democrat	1945
34. Dwight D Eisenhower	Republican	1953
35. John F Kennedy	Democrat	1961
36. Lyndon B Johnson	Democrat	1963
37. Richard M Nixon	Republican	1969
38. Gerald R Ford	Republican	1974
39. James Earl Carter	Democrat	1977
40. Ronald Reagan	Republican	1981
41. George Bush	Republican	1989

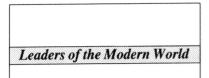

Leaders of the Modern World

Adenauer Konrad 1876–1967. German Christian Democrat politician, chancellor of the Federal Republic 1949–63. With French president de Gaulle he achieved the postwar reconciliation of France and Germany and strongly supported measures designed to strengthen the Western bloc in Europe.

Allende (Gossens) Salvador 1908–1973. Chilean left-wing politician. Elected president 1970 as the candidate of the Popular Front alliance, Allende never succeeded in keeping the electoral alliance together in government. His failure to solve the country's economic problems or to deal with political subversion allowed the army, backed by the CIA, to stage the 1973 coup which brought about the death of Allende and many of his supporters.

Amin Dada Idi 1925– . Ugandan politician, president 1971–79. He led the coup that deposed Milton Obote 1971, expelled the Asian community 1972, and exercised a reign of terror over his people. He fled when insurgent Ugandan and Tanzanian troops invaded the country 1979.

Aquino (Maria) Corazón (born Cojuangco) 1933– . President of the Philippines from 1986, when she was instrumental in the nonviolent overthrow of President Marcos. She has sought to rule in a conciliatory manner, but has encountered opposition from left (communist guerrillas) and right (army coup attempts), and her land reforms have been seen as inadequate.

Attlee Clement (Richard), 1st Earl 1883–1967. British Labour politician. In the coalition government during World War II he was Lord Privy Seal 1940–42, dominions secretary 1942–43, and Lord President of the Council 1943–45, as well as deputy prime minister from 1942. As prime minister 1945–51 he introduced a sweeping programme of nationalization and a whole new system of social services.

Balfour Arthur James, 1st Earl of Balfour 1848–1930. British Conservative politician, prime minister 1902–05 and foreign secretary 1916–19, when he issued the *Balfour Declaration* 1917 in favour of a national home in Palestine for the Jews, and was involved in peace negotiations after World War I.

Banda Hastings Kamuzu *c.* 1902– . Malawi politican. He led his country's independence movement, and was prime minister of Nyasaland from 1963, and first president of Malawi from 1966.

Bandaranaike Sirimavo (born Ratwatte) 1916– . Sri Lankan politician, who succeeded her husband Solomon Bandaranaike to become the world's first woman prime minister 1960–65 and 1970–77, but was expelled from parliament 1980 for abuse of her powers while in office. She was largely responsible for the new constitution 1972.

Bandaranaike Solomon West Ridgeway Dias 1899–1959. Sri Lankan nationalist politician. In 1951 he founded the Sri Lanka Freedom Party and in 1956 became prime minister, pledged to a socialist programme and a neutral foreign policy. He failed to satisfy extremists and was assassinated by a Buddhist monk.

Begin Menachem 1913– . Israeli politician, born in Poland. He was a leader of the extremist Irgun Zvai Leumi organization in Palestine from 1942; prime minister of Israel 1977–83, as head of the right-wing Likud party; and in 1978 shared a Nobel Peace Prize with President Sadat of Egypt for work on the Camp David Agreements for a Middle East peace settlement.

Ben Bella Ahmed 1916– . Algerian leader of the National Liberation Front (FLN) from 1952; he was prime minister of independent Algeria 1962–65, when he was overthrown by Boumédienne and detained until 1980. He founded a new party, Mouvement pour la Démocratie en Algérie, 1985.

Beneš Eduard 1884–1948. Czech politician. President of the republic from 1935 until forced to resign by the Germans, he headed a government in exile in London during World War II. He returned home as president 1945, but resigned again 1948.

Ben-Gurion David. Adopted name of David Gruen 1886–1973. Israeli socialist politician, the country's first prime minister 1948–53 and 1955–63.

Bevan Aneurin 1897–1960. British Labour politician, born in Wales. He was minister of health 1945–51, and inaugurated the National Health Service (NHS); he was minister of labour Jan–Apr 1951, but resigned (with Harold Wilson) on the introduction of NHS charges and led a Bevanite faction against the government. He was noted as an orator.

Bevin Ernest 1881–1951. British Labour politician. Chief creator of the Transport and General Workers' Union, he was its general secretary 1921–40, when he entered the war cabinet as minister of labour and National Service. He was foreign secretary in the Labour government 1945–51.

Bhutto Benazir 1953– . Pakistani politician, leader of the Pakistan People's Party (PPP) from 1984 (in exile until 1986), and prime minister of Pakistan from 1988. She is the first female leader of a Muslim state.

Bhutto Zulfiqar Ali 1928–1979. Pakistani politician, president 1971–73 and then prime minister until the 1977 military coup led by Gen Zia ul-Haq. In 1978 he was sentenced to death for conspiracy to murder a political opponent, and was hanged.

Bismarck Otto Eduard Leopold, Prince von Bismarck 1815–1898. German politician, prime minister of Prussia 1862–90 and chancellor of the German Empire 1871–90. He pursued an aggressively expansionist policy, with wars against Denmark 1863–64, Austria 1866, and France 1870–71, which brought about the unification of Germany.

Bokassa Jean-Bédel 1921– . President and later self-proclaimed emperor of the Central African Republic 1966–79. Commander in chief from 1963, in Dec 1965 he led a military coup which gave him the presidency, and on 4 Dec 1977 he proclaimed the Central African Empire with himself as emperor for life. His regime was characterized by arbitrary state violence and cruelty. In exile 1979–86, he was sentenced to death, but the sentence was commuted to life

imprisonment 1988.

Botha P(ieter) W(illem) 1916– . South African politician. Prime minister from 1978, he initiated a modification of apartheid which later slowed in the face of Afrikaner (Boer) opposition. In 1984 he became the first executive state president. In 1989 he resigned his leadership after suffering a stroke, to be succeeded by F W de Klerk.

Boumédienne Houari. Adopted name of Mohammed Boukharouba 1925–1978. Algerian politician who brought the nationalist leader Ben Bella to power by a revolt 1962, and superseded him as president 1965–78 by a further coup.

Brandt Willy. Adopted name of Karl Herbert Frahm 1913– . West German socialist politician, federal chancellor (premier) 1969–74. He played a key role in the remoulding of the Social Democratic Party (SPD) as a moderate socialist force (chairman 1964–87). As mayor of West Berlin 1957–66, Brandt became internationally known during the Berlin Wall crisis 1961. Nobel Peace Prize 1971.

Brezhnev Leonid Ilyich 1906–1982. Soviet leader. A protégé of Stalin and Khrushchev, he came into power as general secretary of the Soviet Communist Party (CPSU) 1964–82 and was president 1977–82. Domestically he was conservative, abroad he established the USSR as a military and political superpower, extending its influence in Africa and Asia.

Bush George 1924– . US Republican president from 1989. He was director of the Central Intelligence Agency (CIA) 1976–81, and US vice president 1981–89. The evidence in 1987 linking him with the Irangate scandal and the corrupt military ruler of Panama did not prevent Bush from becoming president.

Callaghan (Leonard) James 1912– . British Labour politician. As chancellor of the Exchequer 1964–67, he introduced corporation and capital-gains tax, and resigned following devaluation. He was home secretary 1967–70 and prime minister 1976–79 in a period of increasing economic stress.

Carter Jimmy (James Earl) 1924– . 39th president of the USA 1977–81, a Democrat. In

1976 he narrowly wrested the presidency from Ford. Features of his presidency were the return of the Panama Canal Zone to Panama, the Camp David Agreements for peace in the Middle East, and the Iranian seizure of US embassy hostages. He was defeated by Ronald Reagan 1980.

Castro (Ruz) Fidel 1927– . Cuban Communist politician, prime minister 1959–76 and president from 1976. He led two unsuccessful coups against the right-wing Batista regime and led the revolution that overthrew the dictator 1959. From 1979 he was also president of the non-aligned movement, although promoting the line of the USSR, which subsidized his regime.

Cavour Camillo Benso, Count 1810–1861. Italian nationalist politician, prime minister of Piedmont 1852–59 and 1860–61. With the support of Britain and France, he expelled the Austrians 1859, assisted Garibaldi in liberating S Italy 1860, and achieved a united Italy 1861.

Ceauşescu Nicolae 1918– . Romanian politician, leader of the Romanian Communist Party (RCP), in power from 1967. He has pursued a policy line independent of and critical of the USSR, promoting family members, including his wife, to senior state and party posts. He has increased the power of the secret police, and razed villages in a program of 'modernization'.

Chamberlain (Arthur) Neville 1869–1940. British Conservative prime minister 1937–40. His policy of appeasement towards Mussolini and Hitler (with whom he concluded the Munich Agreement 1938) failed to prevent the outbreak of World War II. He resigned 1940.

Chiang Kai-shek 1887–1975. Chinese Guomindang general and politician, president of China 1928–31 and 1943–49, and of Taiwan from 1949, where he set up a breakaway right-wing government on his expulsion from the mainland by the communist forces. He was a commander in the civil war that lasted from the end of imperial rule 1911 to the Second Sino-Japanese War and beyond, having split with the communist leader Mao Zedong 1927.

Chirac Jacques 1932– . French conservative politician, prime minister 1974–76 and 1986–88. He established the neo-Gaullist Rassemblement pour la République (RPR) 1976, and became mayor of Paris 1977.

Churchill Winston (Leonard Spencer) 1874–1965. British Conservative politician. In Parliament from 1900, as a Liberal until 1923, he held a number of ministerial offices, including 1st Lord of the Admiralty 1911–15 and chancellor of the Exchequer 1924–29. Absent from the cabinet in the 1930s, he returned Sept 1939 to lead a coalition government 1940–45, when he united the nation by his leadership and public speeches, negotiating with Allied leaders in World War II; he was again prime minister 1951–55.

de Gaulle Charles 1890–1970. French conservative politician and general. He organized the Free French troops fighting the Nazis 1940–44, was head of the provisional French government 1944–46, and leader of his own Gaullist party. In 1958 the national assembly asked him to form a government during France's economic recovery, and to solve the crisis in Algeria. He was president 1959–69, having changed the constitution.

Deng Xiaoping formerly *Teng Hsiao-ping* 1904– . Chinese political leader. A member of the Chinese Communist Party (CCP) from the 1920s, he took part in the Long March 1934–36. He was in the Politburo from 1955 until ousted in the Cultural Revolution 1966–69. Reinstated in the 1970s, he gradually took power and introduced a radical economic modernization programme. His future was in doubt after repressing widespread student unrest 1989.

Dubček Alexander 1921– . Czech politician. As first secretary of the Communist Party 1967–69, he launched a liberalization campaign (the Prague Spring). He was arrested by invading Soviet troops, and expelled from the party 1970.

Eden Anthony, 1st Earl of Avon 1897–1977. British Conservative politician, foreign secretary 1935–38, 1940–45, and 1951–55; prime minister 1955–57, when he resigned after the failure of the Anglo-French military intervention in the Suez Crisis.

Eisenhower Dwight D(avid) ('Ike') 1890–1969. 34th president of the USA 1953–60, a Republican. A general in World War II, he commanded the Allied forces in Italy 1943, then the Allied invasion of Europe, and from Oct 1944 all the Allied armies in the West. As president he promoted business interests at home and conducted the Cold War abroad. His vice president was Richard Nixon.

Ershad Hussain Mohammad 1930– . Military ruler of Bangladesh from 1982. He became chief of staff of the Bangladeshi army 1979 and assumed power in a military coup 1982. As president from 1983, Ershad introduced a successful rural-orientated economic programme. He was re-elected 1986 and lifted martial law, but has had to face continuing political opposition and environmental disasters.

Farouk 1920–1965. King of Egypt 1936–52. He succeeded his father Fuad I. In 1952 he was compelled to abdicate, his son Fuad II being temporarily proclaimed in his stead.

Franco (Bahamonde) Francisco 1892–1975. Spanish dictator from 1939. As a general, he led the insurgent Nationalists to victory in the Spanish Civil War 1936–39, supported by Fascist Italy and Nazi Germany, and established a dictatorship. In 1942 Franco reinstated the Cortes (Spanish parliament), which in 1947 passed an act by which he became head of state for life.

Gandhi Indira 1917–1984. Indian prime minister of India 1966–77 and 1980–84, and leader of the Congress Party 1966–77 and subsequently of the Congress (I) Party. She was assassinated by members of her Sikh bodyguard, resentful of her use of troops to clear malcontents from the Sikh temple at Amritsar.

Gandhi Mohandas Karamchand, called *Mahatma* ('Great Soul') 1869–1948. Indian nationalist leader. He was a pacifist, and led the struggle for Indian independence from the UK by nonviolent noncooperation (*satyagraha*, defence of and by truth) from 1915. He was several times imprisoned by the British authorities, and was influential in the nationalist Congress Party and in the independence negotiations 1947. He was assassinated by a Hindu nationalist in the violence which followed Partition.

Gandhi Rajiv 1944– . Indian politician. When his mother Indira Gandhi was assassinated Oct 1984, he was appointed Congress (I)

Party leader and prime minister.

Garibaldi Giuseppe 1807–1882. Italian soldier who played an important role in the unification of Italy by conquering Sicily and Naples 1860. From 1834 a member of the nationalist Mazzini's Young Italy society, he was forced into exile until 1848 and again 1849–54. He fought against Austria 1848–49, 1859, and 1866, and led two unsuccessful expeditions to liberate Rome from papal rule 1862 and 1867.

Giscard d'Estaing Valéry 1926– . French conservative politician, president 1974–81. He was finance minister to de Gaulle 1962–66 and Pompidou 1969–74. As leader of the Union pour la Démocratie Française, which he formed 1978, Giscard has sought to project himself as leader of a 'new centre'.

González Márquez Felipe 1942– . Spanish socialist politician, leader of the Socialist Workers' Party (PSOE), prime minister from 1982.

Gorbachev Mikhail Sergeevich 1931– . Soviet leader. He was a member of the Politburo from 1980 and, during the Chernenko administration 1984–85, was chairman of the Foreign Affairs Commission. As general secretary of the Communist Party (CPSU) from 1985, and president of the Supreme Soviet from 1988, he introduced liberal reforms at home and attempted to halt the arms race abroad.

Hawke Bob (Robert) 1929– . Australian Labor politician, on the right wing of the party. He was president of the Australian Council of Trade Unions 1970–80, and became prime minister 1983.

Heath Edward (Richard George) 1916– . British Conservative politician, party leader 1965–75. As prime minister 1970–74 he took the UK into the European Community, but was brought down by economic and industrial-relations crises at home.

Hitler Adolf 1889–1945. German Nazi dictator, born in Austria. *Führer* (leader) of the Nazi party from 1921, author of *Mein Kampf/My Struggle* 1925–27. Chancellor of Germany from 1933 and head of state from 1934, he created a dictatorship by playing party and state institutions against each other, and continually creating new offices and appointments. His position was not seriously challenged until the 'Bomb Plot' 20 Jul 1944. In foreign affairs, he reoccupied the Rhineland and formed an alliance with Mussolini 1936, annexed Austria 1938, and occupied Sudetenland under the Munich Agreement. The rest of Czechoslovakia was annexed Mar 1939. The Hitler-Stalin pact was followed in Sep by the invasion of Poland and the declaration of war by Britain and France. He committed suicide as Berlin fell.

Ho Chi Minh Adopted name of Nguyen That Tan 1892–1969. North Vietnamese Communist politician, president from 1954. He was trained in Moscow, and headed the communist Vietminh from 1941. Having campaigned against the French 1946–54, he became president and prime minister of the republic at the armistice. Aided by the communist bloc, he did much to develop industrial potential. He relinquished the premiership 1955, but continued as president.

Home Alec Douglas- , Baron Home of the Hirsel 1903– . British Conservative politician. He was foreign secretary 1960–63, and succeeded Macmillan as prime minister 1963. He renounced his peerage (as 14th Earl of Home) to fight (and lose) the general election of 1964, and resigned as party leader 1965. He was again foreign secretary 1970–74.

Honecker Erich 1912– . East German communist politician, in power from 1973, elected chairman of the council of state (head of state) 1976. He has governed in an austere and efficient manner and, while favouring East-West detente, has been a loyal ally of the USSR.

Hoxha Enver 1908–1985. Albanian politician, the country's leader from 1954. He founded the Albanian Communist Party 1941, and headed the liberation movement 1939–44. He was prime minister 1944–54, combining with foreign affairs 1946–53, and from 1954 was first secretary of the Albanian Party of Labour. In policy he was a Stalinist, and independent of both Chinese and Soviet communism.

Jayawardene Junius Richard 1906– . Sri Lankan politician. Leader of the United National Party from 1973, he became prime minister 1977, and the country's first president

1978–88.

Jinnah Muhammad Ali 1876–1948. Indian politician, Pakistan's first governor general from 1947. He became president of the Muslim League 1916 and from 1934 he was elected annually as president. He advised the UK government on the need for a separate state of Pakistan 1942, and at the 1946 conferences in London he insisted on the partition of British India into Hindu and Muslim states.

Johnson Lyndon (Baines) 1908–1973. 36th president of the USA 1963–69, a Democrat. He was elected to Congress 1937–49 and to the Senate 1949–60. He stood as vice president 1960, bringing crucial Southern votes to J F Kennedy, after whose assassination he succeeded as president. After the Tonkin Gulf Incident, the escalation of US involvement in the Vietnam War eventually dissipated the support won by his *Great Society* legislation (civil rights, education, alleviation of poverty), and he declined to stand for re-election 1968.

Kádár János 1912– . Hungarian Communist leader, in power 1956–88, after suppressing the national rising. As Hungarian Socialist Workers' Party (HSWP) leader and prime minister 1956–58 and 1961–65, Kádár introduced a series of market-socialist economic reforms, while retaining close political relations with the USSR.

Kaunda Kenneth (David) 1924– . Zambian politician. Imprisoned 1958–60 as founder of the Zambia African National Congress, he became in 1964 first prime minister of North Rhodesia, then first president of Zambia. In 1973 he introduced one-party rule. He supported the nationalist movement in Southern Rhodesia, now Zimbabwe, and survived a coup attempt 1980 thought to have been promoted by South Africa. He was elected chairman of the Organization of African Unity 1987.

Kennedy John F(itzgerald) 1917–1963. 35th president of the USA 1961–63, a Democrat. Kennedy was the first Roman Catholic and the youngest person to be elected president. In foreign policy he carried through the unsuccessful Bay of Pigs invasion of Cuba, and in 1963 secured the withdrawal of Soviet missiles from the island. His programme for reforms at home, called the ***New Frontier***, was posthumously executed by Lyndon Johnson. Kennedy was assassinated on a visit to Dallas.

Kenyatta Jomo. Assumed name of Kamau Ngengi c. 1889–1978. Kenyan nationalist politician, prime minister from 1963 as well as first president of Kenya from 1964 until his death. He led the Kenya African Union from 1947 (***KANU*** from 1963) and was active in liberating Kenya from British rule.

Khaddhafi or ***Gaddafi*** or ***Qaddafi***, Moamer al 1942– . Libyan revolutionary leader. Overthrowing King Idris 1969, he became virtual president of a republic, although he nominally gave up all except an ideological role 1974. He favours territorial expansion in N Africa reaching as far as Zaïre, has supported rebels in Chad, and proposed mergers with a number of countries. His theories, based on those of the Chinese communist leader Mao Zedong, are contained in a *Green Book*.

Khomeini Ayatollah Ruhollah 1900–1989. Iranian Shi'ite Muslim leader, born in Khomein, central Iran. Exiled for opposition to the Shah from 1964, he returned when the Shah left the country 1979, and established a fundamentalist Islamic republic. His rule was marked by a protracted war with Iraq, and suppression of opposition within Iran.

Khrushchev Nikita Sergeyevich 1894–1971. Soviet politician, secretary general of the Communist Party 1953–64, premier 1958–64. In 1956 he was the first official to denounce Stalin. A personal feud with Mao Zedong led to a breach in Soviet relations with China 1960. Khrushchev's foreign policy was one of peaceful coexistence with the West, marred by the crisis when he attempted to supply missiles to Cuba, and US pressure compelled their withdrawal 1962.

Kim Il Sung 1912– . North Korean communist politician and marshal. He became prime minister 1948 and president 1972, but retained the presidency of the Communist Workers' Party. Known as the 'Great Leader' he has campaigned constantly for the reunification of Korea. His son Kim Jong Il (1942–) known

as the 'Dear Leader', has been named as his successor.

King Martin Luther, Jr 1929–1968. US civil-rights campaigner, black leader, and Baptist minister. He first came to national attention as leader of the Montgomery, Alabama, bus boycott 1955, and was one of the organizers of the massive (200,000 people) march on Washington DC 1963 to demand racial equality. A passionate advocate of nonviolence, he was awarded the Nobel Peace Prize 1964. He was assassinated.

Kinnock Neil 1942– . British Labour politician. Born and educated in Wales, he became an MP in 1970. A noted orator, he was further left than prime ministers Wilson and Callaghan, but as party leader from 1983 (in succession to Michael Foot) adopted a more moderate position, initiating a major policy review 1988–89.

Kissinger Henry 1923– . German-born US diplomat. In 1969 he was appointed assistant for National Security Affairs by President Nixon, and was secretary of state 1973–77. His missions to the USSR and China improved US relations with both countries, and he took part in negotiating US withdrawal from Vietnam 1973 and in Arab-Israeli peace negotiations 1973–75. He shared the Nobel Peace Prize 1973.

Kohl Helmut 1930– . West German conservative politician, leader of the Christian Democratic Union (CDU) from 1976, and chancellor from 1982.

Lange David (Russell) 1942– . New Zealand Labour Party prime minister, party leader from 1983. Labour had a decisive win in the 1984 general election on a non-nuclear defence policy, which Lange immediately put into effect, despite criticism from other Western countries, particularly the USA. He was re-elected 1987.

Lee Kuan Yew 1923– . Singapore politician, prime minister from 1959. Lee founded the anti-communist Socialist People's Action Party 1954 and entered the Singapore legislative assembly 1955. He was elected the country's first prime minister 1959, and took Singapore out of the Malaysian federation 1965.

Lenin Vladimir Ilyich. Adopted name of Vladimir Ilyich Ulyanov 1870–1924. Soviet communist politician and theoretician. Active in the 1905 Revolution, Lenin had to leave Russia when it failed, settling in Switzerland 1914. He returned to Russia after the February revolt in the Russian Revolution. In Nov he became leader of a Soviet government, concluded peace with Germany, and organized a successful resistance to White (pro-tsarist) uprisings and foreign intervention. His modification of traditional Marxist doctrine to fit the objective conditions prevailing in Russia became known as Marxism-Leninism, the basis of communist ideology.

Lincoln Abraham 1809–1865. 16th president of the USA 1861–65. In the US Civil War, his chief concern was the preservation of the Union from which the Confederate (Southern) slave states had seceded on his election. In 1863 he announced the freedom of the slaves with the *Emancipation Proclamation*. He was re-elected 1864 with victory for the North in sight, but was assassinated at the end of the war.

Lloyd George David, 1st Earl Lloyd-George 1863–1945. Welsh Liberal politician, prime minister 1916–22. As chancellor of the Exchequer 1908–15 he introduced old-age pensions 1908 and health and unemployment insurance 1911. High unemployment, intervention in the Russian Civil War, and use of the Black and Tans in Ireland eroded his support as prime minister, and creation of the Irish Free State 1921 and his pro-Greek policy against the Turks caused the collapse of his coalition government.

Lumumba Patrice 1926–1961. Congolese politician, prime minister of Zaïre 1960. Imprisoned by the Belgians, but released in time to attend the conference giving the Congo independence 1960, he led the National Congolese Movement to victory in the subsequent general election. He was deposed in a coup d'état, and murdered some months later.

MacDonald (James) Ramsay 1866–1937. British Labour politician. He joined the Independent Labour Party 1894, and became first secretary of the new Labour Party 1900. In Parliament he led the party 1906–14 and 1922–31, and was prime minister of the first two Labour governments, Jan–Oct 1924 and 1929–31, and of a coalition 1931–35, for which he left the party.

Machel Samora 1933–1986. Mozambique nationalist leader, president 1975–86. Machel was active in the liberation front Frelimo from its conception 1962, fighting for independence from Portugal. He became Frelimo leader 1966, and Mozambique's first president, from independence until his death in a plane crash near the South African border.

Macmillan (Maurice) Harold, 1st Earl of Stockton 1894–1986. British Conservative politician. He became prime minister 1957 on Eden's resignation after the Suez crisis. At home, he furthered domestic expansion. Internationally, he attempted unsuccessfully to negotiate British entry to the European Community, and encouraged the transition to independence of British colonies in Africa.

Makarios III 1913–1977. Cypriot politician, Greek Orthodox archbishop 1950–77. A leader of the Resistance organization EOKA, he was exiled by the British to the Seychelles 1956–57 for supporting armed action to achieve union with Greece (*enosis*). He was president of the republic of Cyprus 1960–77 (briefly deposed by a Greek military coup Jul–Dec 1974).

Mandela Nelson (Rolihlahla) 1918– . South African politician and lawyer. As organizer of the banned African National Congress (ANC), he was acquitted of treason 1961, but was jailed for life 1964 on charges of sabotage and plotting to overthrow the government. In prison he has become a symbol of unity for the anti-apartheid movement. There is strong international pressure to end his incarceration.

Manley Michael 1924– . Jamaican politician, prime minister 1972–80 and from 1989, adopting more moderate socialist policies.

Mao Zedong formerly *Mao Tse-tung* 1893–1976. Chinese political leader and marxist theoretician. A founder of the Chinese Communist Party (CCP) 1921, Mao soon emerged as its leader. He organized the Long March 1934–36 and the war of liberation 1937–49, and headed the CCP and government until his death. His influence diminished with the failure of his 1958–60 Great Leap Forward, but he emerged dominant again during the 1966–69 Cultural Revolution. Mao adapted communism to Chinese conditions, as popularly set out in the *Little Red Book*.

Marcos Ferdinand 1919– . Filipino rightwing politician, president 1965–86, when he was forced into exile. He was backed by the USA when in power, but in 1988 US authorities indicted him for racketeering and embezzlement.

Mazzini Giuseppe 1805–1872. Italian nationalist. He was a member of the revolutionary society, the Carbonari, and founded in exile the nationalist movement *Giovane Italia/Young Italy* 1832. Returning to Italy on the outbreak of the 1848 revolution, he headed a republican government established in Rome, but was forced into exile again on its overthrow 1849. He acted as a focus for the movement for Italian unity.

Meir Golda 1898–1978. Israeli Labour (*Mapai*) politician, born in Russia. She was foreign minister 1956–66 and prime minister 1969–74, resigning after criticism of the Israelis' lack of preparation for the 1973 Arab-Israeli War.

Mitterrand François 1916– . French socialist politician, president from 1981. He held ministerial posts in 11 governments between 1947–1958. He founded the French Socialist Party (PS) 1971. In 1985 he introduced proportional representation, allegedly to weaken the growing opposition from left and right.

Mobutu Seso-Seko-Kuku-Ngbeandu-Wa-Za-Banga 1930– . Zaïrean politician, president from 1965. He assumed the presidency by coup, and created a unitary state under his centralized government. The harshness of some of President Mobutu's policies has attracted widespread international criticism of Zaïre. In 1983 amnesty was offered to all political exiles. Mobutu was re-elected for a third term 1984.

Moi Daniel arap 1924– . Kenyan politician, president from 1978. He became minister of home affairs 1964, vice president 1967, and succeeded Kenyatta as president.

Mugabe Robert (Gabriel) 1925– . Zimbabwe politician, prime minister from 1980 and president from 1987. He was in detention in Rhodesia for nationalist activities 1964–74, then carried on guerrilla warfare from Mozambique. As leader of ZANU he was in alliance with Joshua Nkomo of ZAPU from 1976, and the two parties merged 1987.

Mulroney Brian 1939– . Canadian politician. He replaced Joe Clark as Progressive Conservative party leader 1983, and achieved a landslide in the 1984 election to become prime minister. He won the 1988 election on a platform of free trade with the USA, but with a reduced majority.

Mussolini Benito 1883–1945. Italian dictator 1925–43. As founder of the Fascist Movement 1919 and prime minister from 1922, he became known as *Il Duce* 'the leader'. He invaded Ethiopia 1935–36, intervened in the Spanish Civil War 1936–39 in support of Franco, and conquered Albania 1939. In Jun 1940 Italy entered World War II supporting Hitler. Forced by military and domestic setbacks to resign 1943, Mussolini established a breakaway government in N Italy 1944–45, but was killed trying to flee the country.

Nakasone Yasuhiro 1917– . Japanese conservative politician, leader of the Liberal Democratic Party (LDP) and prime minister 1982–87. He stepped up military spending and increased Japanese participation in international affairs, with closer ties to the USA. His reputation was tarnished by his involvement in the 'Recruit' insider trading scandal.

Napoleon III 1808–1873. Emperor of the French 1852–70, known as *Louis-Napoleon*. After two attempted coups (1836 and 1840) he was jailed and went into exile, returning for the revolution of 1848, when he became president of the Second Republic, but soon turned authoritarian. He had military victories in Europe but in Mexico sponsored the unsuccessful Maximilian. In 1870 he was manoeuvred by the German chancellor into war with Prussia, and was forced to surrender at Sedan, NE France, whereupon the empire collapsed.

Nasser Gamal Abdel 1918–1970. Egyptian politician, prime minister 1954–56 and from 1956 president of Egypt (the United Arab Republic 1958–71). In 1952 he was the driving power behind the Neguib coup, which ended the monarchy. His nationalization of the Suez Canal 1956 and his ambitions for an Egyptian-led Arab union led to disquiet in the Middle East (and in the West).

Ne Win 1911– . Burmese nationalist socialist politician. A general, he was prime minister 1958–60 and, after a military coup 1962, effectively ruled the country until 1988, pursuing an isolationist foreign policy.

Nehru Jawaharlal 1889–1964. Indian nationalist politician, prime minister from 1947. Before partition he led the socialist wing of the Congress Party, and was second in influence only to Mahatma Gandhi. He was imprisoned nine times 1921–45 for political activities. As prime minister from the creation of the dominion (later republic) of India Aug 1947, he originated the idea of nonalignment. His daughter was Indira Gandhi.

Nixon Richard (Milhous) 1913– . 37th president of the USA 1969–74, a Republican. He attracted attention as a member of the Un-American Activities Committee 1948, and was vice president to Eisenhower 1953–61. As president he was responsible for US withdrawal from Vietnam, and forged new links with China, but at home his culpability in the cover-up of the Watergate scandal and the existence of a 'slush fund' for political machinations during his re-election campaign 1972 led to his resignation 1974 after being threatened with impeachment.

Nkrumah Kwame 1909–1972. Ghanaian nationalist politician, prime minister of the Gold Coast 1952–57 and of independent Ghana 1957–60, and Ghana's first president 1960–66. His policy of 'African socialism' led to links with the communist bloc.

Nyerere Julius (Kambarage) 1922– . Tanzanian socialist politician, president 1964–85. From 1954 he devoted himself to the formation of the Tanganyika African National Union and subsequent campaigning for independence. He became chief minister 1960, was prime minister of Tanganyika 1961–62, president of the newly formed Tanganyika Republic 1962–64, first president of Tanzania 1964–85, and head

of the Organization of African Unity 1984.

Obote (Apollo) Milton 1924– . Ugandan politician who led the independence movement from 1961. He became prime minister 1962 and was president 1966–71 and 1980–85, being overthrown first by Idi Amin, and then by Tito Okello.

Ortega (Saavedra) Daniel 1945– . Nicaraguan socialist politician, a member of the Sandinista Liberation Front (FSLN) which overthrew the regime of Anastasio Somoza 1979, and head of state from 1981.

Palme (Sven) Olof 1927–1986. Swedish social-democratic politician. He entered government 1963, holding several posts before becoming leader of the Social Democratic Labour Party (SD) and prime minister 1969–76 and 1982–86. He was assassinated.

Pérez de Cuellar Javier 1920– . Peruvian diplomat. A delegate to the first United Nations general assembly 1946–47, he held several ambassadorial posts and was appointed secretary-general of the UN 1982.

Perón Juan (Domingo) 1895–1974. Argentine politician, dictator 1946–55 and from 1973. He took part in the military pro-fascist coup 1943, and his popularity with the *descamisados*, 'shirtless ones', led to his election as president 1946. He lost popularity after the death of his second wife Eva Perón, and was deposed 1955, but returned from exile to the presidency 1973. He was succeeded by his third wife Isobel Perón.

Pinochet (Ugarte) Augusto 1915– . Military ruler of Chile from 1973, when a CIA-backed coup ousted and killed president Salvador Allende. Pinochet took over the presidency and ruled ruthlessly, crushing all opposition.

Primo de Rivera Miguel 1870–1930. Spanish soldier and politician, dictator from 1923 as well as premier from 1925. He was captain-general of Catalonia when he led a coup against the ineffective monarchy and became virtual dictator of Spain with the support of Alfonso XIII. He resigned 1930.

Ramphal Shridath Surendranath ('Sonny') 1928– . Guyanese politician. He was minister

51

of foreign affairs and justice in Guyana 1972–75, and became secretary-general of the Commonwealth 1975.

Reagan Ronald 1911– . US Republican politician, governor of California 1966–74, president 1981–89. A former Hollywood actor, Reagan was an assertive and popular president. He introduced deregulation of domestic markets and withstood criticism of his interventionist foreign policy, but failed to confront a mounting trade deficit.

Roh Tae-woo 1932–. South Korean right-wing politician and general. He held ministerial office from 1981 under President Chun, and became chairman of the ruling Democratic Justice Party 1985. He was elected president 1987, amid allegations of fraud and despite being connected with the massacre of about 2,000 anti-government demonstrators 1980.

Roosevelt Franklin Delano 1882–1945. 32nd president of the USA 1933–45, a Democrat. He served as governor of New York 1929–33. Becoming president amid the Depression, he launched the *New Deal* economic and social reform programme, which made him popular with the people. After the outbreak of World War II he introduced lend-lease for the supply of war materials to the Allies and drew up the Atlantic Charter of solidarity, and once the USA had entered the war 1941 he spent much time in meetings with Allied leaders.

Sadat Anwar 1918–1981. Egyptian politician. Succeeding Nasser as president 1970, he restored morale by his handling of the Egyptian campaign in the 1973 war against Israel. In 1974 his plan for economic, social, and political reform to transform Egypt was unanimously adopted in a referendum. In 1977 he visited Israel to reconcile the two countries, and shared the Nobel Peace Prize with Menachem Begin 1978. He was assassinated by Islamic fundamentalists.

Salazar Antonio de Oliveira 1889–1970. Portuguese prime minister 1932–68, exercising a virtual dictatorship. A corporative constitution on the Italian model was introduced 1933, and until 1945 Salazar's National Union, founded 1930, remained the only legal party. Salazar was

also foreign minister 1936–47, and during World War II maintained Portuguese neutrality.

Sarney José 1930– . President of Brazil from 1985, member of Brazilian Democratic Movement (PMDB).

Schmidt Helmut 1918– . West German socialist politician, member of the Social Democratic Party (SPD), chancellor 1974–83. As chancellor, Schmidt introduced social reforms and continued Brandt's policy of Ostpolitik. With the French president Giscard d'Estaing, Schmidt introduced annual world and European economic summits. He was a firm supporter of NATO and of the deployment of US nuclear missiles in West Germany during the early 1980s.

Shamir Yitzhak 1915– . Israeli politician, born in Poland; foreign minister under Menachem Begin 1980–83, prime minister 1983–84, and again foreign minister in the Peres unity government from 1984. In Oct 1986, he and Peres exchanged positions, Shamir becoming prime minister and Peres taking over as foreign minister. He was re-elected at the head of a Likud-Labour coalition 1989.

Stalin Adopted name of Joseph Vissarionovich Djugashvili 1879–1953. Soviet politician. A member of the October Revolution Committee 1917, Stalin became General Secretary of the Communist party 1922. After Lenin's death 1924, Stalin sought to create 'socialism in one country' and clashed with Trotsky, who denied the possibility of socialism inside Russia until revolution had occurred in W Europe. Stalin won this ideological struggle by 1927, and a series of five-year plans was launched to collectivize industry and agriculture from 1928. All opposition was eliminated by the Great Purge 1936–38 by which Stalin disposed of all real and fancied enemies. During World War II, Stalin intervened in the military direction of the campaigns against Nazi Germany.

Stroessner Alfredo 1912– . Military leader and president of Paraguay 1954–89. Accused by his opponents of harsh repression, his regime spent heavily on the military in order to preserve his authority. He was overthrown by a military coup and gained asylum in Brazil.

Suharto Raden 1921– . Indonesian politician and general. He ousted Sukarno to become president 1967. He ended confrontation with Malaysia, invaded E Timor 1975, and reached a cooperation agreement with Papua New Guinea 1979. His authoritarian rule has met domestic opposition from the left. He was re-elected 1973, 1978, 1983, and 1988.

Sukarno Achmed 1901–1970. Indonesian nationalist, president 1945–67. During World War II he cooperated in the local administration set up by the Japanese, replacing Dutch rule. After the war he became the first president of the new Indonesian republic, becoming president-for-life 1966; he was ousted by Suharto.

Tambo Oliver 1917– . South African nationalist politician, in exile from 1960, president of the African National Congress (ANC) from 1977.

U Thant 1909–1974. Burmese diplomat, secretary-general of the United Nations 1962–71. He helped to resolve the US-Soviet crisis over the Soviet installation of missiles in Cuba, and he made the controversial decision to withdraw the UN peacekeeping force from the Egypt–Israel border 1967.

Thatcher Margaret Hilda 1925– . British Conservative politician, in Parliament from 1959, party leader from 1975, and prime minister from 1979. Landmarks of the Thatcher government include the Falklands war; the 1984–85 miners' strike; large-scale privatization; the attempt to suppress the publication of *Spycatcher* and other measures to limit civil liberties; the Anglo-Irish Agreement 1985; and rises in unemployment, inflation, interest rates, trade deficit, and homelessness.

Tito Adopted name of Josip Broz 1892–1980. Yugoslav soldier and communist politician. In World War II he organized the National Liberation Army to carry on guerrilla warfare against the German invasion 1941, and was created marshal 1943. As prime minister 1946–53 and president from 1953, he followed a foreign policy of 'positive neutralism'.

Trotsky Leon. Adopted name of Lev Davidovitch Bronstein 1879–1940. Russian revolutionary. He joined the Bolshevik party and took a leading part in the seizure of power and raising the Red Army which fought the Civil War 1918–20. In the struggle for power that followed Lenin's death 1924, Stalin defeated him, and this and other differences with the Communist Party led to his exile 1929. Trotsky settled in Mexico, where he was assassinated with an ice pick, possibly at Stalin's instigation. Trotsky believed in world revolution and in permanent revolution and was an uncompromising, if liberal, idealist.

Trudeau Pierre (Elliott) 1919– . Canadian Liberal politician. He was prime minister 1968–79 and won again by a landslide Feb 1980. In 1980 he defeated the Québec independence movement in a referendum and gained control over the constitution 1982, but by 1984 had so lost support that he resigned.

Truman Harry S 1884–1972. 33rd president of the USA 1945–53, a Democrat. In Jan 1945 he became vice president to F D Roosevelt, and president when Roosevelt died in Apr that year. He used the atom bombs against Japan, launched the Marshall Plan to restore W Europe's economy, and nurtured the European Community and NATO (including the rearmament of West Germany).

Tutu Desmond (Mpilo) 1931– . South African priest, Anglican archbishop of Johannesburg and general secretary of the South African Council of Churches. He is one of the leading figures in the struggle against apartheid in the Republic of South Africa. Nobel Peace Prize 1984.

Ulbricht Walter 1893–1973. East German politician. After exile in the USSR during Hitler's rule, he became first secretary of the Socialist Unity Party in East Germany 1950 and (as chairman of the Council of State 1960–73) was instrumental in the building of the Berlin Wall 1961. He established East Germany's economy and recognition outside the E European bloc.

Waldheim Kurt 1918– . Austrian politician and diplomat. He was secretary general of the United Nations 1972–81, having been Austria's representative there 1964–68 and 1970–71. In 1986 he was elected president of Austria, but his tenure of office was clouded by allegations that during World War II he had been an intelligence officer in an army unit responsible for transporting Jews to death camps.

Walesa Lech 1947– . Polish trade-union leader, founder of Solidarity 1980, which forced substantial political and economic concessions from the Polish government 1980–81 until being outlawed. In 1989 he negotiated a historic agreement with the Polish government, which legalized Solidarity, and set in place a new 'socialist pluralist' political structure. Nobel Peace Prize 1983.

Weizmann Chaim 1874–1952. Zionist leader, born in Russia, who became a naturalized British subject. He conducted the negotiations leading up to the *Balfour Declaration*. He was the first president of the new republic of Israel 1948–52.

Wilson (James) Harold, Baron Wilson of Rievaulx 1916– . British Labour politician, prime minister 1964–70 and 1974–76. His premiership was dominated by the issue of UK admission to EEC membership, the social contract (unofficial agreement with the trade unions), and economic difficulties.

Wilson (Thomas) Woodrow 1856–1924. 28th president of the USA 1913–21, a Democrat. He kept the USA out of World War I until 1917, and in Jan 1918 issued his Fourteen Points as a basis for a just peace settlement. At the peace conference in Paris he secured the inclusion of the League of Nations in individual peace treaties, but these were not ratified by Congress, so the USA did not join the League. Nobel Peace prize 1919.

Zhao Ziyang 1918– . Chinese politician, a member of the Politburo from 1977, prime minister from 1980, and secretary of the Chinese Communist Party (CCP) from 1987. He introduced an economic programme based on self-management and material incentives for workers and factories. He was dismissed 1989 for his liberal views concerning the pro-democracy demonstrations in Beijing ruthlessly crushed by the Chinese authorities.

Zia ul-Haq Mohammad 1924–1988. Pakistani general, in power from 1977 until his assassination. He was a career soldier from a middle-class Punjabi Muslim family, and became army chief of staff 1976. He led the military coup against Zulfiqar Ali Bhutto 1977 and became president 1978. Zia introduced a fundamentalist Islamic regime and restricted political activity.

Economics

Economics seeks to understand how, in a given society, choices are made on the allocation of resources to produce goods and services for consumption, and what mechanisms and principles govern this process. It seeks to apply scientific method to construct theories about the economic process and to test them against what actually happens. Within this broad framework, economics has two central concerns: the efficient allocation of available resources, and the problem of reconciling finite resources with a virtually infinite desire for goods and services. Economics investigates efficient allocation by analysing the ingredients of economic efficiency in the production process, and the implications for practical policies. The economic problem of reconciling scarce resources (for all resources are by definition scarce unless they cost nothing, which virtually nothing does) and limitless demand is studied by examining the conflicting demands and the consequences of whatever choices are made, whether by individuals, enterprises, or governments. Crucial to economics is the concept of opportunity cost, which defines the cost of a particular choice not in terms of money but rather in terms of the value of those options not chosen.

This section contains an introduction to the major *Spheres of Economics*, brief biographies of some of the *Great Economists*, an outline of some important *Economic Institutions*, and short definitions of *Terms*.

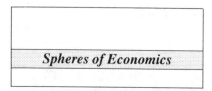

Spheres of Economics

divisions of economics the subject is usually divided into the disciplines of *microeconomics*, studying individual producers, consumers or markets, and *macroeconomics*, studying whole economies or systems. These spheres often overlap, but in practice it is useful to distinguish between the two main levels at which economic phenomena are studied.

Straddling both spheres is the sub-discipline of *econometrics*, which analyses economic relationships using mathematical and statistical techniques. Increasingly sophisticated econometric methods are today being used for such topics as economic forecasting.

Economics aims to be either *positive*, presenting objective and scientific explanations of how an economy works, or *normative*, offering prescriptions and recommendations on what should be done to cure perceived ills. However, it is important to remember that however objective the aim, value judgements are usually involved when economists present particular formulations.

microeconomics the study of individual decision-making units within an economy: a consumer, firm, or industry. It looks at how individual markets work and how individual producers and consumers make their choices and with what consequences. This is done by analysing how relevant prices of goods are determined and the quantities that will be bought and sold.

The operation of the market is therefore a central concern of microeconomics. For simplicity, microeconomics begins by analysing a market in which there is perfect *competition*, a theoretical state which exists only when no individual producer or consumer can influence the market price. In the real world, there is always imperfect competition for various reasons (monopoly practices, barriers to trade, and so on), and microeconomics examines what effect these have on wages and prices.

Underlying these and other concerns of microeconomics is the concept of *optimality*, first advanced by Vilfredo Pareto in the 19th century. Pareto's perception of the most efficient state of an economy, as being when there is no scope to reallocate resources without making someone worse off, has been extremely influential.

macroeconomics the study of whole (aggregate) economies or systems, including such aspects as government income and expenditure, the balance of payments, fiscal policy, inflation, and unemployment. It seeks to understand the influence of all relevant economic factors on each other and thus to quantify and predict aggregate national income.

Modern macroeconomics takes much of its inspiration from the work of Keynes, whose *The General Theory of Employment, Interest and Money* 1936 proposed that governments could prevent financial crises and unemployment by adjusting demand through control of credit and currency. *Keynesian macroeconomics* thus analyses aggregate supply and demand and holds that markets, especially the labour market, do not continuously 'clear' (quickly attain equilibrium between supply and demand) and may require intervention if objectives such as full employment are thought desirable.

Keynesian macroeconomic formulations were generally accepted well into the post-war era and have been refined and extended by the *neo-Keynesian* school, which contends that in a recession the market will clear only very slowly and that full employment equilibrium may never return without significant demand management (by government). At the same time, however, *neo-classical* economics has experienced a recent resurgence, using microeconomic tools to challenge the central Keynesian assumption that resources may be under-employed and that full employment equilibrium requires state intervention.

Another important school is **new classical** economics, which seeks to show the futility of Keynesian demand management policies and stresses instead the importance of **supply-side economics**, believing that the principal factor influencing growth of national output is the efficient allocation and use of labour and capital. A related school is that of the **Chicago monetarists** led by Milton Friedman, who have revived the old idea that an increase in money supply leads inevitably to an increase in prices rather than in output; however, whereas the new classical school contends that wage and price adjustment is almost instantaneous and so the level of employment at any time must be the natural rate, the Chicago monetarists are more gradualist, believing that such adjustment may take some years.

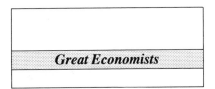

Great Economists

Friedman Milton 1912– . American economist, professor of economics at the University of Chicago since 1948, and Nobel prizewinner 1976. The foremost exponent of monetarism, he argues that a country's economy, and hence inflation, can be controlled through its money supply, although governments lack the 'political will' to control inflation by cutting government spending and thereby increasing unemployment.

Galbraith John Kenneth 1908– . Canadian political economist whose major works include *The Affluent Society* 1958 and *Economics and the Public Purpose* 1974. In the former he argued that advanced industrialized societies like the USA were suffering from private affluence accompanied by public squalor.

Keynes John Maynard, 1st Baron Keynes 1883–1946. British economist, whose *The General Theory of Employment, Interest, and Money* 1936, proposed the prevention of financial crises and unemployment by adjusting demand through government control of credit and currency. Keynes is regarded as the most important economist of the 20th century, responsible for that part of economics now known as macroeconomics. His ideas are today often contrasted with those of monetarism.

Lucas Robert 1937– . US economist, leader of the Chicago University school of new classical macroeconomics which contends that wage and price adjustment is almost instantaneous and that the level of unemployment at any time must be the natural rate (it cannot be reduced by government action except in the short term and at the cost of increasing inflation).

Malthus Thomas Robert 1766–1834. British cleric and economist, whose *Essay on the Principle of Population* 1798 and 1803 argued for population control, since people increase in geometric ratio, and food only in arithmetical ratio. He later suggested 'moral restraints' (delaying marriage and sexual abstinence before it) could keep numbers from increasing too quickly, a statement seized on by later birth-control pioneers (the 'neo-Malthusians').

Marshall Alfred 1842–1924. British economist, professor of economy at Cambridge University 1885–1908. A founder of neo-classical economics, he stressed the power of supply and demand to generate equilibrium prices in markets, introducing the concept of elasticity of demand relative to price. His *Principles of Economics* 1890 remains perhaps the most influential textbook of neo-classical economics.

Marx Karl Heinrich 1818–83. German philosopher, economist and social theorist, whose philosophical system, also known as 'dialectical materialism', proposes that social and political institutions progressively change their nature as economic developments transform material conditions, so that the succession of feudalism, capitalism, and socialism is inevitable. His three-volume *Das Kapital/Capital* 1867–94 is the fundamental text in Marxist economics.

Pareto Vilfredo 1848–1923. Italian economist and political philosopher. He produced the first account of society as a self-regulating and interdependent system which operates independently of human attempts at voluntary control. A founder of welfare economics, he put forward a concept of optimality which contends that optimum conditions exist in an economic system if no one can be made better off without at least one other person becoming worse off. A vigorous opponent of socialism and liberalism, Pareto justified inequality of income on the grounds of his empirical observation (Pareto's law) that income distribution remained constant whatever efforts were made to change it.

Pigou Arthur Cecil 1877–1959. British economist whose notion of the 'real balance effect' (the 'Pigou effect') contended that employment was stimulated by a fall in prices, because the latter increased liquid wealth and thus demand for goods and services.

Ricardo David 1772–1823. British economist, widely regarded as the greatest of the classical economists after Adam Smith. After making a fortune on the London Stock Exchange, he published in 1817 *Principles of Political Economy*, in which 'laws' of rent, value, and wages, long generally accepted, were clearly enunciated, including the important concept of comparative advantage (that countries can benefit by specializing in goods they produce most efficiently and trading internationally to buy others). Ricardo was one of the first to state the law of diminishing returns – that continued increments of capital and labour applied to a given quantity of land will eventually show a declining rate of increase in output.

Schumpeter Joseph A(lois) 1883–1950. Vienna-born US economist and sociologist. In *Capitalism, Socialism and Democracy* 1942 he contended that Western capitalism, impelled by its very success, was evolving into a form of socialism because firms would become increasingly large and their managements increasingly divorced from ownership, while

social trends were undermining the traditional motives for entrepreneurial accumulation of wealth.

Smith Adam 1723–90. Scottish economist and philosopher, regarded as the founder of modern political economy. His *The Wealth of Nations* 1776 defined national wealth in terms of labour, as the only real measure of value, which is expressed in terms of wages. The cause of wealth is explained by the division of labour – dividing a production process into several repetitive operations, each carried out by different workers. Smith advocated the free working of individual enterprise, and especially the necessity of 'free trade' rather than the protection offered by the mercantile system.

Walras Léon 1834–1910. French economist, first holder of the chair of political economy at Lausanne University (Switzerland). In his *Éléments d'économie politique pure* 1874–77, he made a pioneering attempt to develop a unified model for general equilibrium theory (a hypothetical situation in which demands equal supply in all markets). He also originated the theory of marginal utility of a good (the increased value to a person of consuming some more of a product).

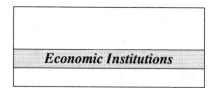

Economic Institutions

Bank of England UK central bank originally founded by Act of Parliament in 1694. It was entrusted with note issue in 1844, and nationalized in 1946. Known by its London site as the 'Old Lady of Threadneedle Street', it is banker to the UK government and assists in implementing the latter's financial and monetary policies.

Brandt Commission officially the Independent Commission on International Development Issues, established in 1977 under the chairmanship of former West German chancellor Willy Brandt. Consisting of 18 eminent persons acting independently of governments, the Commission examined the problems of developing countries in the world economic system and sought to identify corrective measures that would command international support. Its main report, published in 1980 under the title *North-South: A Programme for Survival*, made detailed recommendations for accelerating the development of poorer countries (involving the transfer of resources to the latter from the rich countries). Little government action was taken on the report, however, and the Commission was disbanded in 1983, after producing a second report called *Common Crisis*.

Comecon *(Council for Mutual Economic Co-operation)* established in 1949 in opposition to the Marshall Plan, links the USSR with Bulgaria, Czechoslovakia, Hungary, Poland, Romania, East Germany (from 1950), Mongolia (from 1962), Cuba (from 1972) and Vietnam (from 1978), with Yugoslavia as an associated member. It seeks to promote economic co-operation and development, but has no real central organization and no free trade between members.

European Community an organization which comprises the European Coal and Steel Community 1952; European Atomic Energy Community/Euratom 1957; and European Economic Community/EEC/popularly 'Common Market', both the last-named created under the two *Treaties of Rome* signed there March 1957. Since 1967 they have shared the institutions of the *Commission,* which initiates action (president Jacques Delors from 1986); the Council of Ministers, which decides on the Commission's proposals (both with headquarters in Brussels); *European Parliament*; and *European Court of Justice* (headquarters Luxembourg), which interprets the Rome Treaties. Original members were Belgium, France, West Germany, Italy, Luxembourg, Netherlands; subsequently Denmark, Republic of Ireland, UK 1973 (Norway withdrew its application 1972); Greece 1981; Spain and Portugal 1986.

European Free Trade Association an organization established 1960, currently consisting of Austria, Finland, Iceland, Norway, Sweden, and Switzerland. There are no import duties between members. Of the original members, Britain and Denmark left (end 1972) to join the European Community, as subsequently did Portugal (end 1985).

Federal Reserve System *(Fed)* US central banking system and note issue authority, established in 1913 to regulate the country's credit and monetary affairs and to contribute to its economic well being. The Fed consists of the twelve federal reserve banks and their 25 branches and other facilities throughout the country; it is headed by a board of governors in Washington, appointed by the US President with Senate approval.

International Monetary Fund *(IMF)* specialized agency of the United Nations, established under the 1944 Bretton-Woods agreement and operational since 1947. It seeks to promote international monetary co-operation, the growth of world trade and smooth multilateral payments arrangements among member states. IMF stand-by loans are available to members in balance-of-payments difficulties (the amount being governed by the member's quota), usually on the basis of acceptance of instruction on necessary corrective measures. The Fund also operates other drawing facilities, including several designed to provide preferential credit to developing countries with liquidity problems. Having previously operated in US dollars linked to gold, since 1972 the IMF has used the special drawing right (SDR) as its standard unit of account, valued in terms of a weighted 'basket' of major currencies. Since the 1971 Smithsonian agreement permitting wider fluctuations from specified currency parities, IMF rules have been progressively adapted to the increasing prevalence of fully floating-exchange rates.

Organization for Economic Co-operation and Development *(OECD)* Paris-based intergovernmental organization of 24 industrialized countries active in co-ordinating member states' economic policy strategies. It superseded the Organization for European Economic Co-operation (established 1948 to promote European recovery under the Marshall Plan) in 1961, when the USA and Canada became members and its scope was extended to include development aid. The OECD's subsidiary bodies include the International Energy Agency, set up in 1974 in the face of a world oil crisis.

Organization of the Petroleum Exporting Countries *(OPEC)* 13–nation body established in 1960 to co-ordinate the price and supply policies of oil-producing states. Its concerted action in raising crude oil prices sharply in the 1970s triggered worldwide recession, and generated huge revenues for OPEC members, some of these sums being donated or recycled to poorer developing countries. In the 1980s OPEC's dominant position was undermined by reduced demand for oil in industrialized countries and by rising non-OPEC production, notably from the North Sea. These factors and others caused a sharp fall in world oil prices, forcing OPEC to institute production cutbacks.

Paris Club an international forum dating from the 1950s for the rescheduling of debts granted or guaranteed by official bilateral creditors; it has no fixed membership nor an institutional structure. In the 1980s it has been closely involved in seeking solutions to the major debt crisis affecting many developing countries.

Securities and Exchange Commission *(SEC)* official US agency created in 1934 to ensure full disclosure to the investing public and protection against malpractice in the securities and financial markets (such as insider trading).

Stock Exchange institution for the buying and selling of stocks and shares (securities). London's is the oldest stock exchange, opened 1801. The former division between brokers (who bought shares from jobbers to sell to the public) and jobbers (who sold them only to brokers on commission, the 'jobbers' turn') was abolished in 1986. The major stock

exchanges are London, New York (Wall Street) and Tokyo.

World Bank popular name for the *International Bank for Reconstruction and Development*, established in 1945 under the 1944 Bretton-Woods agreement which also created the International Monetary Fund. The World Bank is a specialized agency of the United Nations which borrows in the commercial market and lends on commercial terms. The International Development Association is an arm of the World Bank.

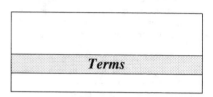

Terms

balance of payments the difference between debits and credits in the buying and selling of goods and services between one country and other countries (usually the rest of the world). A balance-of-payments crisis usually means that more is leaving the country (in paying for imports) than is coming in (in payments for exports).

bank a financial institution which uses funds deposited with it to extend loans to companies or individuals, and also provides financial services to its customers. A central bank issues currency for the government, in order to provide cash for circulation and exchange.

big bang popular term for the major changes instituted in late 1986 to the organization and practices of the City of London as Britain's financial centre. Facilitated in part by computerization and on-line communications, the changes included ending the distinction between jobbers and brokers on the Stock Exchange, allowing non-members of the Stock Exchange to own member firms and opening up the charging of commissions to competition.

capital commonly signifies accumulated or inherited wealth held in the form of assets (such as stocks and shares, property, and bank deposits); in economics, capital is defined as the stock of goods (themselves produced) used in the production of other goods, and may be fixed capital (such as plant and machinery) or circulating capital (raw materials and components). The creation of all forms of capital requires the forgoing of consumption at some point.

comparative advantage law of international trade first elaborated by David Ricardo showing that trade becomes advantageous if the cost of production of particular items differs as between one country and another. At a simple level, if wine is cheaper to produce in country A than in country B, and the reverse is true of cheese, A can specialize in wine and B in cheese and they can trade to mutual benefit.

consumption the purchasing and using of goods and services. In economics, it means the total expenditure, in a given economy and over a given period, on goods and services (including expenditure on raw materials). In Britain consumption accounts for about 80 per cent of the national income, the remainder going to investment.

cost of living the cost of goods and services needed for an average standard of living. In Britain the first cost-of-living index was introduced in 1914 and based on the expenditure of a working-class family of man, woman, and three children; the standard is 100. Known from 1947 as the Retail Price Index (RPI), it is revised to allow for inflation, etc. Supplementary are the Consumer's Expenditure Deflator (formerly Consumer Price Index) and the Tax and Price Index (TPI).

crawling peg also known as a 'sliding party', a method of achieving a desired adjustment in a currency exchange rate (up or down) by small percentages over a given period, rather than by a major one-off revaluation or devaluation.

credit means by which goods or services are obtained without immediate payment. The three main forms are *consumer credit* (usually extended to individuals by retailers), *bank credit* (such as overdrafts or personal loans) and *trade credit* (common in the commercial world both within countries and internationally).

crowding out situation in which an increase in government expenditure, by generating price rises and thus a reduction in the real money supply, results in a fall in private consumption and/or investment. Crowding out has been used in recent years as a justification for privatization of state-owned services and industries.

currency the particular type of money in use in a country. The currency of the United Kingdom is pounds sterling (£).

debt crisis generally any situation in which an individual, company or country owes more to others than they can repay or service when required; more specifically, the term refers to the massive indebtedness of many developing countries which became acute in the 1980s, threatening the stability of the international banking system as many debtor countries became unable to service their debts. The best-known example is Brazil, which in 1987 again 'rescheduled' (announced its incapacity to pay) its debts.

depreciation the decline or erosion of the value of a currency in relation to other currencies; also, the fall in value of an asset (such as factory machinery) resulting from age, wear and tear, or other factors.

deregulation action to abolish or reduce state controls and supervision over private economic activities, as with the deregulation of the US airline industry in 1978. In Britain the major changes in the City of London in 1986 (the big bang) were in part deregulation.

devaluation the lowering of the value of a currency in the international market or against specific other currencies, which makes exports cheaper and imports dearer. It is usually intended that devaluation should improve a country's balance of payments. *Revaluation* is the opposite process.

development aid financial and other assistance given by richer, usually industrialized, countries to developing states. Official development aid (ODA) may be given for idealistic, commercial, or political reasons, or a combination of the three.

disinvestment the practice of withdrawing investment from a country for political reasons. Most generally applied to the removal of funds from South Africa in recent years by such multinational companies as General Motors and Barclays Bank. Disinvestment may be motivated by fear of loss of business in the home market caused by adverse publicity, or by fear of loss of foreign resources if the local government loses power.

exchange rate the price at which one currency is bought, sold or valued in terms of other currencies, gold or accounting units such as the special drawing right of the International Monetary Fund. Exchange rates may be fixed by international agreement or as a matter of government policy, or they may be wholly or (more commonly) partly allowed to 'float' (i.e. find their own level) in world currency markets, as has been the case with most major currencies since the 1970s.

export credits loan, finance, or guarantees provided by government or financial institutions enabling companies to export goods and services in situations where payment for them may be delayed or subject to risk. In Britain the Export Credits Guarantee Department, established in 1930, issues insurance cover in respect of such risks.

exports goods and services produced in one country and sold to another; they may be visible (goods which are physically exported) or invisible (services such as tourism or insurance, provided in the exporting country but paid for in another country).

Financial Times (FT) Index customarily signifying the FT industrial ordinary index measuring the daily movement of 30 major industrial share prices on the London Stock Exchange (1935 = 100). Other FT indices cover government securities, fixed-interest securities, goldmine shares, and Stock Exchange activity.

fiscal policy the range of measures by which government revenue is raised (notably by taxation) and the priorities and purposes governing its expenditure. Post-war British governments have customarily made frequent adjustments to fiscal policy in order to regulate the level of economic activity (although under the post-1979 Conservative administration greater emphasis has been given to monetary policy).

game theory a group of mathematical theories, first developed in 1944 by Oscar Morgenstern and John von Neumann, which seeks to abstract from invented game-playing scenarios and their outcome the essence of situations of conflict and/or co-operation in the real political, business, and social world. A feature of such games is that the rationality of a decision by one player will depend on what the others do; hence game theory has particular application to the study of oligopoly.

gilt-edged stock securities issued by the British government to raise funds and traded on the Stock Exchange. A relatively risk-free investment, gilts bear fixed interest and are usually redeemable on a specified date.

hyperinflation rapid and uncontrolled increases in prices, usually associated with political and/or social instability (as in Germany in the 1920s).

imports goods and services which one country purchases from another for domestic consumption. If an importing country does not have a counterbalancing value of exports, it may experience balance-of-payments difficulties and accordingly consider restricting imports by some form of protection (such as an import tariff or by imposing import quotas).

income tax direct tax levied on personal income, mainly wages and salaries, but which may include the value of receipts other than in cash. In Britain income tax was first introduced in 1799 and has been a permanent fiscal feature since 1842. Indirect taxes are duties payable whenever a specific product is purchased; examples include VAT and customs duties.

incomes policy government-initiated exercise to curb inflation by restraining rises in incomes, on either a voluntary or a compulsory basis; often linked with action to control prices, in which case it becomes a prices and incomes policy. In Britain incomes policies have been applied at various times since the 1950s with limited success. An alternative to incomes policy, employed by the post-1979 Conservative government in Britain, is *monetary policy*, which attempts to manage the economy by controlling the quantity of money in circulation.

inflation a rise in the general level of prices, caused by an excess of demand over supply (*cost-push inflation* such as the world price rise in oil in 1974), and related to an increase in the supply of money (*demand-pull inflation*). *Deflation* is the reverse, a fall in the general level of prices.

insider dealing illegal use of privileged information in trading on the stock exchanges, for example when a company takeover bid is imminent. Insider dealing is in theory detected by the *Securities and Exchange Commission (SEC)* in the USA, and by the *Securities and Investment Board (SIB)* in the UK. Neither agency, however, has any legal powers other than public disclosure.

investment commonly used to signify the purchase of any asset with the potential to yield future financial benefit to the purchaser (such as a house, a work of art, stocks and shares, or even a private education); more strictly, it denotes expenditure on the stock of capital goods or resources of an enterprise or project, with a view to achieving profitable production for consumption at a later date.

laissez-faire theory that the state should refrain from all intervention in economic affairs, originating with the motto of the 18th-century French Physiocrats: *laissez-faire et laissez-passer*, that is 'leave the individual alone, and let commodities circulate freely'. The degree to which intervention should take place is still one of the chief problems of modern economics, both in capitalist and in communist regimes.

monetarism economic policy, advocated by the economist Milton Friedman and others, which proposes control of a country's money supply to keep it in step with the country's ability to produce goods, with the aim of curbing inflation. Cutting government spending is advocated, and the long-term aim is to return as much of the economy as possible to the private sector, allegedly in the interests of efficiency. Additionally, credit is restricted by high interest rates, and industry is not cushioned against internal market forces or overseas competition (with the aim of preventing 'over-manning', 'restrictive' union practices, 'excessive' wage demands, and so on) Unemployment results, but, monetarists claim, less than eventually occurs if Keynesian methods are adopted. The theory was ineffectively applied by Edward Heath in the UK in the early 1970s, and from 1979 the Thatcher government attempted a more complete application of monetarism.

monetary policy an approach by governments which sees control of the money supply and of liquidity as essential to the achievement of desired objectives and thus places less emphasis on tools such as fiscal policy and incomes policy. A monetary policy may not fully embrace all the doctrines of monetarism, but use of it usually indicates that the practitioner gives a higher priority to price stability and balance-of-payments equilibrium than to low unemployment and consumption.

money any common medium of exchange acceptable in payment for goods or services or for the settlement of debts. Today money is usually coinage (first used in the West of Lydia but invented by the Chinese in the second millennium BC) or paper notes (used by the Chinese about 800 AD to avoid imperial messengers being weighed down by coin when pursued by bandits). More recent developments such as the cheque and credit card fulfil many of the traditional functions of money.

money supply term used to denote the amount of money present in an economy at a given moment. In Britain there are several definitions of money supply, none of them totally satisfactory. The **M1** definition encompasses notes and coin in circulation plus current account deposits; **M2**, now rarely used, covers the M1 items plus deposit accounts; and the officially preferred **M3** definition covers M1 and M2 items plus all other deposits held by UK citizens and companies in the UK banking sector.

monopoly in the UK, originally a royal grant of the sole right to manufacture or sell a certain article. In modern commerce, the domination of a particular industry by a cartel or trust (a group of firms) which is large enough to restrict competition against itself and keep prices high.

multinational corporation company or enterprise operating in several countries, often defined as one which has 25 per cent or more of its output capacity located outside its country of origin. Such enterprises, many of them US-based, are seen in some quarters as posing a threat to individual national sovereignty and as exerting undue influence to secure favourable operating conditions.

multiplier theoretical concept, formulated by J M Keynes, of the effect on national income or employment by an adjustment in overall demand. Thus investment by a company in new plant will stimulate new income and expenditure, which will in turn generate new investment, and so on, so that the actual increase in national income may be several times greater than the original investment.

national debt the total amount of money borrowed by the central government of a country, on which it pays interest. In Britain the national debt is managed by the Bank of England, under the control of the Treasury.

newly-industrialized country *(NIC)* term used to denote a former less-developed country which has made a breakthrough into manufacturing and rapid export-led economic growth. The prime examples are South Korea, Singapore, Brazil and Mexico, which on average expanded their gross domestic product (GDP) twice as fast as the older industrialized countries during the 1970s, partly by rapidly increasing the share of manufactured goods in their exports.

oligopoly situation in which a small group of companies controls a large proportion of a particular market and concerts its actions to perpetuate such control. Oligopolies are usu-

ally opposed by governments as being against the general interest.

privatization the selling or transfer into private hands of state-owned assets and services (notably nationalized industries). Privatization of services takes place by the contracting out to private firms of the rendering of services previously supplied by public authorities. The policy has been pursued by several governments in recent years, particularly the post-1979 Conservative administrations in Britain.

profit-sharing a system whereby an employer pays his workers a fixed share of his profits. It originated in France in the early 19th century, and under the influence of the Christian Socialists was widely practised for a time within the co-operative movement.

quantity theory of money theory dating originally from the 17th century and elaborated by the US economist Irving Fisher (1867–1947) to show, in essence, that an increase in the amount of money in circulation will cause a proportionate increase in prices. The quantity theory of money forms the theoretical basis of modern monetarism.

reserves a country's holdings of internationally acceptable means of payment (major foreign currencies or gold); central banks also hold the ultimate reserve of money for their domestic banking sector. On the asset side of company balance sheets, undistributed profits are listed as reserves.

saving the reservation, by individuals or companies, of a portion of income for future needs. Seldom the massing of a money hoard in modern times, because of dangers of fire and theft, but tending to be synonymous with investment.

Say's Law the 'law of markets' enunciated by Jean-Baptiste Say (1767–1832) to the effect that supply creates its own demand and that resources can never be under-used. Widely accepted by classical economists, the 'law' was regarded as erroneous by J M Keynes in his analysis of the depression in Britain during the 1920s and 1930s.

stagflation the condition (experienced in

Britain in the 1970s) in which rapid inflation is accompanied by stagnating, even declining, output and by increasing unemployment. Its cause is often sharp increases in costs of raw materials and/or labour.

stocks and shares broad term for investment holdings in private or public undertakings. Although distinctions have become blurred, in Britain stock usually means fixed-interest securities, especially those issued by central and local government. Shares represent a stake in the ownership of a trading company and, if they are ordinary shares, yield to the owner dividends reflecting the success or otherwise of the company. In the USA the term stock generally signifies what in Britain are ordinary shares.

Treasury bill in Britain, borrowing by the government in the form of a promissory note to repay the bearer 91 days from the date of issue; such bills represent a flexible and relatively cheap way for the government to borrow money for immediate needs.

unemployment the involuntary lack of paid employment. Unemployment is generally subdivided into *frictional* unemployment (the inevitable temporary unemployment of those moving from one job to another); *cyclical* unemployment, caused by a downswing in the trade cycle; *seasonal* unemployment, in an area where there is high demand only during holiday periods, for example; and *structural* unemployment, where changing technology or other long-term change in the economy results in large numbers without work, particularly in certain regions.

Education

In its widest sense, education begins at birth. In the more restricted sense of imparting knowledge and literacy, education has today become almost worldwide. Although highly developed systems of learning emerged early in China, formal education as we know it today is largely of European origin. The earliest known European educational systems are those of ancient Greece, although they were only for the privileged few. Medieval monastic schools gradually admitted other pupils and learning was spread. Compulsory attendance at primary schools was first established in the mid-18th century in Prussia. By the middle of the 20th century, education was free and compulsory in most countries of the world from about 6 to 16.

This section deals with the British education system. It outlines the various *Stages of Education* - pre-school, primary, secondary, post-school, and their aims, such as basic literacy, vocational objectives, graduate and post-graduate work. Then it touches on *Recent Changes* in UK education over the last 20 years, all of which have been paralleled in other countries - the switch to comprehensive secondary, the expansion of higher and further education, the response to the falling birth-rate of the 1970s. It then looks at the major *Areas of Debate* in the 1980s, such as the introduction of the National Curriculum and GCSE examinations. Finally there is a glossary of *Terms* used in education.

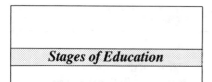

Stages of Education

Education is compulsory and free of charge in the UK from the age of 5 until the age of 16, but in common with most industrialized countries, educational services are provided in various forms from the age of 3 to the stage of post-doctoral research in universities and other higher education colleges, by which time students may be in their mid-20s.

Education up to the age of 18 is provided almost exclusively by *local education authorities* which are run by the local council. The Department of Education and Science had a general oversight of school policy, directly controlling only the universities and the teacher training colleges. During the 1980s it has taken a more central role, introducing the National Curriculum and taking over the funding of polytechnics and some schools. There is also a private fee-paying school sector which attracts 6.5% of school pupils.

pre-school education the UK lags behind many of its industrial neighbours in provision of pre-school education. Only 48% of three and four year olds are provided for in maintained nursery and infants' schools and classes. Another 470,000 children are catered for in playgroups run on a voluntary basis.

school education is divided into *primary* (5 to 11) and *secondary* (11 to 18) sectors. There is a large voluntary sector of schools run co-operatively by the churches and local authorities together, accounting for one-third of primary schools and a smaller proportion of secondary schools. A few local authority areas maintain *middle schools*, which take children from the ages of 8 or 9 to 12 or 13. School transfer in the private sector often also takes place at 13.

education after 16 beyond school-leaving age students have a choice of remaining in school sixth forms, which generally specialize in the A level courses which lead to entrance to higher education, or colleges of further education which specialize in vocational courses, or the Youth Training Scheme which offers a combination of work experience and training. The UK has a very low proportion of 16 to 19 year olds, at just under 40%, remaining in full-time education compared to its industrial competitors. Some local education authorities advocate the closing down of school sixth forms, so that all post-16 education takes place in colleges.

degree level education is divided between 45 universities and the public sector of polytechnics and colleges of higher education. All are now funded directly by the government through various committees. Participation in full-time higher education beyond the age of 18 stands at 25%. Higher education course fees are paid in full for UK students, and there is a system of maintenance grants, on a parental means test basis, to cover students' living expenses while they are studying.

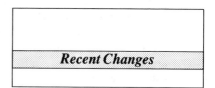

Recent Changes

Education in the UK is going through a period of rapid change. Comprehensive education, introduced during the 1960s and 1970s, was complicated by dramatic changes in the child population, although this has now stabilized. In the late 1980s all schools are adapting to the new GCSE exam and to the National Curriculum.

comprehensive schools the 1960s and 1970s saw a slow but major reform of secondary education, which in the majority of local authority areas replaced selective grammar schools taking only the most academic 20% of children and secondary modern schools for the majority, with comprehensive schools capable of providing suitable courses for children of all abilities. By 1985 only 3.2% of secondary pupils were still in grammar schools. Scotland and Wales have switched completely to comprehensive education, while Northern Ireland retains a largely selective system.

GCSE examinations in 1988 a new exam was introduced, replacing the old O levels and CSE qualifications. The administration of two exams in the same school, with O levels designed only for the most able 20% of pupils, created problems and seemed to work against the spirit of comprehensive education. The new GCSE grades range from A to G, and the exam is suitable for about 80% of school pupils.

National Curriculum the 1988 Education Reform Act has introduced a compulsory National Curriculum which applies to all children of compulsory school age (5-16) in state schools. A compulsory curriculum has not existed before; in the past it has, for instance, been possible to study science only from ages 11-14. There are ten 'core' subjects in the curriculum - English, mathematics, science, technology, history, geography, music, art, physical education, and a foreign language. These subjects are now studied during all stages of schooling by all students. The compulsory curriculum does not apply to private schools or City Technology Colleges.

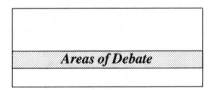

Areas of Debate

The educational debate has moved in new but no less contentious directions in the 1980s. The following are some of the main areas of continuing debate:

central, local, or parental control the Thatcher government has twice strengthened the involvement of parents in the running of the schools by first insisting on the election of parents to governing bodies (1980 Education Act) and then by strengthening that representation and by providing for an annual report by governors to parents (Education Act 1986).

It has given parents greater freedom to select schools within the State system, and to opt into the independent sector, by means of the Assisted Places Scheme. Colleges of Higher Education and Polytechnics are now run and financed by central, rather than local government. The Government has also taken greater powers centrally to influence and fund parts of the curriculum and examination system. Local education authorities fear that the government is engaged in a process of centralization of the education service which could end local political involvement completely.

vocational and technical education the Manpower Services Commission (MSC) has funded a major expansion of technical and vocational education for students over 14 in schools and colleges (TVEI). TVEI funding was originally provided in pilot schemes which reached roughly 3% of secondary school children, but it was announced in 1986 that funding would be extended, at a significantly less generous level, to all secondary schools. The MSC has also become involved with the further education colleges as the Youth Training Scheme for unemployed young people has expanded, but only a minority of YTS trainees attend college.

examination reform the Conservative government since 1979 has initiated a major reform of the public examination system. After a long debate, it authorized the amalgamation of the two 16-plus examinations to create the GCSE, introduced in 1988, and initiated reforms leading to new CPVE and AS level examinations, and a major review of vocational qualifications. These changes have been undertaken with some support from teachers. More contentious are new discussions on the A Level examinations, which it is argued need to be reformed in order to accommodate the GCSE reform, and to broaden the traditional three A Level sixth form programme of study.

higher education 1986 saw a record number of students in higher education, in spite of cuts in university funding which reduced student numbers in the universities after 1981. The extra numbers in higher education are accounted for by the fact that public sector colleges and polytechnics packed in surplus applicants, with minimal extra funding, as the universities contracted. In 1987 the Government conceded that higher education numbers should expand by about 4% by 1990. But plans to rationalize courses, and concentrate on science, technology, and business studies at the expense of the humanities and social sciences, were confirmed.

testing and assessment since 1979 the Conservative government has initiated a major reform of the way in which children are assessed at school. A year after the introduction of GCSE, the Education Act 1988 established that pupils are monitored through a series of nationally organized tests at ages 7, 11, and 14. The results of these tests are to be made available in some form for parents about to choose a school. Critics say that the tests may be unfair, for instance to those who have English as a second language, and that children will be put under exam pressure at too young an age. It is likely however that the testing will be relatively informal so as not to resemble exams. The government has also encouraged new forms of assessment which do not involve testing, such as records of achievement, where pupils compile a portfolio of their best work over a number of years. The CPVE course and the AS level, available for students post-GCSE, have been introduced since 1986 but so far there is no sign that the prestigious A level exams will be reformed.

City Technology Colleges in 1986 Education Secretary Kenneth Baker announced plans to set up a limited number of schools specializing in science and technology, and independent of the local education authorities. The first two CTCs opened in 1988. Most of the costs have been met by central government, although the original plan hoped that private industry would sponsor the colleges. The colleges do not have to follow the National Curriculum, and encourage a market-oriented entrepreneurial philosophy among staff and pupils. Many local education authorities have opposed the setting up of CTCs, claiming that their superior funding will attract the most able students and staff away from comprehensives.

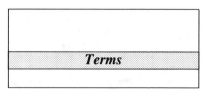

Terms

admission to school legally, in the UK, at the beginning of the term after a child's fifth birthday, but an increasing number of schools now admit children earlier.

A Level General Certificate of Education examinations usually taken in no more than four subjects at the age of 18 after two years' study. Two A Level passes are required for entry onto a degree course.

AS Level Advanced Supplementary GCE examinations introduced in 1988 as the equivalent to 'half an A Level' as a means of broadening the sixth form curriculum.

assessment the means of measuring performance by way of examinations, tests or classwork marking.

Assisted Places Scheme a scheme established in 1980 by which the Government assists parents with the cost of fees at private schools, on a means-tested basis.

Baccalaureate the French school-leaving certificate and qualification for university entrance, also available on an international basis as an alternative to A Levels.

banding the division of school pupils into broad streams by ability. Banding is used by some local authorities to ensure that comprehensive schools receive an intake of children spread right across the ability range, and is used internally by some schools as a means of avoiding groups of very wide mixed ability.

boarding schools schools offering board and lodging as well as tuition. Most boarding education in the UK is provided in the private sector, but there are a number of State schools with boarding facilities.

BTEC Business and Technician Education Council, the examination and validation body formed 1983, which awards diplomas for courses leading to full and part-time qualifications in further and higher education colleges, although some are available to secondary school pupils.

co-education the education of boys and girls together in one institution. There has been a marked switch away from single sex education in favour of co-education over the last 20 years, although there is some evidence to suggest that girls perform better in a single sex institution, particularly in maths and science.

colleges of higher education colleges controlled by the local education authorities in which a large proportion of the work undertaken is at degree level or above.

community schools/education the philosophy which asserts that educational institutions are more effective if closely integrated with, and opened up to all members of, the surrounding community.

comprehensive school a secondary school which admits pupils without regard to ability and therefore without any selection procedure. Secondary education in the USA and the USSR has always been comprehensive, but most western European countries, including France and the UK, have switched from a selective to a comprehensive system within the last 20 years.

CPVE the Certificate of Pre-vocational Education, a qualification introduced in 1986 for students over 16 in schools and colleges who want a one-year course of preparation for work or further vocational study.

credits the system whereby a qualification from one institution is accepted by another. Credit transferability is common in higher education in the USA but is only just beginning to be developed between institutions in the UK. At school level, the equivalence between a BTEC diploma and A Levels is a long-standing one.

CSE Certificate of Secondary Education: the examinations taken by the majority of secondary school pupils, who were not regarded as capable of GCE O Level, before the introduction of the common secondary examination system, GCSE, in 1988.

curriculum the range of subjects offered within an institution or course. The only part

of the school curriculum prescribed by law in the UK is religious education. General responsibility for overseeing the curriculum in England and Wales rests with the local education authority and school governors, although there is increasing central control of the curriculum to ensure that all young people study certain basic subjects such as maths and science.

Department of Education and Science (DES) the Government department responsible for education policy making in England, and for universities throughout the UK.

Education Acts (UK) the foundation for much education policy is still the reforming 1944 Education Act. This was revised by two Acts in 1980, which repealed previous legislation enforcing comprehensive re-organization, and gave new rights to parents, by the 1981 Education Act which made new provisions for the education of children with special needs, and by legislation in 1986, 1987 and 1988, giving further powers to school governors.

Eleven Plus examination the test designed to select children for grammar school education at the time when local authorities provided separate grammar, secondary modern, and occasionally technical schools for children over the age of eleven. The examination became defunct on the introduction of comprehensive schools in Scotland, Wales and most of England during the 1960s and 1970s.

finance education in the UK is funded in two ways: 1. By the local education authorities who, by a combination of government rate support grant and rates directly charged on the local community, support schools, further education and, through a national pool, parts of higher education such as the polytechnics. 2. By direct grant from the DES to the universities, some other colleges of higher education, and for a limited number of specific projects in the schools, and via the Manpower Services Commission, to vocational education in colleges and schools.

further education colleges colleges for students over school-leaving age which provide courses of a vocational or pre-vocational nature and some of general education at a level below that of a degree course.

GCE General Certificate of Education, the public examination usually taken at the age of 16 at Ordinary Level and at 18 at A Level. The GCE O Level examination, aimed at the top 20% of the ability range, was superseded in 1988 by the General Certificate of Secondary Education.

GCSE General Certificate of Secondary Education, the new examination for 16 year old pupils, superseding both GCE O Level and CSE, which offer qualifications for up to 80% of school leavers in any particular subject. The GCSE is more practically biased than O Level and is organized in the light of National Criteria laid down by the Secondary Examinations Council.

governors members of a institution's governing body. Education Acts of 1980 and 1986 have increased elected parental and teacher representation on school governing bodies in England and Wales, and reduced the influence of governors appointed by the local education authorities.

grants allowances made to students to cover the cost of course fees and, in higher education, maintenance costs during term-time. The National Union of Students campaigns for a 'living grant' for all students in further and higher education over the age of 16, with a removal of the present obligation upon parents to contribute on a means tested basis.

health education most secondary schools offer pupils teaching and advice on healthy living, including nutrition, sex education, drink, drugs, and other threats to health. Health education is often included within a course of personal and social education, or alternatively integrated into subjects such as biology, home economics, or physical education. School governors were given specific responsibility for the content of sex education lessons in the 1986 Education Act.

higher education education beyond the age of 18 leading to a degree or similar qualification, provided in the UK in universities, polytechnics, and colleges of higher education, and by distance learning through the Open University.

institutions, survey particular areas of study, comment on standards and levels of provision and advise the Government. Local education authorities also employ their own inspectors, often now called advisers, to advise schools and colleges on their performance at a local level.

independent schools schools run privately without direct assistance from the State. Just over 6% of children in the UK attend private fee-paying schools. The sector includes most boarding education in the UK. Although a majority of independent secondary schools operate a highly selective admissions policy for entrants at the age of 11 or 13, some specialize in the teaching of backward or difficult children and a few follow particular philosophies of progressive education.

inspectors there are two systems of inspection for schools and colleges in the UK. Her Majesty's Inspectors of Schools are a national body, independent of the Department of Education and Science, with authority to visit

integrated studies a course which integrates two or more subjects which can be studied separately. For instance, integrated humanities may include elements of history, geography, social studies, and English; integrated science would normally include elements of physics, chemistry, and biology.

intelligence tests tests which attempt to measure innate intellectual ability, rather than acquired knowledge. Intelligence tests were widely used as part of the eleven plus procedures, in the early days of which it was assumed that inborn intelligence was unalterable. It is now generally believed that children's ability to score at a particular level in an intelligence test can be affected by their environment and teaching. There is also considerably more scepticism now about the accuracy of intelligence tests than there was when they were first introduced in the 1930s, but they are still widely used as a diagnostic tool when children display learning difficulties.

IQ intelligence quotient: the score achieved as the result of an intelligence test, with a score of between 90 and 110 being regarded as average ability.

literacy the ability to read and write at a level to enable an adult to function in the society in which he or she lives. The level at which functional literacy is set rises as society becomes more complex and it becomes increasingly difficult for an illiterate person to find work and cope with the other demands of everyday life.

local education authorities the education committees of metropolitan or county councils which have responsibility for providing educational services locally. There is one directly elected education authority in England, the Inner London Education Authority (which will be abolished by the government 1990), and in Northern Ireland responsibility for education is held by the Education and Library Boards.

local management of schools the increased power schools are given by the Education Act 1988 to run their own budget. From 1989 head teachers will be able to make decisions on staffing and resourcing of the various areas of the curriculum.

mixed ability teaching the practice of teaching children of all abilities in a single class. Mixed ability teaching is normal practice in British primary schools but most secondary schools begin to divide children according to ability, either in sets or, more rarely, streams, as they approach public examinations at 16.

modular courses courses, usually leading to a recognized qualification which are divided into short and often optional units which are assessed as they are completed. An accumulation of modular credits may then lead to the award of a qualification such as a degree, a BTEC diploma or a GCSE pass. Modular schemes are increasingly popular as a means of allowing students to take a wider range of subjects.

National Curriculum Council a committee of educationalists, businesspeople, and parents advising the Secretary of State for Education on the running of the National Curriculum.

O Level the GCE examination formerly taken at 16 plus by the most able children and superseded by the GCSE in 1988.

open learning teaching which is available to students without pre-qualifications by means of flexible attendance at an institution and very often including teaching by correspondence, radio, television or tape.

Open University an institution established in 1969 to enable mature students without qualifications to study to degree level without regular attendance. OU teaching is based on a mixture of correspondence courses, TV and radio lectures and demonstrations, personal tuition organized on a regional basis, and summer schools.

open college an open learning initiative launched by the Manpower Services Commission to enable people to gain and update technical and vocational skills by means of distance teaching.

opting out the process by which a secondary school removes itself from the control of a local education authority. Majority votes are required from both the governing body and the parents, and the Secretary of State for Education must also give his assent. Schools which opt out (numbering 18 by June 1989) are financed directly by the government.

parent teacher associations groups attached to schools consisting of parents and teachers who support the school by fund raising and educational activities amongst the parent body. PTAs are organized into a national federation, the National Confederation of PTAs, which increasingly acts as a pressure group for maintained schools.

parent governors the 1980 Education Act made it mandatory for all state schools to include elected parent representatives on their governing bodies, in line with the existing practice of some local education authorities. The 1986 Education Act increased parental representation.

play-groups voluntary, usually part-time pre-school groups, run either by parents or sometimes by charitable organizations, to provide nursery education for children from three to five. Play-groups sprang up in the 1960s in response to a national shortage of places in maintained nursery education. By the 1980s they were catering for 470,000 children annually, and training and advice services were organized nationally by the Pre-School Playgroups Association.

preparatory schools fee-paying private schools catering for children to the age of 13.

primary education the education of children between 5 and 11 in the state school system in England and Wales, (to 12 in Scotland).

progressive methods a generic term for teaching methods which take as their starting point children's own aptitudes and interests and encourage them to follow their own investigations and lines of enquiry.

racial disadvantage there is considerable evidence that children from some racial groups perform less well than they should in British schools. The Swann Report 1986 recommended methods of combatting racial disadvantage in schools and local authorities are increasingly adopting anti-racist policies and attempting to give their curricula a multi-cultural dimension.

religious education RE is the only compulsory subject. In voluntary aided Church schools, RE syllabuses are permitted to follow the specific teachings of the Church concerned; in other maintained schools the syllabus is agreed jointly between representatives of the local churches and the education authority. The law allows parents to withdraw their children from RE on conscientious grounds.

remedial education special classes, or teaching strategies, which aim to help children with learning difficulties to catch up with children of the normal range of achievement.

school leaving age pupils may leave school in the year in which they reach the age of 16 in the UK, but precise regulations, which differ between England and Wales and Scotland, govern the precise date at which an individual can leave school, depending on his or her birthday.

secondary education education from the age of 11 (12 in Scotland) until school-leaving at 16 or later.

secondary modern school the secondary school which normally takes children who have failed to gain a grammar school place, in those few areas of the UK which retain selection at 11 or 12.

setting the practice of dividing pupils into ability groups for each subject.

sixth form inclusive term used for pupils staying on for one or two years of study beyond school-leaving age in order to gain A Level or other post-15 qualifications. In some areas, sixth form education is concentrated in sixth form colleges.

special education education, often in separate 'special schools', for children with specific problems or disabilities, that is, the blind, deaf, maladjusted. The 1981 Education Act encouraged local authorities to integrate as many children with special needs into mainstream schools as was practicable but did not recommend the complete closure of special schools.

streaming the practice of dividing pupils for all classes according to an estimate of their overall ability, with arrangements for 'promotion' and 'demotion' at the end of each academic year. Rigid streaming is unusual in secondary education in the 1980s and has disappeared from primary education.

teacher training in the UK teachers are trained by means of the four year Bachelor of Education degree, which integrates professional training and the study of academic subjects, or by means of the one year Post Graduate Certificate of Education which offers one year of professional training to follow a normal degree course in a specialist subject.

tertiary college a college for students over 16 which combines the work of a sixth form and a further education college.

TVEI the Technical and Vocational Education Initiative, funded by the Manpower Services Commission, intended to provide secondary schools with equipment and teaching expertise to allow them to expand their vocational and technical courses for 14 to 18 year olds. Initially available in only 3% of schools, it now covers all secondary schools.

vocational education education relevant to a specific job or career and extending from further education courses in craft skills to medical and legal education in the universities.

Language

Language is the general name for human communication through speech or writing, or both, while 'a language' is any expression of language used by one or more communities for everyday purposes (the English language, the Japanese language, and so on). Natural human language has a neurological basis centred on the left hemisphere of the brain and is expressed through two distinct mediums in most present-day societies: through sound, or the phonic medium, and through writing, or the graphic medium. It appears to develop in every normal child under normal circumstances, crucially between the ages of one and five years, and as a necessary interplay of innate and environmental factors. Any human child can learn any human language, under the appropriate conditions.

This section contains an overview of the principal *Languages of the World*, both ancient and modern; notes on *Grammar and Usage*, including parts of speech and punctuation; and definitions of *Terms* people use in the study of language today.

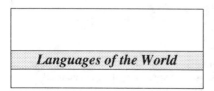

Languages of the World

Afrikaans along with English, an official language of the Republic of South Africa. Spoken mainly by the Afrikaners, descendants of Dutch and other 17th-century colonists, it is a variety of the Dutch language, modified by circumstance and the influence of German, French, and other immigrant and local languages. It became a standardized written language about 1875.

Anglo-Saxon the group of dialects spoken by the Anglo-Saxon peoples who in the 5th to 7th centuries invaded and settled in Britain (in what became England and Lowland Scotland). Anglo-Saxon is traditionally known as Old English.

Arabic a Hamito-Semitic language of W Asia and N Africa, originating among the Arabs of the Arabian peninsula. Arabic script is written from right to left. A feature of the language is its consonantal roots; for example *s-l-m* is the root for *salaam*, a greeting that implies peace, *Islam*, the creed of submission to God and calm acceptance of His will, and *Muslim*, one who submits to that will (a believer in Islam). The *Quran*, the sacred book of Islam, is 'for reading' by a *qari* ('reader') who is engaged in *qaraat* ('reading'). The 7th-century style of the Quran is the basis of *Classical Arabic*. The language has spread as far west as Morocco and as far east as Malaysia, Indonesia and the Philippines. Forms of *Colloquial Arabic* vary in the countries where it is the dominant language: Algeria, Bahrain, Egypt, Iraq, Jordan, Kuwait, Lebanon, Libya, Mali, Mauretania, Morocco, Oman, Sudan, Syria, Tunisia, the United Arab Emirates, and the two Yemens. It is also a language of religious and cultural significance in such other countries as Bangladesh, India, Indonesia, Iran, Malaysia, Pakistan, the Philippines and Somalia.

Aramaic a Hamito-Semitic language of W Asia, the everyday language of Palestine in the time of Christ. In the 13th century BC Aramaean nomads set up states in Mesopotamia, and over the next 200 years spread into N Syria, where Damascus, Aleppo and Carchemish were among their chief centres. Aramaic spread throughout Syria and Mesopotamia, becoming one of the official languages of the Persian Empire under the Achaemenids and serving as a lingua franca of the day. Aramaic dialects survive among small Christian communities in various parts of W Asia.

Aryan languages either the languages of the Aryan peoples of India, or a 19th-century name for the Indo-European languages.

Bantu languages a group of related languages spoken widely over the greater part of Africa south of the Sahara, including Swahili, Xhosa and Zulu. Meaning 'people' in Zulu, the word *Bantu* itself illustrates a characteristic use of prefixes: *mu-ntu*, 'man', *ba-ntu*, 'people'. The Bantu-speaking peoples probably originated in N Central Africa. Until 1978, the black people of the Republic of South Africa were officially designated *bantu(s)*, and the official 'homelands' of the various black ethnic groups were known as *bantustans* ('Bantu lands').

Basic English a simplified form of English devised and promoted by C K Ogden in the 1920s and 1930s as an international auxiliary language, a route into Standard English for foreign learners, and a reminder to the English-speaking world of the virtues of plain language. Its name derives from the letters of *B*ritish, *A*merican, *S*cientific, *I*nternational, *C*ommercial. Basic has a vocabulary of 850 words (plus names, technical terms, etc.), only 18 of which are verbs or 'operators'. *Get* therefore replaces 'receive', 'obtain' and 'become', while *buy* is replaced by the phrase 'give money for'.

Basque a language of W Europe known to its speakers, the Basques, as *Euskara*, and apparently unrelated to any other language on earth. It is spoken by some half a million people in N Spain and SW France, around the Bay of Biscay ('the Basque bay'), as well as by emigrants in both Europe and the Americas. Although officially discouraged in the past, Basque is now accepted as a regional language in both France and Spain, and is of central importance to the Basque nationalist movement.

Bengali a member of the Indo-Iranian branch of the Indo-European language family, the official language of Bangladesh and of the state of Bengal in India.

Bretone a member of the Celtic branch of the Indo-European language family, the language of Brittany in France, related to Welsh and Cornish, and descended from the speech of Celts who left Britain as a consequence of the Anglo-Saxon invasions of the 5th and 6th centuries. Although subject to official neglect for centuries, Breton is now a recognized language of France and has since 1985 received some encouragement from the central government. The Breton Liberation Movement claims equal status in Brittany for Breton and French.

Castilian a member of the Romance branch of the Indo-European language family originating in NW Spain, in the provinces of Old and New Castile. It is the basis of present-day standard Spanish and is often seen as the same language, the terms *castellano* and *español* being used interchangeably in both Spain and the Spanish-speaking countries of the Americas.

Catalan a member of the Romance branch of the Indo-European language family, an Iberian language closely related to Provençal in France. It is spoken in Catalonia in NE Spain, the Balearic Isles, Andorra and a corner of SE France. Since the end of the Franco regime in Spain in 1975, Catalan nationalists have vigorously promoted their regional language as co-equal in Catalonia with Castilian Spanish.

Celtic languages a branch of the Indo-European family, further divided into two groups: the ***Brythonic*** or ***P-Celtic*** (Welsh, Cornish, Breton, and Gaulish) and the ***Goidelic*** or ***Q-Celtic*** (Irish, Scottish and Manx Gaelic). As their names suggest, a major distinction between the two groups is that where Brythonic has 'p' (as in Old Welsh *map*, 'son'), Goidelic has a 'q' sound (as in Gaelic *mac*, 'son'). Celtic languages once stretched from the Black Sea to Britain, but have been in decline for centuries, and are now limited to the so-called 'Celtic Fringe' of W Europe. Gaulish is the long-extinct language of ancient Gaul, Cornish died out as a natural language in the late 18th century and Manx in 1974. All surviving Celtic languages have experienced official neglect in recent centuries and have suffered from emigration; currently, however, governments are more inclined than in the past to encourage their use.

Chinese depending upon definition, a language or group of languages of the Sino-Tibetan family, spoken in China, Taiwan, Hong Kong, Singapore and Chinese communities throughout the world. Varieties of spoken Chinese differ greatly, but share a written form using thousands of ideographic symbols which have changed little in 2,000 years. Because the writing system has a symbolic form (rather like numbers and road signs) it can be read and interpreted regardless of the reader's own dialect. Nowadays, ***putonghua*** ('common speech'), based on the educated Peking dialect known as 'Mandarin' Chinese, is promoted throughout China as the national spoken and written language. The Chinese dialects are tonal (that is, they depend upon the tone of a syllable to indicate its meaning, *ma* with one tone meaning 'mother', with another meaning 'horse'). The characters of Chinese script are traditionally written vertically and read from right to left but are now commonly written horizontally and read from left to right, using 2,000 simplified characters. A variant of the Roman alphabet has been introduced and used in schools to help with pronunciation. Called *Pinyin*, this is prescribed for international use by the People's Republic of China, for personal and place names; for example, Beijing rather than Peking. It is not accepted by the Taiwan government.

77

Coptic a member of the Hamito-Semitic language family and a minority language of Egypt. It is descended from the language of the ancient Egyptians and is the ritual language of the Coptic Christian church. It is written in the Greek Alphabet.

Cornish an extinct member of the Celtic language, branch of the Indo-European language family spoken in Cornwall until 1777. Written Cornish first appeared in 10th-century documents. Some religious plays were written in Cornish in the 15th and 16th centuries, but later literature is scanty, mainly folk-tales and verses. Members of the Cornish nationalist movement have in recent years 'revived' the language for social purposes and for its symbolic value.

Creole languages pidgin languages which have ceased to be simply trade jargons in ports and markets and have become the mother tongues of particular communities. The name 'creole' derives through French from Spanish and Portuguese, in which it originally referred both to children of European background born in tropical colonies and to house slaves on colonial plantations. The implication is that such groups picked up the pidgin forms of languages like Portuguese, Spanish, Dutch, French and English as used in and around the Caribbean, in parts of Africa, and in island communities in the Indian and Pacific Oceans. Having begun with the characteristics of pidgin languages (crudely, the vocabulary of the dominant community arranged in accordance with the syntax or grammar of the dependent groups), many creoles have developed into distinct languages with incipient literatures of their own, such as Jamaican Creole, Haitian Creole, Krio in Sierra Leone, and Tok Pisin in Papua New Guinea.

Danish a member of the N Germanic group of the Indo-European language family, spoken in Denmark and Greenland and related to Icelandic, Faroese, Norwegian and Swedish. As one of the languages of the Vikings, who invaded and settled in parts of Britain during the 9th to 11th centuries, Old Danish had a strong influence on English. *They*, *their* and *them* as well as such *sk-* words as *sky*, *skill*, *skin*, *scrape* and *scrub* are among the language gifts of the Danelaw, along with such place-name endings as *by* (a farm or town) as in Derby, Grimsby and Whitby.

Dutch a member of the W Germanic branch of the Indo-European language family, often referred to by scholars as Netherlandic and taken to include not only the standard language and dialects of the Netherlands (excluding Frisian) but also Flemish (in Belgium and N France) and, more remotely, its off-shoot Afrikaans in S Africa. Many, however, regard Flemish and Afrikaans as distinct languages. Dutch is also spoken in Surinam in S America and the Netherlands Antilles in the S Caribbean.

English a member of the W Germanic branch of the Indo-European language family, traditionally described as having passed through four major stages over about 1,500 years: *Old English* or *Anglo-Saxon* (about 500–1050), *Middle English* (about 1050–1550), *Early Modern English* (about 1550–1700), and *Late Modern English* (from about 1700 onwards). The ancestral forms of English were dialects brought from the NW coastlands of Europe to the island of Britain by Angle, Saxon and Jutish invaders who gained footholds in the SE in the 5th century and over the next 200 years extended and consolidated their settlements from the Channel to the Firth of Forth. Scholars distinguish four main early dialects: of the *Jutes* in Kent, the *Saxons* in the south, the *Mercians* or *S Angles* in the Midlands, and the *Northumbrians* or *N Angles* north of the Humber. For several centuries English was in competition with other languages: first the various Celtic languages of Britain, then Danish (9th–11th centuries), then Norman French after the Conquest of 1066, and Latin as the language of the Catholic church. In 1362 English replaced French as the language of the law courts of England, although the records continued for some time to be kept in Latin. When William Caxton set up his printing press in London in 1477 the new hybrid language (vernacular English mixed with courtly French and learned

Latin) became increasingly standardized, and by 1611, when the Authorized Version of the Bible was published, the educated English of the Home Counties and London had become the core of what is now called 'Standard English'. By the end of the 16th century, English was firmly established in England, Scotland, Wales and Ireland, and with the establishment of the colonies in N America in the early 17th century took root in what are now the United States, Canada and the Caribbean islands. Sea-faring, exploration, commerce and colonial expansion took the language to every corner of the world. By the time of Johnson's *Dictionary* in 1755 and the American Declaration of Independence in 1776, English was recognizably the language we use today. Current English has absorbed material from many other tongues, and is used in varieties from British English, American English, Canadian English, Indian English through to Singapore English and Nigerian English and many pidgins and creoles. It is spoken by more than 300 million 'native speakers', and between 400 and 800 million 'foreign users'. It is the official language of aircraft and shipping, the leading language of science, technology, computers and commerce, and a major medium of education, publishing and international negotiation. For this reason scholars frequently refer to its latest phase as 'World English'.

Erse originally a Scottish form of the word 'Irish', a name applied by Lowland Scots to Scottish Gaelic and also sometimes used as a synonym for Irish Gaelic.

Esperanto an artificial language devised in 1887 by Dr Ludwig L Zamenhof, a Warsaw oculist (1859–1917), as an international auxiliary language. For its structure and vocabulary it draws upon various European languages. Esperantists refer to Esperanto as a 'planned language' and to the natural languages of the world as 'ethnic languages'. Its spelling is phonetic, its accents varying according to the ethnic backgrounds of its users. For its centenary in 1987, Esperantists have claimed some 10 to 15 million users worldwide, and say that

Esperanto estas tre facile lernebla lingvo ('Esperanto is a very easily learnable language').

Finnish a member of the Finno-Ugric language family, the national language of Finland and closely related to neighbouring Estonian, Livonian, Karelian and Ingrian languages. At the beginning of the 19th century Finnish had no official status, Swedish being the language of education, government and literature in Finland. The publication of the *Kalevala*, a national epic poem, in 1835, contributed greatly to the arousal of Finnish national and linguistic feeling.

Finno-Ugric a group or family of more than 20 languages spoken by some 22 million people in scattered communities from Norway in the west to Siberia in the east and to the Carpathian mountains in the south. Speakers of these languages tend to live in enclaves surrounded by Germanic, Slavonic and Turkish speakers, all of whom exercise influence upon the local Finno-Ugric varieties. The best-known members of the family are Finnish, Lapp, and Hungarian.

Flemish a member of the W Germanic branch of the Indo-European language family, spoken in N Belgium and the Nord department of France. It is closely related to Dutch.

French a member of the Romance branch of the Indo-European language family, spoken in France, Belgium, Luxembourg and Switzerland in Europe, Canada (especially the province of Quebec) in N America, such islands as Haiti and Martinique in the Caribbean, Reunion and Mauritius in the Indian Ocean, New Caledonia in the Pacific, and the Francophone (French-speaking) countries of N and W Africa (for example, Mali, Côte d'Ivoire and Senegal). French developed from the Latin spoken in Gaul and was established as a distinct language by the 9th century. Varieties used north of the river Loire formed the *Langue d'oil* (*oui*) while those to the south formed the *Langue d'oc*, according to their word for 'yes'. However, by the 13th century the dialect of the Ile de France was supreme and became in 1539 the official medium of the courts and administration of France. Its literary form still serves as the basis of *le bon français* ('correct French'), which is officially protected by the Académie Française (founded in 1635 at the behest of Cardinal Richelieu) and by occasional legislation in both France and Quebec.

Gaelic a member of the Celtic branch of the Indo-European language family, spoken in Ireland, Scotland and (until 1974) the Isle of Man. It is, along with English, one of the national languages of the Republic of Ireland, with over half a million speakers, and is known there as both Irish and Irish Gaelic. In Scotland, speakers of Gaelic number around 90,000 and are concentrated in the Western Isles, in parts of the NW coast and in the city of Glasgow. Gaelic has been in decline for several centuries, subject until quite recently to neglect within the British state. There is a small Gaelic-speaking community in Nova Scotia, Canada.

German a member of the W Germanic branch of the Indo-European language family, the national language of W Germany, E Germany and Austria, and an official language of Switzerland. There are many spoken varieties of German, the best known distinction being between High German (*Hochdeutsch*) and Low German (*Plattdeutsch*). 'High' and 'low' refer to geography rather than social status, Hochdeutsch originating in the central and southern highlands of Germany, Austria and Switzerland, Plattdeutsch being used in the lowlands of N Germany. However, modern standard and literary German is based on High German, in particular on the Middle German dialect used by Martin Luther for his translation of the Bible in the 16th century. Low German is closer to English in its sound system, the verb 'to make' being *machen* in High German but *maken* in Low German. Such English words as *angst, blitz, frankfurter, hamburger, poltergeist, sauerkraut* and *schadenfreude* are borrowings from High German.

Germanic a branch of the Indo-European language family, divided into *East Germanic*

(Gothic, now extinct), *North Germanic* (Danish, Faroese, Icelandic, Norwegian and Swedish), and *West Germanic* (Afrikaans, Dutch, English, Flemish, Frisian, German and Yiddish). The Germanic languages differ from the other Indo-European languages most prominently in the consonant shift known as Grimm's Law. In it, the sounds *p, t, k* became either (as in English) *f, th, h* or as in Old High German *f, d, h*. Thus, the typical Indo-European of the Latin *pater* is *father* in English and *Fater* in Old High German. In addition, the Indo-European *b, d, g* moved to become *p, t, k*, or in Old High German *f, ts, kh*; compare Latin *duo*, English *two*, and German *zwei* ('tsvai').

Greek a well-documented member of the Indo-European language family which has passed through at least five distinct phases since the second millennium BC: *Ancient Greek*, including Mycenaean, around the 14th to 12th centuries BC; *Archaic Greek*, which included the language of the Homeric epics, coming to an end around 800 BC; the *Classical Greek* of Athens (Attic Greek), Sparta (Doric Greek) and Ionia (Ionian Greek), until around 400 BC; the *Hellenistic Greek* or *Koine* ('common language') of Greece, Asia Minor, W Asia and Egypt from around the 4th century BC to the 4th century AD, first spread by the campaigns of Alexander the Great; *Byzantine Greek*, the language of the Eastern Roman or Byzantine Empire, 5th to 15th centuries AD; and *Modern Greek*, with a variety of dialects but most noticeably divided into the general vernacular (*Demotic Greek* or *Demotiki*) and the so-called 'pure' language of education and traditional literature (*Katharevousa*). In its earlier phases Greek was spoken mainly in Greece proper, the islands, the W coast of Asia Minor and in colonies in Sicily, the Italian mainland and S France. Hellenistic Greek was an important language not only in the Near East but also in the Roman Empire generally, and is the form also known as *New Testament Greek* (in which the Gospels and other books of the New Testament of the Bible were first written). Byzantine Greek was the medium of the Greek Orthodox Church. Modern Greek, in both its forms, is spoken in Greece and in Cyprus, as well as wherever Greeks have settled throughout the world (especially Canada, the United States and Australia). Classical Greek word-forms continue to have a great influence in the world's scientific and technical vocabulary, and make up a large part of the technical vocabulary of English.

Gujarati or **Gujerati** a member of the Indo-Iranian branch of the Indo-European language family, spoken in and around the state of Gujarat in India. It is written in its own script – a variant of the Devanagari script used for Sanskrit and bindi.

Hamito-Semitic languages a family of languages spoken widely throughout the world but commonly associated with N Africa and W Asia. It has two main branches, the *Hamitic* languages of N Africa and the *Semitic* languages originating in Syria and Mesopotamia, Palestine and Arabia but now found from Morocco in the west to the Arabian or Persian Gulf in the east. The Hamitic languages include ancient Egyptian, Coptic and Berber, while the Semitic languages include the most numerous – Arabic, and such other culturally significant languages as Hebrew, Aramaic and Syriac. The scripts of the two best known Hamito-Semitic languages, Arabic and Hebrew, run from right to left.

Hebrew a member of the Hamito-Semitic language family spoken in W Asia by the ancient Hebrews, sustained for many centuries as the liturgical language of Judaism, and revived and developed in the 20th century as Modern Israeli Hebrew, the national language of the State of Israel. It is the original language of the Old Testament of the Bible. Such English words as *bar-mitzvah*, *cherub*, *Hanukkah*, *Jehovah/Yahweh*, *kosher*, *rabbi*, *seraph* and *shibboleth* are borrowings from Hebrew. The Hebrew alphabet is written from right to left.

Hindi a member of the Indo-Iranian branch of the Indo-European language family, the official language of the Republic of India, although resisted as such by the Dravidian-speaking states of the south. Hindi is a north Indian language with many varieties. Hindi proper is used by some 30 per cent of Indians, in such northern states as Uttar Pradesh and Madhya Pradesh. Bihari, Punjabi and Rajasthani, the dominant language varieties in the states of Bihar, Punjab and Rajasthan, are claimed by some to be varieties of Hindi, by others to be distinct languages. Hindi has close historical and cultural links with Sanskrit, the classical language of Hinduism, and is written (from left to right) in Devanagari script.

Hindustani a member of the Indo-Iranian branch of the Indo-European language family, closely related to Hindi and Urdu and originating in the bazaars of Delhi. It serves as a lingua franca in many parts of the Republic of India, and was the contact language during the British Raj between many of the British in India and their servants, shopkeepers, etc. It is sometimes known as Bazaar Hindi.

Hungarian a member of the Finno-Ugric language group, spoken principally in Hungary but also in Czechoslovakia, Romania and Yugoslavia. Known as *Magyar* among its speakers, Hungarian is written in a form of the Roman alphabet in which *s* corresponds to English *sh*, and *sz* to *s*. Like the Turks, the Magyars originated in NE Asia; the term 'Hungarian' appears to derive from the Turkish *on ogur* ('ten arrows'), describing their ten tribes, which may also be the origin of the English 'ogre'.

Icelandic a member of the N Germanic branch of the Indo-European language family, spoken only in Iceland and the most conservative in form of the Scandinavian languages. Its early literature is largely anonymous and seems to have originated in Norse colonies in the British Isles (around 9th–10th centuries). This literature consists mainly of the two Eddas and the more numerous Sagas. Despite seven centuries of Danish rule, Icelandic has remained virtually unchanged since the 12th century, being assured survival by the existence of written law and Bishop Gudbrand's vernacular Bible of 1584. After independence in 1918, Icelandic has experienced a revival, as well as governmental protection against such outside linguistic influences as English-language broadcasting. Halldor Laxness (1902–), writing about Icelandic life in the style of the Sagas, was awarded a Nobel prize in 1955.

Indian languages traditionally, the languages of the subcontinent of India; since 1947, the languages of the Republic of India. These number some 200, depending on whether a variety is classified as a language or a dialect, and divide into five main groups, the two most widespread of which are the *Indo-European* languages (mainly in the north) and the *Dravidian* languages (mainly in the south). The Indo-European languages include the two classical languages, Sanskrit and Pali, and such vernaculars as Bengali, Hindi, Gujarati, Marathi, Oriya, Punjabi and Urdu. The Dravidian languages include Kannada, Malayalam, Tamil and Telugu. A wide range of scripts are used, including Devanagari for Hindi, Arabic for Urdu, and distinct scripts for the various Dravidian languages. The Sino-Tibetan group of languages occurs widely in Assam and along the Himalayas.

Indo-European languages a family of languages whose members are now distributed throughout every inhabited continent of the world but which were once located along a geographical band from India through Iran into NW Asia, E Europe, the northern Mediterranean lands, N and W Europe and the British Isles. When first described in the 19th century this family was known as the Aryan and then the Indo-Germanic language family. However, because of an unwelcome association with ideas of 'Aryan' racial purity and superiority and with the ideology of Nazi Germany, both titles have been abandoned by scholars in favour of the neutral 'Indo-European'. The family includes some of the world's leading classical languages (Sanskrit and Pali in India, Zend Avestan in Iran, and Greek and Latin in Europe) as well as several of the most widely spoken languages of the modern world (English worldwide; Spanish in Iberia, Latin America and elsewhere; and the Hindi group of languages in N India). Eastern Indo-Euro-

pean languages are often called the *satem* group (Zend, 'a hundred') while western Indo-European languages are the *centum* group (Latin, 'a hundred'); this illustrates a split that occurred over 3,000 years ago, between those which had an *s*-sound in certain words and those which had a *k*-sound. Scholars have reconstructed a Proto-Indo-European ancestral language by comparing the sound systems and historical changes within the family, but continue to dispute the original homeland of this ancient form, some arguing for N Europe, others for Russia north of the Black Sea.

Irish Gaelic first official language of the Irish Republic, but much less widely used than the second official language, English.

Irish a common name for Irish Gaelic. At one time, especially in the form 'Erse', also a name for the Gaelic of Scotland.

Italian a member of the Romance branch of the Indo-European language family. Its development parallels the integration of the Italian peninsula and the plains south of the Alps into a cultural and national unity. The standard language originates in the Tuscan dialect of the Middle Ages, particularly as used for literary purposes by Dante Alighieri. With a strong infusion of Latin for religious, academic and educational purposes the written standard has tended to be highly formal and divorced from the many regional dialects (often mutually unintelligible) that are still largely the everyday usage of the general population. Italian has provided English with much of the vocabulary of music *(adagio, arpeggio, cello, crescendo, diminuendo, mezzosoprano, pianoforte)*, Italian cuisine *(lasagne, macaroni, pasta, pizza, ravioli, spaghetti, tagliatelle)*, and an assortment of social comment *(extravaganza, graffiti, imbroglio, mafia, seraglio)*.

Japanese a traditionally isolated language of E Asia, spoken almost exclusively in the islands of Japan. It may be related to Korean. Japanese has a well-defined structure of syllables generally ending with a vowel *(dojo, judo, hiragana, samurai, Honshu, kimono,*

Mitsubishi, teriyaki). Culturally and linguistically influenced by Mandarin Chinese, Japanese is written in a triple system that has evolved from Chinese ideograms: its **Kanji** ideograms are close to their Chinese originals, while the **Hiragana** system is a syllabary for the general language, and **Katakana** a syllabary for foreign borrowings. In print, the three systems blend on the page in a manner comparable to the distinct typefaces of the Roman alphabet. Japanese has an extensive religious and secular literature, including such terse poetic forms as haiku. English words adapted into Japanese belong in *gairaigo.* the foreign vocabulary expressed in the syllable signs of Katakana: *fairu* ('file') *ereganto* ('elegant'), and *purutoniumu* ('plutonium'). Shorter forms are common: *fainda* ('viewfinder') and *wapuro* ('word-processor').

Korean the language of Korea, written from the 5th century AD in Chinese characters until the invention of an alphabet by King Sejong in 1443. This alphabet was, however, discouraged as 'vulgar letters' (*onmun*) and banned by the colonizing Japanese. However, after World War II it has been revived as 'top letters' (*hangul*). The linguistic affiliations of Korean are unclear, but it appears to be distantly related to Japanese.

Lallans a variant of 'lowlands' and a name for Lowland Scots, whether conceived as a language in its own right or as a northern dialect of English. Because of its rustic associations, Lallans has been known since the 18th century as the 'Doric', in contrast with the 'Attic' usage of Edinburgh ('the Athens of the North').

Latin an Indo-European language of ancient Italy, named after the Latini, the inhabitants of Latium ('the broad plain'), the territory around the river Tiber and the city of Rome. Latin has passed through four influential phases: as the language of Republican Rome, the Roman Empire, the Roman Catholic church, and W European culture, science, philosophy and law during the Middle Ages and the Renaissance. It is the parent form of the Romance languages, noted for its highly inflected grammar and conciseness of expression; thus, one word *amabunt* expresses the three English words 'they will love', and *amabuntur* means 'they will be loved'. The influence of Latin in Europe is still considerable, and indirectly both the language and its classical literature still affect many modern languages and literatures. Latin vocabulary has entered English in two major waves: as religious vocabulary from Anglo-Saxon times until the Reformation, and as the vocabulary of science, scholarship and the law from the Middle Ages onwards. In the 17th century the makers of English dictionaries deliberately converted Latin words into English, enlarging the already powerful French component of English vocabulary into the language of education and refinement, placing *fraternity* alongside 'brotherhood', *feline* beside 'cat-like', and so on. Many 'Latin tags' are in regular use in English: *habeas corpus* ('you may have the body'), *ipse dixit* ('he said it himself'), *non sequitur* ('it does not follow'). Nowadays, with fewer students studying Latin in schools and universities, there is a tendency to make Latin words more conventionally English; for example, 'cactuses' rather than *cacti*. There is also some uncertainty about usage, for example whether words like 'data' and 'media' are singular or plural.

Latvian the language of Latvia, one of the two surviving members of the Baltic branch of the Indo-European language family, the other being Lithuanian.

lingua franca any language that is used as a means of communication by groups who do not themselves normally speak that language at home and cannot otherwise do business; for example, English is a lingua franca used by Japanese doing business in Finland, or Swedes in Saudi Arabia. The term derives from Italian (*la lingua franca* 'the Frankish tongue'), referring to French as used around the Mediterranean shores in the Middle Ages. Many of the world's lingua francas are pidgin languages, such as Bazaar Hindi (Hindustani), Bazaar Malay, and Melanesian Pidgin English (also known as Tok Pisin), the official language of

Papua New Guinea.

Lithuanian an Indo-European language spoken by the people of Lithuania that through its geographical isolation has retained many ancient features of the Indo-European language family. It acquired a written form in the 16th century, and is currently spoken by around three to four million people.

Malay a member of the Western or Indonesian branch of the Malayo-Polynesian language family, used in the Malay peninsula and many of the islands of Malaysia and Indonesia. The dialect of the S Malay peninsula is the basis of both standard Malay in Malaysia and Bahasa Indonesia, the official language of Indonesia. Bazaar Malay is a widespread pidgin variety used for trading and shopping. The Malaysian and Indonesian varieties officially employ slightly different versions of the Roman alphabet but are also sometimes written in the Jawi form of Arabic script.

Malayo-Polynesian also known as Austronesian, a family of languages spoken from Malaysia through the Indonesian archipelago, parts of Indo-China, Taiwan, Madagascar, and the Melanesian islands to Polynesia (excluding Australia and most of New Guinea). The group contains some 500 distinct languages, some spoken by only a few hundred people, others the standard languages of millions. The family includes Malay in Malaysia, Bahasa Indonesia, Fijian, Hawaiian and Maori.

Maori a member of the Polynesian branch of the Malayo-Polynesian language family, spoken by the Maori people of New Zealand. Of the approximately 300,000 Maoris today, not more than one third use the language, but efforts are being made to strengthen it after a long period of decline and official indifference. In Maori, New Zealand is *Aotearoa* ('land of the long white cloud') and European settlers are *Pakeha*, a term often used by white New Zealanders when constrasting themselves with the Maori.

Norse generally, the older forms of the Danish, Icelandic, Norwegian and Swedish languages; more particularly, the older common form of Norwegian and Icelandic, in which the Sagas and Eddas were written in the 12th to 14th centuries.

Norwegian a member of the N Germanic branch of the Indo-European language family, spoken in Norway. It is divided into two distinctive but mutually intelligible forms: *Dano-Norwegian* (Bokmal or Riksmal) and *New Norwegian* (Nynorsk). The first arose during the union with Denmark (1380-1814), while the second was created in the 19th century by Ivar Aasen from various rural dialects, to revive the tradition of Old Norse. Both varieties are used in government and education, but Dano-Norwegian dominates the media and literature.

Pali an ancient Indo-European language of N India, related to Sanskrit and a classical language of Buddhism.

Persian a member of the Indo-Iranian branch of the Indo-European language family and the official language of the state once known as Persia but now officially called Iran. Persian is known to its own speakers as *Farsi*, the language of the province of Fars (Persia proper). It is written in the Arabic script, from right to left, and has a large admixture of Arabic religious, philosophical and technical vocabulary. Words in English which derive from Persian include *balcony*, *bazaar*, *paradise*, *sherbet* and *turban*.

Pidgin English commonly and loosely used to mean any kind of 'broken' or 'native' version of the English language, pidgin English proper began as a trade jargon or contact language between the British and the Chinese in the 19th century. *Pidgin* is believed to have been a Chinese pronunciation of the English word 'business' (whence the expression, 'This isn't my pigeon'). There have in fact been many 'pidgin Englishes', often with common elements because of the wide range of contacts made by commercial shipping. The original pidgin English of the Chinese ports combined words of English with a rough-and-ready Chinese grammatical structure, while Melanesian Pidgin English (also known as Tok Pisin) tends to combine English and the syntax of local Melanesian languages. Thus, instead of the

English pronoun 'we', Melanesian pidgin English has both *yumi* (you and me, speaking to each other) and *miffela* (me and fellow, excluding you).

pidgin languages trade jargons, contact languages or lingua francas arising in ports and markets where people of different linguistic backgrounds meet for commercial and other purposes. Generally, a pidgin comes into existence to answer short-term needs, for example Korean Bamboo English as used during the Korean War. Unless there is a reason for extending the life of such a hybrid form (in the case of Korean Bamboo English combining elements of English, Korean and Japanese), it will fade away when the need passes. Usually a pidgin is a rough-and-ready blend of the vocabulary of one (often more dominant) language with the syntax or grammar of one or more other groups (usually in a dependent position). Pidgin English in various parts of the world, *français petit nègre*, and Bazaar Hindi or Hindustani are examples of pidgins which have served long-term purposes, to the extent of being acquired by children as one of their everyday languages.

Polish a member of the Slavonic branch of the Indo-European language family, spoken mainly in Poland. Polish is written in the Roman and not the Cyrillic alphabet and its standard form is based on the dialect of Poznan, in W Poland.

Portuguese a member of the Romance branch of the Indo-European language family, the national language of Portugal, closely related to Spanish and strongly influenced by Arabic. It is also spoken in Brazil, Angola, Mozambique and other ex-Portuguese overseas possessions.

Prakrit a general name for the ancient Indo-European dialects of N India, contrasted with the sacred classical language Sanskrit. The word is itself Sanskrit, meaning 'natural', as opposed to *Sanskrit*, which means 'perfected'. The Prakrits are considered to be the ancestors of such modern N Indian languages as Hindi, Punjabi and Bengali.

Provençal a member of the Romance branch of the Indo-European language family and spoken in and around Provence in SE France. It is now regarded as a dialect or patois but during the Middle Ages was in competition with French, was the language of the troubadours, and had a strong literary influence on such neighbouring languages as Italian, Spanish and Portuguese. Since the 19th century attempts have been made to revive it as a literary language.

Punjabi a member of the Indo-Iranian branch of the Indo-European language family, spoken in the Punjab provinces of India and Pakistan. It is considered by some to be a variety of Hindi, by others to be a distinct language.

Romance languages the branch of the Indo-European languages descended from the Latin of the Roman Empire ('popular' or 'vulgar' as opposed to 'classical' Latin). The present-day Romance languages with national status are French, Italian, Portuguese, Romanian and Spanish. Romansh (or Rhaeto-Romanic) is a minority language of Switzerland which is nevertheless one of the four official languages of the country, while Catalan and Gallego (or Galician) in Spain, Provençal in France and Friulian and Sardinian in Italy are recognised as distinct languages with strong regional and/or literary traditions of their own.

Romanian a member of the Romance branch of the Indo-European language family, spoken in Romania, Macedonia, Albania and parts of N Greece. It has been strongly influenced by the Slavonic languages and by Greek. The Cyrillic alphabet was used until the 19th century, when a variant of the Roman alphabet was adopted.

Romansh a member of the Romance branch of the Indo-European language family, spoken by some 50,000 people in the eastern cantons of Switzerland and accorded official status alongside French, German and Italian in 1937. It is also known among scholars as Rhaeto-Romanic.

Russian a member of the Slavonic branch of the Indo-European language family. The people of Russia proper refer to it as 'Great

Russian', in contrast with Ukrainian (which they call 'Little Russian') and the language of Byelorussia ('White Russian'). It is written in the Cyrillic alphabet and is the standard means of communication throughout the Soviet Union. Words in English which derive from Russian include *apparatchik*, *commissar*, *cosmonaut*, *czar/tsar*, *pogrom*, *samovar* and *vodka*.

Sanskrit the dominant classical language of the Indian subcontinent, a member of the Indo-Iranian group of the Indo-European language family, and the sacred language of Hinduism. The oldest form of Sanskrit is *Vedic*, the variety used in the Vedas and Upanishads (around 1500–700 BC). *Classical Sanskrit* was systematized by Panini and other grammarians in the latter part of the first millennium BC and became fixed as the spoken and written language of culture, philosophy, mathematics, law and medicine. It is written in Devanagari script and is the language of the two great Hindu epics, the *Mahabharata* and the *Ramayana*, as well as many other classical and later works. Sanskrit vocabulary has not only influenced the languages of India, Thailand and Indonesia but has also enriched several European languages, including English, with such words as *bhakti*, *guru*, *karma*, *kundalini*, *mahatma*, *pundit*, *swami* and *yoga*, all relating to Hindu religion and philosophy.

Scots the form of the English language as traditionally spoken and written in Scotland, regarded by some scholars as a distinct language. It is also known as *Inglis* (now archaic, and a variant of 'English'), *Lallans* ('Lowlands'), *Lowland Scots* (in contrast with the Gaelic of the Highlands and Islands), and *the 'Doric'* (as a rustic language in contrast with the 'Attic' or 'Athenian' language of Edinburgh's literati, especially in the 18th century). It is also often referred to as 'Broad Scots' in contrast to the anglicized language of the middle classes. Scots derives from the Northumbrian dialect of Anglo-Saxon or Old English, and has been spoken in SE Scotland since the 7th century. During the Middle Ages it spread from the Central Lowlands northeastwards to Aber-

deenshire and to the far north, where it blended with the Norn dialects of Orkney and Shetland (once distinct varieties of Norse). Scots has been a literary language since the 14th century, with a wide range of poetry, ballads and prose records, including two national epic poems, Barbour's *Bruce* and Blind Harry's *Wallace*. With the transfer of the court to England upon the Union of the Crowns in 1603 and the dissemination of the King James Bible, Scots ceased to be a national and court language in the 17th century, but has retained its vitality among the general population and in various literary and linguistic revivals. In Scotland a wide range of traditional Scots usage intermixes with standard English, such as *advocate* (barrister), *close* (entrance to a staircase of tenement flats), *kirk* (church).

Slavonic or Slavic languages a branch of the Indo-European language family spoken in central and E Europe, the Balkans and parts of N Asia. The family divides into three groups: the *southern group* (Serbo-Croat, Slovene and Macedonian in Yugoslavia, and Bulgarian in Bulgaria); the *western group* (Czech and Slovak in Czechoslovakia, Sorbian in E Germany, and Polish and its related dialects); and the *eastern group* (Russian, Ukrainian, and Byelorussian, in the Soviet Union). There is such a high degree of uniformity among the Slavonic languages that scholars speak of a 'dialect continuum' in which the users of one variety understand tolerably well much of what is said in other varieties. Some Slavonic languages, like Polish, are written in the Roman alphabet while others, like Russian, are written in Cyrillic.

Spanish a member of the Romance branch of the Indo-European language family, traditionally known as Castilian and originally spoken only in NE Spain, in the kingdoms of Castile and Aragon. As the language of the court it has been the standard and literary language of the Spanish state since the 13th century, but has never succeeded in supplanting such regional languages as Basque, Gallego or Galician, and Catalan. Because of the long Muslim dominance of the S Iberian peninsula,

Spanish has been strongly influenced by Arabic. Spanish is now a world language, spoken in all South American and central American countries (save Brazil, Guyana, Surinam and French Guiana), as well as in Mexico and the Philippines. Words in English of Spanish origin include *bronco*, *cargo*, *galleon*, *mosquito*, *ranch* and *sherry*.

Swahili a language of Bantu origin and strongly influenced by Arabic, a widespread lingua franca of E Africa and the national language of Tanzania (1967) and Kenya (1973).

Swedish a member of the N Germanic branch of the Indo-European language family, spoken in Sweden and Finland and closely related to Danish and Norwegian. Words in English of Swedish origin include *ombudsman*, *smorgasbord* and *tungsten*.

Syriac an ancient Semitic language, originally the Aramaic dialect spoken in and around Edessa (now in Turkey) and widely used in W Asia from around 700 BC to 700 AD. From the 3rd to 7th centuries it was an important Christian liturgical and literary language.

Tamil a Dravidian language of SE India, spoken principally in the state of Tamilnadu (formerly, Madras state) and also in N Sri Lanka. It is written in its own distinctive script. Words in English of Tamil origin include *catamaran*, *cheroot*, *mulligatawny* and *pariah*.

Turkish a language of central and W Asia, best known as the national language of Turkey. Originally written in Arabic script, the Turkish of Turkey has since 1928 been written in a variant of the Roman alphabet. Varieties of Turkish are spoken in NW Iran and several of the Asian republics of the Soviet Union, and all have been influenced by Arabic and Persian. Words of Turkish origin in English include *divan*, *coffee*, *cossack*, *horde*, *kiosk* and *yoghourt/yogurt*.

Ukrainian a member of the Slavonic branch of the Indo-European language family, spoken in the Ukraine, a republic of the Soviet Union. It is closely related to Russian and is sometimes referred to by Russians as 'Little Russian', a description which Ukrainians generally do not find appropriate.

Urdu a member of the Indo-Iranian branch of the Indo-European language family, related to Hindi but written not in Devanagari but in Arabic script. Strongly influenced by Persian and Arabic, Urdu is the official language of Pakistan and a language used by Muslims in India.

Welsh a member of the Celtic branch of the Indo-European language family, spoken by over half a million people in Wales out of a total population of just under three million. Among its own speakers it is known as *Cymraeg*. Modern Welsh, like English, is not a highly inflected language, but British, the Celtic ancestor of Welsh, was like Latin and Anglo-Saxon a highly inflected form. The continuous literature of Welsh, from the 6th century onwards, contains the whole range of change from British to present-day Welsh. Although the spoken language is the strongest of the surviving Celtic languages it has been in retreat in the face of English expansion since the accession of the Welsh Henry Tudor (as Henry VII) to the throne of England. Nowadays, few Welsh people speak only Welsh; they are either bilingual or only speak English.

Yiddish a member of the W Germanic branch of the Indo-European language family, deriving from Rhineland German and spoken by Polish and Russian Jews, who have carried it to Israel, the United States and many other parts of the world. In the United States, Yiddish has had a powerful impact on English, especially in the city of New York and in the national media. Such words and expressions as *bagel*, *chutzpa(h)*, *kibbitz*, *mensh*, *nosh*, *schlemiel*, *schmaltz* and *schmuck* are currently acquiring international status in English. Isaac Bashevis Singer (1904–), born in Poland, US citizen 1943, who writes in Yiddish, won the Nobel Prize for Literature in 1978.

THE INDO-EUROPEAN LANGUAGES

Proto-Indo-European
(hypothetical)

```
                    Western Branch                              Eastern Branch
                  (centum languages)                          (satem languages)

 Western      Hellenic¹    Others¹¹       Balto-       Albanian²    Armenian³  Indo-
 European                                 Slavonic                             Iranian

 Celto-      Germanic⁴                    Baltic⁵    Slavonic⁶   Iranian⁷        Indian⁸
 Italic

 Celtic⁹     Italic¹⁰
```

1 Hellenic:	Greek (including *Ancient, *Archaic, *Classical, *Koine, *Byzantine and the modern forms *Demotiki* and *Katharevousa*)
2 Albanian:	Albanian
3 Armenian:	Armenian
4 Germanic:	Afrikaans, *Anglo-Saxon, (Old English), Bavarian, Danish, Dutch/Flemish, English/Scots, Faroese, Frisian, German (Low, High, Swiss, etc), *Gothic, Icelandic, Luxemburgish, *Old Norse, *Old High German, Norwegian, Swedish, Yiddish
5 Baltic:	Latvian, Lithuanian, *Old Prussian
6 Slavonic: (or Slavic)	Bulgarian, Byelorussian, Croatian, Czech, Kashubian, Macedonian, Polish, Pomeranian, Russian, Serbian, Slovak, Slovene, Sorbian, Ukrainian
7 Iranian:	*Avestan (Zend or Zand), *Bactrian, Baluchi, Kurdish, *Median, Ossetic, *Pahlavi, *Parthian, Pashto, Persian (Farsi), Tadzhik
8 Indian:	Assamese, Bengali, Bhili, Bihari, Gujarati, Hindi, Kashmiri, Konkani, Marathi, Oriya, Pahari, *Pali, Punjabi, Rajasthani, *Sanskrit, Sindhi, Sinhalese, Urdu
9 Celtic:	Breton, *Brythonic, *Cornish, Gaelic (Irish, *Manx and Scottish), *Gaulish, *Goidelic, Welsh
10 Italic:	(1) *Latin, *Oscan, *Umbrian (2) Romance: Catalan, French, Gallego (Galician), Italian, Portuguese, Provençal, Romanian (Rumanian), Romansh, Spanish (Castilian)
11 others	*Anatolian (including Hittite), *Tocharian

The Indo-European languages An outline diagram of the historical relationships among the Indo-European languages, followed by lists of languages in each branch of the family tree. Extinct languages are marked with an asterisk (*).

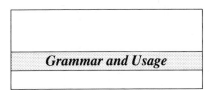

Grammar and Usage

grammar as an aspect of language and the study of language, grammar has traditionally been seen as dealing with the rules of combining words into phrases and clauses, phrases and clauses into sentences, and sentences into paragraphs.

'good grammar', in this view, is the result of an adequate education in one or more classical language, in the mother tongue, in one or more foreign languages, or a combination of these. As a consequence, people with 'bad grammar' have tended to be seen as uneducated, poorly educated, inattentive while being educated, and/or inclined towards sloppy thinking and slovenly style.

classical approach this widespread view has emerged out of 2,500 years of educational procedures and social attitudes relating to the classical Greek *grammatike tekhne* ('art of letters'). This original 'grammar' was an analytical approach to writing, intended to improve the understanding and the skills of scribes, philosophers and litterateurs. Because of a traditional emphasis on writing and (since the 15th century) on the standardizing impact of print, spoken or colloquial language has often been perceived as less grammatical than written – especially literary – language. In addition, when compared with Latin, English has also been widely regarded as having 'less' grammar or at least a simpler grammar; it would be truer, however, to say that English and Latin have *different* grammars, each complex in its own way.

linguistics is the contemporary study of language, in which grammar or syntax is generally understood to refer to the arrangement of the elements in a language, for the purposes of acceptable communication in speech, writing and print. All forms of a language, standard or otherwise, have their grammars or grammatical systems, which children acquire as they mature into that language; indeed, a child may acquire several overlapping systems within one language (especially a non-standard form for everyday life and a standard form linked with writing, school and national life).

natural grammar not even the most comprehensive grammar book (or grammar) of a language like English, French, Arabic or Japanese completely covers or fixes the implicit grammatical system that people use in their daily speech. The rules and tendencies of natural grammar operate largely in non-conscious ways, but can, for many social and professional purposes, be studied and explicitly developed as conscious as well as inherent skills.

part of speech the grammatical function of a word, described in the grammatical tradition of the Western world, based on Greek and Latin. The four major parts of speech are the noun, verb, adjective and adverb; the minor parts of speech vary according to schools of grammatical theory, but include the article, conjunction, preposition and pronoun. In languages like Greek and Latin the part of speech of a word tends to be invariable (usually marked by an ending or inflection); in English, it is much harder to recognise the function of a word simply by its form. Some English words may have only one function (for example, *and* as a conjunction). Others, however, may have several functions (for example, *fancy*, which is a noun in the phrase 'flights of fancy', a verb in 'fancy that', and an adjective in 'a fancy hat').

noun the grammatical part of speech that names (or stands for) such classes of words as persons (*John*), animals (*cat*), places (*London*), things (*hat*), qualities (*love*), actions (*arrest*), ideas and abstractions (*idea, abstraction, reality, Communism, Roman Catholicism*), and so on. *Types of noun* A *common noun* does not begin with a capital letter (*child, cat*), while a proper noun does, because it is the name of a particular person, animal, place, etc (*John, Rover, London*). A *concrete noun* refers to things which can be sensed (*dog*, *box*), while an **abstract noun** relates to generalizations 'abstracted' from life as we observe it (*love*, *illness*). A countable noun can have a plural form (*book*: *books*), while an uncountable noun or mass noun cannot (*dough*). Many English nouns can be used both countably and uncountably (*wine*: 'Have some wine; it's one of our best wines'). A **collective noun** is singular in form but refers to a group (*flock*, *committee*), and a **compound noun** is made up of two or more nouns (*blackbird*, *coffee jug*). A **verbal noun** is formed from a verb (*run*: *running*; *build*:*building*; *regulate*: *regulation*) and in English many simple words are both noun and verb (*crunch*, *jump*, *rain*). Adjectives are often used as nouns (a *local* man: one of the *locals*; a *regular* soldier: an *Army regular*).

verb the grammatical part of speech for what someone or something does (*to go*, *to imagine*), experiences (*to live*, *to die*), or is (*to be*, *to exist*). In the sentences 'They *saw* the accident', 'She *is working* today', and 'He *should have been trying to meet* them', the words in italics are verbs and, in the last case, two verb groups together; these sentences show just how complex the verbs of English can be. Verbs involve the grammatical categories known as number (singular or plural: 'He *runs*; they *run*'), voice (active or passive: 'She *writes* books; it *is written*'), mood (statements, questions, orders, emphasis, necessity, condition, and so on), aspect (completed or continuing action: 'She *danced*; she *was dancing*'), and tense (variation according to time: simple present tense, present continuous/progressive tense, simple past tense, and so on). *Types of verb* A **transitive** verb takes a direct object (he saw *the house*), while an **intransitive verb** has no object ('She laughed'). An **auxiliary** or **helping verb** is used to express tense and/or mood ('He *was* seen'; 'They *may* come'), while a **modal verb** or **modal auxiliary** generally shows only mood; common modals are *may*/*might*, *will*/ *would*, *can*/*could*, *shall*/ *should*, *must*. The infinitive of the verb usually includes 'to' (*to go*, *to run*, and so on), but may be a bare infinitive (for example, after modals, as in 'She

may *go*'). A **regular verb** forms tenses in the normal way (*I walk*: *I walked*: *I have walked*); **irregular verbs** do not (*swim*:*swam*:*swum*; *put*:*put*:*put*, and so on). Because of their conventional nature, regular verbs are also known as weak verbs, while some irregular verbs are strong verbs with special vowel changes across tenses, as in *swim*:*swam*:*swum* and *ride*:*rode*:*ridden*. A **phrasal verb** is a construction in which a particle attaches to a usually one-syllabled verb for certain grammatical and idiomatic purposes (for example, *put* becoming *put up*, as in 'He put up some money for the project', and *put up with*, as in 'I can't put up with this nonsense any longer'). Verbs are formed from nouns and adjectives by adding affixes (prison: *imprison*; light: *enlighten*; fresh: *freshen (up)*; pure: *purify*). Some words function as both nouns and verbs (*crack*; *run*), both adjectives and verbs (*clean*; *ready*), and as nouns, adjectives and verbs (*fancy*).

adjective the grammatical part of speech for words that describe nouns (for example, *new* and *enormous*, as in 'a new hat' and 'an enormous dog'). Adjectives generally have three degrees (grades or levels for the description of relationships): the **positive** degree (*new*; *enormous*), the **comparative** degree (*newer*; *more enormous*), and the **superlative** degree (*newest*; *most enormous*). Some adjectives, however, because of their meanings, do not normally need comparative and superlative forms; one person is not normally 'more asleep' than someone else, a lone action is unlikely to be 'the most single-handed action ever seen', and many people dislike the expression 'most unique', because something unique is supposed to be the only one that there is. However, for purposes of emphasis or style these conventions are often set aside ('I don't know who is more unique; they are both remarkable people'). Double comparatives such as 'more bigger' are unnecessary and not grammatical in Standard English, but Shakespeare is on record as using a double superlative ('the most unkindest cut of all'). Some adjectives may have both of the comparative and superlative forms (*commoner* and *more common*; *commonest* and *most common*), while occasionally shorter words may be given the forms for longer words ('Which of them are the *most clear?*') for emphasis or other reasons. When an adjective comes before a noun it is attributive; if it comes after noun and verb (for example, 'It looks *good*'), it is predicative. Some adjectives can only be used predicatively ('The child was asleep', but not 'the asleep child'). The participles of verbs are regularly used adjectivally ('a *sleeping* child', 'boiled milk') and often in compound forms ('a *quick-acting* medicine', 'a *glass-making* factory', 'a *hard-boiled* egg', '*well-trained* teachers'). Adjectives are often formed by adding suffixes to nouns (sand: sand*y*; nation: nation*al*).

adverb the grammatical part of speech for words that modify or describe verbs ('She ran *quickly*'), adjectives ('a *beautifully* clear day'), and adverbs ('They did it *really* well'). Most adverbs are formed from adjectives or past participles by adding *-ly* (*quick: quickly;*), or *-ally* (*automatic: automatically*). Sometimes they are formed by adding *-wise* (*like: likewise*, and *clockwise*, as in 'moving clockwise'; in 'a clockwise direction', *clockwise* is an adjective). Some adjectives have a distinct form from their partnering adjective, as with good/well ('It was *good* work; they did it *well*'). Others do not derive from adjectives (*very* in 'very nice'; *tomorrow* in 'I'll do it tomorrow'), and some are unadapted adjectives (*pretty*, as in, 'It's pretty good'). Sentence adverbs modify whole sentences or phrases: '*Generally*, it rains a lot here'; '*Usually*, the town is busy at this time of year'. Sometimes there is controversy in such matters. *Hopefully* is universally accepted in sentences like 'He looked at them hopefully' (in a hopeful way), but some people dislike it in, 'Hopefully, we'll see you again next year' (We hope that we'll see you again next year).

article a grammatical part of speech, of which there are two in English: the *definite article* 'the', which serves to specify or identify a noun (for example, 'This is the book I need'), and the *indefinite article* 'a' or 'an (before vowels), which indicates a single unidentified

noun ('They gave me a piece of paper and an envelope'). Some people use the form 'an' before *h* ('an historic building'); this practice dates from the 17th century, when an initial *h* was often not pronounced (as in '*h*onour'), and is nowadays rather grandiose and unnecessary.

conjunction a grammatical part of speech that serves to connect words, phrases and clauses; for example *and* in 'apples and pears' and *but* in 'we're going but they aren't'.

participle a form of the verb, in English either a *present participle* ending in *-ing* (such as 'work*ing*' in 'They were working', 'work*ing* men', and 'a hard-work*ing* team') or a *past participle* ending in *-ed* in regular verbs (such as 'train*ed*' in 'They have been trained well', 'trained soldiers', and 'a well-trained team'). In irregular verbs the past participle has a special form (such as drive/*driven*; light/*lit*, burn/*burned, burnt*). The participle is also used to open such constructions as 'Coming down the stairs, she paused and…', and 'Angered by the news, he…'. Such constructions, however, are not always logically formed, with amusing or ambiguous results. 'Driving along a country road, a stone broke my windscreen' suggests that the stone was driving along the road. This illogical usage is a *misrelated participle*. A *dangling* or *hanging participle* has nothing at all to relate to: 'While driving along a country road there was a loud noise under the car'. Such sentences need to be completely re-expressed, except in some well-established usages where the participle can stand alone (as in 'Taking all things into consideration, your actions were justified').

inflection or **inflexion**. In grammatical analysis, an ending or other element in a word which indicates its grammatical function, (whether it is plural or singular, masculine or feminine, and so on). In a highly inflected language like Latin, nouns, verbs and adjectives have a whole battery of inflectional endings (for example, in the word *amabunt* the base *am* means 'love', and the complex *abunt* indicates the kind of verb, the future tense, indicative mood, active voice, third person and plurality). English is not a highly inflected language, but does have inflections for plural and for certain forms of the verb, (as in the *s* in 'He runs', indicating the third person singular, while in 'the book*s*' it indicates plurality).

preposition a grammatical part of speech coming before a noun or pronoun in order to show a location ('in', 'on'), time ('during'), or some other relationship (such as figurative relationships in phrases like 'by heart' or 'on time'). In the sentence 'Put the book on the table' *on* is a preposition governing the noun 'table' and relates the verb 'put' to the phrase 'the table', indicating where the book should go. Some words of English that are often prepositional in function may, however, be used adverbially, as in the sentences, 'He picked the book up' and 'He picked up the book', in which the ordering is different but the meaning the same. In such cases *up* is called an *adverbial particle* and the form 'pick up' is a *phrasal verb*.

pronoun a grammatical part of speech that is used in place of a noun, usually to save repetition of the noun (such as 'The people arrived around nine o'clock. *They* behaved as though we were expecting *them*'). Words like *they*, *them*, *he*, *she*, and so on, are *personal pronouns* (because they represent people), words like *this*/*these* and *that*/*those* are *demonstrative pronouns* (because they demonstrate or point to something : this book and not that book and so on), words like *that* and *who* can be *relative pronouns* in sentences like 'She said that she was coming' and 'Tell me who did it' (because they relate one clause to another), and words like *myself* and *himself* are *reflexive pronouns* (because they reflect back to a person, as in 'He did it himself').

punctuation the system of conventional signs (*punctuation marks*) and spaces by means of which written and printed language is organized so as to be as readable , clear and logical as possible. It contributes to the effective layout of visual language; if a work is not adequately punctuated there may be problems of ambiguity and unclear association among words. Conventions of punctuation differ from language to language and there are preferred styles in

the punctuation of a language such as English. While some people prefer a fuller use of punctuation, others punctuate more lightly; comparably, the use of punctuation will vary according to the kind of passage being produced, a personal letter, a newspaper article and a technical report all being laid out and punctuated in distinctive ways.

period a punctuation mark (.). The term 'period' is universally understood in English, and is the preferred usage in N America; the term 'full stop' is the preferred form in Great Britain, while the term 'point' is casually used but is not generally considered a technical term. Traditionally, the period has two functions: to mark the end of a properly formed sentence, and to indicate that a word has been abbreviated. In present-day practice these functions continue, but in such contexts as fictional dialogue and advertising, periods often follow phrases and incomplete sentences in order to represent speech more faithfully or for purposes of emphasis. In addition, such abbreviations as acronyms are unlikely to have periods (NATO rather than N.A.T.O.) and certain abbreviations may or may not have periods, according to the stylistic preference of the writer (for example, 'Mr Greene' or 'Mr. Greene'.

comma a punctuation mark (,), intended to provide breaks or pauses inside a properly formed sentence; commas may come at the end of a clause, after a phrase, or in lists (as in apples, pears, plums, and pineapples; or, apples, pears, plums and pineapples). Uncertain where sentences properly end, many occasional writers use a comma instead of a period (or full stop), writing *We saw John last night, it was good to see him again*, rather than *We saw John last night. It was good to see him again*. The meaning is entirely clear in both cases. One solution in such situations is to use a *semicolon* (;), which combines period and comma and serves well in bridging the gap between the close association of the comma and the sharp separation of the period.

colon punctuation mark (:), intended to direct the reader's attention forward, usually because what follows explains or develops what has just been written, for example, *The soldiers carried a variety of weapons: rifles, hand-guns, several machine-guns and an anti-tank weapon.*

semicolon a punctuation mark (;) with a function halfway between the sharp separation of sentence from sentence by means of a period (.) and the gentler separation provided by a comma (,). Although semicolons are not as commonly used as formerly, they provide a useful half-way stage between commas and periods. Rather than the sharpness of *We saw John last night. It was good to see him again*, and the more casual (and often condemned) *We saw John last night, it was good to see him again*, the use of the semicolon both reflects the close link between the two parts of the state-ment and is traditionally considered correct and good style: *We saw John last night; it was good to see him again.*

exclamation mark or exclamation point. A punctuation mark (!), used to indicate emphasis or strong emotion ('What a sur-prise!'). Usually the emphasis or emotion is built directly into the text, as part of a story, dialogue, and so on, but the exclamation can also be placed in brackets to indicate that the writer is surprised by something, especially by something in a quotation. Although the exclamation mark is a natural part of imagina-tive or emotional writing, its use is generally kept to a minimum in serious prose and technical writing.

question mark a punctuation mark (?), used to indicate enquiry or doubt. When indicating enquiry, it is placed at the end of a *direct question* ('Who is coming?') but never at the end of an *indirect question* ('He asked us who was coming'.). When indicating doubt, it usually appears between brackets, to show that a writer or editor is puzzled or uncertain about a statement or quotation.

apostrophe a mark used in the written presentation of English ('). It serves primarily to indicate a missing letter or number (as in *don't* for 'do not' and *'47* for '1947'). It also often precedes the plural *s* used with numbers

and abbreviations (as in *the 1970's* and *a group of P.O.W's*); it is possible, however, to do without the apostrophe in such usages (as in *the 1970s, a group of POWs*). The use of an apostrophe to help indicate a plural (as in a shopkeeper's *Apple's* and *Tomato's*, followed by their prices) is nonstandard and regarded by many as semi-literate. Grammatically, the apostrophe indicates possession (as in *the gen-tleman's hat, the gentlemen's hats, the lady's hat, the ladies' hats*). In the case of certain words ending with *s*, usage is split, as between *James's book* and *James' book*. In current English, the possessive apostrophe is often omitted from such usages as *in ten months' time/in ten months time* and such titles as *Chambers Dictionary*. Many people otherwise competent in writing have great difficulty with the apostrophe, which has never been stable at any point in its history, and some authorities argue that its use will decline over the next few decades, especially as a marker of possession.

asterisk a star-like punctuation mark (*) used to link the asterisked word with a note at the bottom of a page, to mark that certain letters are missing from a word (especially a taboo word such as $f^{**}k$), or to indicate that a word or usage is nonexistent (as in 'In English we say three boys and not *three boy').

hyphen a punctuation mark (-) with two functions: to join words, parts of words, syll-ables, and so on, for particular purposes, and to mark the break in a word continued from the end of one line to the beginning of the next line. The hyphenation of compound words in English is by no means clearcut; the same writer may in one article write, for example, *world view, worldview* and *world-view*. Broadly speaking, conventional hyphenation is a first stage in bringing two words together; if their close association is then generally agreed, the two words are written or printed as one (*teapot*, as opposed to *tea-pot* or *tea pot*), or are kept apart for visual and aesthetic reasons (*coffee pot* rather than *coffee-pot* or *cof-feepot*). Practice does, however, vary wildly. There is a growing tendency in the use of prefixes towards omitting the hyphen.

93

Terms

accent a way of speaking that identifies a person with a particular country ('a New Zealand accent'), region ('a Northern Irish accent'), language ('a French accent'), social class ('an upper-class accent'), linguistic style ('a Country and Western accent'), or some mixture of these ('a French-Canadian accent'; 'a working-class Glasgow accent'; 'a middle-class south-east of England accent'). People often describe only those who belong to groups other than their own as having accents ('She spoke with a funny accent'; 'He had a harsh foreign accent'), and may give them special names, such as an Irish brogue or a Northumbrian burr.

acronym a word formed from the initial letters and/or syllables of other words, intended as a pronounceable abbreviation, such as *NATO* (*N*orth *A*tlantic *T*reaty *O*rganization), *radar* (*ra*dio *d*etecting *a*nd *r*anging), and *Asda* (*As*sociated *Dai*ries). Many acronyms are so successfully incorporated into everyday language that their original significance is widely overlooked.

acrostic a number of lines of writing, especially verse, whose initial letters (read downwards) form a word, phrase or sentence. A *single acrostic* is formed by the initial letters of lines only, while a *double acrostic* is formed by both initial and final letters. In the original Greek, acrostic means 'at the extremity of a line or row'.

alphabet a set of conventional symbols for the purpose of writing, so-called from *alpha* and *beta*, the names of the first two letters of the classical Greek alphabet. Alphabetic writing began in W Asia during the second millennium BC among the northern Semitic peoples, and now takes many forms, including the Arabic script, written from right to left, the

Devanagari script of the Hindus, in which the symbols 'hang' from a line common to all the symbols, and the Greek alphabet, with the first clearly delineated vowel symbols. Each letter of the alphabets descended from Greek represents a particular sound or sounds, usually described as *vowels* (*a, e, i, o, u*, in the English version of the Roman alphabet), *consonants* (*b, p, d, t*, and so on) and *semi-vowels* (*w, y*). Letters may operate in special arrangements to produce distinct sounds (for example *a* and *e* together in words like *tale* and *take*, or *o* and *i* together to produce a 'wa' sound in the French *loi*), or may have no sound whatsoever (for example the silent letter *gh* in 'high' and 'through').

antonymy near or precise oppositeness between or among words. 'Good' and 'evil' are antonyms, 'good' and 'bad' are also antonyms, and therefore 'evil' and 'bad' are synonyms in this context. Antonymy may vary with context and situation; in discussing the weather, 'dull' and 'bright' are antonymous, but when talking about knives and blades the opposite of 'dull' is 'sharp'.

dialect a variety of a language, either as spoken in a particular area ('Yorkshire dialect'), by a particular social group ('the dialect of educated Standard English'), or both ('the black American dialects of English'). The term is used both neutrally, as above, and in a judgemental and often dismissive way ('the locals have a harsh, ugly dialect; few of them have been properly educated'). In the latter case, the standard language of a community is not seen as a dialect itself, but as the 'proper' form of that language, dialects being considered in some way corrupt. This is a matter of social attitude, not of scientific study.

dictionary a book that contains a selection of the words of a language, with their pronunciations and meanings, usually arranged in alphabetic order. The first dictionaries of English (in the 17th century) served to explain 'hard' Latin and Greek words in everyday English. Samuel Johnson's dictionary of 1755 was one of the first dictionaries of standard English, to which Noah Webster in 1828 offered an American alternative. The term dictionary is also applied to any usually alphabetic work of reference containing specialized information about a particular subject, art or science, such as a dictionary of music.

etymology the study of the origin and history of words within and across languages. It has two major aspects: the study of the *phonetic* or the written forms of words, and the *semantics* or meanings of those words. Etymological research has been particularly successful in tracing the development of words and word elements within the Indo-European language family. Standard dictionaries of a language like English usually contain etymological information within square brackets at the end of each entry.

homonymy an aspect of language in which, through historical accident, two or more words may sound and look alike (*homonymy* proper, as in a farmer's bull and a papal bull), may sound the same but look different (*homophony*; as in *air* and *heir*; *gilt* and *guilt*), and may look the same but sound different (*homography*, as in the wind in the trees and roads that *wind*). Homonyms, homophones and homographs seldom pose problems of comprehension, because they usually belong in different contexts. They may, however, be used to make puns (such as talking about a papal bull in a china shop).

jargon language usage that is complex and hard to understand, usually because it is technical or occupational, more technical and complicated than necessary, used in the wrong contexts, or intended to impress or confuse ('technical jargon'; 'writing in pseudoscientific jargon'; 'using a meaningless and barbarous jargon'). Jargon is often also known as *gobbledygook/gobbledegook* and *bafflegab*, and is sub-categorized as *bureaucratese* and *officialese* (the usage of bureaucrats and officials), *journalese* (the languages of newspapers), and *medicalese* (the often impenetrable usage of doctors), and so on. In writing, jargon may be highly formal, while in speech it often contains slang expressions.

rhetoric traditionally, the art of the orator (in Greek, *rhetor*) or of public speaking and debate. Rhetorical skills are valued in such occupations as politics, the law, preaching and broadcasting. Accomplished rhetoricians need not be sincere in what they say; they should, however, be effective, or at least entertaining. Nowadays, 'rhetoric' is often a pejorative term ('Cut the rhetoric and tell us what you really think!').

rhetorical question a question, often used by public speakers and debaters, which either does not require an answer or for which the speaker intends to provide his or her own answer ('Where else in the world can we find such brave young men as these?').

slang extremely informal language usage that often serves to promote a feeling of group membership. Slang is not usually accepted in serious, formal speech or writing, and includes expressions that may be impolite or taboo in conventional terms. Some types of slang are highly transient; others may last across generations, and gain currency in the standard language. Because slang is often vivid, suggestive and linked with such subjects as defecation, urination, sex, blasphemy, and getting drunk, many people find it offensive. It is, however, pervasive in its influence and effects. Thus, the standard French *tête* ('head') derives from *testa* ('nutshell' or 'pot'), probably the slang of the Roman legions. It can be compared with the English expression 'Use your nut'.

synonymy near or identical meaning between or among words. There are, however, very few strict synonyms in any language, although there may be many near-synonyms, depending upon the contexts in which the words are used. Thus, 'brotherly' and 'fraternal' are synonyms in English, but a 'brotherhood' is not exactly the same as a 'fraternity'; people talk about the brotherhood of man but seldom if ever about the 'fraternity of man'. *Brotherhood* and *fraternity* are not therefore strictly synonymous.

Philosophy

Philosophy, from the Greek 'love of wisdom', is a difficult subject to define, since unlike biology or history, for example, it does not possess a specific object of enquiry. Rather, philosophy is concerned with fundamental problems which arise in every area of human thought and activity, and which cannot be resolved by a specific method. In thinking about morality, for example, we are likely to wonder whether human beings are responsible for their actions, or whether everything which we do is determined. Similarly, in considering the development of science, we may be led to ask whether there can be any final scientific truth. In the past there have been many philosophical systems which attempt to give a comprehensive account of the world and of the place of human beings within it. Contemporary philosophers, however, are more inclined to think of philosophy as an activity – an investigation of the fundamental assumptions which govern our ways of understanding and acting in the world.

This section begins with a table of *Great Philosophers*, from the ancient Greeks to the present day, followed by brief individual accounts of each philosopher and his leading ideas. This is inevitably selective, but an attempt has been made to include those philosophers who are most representative of historical periods and major trends in philosophy. The section concludes with a glossary of the most frequently encountered philosophical *Terms.*

GREAT PHILOSOPHERS

name	dates	nationality	representative work
Heraclitus	c.544–483 BC	Greek	*On Nature* (fragments)
Parmenides	c.510–c.450 BC	Greek	fragments
Socrates	469–399 BC	Greek	———
Plato	428–347 BC	Greek	*Republic*
			Phaedo
Aristotle	384–322 BC	Greek	*Nicomachean Ethics*
			Metaphysics
Epicurus	341–270 BC	Greek	fragments
Lucretius	c.99–55 BC	Roman	*On the Nature of Things*
Plotinus	205–270 AD	Greek	*Enneads*
Augustine	354–430	N African	*Confessions*
			City of God
Aquinas	c.1225–1274	Italian	*Summa Theologica*
Duns Scotus	c.1266–1308	Scottish	*Opus Oxoniense*
William of Occam	c.1285–1349	English	*Commentary of the Sentences*
Nicholas of Cusa	1401–1464	German	*De Docta Ignorantia*
Giordano Bruno	1548–1600	Italian	*De la Causa, Principio e Uno*
Bacon	1561–1626	English	*Novum Organum*
			The Advancement of Learning
Hobbes	1588–1679	English	*Leviathan*
Descartes	1596–1650	French	*Discourse on Method*
			Meditations on the first Philosophy
Pascal	1623–1662	French	*Pensées*
Spinoza	1632–1677	Dutch	*Ethics*
Locke	1632–1704	English	*Essay Concerning Human*
			Understanding
Leibniz	1646–1716	German	*The Monadology*
Vico	1668–1744	Italian	*The New Science*
Berkeley	1685–1753	Irish	*A Treatise Concerning the Principles*
			of Human Knowledge
Hume	1711–1776	Scottish	*A Treatise of Human Nature*
Rousseau	1712–1778	French	*The Social Contract*
Diderot	1713–1784	French	*D'Alembert's Dream*
Kant	1724–1804	German	*The Critique of Pure Reason*
Fichte	1762–1814	German	*The Science of Knowledge*
Hegel	1770–1831	German	*The Phenomenology of Spirit*
Schelling	1775–1854	German	*System of Transcendental Idealism*
Schopenhauer	1788–1860	German	*The World as Will and Idea*
Comte	1798–1857	French	*Cours de philosophie positive*
Mill	1806–1873	English	*Utilitarianism*
			On Liberty
Kierkegaard	1813–1855	Danish	*Either Or*
			Concept of Dread

name	dates	nationality	representative work
Marx	1818–1883	German	*Economic and Philosophical Manuscripts* *The German Ideology*
Dilthey	1833–1911	German	*The Rise of Hermeneutics*
Peirce	1839–1914	American	*How to Make our Ideas Clear*
Nietzsche	1844–1900	German	*Thus Spake Zarathustra* *Beyond Good and Evil*
Bergson	1859–1941	French	*Creative Evolution*
Husserl	1859–1938	German	*Logical Investigations* *Ideas*
Russell	1872–1970	English	*Principia Mathematica*
Lukács	1885–1971	Hungarian	*History and Class Consciousness*
Collingwood	1889–1943	English	*An Essay on Philosophical Method* *The Principles of Art*
Wittgenstein	1889–1951	Austrian	*Tractatus Logico–Philosophicus* *Philosophical Investigations*
Heidegger	1889–1976	German	*Being and Time*
Gadamer	1900–	German	*Truth and Method*
Sartre	1905–1980	French	*Being and Nothingness* *Critique of Dialectical Reason*
Merleau-Ponty	1908–1961	French	*The Phenomenology of Perception* *The Visible and the Invisible*
Quine	1908–	American	*Word and Object*
Foucault	1926–1984	French	*The Order of Things*

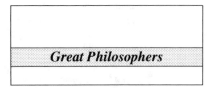

Great Philosophers

Aquinas St Thomas c.1225–74. Italian Dominican scholastic philosopher, monk, and theologian, known as the 'Angelic Doctor'; canonized in 1323. His *Summa Contra Gentiles* (1259-64) argues that reason and faith are compatible. His unfinished *Summa Theologica*, begun 1265, deals with the nature of God, morality, and the work of Christ. His works embodied the world view taught in universities up to the mid-17th century, and include scientific ideas derived from Aristotle. In 1879 they were recognized as the basis of Catholic theology by Pope Leo XIII, who had launched a modern edition of his works.

Aristotle 384–322 BC. Greek philosopher, pupil of Plato, founder of the Lyceum, and tutor to Alexander the Great. Aristotle turned away from Platonic mysticism, placing great emphasis on classification and knowledge through the experience of the senses. He is responsible for pioneering work in natural science, metaphysics, logic, ethics, politics, and literary criticism. His notion of the Unmoved Mover was to have a profound effect upon subsequent thinkers and the idea was incorporated into Christian theology.

Augustine 354–430. Christian saint, theologian, and a Father of the Church. He wrote about 230 works as well as many sermons and pastoral letters. Augustine's most famous writings are his *Confessions*, his spiritual autobiography, and the influential *De Civitate Dei/ City of God* vindicating the Christian Church and Divine Providence in 22 books.

Bacon Francis 1561–1626. English philosopher, who became Lord Chancellor and later Viscount St Albans. Bacon's most significant contribution to philosophy was a new conception of science which broke away from Aristotle. In the *Novum Organum* 1620 he redefined

the task of natural science, seeing it as a means of empirical discovery and a method of increasing human power over nature. He laid the foundations for scientific induction and the British empiricism of the 18th century.

Bergson Henri 1859–1941. French philosopher. He was professor of philosophy at the Collège de France (1900–21) and in 1928 was awarded the Nobel Prize for Literature. For Bergson time, change, and development were the essence of reality and he considered that time was not a succession of distinct and separate instants, but a continuous process in which one period merged imperceptibly into the next. In *Creative Evolution* 1907 he expressed his dissatisfaction with the materialist account of evolution popularized by such thinkers as Herbert Spencer, and attempted to prove that all evolution and progress are due to the working of the *élan vital* or life-force.

Berkeley George 1685–1753. Irish philosopher, who became Bishop of Cloyne. He is best known for his immaterialism, the belief that there is no such thing as material substance. This is not a denial that things exist, merely that they lack substantiality. For Berkeley, everyday objects are collections of ideas or sensations, hence the dictum *esse est percipi* ('to exist is to be perceived').

Bruno Giordano 1548–1600. Italian philosopher. He became a Dominican in 1563, but his sceptical attitude to Catholic doctrines forced him to flee from Italy in 1577. After visiting Geneva and Paris, he lived in England 1583–85, where he wrote some of his finest works. After returning to Europe, he was arrested by the Inquisition in 1593 in Venice, and burned at the stake for his adoption of Copernican astronomy and his heretical religious views.

Collingwood Robin George 1889–1943. English philosopher, professor of philosophy at Oxford. Collingwood stressed the importance of 'doing philosophy historically'. In effect this meant that any philosophical theory or position could only be properly understood within its own historical context and not from the point of view of the present. He is also significant for his aesthetic theory, outlined in

The Principles of Art 1938.

Comte Auguste 1798–1857. French philosopher, one of the first to consider the development of science in a historical perspective. He argued that human thought passed through three stages: theological, metaphysical, and positive. In the first, events were explained by reference to deities, and in the second by reference to occult forces. In the positivist phase, science relies only on the correlation of observed facts. He announced the emergence of sociology as the culmination of this development.

Descartes René 1596–1650. French philosopher, who exposed the doubtful nature of commonly accepted 'knowledge' (such as that acquired through the senses). He then attempted to rebuild human knowledge using as his foundation *Cogito ergo sum* ('I think, therefore I am'). The 'thinking thing' (*res cogitans*) or mind, Descartes identified with the human soul or consciousness; the body, though somehow interacting with the soul, was a physical machine, secondary to, and in principle separable from the soul.

Diderot Denis 1713–84. French philosopher of the Enlightenment and editor of the celebrated Encyclopaedia. He exerted an enormous influence on contemporary social thinking with his materialism and anti-clericalism. His materialism, most articulately expressed in *D'Alembert's Dream*, sees the natural world as nothing more than matter and motion. He gave an account of the origin and development of life which is purely mechanical.

Dilthey Wilhelm 1833–1911. German philosopher, a major figure in the tradition of hermeneutics. He argued that the 'human sciences' (*Geisteswissenschaften*) could not employ the same methods as the natural sciences, but must use the procedure of 'understanding' (*Verstehen*) to grasp the inner life of an alien culture or past historical period. Thus Dilthey extended the significance of hermeneutics far beyond the interpretation of texts to the whole of human history and all of human culture.

Duns Scotus c.1266–1308. Franciscan monk, born in Scotland, and an important figure of medieval scholasticism. On many points he turned against the orthodoxy of Aquinas; for example, he rejected the idea of a necessary world, favouring a conception of God as absolute freedom capable of spontaneous activity. In the medieval controversy over universals he advocated nominalism.

Epicurus 341–270 BC. Greek materialist philosopher of the Hellenic period. He believed the world was made up of atoms moving in empty space; the unpredictability of the movement of the atoms accounted for chance and human freedom. In ethics he advocated ataraxia, a blissful state of peace, which came about through the avoidance of suffering. For Epicurus, the purpose of knowledge was to free people from ignorance and superstition.

Fichte Johann Gottlieb 1762–1814. German philosopher, pupil of Kant, who later taught at the universities of Jena and Berlin. Fichte criticized the Kantian doctrine of the thing-in-itself as dogmatic, and developed a comprehensive form of subjective idealism, expounded in his *The Science of Knowledge* 1794. For Fichte, the absolute ego posits both the external world (the non-ego) and the finite self. Morality consists in a striving of this finite self to rejoin the absolute.

Foucault Michel 1926–84. French philosopher, one of the generation that came to maturity in the 1950s, and who rejected phenomenology and existentialism. His work is concerned with how forms of knowledge and forms of human subjectivity are constructed by specific institutions and practices, and is largely historical in character. Foucault was deeply influenced by Nietzsche, and developed a novel analysis of the operation of power in modern society using Nietzschean concepts.

Gadamer Hans-Georg 1900– . German philosopher, a major contributor to the tradition of hermeneutics in the 20th century. In his masterpiece, *Truth and Method* 1960, he argued that 'understanding' is fundamental to human existence, and that all understanding takes place within a tradition. The relation between text and interpreter can be viewed as a dialogue, in which the interpreter must remain open to the truth of the text. The historical nature of this dialogue excludes the possibility of a definitive interpretation.

Hegel Georg Wilhelm Friedrich 1770–1831. German philosopher, author of *The Phenomenology of Spirit* 1807, *Encyclopaedia of the Philosophical Sciences* 1817, and *Philosophy of Right* 1821. He was professor of philosophy at Heidelberg 1817–18, and at Berlin 1818–31. Hegel conceived of consciousness and the external object as forming a unity, in which neither factor can exist independently. Mind and nature are two abstractions of one indivisible whole. Thus the world is the unfolding and expression of one all-embracing absolute idea, an organism constantly developing by its own internal necessity so as to become the gradual embodiment of reason. Each system by its own development brings about its opposite (antithesis), and finally a higher synthesis unifies and embodies both.

Heidegger Martin 1889–1976. German philosopher, one of the most influential of the 20th century. In his major work, *Being and Time* 1927, he used the methods of Husserl's phenomenology to develop an account of the concrete structures of human existence, *Dasein*. Throughout his work, he argued that Western philosophy had forgotten the basic question of the 'meaning of being', and in his later writings meditated on the fate of a world dominated by science and technology.

Heraclitus c. 544–483 BC. Greek pre-Socratic philosopher, who saw everything in the universe as fire. Fire was the fundamental material which accounted for all change and motion in the world; it also explained the contradictory, ever-changing, nature of things. Nothing in the world ever stays the same, hence the famous dictum 'one cannot step in the same river twice'.

Hobbes Thomas 1588–1679. English philosopher, best known for his political philosophy, notably his notion of the social contract. In the state of nature man is in a state of

perpetual war of all against all. The social contract is enacted to bring about civil peace; the state comes into existence as a result of the individual's voluntary submission to established power. Without the state the life of the individual would be 'solitary, poor, nasty, brutish and short' (*Leviathan* 1651).

Hume David 1711–76. Scottish moral and political philosopher, a figure of the Enlightenment, whose indifferently-received philosophical work *A Treatise of Human Nature* 1740 has proved to be a lasting stimulus. He shared many of the beliefs of the British Empiricist school, especially those of Locke.

Husserl Edmund Gustav Albrecht 1859–1938. German philosopher, founder of phenomenology, one of the most influential movements in 20th-century philosophy. His aim was to grasp the essence of phenomena through a close descriptive analysis of the structures of experience. In order to achieve this the philosopher must carry out a 'transcendental reduction', a suspension of all accepted beliefs, including the belief in a world independent of consciousness.

Kant Immanuel 1724–1804. German philosopher. In his *The Critique of Pure Reason* 1781 he argued that our knowledge of the world cannot be the mere aggregate of impressions impinging on our consciousness from our senses (roughly the view of Locke), but that it is dependent upon the conceptual apparatus of the human understanding – which is not itself derived from experience. In ethics, Kant stressed that the right action is objectively determinable and must conform to a moral law he called the 'Categorical Imperative'; feelings and inclinations are not a basis for moral decisions.

Kierkegaard Soren Aabye 1813–55. Danish philosopher, usually considered to be the founder of existentialism. He was a consistent opponent of Hegel's philosophy, arguing that no system of thought could explain the unique experience of the individual. He defended Christianity, suggesting that God cannot be known through reason, but only through a 'leap of faith'.

Leibniz Gottfried Wilhelm 1646–1716. German philosopher and mathematician. In his metaphysical works (such as *The Monadology* 1714) he argued that the world (that is, the totality of everything there is) consisted of innumerable units – 'monads'. Each monad's properties determined its past, present, and future, and were selected by God so that monads, though independent of each other, interacted predictably; this meant that Christian faith and scientific reason need not be in conflict, and that 'this is the best of all possible worlds'.

Locke John 1632–1704. English philosopher. His great works are *Treatises on Government* (from a Whig viewpoint) and *Essay Concerning Human Understanding*, both 1690. The former, influential also in America and France, supposed governments to derive authority from popular consent (regarded as a 'contract'), so that a government may be rightly overthrown if it infringes such fundamental rights of the people as religious freedom. The latter maintained that experience was the only source of knowledge (empiricism), and that 'we can have knowledge no farther than we have ideas' prompted by such experience.

Lucretius (Titus Lucretius Carus) c. 99–55 BC. Roman poet and Epicurean philosopher, whose *De Rerum Natura/On the Nature of Things* envisaged the whole universe as a combination of atoms, and had some concept of evolutionary theory: animals were complex but initially quite fortuitous clusters of atoms, only certain combinations surviving to reproduce.

Lukács Georg 1885–1971. Hungarian philosopher, generally considered to be the founder of the tradition of Western Marxism, a philosophical current opposed to the Marxism of the official communist movement. In his book *History and Class Consciousness* 1923 he emphasized the Hegelian aspects of Marxism, arguing that the working class was both subject and object of history, and could therefore grasp society as a 'totality'. However, Lukács himself repudiated the book, and spent much of the rest of his life as an orthodox communist.

He also made major contributions to Marxist aesthetics and literary theory.

Marx Karl 1818–83. German philosopher and social theorist, whose account of change through conflict is known as historical materialism. The theory demonstrates the material basis of all human activity: 'Life is not determined by consciousness, but consciousness by life' (*German Ideology* 1845). Marx also developed a powerful critique of capitalist society, which he saw as giving rise to alienation, and as ultimately a self-destructive system. The collapse of capitalism would usher in a period of socialism and eventually communism. Marx's philosophical work owes much to the writings of Hegel.

Merleau-Ponty Maurice 1908–61. French philosopher, one of the most significant contributors to phenomenology after Husserl. He attempted to move beyond the notion of a pure experiencing consciousness, arguing in *The Phenomenology of Perception* 1945 that perception is intertwined with bodily awareness and with language. In his posthumous work, *The Visible and the Invisible* 1964, he argued that our experience is inherently ambiguous and elusive, and that the traditional concepts of philosophy are therefore inadequate to grasp it.

Mill John Stuart 1806–73. English philosopher, celebrated for his work in logic, economics, political theory, and ethics. He is identified with the ethical theory known as utilitarianism, formulated in his book *Utilitarianism* 1863, which puts forward the 'greatest happiness' principle. This states that actions are right if they bring about happiness and wrong if they bring about the reverse of happiness. Mill's *On Liberty* 1859 is often seen as the classic philosophical defence of liberalism.

Nicholas of Cusa 1401–64. German philosopher, important in the transition from scholasticism to the philosophy of the modern period. He argued that knowledge is learned ignorance (*docta ignorantia*), since God, the ultimate object of knowledge, stands above the opposites in terms of which human reason grasps the objects of nature. Nicholas also asserted that the universe is boundless and that it has no circumference, thereby breaking with the cosmology of the Middle Ages.

Nietzsche Friedrich Wilhelm 1844–1900. German philosopher whose thought is a sustained attack on the illusions of metaphysics and religion, and on the moral values upheld by these forms of thought. He argued that 'God is dead', and that man is therefore free to create his own values. Nietzsche claimed that knowledge is never objective, but always serves some interest or unconscious purpose. His insights into the relation between thought and language have had an important influence on contemporary philosophy.

Parmenides c. 510–c. 450 BC. Greek philosopher, head of the Eleatic School (so called after Elea in S Italy). Against Heraclitus's doctrine of becoming Parmenides presented the world in a state of being. He saw the world as immobile and dense with matter. Motion was impossible because it implied a contradiction. Parmenides saw speculation and reason as more important than the evidence of the senses.

Pascal Blaise 1623–62. French philosopher-mathematician. He contributed to the development of hydraulics, the calculus, and the mathematical theory of probability. After a mystical experience 1654, he took refuge in the Jansenist monastery of Port Royal and defended the Jansenists against the Jesuits in his *Lettres Provinciales* 1656. His influential *Pensées* 1670 was part of an unfinished defence of the Christian religion.

Peirce Charles Sanders 1839–1914. American philosopher, the founder of pragmatism, who argued that genuine conceptual distinctions must be correlated with some difference of practical effect. He wrote extensively on the logic of scientific enquiry, suggesting that truth could be conceived of as the object of an ultimate consensus. His writings on the theory of signs have also had an influence on 20th-century developments in this area.

Plato 428–347 BC. Greek philosopher, pupil of Socrates and founder of the educational establishment, the Academy. He was the author of more than 20 philosophical dialogues on such topics as metaphysics, ethics and politics. Central to his teaching is the notion of forms: located outside the everyday world, these are timeless, motionless, and absolutely real. True knowledge can only be knowledge of the forms; the senses can only give us opinion or illusion. Plato and his pupil Aristotle were the most influential thinkers of the ancient world.

Plotinus 205–270. Greek philosopher, who was born in Egypt and lived in Rome. He was the founder of Neo-Platonism, a revival of Plato's teaching which placed strong emphasis upon mysticism. In his principal work, the *Enneads*, Plotinus expounded the notion of the three realities, a religious reworking of Plato's form of the Good.

Quine Willard Van Orman 1908– . American philosopher and logician, professor of philosophy at Harvard. In his important paper *Two Dogmas of Empiricism* 1951, Quine argued against the analytic/synthetic distinction. In *Word and Object* 1960, he put forward the thesis of radical untranslatability, the view that a sentence can always be regarded as referring to many different things.

Rousseau Jean Jacques 1712–78. French philosopher, born in Geneva. He published an examination of the *Origin and Foundations of Inequality Amongst Men* 1754 and *Emile* 1762, outlining a new theory of education to elicit the unspoilt nature and abilities of children. His revolutionary *The Social Contract* 1762, which saw governments as given authority by the people, who could also withdraw it, was immensely influential.

Russell Bertrand Arthur William 1872–1970. English philosopher and mathematician, who contributed greatly to the development of modern mathematical logic. He is also significant in the early 20th-century revival of British empiricism. In later life, Russell moved away from technical philosophy, writing works on education, ethics and the dangers of nuclear war.

Sartre Jean-Paul 1905–80. French philosopher, one of the leading proponents of existentialism in post-war philosophy. His first major work, *Being and Nothingness* 1943, propounds a radical doctrine of human freedom. Our awareness of our own freedom takes the form of anxiety, and we therefore attempt to flee from this awareness into what Sartre terms 'bad faith'. In his later work, Sartre became more sensitive to the social constraints on our action, and in *Critique of Dialectical Reason* 1960 he tried to produce a monumental synthesis of existentialism and Marxism.

Schelling Friedrich Wilhelm Joseph 1775–1854. German philosopher, who began as a follower of Fichte, but moved away from subjective idealism towards a 'philosophy of identity' ('Identitätsphilosophie'), in which subject and object are seen as united in the absolute. His early philosophy influenced Hegel, but in his later work he became one of the first critics of Hegel, arguing that *being* necessarily precedes *thought*.

Schopenhauer Arthur 1788–1860. German philosopher, whose chief work *The World as Will and Idea* 1818 expounded an atheistic, pessimistic theory akin to Buddhism. The driving force of irrational will in human beings results in an ever-frustrated cycle of desire, from which the only escape is a contemplative existence inspired by the arts, and eventual absorption into nothingness. This theory struck a responsive chord in Nietzsche, Wagner, Thomas Mann, and Hardy.

Socrates 469–399 BC. Greek philosopher, who wrote nothing but was immortalized in the dialogues of his pupil, Plato. In his desire to combat the scepticism of the sophists, Socrates asserted the possibility of true knowledge. In the sphere of morality he put forward the view that the good person never knowingly does wrong. True knowledge emerges through dialogue and an abandoning of uncritical claims to knowledge. The effect of Socrates's teaching was disruptive and he was executed by the Athenian authorities.

Spinoza Benedict or Baruch 1632–77.

Dutch philosopher, who abandoned Judaism for a rationalistic pantheism that owed much to Descartes. He taught that all that we know, mind and matter, is a manifestation of the all-embracing substance that is God, good and evil being relative. His *Ethics* 1677 is his chief work.

Vico Giambattista 1668–1744. Italian philosopher, usually considered to be the founder of the modern philosophy of history. He argued that history develops according to inner laws, and that society passes through a cycle of three phases: the divine, the heroic, and the human. He was critical of Descartes' emphasis on the mathematical and natural sciences, and argued that we can understand history more adequately than nature, since it is we who have made it. This is expressed in his celebrated dictum *verum et factum convertuntur* ('the true and the made are convertible').

William of Occam c. 1285–1349. Medieval English theologian, scholastic philosopher, and critic of Aquinas. A tutor at Oxford university, he was accused of heresy and escaped from prison to Bavaria. On the matter of universals he was, like Duns Scotus, an advocate of nominalism. His abiding contribution to philosophy is a principle of simplicity and economy, known as Occam's razor. This states that 'entities are not to be multiplied beyond necessity'.

Wittgenstein Ludwig 1889–1951. Viennese philosopher, who taught at Cambridge in the 1930s and 1940s and whose work has been very influential. *Tractatus Logico-Philosophicus* 1922 was a detailed working out of a 'picture theory' of language: a sentence must be analysable into 'atomic propositions' whose elements stand for elements of the real world; otherwise, the sentence is not stating any fact. Wittgenstein's later philosophy as presented, for example, in *Philosophical Investigations*, published in 1954, developed a quite different, anthropological, view of language: words are used according to different rules in a variety of human activities – different 'language games' are played with them.

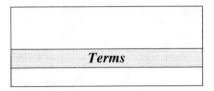

Terms

aesthetics that branch of philosophy which deals with the nature of beauty, especially in art. Aesthetics only emerged as a distinct branch of enquiry in the mid-18th century, the term first being used by the German philosopher Baumgarten (1714–62).

alienation in Hegel's philosophy, a term describing the process whereby consciousness becomes 'lost' to itself through taking on an objective form. Marx denied that alienation was purely a matter of consciousness, and employed the term to describe the condition of the worker in capitalist society.

analytic a term derived from Kant's philosophy: the converse of synthetic. In an analytic judgement the subject is contained in the predicate, and the judgement therefore provides no new knowledge. For example: 'All bachelors are unmarried'.

a posteriori a Latin term meaning 'from what comes after'. A posteriori propositions are true or false in relation to known and established facts of experience.

a priori a Latin term meaning 'from what comes before'. An a priori proposition is one that is known to be true, or false, without reference to experience.

category a fundamental concept applied to being, which cannot be reduced to anything more elementary. Aristotle listed ten: substance, quantity, quality, relation, place, time, position, state, action, passion. Kant derived a table of 12 categories that are applied in experience, although they do not derive from it.

deduction a form of argument in which the conclusion necessarily follows from the premises: it would be inconsistent to accept the premises but deny the conclusion.

dialectic a Greek term, originally associated with Socrates's method of argument through dialogue and conversation. The word was taken over by 19th-century German thinkers, notably Hegel and Marx. For Hegel, dialectic refers to thought which develops through contradiction.

determinism the view that denies human freedom of action, arguing that because everything in the natural world is strictly governed by the principle of cause and effect, human action is no exception.

dualism the belief that reality is essentially dual in nature. Descartes, for example, refers to thinking and material substance. These entities interact, but are fundamentally separate and distinct. Dualism is contrasted with monism.

emotivism a position in the theory of ethics which came to prominence during the 1930s, largely under the influence of A J Ayer's *Language, Truth and Logic* 1936. Emotivists deny that moral judgements can be true or false: they merely express an attitude or an emotional response.

empiricism a long-established tradition in British philosophy, frequently contrasted with rationalism. The principal tenet of empiricism is the belief that all knowledge is ultimately derived from sense experience. It is only through experience that we can come to understand the world.

Enlightenment a broad intellectual movement, reaching its high point in the 18th century. Enlightenment thinkers were believers in social progress and in the liberating possibilities of science. They were often critical of existing society and were hostile to religion, which they saw as keeping the human mind chained down by superstition. Leading representatives of the Enlightenment are Voltaire (1694–1778), Lessing (1729–81), and Diderot (1713–84).

epistemology the study of knowledge. It examines the nature of knowledge and attempts to determine the limits of human understanding. How knowledge is derived, how it is to be validated and tested are central issues in epistemology.

ethics the area of philosophy concerned with human conduct, also referred to as moral philosophy. As well as investigating the meanings of moral terms, ethics studies theories of conduct and goodness.

existentialism a trend in modern philosophy, whose origins are usually traced back to Kierkegaard. Existentialists argue that philosophy must begin from the concrete situation of the individual in the world, and that this situation cannot be comprehended by any purely rational system.

hermeneutics a philosophical tradition concerned with the nature of understanding and interpretation. From its origins in problems of biblical interpretation, hermeneutics has expanded to cover many fields of enquiry, including aesthetics, literary theory, and social science. Dilthey, Heidegger, and Gadamer are influential contributors to this tradition.

idealism a philosophical theory which states that what we ordinarily refer to as the external world is fundamentally immaterial and a dimension of the mind. Objects in the world exist but, according to this theory, they lack substance.

induction by examining and observing particular instances of things, induction derives general statements and laws. It is the opposite of deduction which moves from general statements and principles to the particular. The principle of induction was criticized by Hume because it relied upon belief rather than valid reasoning.

intentionality the property of consciousness whereby it is directed towards an object, even when this object does not exist in reality (such as 'the golden mountain'). Intentionality is a key concept in Husserl's philosophy.

irrationalism a feature of many philosophies rather than a philosophical movement. Irrationalists deny that the world can be comprehended by conceptual thought, and often see the human mind as determined by unconscious forces.

logic a branch of philosophy which studies the structure and principles of valid reasoning and argument. It is also the study of those relations by virtue of which one thing may be said to follow from or be a consequence of another.

materialism the theory that there is nothing in existence over and above matter and matter in motion. Such a theory excludes the possibility of deities. It also sees mind as an attribute of the physical, denying idealist theories which see mind as something independent of body, for example, Descartes' theory of 'thinking substance'.

mediation a technical term in Hegel's philosophy, and in Marxist philosophy influenced by Hegel, describing the way in which an entity is defined through its relations to other entities.

metaphysics a branch of philosophy that deals with first principles, especially 'being' and 'knowing', and which is concerned with the ultimate nature of reality.

monad a technical term deriving from the philosophy of Leibniz, suggesting a soul or metaphysical unit which has a self-contained life. In Leibniz the monads were independent of each other, but were co-ordinated by a 'pre-established harmony'.

monism the theory that reality is made up of one, and only one, substance. This view is usually contrasted with dualism, which divides reality into two substances, matter and mind. Spinoza (1632–77), the celebrated monist, saw the one substance as God or Nature.

Neo-Platonism a school of philosophy which flourished during the declining centuries of the Roman Empire (3rd–6th centuries AD). Neo-Platonists argued that the highest stage of philosophy is attained not through reason and experience, but through a mystical ecstasy. Many later philosophers, including Nicholas of Cusa, were influenced by Neo-Platonism.

nominalism a philosophical position which argues that universals have no objective reality, and that all that truly exists are particular things. William of Occam was a leading medieval exponent of nominalism.

ontology that branch of philosophy concerned with the study of being as such. In the 20th century, Heidegger distinguished between an 'ontological' enquiry (an enquiry into being) and an 'ontic' enquiry (an enquiry into a specific kind of entity).

phenomena a technical term in Kant's philosophy, describing things as they appear to us, rather than as they are in themselves.

phenomenalism a philosophical position which argues that statements about objects can be reduced to statements about what is perceived or perceivable.

phenomenology an influential tradition in 20th-century philosophy, founded by Husserl. Phenomenology attempts to describe the nature of experience from the standpoint of the experiencing subject, without any metaphysical assumptions. It has been practised by Heidegger, Sartre, and Merleau-Ponty.

positivism a theory, frequently associated with Comte and empiricism, which confines genuine knowledge within the bounds of science and observation. The theory is especially hostile to theology and metaphysics which oversteps this boundary. In the 20th century 'logical positivism' was influential through the work of A J Ayer (1910–   ).

pragmatism a philosophical tradition which interprets truth in terms of the practical effects of what is believed, and in particular the usefulness of these effects.

rationalism in the most common sense of the term, the philosophical view that knowledge of the world is derived from reason, not dependent upon perception and experience.

realism in the medieval philosophy known as scholasticism, the theory that the only truly real things are 'universals'; it is thus opposed to nominalism. In modern philosophy, the doctrine that what is experienced through the senses has an independent existence. As such it is opposed to idealism.

relativism a philosophical position which denies the possibility of objective truth, independent of some specific social or historical context or conceptual framework.

scepticism an ancient philosophical view which doubts the possibility of genuine knowledge. Its most radical form is known as solipsism; the solipsist sees himself/herself as the only real person, assuming other people to be a reflection of their own consciousness.

scholasticism the name given to medieval philosophy, as studied in the schools or universities. Principally scholasticism sought to integrate Christian teaching with Platonic and Aristotelean philosophy.

sophists an assortment of Greek teachers and philosophers, contemporaries of Socrates. They were noted for their bogus reasoning, sophistry being more to do with winning arguments than establishing truth.

structuralism a 20th-century movement which has also been influential in linguistics and literary criticism. Inspired by the work of the Swiss linguist, Ferdinand de Saussure (1857–1913), structuralists believe that objects should be analysed as systems of relations, rather than as positive entities.

syllogism a set of statements devised by Aristotle in his pioneering work on logic. Its purpose is to establish the conditions under which a valid conclusion follows or does not follow from given premises: 'All men are mortal, Socrates is a man, therefore Socrates is mortal,' is a valid syllogism.

synthetic a term employed in Kant's philosophy, and subsequently, to describe a judgement in which the predicate is not contained within the subject, for example: 'The flower is blue'.

thing-in-itself *ding-an-sich* a technical term in the philosophy of Kant, employed to denote the unknowable source of the sensory component of our experience. Later thinkers, including Fichte and Hegel, rejected this concept.

universal a property which is instantiated by all the individual things of a specific class: for example, all red things instantiate 'redness'. Many philosophical debates have centred on the status of universals, including the debate between nominalism and realism.

utilitarianism a theory of ethics, associated with Bentham (1748–1832) and Mill (1806–73). According to utilitarianism, an action is morally right if it has consequences which lead to happiness, and wrong if it brings about the reverse of happiness.

Politics and Government

Until relatively recently the study of politics was almost exclusively concerned with three things: the reasons why people should choose to associate together in communities which accepted common governments and rules; the nature and most appropriate form of such associations; and the precise meaning of terms such as freedom, democracy, and justice that were constantly employed in political dialogue. In the last 50 years the study of politics has widened to embrace such matters as the formal and informal processes of politics, with terminology, concepts, and theories being borrowed from many other disciplines, including sociology, anthropology, and economics.

The six parts of this section comprise an introduction to the *Language of Politics*, which defines some of the most frequently used expressions in politics; brief biographies of the 14 most important *Political Thinkers* since Plato; a section defining some of the most commonly used expressions in *International Politics*, a discussion of the principal *Political Ideologies* of 20th-Century politics; an outline of the *Process of Government*, which considers the ways in which governments may be classified, the main voting systems currently in operation, and the machinery of government in two of the leading Western democracies, Britain, and the USA, and a *Chronology of Major Political Events*, which reviews some of the decisive political developments since the ancient Greeks. Political systems of individual countries are treated in the Gazetteer section and a historical approach to world political events can be found in the History section.

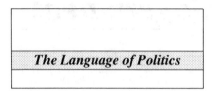

The Language of Politics

authority the capacity to take and enforce decisions within a political system. The nature, sources, and limitations of political authority have been much debated questions since the ancient Greeks.

coalition an association of political groups, usually for some limited or short term purpose, such as fighting an election or forming a government where one party has failed to secure a majority in a legislature following an election.

communication the circulation of information and attitudes within a political system. The importance of mass media such as television has led some thinkers (such as Marshall McLuhan) to develop sophisticated theories of communication.

corporatism the belief that the state in modern capitalist democracies should intervene to a large extent in the economy in order to ensure social harmony.

elite the most influential individuals and groups in a political system. Also called 'the establishment' or 'the governing circles', their identification, selection, and methods of operation have been much discussed issues.

hegemony from Greek 'leadership', in modern political thought it refers to the Marxist approach of thinkers such as Gramsci that sees the state as a means of maintaining the predominance of bourgeois values and ideas over other classes.

ideology a system of basic values, ideas about the nature of the world, and beliefs about ultimate human purposes. All political activity has an ideological base but in some groups, such as Marxists, this is more explicit or self-conscious than in others.

justice a goal of political activity and a subject of political inquiry since Plato. The term has been variously defined as fairness, equity, rightness, the equal distribution of resources and positive discrimination in favour of underprivileged groups.

legitimacy the justification of a ruling group's right to exercise power. Principles of legitimacy have included divine right, popular approval and, in the case of Communist parties, an insight into the true meaning of history.

mandate the right of a government to carry out a programme of policies to which the people are assumed to have given their consent by electing the government to office.

nationalism any movement aimed at strengthening national feeling, especially when aimed at unification of a nation or its liberation from foreign rule. Stimulated by the French Revolution, such movements were widespread in Europe in the 19th century, and subsequently became potent in Asia and Africa.

nationalization policy of bringing essential services and industries under public (government) ownership (as pursued in the UK especially under the Labour government 1945–51) and also taking over assets in the hands of foreign governments or companies. In recent years the trend towards nationalization has slowed and in some countries (Britain, France, and Japan) reversed.

obligation the duty of individuals to obey the laws of their state and, generally, to accept the authority of its government. The basis of political obligation has been depicted as a contract between ruler and people or as arising from the state's ability to provide for the welfare of its citizens.

opinion poll attempt to measure public opinion as a whole by taking a survey of the views of a small, representative sample of the electorate. The first accurately sampled opinion poll was carried out by George Gallup during the US presidential election of 1936. Opinion polls have encountered criticism on the grounds that they may actually influence the outcome of an election, rather than simply predicting it.

order a pattern of behaviour by the members of a society that is conducive to stability and coexistence. Normally associated with some system of rules, as implied by the phrase 'law and order'. Like justice, it has been one of the major concerns of political analysis, but in practice order and justice may sometimes be conflicting goals.

pluralism the view that decision making in contemporary liberal democracies is the outcome of competition among several interest groups in a political system characterized by free elections, representative institutions and open access to the organs of power. This conception is opposed by corporatist and other approaches that perceive power to be centralized in the state and its principal elites.

pressure group (also called 'interest group' or 'lobby') group which puts pressure on parties or governments to ensure laws and treatment favourable to its own interest. Pressure groups have played an increasingly prominent role in contemporary Western democracies. In general they fall into two types: groups concerned with a single issue, such as nuclear disarmament, and groups attempting to promote their own interests, such as oil producers.

privatization reconversion of nationalized services and industries to private ownership, as under the Conservative governments in the UK from 1953, especially the Thatcher government from 1979, and in France since 1986.

propaganda literally the spreading of information, used particularly with reference to the promotion of a religious or political doctrine. This century the word has acquired pejorative connotations because of its association with the use of propaganda by Nazi Germany.

rights an individual's automatic entitlement to certain freedoms and other benefits, usually, in liberal democracies such as the UK, in the context of the individual's relationship with the government of the country. The struggle to assert political and civil rights against arbitrary government has been a major theme of Western political history.

rule of law the doctrine that no individual, however powerful, is above the law. The principle had a significant influence on

attempts to restrain the arbitrary use of power by rulers and on the growth of legally enforceable human rights in many Western countries. It is often used as a justification for separating legislative from judicial power.

separation of powers an approach to limiting the powers of government by separating governmental functions into the executive, legislative, and judiciary. The concept has its fullest practical expression in the constitution of the USA.

social contract the idea that government authority derives originally from an agreement between ruler and ruled in which the former agrees to provide order in return for obedience from the latter. Social contract theories are associated particularly with the work of Hobbes, Locke, and Rousseau.

sovereignty absolute authority within a given territory. The possession of sovereignty is taken to be the distinguishing feature of the state, as against other forms of community. The term has an internal aspect, in that it refers to the ultimate source of authority within a state such as Parliament or a monarch, and an external aspect, where it denotes the independence of the state from any outside authority.

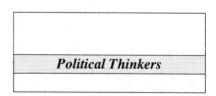

Political Thinkers

Aquinas Saint Thomas 1225–74. Italian theologian and political philosopher, born of aristocratic parentage, and canonized in 1323. His *Summa Contra Gentiles* 1259–64 and the incompleted *Summa Theologica* 1266–73 are designed to show that reason and faith are compatible. His works embodied the world view taught in universities up till the mid-17th century, and include scientific ideas derived from Aristotle. In politics he insisted that government should be morally directed and subject to law.

Aristotle 384–322 BC. Greatest of Greek philosophers. He studied under Plato, and became tutor to Alexander the Great. He stressed the value of reason. Amongst his many contributions to political thought were the first systematic attempts to distinguish between different forms of government, ideas about the role of law in the state and the purpose of political activity, an early discussion of social classes and, in general, the very conception of a science of politics.

Bentham Jeremy 1748–1832. British philosopher and legal reformer. His *Fragments on Government* 1776 and *Principles of Morals and Legislation* 1789 outline his Utilitarian philosophy that laws should be 'for the greatest happiness of the greatest number' and he later contended that 'utility' was best served by allowing each individual to pursue their own interests unhindered by restrictive legislation.

Gandhi Mohandas Karamchand 1869–1948. He led the struggle for Indian independence using his philosophy of nonviolence. He proposed that Third World countries like India should develop their own village based, noncapitalist economic system rather than pursuing Western-style industrialization, but this idea has few adherents today.

Hegel Georg Wilhelm Friedrich 1770–1831. German philosopher, author of *The Phenomenology of Mind* 1807, *Encyclopedia of the Philosophical Sciences* 1817, and *Philosophy of Right* 1821. As a 'rightist' he championed religion, the Prussian state and the existing order, but 'leftist' followers include Marx, who used Hegel's dialectic to attempt to show the inevitability of radical change and attacked both religion and the social order.

Hobbes Thomas 1588–1679. English political philosopher, tutor to the exiled Prince Charles. The first thinker since Aristotle to attempt to develop a comprehensive theory of nature, including human behaviour. His political thinking was much influenced by the anarchic age in which he lived and he is best remembered for *The Leviathan* 1651, in which he advocates absolutist government as the only means of ensuring order and security.

Lenin pseudonym of Vladimir Ilyich Ulyanov 1876–1924. Russian statesman who after 1893 devoted himself entirely to revolutionary propaganda. In *What is to be Done* 1902, he maintained that the revolution must be led by a disciplined party of professional revolutionaries; at the 1903 Social Democratic Party congress in London this theory was accepted by the majority of the delegates, who hence became known as the Bolsheviks (Russian: 'majority'). He later attacked those socialists who supported World War I, which in his view was a purely 'imperialist' struggle, as expounded in his most important book, *Imperialism* 1917. He led the Bolsheviks to power on 7 November 1917.

Locke John 1632–1704. English philosopher. His *Two Treatises on Government* 1690 supply the classical statement of Whig theory and enjoyed great influence in America and France. He maintains that governments derive their authority from the people's consent, and that they may overthrow any government threatening their fundamental rights. Among these rights he includes freedoms, although he would deny toleration to Catholicism and atheism as dangerous to society.

Machiavelli Niccoló 1469–1527. Italian statesman and author whose name is now synonymous with cunning and ruthless statesmanship. In his most important political works, *The Prince* 1513 and *The Discourses* 1531, he discusses ways in which rulers can advance the interests of their states (and themselves) through an often cynical and amoral manipulation of other people.

Mao Zedong 1893–1976. Chinese statesman, founder member of the Chinese Communist Party. He led it to victory in 1949 after a long civil war, and was the effective ruler of China until his death. He is credited with having developed Marxism-Leninism and applied it to the circumstances of a poor Third World country with a huge peasant population but small industrial working class. The Cultural Revolution of 1966–76, which he inspired, was an attempt to keep alive revolutionary fervour, but the disruption and hardship caused by his attempts to put his theories into practice are now strongly criticized in China.

Marx Karl Heinrich 1818–83. German philosopher and socialist. In 1844 he began his lifelong collaboration with Friedrich Engels, with whom he developed the Marxist philosophy, first formulated in their joint works *The Holy Family* 1844 and *German Ideology* 1846 and Marx's *Poverty of Philosophy* 1847. Both joined the Communist League, a German refugee organization, and in 1847–48 they prepared its programme, 'The Communist Manifesto'. In 1849 he settled in London, where he wrote *Class Struggles in France* 1849, *The 18th Brumaire of Louis Bonaparte* 1852, *Critique of Political Economy* 1859 and his monumental work *Das Kapital* (*Capital*) 1867. His systematic theses on class struggle, history and the importance of economic factors in politics have exercised an enormous influence on later thinkers and political activists.

Mill John Stuart 1806–73. British philosopher and economist. In his most important work, *On Liberty* 1859, he moved away from the Utilitarian notion that individual liberty was necessary for economic and governmental efficiency and advanced the classical defence of individual freedom as a value in itself and the mark of a mature society. He sat in parliament as a Radical 1865–8 and introduced a motion for women's suffrage. His feminist views inspired his *On the Subjection of Women* 1869.

Plato 428–c348 BC. Athenian philosopher, disciple of Socrates and teacher of Aristotle. In his major political works, *The Republic* and *The Laws*, he discusses theories of justice and conceptions of the ideal state, arguing in favour of a state governed by a special class of 'philosopher kings' specially trained for that purpose.

Rousseau Jean Jacques 1712–78. French philosopher. His *Discourses on the Origins of Inequality* 1754 denounced civilized society and made him famous but his most important work was the *Social Contract* 1762, which emphasized the rights of the people over those of the government and was a significant influence on the French Revolution.

International Politics

alliance an agreement between two or more states to come to each other's assistance in the event of war. Alliances were criticized after World War I as having contributed to the outbreak of war but NATO and the Warsaw Pact have been major parts of the post-1945 structure of international relations.

arms control attempts to limit the arms race between the superpowers by reaching agreements to restrict the production of certain weapons, as in the Strategic Arms Limitation Talks (SALT) of the 1970s and the Geneva and Helsinki negotiations of the 1980s.

balance of power in politics, the theory that the best way of ensuring international order is to have power so distributed among states that no single state is able to achieve a preponderant position. The term, which may also refer more simply to the actual distribution of power, is one of the most enduring concepts in international relations. Since the development of nuclear weapons, it has been asserted that the balance of power has been replaced by a balance of terror.

Cold War the tensions from about 1945 between the USSR and Eastern Europe on the one hand, and the USA and Western Europe on the other. The Cold War has been exacerbated by propaganda, covert activity by intelligence agencies, and economic sanctions, and has intensified at times of conflict.

collective security a system for achieving international stability by an agreement among all states to unite against any aggressor. Such a commitment was embodied in the post–World War I League of Nations and also in the United Nations Organization, although neither body was able to live up to the ideals of its founders.

Commonwealth, the (British) voluntary association of 48 states that have been or still are ruled by Britain. Independent states are full 'members of the Commonwealth', while dependent territories, such as colonies and protectorates, rank as 'Commonwealth countries'. Very small self-governing countries may have special status, for example, Nauru. The Commonwealth is founded more on tradition and sentiment than political or economic factors. Queen Elizabeth II is the formal head, and its secretariat, headed by Sonny Ramphal, is based in London.

détente an easing of political tension between nations.

deterrence the underlying conception of the nuclear arms race: the belief that a potential aggressor will be deterred from launching a 'first strike' nuclear attack by the knowledge that the adversary is capable of striking back. This doctrine is widely known as that of mutual assured destruction (MAD). Three essential characteristics of deterrence are: the 'capability to act', 'credibility', and the 'will to act'.

diplomacy the process by which states attempt to settle their differences through peaceful means such as negotiation or arbitration. See foreign relations.

European Community (EC) political and economic alliance consisting of the European Coal and Steel Community (1952), European Economic Community (EEC, popularly called the Common Market, 1957), and the European Atomic Energy Commission (Euratom, 1957). The original six members – Belgium, France, West Germany, Italy, Luxembourg, and the Netherlands – were joined by the UK, Denmark, and the Republic of Ireland 1974, Greece 1981, Spain and Portugal 1985.

Green Party political party aiming to 'preserve the planet and its people', based on the premise that incessant economic growth is unsustainable. The leaderless party structure reflects a general commitment to decentralization. Green parties sprung up in W Europe in the 1970s and spread in the 1980s. Parties in different countries are linked to one another but unaffiliated to any pressure group, and had a number of parliamentary seats in 1989: Austria 8, Belgium 11, Finland 4, Italy 20, Luxembourg 2, Republic of Ireland 1, Sweden 20, Switzerland 9, West Germany 42; and 24 members of

the European Parliament (Belgium 3, France 9, Italy 3, Portugal 1, West Germany 6). The British Green Party was founded 1973 as the Ecology Party (initially solely environmental). In the 1989 European elections, the British Greens polled over 2 million votes but received no seats in the parliament because Britain was the only country in Europe not to have some form of proportional representation.

imperialism the attempt by one country to dominate others, either by direct rule or by less obvious means such as control of markets for goods or raw materials. The latter is often called neo-colonialism. In the 19th century imperialism was synonymous with the establishment of colonies. Many socialist thinkers believe that the role of Western (especially US) finance capital in the Third World constitutes a form of imperialism.

international law body of rules generally accepted as governing the relations between countries, pioneered by Hugo Grotius, especially in matters of human rights, territory, and war. Neither the League of Nations nor United Nations proved able to enforce it, successes being achieved only when the law coincided with the aims of a predominant major power, for example the Korean War. The scope of the law is now extended to space, for example the 1967 treaty which (among other things) banned nuclear weapons from space.

International Monetary Fund (IMF) specialized agency of the United Nations, headquarters Washington DC, established under the 1944 Bretton Woods agreement and operational since 1947. It seeks to promote international monetary cooperation, the growth of world trade, and to smooth multilateral payment arrangements among member states. IMF stand-by loans are available to members in balance of payments difficulties (the amount being governed by the member's quota), usually on the basis of acceptance of instruction on stipulated corrective measures.

neutrality the legal status of a country that decides not to take part in a war. Certain states, notably Switzerland and Austria, have opted for permanent neutrality. Neutrality always has a legal connotation. Neutrality towards the big power alliances is usually called *non-alignment*.

nonaligned movement strategic and political position of neutrality ('nonalignment') towards major powers, specifically the USA and USSR. Although originally used by poorer states, the nonaligned position came later to be adopted by oil-producing nations as well.

North Atlantic Treaty Organization (NATO) association set up 1949 to provide for the collective defence of the major W European and North American states against the perceived threat from the USSR. Its chief body is the Council of Foreign Ministers (who have representatives in permanent session), and there is an international secretariat in Brussels, Belgium, and also the Military Committee consisting of the Chiefs of Staff. The military headquarters SHAPE (Supreme Headquarters Allied Powers, Europe) is in Chièvres, near Mons, Belgium. US dominance and nuclear weapons have caused controversy.

Organization of African Unity (OAU) association established 1963 to eradicate colonialism and improve economic, cultural, and political cooperation in Africa; headquarters Addis Ababa, Ethiopia. The French-speaking Joint African and Mauritian Organization/Organisation Commune Africaine et Mauritienne: OCAM (1962) works within the framework of the OAU for African solidarity; headquarters Yaoundé, Cameroon.

Organization of American States (OAS) association founded 1948 by a charter signed by representatives of 30 North, Central, and South American states (except for Canada). It aims to maintain peace and solidarity within the hemisphere, and is also concerned with the social and economic development of Latin America. Its headquarters are in Washington, DC, USA. It is based on the International Union of American Republics 1890–1910 and Pan-American Union 1910–1948, set up to encourage friendly relations between countries of North and South America.

Organization of the Petroleum Exporting Countries (OPEC) body established 1960 to coordinate price and supply policies of oil-producing states, and also to improve the position of Third World states by forcing Western states to open their markets to the resultant products. Its concerted action in raising prices in the 1970s triggered worldwide recession but also lessened demand so that its influence was reduced by the mid-1980s. OPEC members in 1986 were: Algeria, Ecuador, Gabon, Indonesia, Iran, Iraq, Kuwait, Libya, Nigeria, Qatar, Saudi Arabia, United Arab Emirates, and Venezuela.

Strategic Defence Initiative (SDI) also called *Star Wars*. An attempt by the USA to develop a defence system against foreign nuclear missiles based in part outside Earth's atmosphere. It was announced by President Reagan Mar 1983, and has cost to date over $16.5 billion.

superpower term used to describe the USA and the USSR from the end of World War II, when they emerged as significantly stronger than all other countries.

Warsaw Pact military alliance established 1955 between the USSR and E European communist states as a response to the admission of West Germany into NATO.

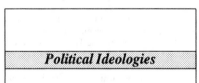

Political Ideologies

anarchism a term derived from the Greek *anarkhos* ('without ruler'). It does not mean 'without order', since most theories of anarchism imply an order of a very strict and symmetrical kind, but they maintain that such order can be achieved by cooperation, claiming that other methods of achieving order, which rely on authority, are both morally reprehensible and politically unstable. The religious type of anarchism, claimed by many anarchists to be exemplified in the early organization of the Christian church, has found expression in modern times in the social philosophy of Tolstoy and Gandhi. The theory of anarchism is best expressed in the works of Peter Alexeivich Kropotkin 1842–1921.

communism the revolutionary socialist movement basing its theory and practice on the teachings of Marx. At its heart is a theory which combines with a belief in economic determinism to form the central communist concept of 'dialectical materialism'. According to this, human society has passed through successive stages - primitive society, slavery, feudalism and capitalism. Each phase was at first progressive, but later hindered progress and had to be superseded by a higher phase through the taking of power by a new class. Marx believed that capitalism, progressive in its earlier stage had become a barrier to progress and needed to be replaced by a dictatorship of the proletariat (working class), which would build a socialist society. The movement was increasingly dominated after the Bolshevik Revolution 1917 by Stalin's Russia but beginning in 1948 with the development of a distinctive approach to socialism in Yugoslavia a number of divergent paths to socialism emerged in China, Romania and Hungary and among 'Euro-Communist' parties in France, Italy, Spain, and elsewhere.

conservatism an approach to government and economic management identified with a number of Western political parties such as the British Conservative, West German Christian Democratic and Australian Liberal Parties. It tends to be explicitly non-doctrinaire and pragmatic but its central themes may be identified as an emphasis on the importance of national traditions, a belief in free enterprise capitalism, a minimalist approach to governmental intervention in the economy, and a stress on law and order.

fascism the totalitarian nationalist movement founded in Italy by Mussolini. It was essentially a product of the economic and political crisis of the years after World War I. It protected the existing social order by its forcible suppression of the working class movement and by providing scapegoats for popular anger in the Jew, the foreigner, or the black person; it also provided the machinery for the economic and psychological mobilization of the nation for war. Its ideology denied all rights to the individual in his relations with the state, personified in the infallible 'leader' (*Duce, Führer*). The atrocities committed by Nazi Germany and other fascist countries discredited fascism, but small neofascist groups still exist in many Western European states.

Islam one of the great world religions (Arabic 'submission', that is, to the will of Allah). The Oneness of God is emphasised as are his omnipotence, benificence and inscrutability. Beliefs are drawn from a succession of scriptures, including parts of the Old and New Testaments of the Christian bible. The ultimate and perfect revelation is the Koran of Muhammad (*c.* 570-632). Islam is a major force in the Arab world and is also a focus for nationalism among the peoples of Soviet Central Asia. It is also a significant factor in Pakistan, Indonesia, Malaysia and parts of Africa. Since World War II a resurgence of fundamentalist Islam, often fanatically opposed to the ideas of the West, has become a potent factor in modern politics in Iran, Libya, Pakistan, and elsewhere.

liberalism the political and social theory associated with the Liberal Party in Britain and similar parties elsewhere. Liberalism developed during the 17th-19th centuries as the distinctive theory of the industrial and commercial classes in their struggle against the power of the monarchy, the Church and the feudal landowners. In politics it stood for parliamentary government, freedom of the press, speech and worship, and the abolition of class privileges; economically it was associated with laissez faire, a minimum of state interference in economic life and international free trade. These ideas were modified in the late 19th and early 20th centuries by the acceptance of a certain amount of state intervention in order to ensure a minimum standard of living and to remove extremes of poverty and wealth.

socialism a movement aiming at the establishment of a classless society through the substitution of common for private ownership of the means of production, distribution and exchange. The term is used both to cover all movements with this aim, such as Communism and Anarchism, and more narrowly for evolutionary socialism or democracy. In general the tendency since 1917 has been for a clear distinction, if not opposition, to exist between parties governed by Marx's revolutionary, 'scientific' socialism and the gradualist, reforming approach of the British Labour Party and Western European Social Democratic Party.

The Process of Government

classification of governments political theorists have made many attempts to divide governments (and political systems generally) into different types. Such endeavours have seldom been completely satisfactory because few, if any, societies have conformed exactly to the 'ideal type'; such typologies are inadequate and simplistic as means of describing where power is located in any society; and many of the words used (dictatorship, tyranny, totalitarian, democratic) have acquired negative or positive connotations which makes it difficult to use them in any objective fashion. Aristotle was the first to attempt a systematic classification of governments. His main distinctions were between government by one person, by few and by many (monarchy, oligarchy, and democracy), although the characteristics of each may vary between states and each may degenerate into tyranny (rule by an oppressive elite in the case of oligarchy or by the mob in the case of democracy). Later writers attempted a refinement of Aristotle's definitions, including the French philosopher Montesquieu 1689–1775 who distinguished between constitutional governments – whether monarchies of republics – which operated under various legal and other constraints, and despotism, which was not constrained in this way. A more modern distinction is between liberal democracies, totalitarian states, and autocracies. *Liberal democracy* was

a term coined to distinguish Western types of democracy from the many other political systems that claimed to be 'democratic'. Its principal characteristics are the existence of more than one political party, open processes of government and political debate and a separation of powers. *Totalitarian* is a more disputed term. It has been applied to both fascist and communist states and denotes a system where all power is centralized in the state, which in turn is controlled by a single party deriving its legitimacy from an exclusive ideology. *Autocracy* describes a form of government that has emerged in a number of Third World countries, where state power is in the hands either of an individual or of the army; normally ideology is not a central factor, individual freedoms tend to be suppressed where they many constitute a challenge to the authority of the ruling group and there is a reliance upon force. Other useful distinctions are between *federal* governments (where important powers are dispersed among regions which in certain respects are self-governing) and *unitary* governments (where powers are concentrated in a central authority); and between *presidential* (where the head of state is also the directly elected head of government, not part of the legislature) and *parliamentary systems* (where the government is drawn from an elected legislature which can dismiss it).

voting systems Western democracies employ many different voting systems of which the many variants are: *1* Where the electorate is divided into constituencies, each of which elects one member of the legislature, with the candidate who receives the largest number of votes winning, (Britain and the USA). *2* Similar to the above except that a second ballot may be held, with those receiving the lowest number of votes eliminated, in order that one candidate may receive an absolute majority of votes cast, (France). *3* A single member constituency system but with the electorate entitled to list all candidates in order of preference so that the votes of the weaker candidates may be distributed among the stronger until one candidate receives an absolute majority, (Australia). *4* Proportional Representation. This may take many forms but essentially involves systems where legislative seats are distributed among parties in such a way as to correspond to the votes cast for each party. Some countries also make use of a referendum on specific issues. This is the procedure whereby a decision on proposed legislation is referred to the electorate for settlement by direct popular vote. It is most frequently employed in Switzerland but has also been used in Canada, Australia, New Zealand and certain states of the USA. It was used for the first time in the UK in 1975 on the issue of British membership of the European Community.

Cabinet in Britain, the committee of ministers holding the most important executive offices who decide the government's policy. Cabinet policy is a collective one, and a vote of censure on one minister usually involves the whole Cabinet. In the USA a Cabinet system developed early, the term being used from 1793, though it is not responsible as in Britian for initiating legislation. Members are selected by the President and, again contrary to British practice, may neither be members of Congress nor speak there, being responsible to the president alone.

Congress national legislature of the USA, consisting of a House of Representatives (435 members, apportioned to the States of the Union on the basis of population, and elected for two-year terms) and the Senate (100 Senators, two for each state, elected for six years, one third elected every two years). Both representatives and senators are elected by direct popular vote. Congress meets at Washington in the Capitol. An Act of Congress is a bill or resolution that has been passed by the Senate and the House of Representatives and has received the President's assent. Even if the President vetoes it, it may become an Act of Congress if it is returned to Congress again and passed by a majority of two-thirds in each House.

Parliament the supreme legislature of Great Britain comprising the House of Commons

and the House of Lords. Parliament originated under the Norman kings as the Great Council of royal tenants-in-chief, to which in the 13th century representatives of the shires were sometimes summoned. De Montfort's parliament (1265) set a precedent by including representatives of the boroughs as well as the shires. Under Edward III the burgesses and knights of the shires began to meet separately from the barons, thus forming the House of Commons. By the 15th Century Parliament had acquired the right to legislate, vote and appropriate supplies, examine public accounts and impeach royal ministers. The powers of Parliament were much diminished under the Yorkists and Tudors but under Elizabeth I a new spirit of independence appeared. The revolutions of 1640 and 1688 established parliamentary control over the executive and judiciary, and finally abolished all royal claim to tax or legislate without parliamentary consent. During these struggles the two great parties appeared and after 1688 it became customary for the king to choose his ministers from the party dominant in the Commons. The duration of Parliaments was fixed at five years in 1911 but any Parliament may extend its own life, as happened during both World Wars. The House of Lords comprises the temporal peers (all hereditary peers and all life peers: both the Law Lords and those created under the Life Peerage Act of 1958) and the spiritual peers (the two archbishops and 24 of the bishops). Since the Parliament Act of 1911 the powers of the Lords have been restricted in that they may delay a bill passed by the Commons but not reject it. The Lords are presided over by the Lord Chancellor, and the Commons by the Speaker. A public bill is given a preliminary first reading and discussed in detail at the second reading; it is then referred to a select or standing committee, after which it is considered by a committee of the whole House. After the third reading it is sent to the Lords, whose procedure is similar. If it passes both houses, it receives the royal assent and so becomes law.

479 BC   Greeks defeated Persians at battle of Plataea: beginning of golden age of Athenian democracy under Pericles (c 490–429 BC).

431–404   Peloponnesian War, ending in the defeat of Athens by Sparta.

207   Unification of China under the Han dynasty.

49–46   Civil war in Italy ended with victory of Julius Caesar and his establishment as dictator, effectively marking the end of the Roman Republic and the start of the Imperial era.

330 AD   Byzantium renamed Constantinople (after Constantine the Great) and declared the Christian capital of the Roman Empire, as distinct from the non-Christian Rome.

634–643   Omar, the great Caliph (successor to Muhammad) conquered the whole Middle East and imposed the Islamic religion upon it.

800   Charlemagne (768–814) declared first Holy Roman Emperor by Pope Leo III.

878   Alfred the Great, King of Wessex, defeated the Danes at the battle of Edington.

980   Dynastic struggles in Russia ended with the victory of Prince Vladimir, who established Christianity there.

1066   Battle of Hastings ended in the imposition of Norman rule under William the Conqueror upon England.

1073–85   Gregory VII (Hildebrand) became pope. Asserted the authority of Church over Emperor, beginning a long struggle for primacy between secular and religious heirs of Roman Empire.

1206   Temujin chosen to be Genghis Khan ('supreme king') of the Mongolian people. Beginning of Mongol conquests of China, Central Asia and Eastern Europe

1215   King John I of England forced to sign the Magna Carta, the most famous of a number of charters of liberties that appeared in Europe at this time. With such affirmations by the King as 'To no one will we sell, to no one will we deny, or delay right or justice' it laid the foundations for the protection of political and civil rights.

1378– 1415   The Great Schism in the Roman Catholic church, when two and later three popes were in existence at the same time. This marked the effective end of the dreams of a universal European order under the pope and the beginning of the modern European states system.

1517   Martin Luther (1483–1546) nailed his 95 theses criticizing certain practices of the papacy to the church at Wittenburg, unleashing the Protestant Reformation.

1534   Act of Supremacy of Henry VIII (1491–1547) declared the king to be 'the only supreme head in earth of the Church of England'.

1555   Peace of Augsburg established principle that each German state should adopt the religion of its ruler.

1640   Establishment of Long Parliament in England.

1642   Outbreak of English Civil War.

1648	Peace of Westphalia ended Thirty Years War and established the sovereign equality of states as the basic principle of the international order, finally discarding the special political role of the papacy.
1649	Charles I executed. English Commonwealth established.
1653	Oliver Cromwell (1599–1658) Lord Protector of the United Kingdom.
1660	Restoration of monarchy in England.
1661–1715	Louis XIV of France (1638–1715), king since 1643, assumed absolute power. Period of French ascendancy.
1679	Habeas Corpus act established freedom from arbitrary arrest in England.
1688	William of Orange landed in England, displacement of James II in the 'Glorious Revolution'.
1689	English Bill of Rights laid down the political and civil rights achieved by the 'Glorious Revolution'.
1689–1725	Rise of Russia to major power status under Peter the Great (1672–1725).
1707	Union of England and Scotland.
1776	American Declaration of Independence asserted the basic rights of all to 'life, liberty and the pursuit of happiness': the first affirmation of human rights of the modern era.
1787	Constitution of the United States of America established the basic features of the American political system: the first modern democracy.
1789	French Revolution began. Declaration of the Rights of Man (liberty, equality and fraternity).
1791	Adoption of French constitution (constitutional monarchy with guarantees of human rights).
1804	Napoleon Bonaparte (1769–1821) emperor of France.
1815	Defeat of Napoleon.
1832	First Reform Bill in England extended franchise.
1848	Nationalist and liberal revolutionary movement throughout Europe.
1861–5	American Civil War.
1868	Beginning of Meiji Restoration which transformed Japan into a major power within thirty years.
1911	Establishment of Chinese Republic
1914–18	World War I.
1917	Russian Revolution.
1933	Adolf Hitler (1889–1945) Chancellor of Germany.
1939–45	World War II.
1945	First use of atomic bomb against Japan. Establishment of United Nations Organization.

1947   Indian independence marked the start of decolonisation and the emergence of the 'Third World'.

1948   Proclamation of State of Israel. Yugoslavia expelled from Cominform (the Soviet dominated alliance of Communist parties).

1949   Communist victory in China.

1958   European Economic Community (EEC) came into being.

1959   Fidel Castro established communist government in Cuba.

1960   Many African states gained independence.

1961   Berlin Wall erected.

1964   Major civil rights bill passed in USA aimed at implementing a programme of equal rights for black people.

1965   Crisis in the EEC caused by French opposition to relinquishing sovereign powers to Community institutions.

1966   Outbreak of 'Cultural Revolution' in China, which aimed at restoring ideological purity to the country and sanctifying the 'Thought' of Mao Zedong.

1968   Violent unrest in France; Britain announced a policy of ending its role as a world power; USSR invaded Czechoslovakia to stamp out liberal reforms.

1970   Moscow Treaty between West Germany and USSR renounced force and recognised the inviobility of all existing European borders.

1972   US President Nixon's visit to China ended more than 20 years of Sino-American hostility; Britain entered EEC.

1974   Nixon forced to resign over Watergate affair.

1977   Historic meeting of Israeli and Egyptian leaders, Menachem Begin and President Sadat, after nearly 30 years of conflict.

1979   Margaret Thatcher became first woman prime minister of Britain; Islamic fundamentalist revolution in Iran.

1981   Imposition of martial law in Poland.

1982   War between United Kingdom and Argentina over Falkland Islands.

1985   Mikhail Gorbachev became leader of the Soviet Union and embarked on an ambitious programme of political and economic reform; signing of Single European Act.

1986   Ferdinand Marcos ousted in the Philippines by Corazon Aquino.

1987   Signing of Intermediate Nuclear Forces (INF) treaty.

1988   Ceasefire in Iran–Iraq war.

1989   Death of Ayatollah Khomeini; ruthless suppression of pro-democracy movement in China; Soviets withdraw from Afghanistan.

Psychology

The scope of psychology is large, and attempts to define it have been varied. For example, William James saw psychology as the 'science of mental life', while J B Watson regarded it as the study of human and animal behaviour. Differing views of psychology are reflected in the diverse areas of study and application.

This section comprises an overview of the main *Areas of Study* and the main *Areas of Application* of psychology; definitions of *Terms and Concepts* used in psychology; *Biographies* of key people who have made important contributions to psychology; and a *Chronology* of major events in the development of psychology.

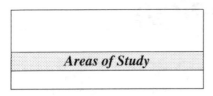

Areas of Study

experimental psychology emphasizes the application of rigorous and objective scientific methods to the study of mental processes and behaviour. This covers a wide range of fields of study including:

human and animal learning in which learning theories describe how new behaviours are acquired and modified.

cognitive processes the study of cognition covers a number of functions; for example, perception, attention, memory and language.

physiological psychology relates the study of cognition to different regions of the brain.

artificial intelligence refers to the computer simulation of cognitive processes, such as language and problem-solving.

developmental psychology is the study of development of cognition and behaviour from birth to adulthood.

social psychology concerns the study of individuals within their social environment; for example, within groups and organizations. This has led to the development of occupational and organizational psychology.

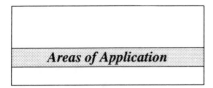

Areas of Application

clinical psychology concerns the understanding and treatment of health problems, particularly mental disorders. The main problems dealt with include anxiety, phobias, depression, obsessions, sexual and marital problems, drug and alcohol dependence, childhood behavioural problems, psychoses (such as schizophrenia), mental handicap and brain damage (such as dementia). Other areas of work include forensic psychology (concerned with criminal behaviour) and health psychology. The main approaches include:

assessment procedures which assess intelligence and cognition, for example, in detecting the effects of brain damage. Assessment procedures usually involve the use of psychometric tests.

behavioural approaches are methods of treatment which apply learning theories to clinical problems. *Behaviour therapy* helps clients change unwanted behaviours (such as phobias, obsessions, sexual problems) and to develop new skills (such as improve social interactions). *Behaviour modification* relies on operant conditioning, and makes selective use of rewards (such as praise) to change behaviours. This is particularly useful for children, the mentally handicapped and for patients in institutions, such as mental hospitals.

cognitive therapy is a new approach to treating emotional problems, such as anxiety and depression, by teaching clients to change negative thoughts and attitudes.

counselling, developed by Rogers, is widely used in order to help clients to solve their own problems.

psychoanalysis, as developed by Freud and Jung, is little used by clinical psychologists today. It emphasizes childhood conflicts in leading to adult problems.

educational psychology concerns work primarily in schools, including the assessment of children with achievement problems and advising on problem behaviours in the classroom.

occupational psychology studies human behaviour at work. It includes dealing with problems in organizations, advising on management difficulties and investigating the relationship between humans and machines (as in the design of aircraft controls). Another important area is the use of psychometric assessment procedures to assist in selection of personnel.

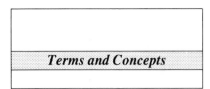

Terms and Concepts

anxiety an emotional state of fear or apprehension. Normal anxiety is a response to dangerous situations. Abnormal anxiety can either be free-floating, when the person may feel anxious much of the time in a wide range of situations, or it may be phobic, when the person is excessively afraid of an object or situation.

behaviour therapy the application of behavioural principles, derived from learning theories, to the treatment of clinical conditions such as phobias, obsessions, sexual and interpersonal problems. For example, in treating agoraphobia the person is taken into the situation which he or she is afraid of, in gradual steps. Over time, the fear typically reduces, and the problem improves.

behaviourism an influential approach, first systemically described by Watson. It concentrates on observable behaviour in human and other animals.

brain damage this can be caused by trauma (for example, accidents) or disease (such as encephalitis), or it may be present at birth. Depending on the area of the brain which is affected, language, movement, sensation, judgement, or other abilities may be impaired.

cognition a general term covering the functions involved in dealing with information, for example, perception (seeing, hearing, etc.) attention, memory and reasoning.

cognitive therapy a treatment for emotional disorders, particularly depression and anxiety, developed by Professor Aaron T Beck in the USA. This approach encourages the client to challenge the distorted and unhelpful thinking that is characteristic of these problems. The treatment includes behavioural methods, and has been particularly helpful for people suffering from depression.

conditioning there are two major principles of conditioning. In *classical conditioning*, described by Pavlov, a new stimulus can evoke an automatic response by being repeatedly associated with a stimulus that naturally provokes that response. For example, a bell repeatedly associated with food will eventually trigger salivation, even if presented without food. In *operant conditioning*, described by Thorndike and Skinner, the frequency of a voluntary response can be increased by following it with a reinforcer or reward. For example, children will be more likely to say 'Thank you' if they have been repeatedly praised for doing so when given something.

counselling an approach in which clients are encouraged to solve their own problems with support from a counsellor. The importance of qualities of the counsellor, such as empathy, warmth and genuineness, was emphasized by Rogers.

dementia a progressive loss of mental abilities such as memory and orientation. Typically a problem of old age, it can be accompanied by depression.

depression an emotional state characterized by sadness, unhappy thoughts, apathy and dejection. Sadness is a normal response to important losses (bereavement, unemployment, and other major losses). However, clinical depression, which is prolonged or unduly severe, often requires treatment, such as antidepressant medication, cognitive therapy or in some cases, electro-convulsive therapy (ECT), in which an electrical current is passed through the brain.

drug and alcohol dependence individuals can become dependent on addictive drugs such as alcohol, nicotine (in cigarettes), tranquillizers, heroin, or solvents (as in for example, glue sniffing). Such substances can alter mood or behaviour. When dependence is established, sudden withdrawal from the drug can cause an unpleasant reaction, which can be dangerous for some drugs.

extraversion a personality dimension described by Jung and later by Eysenck. The typical extravert is sociable, impulsive and carefree. The oppositie of extraversion is introversion; the typical introvert is quiet, inward-looking and reliable.

health psychology a new development within clinical psychology which applies psychological principles to promote physical well-being. For example, people with high blood pressure can learn methods such as relaxation, meditation, and life-style changes.

intelligence a general concept that summarizes the abilities of an individual in reasoning and problem solving, particularly in novel situations. These consist of a wide range of verbal and non-verbal skills and therefore some psychologists dispute a unitary concept of intelligence.

learning theories these describe how an organism acquires new behaviours. Two main theories are classical and operant conditioning.

mental handicap impairment of intelligence which can be very mild, but in the more severe cases is associated with social problems and difficulties in living independently. Individuals may be born with mental handicap or may acquire it through brain damage. Mental handicap is also known as pervasive learning difficulty.

neurosis a general term referring to emotional disorders, such as anxiety, depression and obsessions. The main disturbance tends to be one of mood, whereas contact with reality is relatively unaffected, in contrast to psychosis.

neuroticism a personality dimension described by Eysenck. People with high neuroticism are worriers, emotional and moody. The opposite to neuroticism is emotional stability.

obsession repetitive unwanted thought that is often recognized by the sufferer as being irrational, but which nevertheless causes distress. It can be associated with a compulsion where the individual feels an irresistible urge to carry out a repetitive series of actions. For example, a person excessively troubled by fears of contamination by dirt or disease may engage in continuous hand-washing for four or five hours every day.

personality an individual's characteristic

way of behaving across a wide range of situations. Two broad dimensions of personality are extraversion and neuroticism. A number of more specific personal traits have also been described, including psychopathy (anti-social behaviour).

phobia excessive irrational fear of an object or situation, for example, agoraphobia (fear of open spaces and crowded places), acrophobia (fear of heights), claustrophobia (fear of enclosed places). Behaviour therapy is one form of treatment.

psychoanalysis a theory and treatment method for neuroses, developed by Freud. It emphasizes the impact of early childhood sexuality and experiences which are stored in the unconscious and can lead to the development of adult emotional problems. The main treatment method involves the free association of ideas, and interpretation. Treatment typically is expensive and prolonged and there are serious doubts about its effectiveness. Modern approaches, drawing from Freud's ideas, are briefer and problem-focussed.

psychometrics the measurement of mental processes. This includes intelligence and aptitude testing to help in job selection and in the clinical assessment of cognitive deficits resulting from brain damage.

psychosis a general term for a serious mental disorder where the individual commonly loses contact with reality and may experience hallucinations (seeing or hearing things that do not exist) or delusions (fixed false beliefs). For example, in a paranoid psychosis, an individual may believe that others are plotting against him or her. A major type of psychosis is schizophrenia.

psychotherapy treatment approaches for mental problems which involve talking rather than physical methods such as drugs. Examples of such approaches include behaviour therapy, cognitive therapy and psychoanalysis.

schizophrenia one of the psychoses which is of unknown origin. This may develop in early adulthood and can lead to profound changes in personality and behaviour. Modern treatment approaches use drugs, and can include family therapy, stress reduction and rehabilitaion.

stress a wide range of situations or events which can tax the individual's physical or mental coping abilities. Examples of stress include excessive noise, marital conflict and overwork. Individual reactions to stress are varied, including irritability, fatigue, anxiety or physical health problems, such as stomach ulcers, high blood pressure. Stress is now treated by health psychology.

unconscious an absence of awareness. In psychoanalysis it refers to part of the personality of which the individual is unaware. This contains impulses or urges which are held back, or repressed, from conscious awareness. Emotional problems and irrational actions are believed by psychoanalysts to stem from unconscious conflicts.

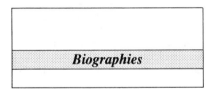

Biographies

Eysenck Hans 1916–. German-born British psychologist who was appointed Professor of Psychology at London University's Institute of Psychiatry in 1955. He promoted behaviour therapy, attacked psychoanalysis, and devised scientific measures of extraversion and neuroticism, key dimensions of personality.

Freud Sigmund 1856–1939. Austrian psychiatrist who developed psychoanalysis. He held that the repression of infantile sexuality caused adult neuroses. His treatment involved making the patient aware of unconscious conflicts. Books include *Studies in Hysteria*, and *The Interpretation of Dreams*.

James William 1842–1910. American psychologist and philosopher; brother of the novelist Henry James. He published *Principles of Psychology* an influential early text. He emphasized the physiological aspects of memory and emotion and advocated a scientific approach.

Jung Carl 1875–1961. Swiss psychiatrist who collaborated with Freud until their disagreement in 1912 about the importance of sexuality in causing psychological problems. He studied religion and dream symbolism and saw the unconscious as a source of spiritual insight. He also distinguished between introversion and extraversion.

Pavlov Ivan 1849–1936. Russian physiologist who studied conditioned reflexes in animals. His work greatly influenced behavioural and learning theory.

Piaget Jean 1896–1980. Swiss psychologist who studied the development of thought, concepts of space and movement, logic and reasoning in children. He wrote *The Child's Construction of Reality* and *The Child's Construction of Intelligence.*

Rogers Carl 1902– . US psychologist who developed the client-centred approach to counselling and psychotherapy. This stressed the importance of clients making their own decisions and developing their own potential (self-actualization).

Skinner Burrhus 1903– . American radical behaviourist who rejects mental concepts, seeing the organism as a 'black box' (internal processes are not important in predicting behaviour). He studied operant conditioning and stresses that behaviour is shaped and maintained by its consequences. His radical approach rejected almost all previous psychology; his text *Science and Human Behaviour* contains no references and no bibliography.

Watson John B 1878–1958. American founder of behaviourism. He rejected introspection (observation by an individual of his or her own mental processes) and regarded psychology as the study of observable behaviour, within the scientific tradition.

Wundt Wilhelm 1832–1920. German physiologist who regarded psychology as the study of internal experience or consciousness. His main psychological method was introspection; he also studied sensation, perception of space and time, and reaction times.

1879 Wilhelm Wundt founded the first psychological laboratory, in Leipzig.

1890 William James published the first comprehensive psychology text, *Principles of Psychology*.

1895 Freud's first book on psychoanalysis was published.

1896 The first clinical psychology clinic was founded by Witner at the University of Pennsylvania.

1903 Pavlov reported his early study on conditioned reflexes in animals.

1905 Binet and Simon developed the first effective intelligence test.

1908 A first textbook of social psychology was published by William McDougall.

1913 J B Watson published his influential work *Behaviourism*.

1926 Jean Piaget presented his first book on child development.

1947 Eysenck published *Dimensions of Personality*: a large scale study of neuroticism and extraversion.

1953 Skinner's *Science of Human Behaviour*, a text of operant conditioning, was published.

1957 Chomsky's *Syntactic Structures*, which stimulated the development of psycholinguistics, the study of language processes, was published.

1963 Milgram's studies of compliance with authority indicated conditions under which individuals behave cruelly to others when instructed to do so.

1967 Neisser's *Cognitive Psychology* marked renewed interest in the study of cognition after years in which behaviourism had been dominant.

1972 Newell and Simon simulated human problem solving abilities by computer; an example of artificial intelligence.

1989 Jeffrey Masson attacked the fundamental principles of Freudian analytic psychotherapy in his book *Against Therapy*.

Religion and Mythology

The term religion is probably derived from the Latin *religāre*, 'to bind', and is used to describe people's attitude towards the gods or God. In original Buddhism, there is no Deity; yet Buddhism, like atheistic Jainism, and Confucianism, which is primarily a code of good behaviour, is always included in a list of the world's religions. A great many prominent thinkers have attempted to define religion: as a belief in spiritual beings; as morality touched with emotion; as a feeling of harmony between oneself and the universe; or as a feeling of awe or reverence for an Unseen Power.

In addition to the main religions of the world, there are also a great many 'new religions' and offshoots. In some parts of the world, for example Africa and North America, indigenous religions still survive despite contact with modern westernized society.

Religion and mythology are closely linked. When we talk about, for example, Greek or Roman mythology, we are talking of what was once the sacred history of a living religion. The stories of mythology often concern themselves with the great religious questions, such as 'How did everything begin?' and 'What happens after death?', and try to answer them in terms familiar to the hearer.

This section contains an overview of living ***Religions of the World*** and their tenets; details of ***Rites of Passage*** in various religions; a look at the ***Holy Books*** of different religions; biographies of major ***Religious Figures***; a list of ***Holy Places*** in different religions; and the main religious ***Festivals*** with a table. Finally, ***Mythological Figures*** looks at the gods, goddesses, and other main figures of ancient religions.

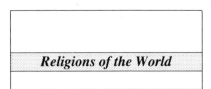

Religions of the World

African religions there is a wide variety of belief and practice in African religion. Most indigenous African religions are basically polytheistic (believing in a number of gods), but there is often a concept of one High God, generally a creator who has withdrawn from interaction with the world. There are also many spirits, which are present in all natural objects: water is seen as a particularly powerful force. Dead ancestors are very important in African religions, and are consulted before major undertakings. If offended, they can cause natural disasters and sterility, so they must be placated with offerings. In society, healers are regarded highly, since they deal with supernatural powers, as do diviners, but the most powerful human figure is the chief-king, who is surrounded by prohibitions because he is so dangerous: he is the life of the tribe incarnate, though because of this he may be required to sacrifice himself to preserve the health of his people.

American Indian religions these form a wide variety, but have some features in common, especially a belief that everything in nature is alive and contains powerful forces which can be helpful or harmful to humans. If the forces are to be helpful, they must be treated with respect, and so hunting and other activities require ritual and preparation. Certain people are believed to be in contact with or possessed by the spirit world and so to have special powers; but each individual can also seek power and vision through ordeals and fasting.

Baha'i religion forshadowed by the teachings of Iranian Mirza Ali Muhammad 1819–50 known as the Bab, 'the Gate'. His claim that Islam was not God's final revelation ended in his being shot by the government at Tabriz.

Another of his countrymen, Husayn Ali, known as Baha'u'llah, 'God's Glory' proclaimed himself as the prophet the Bab had foretold. The most important principle of his message was that all great religious leaders, including the Bab and Baha'u'ullah, are manifestations of the unknowable God; therefore all founders of religions are to be honoured and all scriptures are sacred. Baha'is are expected to work towards world unification, and great stress is laid on equality regardless of religion, race or gender. Drugs and alcohol are forbidden, as is monastic celibacy. Marriage is strongly encouraged; there is no arranged marriage, but parental approval must be given. Baha'is are expected to pray daily, but there is no set prayer. From 2nd to 20th March, adults under 70 fast from sunrise to sunset. There is no priesthood: all Baha'is are expected to teach, and administration is carried out by an elected body, the Universal House of Justice.

Buddhism one of the great world religions, which originated in India. It derived from the teaching of Buddha, who is regarded as one of a series of such enlightened beings, the next incarnation being due c. 3000 AD. *scriptures* The only complete canon of the Buddhist scriptures is that of the Sinhalese (Sri Lanka) Buddhists, in Pali, but other schools have essentially the same canon in Sanskrit. The scriptures are known as Pitakas or 'baskets'. They are three divisions: *Vinaya* or Discipline, listing offences and rules of life; *Sutta* or Discourse or *Dhamma* or Doctrine, the exposition of Buddhism by Buddha and his disciples; *Abhidhamma* or Further Doctrine, later discussions on doctrine. The most important belief doctrine is that of *karma*, good or evil deeds meeting an appropriate reward or punishment either in this life or (through transmigration or rebirth) in a long succession of lives. The self is not regarded as permanent, and the aim of the Noble Eightfold Way is to break the chain of karma, and achieve dissociation from the body by attaining *Nirvana* 'blowing out', the eradication of all desires, either in annihilation, or by absorption of the self in the infinite. There are no gods, but great reverence is accorded to

Buddha, and other such advanced incarnations.

divisions: Theraveda Buddhism, the School of the Elders, which is also known as *Hinayana* or Base Career, prevails in southern Asia (Sri Lanka, Thailand, and Burma), and its scriptures are written in *Pali* an Indo-Aryan language with its roots in N India; *Mahayana* or Great Career, which arose at the beginning of the Christian era, exhorts the individual not merely to attain Nirvana as an individual, but to become a trainee Buddha (or Boddhisattva), and so save others. This prevails in northern Asia (China, Korea, Japan, and Tibet). The form established in Tibet, *Lamaism,* dates from 750 AD when the Dalai Lama became both spiritual and temporal ruler; its outward forms include prayer wheels and it had strong magical elements. In India itself Buddhism was replaced by Hinduism, but still has five million devotees, and is growing. *Zen* originated with a Mahayana monk, Bodhidharma, c. 520 AD, in China, and from the 12th century was adopted in Japan; it is characterized by anecdotes giving rise to exchanges between master and pupil which result in sudden enlightenment. Japan is also noted for such lay organizations as *Soka Gakkai* (Value Creation Society), founded 1937, which equates absolute faith with immediate material benefit, and by the 1980s was followed by more than seven million households.

Christianity world religion derived from the teaching of Jesus Christ in the first third of the first Christian century; overall membership c. 944 million. Belief in an omnipotent God the Father is the fundamental concept, together with the doctrine of the Trinity, that is the union of the three Persons of the Father Son and Holy Spirit in one Godhead. Like Buddhism and Islam it is a universal religion, and has always had a missionary element. In the late 20th century it is spreading most rapidly in Africa and South America. The chief commandment is love of God, and of one's neighbour as of oneself.

divisions:

Roman Catholicism which acknowledges the supreme jurisdiction of its head the Pope, infallible when he speaks *ex cathedra* 'from the throne', a tenet which remains the chief stumbling block in attempted reunion with other churches; the doctrine of the Immaculate Conception (which states that the Virgin Mary was conceived without the original sin which all other human beings are born with), and an allotment of a special place to the Virgin Mary (the mother of Jesus) is also at issue. The final split between Eastern and Western churches was in 1054, and a further schism came with the Reformation in the 16th century, to which the Counter-Reformation provided only a partial answer. An attempt to update its doctrines in the late 19th century was condemned by Pope Pius X in 1907, and more recent moves have been stifled by Pope John Paul II. Membership 585 million.

Eastern Orthodox a federation of self-governing churches (some founded by the Apostles and their disciples). There is elaborate ritual and singing (no instrumental music) in services, and in the marriage service the bride and groom are crowned. There is a married clergy, except for bishops; the Immaculate Conception is not accepted.

Protestantism originating with the Reformation, and named from the protest of Luther and his supporters at the Diet of Spires 1529 against the decision to reaffirm the Edict of the Diet of Worms against the Reformation. The chief sects are the Anglican Communion, Baptists, Christian Scientists, Lutherans, Methodists, Pentecostal Movement, Presbyterians, Unitarians. Membership c. 320 million. There has been a move this century to reunite various Protestant sects and, to some extent, the Roman Catholic church, for example the World Council of Churches 1948. In the 1970s and 80s there has been a revival of interest in Christianity among young people which is not necessarily connected to the established churches, for example the so-called Jesus Freaks and Children of God.

Confucianism the body of beliefs and practices that are based on the Chinese classics and are supported by the authority of Confucius, although he himself maintained that he was a transmitter rather than a creator. For some 2,500 years Confucianism has been the religion of the great masses of Chinese. The scriptures of Confucius are the five Chinese classics or canonical books, namely the **Shu King**, or book of historical documents; the **Shih King**, or ancient poems; the **Li Ki**, or book of rites and ancient ceremonies and institutions; the **Yi King**, or book of changes; and the **Annals** of **Lu**, otherwise known as Spring and Autumn. Only the last may be attributed with any confidence to Confucius's authorship, but the material in the other books may owe something to his editing. From these scriptures the Chinese in countless generations have derived their ideas of cosmology, political government, social organization, and individual conduct. The origin of things is seen in the union of **Yin** and **Yang**, the negative and positive principles. Human relationships follow the patriarchal pattern; until 1912 the emperor was regarded as the father of his people, appointed by heaven to rule. The Superior Man was the ideal human, filial piety was the virtue of virtues, and in general human relationships were to be regulated by the Golden Rule. Accompanying this lofty morality is a kind of ancestor worship. Under the emperor, sacrifices were offered to heaven and earth, the heavenly bodies, the imperial ancestors, various nature gods, and Confucius himself. These were abolished at the Revolution in 1912, but ancestor worship (better expressed as reverence and remembrance) remained a regular practice in the home. Under Communism Confucianism continued, Lin Piao being associated with the cult, but Mao Zedong undertook an anti-Confucius campaign 1974–76, which was not pursued by the succeeding regime.

Hinduism religion of the Hindus, which has a triad of three chief gods (the Trimurti):
Brahma the Supreme Spirit, or **Atman**, who works creatively, as one of the triad, and brought into being the cosmos which is both real and an illusion (*'maya'*), since its reality is not lasting; the cosmos is itself personified as the goddess Maya.

Vishnu the preserver, who is thought to have taken various human forms including **Krishna** (hero of the epic *Mahabharata*, the guise in which he receives most popular adoration) and **Rama**. As **Jagganath** 'Lord of the World' he has a famous temple at Puri.
Shiva, the destroyer and re-creator, who represents the force for change in the universe and is depicted both as the supreme ascetic and as the supreme lover.

There are numerous lesser divinities, for example Ganesa, Hanuman, and Lakshmi, demons, ghosts, and spirits, who are also reverenced. Important ideas in Hinduism include the transmigration of souls and karma. The practice of Hinduism is a complex of rites and ceremonies performed within the framework of the caste system under the supervision of the Brahman priests and teachers. Temple worship is almost universally performed, and there are many festivals. In India and the rest of Asia there are over 475 million Hindus.
karma (Sanskrit 'fate'). In Hinduism the sum of a human being's actions, carried forward from one life to the next to result in an improved or worsened fate. Buddhism has a similar belief, except that no permanent personality is envisaged, the karma relating only to the physical and mental elements carried on from birth to birth, until the power holding them together disperses in the attainment of Nirvana.

caste a term generally used to denote the component groups of Indian or more particularly Hindu society. In India the caste system is derived traditionally from the four classes of early Hindu society – Brahmans (priests),. Kshatriyas (nobles and warriors), Vaisyas (traders and cultivators), and Sudras (servants), which were said to have originated from the head, arms, thighs, and feet respectively of Brahma, the Creator. A fifth class, the Untouchables, seen as polluting in its origin, its occupations, or its mode of life, remained and still largely remains outside the pale of Hindu society, for although the Indian Constituent Assembly of 1947 abolished 'untouchability', and made discrimination against the Scheduled

Castes or Depressed Classes illegal, and attempts have been made to enforce this, strong prejudice continues. The existing castes, which number probably some 3,000, exclusive of sub-castes, are regarded as having come into being by the interbreeding of these original groups.

International Society for Krishna Consciousness (ISKON) a Hindu sect introduced to the West by Swami Prabhupada (1896–1977), based on the demonstration of intense love for Krishna, especially by chanting the mantra 'Hare Krishna'. Members believe that by chanting the mantra and meditating on it, they may achieve enlightenment and so remove themselves from the cycle of reincarnation. They wear distinctive yellow robes and men often have most of their head shaven. Members of the movement are expected to live ascetic lives, avoiding meat and eggs, alcohol, tea, coffee and other drugs and gambling; sexual relationships should only take place within marriage and solely for procreation. Their holy books are the Hindu scriptures and particularly the *Bhagavad Gita*, which they study daily.

Islam religion (Arabic 'submission' to the will of Allah, the Muslim name for God), of which the creed declares: there is no God but Allah, and Muhammad is the Prophet or Messenger of Allah. Beliefs include Creation, Fall of Adam, Angels and the Jinn, Heaven and Hell, Day of Judgment, God's predestination of good and evil, and the succession of scriptures revealed to the prophets, including Moses and Jesus, but of which the perfect, final form is the *Koran* or *Quran* divided into 114 *suras* or chapters, said to have been divinely revealed to Muhammad, the original being preserved beside the throne of Allah in heaven. *sects* there are two main Muslim sects: *Sunni* whose members hold that the first three caliphs were all Muhammad's legitimate successors, and are in the majority. The name derives from the *Sunna* Arabic 'rule', the body of traditional law evolved from the teaching and acts of Muhammad. *Shi'ite* or *Shia* whose members believe that Ali was Muhammad's

first true successor; they number c 85 million, and are found in Iran, Iraq, Lebanon, and Bahrain. Holy men have greater authority in the Shi'ite sect. Breakaway sub-sects include the *Alawite* sect to which the ruling party in Syria belongs; and the *Ismaili* sect with the *Aga Khan* IV 1936– as its spiritual head. There is an Ismaili Centre (1985) in Kensington, London. Later schools include *Sufism*, a mystical movement in 17th century Iran. Generally speaking, Islam has not been a missionary religion, but after World War II a missionary movement, backing the militant organizations for the 'true Islamic state', developed. *Islamic law* Islam differs from Christianity in embodying a secular Islamic Law (the Shari'a or 'Highway'), which is clarified for Shi'ites by reference to their own version of the *sunna,* 'practice' of the Prophet as transmitted by his companions; the Sunni sect also take into account *ijma'*, the endorsement by universal consent of practices and beliefs among the faithful. A *mufti* is a legal expert who guides the courts in their interpretation, and in Turkey (until the establishment of the republic in 1924) had supreme spiritual authority. *organization* there is no organized church or priesthood, though Muhammad's descendants (the Hashim family) and popularly recognized holy men, mullahs and ayatollahs are accorded respect. *observances* the 'Five Pillars of the Faith' are: recitation of the creed, worship five times a day (facing the holy city of Mecca; the call to prayer is given by a muezzin, usually from the minaret or tower of a mosque), almsgiving, fasting sunrise to sunset through Ramadan (ninth month of the year, which varies with the calendar), and the pilgrimage to Mecca at least once in a lifetime.

Jainism a religion professed by about two and a half million Hindus, and sometimes regarded as an offshoot from Hinduism. Its sacred books record the teachings of Mahavira 599–527 BC, the latest of a long series of Tirthankaras, or omniscient saints and seers. Born in Vessali, now Bessarh, he became an ascetic at the age of 30, became omniscient (all-knowing) at 42, and preached for 30 years.

Jains believe that non-injury to living beings is the highest religion and their code of ethics is based on sympathy and compassion. They also believe in 'karma'. In Jainism there is no deity, and like Buddhism it is a monastic religion. There are two main sects: the *Digambaras*, who originally went about completely nude, and the *Swetambaras*.

Jehovah's Witnesses religious organization originated in the USA in 1872 by Charles Taze Russell 1852–1916. They attach great importance to Christ's second coming, which Russell predicted would occur in 1914, and which Witnesses still believe is imminent. The ensuing Armageddon and Last Judgment, which entail the destruction of all except the faithful, is to give way to the Theocratic Kingdom. Earth will continue to exist as the home of mankind, apart from 144,000 chosen believers who will reign with Christ in heaven. When Russell died in 1916, he was succeeded by Joseph Rutherford (d. 1942). Witnesses believe that they should not become involved in the affairs of this world, and their tenets, involving rejection of obligations such as military service, have often brought them into conflict with authority. Because of Biblical injunction against eating blood, Witnesses will not give or receive blood transfusions. Adults are baptized by total immersion. All Witnesses are expected to take part in house to house preaching; there are no clergy. The Watch Tower Bible and Tract Society and the Watch Tower Students' Association form part of the movement. Membership c. 1,000,000.

Judaism the religion of the Jews, founded on the Torah ('direction for living'), combining the Mosaic code and its oral interpretation. It was retained when the Jews were in exile in Babylon from 586 BC, and was reconstituted by Ezra on the return to Jerusalem. The ultimate destruction of the Temple at Jerusalem was countered by greater stress on the synagogue (in continental and US usage 'temple'), the local building for worship (originally simply the place where the Torah was read and expounded; its characteristic feature is still the Ark, or cupboard, where the Torah scrolls are

kept) and home observance. The work of lay rabbis (teachers), skilled in the Jewish law and ritual, also grew in importance, and in modern times they either act as spiritual leaders and pastors of their communities, or devote themselves to study. The *Talmud* compiled c. 200 AD combines the *Mishnah,* rabbinical commentary on the law handed down orally from 70 AD, and the *Gemara,* legal discussions in the schools of Palestine and Babylon. The *Haggadah* is that part of the Talmud which deals with stories of heroes. The *Midrash* is the collection of commentaries on the scriptures written 400–1200 AD, mainly in Palestine. The *creed* rests on the concept of one God, whose will is revealed in the Torah, and who has a special relationship with the Jewish people. Observances include: circumcision, daily services in Hebrew, and observance of the *Sabbath* (sunset on Friday to sunset Saturday), as a day of rest. Observed with more solemnity are *Rosh Hashanah* Jewish New Year (first new moon after the autumn equinox, announced by blowing a ram's horn) and, a week later, the religious fast *Yom Kippur*.

Mormon or 'Church of Jesus Christ of Latter-Day Saints'. Religious organization founded by Joseph Smith 1805–44. Born in Vermont, he received his first call in 1820, and in 1827 claimed to have been granted the revelation of the *Book of Mormon* (an ancient prophet), inscribed on gold plates and concealed a thousand years before in a hill near Palmyra, New York state. Christ is said to have appeared to an early American people after His ascension to establish His church in the New World, and the Mormon Church is a re-establishment of this by divine intervention. The Church was founded at Fayette, New York in 1830 and accepted the book as supplementing the Christian scriptures. Further settlements were rapidly established despite persecution, and Brigham Young and the Twelve Apostles undertook the first foreign Mormon mission in England, the earliest European converts reaching the USA in 1840. Their doctrines met with persecution, and Smith was killed in Illinois. To escape further persecution, Brigham Young led an emigration to the Valley of the Great Salt Lake in 1847 and in 1850 Utah was created a territory with Young as governor 1851–58. Most of the Mormons who remained in the Middle West (headquarters Independence, Missouri) accepted the founder's son Joseph Smith 1832–1914 as leader, adopted the name Reorganized Church of Jesus Christ of Latter-Day Saints, and claim to be the true successor of the original church. They do not accept the non-Christian doctrines later proclaimed by Young in 1852, notably that of polygamy, which Young attributed to the original founder in 1843 on no verifiable evidence: Smith is on record as condemning plural wives. The doctrine was formally repudiated by the Utah Mormons in 1890, and Utah was recognized as a State of the Union in 1896. Mormons believe that marriage is eternal and a necessary step to godhood, and that parenthood is both an obligation and a blessing. Entrance into the church is through baptism by total immersion; children are baptized at about eight years of age. Mormons believe that it is possible for the dead to be baptized vicariously and so enter heaven; because of this they make every effort to trace their ancestors for baptism. Members of the church are known as Saints, and are expected to donate one tenth of their income to the church; they must abstain from alcohol, tobacco, tea and coffee. Women cannot become priests; they are expected to be modest in dress and obedient to their husbands. The Mormons number c. 3,250,000; the Re-organized Church c. 205,000; both have branches in Britain.

Parseeism the religion of the followers of Zoroaster who fled from Persia after its conquest by the Arabs, and settled in India in the eighth century AD. They now live mainly in Bombay state, maintaining their rituals of the sacred fire and the exposure of their dead. They are noted for their success in business and philanthropy. They number about 100,000.

Rajneesh Meditation a form of meditation based on the teachings of Bhagwan Shree Rajneesh, who established an ashram or religious community in Poona, NW India, in the early 1970s. He gained many followers, both Indian and Western, but his teachings also created considerable opposition, and in 1981 the Bhagwan moved his ashram to Oregon, USA. Followers of the Bhagwan regard themselves as *Sannyas*, a term used for Hindu ascetics: they wear orange robes and carry a string of prayer beads. The Bhagwan teaches that there is a basic energy in the world, bioenergy, and that individuals can release this by Dynamic Meditation, which involves breathing exercises and explosive physical activity. Followers of Rajneesh, who now number about 500,000, are not expected to observe any specific prohibitions, but to be guided by their instincts. They are encouraged to live in large groups, so their children may grow up in contact with a variety of people.

Rastafarianism West Indian religion based on the ideas of Marcus Garvey, who preached that the only way for black people to escape their poverty and oppression was to return to Africa. When Haile Selassie (Ras Tafari, the Lion of Judah) was crowned Emperor of Ethiopia in 1930, this was seen as a fulfilment of prophecy, and Rastafarians acknowledged him as the Messiah, the incarnation of God (Jah). Rastafarians identify themselves with the Chosen People, the Israelites, of the Bible: Ethiopia is seen as the promised land, while all countries outisde Africa, and their cultures and institutions, are 'Babylon', the place of exile. Rastafarians use a distinct language, in particular using the term 'I and I' for 'we' to stress unity. Many Rastafarians do not cut their hair, because of Biblical injunctions against this, but wear their hair in long dreadlocks, often covered in woollen hats in the Rastafarian colours of red, green and gold. Food laws are very strict: for example, no pork or shellfish, no salt, milk or coffee. The term I-tal is used for food as close as possible to its natural state. Medicines should be made from natural herbs, and the use of ganja (marijuana) is seen as a sacrament. There are no churches, but meetings are held regularly for prayer, discussion and celebration, and at intervals there is a very large meeting or Nyabingi. There are currently about one million Rastafarians.

Scientology an 'applied religious philosophy', its name derived from Latin *scire* 'to know' and Greek *logos* 'branch of learning', founded in California in 1954 by Lafayette Ronald Hubbard 1911– as the Church of Scientology, its headquarters from 1959 being at Saint Hill Manor, East Grinstead, Sussex. It claims to 'increase man's spiritual awareness', but the movement has met with criticism.

Dianetics a form of psychotherapy developed by L Ron Hubbard in the USA, which formed the basis for Scientology. Hubbard believed that all mental illness and certain forms of physical illness are caused by engrams or incompletely assimilated traumatic experiences, both pre- and post-natal. These engrams can be confronted during therapy with an auditor and thus exorcised. An individual free from engrams would be a 'Clear' and perfectly healthy. Hubbard later developed this theory: behind each mind is a non-physical and immortal being, the Thetan, which has forgotten its true nature and is therefore trapped in a cycle of reincarnation, accumulating engrams with each lifetime. If these engrams are cleared, the individual will become an Operating Thetan, with quasi-miraculous powers.

Shinto the Chinese transliteration of the Japanese for Kami-no-Michi, the Way or Doctrine of the Gods, the indigenous religion of Japan. This is a mixture of nature-worship and loyalty to the reigning dynasty as descendants of the Sun-goddess, Amaterasu-Omikami. State Shinto was the national faith of Japan; its holiest shrine is at Ise, where in the temple of the Sun-goddess is preserved the mirror that she is supposed to have given to Jimmu, the first emperor, in the seventh century BC. *Sects* Shinto consists of 130 sects, each founded by an historical character; the sects are officially recognized, but are not State-supported, as was State Shinto until its disestablishment by General MacArthur's decree after World War II. Unquestioning obedience and devotion to the emperor is inculcated, but there is also an exemplary ethic.

Sikhism the religion professed by some ten million Indians living for the most part in the Punjab. It was founded by Nanak 1469–c. 1539. Its basis is the Unity of God and the Brotherhood of Man: Sikhism is strongly opposed to caste divisions. On Nanak's death he was followed as Guru – teacher – by a succession of leaders who converted the Sikhs – the word means disciple – into a military confraternity which established itself as a political power. Guru Gobind Singh instituted the Khanda-di-Pahul, the Baptism of the Sword, and established the Khalsa ('the pure'), the Brotherhood of the faithful, the Singhs. The Singhs wear the five Ks: *kes*, long hair; *kangha*, a comb; *kirpan*, a sword; *kachh*, short trousers; and *kara*, a steel bracelet. The last of the Gurus, Gobind Singh, was assassinated by a Muslim in 1708, and since then the Granth Sahib, the holy book of the Sikhs, has taken the place of a leader. On the partition of India many Sikhs migrated from W to E Punjab, and in 1966 the efforts of Sant Fateh Singh c. 1911–72 led to the creation of a separate Sikh state by partition of Punjab. However, the Alkali separatist movement agitates for a completely independent Sikh state, Khalistan, and a revival of fundamentalist belief was headed from 1978 by Sant Jarnail Singh Bhindranwale 1947–84, killed in the siege of the Golden Temple, Amritsar. In retaliation for this, the Indian Prime Minister, Indira Gandhi, was assassinated in October of the same year by her Sikh bodyguard. Heavy rioting followed, in which 1,000 Sikhs were killed. Mrs Gandhi's successor, Rajiv Ghandi, reached an agreement for the election of a popular government in the Punjab and for state representatives to the Indian Parliament with the moderate Sikh leader Sant Harchand Singh Longowal, who was himself killed in 1985 by Sikh extremists. The agreement did not mean an end to conflict, which still continues.

Taoism Chinese philosophical system, traditionally founded by Lao-zi in the sixth century BC, though the scriptures, *Tao Te Ching* were apparently compiled in the third century BC. The 'tao' or 'way' denotes the hidden

Principle of the Universe, and less stress is laid on good deeds than on harmonious interaction with the environment, which automatically ensures right behaviour. The second important work is that of Zhuangzi c. 389–286 BC, *The Way of Zhuangzi*. The later magical side of Taoism is illustrated by the *I Ching* or *Book of Changes*, a book of divination.

Transcendental Meditation (TM) a technique of focusing the mind based in part on Hindu meditation, introduced to Britain by the Maharishi Mahesh Yogi and popularized by the Beatles in the late 1960s. Such meditation is believed to bring benefit to the practitioner in the form of release from stress; devotees claim that if even as few as one per cent of the population meditated in this way, it would create peace in the world. Meditators are given a mantra (a special word or phrase) to chant. This mantra is never written down or divulged to anyone else. The Maharishi believes that through the practice of meditation special powers such as levitation, precognition and control over bodily functions can be developed.

Unification Church (Moonies) Church founded in Korea in 1954 by the Reverend Sun Myung Moon. World membership is about 200,000. The theology unites Christian and Taoist ideas, and is based on the book *Divine Principle* which teaches that the original purpose of creation was to set up a perfect family, in a perfect relationship with God; this was thwarted by the Fall of Man. Throughout history there have been attempts to renew this plan, which is now said to have found its fulfilment in Reverend and Mrs Moon. The Unification Church believes that marriage is essential for spiritual fulfilment, and marriage partners are chosen for members by Reverend Moon, though individuals are free to reject a chosen partner. Marriage, which takes the form of mass blessings by Reverend and Mrs Moon, is the most important ritual of the church; it is preceded by the wine or engagement ceremony. There are few other rituals, though there is a weekly pledge, which is a ceremony of rededication. The role of women

in the church is to some extent still influenced by its Korean origins, but this, like the church's extreme anti-Marxist stance, is undergoing change.

Zen abbreviation of Japanese *zenna*, 'quiet mind concentration', a variant of Buddhism introduced from India to Japan via China in the 12th century. *Zazen* or 'sitting meditation' involves periods in the cross-legged lotus position, during which all worldly concerns are banished and a state of selflessness reached which ultimately leads to 'enlightenment'.

Zoroastrianism the religion founded by Zoroaster, represented today by the Parsees. Its theology is dualistic, the Good God Ahura Mazda or Ormuzd being opposed by the Evil God, Angra Mainyu or Ahriman. These are represented in the Avesta as being perpetually in conflict, but ultimately the victory will be Ormuzd's. A ceremonial was devised for purifying and keeping clean both soul and body. Worship was at altars on which burnt the sacred fire. A priestly caste was instituted. The dead were exposed to vultures.

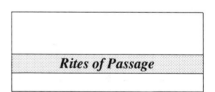

Rites of Passage

Most religions mark certain important stages in a person's life, such as birth, initiation, marriage, and death, by special ceremonies or rites of passage. These rituals provide a way of publicly recognizing a change of status; they are also a time for the whole community to reaffirm its faith.

Birth rites

Birth is often a time of rejoicing, but it is also a time of new responsibility and, especially in communities with a high infant mortality rate, a time of worry and danger. This ambivalence is reflected in some of the rituals associated with birth.

Hindu birth rites begin with the choice of a

suitable day for conception, and continue through pregnancy; the mother-to-be must avoid certain foods and recite verses from the Hindu holy books. When the baby is born, there are a number of further ceremonies including naming the child, the last of which, the shaving of the child's hair, may take place up to two years after the birth. Hindus believe that these ceremonies will help the child towards a better rebirth.

Sikh birth rites Sikhs believe that the first words a child should hear are those of the Mool Mantra, the beginning of the Sikh holy book, and so, as soon as the baby is born, it is washed and the words of the Mool Mantra whispered into its ear. A few weeks later the child is taken to the Gurdwara, the Sikh place of worship, to be named. The initial of the name is chosen by opening the Guru Granth Sahib at random.

Muslim birth rites the first words which a Muslim baby will hear are those of the call to prayer, which is used to call Muslims to the mosque or place of worship each day; these words, which contain the basic beliefs of Islam, are whispered into its ears. Seven days later, the child is named. This ceremony involves the shaving of the baby's head. If the child is a boy, he will also be circumcised (see below) at this time.

Jewish birth rites the surgical operation of *circumcision* consists of the removal of a small part of the foreskin. All Jewish boys must be circumcised on the eighth day after birth, as long as health permits. This is a reminder of the covenant or agreement which God made with Abraham. If the child is a girl, her name is announced in the synagogue (the Jewish place of worship) by the father on the week of her birth.

Christian birth rites universal in the Christian Church from its beginning has been the religious initiation rite of *baptism* (Greek 'to dip'), involving immersion in or sprinkling with water. In the baptismal ceremony, sponsors or godparents make vows on behalf of the child which are renewed by the child at confirmation. Baptism was originally administered to adults by immersion, and infant baptism has

been common only since the 6th century. In some of the Protestant churches, adults are still baptized by immersion in a pool of water. The immersion symbolizes death and new life.

Chinese birth rites Chinese babies are not named for the first month after birth; then the Full Month ceremony is held, with special foods, including red eggs which are symbols of luck and new life. The name given to the baby is a nickname designed to convince any malevolent spirits that the child is not worth stealing.

Initiation Rites

Initiation is a passage into full membersip of a group, whether religious or social. It gives the individual both rights and responsibilities.

Sikh initiation rites the tenth guru of Sikhism, Guru Gobind Singh, set up a group of dedicated Sikhs, the Khalsa; any sufficiently mature Sikh may apply to join the Khalsa. The ceremony is conducted by five members of the Khalsa in the presence of the Guru Granth Sahib, the Sikh holy book; it involves the drinking and sprinkling of amrit (sugar and water). Those initiated in the Khalsa must always wear five things known as the Five K's: uncut hair; a steel bracelet; a short sword; a comb and kachh, a type of shorts.

Jewish initiation is marked by the *bar mitzvah* (Hebrew 'son of the commandment'), initiation of a boy at the age of 13 into the adult Jewish community; less common is the bat mitzvah for girls. The boy reads a passage from the Torah in the synagogue on the Sabbath. After this, he is regarded as a full member of the congregation.

Christian initation is marked by *confirmation*, a rite by which a previously baptized person is admitted to full membership of the Christian Church. It consists in the laying on of hands by a bishop, in order that the confirmed person may receive the gift of the Holy Spirit.

Among Anglicans, the rite is deferred until the child is able to learn a catechism or series of questions and answers, containing the fundamentals of Christian doctrine, and an unconfirmed person is not usually allowed to receive Holy Communion. A child's first Holy Communion is also an initiation rite.

Marriage Rites

Marriage involves not only a change in status for the two people concerned, but also a new set of relationships for their families and the probability of children. In many cultures the choice of marriage partner is made by the parents.

Hindu marriage rites Hindu weddings may take place at the bride's home, or in a temple. The bride usually wears a red sari, and her hands and feet are painted with patterns in henna, an orange dye. The most important part of the ceremony is the seven steps which the bride and groom take round a sacred fire, which symbolize food, strength, wealth, good fortune, the seasons, and everlasting friendship.

Sikh marriage rites a Sikh wedding may be held anywhere, as long as the Guru Granth Sahib is present. During the ceremony, the couple show their assent to the marriage by bowing to the holy book. The couple walk together round the Guru Granth Sahib as a hymn written by the fourth Guru is sung: this hymn contains all the basic teachings of Sikhism.

Jewish marriage rites marriage is important in Judaism, since the Torah, the Jewish holy book, says that humanity should 'be fruitful and multiply'. The ceremony usually takes place in the synagogue, the place of worship. The bride and groom, with their parents, stand under a canopy or chupah. Blessings are recited by the rabbi, the religious leader, and the groom gives the bride a ring. At the end of the ceremony the groom steps on and shatters a glass as a reminder, amidst the happiness, of the destruction of the Temple at Jerusalem.

Christian marriage rites Christian marriages are usually celebrated at the place of worship (church or chapel). The groom is accompanied by a helper, or best man, while the bride is escorted by her father, who officially 'gives' her to her new husband, and by attendants (bridesmaids). The couple make promises to love, honour and care for each other and exchange rings.

Muslim marriage rites Muslim weddings may take place in the bride's home or in the place of worship, the mosque. The bride and groom are normally in separate rooms throughout the short ceremony. There is often a reading from the Koran, and a talk on the duties of marriage. The couple must consent to the marriage three times, and rings are exchanged.

Chinese marriage rites in Chinese weddings, the concept of yin and yang, the two complementary forces which make up the universe, plays a prominent part; among their other attributes yin is seen as female and yang as male. There is a series of rituals leading up to the wedding, including the giving of gifts, an exchange of horoscopes (a prediction of a person's fortune) and a payment to the bride's family. The ceremony itself involves offerings and prayers to the bridegroom's ancestors and the household gods.

Death Rites

Death rites fulfil three main purposes: to comfort and strengthen the dying person, to comfort those left behind, and to ensure the best possible outcome for the deceased person in the next world or next birth. In several religions, such as Sikhism, Judaism, and Islam, people are encouraged to speak a declaration of faith before death, and Sikhs and Muslims read from their holy books to the dying person. Some religions discourage mourning, because they feel that death should not be regarded as a tragedy for the individual, especially after a long life, while others, such as Judaism, set time aside for the family to grieve. There are many ways in which religions try to help the deceased in the afterlife. The Chinese offer practical help: since the afterlife may have resemblances to this life, replicas of useful goods, cars, washing machines, and money, are burnt at the funeral for the use of the deceased who will, with the other ancestors, now watch over the family.

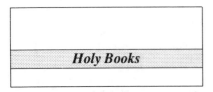

Many religions have a book or books which are regarded as holy or as providing especial wisdom. These books are treated with great reverence and copies may be kept in a place particularly set aside or have specific ceremonies associated with them. Such books are sometimes referred to as scriptures.

Buddhist

Buddhism has a vast number of books which are revered because they contain the teachings of the Buddha. Since Buddhism was transmitted by word of mouth for about 500 years after the death of the Buddha, it is impossible to say which of these writings contain the original words of the Buddha and which are later additions. The main group of texts is known as the *Tipitaka* or *Tripitaka* (literally 'three baskets'), which are divided into three sections; however, the contents of these sections vary among the different schools of Buddhism.

Chinese

Since Chinese religion is a mixture of Buddhism, Confucianism and Taoism, the Chinese generally respect the writings of all three. The main text of Taoism is the *Tao Te Ching*, attributed to the traditional founder of Taoism, Lao-zi. Confucianism's main writings are those of Confucius himself, especially the Analects or 'selected sayings'.

Christian

Bible the authorized documentation (Greek *ta biblia* 'the books') of the Christian and Jewish religions. It comprises the *Old Testament* books recognized by both Jews and Christians (the first five are traditionally ascribed to Moses and known as the Pentateuch); *Apocryrypha* books not included in the final Hebrew canon, but recognized by Roman Catholics, though segregated or omitted in Protestant bibles, and the *New Testament* books recognized by the Chris-

tian Church from the fourth century as canonical. The latter include the Gospels, which tell of the life and teachings of Jesus, the history of the early church, teachings of St Paul, and mystical writings.

Hindu

Veda (Sanskrit, 'divine knowledge'). The most sacred of the Hindu scriptures, hymns written in an old form of Sanskrit; the oldest may date from 1500 or 2000 BC. The four main collections are: the Rigveda (hymns and praises); Yajurveda (prayers and sacrificial formulae); Sâmaveda (tunes and chants); and Atharvaveda, or Veda of the Atharvans, the officiating priests at the sacrifices.

Bhagavad-gita religious and philosophical poem (The Song of the Blessed) which is the supreme religious work of Hinduism.

Ramayana Sanskrit epic c. 300 BC, in which Rama, an incarnation of the god Vishnu, and his friend Hanuman (the monkey chieftain) strive to recover Rama's wife, Sita, abducted by demon king Ravana.

Jewish

The *Torah*, the Jewish holy book, is made up of five books attributed to Moses. They contain a traditional account of history from the creation of the world up to the death of Moses, as well as the laws by which Jews believe they should live. Other books which are important are the *Talmud*, compiled by rabbis or religious teachers between the first and fifth centuries AD, which interprets and expands on the Torah; and the books containing the Psalms (sacred songs) and the messages of prophets (people who speak on behalf of God).

Muslim

Koran more properly, *Quran*, though both are transliterations; the sacred book of Islam. Written in the purest Arabic, it contains 114 suras or chapters, and is stated to have been divinely revealed to the prophet Muhammad; the original is supposed to be preserved beside the throne of Allah in heaven.

Sikh

The Sikh holy book is the *Guru Granth Sahib*, also known as the Adi Granth or 'first book'. It is a collection of hymns by the Sikh gurus or teachers, as well as by Muslim and Hindu writers, which was compiled largely by the fifth guru, Guru Arjan, and completed by the tenth guru, Guru Gobind Singh. On the death of the tenth guru, the Guru Granth Sahib took over the role of teacher and leader of the Sikhs. Guidance is sought by opening the holy book at random and reading verses. Any copy of the Guru Granth Sahib must have a special room to itself; people entering the room must cover their heads and remove their shoes. All copies of the holy book are idential, having 1,430 pages, and written in Gurmukhi, the written form of Punjabi.

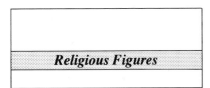

Religious Figures

Abraham founder of the Jewish nation. Born at Ur, Abram was the son of Terah, and migrated to Haran, N Mesopotamia, with his father, his wife Sarah, and his nephew Lot. Proceeding to Canaan, he received Jehovah's promise of the land to his descendants, and after sojourning in Egypt during a famine, separated from Lot at Bethel before settling in Hebron. On re-naming him Abraham, 'father of many nations', Jehovah promised him a legitimate heir, and then tested him by a command to slay the boy Isaac in sacrifice. By his second wife, Keturah, Abraham had six sons. He was buried in Machpelah cave, Hebron.

Abu Bakr c. 573–634 AD. A close friend of Muhammad and caliph (teacher and leader of the Muslim community) 632–634 AD. Traditionally, it was Abu Bakr who encouraged those who had been companions of the prophet to memorize his teachings, which were later written down to form the Koran.

Al-Ghazzali 1058–1111 AD. Muslim philosopher and one of the most famous Sufis (Muslim mystics). Initially, he believed that God's exis-

tence could be proved by reason, but later he became a wandering Sufi, seeking God through mystical experience; he did not, however, turn his back on scholarly work, and his best-known book, *The Alchemy of Happiness* , was written on his travels. He was also responsible for easing the conflict between the Sufi and the Ulema, a body of Muslim religious and legal scholars.

Ali born 600 AD. Cousin and son-in-law of Muhammad, and elected fourth caliph of Islam in 656. Ali was opposed by Muhammad's wife Aisha, who accused him of plotting the death of his predecessor. This led to civil war, and Ali was finally assassinated in 661. Shi'ite Muslims believe that the caliphate passed to the descendants of Ali.

Asoka reigned 264–228 BC. Indian emperor, who was a Buddhist convert, he had edicts enjoining the adoption of his new faith carved on pillars and rock faces throughout his dominions, and many survive. In Patna, there are the remains of a hall built by him.

Augustine 354-430 AD. Christian saint, theologian, and a Father of the Church. Born at Tagaste, Numidia, of Roman descent, he studied rhetoric in Carthage where he became the father of a natural son, Adeodatus. He lectured at Tagaste and Carthage and for ten years was attached to the Manichaean heresy. In 383 he went to Rome, and on moving to Milan came under the influence of Ambrose. After prolonged study of Neo-Platonism Augustine was converted to Christianity and was baptized by Ambrose together with his son. Resigning his chair in rhetoric, he returned to Africa, his mother St Monica dying at Ostia on the journey, and settled at Tagaste. His son died at 17. In 391, while visiting Hippo, Augustine was ordained priest. In 395 he was given the right of succession to the bishopric of Hippo, and in 396 succeeded to the office. He died at Hippo during its siege by the Vandals.

Many of Augustine's books resulted from his share in three great controversies: he refuted Manichaeism; attacked and did much to eliminate Donatism (conference of Carthage, 411); and devoted the last 20 years of his life to the Pelagian controversy, in which he maintained the doctrine of original sin and the necessity of divine grace. He estimated the number of his works at 230, and also wrote many sermons, as well as pastoral letters. Augustine's most famous productions are his 'Confessions', his spiritual autobiography, and the influential *De Civitate Dei*/*The City of God* vindicating the Christian Church and Divine Providence in 22 books.

Bodhidharma 6th century BC Indian Buddhist. He entered China from S India c. 520, and was the founder of Zen ('religious meditation', Japanese word derived from Chinese *cha'an*), the school of Mahayana Buddhism in which intuitive meditation, prompted by contemplation of the beautiful, leads to enlightenment. It passed to Japan in the 12th century, where it is the best-known school.

Buddha title of prince Gautama Siddhartha c. 563–483 BC born at Lumbini in Nepal. At the age of 29, he left his wife and son to seek a way of escape from the burdens of existence, and after six years of austerity became enlightened (Buddha means 'enlightened one') under a Banyan or bo tree near Buddh Gaya. He acquired the Four Truths: the fact of pain or ill; that pain has a cause; that pain can be ended; and that it can be ended by following the Eightfold Way of right views, right intention, right speech, right action, right livelihood, right effort, right mindfulness, and right concentration, and so arriving at Nirvana, the extinction of all craving for things of the senses. He began teaching at Varanasi, and founded the Sangha, or order of monks, eventually dying at Kusinagara in Uttar Pradesh.

Confucius Latinized name (meaning 'Kong the Master') of Chinese sage Kong Zi 550–478 BC. Born in Lu, a small state in what is now the province of Shandong, at Qufu, he became a minor official. Taking to teaching, he gathered disciples, and was for a time so excellent a governor of a small town that he became prime minister of Lu. However, he went into exile when his advice was ignored, returning only in the last years of his life under a new ruler. He was buried at Qufu.

Jesus Christ c. 4 BC-c.30 AD. Jesus (Hebrew *Messiah*, Greek *the Christ*) was the founder of Christianity, based on the account of his life in the four Gospels, (which form part of the Bible, the Christian holy book). Born in Bethlehem (a town in Israel), son of the Virgin Mary (of the peoples of Judah and the family of David), he was brought up as a carpenter by Mary's husband Joseph at Nazareth. In 26/27 AD his cousin John the Baptist began a preparatory mission, and baptized Jesus, whose Galilean ministry included two missionary journeys through the district, and the calling of 12 apostles or followers. His teaching, summarized in the Sermon on the Mount, aroused both religious opposition from the Pharisees, Jewish leaders, and secular opposition from the government of the day, the Herodian party. When he returned to Jerusalem a week before the Passover, he was greeted by the people as the Messiah or coming saviour, and the Jewish authorities (aided by one of his followers, Judas) had him arrested and condemned to death (after a hurried trial) by the religious court of Sanhedrin. The sentence was confirmed by the Roman procurator, Pontius Pilate, but three days after the Crucifixion (death by hanging on a cross), came reports of his resurrection, and later ascension to heaven.

Luther Martin 1483–1546. German Protestant reformer. Originally a monk, he became convinced of the primacy of grace (the freely given gift of God) over merit, 'justification by faith'. In 1517 he nailed on the church door at Wittenberg his 'Ninety-five Theses against Indulgences' (an abuse of power common in the church at the time), following this in 1519 with opposition to the infallibility and primacy of the Pope, and becoming an outlaw before the Empire and an apostate before the Church. In 1525 he married an ex-nun, and in 1530 formulated the Augsburg Confession, the basis of Lutheranism. His translation of the scriptures marks the emergence of modern German. Formerly condemned by Communism, he had by the 1980s been rehabilitated as a revolutionary socialist hero, and was claimed as patron saint by both East and West

Germany.

Maimonides 1135–1204 AD. Jewish rabbi (teacher) and philosopher influenced by the ideas of the Greek philosopher Aristotle. He drew up the *Thirteen Principles,* a summary of the basic beliefs of Judaism. His approach to reasoning aroused hostility in his lifetime, but he is now thought of as one of the great teachers of Judaism.

Mencius 371–289 BC. Confucian philosopher who developed and elaborated on the teachings of Confucius. He put great emphasis on the idea that human nature was basically good, and that failure to act in a virtuous way was a result of wrong environment. He believed that rulers should act in accordance with the will of heaven, and was outspoken in his condemnation of those who failed to live up to this ideal.

Moses Jewish lawgiver and judge who led the Israelites out of Egypt to the promised land of Canaan. According to the Torah, Moses was hidden among the bulrushes on the banks of the Nile when the Pharaoh commanded that all new-born male Hebrew children should be destroyed. He was found by a daughter of Pharaoh, who reared him. Eventually he became the leader of the Israelites in the Exodus, and the 40 years' wandering in the wilderness. On Mt Sinai he received from Jehovah the Ten Commandments engraved on tablets of stone, and died at the age of 120, after having been allowed a glimpse of the Promised Land from Mount Pisgah.

Muhammad or Mohammed, Mahomet, Mahound (Arabic 'praised') c. 570–632 AD. Founder of Islam, born in Mecca. Originally a shepherd and caravan conductor, he found leisure for meditation by his marriage with a wealthy widow in 595, and received his first revelation in 610. After some years of secret teaching, he openly declared himself the prophet of God in about 616, the Koran (revealed to him by God and later written down by his followers) being the basis of his teaching. Persecuted as the number of his followers increased, he fled to the town now known as Medina in 622 (the flight, *Hegira,*

which marks the beginning of the Islamic era). After the battle of Badr in 623, he was continuously victorious, entering Mecca as the recognized prophet of Arabia 630. The succession was troubled.

Nanak 1469–c. 1539. Indian guru, strongly opposed to caste divisions, founder of Sikhism on the basis of the Unity of God and the Brotherhood of Man.

Paul St c. 3–64 or 68 AD. One of the Apostles (the Jewish form of his name being Saul), he was born in Tarsus, son of well-to-do Pharisees, and had Roman citizenship. Opposed to Christianity, he took part in the stoning of the first Christian martyr Stephen, but was converted by a vision on the road to Damascus. He made great missionary journeys, for example to Philippi, Ephesus, hence becoming known as the 'Apostle of the Gentiles' (non-Jews). On his return to Jerusalem, he was arrested, appealed to Caesar, and (as a citizen) was sent to Rome for trial c. 57 or 59. After two years in prison, he may have been released before his final arrest and execution under Nero. Thirteen epistles in the New Testament are attributed to him. His theology was rigorous on such questions as sin and atonement, and his views on the role of women became those of the Church generally.

Ramakrishna 1834–86 AD. A teacher and mystic (one dedicated to achieving oneness with or a direct experience of God or some force beyond the normal world). Ramakrishna claimed that mystical experience was the ultimate aim of religions, and that all religions which led to this goal were equally valid.

Ranjit Singh Maharaja 1780–1839 AD. A military leader of the Sikhs who became ruler of the Punjab at the age of 20, and preserved it from capture by the British until his death.

Shankara 799–833 AD. Hindu philosopher who wrote commentaries on some of the major Hindu scriptures, as well as hymns and essays on religous ideas. Shankara was responsible for the final form of the Advaita Vedanta school of Hindu philosophy, which teaches that Brahman, the supreme being, is all that exists in the universe; everything else is illusion. Shankara was fiercely opposed to Buddhism, and may have been largely responsible for its decline in India.

Zoroaster or Zarathustra c. 628–c. 551 BC. Persian founder of Zoroastrianism, who was assassinated by rival prophets.

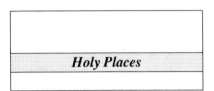

Holy Places

The concept of *pilgrimage*, a journey to sacred places inspired by religious devotion, is common to many religions. For Hindus the holy places include Benares and the purifying Ganges; for Buddhists the places connected with the crises of Buddha's career; for the ancient Greeks the shrines at Delphi, Ephesus, among others; for the Jews, the sanctuary at Jerusalem; and for Muslims, Mecca. Among Christians, pilgrimages were common by the second century, and as a direct result of the established necessity of making pilgrimages there arose the numerous hospices catering for pilgrims, the religious orders of knighthood, and the Crusades. The great centres of Christian pilgrimages have been, or are, Jerusalem, Rome, the tomb of St James of Compostella in Spain, the shrine of Becket at Canterbury, and the holy places at La Salette and Lourdes in France.

Amritsar city in the Punjab, India, founded 1577. It is the religious centre of the Sikhs and contains the *Golden Temple* and Guru Nanak University 1969, named after the first Sikh Guru.

Jerusalem ancient city of Palestine, which is a holy place for Jews, Christians and Muslims. It was divided in 1948 between the new republic of Israel and Jordan. In 1950 the western New City was proclaimed as the Israeli capital, and following the Israeli capture of the eastern Old City in 1967 from the Jordanians, it was affirmed in 1980 that the united city was the

country's capital, but the United Nations does not recognize the claim.

history by 1400 BC Jerusalem was ruled by a king subject to Egypt, but c. 1000 BC David, the second king of Israel, made it the capital of a united Jewish kingdom. It was captured by Nebuchadnezzar 586 BC, who deported its population. Later conquerors include Alexander the Great and Pompey (63 BC), and it was under Roman rule that Jesus Christ was executed. In 70 AD a Jewish revolt led to its complete destruction by Titus. It was first conquered by Islam in 637; was captured by Crusaders, Christians who were fighting the Muslims in Israel, 1099, and recaptured by Saladin 1187, to remain under almost unbroken Islamic rule until the British occupation of Palestine in 1917.

Notable buildings include the *Church of the Holy Sepulchre* (built 335), and the mosque of the *Dome of the Rock*. The latter was built on the site of Solomon's Temple, and the *Western* ('wailing') *Wall*, held sacred by Jews, is part of the walled platform on which the Temple once stood.

Temple the centre of Jewish national worship at Jerusalem. Three temples occupied the site: *Solomon's Temple*, which was destroyed by Nebuchadnezzar; *Zerubbabel's Temple*, built after the return from Babylon; and *Herod's Temple*, which was destroyed by the Romans in 70 AD. The Mosque of Omar occupies the site. The *Wailing Wall* is the surviving part of the western wall of the platform of the enclosure of the Temple of Herod, so-called by tourists because of the oriental chanting style of the Jews in their prayers there. Under Jordanian rule Jews had no access to the place, but took this part of the city in the 1967 campaign.

Kyoto a city in S Honshu, Japan, which was the capital of Japan 794–1868, and has famous temples; to the south east is Ise, site of the most sacred Shinto shrine, rebuilt every 20 years in the form of a thatched seventh-century house, and containing the octagonal mirror of the sun-goddess Amaterasu.

Mecca city of Saudi Arabia, the holiest city of the Muslim world, where the Prophet was born. It stands in the desert, in a valley about 72 km/45 mi east of Jidda, its port on the Red Sea, with which it is linked by an asphalted road, and long before the time of Muhammad was a commercial centre, caravan junction, and place of pilgrimage. In the centre of Mecca is the *Great Mosque*, in whose courtyard is the *Kaaba*; it also contains the well *Zam-Zam*, associated by tradition with Ishmael, the son of Abraham, and his mother Hagar, and the *Maqām Ibrāhīm*, a holy stone supposed to bear the imprint of Abraham's foot.

kaaba the oblong building in the quadrangle of the Great Mosque at Mecca into the north-east corner of which is built the black stone declared by Muhammad to have been given to Abraham by Gabriel, and devoutly revered by Muslim pilgrims. The name means chamber.

Medina city in Saudi Arabia, about 355 km/220 mi north of Mecca. To Muslims it is a holy city second only to Mecca, since Muhammad lived here for many years after he fled from Mecca, and died here. The *Mosque of the Prophet* contains his reputed tomb, and those of the caliphs or Muslim leaders Abu Bakr, Omar, and Fatima, Muhammad's daughter.

Varanesi Indian city on the sacred Ganges river in Uttar Pradesh, more familiar in the West under the form Benares. It is holy to Hindus with a 5 km/3 mi frontage of stairways (ghats), leading up from the river to innumerable streets, temples, and the 1,500 golden shrines. The ritual of purification is daily practised by thousands of devout Hindus, who bathe from the ghats in the sacred river. At the burning ghats, the ashes, following cremation, are scattered on the river, a ritual supposed to ensure a favourable reincarnation.

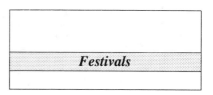

Festivals

Buddhist festivals

Wesak the day of the Buddha's birth, enlightenment and death. A large act of worship is held and gifts given to monks; captive animals may be freed.

Dhammacakka celebrates the preaching of the Buddha's first sermon. Visits are made to monasteries and gifts are given to the monks.

Bodhi Day Mahayana Buddhist celebration of the Buddha's enlightenment.

Chinese festivals

New Year time when the Kitchen God, whose picture is in every home, returns to heaven to report on the family's behaviour during the year. There are elaborate lion dances and fireworks, and vegetarian feasts are eaten.

Chin Ming a time for visiting ancestral tombs, making offerings and remembering the dead.

Dragon Boat Festival celebrates the story of a brave official who persuaded a harsh emperor to relent over his crippling taxation of the people by drowning himself. Races are held between boats carved to resemble dragons, in memory of the boat chase to save the official's body from being eaten by dragons and demons.

Moon Festival commemorates the story of a brave woman who defied her husband, a wicked king, to stop him obtaining immortality, and was carried off by the gods to live on the moon. The festival is held at full moon and the moon is greeted with incense, lanterns and feasting.

Winter Festival time of feasting to build up strength for the winter ahead.

Christian festivals

Epiphany annual festival (6 Jan) of the Christian Church, celebrating the coming of the Magi or wise men to Bethlehem with gifts for the infant Christ, and symbolizing the manifestation of Christ to the world. It is the twelfth day after Christmas, and marks the end of the Christmas festivities. In many countries the night before, called *Twelfth Night*, is marked by the giving of gifts.

Shrove Tuesday the day before Ash Wednesday. The name comes from the Anglo-Saxon *scrifan*, to shrive, and in former times it was the time for confession before Lent. Another name for it is Pancake Tuesday; the pancakes are a survival of merrymaking in anticipation of Lenten abstinence.

Ash Wednesday first day of Lent, the period in the Christian calendar leading up to Easter; in the Catholic Church the foreheads of the congregation are marked with a cross in ash, as a sign of penitence.

Lent in the Christian Church, the forty days' period of fasting which precedes Easter, beginning on Ash Wednesday, but omitting Sundays.

Palm Sunday the Sunday before Easter, and first day of Holy Week; so-called to commemorate Christ's entry into Jerusalem, when the crowd strewed palm leaves in his path.

Good Friday (probably a corruption of God's Friday). In the Christian Church, the Friday before Easter, which is kept in memory of the Crucifixion (the death of Jesus).

Easter feast of the Christian Church, commemorating the Resurrection of Christ. It developed from the Jewish Passover, but the English name derives from Eostre, Anglo-Saxon goddess of spring, who was honoured in Apr. Eggs are given at this time as a symbol of new life.

Whitsun celebrates the filling of the followers of Jesus with the Holy Spirit, which Christians believe to be the third aspect of God, after Jesus had returned to heaven. As the disciples went out and told everyone about Jesus, so at Whitsun Christians go on processions around the parish boundaries.

Advent the time leading up to Christmas; a time of preparation for Christians.

Christmas day on which the birth of Christ is celebrated by Christians. Although the actual birth date is unknown, the choice of a date near the winter solstice owed much to missionary desire to facilitate conversion of pagans, for example in Britain 25 Dec had been kept as a festival long before the introduction of Christianity. Many of its customs also have a non-Christian origin.

Hindu festivals

Mahashivaratri Festival of Siva, who is celebrated as lord of the dance, dancing on the demon of ignorance.

Holi a harvest time festival in honour of Krishna, when bonfires are lit; people throw coloured water at each other and play games and tricks as a reminder of Krishna's mischievous behaviour.

Rama Naumi celebration of the Birth of Rama. An eight-day fast during which the Ramayana is recited; the fast is broken on the ninth day with fruit and nuts, and offerings are made to Rama.

Raksha Bandhan a family festival in which sisters present their brothers with a bracelet of thread to protect them from harm, in return for which the brothers promise to look after their sisters.

Janmashtami celebration of the birthday of Krishna. Children act out stories of Krishna, and a statue of the young Krishna is used in the celebrations.

Dusshera a festival (also known as Durga Puja) which lasts ten days; the great goddess Devi is worshipped in her many forms.

Divali a new year festival which honours Lakshmi, goddess of fortune. Lights are lit in every window.

Jewish festivals

Purim celebrates the story of Esther, a Jewish woman who risked her life to save her people from treacherous slaughter. The story is read from a scroll in the synagogue, and the congregation boo and hiss when the villain's name is read out. It is a time for noisy parties and merriment.

Passover (Pesach) an ancient Jewish spring festival which commemorates the escape from slavery in Egypt. A special meal, the seder meal, is eaten and the story of how the Jews were saved by God from this bondage is told.

Shavuot or Pentecost commemorates the giving of the ten commandments to Moses.

Rosh Hashana the two-day holiday at the start of the Jewish New Year (first new moon after the autumn equinox).

Yom Kippur (Day of Atonement) day of Jewish religious fast held on the tenth day of Tishri (Sept-Oct), the seventh month of the Jewish year.

Succot the feast of Tabernacles (tents), a reminder of the time the Israelites spent wandering in the wilderness. Temporary homes of branches are built at the synagogue and sometimes at home.

Hanukkah celebrates the recapture and rededication of the Temple of Jerusalem by Judas Maccabeus in 164 BC. The festival lasts eight days; each day, a new candle is lit on a special candlestick or menorah.

Muslim festivals

The Muslim calendar is lunar, and correspondences with the Western calendar cannot be given; festivals fall 11–12 days earlier each year.

Lailat ul-Isra Wal Mi'raj celebrates Muhammad's night journey by horse to Jerusalem and up to heaven.

Lailat ul-Barah the night of forgiveness; a time to prepare for Ramadan.

Ramadan the ninth month of the Muslim year, throughout which a strict fast is observed during the hours of daylight.

Lailat ul-Qadr commemorates the night the Quran was first revealed to Muhammad.

Eid ul-Fitr the end of the fast of Ramadan. Gifts are given to charity, new clothes are worn and sweets are given.

Eid ul-Adha celebrates the faith of the prophet Abraham, who was prepared to sacrifice his son Ismail when Allah asked him to. Lamb is eaten and shared with the poor, as a reminder of the sheep which Allah provided as a sacrifice instead of Ismail.

Day of Hijra commemorates the journey of Muhammad from Mecca to Medina.

Sikh festivals

Hola Mohalla a three-day festival held at the time of the Hindu festival Holi. Sporting competitions and other tests of skill take place.

Baisakhi originally a harvest festival, it now celebrates the founding of the Khalsa, the Sikh brotherhood, and commemorates those Sikhs killed by British troops in Amritsar on Baisakhi, 1919.

Martyrdom of Guru Arjan commemorates the death of the fifth guru, Guru Arjan, who built the Golden Temple at Amritsar and compiled the main part of the Sikh holy book.

Divali celebrates the release from prison of the sixth guru, Guru Hargobind, who also managed to secure the release of 51 Hindu princes who were imprisoned with him.

Guru Nanak's birthday celebrates the birth of the founder of the first guru of Sikhism.

Martyrdom of Guru Tegh Bahadur commemorates the birth of the ninth guru, martyred for the faith.

Birthday of Guru Gobind Singh celebrates the birth of the tenth and last human guru of Sikhism, and the founder of the Khalsa.

month	festival	religion	commemorating
Jan			
6th	Epiphany	Western Christian	coming of the Magi
6th-7th	Christmas	Orthodox Christian	birth of Christ
18th-19th	Epiphany	Orthodox Christian	coming of the Magi
Jan-Feb	New Year	Chinese	Return of Kitchen God to heaven
Feb-Mar	Shrove Tuesday	Christian	day before Lent
	Ash Wednesday	Christian	first day of Lent
	Purim	Jewish	story of Esther
	Mahashivaratri	Hindu	Siva
Mar-Apr	Palm Sunday	Western Christian	first day of Holy Week
	Good Friday	Western Christian	Crucifixion of Christ
	Easter	Western Christian	Resurrection of Christ
	Passover	Jewish	escape from slavery in Egypt
	Holi	Hindu	Krishna
	Holi Mohalla	Sikh	(coincides with Holi)
	Rama Naumi	Hindu	birth of Rama
	Ching Ming	Chinese	remembrance of dead
Apr			
13th	Baisakhi	Sikh	founding of the Khalsa
Apr-May	Easter	Orthodox Christian	Resurrection of Christ
May-Jun	Shavuot	Jewish	giving of Ten Commandments to Moses
	Whitsun	Western Christian	filling of Jesus's followers with Holy Spirit
	Wesak	Buddhist	day of Buddha's birth, enlightenment and death
	Martyrdom of Guru Arjan	Sikh	death of fifth guru of Sikhism
Jun	Dragon Boat Festival Whitsun Orthodox Christian	Chinese	Chinese martyr
Jul	Dhammacakka	Buddhist	preaching of Buddha's first sermon
Aug	Raksha Bandhan	Hindu	family
Aug-Sept	Janmashtami	Hindu	birthday of Krishna
Sept	Moon Festival	Chinese	Chinese hero
Sept-Oct	Rosh Hashana	Jewish	start of Jewish New Year
	Yom Kippur	Jewish	day of fasting
	Succot	Jewish	Israelites' time in the wilderness

month	festival	religion	commemorating
Oct	Dusshera	Hindu	goddess Devi
Oct-Nov	Divali	Hindu	goddess Lakshmi
	Divali	Sikh	release of Guru Hargobind from prison
Nov	Guru Nanak's Birthday	Sikh	founder of Sikhism
	Advent	Western Christian	preparation for Christmas
Nov-Dec	Bodhi Day	Buddhist (Mahayana)	Buddha's enlightenment
Dec	Hanukkah	Jewish	recapture of Temple of Jerusalem
	Winter Festival	Chinese	time of feasting
25th	Christmas	Western Christian	birth of Christ
Dec-Jan	Birthday of Guru Gobind Singh	Sikh	last (tenth) human guru of Sikhism
	Martyrdom of Guru Tegh Bahadur	Sikh	ninth guru of Sikhism

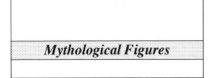

Mythological Figures

Achilles Greek hero of Homer's *Iliad*, the son of the sea nymph Thetis. She rendered him invulnerable, except for the heel by which she held him, by dipping him in the River Styx. He killed Hector in the Trojan War, and was himself killed by Paris with a poisoned arrow in the heel.

Actaeon in Greek mythology, a hunter who surprised Artemis bathing; she changed him to a stag and he was torn to pieces by his own hounds.

Adonis in Greek mythology, a youth beloved by Aphrodite. He was killed while boar-hunting, but was allowed to return from the lower world for six months every year to rejoin her. Worshipped as a god of vegetation, he was known as *Tammuz* in Babylonia, Assyria, and Phoenicia (where it was his sister, Ishtar, who brought him from the lower world). He seems also to have been identified with Osiris.

Aegir in Scandinavian mythology, the god of the sea.

Aeolus in Greek mythology, the god of the winds, who kept them imprisoned in a cave on the Lipari Islands.

Aesculapius in Greek and Roman mythology, the god of medicine; his emblem was a staff with a snake coiled round it, since snakes were believed to renew life by sloughing their skin. Sacred snakes were kept in the sanctuaries of Aesculapius at Epidaurus and elsewhere. The customary offering to Aesculapius was a cock.

Agamemnon in Greek mythology, a Greek hero, son of Atreus, King of Mycenae. He married Clytemnestra, and their children included Electra, Iphigenia, and Orestes. Setting out from Aulis to the Trojan War, he would have sacrificed Iphigenia to Artemis to secure fair winds (she was saved by the goddess and made a priestess). He led the capture of

Troy, received Priam's daughter Cassandra as a prize, and was murdered by Clytemnestra and her lover, Aegisthus, on his return home. Orestes and Electra later killed the guilty couple. Aeschylus, Euripides, T S Eliot, O'Neill and Sartre all based plays on the theme.

Agni in Hindu mythology, the god of fire, the protector of humans against the powers of darkness, and the guardian of their homes.

Amaterasu in Japanese mythology, the sun-goddess, grandmother of Jimmu Tenno, first ruler of Japan, from whom the emperors claimed to be descended.

Amazon in Greek mythology, a member of a group of legendary female warriors living near the Black Sea, who cut off their right breasts to use the bow more easily; their queen, Penthesilea, was killed by Achilles at the siege of Troy.

Ammon in Egyptian mythology, the king of the gods, the equivalent of Zeus/Jupiter; the name is also spelt Amen/Amun, as in the name of the pharaoh Tutankh*amen*. In art, he is represented as a ram, as a man with a ram's head. or as a man crowned with feathers. He had famous temples at Siwa oasis, Libya and Thebes, Greece.

Andromeda in Greek mythology, a princess chained to a rock as a sacrifice to a sea monster. She was rescued by Perseus.

Anubis in Egyptian mythology, the jackal-headed god of the dead.

Aphrodite in Greek mythology, the goddess of love (Roman Venus, Phoenician Astarte, Babylonian Ishtar); said to be either a daughter of Zeus or sprung from the foam of the sea. She was the unfaithful wife of Hephaestus, the mother of Eros, and was awarded the prize for beauty by Paris; centres of her worship were Cyprus (Paphos) and Cythera.

Apollo in Greek mythology, the god of sun, music, poetry, and prophecy, agriculture and pastoral life, and leader of the Muses. He was the twin child (with Artemis), of Zeus and Leto. His chief cult centres were his supposed birthplace on the island of Delos, and Delphi. Ancient statues show Apollo as the embodiment of the Greek ideal of male beauty.

Arachne in Greek mythology, a girl weaver who beat Athena in a contest, and was transformed by her into a spider (Greek *arachne*).

Ares in Greek mythology, the god of war (Roman Mars). The son of Zeus and Hera, he was worshipped chiefly in Thrace.

Argus in Greek mythology, a giant with a hundred eyes, which Hera eventually transplanted to the tail of her favourite bird, the peacock.

Ariadne in Greek mythology, the daughter of Minos, king of Crete. When Theseus came from Athens as one of the victims offered to the Minotaur, she fell in love with him and gave him the ball of thread which enabled him to find his way out of the labyrinth.

Artemis in Greek mythology, the goddess (Roman Diana) of chastity, childbirth, and the young; she was envisaged as a virgin huntress; her cult centre was at Ephesus. She was later also identified with Selene, goddess of the moon.

Atalanta in Greek mythology, a huntress who challenged all her suitors to a foot race; if they lost they were killed. Milanion was given three golden apples to drop by Aphrodite; this ensured that when Atalanta stopped to pick them up, she lost the race.

Athena in Greek mythology, the goddess (Roman Minerva) of war, wisdom, and the arts and crafts, who was supposed to have sprung fully-armed from the head of Zeus. Her chief cult centre was Athens, where the Parthenon was dedicated to her. In Rome a statue of her (the 'Palladium'), allegedly brought by Aeneas from Troy, was kept in the temple of Vesta.

Atlas in Greek mythology, a N African king, transformed for his sins to a peak of the Atlas mountains, which were envisaged by the Greeks as supporting the heavens.

Aurora in Roman mythology, the goddess of dawn (Greek Eos).

Avalon in Celtic legend, the island of the blest or paradise, and in the Arthurian legend the land of heroes, to which the dead king was conveyed. It has been associated with Glastonbury.

Avatar in Hindu mythology, the descent of a deity to earth in a visible form. Most famous are the ten Avatars of Vishnu.

Bacchus in Greek and Roman mythology, the god of fertility (identified with Dionysus) and of wine; his rites were orgiastic.

Balder in Norse mythology, the son of Odin and Frigga and husband of Nanna, and the best, wisest, and most loved of all the gods. He was killed, at Loki's instigation, by a twig of mistletoe shot by the blind god Hodur.

Bes in Egyptian mythology, the god of music and dance, usually shown as a grotesque dwarf.

Calliope in Greek mythology, the Muse of epic poetry, and chief of the Muses.

Callisto in Greek mythology, the nymph beloved by Zeus (Jupiter).

Calypso in Greek mythology, a sea nymph who waylaid the homeward-bound Odysseus for seven years.

Cassandra in Greek mythology, the daughter of Priam, whose prophecies (for example of the fall of Troy) were never believed, because she had rejected the love of Apollo. She was murdered with Agamemnon.

Cassiopeia in Greek mythology, the mother of Andromeda.

Castor and Pollux/Polydeuces in Greek mythology, twin sons of Leda (by Zeus), brothers of Helen and Clytemnestra. Protectors of seamen, they were transformed at death to the constellation Gemini.

centaur in Greek mythology, a creature half human and half horse. They were supposed to live in Thessaly, and be wild and lawless: the mentor of Hercules, Chiron, was an exception.

Cerberus in Greek mythology, the three-headed dog guarding the entrance to Hades.

Ceres in Roman mythology, the corn goddess, identified with the Greek goddess Demeter.

Charon in Greek mythology, the boatman who ferried the dead over the river Styx.

Chiron in Greek mythology, the son of Kronos by a sea nymph. A centaur, he was the wise tutor of Jason and Achilles among others.

Circe in Greek mythology, an enchantress. In the *Odyssey* of Homer she turned the followers of Odysseus into pigs when she held their leader captive.

Clio in Greek mythology, one of the muses, the inventor of epic poetry and history.

Clytemnestra in Greek mythology, the wife of Agamemnon.

Cupid in Roman mythology, the god of love, identified with the Greek god Eros.

Cybele in Phrygian mythology, an earth goddess, identified by the Greeks with Rhea and honoured in Rome. The Corybantes (eunuch priests) celebrated her worship with orgiastic dances.

cyclopes in Greek mythology, giants who lived in Sicily, had a single eye, and lived as shepherds; Odysseus encountered them.

Daedalus in Greek mythology, an Athenian craftsman supposed to have constructed for King Minos the labyrinth in which the Minotaur was imprisoned. He fled from Crete with his son Icarus using wings made from feathers fastened with wax; Icarus flew too near the sun, and fell into the Aegean and was drowned.

Daphne in Greek mythology, a nymph, changed into a laurel tree to escape from Apollo's amorous pursuit.

Deirdre in Celtic mythology, beautiful intended bride of Conchobar.

Demeter in Greek mythology, goddess of agriculture (identified with Roman Ceres), daughter of Kronos and Rhea, and by Zeus mother of Persephone. She is identified with the Egyptian goddess Isis and had a temple dedicated to her at Eleusis where mystery religions were celebrated.

Diana in Roman mythology, goddess of hunting and the moon (Greek Artemis), daughter of Jupiter and twin-sister of Apollo.

Dionysus in Greek mythology, god of wine (son of Semele and Zeus), and also of orgiastic excess (an animal, or on occasion a child, being torn to pieces alive and eaten). He was identified with Bacchus, whose rites were less savage. His festivals, the *Dionysia*, were particularly associated with Athens; see theatre. Attendant on him were wild women (*maenads*) and goatlike men (*satyrs*) with pointed ears, horns and a tail.

Dis in Roman mythology, god of the underworld (Greek Pluto); ruler of Hades.

Erebus in Greek mythology, the god of darkness and the intermediate region between upper earth and Hades.

Eros in Greek mythology, boy-god of love (Roman *Cupid*), son of Aphrodite, and armed with bow and arrows; he fell in love with Psyche.

Europa in Greek mythology, princess of Tyre, carried off by Zeus (in the form of a bull); she personifies the continent of Europe.

Fates in Greek mythology, the three female figures, Atropos, Clotho and Lachesis, envisaged as elderly spinners, who decided the length of human life, and analogous to the Roman Parcae and Norse Norns.

Faunus in Roman mythology, god of fertility and prophecy, with goat's ears, horns, tail and hind legs, identified with the Greek Pan; in 1979 archaeological evidence showed that he was also worshipped in Britain.

Flora in Roman mythology, goddess of flowers, youth, and of spring.

Fortuna in Roman mythology, goddess of chance and good fortune. (Greek *Tyche*).

Frigga or *Freya* in Scandinavian mythology, wife of Odin and mother of Thor, goddess of married love and the hearth. Friday is named after her.

Furies in Greek mythology, the Erinyes, winged women with snake-like hair, spirits of vengeance, sometimes referred to appeasingly as the 'Kindly ones' (Eumenides).

Gaia or *Ge*. In Greek mythology, the goddess of the Earth. She sprang from primordial Chaos and herself produced Uranus, by whom she was the mother of the Cyclopes and Titans.

Galatea in Greek mythology, a Nereid. In legend, Pygmalion made a statue (later named Galatea) which was brought to life by Aphrodite.

Ge in Greek mythology, an alternative name for Gaia, goddess of the earth.

Gorgon in Greek mythology, any of three sisters, Stheno, Euryale and Medusa, who had wings, claws, enormous teeth, and snakes for hair. Medusa, the only one who was mortal, was killed by Perseus, but her head was still so frightful, it turned the onlooker to stone. The winged horse Pegasus was supposed to have sprung from her blood.

Graces in Greek mythology, three goddesses (Aglaia, Euphrosyne, and Thalia), daughters of Zeus and Hera, the personification of grace and beauty and the inspirers of the arts and the sciences.

Hades in Greek mythology, the underworld where the spirits of the departed went after death, usually depicted as a cavern or pit underneath the earth. It was presided over by the god Hades or Pluto (Roman Dis). He was the brother of Zeus, and married Persephone, daughter of Demeter and Zeus. She was allowed to return to the upper world for part of the year, bringing spring with her. The entrance to Hades was guarded by the three-headed dog Cerberus. *Tartarus* was the section where the wicked were punished, for example Tantalus.

Harpies in early Greek mythology, wind spirits; in later legend they have horrific women's faces and the bodies of vultures.

Hathor in ancient Egyptian mythology, the sky-goddess, identified with Isis.

Hebe in Greek mythology, the goddess of youth, daughter of Zeus and Hera, and hand-maiden of the gods.

Hecate in Greek mythology, the goddess of witchcraft and magic, sometimes identified with Artemis and the moon.

Hector in Greek mythology, a Trojan prince, son of Priam, who, in the siege of Troy, was the foremost warrior on the Trojan side until he was killed by Achilles.

Hecuba in Greek mythology, the wife of Priam, and mother of Hector and Paris, captured by the Greeks after the fall of Troy.

Hel or *Hela* in Norse mythology, the goddess of the underworld.

Helen in Greek mythology, the daughter of Zeus and Leda, the most beautiful of women. Married to Menelaus, king of Sparta, she eloped with Paris in his absence, which precipitated the Trojan War. Afterwards she returned home with her husband.

Helios in Greek mythology, the sun-god and father of Phaethon, thought to make his daily journey across the sky in a chariot.

Hephaestus in Greek mythology, the god of fire and metalcraft (Roman Vulcan), son of Zeus and Hera; he was lame, and married Aphrodite.

Hera in Greek mythology, a goddess, sister-consort of Zeus, mother of Hephaestus, Hebe, and Ares; protector of women and marriage, and identified with Roman Juno.

Heracles in Greek mythology, a hero (Roman *Hercules*), son of Zeus and Alcmene, famed for strength. While serving Eurystheus, king of Argos, he performed 12 Labours, including the cleansing of the Augean stables.

Hermaphroditus in Greek mythology, the son of Hermes and Aphrodite. He was loved by a nymph who prayed for eternal union with him, so that they became one body with dual sexual characteristics, hence the term hermaphrodite.

Hermes in Greek mythology, a god, son of Zeus and Maia, and messenger of the gods; he has winged sandals and a staff around which serpents coil. Identified with the Roman Mercury and ancient Egyptian Thoth, he protected thieves, travellers, and merchants.

Hero and Leander in Greek mythology, a pair of lovers. Hero was a priestess of Aphrodite at Sestos on the Hellespont, in love with Leander on the opposite shore at Abydos. When he was drowned while swimming across during a storm, she threw herself into the sea out of grief.

Hesperides in Greek mythology, the mythical Greek maidens who guarded a tree bearing golden apples in the Islands of the Blessed.

Hestia in Greek mythology, the goddess (Roman Vesta) of the hearth, daughter of Chronos (Roman Saturn) and Rhea.

Hippolytus in Greek mythology, the son of Theseus, who cursed him for his supposed dishonourable advances to his stepmother Phaedra. Killed by Poseidon as he rode near the sea in his chariot, he was restored to life when his innocence was proved.

Horus in ancient Egyptian mythology, the

hawkheaded sun god, son of Isis and Osiris, of whom the pharaohs were thought the incarnation.

Hydra in Greek mythology, a monster with nine heads. Whenever a head was cut off, two new ones grew in its place. It was finally killed by Heracles.

Hygieia in Greek mythology, the goddess of health (Roman Salus), daughter of Aesculapius.

Hymen in Greek mythology, the god of marriage, shown as a youth with a bridal torch.

Io in Greek mythology, a princess loved by Zeus, who transformed her to a heifer to hide her from the jealousy of Hera.

Iphigenia in Greek mythology, the daughter of Agamemnon.

Irene in Greek mythology, goddess of peace (Roman Pax).

Janus in Roman mythology, god of doorways and passageways, the patron of the beginning of the day, month, and year, after whom January is named; he is represented as two-faced, looking in opposite directions.

Jason in Greek mythology, leader of the *Argonauts* who sailed in the Argo to Colchis in search of the Golden Fleece.

Jinn in Muslim mythology, a spirit able to assume human or animal shape.

Juno in Roman mythology, queen of the gods. Greek equivalent: Hera.

Jupiter in Roman mythology, king of the gods (Greek Zeus), son of Saturn. A sky god, he was associated with lightning and thunder bolts, and victory in war; he married his sister Juno.

Kali in Hindu mythology, the wife of Siva. She is the goddess of destruction and death.

Kronos or *Cronus* in Greek mythology, one of the Titans, ruler of the world, and father of Zeus, who overthrew him.

Lares and Penates in Roman mythology, spirits of the farm and of the store cupboard, often identified with the family ancestors, whose shrine was the centre of family worship in Roman homes.

Leda in Greek mythology, wife of Tyndareus, by whom she was the mother of Clytemnestra.

By Zeus, who came to her as a swan, she was the mother of Helen of Troy, Castor and Pollux.

Lethe in Greek mythology, a river of the underworld. To drink its waters was to forget the past.

Loki in Norse mythology, the god of evil, the slayer of Baldur, whose children were the Midgard serpent Jörmungander which girdles the Earth, the wolf Fenris, and Hela, goddess of the underworld.

Manu in Hindu mythology, the founder of the human race, who was saved by Brahma from a deluge.

Marduk in Babylonian mythology, the sun-god, creator of earth and man.

Mars in Roman mythology, the god of war, after whom the month of March is named.

Medea in Greek mythology, the sorceress daughter of the king of Colchis. When Jason reached the court, she fell in love with him, helped him acquire the Golden Fleece, and fled with him. When Jason married Creusa, Medea killed his bride with the gift of a poisoned garment, and also killed her own two children by Jason.

Medusa in Greek mythology, a mortal woman who was transformed into a Gorgon.

Melpomene in Greek mythology, the Muse of tragedy.

Mercury in Roman mythology, the messenger of the gods, identified with Greek Hermes.

Minerva in Roman mythology, the goddess of wisdom. Greek counterpart: Athena.

Minos in Greek mythology, a King of Crete (son of Zeus and Europa).

Minotaur in Greek mythology, a monster, half man-half bull, offspring of Pasiphaë, wife of King Minos of Crete and a bull. It lived in the labyrinth at Knossos and its victims were seven girls and seven youths, sent in annual tribute by Athens, until Theseus slew it, with the aid of Ariadne, the daughter of Minos.

Mithras in Persian mythology, the god of light.

Morpheus in Greek mythology, the god of dreams, son of Somnus, god of sleep.

Muses in Greek mythology, the nine daughters of Zeus and Mnemosyne (goddess of memory) and inspirers of creative arts: *Calliope* epic poetry; *Clio* history; *Erato* love poetry; *Euterpe* lyric poetry; *Melpomene* tragedy; *Polyhymnia* hymns; *Terpsichore* dance; *Thalia* comedy; *Urania* astronomy.

Naiad in classical mythology, a water-nymph.

Narcissus in Greek mythology, a beautiful youth who rejected the love of the nymph Echo. Condemned to fall in love with his own reflection, he pined away.

Nemesis in Greek mythology, the goddess of retribution, especially punishing hubris (Greek *hybris*), arrogant self-confidence.

Neptune in Roman mythology god of the sea, the equivalent of the Greek Poseidon.

Nereid in Greek mythology, a minor sea goddess who sometimes mated with mortals.

Nike in Greek mythology, goddess of victory, represented as 'winged', as in the statue from Samothrace in the Louvre. One of the most beautiful architectural monuments of Athens was the temple of Nike Apteros.

Niobe in Greek mythology, the daughter of Tantalus and wife of Amphion, the king of Thebes. Contemptuous of the mere two children of the goddess Leto, Apollo and Artemis, she died of grief, and was changed to stone by Zeus, when her own twelve offspring were killed by them in revenge.

nymph in Greek mythology, a guardian spirit of nature; *hamadryads* or *dryads* guarded trees; *naiads*, springs and pools; *oreads*, hills and rocks; *nereids*, the sea.

Oceanus in Greek mythology, the god (one of the Titans) of a river supposed to encircle the earth, and progenitor of other river gods, and the nymphs of the seas and rivers.

Odin chief god of Scandinavian mythology, the Woden or Wotan of the Germanic peoples. A sky god, he is resident in Asgard, at the top of the world-tree, and receives the souls of heroic slain warriors from the Valkyries, the 'divine maidens', feasting with them in his great hall, Valhalla. At Ragnarök (doomsday) the warriors were envisaged as fighting a final battle in support of Odin against the evil giants, a new order arising from the ensuing general destruction. The wife of Odin is Frigga or Freya, and

Thor is their son. Wednesday is named after him.

Orestes in Greek mythology, one of the children of Agamemnon and Clytemnestra.

Orion in Greek mythology, a giant of Boeotia, famed as a hunter.

Pan in Greek mythology, god (Roman Sylvanus) of flocks and herds, shown as a man with the horns, ears and hooves of a goat, and playing a shepherd's pipe.

Pandora in Greek mythology, the first woman. Zeus sent her to earth with a box of evils (to counteract the blessings brought to mortals by Prometheus's gift of fire); she opened it, and they all flew out. Only hope was left inside as a consolation.

peri in Persian myth, beautiful, harmless beings, ranking between angels and evil spirits, and ruled by Eblis, greatest of the latter.

Perseus in Greek mythology, son of Zeus and Danae. He slew Medusa, the Gorgon; rescued Andromeda; and became king of Tiryns.

Pleiades in Greek mythology, seven daughters of Atlas, who asked to be changed to a cluster of stars to escape the pursuit of Orion.

Polyhymnia in Greek mythology, the Muse of singing, mime and sacred dance.

Procrustes (Greek 'the stretcher') in Greek mythology, a robber who tied his victims to a bed; if they were too tall for it, he cut off the ends of their legs, and if they were too short stretched them.

Prometheus in Greek mythology, a Titan who stole fire from heaven for the human race. In revenge, Zeus had him chained to a rock with an eagle preying on his liver, until he was rescued by Hercules.

Romulus in Roman mythology, the legendary founder and first king of Rome, the son of Mars by Rhea Silvia. He and his twin brother Remus were exposed by their great-uncle Amulius, but were suckled by a she-wolf and rescued by a shepherd. On reaching manhood they killed Amulius and founded Rome. Having murdered Remus, Romulus reigned alone until he disappeared in a storm, and thereafter was worshipped as a god under the name of Quirinus.

Saturn in Roman mythology, an ancient god (possibly the god of agriculture, also identified with the Greek god Kronos). He was dethroned by his sons Jupiter, Neptune, and Pluto. At his festival in Dec gifts were exchanged, and slaves were briefly treated as their masters' equals.

satyr in Greek mythology, a cross between a man and a goat.

Selene in Greek mythology, the goddess of the moon; in later times identified with Artemis.

Semele in Greek mythology, mother of Dionysus by Zeus. She was consumed by lightning when jealous Hera suggested she ask her lover to appear in his full glory.

Sibyl in Roman mythology, a priestess of Apollo, especially the Cumaean Sibyl living in a cave near Naples, Italy. She offered to sell Tarquinius nine collections of prophecies, the *Sibylline Books*, but the price was too high. When she had destroyed all but three, he bought those for the identical price, and these were kept for consultation in emergency at Rome.

Siren in Greek mythology, a sea nymph who lured sailors on to rocks by her singing. Odysseus, in order to hear the Sirens safely, tied himself to the mast and stuffed his crews' ears with wax; the Argonauts escaped them because the singing of Orpheus surpassed that of the sirens.

Sisyphus in Greek mythology, king of Corinth who, after his evil life, was condemned to roll a huge stone uphill, which always fell back before reaching the top.

Styx in Greek mythology, the river surrounding the underworld.

Surya in Hindu mythology, the personification of the Sun.

Tantalus in Greek mythology, a king whose crimes were punished in Tartarus by food and drink he could not reach.

Tartarus in Greek mythology, the part of Hades where the wicked were punished.

Thalia in Greek mythology, the Muse of comedy and pastoral poetry.

Thor in Norse mythology, son of Odin and Frigga, god of thunder (his hammer), and represented as a man of enormous strength defending humans against demons. Thursday is named after him.

Thoth in Egyptian mythology, god of wisdom and learning, scribe of the gods.

Titan in Greek mythology, any of the giant children of Uranus and Gaia, who included Kronos, Rhea, Themis (mother of Prometheus and personification of law and order) and Oceanus. Kronos and Rhea were in turn the parents of Zeus, who ousted Kronos as the ruler of the world.

Triton in Greek mythology, a merman sea-god, the son of Poseidon and the sea-goddess Amphitrite. He is shown blowing on a conch.

Tyr in Norse mythology, the god of battles, whom the Anglo-Saxons called Týw, hence 'Tuesday'.

Uranus in Greek mythology, the sky-god, responsible both for the sun and rain. He was the son and husband of Gaia, by whom he fathered the Titans.

Valhalla in Norse mythology, the hall in Odin's palace where he feasts with the souls of the dead heroes of mortal battles.

Venus in Roman mythology, the goddess of love (Greek Aphrodite).

Vesta in Roman mythology, the goddess of the hearth (Greek *Hestia*). The sacred flame in her shrine in the Forum was kept constantly lit by the six *Vestal Virgins*.

Vulcan in Roman mythology, the god of fire and destruction, later identified with the Greek god Hephaestus.

Zeus in Greek mythology, chief of the gods (Roman Jupiter). He was the son of Kronos, whom he overthrew: his brothers and sisters included Demeter, Hades, Hera, and Poseidon. His offspring, either gods and goddesses, or godlike humans, included Apollo, Athena, Artemis, Castor and Polydeuces/Pollux, Dionysus, Hebe, Heracles, Hermes, Minos, Perseus, Persephone. As the supreme god he dispersed good and evil and was the father and ruler of all mankind. His emblems are the thunderbolt and aegis (shield), representing the thunder cloud.

Resources

Resources are things that can be used to provide the means to satisfy wants – in other words, they are not resources until people are able to use them. Because human wants are very diverse and extend from basic physical requirements such as food and shelter, through to ill-defined aesthetic needs, resources encompass a vast range of items. It is the intellectual resources of a society – its ideas and technologies – that determine which aspects of the environment meet that society's needs, and therefore become resources. In the 19th century uranium was simply a curiosity used only in the manufacture of coloured glass. Today, with the advent of nuclear technology, it is a vital energy resource. Though minerals such as coal and iron ores tend to dominate the perception of resources, the concept also embraces less tangible things such as beautiful landscapes and pleasant climates.

This section contains an overview of *Types of Resources,* and information on particular resources – *Minerals, Crops,* and *Commodities.*

Types of Resources

resources are often categorized into *human resources,* such as labour supplies and skills, and *natural resources,* such as climate, fossil fuels, and water. Natural resources are divided into those which are non-renewable and others which can be replenished (renewable). *Non-renewable resources* are things like coal, copper ores, and diamonds, which exist in strictly limited quantities. Once consumed they will not be replenished within the time-span of human history. In contrast, water supplies, timber, food crops, and solar power and similar resources can, if managed properly, provide a steady yield virtually for ever. These are termed replenishable or *renewable resources,* which may, in turn, be continuous (where supply is largely independent of people's actions) or flow (where supply is dependent on people's actions). However, inappropriate use of renewable resources can lead to their destruction, as for example when a fishery or forest is over-utilized and totally consumed.

demands for resources made by present-day societies are causing concern among many people, who consider that the present and future demands of industrial societies cannot be sustained for more than a century or two, and that once a resource base fails to meet a society's needs that society will collapse. However this view is not universally held, and other authorities contend that such analyses misunderstand the nature of resources.

resources for future generations will, they believe, be determined by the level of knowledge of future societies, and cannot be properly assessed by our current perceptions. As knowledge increases, new technologies will emerge, enabling materials which are currently of little importance to become valuable resources. The resource base can therefore expand as societies become better able to harness their environment to meet their needs.

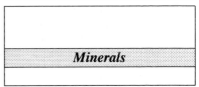

Minerals

minerals are substances with a regular atomic structure and a composition which lies within defined limits. The term is also used loosely to mean any material which is extracted from the earth. Minerals are the materials which form rocks. They provide the oil, coal, metals, fertilizers, and building materials on which industrial societies depend. Many industrial nations are dependent on imports of

Resources
NATURAL RESOURCES

Renewable		Non-Renewable
Continuous Resources Supply is largely independent of people's actions:	*Flow Resources* Supply is very dependent upon people's actions:	Supply is permanently depleted if they are worked. They are mostly minerals:
solar power	timber	
climates	wildlife	coal
tidal power	attractive landscape	copper ores
	water resources	oil
		phosphates

minerals from primary producer countries. The EEC imports over 95% of its chrome, copper and manganese. Many Third World countries are dependent on mineral exports to finance their economies. Conflict between the interests of exporting nations was highlighted in the 1970s by the restriction of oil exports by producers. Attention has been focussed on the adequacy of mineral resources to meet future needs, but the issue is complex; availability depends on the interaction of technology, price, and political factors as well as on the disposition of minerals within the earth's crust. *mineral ores* are concentrations of minerals which can be profitably worked. Concentration arises from specific geological processes, and consequently particular minerals are commonly associated with certain types of geological formation.

mineral reserves and mineral resources in casual conversation the terms reserves and resources are often interchanged. However, when discussing mineral resources the two refer to quite different things. *Mineral reserves* are the deposits which are known to exist, which are accessible and are of such quality

that under prevailing economic and technical conditions it is likely that they can be profitably extracted. *Mineral resources* include reserves plus deposits that are known but cannot currently be economically worked and deposits that have yet to be found. An increase in the price of a mineral or a change in technology or other conditions which lower the cost of extraction will make some marginally economic resources into reserves.

Mineral reserves may be increased by either the discovery of new deposits which can be economically worked, or by a favourable change in the economics associated with working deposits which were previously sub-economic. Such favourable changes may result from new lower cost extraction technologies or from a rise in the price of the mineral.

Reserves can also be reduced by events which make it unprofitable to work them (an example is the way tin deposits in Cornwall became uneconomic to mine after a collapse in tin prices in 1986). Because of this, mineral reserves constantly fluctuate in quantity and published figures should be interpreted with great caution.

MAJOR ECONOMIC MINERALS

Minerals and their sources

Major Metals	Minor Metals	Fuels	Chemicals	Miscellaneous
Iron	Nickel	Coal	Sulphur	Talc
Hematite	*Pentlandite*	Oil	*Pyrites*	*Talc*
Magnetite	Chrome	Gas	*Anhydrite*	Mica
Limotite	*Chromite*		*Native Sulphur*	*Muscivite*
Aluminium	Tin		Salt	*Biotite*
Bauxite	*Cassiterite*		*Halite*	Asbestos
Copper	Tungsten		Potash	*Chrysotile*
Calcocite	*Wolframite*		*Sylvite*	Kaolin
Chalcopyrite	Titanium		Phosphate	*Kaolinite*
Zinc	*Rutile*		*Apatite*	Diamond
Sphalerite	*Ilmenite*			*Diamond*
Calamine	Silver			
Lead	*Argenite*			
Galena				

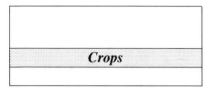

Crops

crops are plants grown for human use. Over 80 crops are grown worldwide, providing people with the majority of their food, and supplying fibres, rubber, pharmaceuticals, dyes and other materials. Four main groups of crops are readily identifiable: food crops, forage crops, fibre crops, and miscellaneous crops.

food crops are grown specifically to feed people, and provide the bulk of people's food worldwide. The major types are cereals, roots, pulses, vegetables, fruits, oil crops, tree nuts, sugar, beverages, and spices. Cereals make the most important contribution to human nutrition. Though most food crops are carefully cultivated, crop production techniques and yields vary enormously from one part of the world to another.

cereal crops are grasses which are grown for their edible starch seeds. All major civilizations have depended upon them for food, and in 1985 world production exceeded 1.8 billion tonnes. Cereals are an attractive foodstuff as they are easy to store and contain about 75% carbohydrate and 10% protein. In recent years research has led to dramatic increases in cereal yields; in the decade 1975–85 cereal yields in Britain almost doubled and now commonly exceed six tonnes per hectare. If all the world's cereal crop was consumed directly by humans everybody could obtain an adequate dietary intake of protein and carbohydrate. However a large proportion of cereal production, particularly in affluent nations, is used as animal feeds to boost the production of meat, milk, butter, and eggs.

root crops in agriculture the term refers to turnips, swedes, and beets which are actually enlarged hypocotyls and contain little root, whilst in trade statistics it refers essentially to the tubers of potatoes, cassava, and yams.

These three crops are second in importance to cereals as human food and in the mid-1980s world production was just under 600 million tonnes. Food production per hectare from roots is higher than for cereals. Roots have a high carbohydrate content, but their protein content rarely exceeds 2%. Consequently communities relying too heavily upon roots may suffer from protein deficiency. *Potatoes* are the major temperate food crop. The major tropical root crops are cassava – a shrub which produces starchy tubers, yams, and sweet potatoes. Root crops are also widely used as animal feeds and may be processed to produce starch, glues, and alcohol.

pulses are crops such as peas and beans. They are grown primarily for their seeds which provide a concentrated source of vegetable protein and make a vital contribution to human diets, especially in poor countries where meat is scarce. In the mid-1980s world production was about 50 million tonnes a year. *Soyabeans* are the major temperate protein crop. Most are used for oil production or for animal feeds, though some are processed into 'meat substitutes'. Peanuts dominate pulse production in the tropical world, and are mostly consumed directly as human food. Pulses play a useful role in crop rotations as they help to raise soil nitrogen levels as well as acting as break crops.

vegetable crops are a diverse group of plants eaten for their leaves, stems, flower clusters, and buds. Some fruits such as pumpkins and tomatoes are also considered as vegetables because of the manner in which they are consumed. Most vegetables are annuals, that is plants that live for one year or less. Though vegetables are not major sources of protein or energy, they add variety to human diets and are an important source of vitamins A and C, as well as providing dietary fibre and minerals. Vegetables are succulent, easily damaged, and rapidly decompose. Consequently until recent years there was little international trade in them, and even today the bulk of production will be consumed close to where it is grown. As a high proportion never enters the commercial market, statistics probably underestimate the

CROPS USAGE

Group	Types	Major Plants
Food Crops	Cereals	Wheat, Rice, Maize, Sorghum
	Roots	Potatoes, Cassava, Yams, Sweet Potatoes
	Pulses	Soyabeans, Groundnuts, Lentils, Peas
	Vegetables	Cabbage, Carrots, Okra, Lettuce
	Fruits	Apples, Citrus, Plums, Mangoes
	Oil Crops	Olives, Sunflower, Rapeseed, Oil Palm
	Tree Nuts	Brazil nuts, Hazlenuts, Cashew nuts, Almonds
	Sugar	Sugar Cane, Sugar Beet, Sorghum
	Beverages and Spices	Tea, Coffee, Cocoa, Ginger, Mace
Forage Crops	Pure Stands	Kale, Rape, Mustard
	Mixed Crops	Grasses, Vetches, Lucerne, Clover
Fibre Crops	Coarse Fibres	Jute, Sisal, Hemp, Coir
	Fine Fibres	Cotton, Flax, Kapok, Ramie
Miscellaneous Crops	Rubber	Rubber Trees
	Tobacco	Tobacco
	Pharmaceuticals	Foxglove, Evening Primrose, Poppy
	Ornamentals and Fragrants	Orchids, Carnations, Roses, Lavender

amount grown. In the mid-1980s world production certainly exceeded 380 million tonnes.

fruits the seeds of plants together with the tissues which enclose them. These fleshy tissues have evolved to aid seed dispersal and are often colourful, sweet, juicy, and very palatable. The word fruit comes from the Latin *frui* meaning 'to enjoy'. Most fruits are borne by perennial plants. Like vegetables, they provide vitamins and minerals but little protein, and are often regarded as a semi-luxury. Recorded world production in the mid-1980s was approximately 300 million tonnes per year. Broadly fruits are divided into three types: *temperate fruits,* which require a cold season for satisfactory growth; *sub-tropical fruits,* which require warm conditions but can survive light frosts; and *tropical fruits,* which succumb if temperatures drop close to freezing point. In order of abundance the principal temperate fruits are apples, pears, plums, peaches and apricots, cherries, and soft fruits like raspberries and strawberries. Sub-tropical fruits include oranges and other citrus fruits, dates, pomegranates, and avocados, while bananas, mangoes, pineapples, papaya, and litchis are typical tropical fruits. In recent decades technical advances have improved the storage and transportability of fruits and increasingly new trade routes are being established. Consequently 'exotic' tropical fruits are now available to consumers in temperate areas, and fresh temperate fruits are also available all year round.

oil crops vegetable oils are pressed from the seeds of many crops. All arable agricultural regions have their characteristic oil crops. Cool temperate areas grow rapeseed and linseed; warm temperate regions produce sunflowers, olives and soyabeans; tropical areas produce groundnuts, oil palm and coconuts. Some of the major vegetable oils such as soyabean oil,

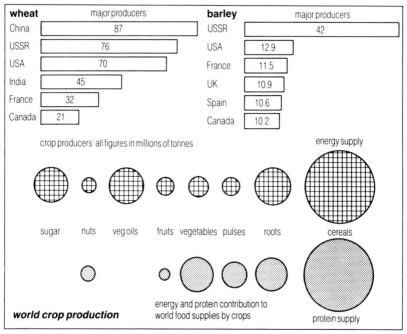

wheat	major producers
China	87
USSR	76
USA	70
India	45
France	32
Canada	21

barley	major producers
USSR	42
USA	12.9
France	11.5
UK	10.9
Spain	10.6
Canada	10.2

crop producers all figures in millions of tonnes

energy supply

sugar nuts veg oils fruits vegetables pulses roots cereals

world crop production

energy and protein contribution to world food supplies by crops

protein supply

groundnut oil, and cottonseed oil are derived from crops grown primarily for other purposes. Most vegetable oils are used as both edible oils and ingredients in industrial products such as soaps and varnishes, printing inks, and paints.

tree nuts nut is the common name for seeds which are enclosed in 'woody' shells. The kernels of most nuts provide a concentrated food with about 50% fat and a protein content of 10% to 20%, though a few, such as chestnuts, are high in carbohydrates and have only a moderate (5%) protein content. Most nuts are produced by perennial trees and bushes. Whilst the majority are obtained from plantations, considerable quantities of Brazil and pecan nuts are still collected from the wild. Records of production are incomplete but current estimates suggest that world production in the mid-1980s was only about four million tonnes per year. Besides being a useful food for people, nuts also provide edible and industrial oils.

sugar in the mid-1980s world production of refined sugar averaged approximately 100 million tonnes per year. The major sources are tropical cane sugar which accounts for about two-thirds of production, and temperate sugar beet. Sugar cane, which is a tropical grass, commonly yields over 20 tonnes of sugar per hectare per year, whereas sugar beet rarely exceeds seven tonnes per hectare per year. Beet sugar is more expensive to produce and its cultivation is often subsidised by governments which wish to support the agricultural sector and avoid over-dependence on the volatile world sugar market. Minor quantities of sugar are produced from maple trees (maple syrup) and from sorghum and date palms.

beverages and spices tea, coffee, cocoa, cola nuts, and hops are plant products which are

INTERNATIONALLY TRADED COMMODITIES

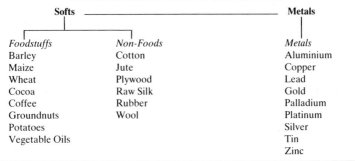

Foodstuffs	*Non-Foods*	*Metals*
Barley	Cotton	Aluminium
Maize	Jute	Copper
Wheat	Plywood	Lead
Cocoa	Raw Silk	Gold
Coffee	Rubber	Palladium
Groundnuts	Wool	Platinum
Potatoes		Silver
Vegetable Oils		Tin
		Zinc

widely used to impart pleasant flavours and stimulants to people's fluid intake. The juice of grapes and other fruits is fermented to produce wines, whilst fermented cereals form the basis of most beers. The alcoholic content of beers and wines can provide a useful addition to some people's energy intake. Spices are used to impart flavours and aromas to food. They have little food value, but increase the appetite and may facilitate digestion.

forage crops are crops like grass, clover and kale which are grown to feed livestock. Forage crops cover a greater area of the world than food crops, and grass, which dominates this group, is the world's most abundant crop, though much of it is still in an unimproved state. In areas where intense agriculture occurs forage crops often form break crops in a predominantly arable rotation.

fibre crops produce vegetable fibres. Temperate areas produce flax and hemp, but the most important fibre crops are cotton, jute, and sisal which are grown mostly in the tropical world. Cotton dominates fibre crop production.

miscellaneous crops are a diverse group of crops including tobacco, rubber, ornamental flowers, and perfume, pharmaceutical and dye-producing plants.

Commodities

commodities are essentially things produced for sale. They may be *consumer goods* like radios, or *producer goods* such as copper bars. *Commodity markets* deal in raw or semi-raw materials which are amenable to grading and which can be stored for considerable periods without deterioration. They developed to their present form in the 19th century, when industrial growth facilitated trading in large, standardized quantities of raw materials. Most markets encompass trading in 'commodity futures', that is trading for delivery several months ahead. Major commodity markets exist in Chicago, Tokyo, London, and elsewhere. Though specialized markets exist, such as silkworm cocoons in Tokyo, most trade relates to cereals and metals. 'Softs' is a term used for most materials other than metals.

Sociology

Sociology is the study of society, in particular of social order and social change, social conflict, and social problems. It studies social institutions, such as the family, law, and the church, as well as social concepts such as norm, role, and culture. What distinguishes sociology from other disciplines studying human behaviour is its emphasis on social factors, its attempt to study people in their social environment according to certain underlying moral, philosophical, and political codes of behaviour. Auguste Comte, who coined the term in 1830, is generally seen as the founder of modern sociology as a distinct and systematic discipline. He attempted to use the same philosophy (positivism) and research methods as the natural sciences to try to discover the underlying laws of social evolution and to make social knowledge more reliable, precise and systematic, capable of predicting social change and solving social problems.

Sociology today reflects a variety of perspectives and traditions. Its focus tends to be on contemporary industrial society, sometimes comparing it with pre-industrial society, and occasionally drawing on such related disciplines as history, geography, politics, economics, psychology, and anthropology. It concerns range from theories of social order and change to detailed analyses of small groups, individuals, and the routines of daily life. The relation between theory and method is one part of the current debate about whether sociology is or should be a science, and whether it can or should be free of ideology.

This section contains an overview of key *Perspectives* in sociology, definitions of *Terms and Concepts*, and biographical notes on *Key Thinkers* whose work has influenced the development of modern sociology.

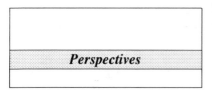

Perspectives

ethnomethodology the study of social order and routines used by people in their daily lives, to explain how everyday reality is created and perceived. Ethnomethodologists tend to use small-scale studies and experiments to examine the details of social life and structure (such as conversations) that people normally take for granted, rather than construct large-scale theories about society.

functionalism the view of society as a system comprising a number of interrelated parts, all functioning on the basis of a common value system or consensus about basic values and common goals. Every social custom and institution is seen as having a function in ensuring that society works efficiently; deviance and crime are seen as a form of social sickness. Functionalists often describe society as an organism with a life of its own, above and beyond the sum of its members. Comte, Durkheim, and Parsons have taken functionalist approaches.

Marxism the social, economic, and political theory, also known as dialectical or historical materialism, developed by Marx and Engels, which sees social and political institutions progressively changing their nature as economic developments transform material conditions. The evolution from feudalism, through capitalism, to socialism as modes of production is seen as inevitable, and resistance of an existing system to change requires its overthrow in the class struggle. Marxism has proved one of the most powerful and controversial theories in modern history, and a key focussing point in the social sciences, inspiring both dedicated exponents and bitter opponents.

phenomenology the philosophical perspective, founded by Husserl, which in the social sciences concentrates on phenomena as objects of perception (rather than as facts or occurrences which exist independently) in attempting to examine the ways people think about and interpret the world around them. In contrast to positivism or 'scientific' philosophy, phenomenology sees reality as essentially relative and subjective, and uses such tools as ethnomethodology and symbolic interactionism to focus on the structure of everyday life.

positivism the philosophical perspective, founded by Comte, which argues that only that which can be seen really exists and that the only valid form of knowledge is that gathered by empirical scientific method. Also called *scientific philosophy*, it assumes that there is a fixed and objective reality whose underlying laws of cause and effect can be discovered and then used to predict and control natural phenomena. Positivism sees phenomena as facts or occurrences which exist independently, rather than as objects of perception.

symbolic interactionism sociological method, founded by G H Mead, that studies the behaviour of individuals and small groups through observation and description, viewing people's appearance, gestures, and language as symbols they use to interact with others in social situations. In contrast to theories such as Marxism or functionalism, which attempt to analyse society as a whole through economic or political systems, it takes a perspective of society from within, as created by people themselves.

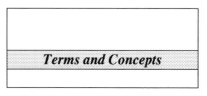

Terms and Concepts

alienation a sense of frustration, isolation, and powerlessness; a feeling of loss of control over one's life; a sense of estrangement either from society or from oneself. As a sociological concept it was developed by Hegel and Marx, who used it as a description and criticism of the condition of workers in capitalist society. The term has also been used by non-Marxist writers to explain, for example, industrial unrest in modern factories.

anomie a state created by the breakdown of commonly agreed standards of behaviour and morality; the term is often used to refer to situations where the social order appears to have collapsed. It was developed as a sociological concept by Durkheim to describe societies in transition, particularly during industrialization.

bureaucracy an organization whose structure and operations are governed to a high degree by written rules and a hierarchy of offices: in its broadest sense, all forms of administration; in its narrowest, rule by officials. Contemporary writers have highlighted the problems of bureaucracy, such as its inflexibility and rigid adherence to rules, and the term today is often used critically rather than in its original neutral sense.

class the main form of social stratification in industrial societies, based primarily on economic and occupational factors, but also referring to people's style of living or sense of group identity. Within the social sciences, class has been used both as a descriptive category and as the basis of theories about industrial society. The most widely used descriptive classification in the UK, that of the Registrar-General, divides the population into five main classes (see next page). The main division is that between the manual and non-manual occupations being made. Such classifications have been widely criticized, however, on several grounds: that they reflect a middle-class bias that brain is superior to brawn; that they classify women according to their husband's occupation rather than their own; that they ignore the upper class, the owners of land and industry. Theories of class may see such social divisions either as a source of social stability (Durkheim) or social conflict (Marx).

community the sense of identity, purpose, and companionship that comes from belonging to a particular place, organization, or social group. The concept dominated sociological thinking in the first half of the 20th century, and inspired the academic discipline of ***community studies***.

culture the way of life of a particular society or group of people, including patterns of thought, beliefs, behaviour, customs, traditions and rituals, dress, language, as well as art, music, and literature. Sociologists and anthropologists see culture as a key concept in describing and analysing human societies.

demography the study of the size, structure, and development of human populations to establish reliable statistics on such factors as birth and death rates, marriages and divorces, life expectancy, and migration. Demography is important in the social sciences as the basis for government planning in such areas as education, housing, welfare, transport, and taxation.

development in the social sciences, the term generally refers to economic development, the acquisition by a society of industrial techniques and technology; hence the common classification of the 'developed' nations of the First World and the poorer 'developing' or 'underdeveloped' nations of the Third World. The assumption that development in the sense of industrialization is inherently good has been increasingly questioned since the 1960s. Many universities today have academic departments of ***development studies*** which address the theoretical questions involved in proposing practical solutions to the problems of development in the Third World.

deviance abnormal behaviour; that is, behaviour that deviates from the norms or laws of a particular society or group, and so invokes social sanctions, controls, or stigma. The term may refer to minor abnormalities (such as nail-biting) as well as to criminal acts. Deviance is a relative concept: what is considered deviant in some societies is normal in others; and in a particular society the same act (killing someone, for example) may be either normal or deviant depending on the circumstances (in wartime or for money, for example). Some sociologists argue that the reaction of others, rather than the act itself, is what determines

SOCIAL CLASSES IN BRITAIN

	Middle Class
I	professional occupations: accountant, lawyer
II	intermediate occupations: managers, senior administrators
IIIN	skilled occupations (non-manual): policeman, nurse
	Working Class
IIIM	skilled occupations (manual): plumber, electrician
IV	semi-skilled occupations: machinist, mechanic
V	unskilled occupations: dustman, cleaner
	Other
	residual groups: students, armed forces

Social Classes in Britain as classified by the Registrar-General

whether an act is deviant.

elite a small group in a society with power, privileges, and status above others. An elite may be cultural, educational, religious, political, or social. Sociological interest has centred on how such minorities get, use, and hold on to power, and on what distinguishes elites from ordinary members of society.

ethnicity from Greek *ethnos*, 'a people', a term that overlaps with such social concepts as race, nation, class, and religion. Social scientists use the term ethnic group to refer to groups or societies who feel a common sense of identity, often based on a similar culture, language, religion, and customs. It may or may not include common territory, skin colour, or common descent. Whereas the concept of race was used from the outside to label people according to perceived biological features, ethnicity refers to people's own sense of cultural identity. The US, for example, is often described as a *multi-ethnic society* because many members would describe themselves as members of an ethnic group (Jewish, black, or Irish, for example) as well as their national one (American).

feudalism the main form of social stratification in medieval Europe. A system based primarily on land, it involved a hierarchy of authority, rights, and power that extended from the king downwards. An intricate network of duties and obligations linked royalty,

nobility, lesser gentry, free tenants, villeins, and serfs. Feudalism was reinforced by a complex legal system and supported by the Christian church. With the growth of commerce, trade and industry in the 13th century, feudalism gradually gave way to class as the dominant form of social ranking.

Gemeinschaft and **Gesellschaft** German terms (roughly, 'community' and 'association') used by Ferdinand Tönnies (1855–1936) to contrast social relationships in traditional rural societies with those in modern industrial societies. He saw Gemeinschaft as intimate and positive, and Gesellschaft as impersonal and negative. In small-scale societies, where everyone knows everyone else, the social order is stable and the culture homogeneous. In large urban areas life is faster and more competitive, and relationships are more superficial, transitory, and anonymous.

ideology a set of ideas, beliefs, and opinions about the nature of people and society providing a framework for a theory about how society is or should be organized. The term is used by philosophers and social scientists in an analytical and neutral way, but it has more popularly been used to describe beliefs based on fanatical faith rather than rational argument.

kinship human relationship based on blood or marriage, and sanctified by law and custom. Kinship forms the basis for most human societies and for such social groupings as the family, clan, or tribe. Kinship is universal, although its social significance varies from society to society. Most human societies have evolved strict social rules, customs, and taboos regarding kinship, particularly to do with sexual behaviour (such as the prohibition of incest).

labelling defining or describing a person in terms of his or her behaviour; for example, describing someone who has broken a law as a criminal. In sociology, labelling theory deals with human interaction, behaviour, and control, particularly in the field of deviance. Social labelling has been seen as a form of social control in that labels affect both a person's self-image and other people's reactions. Crucial factors include who labels a person, and whether the label sticks.

marriage the legally or culturally sanctioned union of one man and one woman (monogamy); one man and two or more women (polygyny); one woman and two or more men (polyandry). The basis of marriage varies considerably in different societies (romantic love in the West; arranged marriages in some other societies), but most marriage ceremonies, contracts, or customs involve a set of rights and duties such as care and protection, and there is generally an expectation that children will be born of the union to continue the family line.

norms informal guidelines about what is, or is not, considered normal social behaviour (as opposed to rules and laws, which are formal guidelines). Such shared values and expectations vary from one society to another and from one situation to another, and range from crucial taboos such as incest or cannibalism to trivial customs and traditions, such as the correct way to hold a fork. Norms are an integral part of any society's culture and of any group or organization's subculture, and a key part of social control and social order.

peer group in the social sciences, a term used to refer to groups or collections of people who have a common identity based on such characteristics as similar social status, interests, age, or ethnic group. The concept has proved useful in analysing the power and influence of workmates, schoolfriends, and ethnic and religious groups in socialization and social behaviour. In particular the term has become associated with the study of children and adolescents.

role in the social sciences, a term used to mean the part a person plays in society, either in helping the social system to work or in fulfilling social responsibilities towards others. Sociologists distinguish between formal roles, such as those of a doctor or politician, and informal roles, such as those of mother or husband, which are based on personal relationships. Social roles involve mutual expectations: a doctor can fulfil that role only if the patients play their part; a father requires the support of his children. *Role play* refers to the way children learn adult roles by acting them out in play (mothers and fathers; cops and robbers). Everyone has a number of roles to play in a society: a woman may be a mother, a wife, and a doctor at the same time, for example. *Role conflict* arises where two or more of a person's roles are seen as incompatible.

sect a small, voluntary, ideological group, usually religious in nature, aspiring to personal perfection and claiming a monopoly of access to truth or salvation. Sects are usually highly exclusive. They demand strict conformity, total commitment to their code of behaviour, and complete personal involvement, sometimes to the point of rejecting mainstream society altogether in terms of attachments, names, possessions and family. Most sects are short-lived, either because their appeal dies out and their members return to mainstream society, or because their appeal spreads and they become part of mainstream society (for example, Christianity). Sects are sociologically important as indicators of social change.

secularization the process through which religious thinking, practice, and institutions lose their social significance. The concept is based on the theory, held by some sociologists, that as societies become industrialized their religious morals, values, and institutions give way to secular ones.

socialization the process, beginning in childhood, by which a person learns how to become a member of a particular society, learning its norms, customs, laws, and ways of living. The main agents of socialization are the family, school, peer groups, work, religion, and the mass media. The main methods of socialization are direct instruction, rewards and punishment, imitation, experimentation, role play, and interaction. Some agents of socialization, such as the family and the peer group, may conflict with each other, offering alternative goals, values, and styles of behaviour.

social mobility the movement of groups and individuals up and down the social scale. The extent or range of social mobility varies in different societies. The caste system of India and the feudalism of medieval Europe are often cited as examples of closed societies, where little social mobility was possible; the class system of Western industrial societies is considered relatively open and flexible. Individual social mobility may occur through education, marriage, talent, and so on; group mobility usually occurs through change in the occupational structure caused by new technological or economic developments.

status an individual's social position, or the esteem in which he or she is held by others in society. These two forms of social prestige may be separate or interlinked. Formal social status is attached to a particular social position, occupation, role, or office. Informal social status is based on an individual's own personal talents, skills, or personality. Both within and between most occupations or social positions there is a status hierarchy. Accompanying high status are usually *status symbols*, such as insignia of office or an expensive car. Sociologists distinguish between *ascribed status*, which is bestowed by birth, and *achieved status*, the result of one's own efforts. Status is seen as a key influence on human behaviour, on the way people evaluate themselves and others.

stereotype (Greek 'fixed impression') a one-sided, irrational, and preconceived idea about a particular group or society. It is based on prejudice rather than fact, but by repetition stereotypes become fixed in people's minds, resistant to change or to factual evidence to the contrary. Stereotypes can prove dangerous when used to justify persecution and discrimination. Some sociologists believe that stereotyping reflects a power structure in which one group in society uses labelling to keep another group 'in its place'.

trade union an organized association of workers in a particular trade, formed to protect their interests and improve their conditions of work and wages. Sociological interest in trade unions has concentrated on the extent to which they have contributed to the stability of modern industrial societies or to social and industrial conflict.

urbanization the process by which the proportion of a population living in or around towns and cities increases. The growth of urban concentrations is a relatively recent phenomenon, dating back only about 150 years, although the world's first cities date back more than 5,000 years. Urbanization has had a major effect on the social structures of industrial societies, affecting not only where people live but how they live, and *urban sociology* has emerged as a distinct area of study.

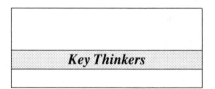

Key Thinkers

Althusser Louis 1918– . French Marxist philosopher. Arguing against a view that the economic system determines the way we live, he divided each mode of production into four interacting elements – the economic, political, ideological and theoretical. He attempted to show how the ruling class ideology of a particular era is a crucial form of class control. Works include *For Marx* 1965 and *Lenin and Philosophy* 1969.

Chicago School of Sociology the first university department of sociology was founded in Chicago, Illinois, USA, in 1892. In the 1920s and 1930s, under Robert E Park, with W I Thomas, Ernest Burgess, Louis Wirth, and R McKenzie, it became an important centre for social science, studying modern urban life including crime and deviance in Chicago.

Comte Auguste 1798–1857. French philosopher and founder of sociology, a term he coined in 1830. He sought to establish sociology as a 'scientific' discipline, using positivism as the basis of a new science of social order and social development. In his six-volume *Cours de philosophie positive* 1830–42 he argued that human thought and social development evolve through three stages: the theological, the metaphysical and finally the positive or scientific. His early radical ideas were increasingly tempered by the political and social upheavals of his time.

Durkheim Emile 1858–1917. French sociologist. He analysed the bases of social order and the effects of industrialization on traditional social and moral order, and attempted to establish sociology as an academic discipline. Key works are *The Division of Labour in Society* 1893, comparing small-scale societies with industrial ones; *The Rules of Sociological Method* 1895, proclaiming positivism as the way forward for sociology as a science; and *Suicide* 1897, showing social causes of this apparently individual act.

Engels Friedrich 1820–95. German social and political philosopher. He wrote *The Condition of the Working Class in England* 1845, and collaborated with Marx on *The Communist Manifesto* 1848. His later works, such as *Origins of the Family, Private Property, and the State* 1884, helped popularize Marxism as well as using Darwinian ideas to give Marxism a scientific and deterministic flavour which was to influence later Soviet thinking.

Frankfurt School term for the Institute of Social Research, set up at Frankfurt University in Germany in 1923 as the first Marxist research centre. In the 1930s, under Max Horkheimer, a group which included Erich Fromm, Herbert Marcuse and T W Adorno tried to integrate the ideas of Marx and Freud in a synthesis known as **critical theory**. With the rise of Hitler, many of its members went to the USA and set up the Institute at Columbia University, New York.

Gramsci Antonio 1891–1937. Italian Marxist theorist who helped to found the Italian Communist Party in 1921, but was imprisoned by Mussolini in 1926 and spent virtually the rest of his life in prison. His *Prison Notebooks* include his famous concept of **hegemony**, a belief that real class control in capitalist societies is ideological and cultural rather than physical, and that bourgeois propaganda can only be revealed by radical education of the working class. His approach influenced European Marxists in their attempt to distance themselves from orthodox Soviet communism.

Husserl Edmund 1859–1938. German philosopher, whose theory of **phenomenology** concentrating on what is consciously experienced (phenomena), was influential in the development of sociology. His main works are *Logical Investigations* 1900, 1901, and *Phenomenological Philosophy* 1913.

Illich Ivan 1926– . Viennese-born social critic, who believes that modern technology and bureaucratic institutions are destroying individual skills and self-sufficiency, particularly in the Third World, and creating a new form of dependency, on experts and professionals. His solution is to abolish the institutions on which authority rests. Works include *Deschooling Society* 1971 and *Towards a History of Need* 1978.

Kuhn Thomas S 1922– . American historian of science, whose *The Structure of Scientific Revolutions* 1962 argued that all knowledge, even scientific knowledge, is relative, dependent on the paradigm (theoretical framework) that dominates a particular subject at a particular point in time. Such paradigms (such as Darwinism or Newtonian theory) are uncritically accepted as true, until a 'scientific revolution' creates a new orthodoxy.

Mannheim Karl 1893–1947. Hungarian sociologist, who settled in the UK in 1933. In *Ideology and Utopia* 1929 he argued that all knowledge except mathematics and physics is ideological, a reflection of class interests and values. He distinguished between ruling class ideologies and those of utopian or revolutionary groups, arguing that knowledge is thus created by a continual power struggle between rival groups and ideas.

Marx Karl (Heinrich) 1818–83. German philosopher, economist and social theorist. His large body of work, much of it in collaboration with Engels, including *The Communist Manifesto* 1848 and *Capital* 1867–94, helped give birth to communist revolutions in Russia, China, and the Third World. His materialist conception of history and his analysis of capitalist society have made him possibly the single most influential thinker over the whole range of the social sciences in the 20th century.

Mead George Herbert 1863–1931. American philosopher and social psychologist, who helped to found the philosophy of pragmatism. His work on group interaction stimulated the development of role theory, phenomenology, and ethnomethodology.

Michels Robert 1876–1936. German social and political theorist. Originally a radical, he became a severe critic of socialism and Marxism, and in his last years was a supporter of Hitler and Mussolini. In *Political Parties* 1911 he propounded the 'Iron Law of Oligarchy', arguing that in any society there is a tendency towards rule by the few in the interests of the few, and that ideologies such as socialism and communism were merely propaganda to control the masses.

Mills C Wright 1916–62. American sociologist, whose concern for humanity, ethical values, and individual freedom led him to criticize the US establishment as well as analyse it. Originally in the liberal tradition, he later adopted a more radical standpoint. Works include *White Collar* 1951 and *The Power Elite* 1956.

Parsons Talcott 1902–79. American sociologist, professor of sociology at Harvard University from 1931 until his death. He was the author of over 150 books and articles, and put forward the influential theory of structural functionalism. Works include *The Structure of Social Action* 1939 and *The Social System* 1951.

Popper Karl (Raimund) 1902– . Austrian philosopher of science, and social theorist critic of Marxism. He views scientific discovery as a process of falsification rather than verification – that ideas and theories can only be proved false, not correct. There is no such thing as objective knowledge, and good science involves a process of conjecture and refutation (trial and error) whereby ideas are tested, and in most cases rejected. A good theory is one that is falsifiable; a bad one (such as Marxism, in his view) is one that is not logically testable. Works include *The Logic of Scientific Discovery* 1934, *Conjectures and Refutations* 1963, and *Objective Knowledge* 1972.

Taylor Frederick Winslow 1856–1915. American management consultant, the founder of scientific management, which aims at improving working efficiency and industrial discipline. His ideas, published in *Principles of Scientific Management* 1911, were based on the breakdown of work to the simplest tasks, and the introduction of time and motion studies. His methods were most clearly expressed in 'assembly line' factories, but his ideas have been criticized for alienating workers.

Tönnies Ferdinand 1855–1936. German social theorist and philosopher. His main work *Gemeinschaft-Gesellschaft* 1887 contrasted traditional societies and small organizations with modern industrial societies and large organizations. He saw industrialization as a threat to traditional society's sense of community.

Weber Max 1864–1920. German sociologist, who emphasized cultural and political factors as key influences on economic development and individual behaviour. He undertook comparative analyses of ancient and modern civilizations and religions and he argued for the possibility of a scientific and value-free approach to research. Key works include *The Protestant Ethic and the Spirit of Capitalism* 1902 and *The Sociology of Religion* 1920.

Sport

Many sports can be traced to ancient Egyptian or Greek times. Coursing, for example, was believed to have taken place in Egypt in 3000 BC, using Saluki dogs. Wrestling certainly took place in Egypt more than 4,000 years ago, and the Greeks participated in boxing around 1500 BC.

The real development of the majority of today's sport as competitions, rather than pastimes, was in the 18th and 19th centuries, when sports such as cricket, football, rugby, golf, tennis, and many more became increasingly popular.

The traditional sports have changed very little over the years but the advent of television has led to more and more competitions within each sport. Television has also helped the growth and development of some sports; darts, snooker and bowls are three prime examples.

Thanks to large sums of money through sponsorship, most sports can look forward to a healthy future, and their superstars can continue to be among the highest-paid people in the world. But, when one sees the delicate skills of champions such as Steve Davis, Jack Nicklaus, Martina Navratilova, and John Lowe, there is no denying them such rewards for years of dedication to their sport.

This section begins with *Events and Records*, a brief history and description of many sports, with lists of recent champions and winners in each. It concludes with *Biographies* of a selection of the many sporting greats that have made the headlines and broken records over the years.

Events and Records

angling fishing with rod and line in many popular forms. *Freshwater* and *sea-fishing* are the most popular forms. Fishing is the biggest participant sport in the UK. *Freshwater* coarse fishing includes members of the carp family, and pike (not usually eaten but thrown back into the water); freshwater game fish include salmon and trout. In *seafishing* the catch includes flatfish, bass, mackerel; big-game fish (again usually not eaten) including shark, tuna or tunny, marlin, and swordfish. Competition angling exists and world championships take place for most branches of the sport. The oldest is the World Freshwater Championship, inaugurated 1957.

World Freshwater Championship
individual
1982	Kevin Ashurst *(England)*
1983	Rudiger Kremkus *(West Germany)*
1984	Bobby Smithers *(England)*
1985	Dave Roper *(England)*
1986	Lud Wever *(Holland)*
1987	Clive Branson *(Wales)*
1988	J P Fouquet *(France)*

team
1982	Holland
1983	Belgium
1984	Luxembourg
1985	England
1986	Italy
1987	England
1988	England

archery the use of the bow and arrow originally in war and hunting, but now as a competitive sport. Organizations include the world governing body, the Fédération Internationale du Tir à L'Arc 1931, and the British Grand National Archery Society 1861. In competitions, results are based on double FITA rounds, 72 arrows at each of four targets at 90, 70, 50, and 30 metres (70, 60, 50, and 30 for women). The highest possible score is 2,880.

CHAMPIONS
World Championships first held 1931; formerly an annual event, now biennial
men – individual
1979	Darrell Pace *(USA)*
1981	Kyöti Laasonen *(Finland)*
1983	Richard McKinney *(USA)*
1985	Richard McKinney *(USA)*
1987	Vladimir Asheyer *(USSR)*

men – team
1979	USA
1981	USA
1983	USA
1985	South Korea
1987	South Korea

women – individual
1979	Jin-Ho Kim *(South Korea)*
1981	Natalia Butuzova *(USSR)*
1983	Jin-Ho Kim *(South Korea)*
1985	Irina Soldatova *(USSR)*
1987	Ma Xiagjuan *(China)*

women – team
1979	South Korea
1981	USSR
1983	South Korea
1985	USSR
1987	China

athletics competitive track and field events consisting of running, throwing, and jumping disciplines. *Running events* range from sprint races (100 metres) to the marathon (26 miles 385 yards). *Jumping events* are the high jump, long jump, triple jump, and pole vault (men only). *Throwing events* are javelin, discus, shot put, and hammer throw (men only).

OLYMPIC CHAMPIONS
track and field champions the 24th Olympics were held in Seoul, S Korea, Sep 17-Oct 2 1988
men/women
100 metres Carl Lewis *(USA)*/Florence Griffith-Joyner *(USA)*
200 metres Joe Deloach (USA)/Florence Griffith-Joyner*(USA)*
400 metres Steve Lewis *(USA)*/Olga Bryzgina *(USSR)*
800 metres Paul Ereng *(Kenya)*/Sigrun Wodars *(East Germany)*
1,500 metres Peter Rono *(Kenya)*/Paula Ivan *(Romania)*
3,000 metres – /Tatyana Samolenko*(USSR)*
5,000 metres John Ngugi *(Kenya)*/ –
10,000 metres Brahim Boutaib *(Morocco)*/ Olga Bondarenko *(USSR)*

Marathon Gelindo Bordin*(Italy)*/ Rosa Mota *(Portugal)*
100 metres hurdles – /Jordanka Donkova *(Bulgaria)*
110 metres hurdles Roger Kingdom *(USA)*/-
400 metres hurdles Andre Phillips *(USA)*/ Debbie Flintoff-King*(Australia)*
3,000 metres steeplechase Julius Kariuki *(Kenya)*/ –
20,000 metres walk Joseph Pribilinec *(Czechoslovakia)*/–
50,000 metres walk Viacheslav Ivanenko *(USSR)*–
4 × 100 metres relay USSR/USA
4 × 400 metres relay USA/USSR
high jump Guennadi Avdeyenko *(USSR)*/ Louise Ritter *(USA)*
long jump Carl Lewis *(USA)*/Jackie Joyner-Kersee *(USA)*
triple jump Hristo Markov *(Bulgaria)*/–
pole vault Sergey Bubka *(USSR)*/–
javelin Tapio Korjus *(Finland)*/Petra Felke *(East Germany)*
hammer Sergey Litvinov *(USSR)*
discus Jurgen Schult *(East Germany)*/ Martina Hellmann *(East Germany)*
shot put Ulf Timmermann *(East Germany)*/ Natalya Lisovaskaya *(USSR)*
decathlon Christian Schenk *(East Germany)*/–
heptathlon –/Jackie Joyner-Kersee *(USA)*
World Cross Country Championships
men - individual
1988   John Ngugi *(Kenya)*
1989   John Ngugi *(Kenya)*
women - individual
1988   Ingrid Kristiansen *(Norway)*
1989   Annette Sergant *(France)*
men - team
1988   Kenya
1989   Kenya
women - team
1988   USSR
1989   USSR
World Records (at 15 June 1989)
men
400 metres   43,29 Butch Reynolds *(USA)*
5,000 metres   12:58,39 Said Aouita *(Morocco)*
high jump   2.42m Patrick Sjoeberg *(Sweden)* /Carlo Thranhardt *(West Germany)*
pole vault   6.06m Sergey Bubka *(USSR)*
women
100 metres   10.49 Florence Griffith-Joyner *(USA)*
200 metres   Heike Dreschler *(East Germany)*
100 metres hurdles   12.25 Ginka Zagorcheva *(Bulgaria)*

high jump   2.09m Stefka Kostadinova *(USSR)*
long jump   7.52m Galina Chistyakova *(USSR)*
javelin   78.90m Petra Felke *(East Germany)*

badminton indoor racket game played on a court with a feathered shuttlecock instead of a ball. Similar to lawn tennis but played on a smaller court, the object is the same: to force the opponent(s) to be unable to return the shuttlecock.

CHAMPIONS
World Championships have existed since 1977 at singles, doubles, and mixed doubles
men
1980   Rudy Hartono *(Indonesia)*
1983   Icuk Sugiarto *(Indonesia)*
1985   Han Jian *(China)*
1987   Yang Yang *(China)*
women
1980   Wiharjo Verawaty *(Indonesia)*
1983   Li Lingwei *(China)*
1985   Han Aiping *(China)*
1987   Han Aiping *(China)*
Thomas Cup; an international team championship for men's international teams, first held
1949
1970   Indonesia
1973   Indonesia
1976   Indonesia
1979   Indonesia
1982   China
1984   Indonesia
1986   China
1988   China
Uber Cup; a women's international team competition, first held
1957
1972   Japan
1975   Indonesia
1978   Japan
1981   Japan
1984   China
1986   China
1988   China

baseball national summer game of USA, possibly derived from the English game of rounders. According to tradition it was invented in Cooperstown, New York, by Abner Doubleday in 1839.

World Series first held 1903 as an end-of-season game between the winners of the two professional leagues, the National League and the American League; established as a series of seven games 1905

1978	New York Yankees
1979	Pittsburgh Pirates
1980	Philadelphia Phillies
1981	Los Angeles Dodgers
1982	St Louis Cardinals
1983	Baltimore Orioles
1984	Detroit Tigers
1985	Kansas City Royals
1986	New York Mets
1987	Minnesota Twins
1988	Los Angeles Dodgers

basketball ball game between two teams of five players on an indoor enclosed court. The aim is, via a series of passing moves, to throw the large inflated ball through one of two circular hoops and nets which are 3.05m/10ft above the ground and positioned at each end of the court. Basketball was invented by YMCA instructor Dr James Naismith at Springfield, Massachusetts, in 1891. The most famous basketball team is the *Harlem Globetrotters*.

CHAMPIONS
World Championships first held 1950 for men, 1953 for women; held every four years
men
1950	Argentina
1954	USA
1959	Brazil
1963	Brazil
1967	USSR
1970	Yugoslavia
1974	USSR
1978	Yugoslavia
1982	USSR
1986	USA

women
1953	USA
1957	USA
1964	USSR
1967	USSR
1971	USSR
1975	USSR
1979	USA
1983	USSR
1987	USA

billiards indoor game played with cues (tapered poles) and composition balls (one red, two white) on a rectangular green baize table with six pockets, one at each corner and one in the middle of each of the long sides. There are normally two players, who score strokes by potting the red ball, potting the opponent's ball, or potting another ball off one of these two.

CHAMPIONS
World Professional Championship instituted 1870, organized on a challenge basis; restored as an annual tournament 1980

1980	Fred Davis *(England)*
1981	not held
1982	Rex Williams *(England)*
1983	Rex Williams *(England)*
1984	Mark Wildman *(England)*
1985	Ray Edmonds *(England)*
1986	Robert Foldvari *(Australia)*
1987	Norman Dagley *(England)*
1988	Norman Dagley *(England)*

bobsleighing or **bobsledding** the sport of racing steel-bodied, steerable toboggans, manned by two or four people, down mountain ice-chutes at speeds of up to 130 kmph/80 mph.

CHAMPIONS
Olympic Champions four-man event introduced 1924, two-man 1932
two-man/four-man
1968	Italy/Italy
1972	West Germany/Switzerland
1980	Switzerland/East Germany
1984	East Germany/East Germany
1988	USSR/Switzerland

World Championship four-man championship introduced 1924, two-man 1931; in Olympic years winners automatically become world champions
two-man/four-man
1980	Switzerland/East Germany
1981	East Germany/East Germany
1982	Switzerland/Switzerland
1983	Switzerland/Switzerland
1984	East Germany/East Germany
1985	East Germany/East Germany
1986	East Germany/Switzerland
1987	Switzerland/Switzerland
1988	USSR/Switzerland

bowls outdoor and indoor game popular in England and Commonwealth countries, and played in Britain since the 13th century. It is played on *flat* or *crown greens* with biased bowls of lignum vitae (13 cm/5 in in diameter), and the aim is to draw each bowl as near as possible to the small white jack. The game can be played as singles, pairs, triples, or rinks (four players a side).

CHAMPIONS
World Championship first held 1966 for men, 1969 for women
men - singles/pairs
1972	Malwyn Evans(Wales)/Hong Kong
1976	Doug Watson *(South Africa)*/South Africa
1980	David Bryant *(England)*/Australia
1984	Peter Bellis *(New Zealand)*/USA
1988	Peter Bryant *(England)*/New Zealand

triples/fours
1972	USA/England
1976	South Africa/South Africa
1980	England/Hong Kong
1984	Ireland/England
1988	New Zealand/Ireland

women - singles/pairs
1973	Elsie Wilke *(New Zealand)*/Australia
1977	Elsie Wilke *(New Zealand)*/Hong Kong
1981	Norma Shaw *(England)*/Ireland
1985	Merle Richardson *(Australia)*/Australia
1988	Janet Ackland *(Wales)*/Ireland

triples/fours
1973	New Zealand/New Zealand
1977	Wales/Australia
1981	Hong Kong/England
1985	Australia/Scotland
1988	Australia/Australia

Crown Green Bowls Waterloo Handicap first held 1907
1979	Brian Duncan
1980	Vernon Lee
1981	Roy Nicholson
1982	Dennis Mercer
1983	Stan Frith
1984	Steve Ellis
1985	Tommy Johnstone
1986	Brian Duncan
1987	Brian Duncan
1988	Ingham Gregory

boxing fighting with fists. The modern sport dates from the 18th century when fights were fought with bare knuckles and with untimed rounds. Each round ended with a knockdown.

Fighting with gloves became standard after the formulation of the Queensberry Rules in 1867. The last bare-knuckle fight was in 1889 between John L Sullivan and Jake Kilrain. Jack Broughton (1704-89) was one of the early champions and in 1743 drew up the first set of boxing rules. All modern boxing follows the original Queensberry Rules, but with modifications. Contests take place in a roped ring 4.3–6.1 m/ 14–20 ft square. All rounds last for 3 minutes. Amateur bouts last for 3 rounds and professional bouts for 12 rounds. Boxers are classified according to weight and can fight opponents from the same weight division or a heavier division. The weight divisions in professional boxing range from *mini-flyweight* (also known as paperweight and minimum weight), under 49kg/108lb to *heavyweight*, over 88kg/195lb.

CHAMPIONS
World Champions
WBC = World Boxing Council
WBA = World Boxing Association
IBF = International Boxing Federation
WBO = World Boxing Organization
heavyweight (since 1979)
1979	John Tate *USA (WBA)*
1980	Mike Weaver *USA (WBA)*
1982	Mike Dokes *USA (WBA)*
1983	Gerry Coetzee *South Africa (WBA)*
1984	Larry Holmes *USA (IBF)*
1984	Tim Witherspoon *USA (WBC)*
1984	Pinklon Thomas *USA (WBC)*
1984	Greg Page *USA (WBA)*
1985	Michael Spinks *USA (IBF)*
1985	Tony Tubbs *USA (WBA)*
1986	Tim Witherspoon *USA (WBA)*
1986	Trevor Berbick *Canada (WBC)*
1986	Mike Tyson *USA (WBC/WBA)*
1986	James Smith *USA (WBA)*
1987	Mike Tyson *USA (WBC)*
1987	Tony Tucker *USA (IBF)*
1987	Mike Tyson *USA* (Undisputed)

world champions at five different weights
Sugar Ray Leonard *USA*
1979	WBC welterweight
1981	WBA junior-middleweight
1987	WBC middleweight
1988	WBC light-heavyweight, WBC super-middleweight

Thomas Hearns *USA*
1980	WBA welterweight
1982	WBC junior-middleweight
1987	WBC middleweight

1988   WBO super-middleweight, WBC light-heavyweight

great heavyweights

1882-92	John L Sullivan
1992-97	Jim Corbett
1919-28	Jack Dempsey
1937-49	Joe Louis
1952-56	Rocky Marciano
1964-67	Muhammad Ali
1974-78	Muhammad Ali
1978-79	Muhammad Ali
1978-85	Larry Holmes
1986-	Mike Tyson

canoeing sport of propelling a lightweight, shallow boat, pointed at both ends, by paddles or sails. Modern canoes are made from fibre-glass, but original boats were of wooden construction covered in bark or skin. Canoeing became a sport in the 19th century and the Royal Canoe Club in Britain was founded in 1866.

CHAMPIONS
introduced into the *Olympic Games* 1936
men - Kayak singles
500 metres

1980	Vladimir Parfenovich *(USSR)*
1984	Ian Ferguson *(New Zealand)*
1988	Zsolt Gyulay *(Hungary)*

1,000 metres

1980	Rudiger Helm *(East Germany)*
1984	Alan Thompson *(New Zealand)*
1988	Greg Barton *(USA)*

Kayak pairs
500 metres

1980	USSR
1984	New Zealand
1988	New Zealand

1,000 metres

1980	USSR
1984	Canada
1988	USA

Kayak fours
1,000 metres

1980	East Germany
1984	New Zealand
1988	Hungary

Canadian singles
500 metres

1980	Sergey Postrekhin *(USSR)*
1984	Larry Cain *(Canada)*
1988	Olaf Heukrodt *(East Germany)*

1,000 metres

1980	Lubomir Lubenov *(Bulgaria)*
1984	Ulrich Eicke *(West Germany)*
1988	Iavn Klementiev *(USSR)*

Canadian pairs
500 metres

1980	Hungary
1984	Yugoslavia
1988	USSR

1,000 metres

1980	Romania
1984	Romania
1988	USSR

women - Kayak singles
500 metres

1980	Birgit Fischer *(East Germany)*
1984	Agneta Anderson *(Sweden)*
1988	Vania Guecheva *(Bulgaria)*

Kayak pairs
500 metres

1980	East Germany
1984	Sweden.
1988	East Germany

chess board game originating as early as the 2nd century AD. Two players use 16 pieces each, on a board of 64 squares of alternating colour, to try and force the opponent into a position where the main piece (the king) is threatened, and cannot move to another position without remaining threatened.

CHAMPIONS
World Championships first official world champion recognized 1886
men

1957	Vassiliy Smyslov *(USSR)*
1958	Mikhail Botvinnik *(USSR)*
1960	Mikhail Tal *(USSR)*
1961	Mikhail Botvinnik *(USSR)*
1963	Tigran Petrosian *(USSR)*
1969	Boris Spassky *(USSR)*
1972	Bobby Fischer *(USA)*
1975	Anatoliy Karpov *(USSR)*
1985	Gary Kasparov *(USSR)*

women

1950	Lyudmila Rudenko *(USSR)*
1953	Elizaveta Bykova *(USSR)*
1955	Olga Runtsova *(USSR)*
1958	Elizaveta Bykova *(USSR)*
1962	Nona Gaprindashvili *(USSR)*
1978	Maya Chiburdanidze *(USSR)*

cricket the national summer sport in England. The game is played between two sides of 11 players each on a pitch 20 m/22 yds long with a wicket at each end. The object of the game is to score more runs than the opposing side. A run is normally scored by the batsman after striking the ball and exchanging ends with his partner, or by hitting the ball to the boundary line for an automatic four or six runs.

CHAMPIONS
County Championship first officially held 1890
1980   Middlesex
1981   Nottinghamshire
1982   Middlesex
1983   Essex
1984   Essex
1985   Middlesex
1986   Essex
1987   Nottinghamshire
1988   Worcestershire
Refuge Assurance League (formerly John Player League) first held 1969
1980   Warwickshire
1981   Essex
1982   Sussex
1983   Yorkshire
1984   Essex
1985   Essex
1986   Hampshire
1987   Worcestershire
1988   Worcestershire
NatWest Cup (formerly the *Gillette Cup*) first held 1963
1980   Middlesex
1981   Derbyshire
1982   Surrey
1983   Somerset
1984   Middlesex
1985   Essex
1986   Sussex
1987   Nottinghamshire
1988   Middlesex
Benson and Hedges Cup first held 1972
1980   Northamptonshire
1981   Somerset
1982   Somerset
1983   Middlesex
1984   Lancashire
1985   Leicestershire
1986   Middlesex
1987   Yorkshire
1988   Hampshire
World Cup first held 1975, contested every four years
1975   West Indies
1979   West Indies
1983   India
1987   Australia

cycling cycle racing takes place on oval artificial tracks; or on the road, as in the French Tour de France, and the British Milk Race; or across country. There are several types of race.

Stage races are held over gruelling terrain and can last from three days up to three weeks, as in the Tour de France, Tour of Italy, and Tour of Spain. *Criteriums* are fast races around the closed streets of city centres. *Road races* are run over a prescribed circuit, which the riders lap several times, usually covering a distance of about 100 miles. *Track racing* takes place on a concrete or wooden banked circuit, either indoors or outdoors. In *Time trialing* each rider races against the clock, with all the competitors starting at different intervals.

CHAMPIONS
Tour de France first held 1903
1981   Bernard Hinault *(France)*
1982   Bernard Hinault *(France)*
1983   Laurent Fignon *(France)*
1984   Laurent Fignon *(France)*
1985   Bernard Hinault *(France)*
1986   Greg LeMond *(USA)*
1987   Stephen Roche *(Ireland)*
1988   Pedro Delgado *(Spain)*
1989   Greg LeMond *(USA)*
Tour of Britain (Milk Race) first held 1951
1980   Ivan Mitchtenko *(USSR)*
1981   Sergei Krivocheyev *(USSR)*
1982   Yuri Kashirin *(USSR)*
1983   Matt Eaton *(USA)*
1984   Oleg Czougeda *(USSR)*
1985   Erik van Lancker *(Belgium)*
1986   Joey McLoughlin *(Great Britain)*
1987   Malcolm Elliott *(Great Britain)*
1988   Vasiliy Zhdanov *(USSR)*
World Professional Road Race Champions first held 1927
1980   Bernard Hinault *(France)*
1981   Freddie Maertens *(Belgium)*
1982   Giuseppe Saroni *(Italy)*
1983   Greg LeMond *(USA)*
1984   Claude Criquielon *(Belgium)*
1985   Joop Zoetemelk *(Holland)*
1986   Moreno Argentin *(Italy)*
1987   Stephen Roche *(Ireland)*
1988   Maurizio Fondriest *(Italy)*

darts indoor game played on a circular board. Darts (like small arrow shafts) approx 13cm/5in in length are thrown at segmented targets and score points values according to their landing place.

CHAMPIONS
World Championship inaugurated 1978; held annually

1980	Eric Bristow *(England)*
1981	Eric Bristow *(England)*
1982	Jocky Wilson *(Scotland)*
1983	Keith Deller *(England)*
1984	Eric Bristow *(England)*
1985	Eric Bristow *(England)*
1986	Eric Bristow *(England)*
1987	John Lowe *(England)*
1988	Bob Anderson *(England)*
1989	Jocky Wilson *(England)*

equestrianism skill in horse riding as practised under International Equestrian Federation rules. An Olympic sport, there are three main branches of equestrianism: *show jumping, three-day eventing* and *dressage.*

CHAMPIONS
World Championship first held 1953 for men, 1965 for women; since 1978 they have competed together
men

1953	Francisco Goyoago *(Spain)*
1954	Hans-Gunter Winkler *(West Germany)*
1955	Hans-Gunter Winkler *(West Germany)*
1956	Raimondo D'Inzeo *(Italy)*
1960	Raimondo D'Inzeo *(Italy)*
1966	Pierre d'Oriola *(France)*
1970	David Broome *(UK)*
1974	Hartwig Steenken *(West Germany)*

women

1965	Marion Coakes *(UK)*
1970	Janou Lefebvre *(France)*
1974	Janou Tissot (born Lefebvre) *(France)*

mixed

1978	Gerd Wiltfang *(West Germany)*
1982	Norbert Koof *(West Germany)*
1986	Gail Greenough *(Canada)*

European Championship first held 1957 as a separate competition for men and women; since 1975 they have competed together

1975	Alwin Schockemohle *(West Germany)*
1977	Johan Heins *(Holland)*
1979	Gerd Wiltfang *(West Germany)*
1981	Paul Schockemohle *(West Germany)*
1983	Paul Schockemohle *(West Germany)*
1985	Paul Schockemohle *(West Germany)*
1987	Pierre Durand *(France)*

British Showjumping Derby first held 1961 and staged annually at Hickstead, Sussex

1979	Eddie Macken *(Ireland)*
1980	Michael Whitaker *(UK)*
1981	Harvey Smith *(UK)*
1982	Paul Schockemohle *(West Germany)*
1983	John Whitaker *(UK)*
1984	John Ledingham *(Ireland)*
1985	Paul Schockemohle *(West Germany)*
1986	Paul Schockemohle *(West Germany)*
1987	Nick Skelton *(UK)*
1988	Nick Skelton *(UK)*

Three-Day Eventing World Championships first held 1966

1966	Carlos Moratorio *(Argentina)*
1970	Mary Gordon-Watson *(UK)*
1974	Bruce Davidson *(USA)*
1978	Bruce Davidson *(USA)*
1982	Lucinda Green *(UK)*
1986	Virginia Leng *(UK)*

Badminton Horse Trials first held 1949

1980	Mark Todd *(New Zealand)*
1981	Captain Mark Phillips *(UK)*
1982	Richard Meade *(UK)*
1983	Lucinda Green *(UK)*
1984	Lucinda Green *(UK)*
1985	Virginia Holgate *(UK)*
1986	Ian Stark *(UK)*
1987	cancelled
1988	Ian Stark *(UK)*
1989	Virginia Leng *(UK)*

fencing sport using the *foil,* derived from the light weapon used in practice duels; *épée,* a heavier weapon derived from the duelling sword proper; and *sabre,* in which cuts (it has two cutting edges) count as well as thrusts. Masks and protective jackets are worn, and hits are registered electronically in competitions.

CHAMPIONS
World Championships men's fencing has been part of the Olympic programme since 1896 (women first competed 1924, but contest only the foil)
foil - men

1968	Ion Drimba *(Romania)*
1972	Witold Woyda *(Poland)*
1976	Fabio Dal Zotto *(Italy)*
1980	Vladimir Smirnov *(USSR)*
1984	Mauro Numa *(Italy)*
1988	Stefano Ceriomni *(Italy)*

foil - women

1968	Elena Novikova *(USSR)*
1972	Antonella Ragno-Lonzi *(Italy)*
1976	Ildiko Schwarczenberger *(Hungary)*
1980	Pascale Trinquet *(France)*
1984	Jujie Luan *(China)*
1988	Anja Fichtel *(West Germany)*

épée

1968	Gyozo Kulcsar *(Hungary)*
1972	Csaba Fenyvesi *(Hungary)*

1976	Alexander Pusch *(West Germany)*
1980	Johan Har**men**berg *(Sweden)*
1984	Phillipe Boisse *(France)*
1988	Arnd Schmitt *(West Germany)*

sabre
1968	Jerzy Pawlowski *(Poland)*
1972	Viktor Sidiak *(USSR)*
1976	Viktor Krovopouskov *(USSR)*
1980	Viktor Krovopouskov *(USSR)*
1984	Jean-Francois Lamour *(France)*
1988	Jean-Francois Lamour *(France)*

football, American a contact sport similar to the English game of rugby. The players wear protective suits against rough tackling, and games are divided into four fifteen-minute periods. The first match under Harvard rules was between Harvard University and McGill University, Montreal in 1874.

CHAMPIONS
Super Bowl first held 1967
1980	Pittsburgh Steelers
1981	Oakland Raiders
1982	San Francisco 49ers
1983	Washington Redskins
1984	Los Angeles Raiders
1985	San Francisco 49ers
1986	Chicago Bears
1987	New York Giants
1988	Washington Redskins
1989	San Francisco 49ers

football, association a form of football also called soccer. Played in England since the 14th century, the first set of rules were drawn up at Cambridge University in 1848. The modern game is played according to the rules laid down by the Football Association (founded 1863). Slight amendments to the rules take effect in certain competitions and overseas matches laid down by the sport's world governing body Fédéreation Internationale de Football Association (FIFA). It is played between two teams each of 11 players, on a field 90–120 m/100–130 yds long and 45–90 m/50–100 yds wide with a spherical, inflated (traditionally leather) ball, circumference 0.71–0.68 m/27–28 in.

CHAMPIONS
World Cup first contested 1930; held every four years
1950	Uruguay
1954	West Germany
1958	Brazil
1962	Brazil
1966	England
1970	Brazil
1974	West Germany
1978	Argentina
1982	Italy
1986	Argentina

European Championship instituted 1958, first final 1960; held every four years
1960	USSR
1964	Spain
1968	Italy
1972	West Germany
1976	Czechoslovakia
1980	West Germany
1984	France
1988	Holland

European Champions Cup first held 1955
1979	Nottingham Forest *(England)*
1980	Nottingham Forest *(England)*
1981	Liverpool *(England)*
1982	Aston Villa *(England)*
1983	SV Hamburg *(West Germany)*
1984	Liverpool *(England)*
1985	Juventus *(Italy)*
1986	Steau Bucharest *(Romania)*
1987	FC Porto *(Portugal)*
1988	PSV Eindhoven *(Holland)*
1989	AC Milan *(Italy)*

European Cup Winners Cup first held 1960
1979	Barcelona *(Spain)*
1980	Valencia *(Spain)*
1981	Dinamo Tbilisi *(USSR)*
1982	Barcelona *(Spain)*
1983	Aberdeen *(Scotland)*
1984	Juventus *(Italy)*
1985	Everton *(England)*
1986	Dinamo Kiev *(USSR)*
1987	Ajax *(Holland)*
1988	Mechelen *(Belgium)*
1989	Barcelona *(Spain)*

UEFA Cup (formerly Inter Cities Fairs Cup) first held 1955
1979	Borussia Moenchengladbach *(West Germany)*
1980	Eintracht Frankfurt *(West Germany)*
1981	Ipswich Town *(England)*
1982	IFK Gothenburg *(Sweden)*
1983	Anderlecht *(Belgium)*
1984	Tottenham Hotspur *(England)*
1985	Real Madrid *(Spain)*
1986	Real Madrid *(Spain)*
1987	IFK Gothenburg *(Sweden)*
1988	Bayer Leverkusen *(West Germany)*
1989	Napoli *(Italy)*

FA Cup a knockout club competition, first

held 1872; held annually in England and Wales

1979	Arsenal
1980	West Ham United
1981	Tottenham Hotspur
1982	Tottenham Hotspur
1983	Manchester United
1984	Everton
1985	Manchester United
1986	Liverpool
1987	Coventry City
1988	Wimbledon
1989	Liverpool

Football League Cup or **Littlewoods Cup**, (formerly the *Milk Cup*) first final 1961 in two stages, now a single game

1979	Nottingham Forest
1980	Wolverhampton Wanderers
1981	Liverpool
1982	Liverpool
1983	Liverpool
1984	Liverpool
1985	Norwich City
1986	Oxford United
1987	Arsenal
1988	Luton Town
1989	Nottingham Forest

Division One Champions Football League founded 1888–9

1981–82	Liverpool
1982–83	Liverpool
1983–84	Liverpool
1984–85	Everton
1985–86	Liverpool
1986–87	Everton
1987–88	Liverpool
1988–89	Arsenal.

Scottish Premier Division Champions Scottish League formed 1890–91, reformed into three divisions in 1979–80

1980–81	Celtic
1981–82	Celtic
1982–83	Dundee United
1983–84	Aberdeen
1984–85	Aberdeen
1985–86	Celtic
1986–87	Rangers
1987–88	Celtic
1988–89	Rangers

Scottish FA Cup first final held 1874

1979	Rangers
1980	Celtic
1981	Rangers
1982	Aberdeen
1983	Aberdeen
1984	Aberdeen

1985	Celtic
1986	Aberdeen
1987	St Mirren
1988	Celtic
1989	Celtic

golf outdoor game in which a small rubber-cored ball is hit with a club (either wooden- or iron-faced). The club faces have varying angles and are styled for different types of shot. The ball is hit from a tee, which elevates the ball slightly off the ground, and the object of the game is to putt the ball in a hole than can be anywhere between 90 m/100 yd and 457 m/500 yd away, using the least number of strokes.

Most courses consist of 18 holes and are approximately 5,500 m/6,000 yd in length. Each hole is made up of three distinct areas: *tee* from where plays start at each hole; *green*, a finely manicured area in which is positioned the hole, and the *fairway*, the grassed area between the tee and the green. The perimeter of the fairway is often left to grow naturally, thus creating a 'rough'. Natural hazards like trees, bushes and streams make play more difficult, and there are additional hazards in the form of sand-filled bunkers.

CHAMPIONS
British Open first held 1860

1979	Severiano Ballesteros, Spain
1980	Tom Watson, USA
1981	Bill Rogers, USA
1982	Tom Watson, USA
1983	Tom Watson, USA
1984	Severiano Ballesteros, Spain
1985	Sandy Lyle, Great Britain
1986	Greg Norman, Australia
1987	Nick Faldo, Great Britain
1988	Severiano Ballesteros, Spain

US Open first held 1895

1979	Hale Irwin, USA
1980	Jack Nicklaus, USA
1981	David Graham, Australia
1982	Tom Watson, USA
1983	Larry Nelson, USA
1984	Fuzzy Zoeller, USA
1985	Andy North, USA
1986	Ray Floyd, USA
1987	Scott Simpson, USA
1988	Curtis Strange, USA

Masters first held 1934

1980	Severiano Ballesteros, Spain
1981	Tom Watson, USA

1982	Craig Stadler, USA
1983	Severiano Ballesteros, Spain
1984	Ben Crenshaw, USA
1985	Bernhard Langer, West Germany
1986	Jack Nicklaus, USA
1987	Larry Mize, USA
1988	Sandy Lyle, Great Britain
1989	Nick Faldo, Great Britain

United States PGA first held 1916

1979	David Graham, Australia
1980	Jack Nicklaus, USA
1981	Larry Nelson, USA
1982	Ray Floyd, USA
1983	Hal Sutton, USA
1984	Lee Trevino, USA
1985	Hubert Green, USA
1986	Bob Tway, USA
1987	Larry Nelson, USA
1988	Jeff Sluman, USA

horse racing the sport of racing mounted or driven horses. Two forms in Britain are *flat racing* for thoroughbred horses over a flat course, and *National Hunt* racing, in which the horses have to clear obstacles. *Steeplechasing* is a developm*en*t of foxhunting, of which *point-to-point* is the amateur version, and *hurdling* a version with less severe, and movable, fences. Steeplechases include the Grand National at Aintree, Liverpool. and Cheltenham Gold Cup. The leading hurdling race is the Champion Hurdle. *Harness racing* is popular in North America. Races such as the Hambletonian and the Little Brown Jug are for standard-bred horses pulling a two-wheeled 'sulky' on which the driver sits.

CHAMPIONS
The Derby
horse/jockey

1979	Troy/Willie Carson
1980	Henbit/Willie Carson
1981	Shergar/Walter Swinburn
1982	Golden Fleece/Pat Eddery
1983	Teenoso/Lester Piggott
1984	Secreto/Christy Roche
1985	Slip Anchor/Steve Cauthen
1986	Shahrastani/Walter Swinburn
1987	Reference Point/Steve Cauthen
1988	Kahyasi/Ray Cochrane
1989	Nashwan/Willie Carson

The Oaks
horse/jockey

1979	Scintillate/Pat Eddery
1980	Bireme/Willie Carson
1981	Blue Wind/Lester Piggott
1982	Time Charter/Billy Newnes
1983	Sun Princess/Willie Carson
1984	Circus Plume/Lester Piggott
1985	Oh So Sharp/Steve Cauthen
1986	Midway Lady/Ray Cochrane
1987	Unite/Walter Swinburn
1988	Diminuendo/Steve Cauthen
1989	Aliysa/Walter Swinburn

1,000 Guineas
horse/jockey

1979	One in a Million/Joe Mercer
1980	Quick As Lightning/Brian Rouse
1981	Fairy Footsteps/Lester Piggott
1982	On The House/John Reid
1983	Ma Biche/Fredd Head
1984	Pebbles/Philip Robinson
1985	Oh So Sharp/Steve Cauthen
1986	Midway Lady/Ray Cochrane
1987	Miesque/Fredd Head
1988	Ravinella/Gary Moore
1989	Musical Bliss/Walter Swinburn

2,000 Guineas
horse/jockey

1979	Tap On Wood/Steve Cauthen
1980	Known Fact/Willie Carson
1981	To-Agori-Mou/Greville Starkey
1982	Zino/Fredd Head
1983	Lomond/Pat Eddery
1984	El Gran Senor/Pat Eddery
1985	Shadeed/Lester Piggott
1986	Dancing Brave/Greville Starkey
1987	Don't Forget Me/Willie Carson
1988	Doyoun/Walter Swinburn
1989	Nashwan/Walter Swinburn

St Leger the oldest English classic, dating to 1776
horse/jockey

1979	Son of Love/Alain Lequeux
1980	Light Cavalry/Joe Mercer
1981	Cut Above/Joe Mercer
1982	Touching Wood/Paul Cook
1983	Sun Princess/Willie Carson
1984	Commanche Run/Lester Piggott
1985	Oh So Sharp/Steve Cauthen
1986	Moon Madness/Pat Eddery
1987	Reference Point/Steve Cauthen
1988	Minster Son/Willie Carson

Grand National first held 1836
horse/jockey (amateurs are shown as Mr)

1979	Rubstick/Maurice Barnes
1980	Ben Nevis/Mr Charles Fenwick
1981	Aldaniti/Bob Champion
1982	Grittar/Mr Dick Saunders
1983	Corbiere/Ben De Haan
1984	Hallo Dandy/Neale Doughty

1985	Last Suspect/Hywel Davies
1986	West Tip/Richard Dunwoody
1987	Maori Venture/Steve Knight
1988	Rhyme N'Reason/Brendan Powell
1989	Little Polveir/Jimmy Frost

Prix de L'Arc de Triomphe
horse/jockey

1979	Three Troikas/Freddy Head
1980	Detriot/Pat Eddery
1981	Gold River/Gary Moore
1982	Akiyda/Yves Saint-Martin
1983	All Along/Walter Swinburn
1984	Sagace/Yves Saint-Martin
1985	Rainbow Quest/Pat Eddery
1986	Dancing Brave/Pat Eddery
1986	Lieutenant's Lark/Robbie Davis
1987	Trempolino/Pat Eddery
1988	Tony Bin/John Reid

judo a type of wrestling of Japanese origin. The two combatants wear loose-fitting, belted jackets and trousers to facilitate holds, and the falls are broken by a square mat; when one has established a painful hold that the other cannot break, the latter signifies surrender by slapping the ground with a free hand. Degrees of proficiency are indicated by the colour of the belt: for novices white; after examination, brown (three degrees); and finally, black (nine degrees).

CHAMPIONS
World Championships first held 1956, now contested biennially

open class

1971	Masatoshi Shinomaki *(Japan)*
1972	Kazuhiro Ninomiya *(Japan)*
1975	Haruki Uemura *(Japan)*
1979	Sumio Endo *(Japan)*
1981	Yasuhiro Yamashita *(Japan)*
1983	Angelo Parisi *(France)*
1985	Yoshimi Masaki *(Japan)*
1987	N Ogawa *(Japan)*

over 95 kg

1979	Yasuhiro Yamashita *(Japan)*
1981	Yasuhiro Yamashita *(Japan)*
1983	Yasuhiro Yamashita *(Japan)*
1985	Yong-Chul Cho *(South Korea)*
1987	Grigori Vertichev *(USSR)*

under 95 kg

1971	Fumio Sasahara *(Japan)*
1973	Nobuyaki Sato *(Japan)*
1975	Jean-Luc Rouge *(France)*
1979	Tengiz Khubuluri *(USSR)*
1981	Tengiz Khubuluri *(USSR)*
1983	Valeriy Divisenko *(USSR)*

1985	Hitoshi Sugai *(Japan)*
1987	Hitoshi Sugai *(Japan)*

under 86 kg

1979	Detlf Ultsch *(East Germany)*
1981	Bernard Tchoullouyan *(France)*
1983	Detlef Ultsch *(East Germany)*
1985	Peter Seisenbacher *(Austria)*
1987	Fabien Canu *(France)*

under 78 kg

1979	Shozo Fujii *(Japan)*
1981	Neil Adams *(Great Britain)*
1983	Nobutoshi Hikage *(Japan)*
1985	Nobutoshi Hikage *(Japan)*
1987	H Okada *(Japan)*

under 71 kg

1979	Kyoto Katsuki *(Japan)*
1981	Chon Hak Park *(South Korea)*
1983	Hidetoshi Nakanichi *(Japan)*
1985	Ahn Byeong-Keun *(South Korea)*
1987	Mike Swain *USA*

under 65 kg

1979	Nikolai Soludkhin *(USSR)*
1981	Katsuhiko Kashiwazaki *(Japan)*
1983	Nikolai Soludkhin *(USSR)*
1985	Yuri Sokolov *(USSR)*
1987	H Yamamto *(Japan)*

under 60 kg

1975	Yoshiharu Minamo *(Japan)*
1979	Thierry Ray *(France)*
1981	Yasuhiko Mariwaki *(Japan)*
1983	Khazret Tletseri *(USSR)*
1985	Shinji Hosokawa *(Japan)*
1987	Jae Yup Kim *(South Korea)*

lacrosse Canadian ball game, adopted from the North American Indians, and named from a supposed resemblance of the lacrosse stick to a bishop's crozier. Thongs across its curved end form a pocket to carry the small rubber ball. The pitch is about 100 m/110 yd long and a minimum 55 m/60 yd wide in the men's game, which is played ten a side; the women's pitch is larger, and they play twelve a side. The goals are just under 2 m/6 ft square, with loose nets.

CHAMPIONS
World Championship first held 1967 for men, 1969 for women

men

1967	USA
1974	USA
1978	Canada
1982	USA
1986	USA

women

1969	Great Britain

1974	USA
1978	Canada
1982	USA
1986	Australia

motor racing competitive racing of motor vehicles. It has many forms as diverse as hill-climbing, stock-car racing, rallying, sports car racing, and Formula One Grand Prix racing. The first race was held in 1894 from Paris to Rouen.

CHAMPIONS
World Driver's Championship first held 1950

1979	Jody Scheckter *(South Africa)*
1980	Alan Jones *(Australia)*
1981	Nelson Piquet *(Brazil)*
1982	Keke Rosberg *(Finland)*
1983	Nelson Piquet *(Brazil)*
1984	Niki Lauda *(Austria)*
1985	Alain Prost *(France)*
1986	Alain Prost *(France)*
1987	Nelson Piquet *(Brazil)*
1988	Ayrton Senna *(Brazil)*

Le Mans Grand Prix d'Endurance ('Le Mans 24-Hour Race') first held 1923

1979	Klaus Ludwig *(West Germany)*/Bill Whittington *(USA)*/Don Whittington *(USA)*
1980	Jean-Pierre Jassuad *(France)*/Jean Rondeau *(France)*
1981	Jacky Ickx *(Belgium)*/Derek Bell *(UK)*
1982	Jacky Ickx *(Belgium)*/Derek Bell *(UK)*
1983	Vern Schuppan *(Austria)*/Al Holbert *(USA)* /Hurley Haywood *(USA)*
1984	Klaus Ludwig *(West Germany)*/Henri Pescarolo *(France)*
1985	Klaus Ludwig *(West Germany)*/'John Winter'*(West Germany)*/Paolo Barilla *(Italy)*
1986	Hans Stuck *(West Germany)*/Derek Bell *(UK)* /Al Holbert *(USA)*
1987	Hans Stuck *(West Germany)* Derek Bell *(UK)* Al Holbert *(USA)*
1988	Jan Lammers *(Holland)*/Johnny Dumfries *(UK)*/Andy Wallace *(UK)*
1989	Jochen Mass *(West Germany)*/Manuel Reuter *(West Germany)*/Stanley Dickens *(Sweden)*

Indianapolis 500 first held 1911

1980	Johnny Rutherford *(USA)*
1981	Bobby Unser *(USA)*
1982	Gordon Johncock *(USA)*
1983	Tom Sneva *(USA)*
1984	Rick Mears *(USA)*
1985	Danny Sullivan *(USA)*

1986	Bobby Rahal *(USA)*
1987	Al Unser *(USA)*
1988	Rick Mears *(USA)*
1989	Emerson Fittipaldi *(Brazil)*

orienteering sport of cross-country running and route-finding. Competitors set off at one minute intervals and have to find their way, using map and compass, to various check points (approximately 0.8 km/0.5 mi apart), where their control cards are marked.

CHAMPIONS
World Championships first held 1966
individual - men/women

1979	Oyvin Thon *(Norway)*/Outi Bergonstrom *(Finland)*
1981	Oyvin Thon *(Norway)*/Annichen Kringstad *(Norway)*
1983	Morten Berglia *(Norway)*/Annichen Kringstad *(Norway)*
1985	Kari Sallinen *(Finland)*/Annichen Kringstad *(Norway)*
1987	Kent Olsson *(Sweden)*/Arja Hannus *(Sweden)*

relay men/women

1979	Sweden/Finland
1981	Norway/Sweden
1983	Norway/Sweden
1985	Norway/Sweden
1987	Norway/Norway

rowing propulsion of a boat by oars, either by one rower with two oars (sculling), or by crews (two, four, or eight persons) with one oar each, often with a coxswain (steersman).

CHAMPIONS
World Championship first held 1962 for men, 1974 for women
men – single sculls

1979	Pertti Karppinen *(Finland)*
1981	Peter-Michael Kolbe *(West Germany)*
1982	Rudiger Reiche *(East Germany)*
1983	Peter-Michael Kolbe *(West Germany)*
1985	Pertti Karppinen *(Finland)*
1986	Peter-Michael Kolbe *(West Germany)*
1987	Thomas Lange *East Germany*

women – single sculls

1979	Sanda Toma *(Romania)*
1981	Sanda Toma *(Romania)*
1982	Irina Fetisova *(USSR)*
1983	Jutta Hampe *(East Germany)*
1985	Cornelia Linse *(East Germany)*
1986	Jutta Hampe *(East Germany)*
1987	Magdalena Georgeyeva *Bul-*

garia
The Boat Race first held 1829, rowed annually between Putney and Mortlake by crews from the Oxford and Cambridge University rowing clubs

1986	Cambridge
1987	Oxford
1988	Oxford

wins
Cambridge 69
Oxford 64

Doggett's Coat and Badge first held 1715

1979	F K Bearwood
1980	W R Woodward-Fisher
1981	W Hickman
1982	G Anness
1983	P Hickman
1984	S McCarthy
1985	R B Spencer
1986	C Woodward-Fisher
1987	C Spencer
1988	G Hayes

Rugby League the professional form of Rugby football founded in England 1895 as the Northern Union, when a dispute about pay caused northern clubs to break away from the Rugby Football Union. The game is similar to Rugby Union but the number of players was reduced from 15 to 13 in 1906, and the scrum now plays a less important role as rule changes have made the game more open and fast-moving.

CHAMPIONS
Challenge Cup final first held 1897, at Wembley Stadium since 1929

1980	Hull Kingston Rovers
1981	Widnes
1982	Hull
1983	Featherstone Rovers
1984	Widnes
1985	Wigan
1986	Castleford
1987	Halifax
1988	Wigan
1989	Wigan

Premiership Trophy introduced at the end of the 1974–75 season; a knockout competition involving the top eight clubs in the first division

1980	Widnes
1981	Hull Kingston Rovers
1982	Hull Kingston Rovers
1983	Widnes
1984	Hull Kingston Rovers
1985	St Helens
1986	Warrington
1987	Wigan
1988	Widnes
1989	Widnes

Rugby Union the amateur form of Rugby football, in which there are 15 players on each side. 'Tries' are scored by 'touching down' the ball beyond the goal-line or by kicking goals from penalties. The Rugby Football Union was formed 1871 and has its headquarters at Twickenham, Middlesex. The first World Cup was held in Australia and New Zealand 1987, and was won by New Zealand.

CHAMPIONS
World Cup; the William Webb Ellis trophy

1987	New Zealand

International championship instituted 1884, now a tournament between England, France, Ireland, Scotland, and Wales

1980	England
1981	France
1982	Ireland
1983	France and Ireland
1984	Scotland
1985	Ireland
1986	France
1987	France
1988	France and Wales
1989	France

County championship inaugurated 1889

1980	Lancashire
1981	Northumberland
1982	Lancashire
1983	Gloucestershire
1984	Gloucestershire
1985	Middlesex
1986	Warwickshire
1987	Yorkshire
1988	Lancashire
1989	Durham

Pilkington Cup formerly the **John Player Special Cup** the English club knockout tournament, first held 1971–72

1980	Leicester
1981	Leicester
1982	Gloucester/Moseley
1983	Bristol
1984	Bath
1985	Bath
1986	Bath
1987	Bath
1988	Harlequins
1989	Bath

skating self-propulsion on ice by means of bladed skates, or on other surfaces by skates with four small rollers. The chief competitive events are figure skating, for singles or pairs, ice-dancing, and simple speed skating.

CHAMPIONS
Ice Skating World Championships first world figure skating championships held 1896
men
1980	Jan Hoffman *(East Germany)*
1981	Scott Hamilton *(USA)*
1982	Scott Hamilton *(USA)*
1983	Scott Hamilton *(USA)*
1984	Scott Hamilton *(USA)*
1985	Alexsander Fadeev *(USSR)*
1986	Brian Boitano *(USA)*
1987	Brian Orser *(Canada)*
1988	Brian Boitano *(USA)*
1989	Kurt Browning *(Canada)*

women
1980	Annett Potzsch *(East Germany)*
1981	Denise Beillmann *(Switzerland)*
1982	Elaine Zayak *(USA)*
1983	Rosalynn Sumners *(USA)*
1984	Katerina Witt *(East Germany)*
1985	Katerina Witt *(East Germany)*
1986	Debi Thomas *(USA)*
1987	Katerina Witt *(East Germany)*
1988	Katerina Witt *(East Germany)*
1989	Midoria Ito *(Japan)*

pairs
1980	Sergei Shakrai/Marina Tcherkasova *(USSR)*
1981	Igor Lisovsky/ Irina Vorobyeva *(USSR)*
1982	Tassilo Thierbach/Sabine Baess *(East Germany)*
1983	Oleg Vasiliev/Yelena Valova *(USSR)*
1984	Paul Martini/Barbara Underhill *(Canada)*
1985	Oleg Vasiliev/Yelena Valova *(USSR)*
1986	Sergei Grinkov/Ekaterina Gordeeva *(USSR)*
1987	Sergei Grinkov/Ekaterina Gordeeva *(USSR)*
1988	Oleg Vasilyev/Yelena Valova *(USSR)*
1989	Sergei Grinkov/Ekaterina Gordeeva *(USSR)*

ice dance
1980	Andras Sallay/Krisztine Regoczy *(Hungary)*
1981	Christopher Dean/Jayne Torvill *(Great Britain)*
1982	Christopher Dean/Jayne Torvill *(Great Britain)*
1983	Christopher Dean/Jayne Torvill *(Great Britain)*
1984	Christopher Dean/Jayne Torvill *(Great Britain)*
1985	Andrei Bukin/Natalia Bestemianova *(USSR)*
1986	Andrei Bukin/Natalia Bestemianova *(USSR*
1987	Andrei Bukin/Natalia Bestemianova *(USSR)*
1988	Andrei Bukin/Natalia Bestemianova *(USSR)*
1989	Sergei Ponamarenko/Marina Klimova *(USSR)*

skiing self-propulsion on snow by means of elongated runners for the feet, slightly bent upward at the tip. Events include downhill (with speeds up to 80 km/50 mi per hour); slalom, in which a series of turns between flags have to be negotiated; cross-country racing; and ski jumping, where jumps of over 150 m/400 ft are achieved from ramps up to 90 m/295 ft high.

CHAMPIONS
Alpine World Cup first held 1967
men – overall
1980	Andreas Wenzel *(Liechtenstein)*
1981	Phil Mahre *(USA)*
1982	Phil Mahre *(USA)*
1983	Phil Mahre *(USA)*
1984	Pirmin Zurbriggen *(Switzerland)*
1985	Marc Girardelli *(Luxembourg)*
1986	Marc Girardelli *(Luxembourg)*
1987	Pirmin Zurbriggen *(Switzerland)*
1988	Pirmin Zurbriggen *(Switzerland)*
1989	Marc Giradelli *(Luxembourg)*

women
1980	Hanni Wenzel *(Leichtenstein)*
1981	Marie-Therese Nadig *(Switzerland)*
1982	Erika Hess *(Switzerland)*
1983	Tamara Mckinney *(USA)*
1984	Erika Hess *(Switzerland)*
1985	Michela Figini *(Switzerland)*
1986	Maria Walliser *(Switzerland)*
1987	Maria Walliser *(Switzerland)*
1988	Michela Figini *(Switzerland)*
1989	Vreni Schneider *(Switzerland)*

snooker indoor game derived from billiards. It is played with 22 balls: 15 reds, one each of yellow, green, brown, blue, pink, and black, and a white cue-ball. Red balls when potted are worth one point while the coloured balls have ascending values from two points for the yellow to seven points for the black.

CHAMPIONS
World Professional Championship first held 1927

1980	Cliff Thorburn *(Canada)*
1981	Steve Davis *(England)*
1982	Alex Higgins *(Northern Ireland)*
1983	Steve Davis *(England)*
1984	Steve Davis *(England)*
1985	Dennis Taylor *(Northern Ireland)*
1986	Joe Johnson *(England)*
1987	Steve Davis *(England)*
1988	Steve Davis *(England)*
1989	Steve Davis *(England)*

World Amateur Championship instituted 1963

1974	Ray Edmonds *(England)*
1976	Doug Mountjoy *(Wales)*
1978	Cliff Wilson *(Wales)*
1980	Jimmy White *(England)*
1982	Terry Parsons *(Wales)*
1984	O B Agrawal *(India)*
1985	Paul Mifsud *(Malta)*
1986	Paul Mifsud *(Malta)*
1987	Darren Morgan *(Wales)*
1988	James Wattana *(Thailand)*

speedway the sport of motorcycle racing on a dirt track. Four riders compete in each heat over four laps. A series of heats make up a match or competition. In Britain there are two Leagues, the British League and the National League. World championships exist for individuals, pairs, four-man teams, long-track racing, and ice speedway.

CHAMP[IONS
World Championships first held 1936
individual

1979	Ivan Mauger *(New Zealand)*
1980	Mike Lee *(England)*
1981	Bruce Penhall *(USA)*
1982	Bruce Penhall *(USA)*
1983	Egon Muller *(West Germany)*
1984	Erik Gundersen *(Denmark)*
1985	Erik Gundersen *(Denmark)*
1986	Hans Nielsen *(Denmark)*
1987	Hans Nielsen *(Denmark)*
1988	Erik Gundersen *(Denmark)*

Pairs first held 1970

1979	Ole Olsen/Hans Nielson *(Denmark)*
1980	Dave Jessup/Peter Collins *(England)*
1981	Bruce Penhall/Bobby Schwartz *(USA)*
1982	Dennis Sigalos/Bobby Schwartz *(USA)*
1983	Kenny Carter/Peter Colins *(England)*
1984	Peter Collins/Chris Morton *(England)*
1985	Erik Gundersen/Tommy Knudsen *(Denmark)*
1986	Erik Gundersen/Hans Neilson *(Denmark)*
1987	Erik Gundersen/Hans Nielsen *(Denmark)*
1988	Erik Gundersen/Hans Nielsen *(Denmark)*

Team first held 1960

1979	New Zealand
1980	England
1981	Denmark
1982	USA
1983	Denmark
1984	Denmark
1985	Denmark
1986	Denmark
1987	Denmark
1988	Denmark

squash game played on an enclosed court and derived from rackets. Usually played by two players, it became popular in the 1970s and is now a fitness craze as well as a competitive sport.

CHAMPIONS
World Open championship first held 1975
men

1979	Geoff Hunt *Australia)*
1980	Geoff Hunt *(Australia)*
1981	Jahangir Khan *(Pakistan)*
1982	Jahangir Khan *(Pakistan)*
1983	Jahangir Khan *(Pakistan)*
1984	Jahangir Khan *(Pakistan)*
1985	Jahangir Khan *(Pakistan*
1986	Ross Norman *(New Zealand)*
1987	Jansher Khan *(Pakistan)*
1988	Jahangir Khan *(Pakistan)*

women

1979	Heather McKay *(Australia)*
1981	Rhonda Thorne *(Australia)*
1983	Vicky Cardwell *(Australia)*
1985	Sue Devoy(New Zealand)
1987	Sue Devoy *(New Zealand)*
1989	Martine Le Moignan *(Great Britain)*

swimming self-propulsion of the body through water. As a competitive sport there are four strokes; freestyle, breaststroke, backstroke and butterfly. Distances of races vary between 50-1,500m. Olympic-size pools are 50 m/55 yd long and have eight lanes. A recent innovation for wo***men*** is synchronised swimming.

CHAMPIONS
Olympic Games Swimming has been included in the Olympics since 1896 for men and 1912 for women
most gold medals
9   Mark Spitz *(USA)* 1968, 1972
5   Charles Daniels *(USA)* 1904, 1908
5   Johnny Weissmuller *(USA)* 1924, 1928
5   Don Schollander *(USA)* 1964, 1968
4   Henry Taylor *(UK)* 1906, 1908
4   Pat McCormick *(USA)* 1952, 1956*
4   Murray Rose *(Australia)* 1956, 1960
4   Dawn Fraser *(Australia)* 1956, 1960, 1964
4   Roland Matthes *(East Germany)* 1968, 1972
4   John Naber *(USA)* 1976
4   Kornelia Ender *(East Germany)* 1976
* McCormick won all her medals at diving
most medals
11   Mark Spitz *(USA)* 1968, 1972
8   Charles Daniels *(USA)* 1904, 1908
8   Roland Matthes *(East Germany)* 1968, 1972
8   Henry Taylor *(UK)* 1906, 1908, 1912, 1920
8   Dawn Fraser *(Australia)* 1956, 1961, 1964
8   Kornelia Ender *(East Germany)* 1972, 1976
8   Shirley Babashoff *(USA)* 1972, 1976
World Championships introduced 1973, next held 1975, 1978, and every four years since
most gold medals
8   Kornelia Ender *(East Germany)* 1973, 1975
7   Kristin Otto *(East Germany)* 1982, 1986
6   Jim Montgomery *(USA)* 1973, 1975
5   Greg Louganis *(USA)* 1978, 1982, 1986*
5   Rowdy Gaines *(USA)* 1978, 1982
* All Louganis' medals were at diving
most medals
10   Kornelia Ender *(East Germany)* 1973, 1975
9   Kristin Otto *(East Germany)* 1982, 1986
9   Mary Meagher *(USA)* 1978, 1982
8   Rowdy Gaines *(USA)* 1978, 1982

table tennis indoor ball game played on a rectangular table by two or four players. It was developed in Britain about 1880 and derived from lawn tennis. It is popularly known as *ping-pong*.

CHAMPIONS
World Championships first held 1926
Swaythling Cup (men's team)
1971   China

1973	Sweden
1975	China
1977	China
1979	Hungary
1981	China
1983	China
1985	China
1987	China
1989	Sweden

Corbillon Cup (women's team)
1971   Japan
1973   South Korea
1975   China
1977   China
1979   China
1981   China
1983   China
1985   China
1987   China
1989   China
men's singles
1971   Stellan Bengtsson *(Sweden)*
1973   Hsi En-Ting *(China)*
1975   Istvan Jonyer *(Hungary)*
1977   Mitsuru Kohno *(Japan)*
1979   Seiji Ono *(Japan)*
1981   Guo Yue-Hua *(China)*
1983   Guo Yue-Hua *(China)*
1985   Jiang Jialiang *(China)*
1987   Jiang Jialiang *(China)*
1989   Jan-Ove Waldnet *(Sweden)*
women's singles
1971   Lin Hui-Ching *(China)*
1973   Hu Yu-Lan *(China)*
1975   Pak Yung-Sun *(North Korea)*
1977   Pak Yung-Sun *(North Korea)*
1979   Ke Hsin-Ai *(China)*
1981   Ting Ling *(China)*
1983   Cao Yan-Hua *(China)*
1985   Cao Yan-Hua *(China)*
1987   He Zhili *(China)*
1989   Qiao Hong *(China)*

tennis, lawn a racket and ball game invented in England towards the end of the 19th century It derived from real tennis. Although played on different surfaces (grass, wood, shale, clay, concrete etc) it is still called 'lawn tennis'.

The aim of the two or four players is to strike the ball into the prescribed area of the court, with oval-headed rackets (strung with gut or nylon), in such a way that it cannot be returned. The game is won by those first winning four points (called 15, 30, 40, game), unless both sides reach 40 (deuce) when two consecutive points are needed to win. A set is won by winning six games with a margin of two over opponents, although a tie-break system operates, that is at six games to each side (or in some cases eight) excepting in the final set. Major events include the *Davis Cup* 1900 for international men's competition, and *Wightman Cup* 1923 for US and UK women's teams, and the annual All England Tennis Club championships, an open event for players of both sexes at Wimbledon.

CHAMPIONS
Wimbledon Championships first held 1877
men's singles
1980   Björn Borg *(Sweden)*
1981   John McEnroe *(USA)*
1982   Jimmy Connors *(USA)*
1983   John McEnroe *(USA)*
1984   John McEnroe *(USA)*
1985   Boris Becker *(West Germany)*
1986   Boris Becker *(West Germany)*
1987   Pat Cash *(Australia)*
1988   Stefan Edberg *(Sweden)*
1989   Boris Becker *(West Germany)*
women's singles
1980   Evonne Goolagong-Cawley *(Australia)*
1981   Chris Evert-Lloyd *(USA)*
1982   Martina Navratilova *(USA)*
1983   Martina Navratilova *(USA)*
1984   Martina Navratilova *(USA)*
1985   Martina Navratilova *(USA)*
1986   Martina Navratilova *(USA)*
1987   Martina Navratilova *(USA)*
1988   Steffi Graf *(West Germany)*
1989   Steffi Graf *(West Germany)*
United States Open first held 1881 as the United States Championship, and became the United States Open 1968
men's singles
1979   John McEnroe *(USA)*
1980   John McEnroe *(USA)*
1981   John McEnroe *(USA)*
1982   Jimmy Connors *(USA)*
1983   Jimmy Connors *(USA)*
1984   John McEnroe *(USA)*
1985   Ivan Lendl *(Czechoslovakia)*
1986   Ivan Lendl *(Czechoslovakia)*
1987   Ivan Lendl *(Czechoslovakia)*
1988   Mats Wilander *(Sweden)*
women's singles
1979   Tracy Austin *(USA)*

1980   Chris Evert-Lloyd *(USA)*
1981   Tracy Austin *(USA)*
1982   Chris Evert-Lloyd *(USA)*
1983   Martina Navratilova *(USA)*
1984   Martina Navratilova *(USA)*
1985   Hana Mandlikova *(Czechoslovakia)*
1986   Martina Navratilova *(USA)*
1987   Martina Navritilova *(USA)*
1988   Steffi Graf *(West Germany)*
Davis Cup first contested 1900
1979   USA
1980   Czechoslovakia
1981   USA
1982   USA
1983   Australia
1984   Sweden
1985   Sweden
1986   Australia
1987   Sweden
1988   West Germany

trampolining gymnastics performed on a sprung canvas sheet which allows the performer to reach great heights before landing again. Marks are gained for carrying out difficult manoeuvres. Synchronized trampolining and tumbling are also forms of the sport.

CHAMPIONS
World championships first held 1964
men
1970   Wayne Miller *(USA)*
1972   Paul Luxon *(Great Britain)*
1974   Richard Tisson *(France)*
1976   Richard Tisson *(France)*/Evgeni Janes
1978   Evgeni Janes *(USSR)*
1980   Stewart Matthews *(Great Britain)*
1982   Carl Furrer *(Great Britain)*
1984   Leon Pioline *(France)*
1986   Leon Pioline *(France)*
1988   V Crasonshapka *(USSR)*
women
1970   Renee Ransom *(USA)*
1972   Alexandra Nicholson *(USA)*
1974   Alexandra Nicholson *(USA)*
1976   Svetlana Levina *(USSR)*
1978   Tatyana Anisimova *(USSR)*
1980   Ruth Keller *(Switzerland)*
1982   Ruth Keller *(Switzerland)*
1984   Sue Shotton *(Great Britian)*
1986   Tatyana Lushina *(USSR)*
1988   K Roussoudan *(USSR)*

volleyball an indoor team game played on a court between two teams of six players each. A net is placed across the centre of the court, and players hit the ball over the net with their hands, the aim being to ground it in the opponents' court.

CHAMPIONS
World Championships first held 1949 for men, 1952 for women

men

1970	East Germany
1972	Japan
1974	Poland
1976	Poland
1978	USSR
1980	USSR
1982	USSR
1984	USA
1986	USA
1988	USA

women

1970	USSR
1972	USSR
1974	Japan
1976	Japan
1978	Cuba
1980	USSR
1982	China
1984	China
1986	USA
1988	USSR

water polo a water sport developed in England 1869, originally called 'soccer-in-water'. The Swimming Association of Great Britain recognized the game in 1885. The aim is to score goals, as in soccer, at each end of a swimming pool.

CHAMPIONS
World championships first held 1973; they are held during the world swimming championships.

1973	Hungary
1975	USSR
1978	Italy
1982	USSR
1986	Yugoslavia.

water skiing a watersport in which a person is towed across water on a ski, or skis, wider than those used for skiing on snow, by means of a rope (23 m/75 ft long) attached to a speedboat. In competitive water skiing, competitions are for overall performances, slalom, tricks, and jumping.

CHAMPIONS

World Championships first held 1949

men – overall

1971	George Athans *(Canada)*
1973	George Athans *(Canada)*
1975	Carlos Suarez *(Venezuela)*
1977	Mike Hazelwood *(Great Britain)*
1979	Joel McClintock *(Canada)*
1981	Sammy Duvall *(USA)*
1983	Sammy Duvall *(USA)*
1985	Sammy Duvall *(USA)*
1987	Sammy Duvall *(USA)*

women - overall

1971	Christy Weir *(USA)*
1973	Lisa StJohn *(USA)*
1975	Liz Allan-Shetter *(USA)*
1977	Cindy Todd *(USA)*
1979	Cindy Todd *(USA)*
1981	Karin Roberge *(USA)*
1983	Ana-Maria Carrasco *(Venezuela)*
1985	Karen Neville *(Australia)*
1987	Deena Brush *(USA)*

weightlifting the sport of lifting the heaviest possible weight above the head to the satisfaction of judges. In international competitions there are two standard lifts, the *snatch* and the *jerk*.

CHAMPIONS
World and Olympic champions
weight 1987 World champions/1988 Olympic champions
52kg Sevdalin Marinov *(Bulgaria)*/Sevdalin Marinov *(Bulgaria)*
56kg Nerno Terziiski *(Bulgaria)*/Oxen Mirzoian *(USSR)*
60kg Stefan Topurov *(Bulgaria)*/Naim Suleymanoglu *(Turkey)*
67.5kg Michail Petrov *(Bulgaria)*/Joachim Kunz *East Germany)*
75kg Borislav Guidikov *(Bulgaria)*/Borislav Guidikov *(Bulgaria)*
82.5kg L Barsi *(Hungary)*/Israil Arsanmakov *(USSR)*
90 kg Anatoliy Khrapati *(USSR)*/Anatoliy Khrapati *(USSR)*
100kg Pavel Kouznetsov *(USSR)*/Pavel Kouznetsov *(USSR)*
110kg Yuriy Zacharovich *(USSR)*/Yuriy Zacharovich *(USSR)*
110+kg Alexandre Kurlovich *(USSR)*/Alexandre Kurlovich *(USSR)*

yachting pleasure cruising or racing a small and light vessel, whether sailing or power-driven. At the Olympic Games, seven categories exist Soling, Flying Dutchman, Star, Finn,

Tornado, 470, and Windglider (Boardsailing), which was introduced at the 1984 Los Angeles games. The Finn and Windglider are solo events, the Soling Class is for three-person crews, while all other classes are for crews of two.

CHAMPIONS

America's Cup first contested 1870. All winners have been US boats, except the Australia II in 1983

1903	Reliance
1920	Resolute
1930	Enterprise
1934	Rainbow
1937	Ranger
1958	Columbia
1962	Weatherly
1964	Constellation
1967	Intrepid
1970	Intrepid
1974	Courageous
1977	Courageous
1980	Freedom
1983	Australia II
1987	Stars and Stripes

Admiral's Cup first contested 1957; a team event in which each country is represented by three boats comprising six races

1969	USA
1971	Great Britain
1973	West Germany
1975	Great Britain
1977	Great Britain
1979	Australia
1981	Great Britain
1983	West Germany
1985	West Germany
1987	New Zealand

Sporting Greats

Agostini Giacomo 1943– . Italian motor cyclist. He won a record 122 grands prix and 15 world titles. His world titles were at 350cc and 500cc and he was five times a dual champion.

CAREER HIGHLIGHTS
World titles:
350cc: 1968-73 (MV Agusta), 1974 (Yamaha)
500cc: 1966-72 (MV Agusta), 1975 (Yamaha)

Isle of Man
TT wins:
Junior TT: 1966, 1968-70, 1972 (all MV Augusta)
Senior TT: 1968-72 (all MV Agusta)

Alexeev Vasiliy 1942– . Soviet weightlifter who broke 80 world records 1970-77, a record for any sport. He was Olympic super-heavyweight champion twice, world champion seven times, and European champion on eight occasions.

CAREER HIGHLIGHTS
Olympic Champion: 1972, 1976
World Champion: 1970-71, 1973-75, 1977
European Champion: 1970-78.

Ali Muhammad 1942– . US boxer. Olympic light-heavyweight champion 1960, he went on to become world professional heavyweight champion 1964, and was the only man to regain the title twice. He was known for his quickness and extroversion.

Aouita Said 1960– . Moroccan runner. Outstanding at middle and long distances, he won the 1984 Olympic and 1987 World Championship 5000 metres title, and has set many world records.

CAREER HIGHLIGHTS
Olympic Games - gold: 5000 metres 1984
World Records: 1500 metres: 1985
Two Miles: 1987
2000 metres: 1987
5000 metres: 1985; 1987

Archer Frederick 1857–1886. English jockey. He rode 2,748 winners in 8,084 races 1870–86, including 21 classic winners.

Ballesteros Severiano 'Seve' 1957– . Spanish golfer who came to prominence 1976 and has been dominant in Europe, as well as winning leading tournaments in the US. He has won the British Open three times 1979, 1984, 1988.

Bannister Roger Gilbert 1929– . English athlete who became the first man to run the mile in under four minutes. He achieved this feat at Oxford, England on 6 May 1954 in a time of 3 min 59.4 sec. He was knighted 1975.

Becker Boris 1967– . West German lawn tennis player. In 1985 he became the youngest winner of a singles title at Wimbledon at the age of 17 years 227 days. He has won the title three times and helped West Germany to win the Davis Cup 1988.

CAREER HIGHLIGHTS
Wimbledon:
singles: 1985–86, 1989
Davis Cup: 1988

Border Allan 1955– . Australian cricketer, who has played for New South Wales, Queensland, Gloucestershire, and Essex. He made his test debut for Australia 1978–79, and was appointed captain 1985.

CAREER HIGHLIGHTS
Test Cricket:
Appearances (up to 1989): 102
Runs: 7,831
Average: 52.55
Best: 205 v. New Zealand 1987–88
Wickets: 27
Average: 32.14
Best: 7-46 v. West Indies 1988–89

Borg Bjorn 1956– . Swedish lawn tennis player who won the men's singles title at Wimbledon five times 1976-80, a record since the abolition of the challenge system in 1922.

Botham Ian Terrence 1955– . English cricketer. A prolific all-rounder, he is often controversial. He has played county cricket for Somerset and Worcestershire as well as playing in Australia. His 373 test wickets, 109 catches, and 5,057 runs in 94 appearances by the end of the 1988 English season was a record until equalled by Richard Hadlee (New Zealand) later in the same year.

CAREER HIGHLIGHTS
All First Class Matches
Runs: 15,758
Average: 35.09
Best: 228 Somerset v. Gloucestershire, 1980
Wickets: 975
Average: 26.71
Best: 8-34 England v. Pakistan, 1978
Test Cricket
Runs: 5,057
Average: 34.87
Best: 208 v. India, 1982
Wickets: 373
Average: 27.86
Best: 109

Bradman Donald George 1908– . Australian test cricketer with the highest average in test history. From 52 test matches he averaged 99.94 runs per innings. He only needed four runs from his final test innings to average 100 but was dismissed at second ball.

CAREER HIGHLIGHTS
All First Class Matches Runs: 28,067
Average: 95.14
Best: 452 not out New South Wales v. Queensland, 1930
Test Cricket Runs: 6,996
Average: 99.94
Best: 334 v. England, 1930

Bristow Eric 1957– . English darts player nicknamed 'the Crafty Cockney'. He has won all the game's major titles, including the world professional title a record five times between 1980-86.

CAREER HIGHLIGHTS
World professional champion: 1980-81, 1984-86
World Masters: 1977, 1979, 1981, 1983-84,
World Cup (Team): 1979, 1981, 1983, 1985, 1987
World Cup (Ind): 1983, 1985
British Open: 1978, 1981, 1983, 1985-86
News of the World: 1983-84
World Pairs: 1987 (with Peter Locke)

Budge Donald 1915– . US tennis player. The first person to perform the Grand Slam when he won Wimbledon, French, US, and Australian championships in 1938.

Caslavska Vera 1943– . Czechoslovakian gymnast, the first of the great modern-day stylists. She won a record 21 world, Olympic and European gold medals 1959-68; she also won 8 silver medals and 3 bronze medals.

CAREER HIGHLIGHTS
Olympic champion
overall individual: 1964, 1968
beam: 1964, 1968
vault: 1964, 1968
floor exercise: 1968
World champion
overall individual: 1966
vault: 1962, 1966.

Cauthen Steve 1960– . US jockey. He rode

Affirmed to the US Triple Crown in 1978 at the age of 18 and won 487 races in 1977. He has ridden in England since 1979 and has twice won the Derby, on *Slip Anchor* in 1985 and on *Reference Point* in 1987. He was champion jockey in 1984, 1985 and 1987.

Charlton Robert 'Bobby' 1937– . English footballer who scored a record 49 goals in 106 appearances. He spent most of his playing career with Manchester United.

CAREER HIGHLIGHTS
Football League appearances 644, goals 206
International appearances 106, goals 49
World Cup 1966
Football League championship 1965, 1967
FA Cup 1963
European Cup 1968
Footballer of the Year 1966
European Footballer of the Year 1966.

Clark James 'Jim' 1936–1968. Scottish-born motor racing driver, who was regarded as one of the finest in the post-war era. He was twice world champion in 1963 and 1965. He spent all his formula one career with Lotus.

CAREER HIGHLIGHTS
World Champion: 1963, 1965 (both Lotus)
Formula One Grand Prix: races 72, wins 25
1st Grand Prix: 1960
Dutch GP: (Lotus)
Last Grand Prix: 1968
South African GP: (Lotus).

Cobb Ty(rus Raymond). Nickname 'the Georgia Peach' 1886–1961. US baseball player, one of the greatest batters and base runners of all time. He played for Detroit and Philadelphia 1905–28, and won the American League batting average championship 12 times. He holds the all-time record for runs scored, 2,254, and batting average, .367. He had 4,191 hits in his career, a record which held for almost 60 years.

Coe Sebastian 1956– . English middle-distance runner. He was Olympic 1500 metre champion 1980 and 1984. Between 1979–81 he broke eight individual world records at 800, 1000, 1500 metres, and one mile.

CAREER HIGHLIGHTS
Olympic Games:
gold 1,500 Metres 1980, 1984

silver 800 Metres 1980, 1984
World Records:
800 Metres 1979, 1981
1,000 Metres 1980, 1981
One Mile 1979, 1981 (twice)
1,500 Metres 1979
4x800 Metres Relay 1982.

Comaneci Nadia 1961– . Romanian gymnast. She won three gold medals at the 1976 Olympics at the age of 14, and was the first gymnast to record a perfect score of 10 in international competition.

CAREER HIGHLIGHTS
Olympic Games gold medals: 1976 beam, vault, floor exercise
1980 beam, parallel bars

Connors Jimmy 1952– . US lawn tennis player. Very popular and entertaining, he became well-known for his 'grunting' during play. He won the Wimbledon title 1974, and has since won 10 Grand Slam events. He was one of the first players to popularize the two-handed backhand.

CAREER HIGHLIGHTS
Wimbledon:
singles: 1974, 1982
doubles: 1973
US Open:
singles: 1974, 1976, 1978, 1982–83
doubles: 1975
Australian Open:
singles: 1974

Court Margaret (born Smith) 1942– . Australian tennis player. The most prolific winner in the women's game, she won a record 66 Grand Slam titles, including a record 24 at singles.

Davis Steve 1957– . English snooker player, the greatest player of modern times. He has won every major honour in the game since turning professional 1978. He has been world champion six times, including 1989. He has won as many major titles as all the other professionals between them.

CAREER HIGHLIGHTS
World Professional champion:
1981, 1983-84, 1987-89
World Pairs Championship (with Tony

Meo):
1982-83, 1985-86
World Team Championship:
1981, 1983, 1988.

Dempsey Jack. Nickname 'the Manassa Mauler' 1895–1983. US heavyweight boxing champion. He beat Jess Willard 1919 to win the title and held it until losing to Gene Tunney 1926. He engaged in the 'Battle of the Long Count' with Tunney 1927.

CAREER HIGHLIGHTS
Fights: 79
Wins: 64
Draws: 9
Defeats: 6

DiMaggio Joe 1914– . US baseball player with the New York Yankees 1936–51. In 1941 he set a record by getting hits in 56 consecutive games. He was an outstanding fielder, hit 361 home runs and had a career average of .325. He was once married to the actress Marilyn Monroe.

Eusebio Full name of Eusebio Ferreira da Silva. 1942– . Portuguese footballer, born in Lourenco Marques. He made his international debut 1961 and played for his country 77 times. He spent most of his league career with Benfica, and also played in the USA.

CAREER HIGHLIGHTS
European Cup: 1962
European Footballer of the Year:
1965

Evert Chris 1954– . US lawn tennis player. She won her first Wimbledon title 1974, and has since won 21 Grand Slam titles. She became the first woman to win $1 million in prize money.

CAREER HIGHLIGHTS
Wimbledon:
singles: 1974, 1976, 1981
doubles: 1976
US Open:
singles: 1975–78, 1980, 1982
French Open:
singles: 1974–75, 1979–80, 1983, 1985–86
doubles: 1974–75
Australian Open:
singles: 1982, 1984

Ferrari Enzo 1898–1988. Founder of the Ferrari car empire which specializes in Grand Prix racing cars and high quality sports cars. He was a former racing driver for Alfa Romeo in the 1920s and then became one of their designers. He took over their racing division 1929, and in 1947 the first 'true' Ferrari was seen. The Ferrari car has won more world championship Grands Prix than any other car.

Finney Thomas 'Tom' 1922– . English footballer, known as the 'Preston Plumber'. He played for England 76 times, and in every forward position. He was noted for his ball control and goal-scoring skills, and was the first man to win the Footballer of the Year award twice.

Gavaskar Sunil Manohar 1949– . Indian cricketer. Between 1971-87 he scored a record 10,122 test runs in a record 125 matches (including 106 consecutive).

CAREER HIGHLIGHTS
All First Class Matches Runs: 25,834
Average: 51.46
Best: 340 Bombay v Bengal, 1981-82
Test Cricket Runs: 10,122
Average: 51.12
Best: 236 not out v. West Indies, 1983-84

Gower David 1957– . English left-handed cricketer. He made his debut for Leicestershire 1975 and has scored over 20,000 first class runs. He made his England debut 1978, was appointed captain 1984, and was re-appointed captain 1989.

CAREER HIGHLIGHTS
Test Cricket:
Appearances (up to 1989): 100
Runs: 7,000
Average: 44.02
Best: 215 v. Australia 1985

Grace W(illiam) G(ilbert) 1848–1915. English cricketer. By profession a doctor, he became the best batsman in England. He began playing first class cricket at the age of 16, scored 152 runs in his first Test match, anad scored the first triple century 1876.

CAREER HIGHLIGHTS
All First Class Matches
Runs: 54,896
Average: 39.55
Best: 344 MCC v. Kent, 1876
Wickets: 2,876
Average: 17.92
Best: 10-49 MCC v. Oxford University, 1886
Test Cricket
Runs: 1,098
Average: 32.29
Best: 170 v. Australia, 1886
Wickets: 9
Average: 26.22
Best: 2-12 v Australia, 1890.

Graf Steffi 1969– . West German lawn tennis player, who succeeded Martina Navratilova as the world's number one female player. She reached the semi-final of the US Open 1985 at the age of 16, and won five consecutive Grand Slam singles titles 1988–89.

CAREER HIGHLIGHTS
Wimbledon:
singles: 1988–89
doubles: 1988
US Open:
singles: 1988
French Open:
singles: 1987–88
Australian Open:
singles: 1988–89

Hadlee Richard John 1951– . New Zealand cricketer. In 1987 he equalled Ian Botham's world record of 373 wickets in test cricket.

CAREER HIGHLIGHTS
All First Class Matches
Runs: 11,349
Average: 31,78
Best: 210 not out Nottinghamshire v. Middlesex, 1984
Wickets: 1,384
Average: 17.94
Best: 9-52 New Zealand v. Australia, 1985-86
Test Cricket Runs: 2,770
Average: 27.42
Best: 151 not out v. Sri Lanka, 1986-87
Wickets: 373
Average: 22.46
Best: 9-52 v. Australia, 1985-86

Hick Graeme 1966– . Rhodesian-born cricketer who became Zimbabwe's youngest cricketer at the age of 17. A prolific batsman, he joined Worcestershire, England 1984. He achieved the highest batting score in England this century in 1988 against Somerset, 405 not out.

Howe Gordie 1926– . Canadian ice hockey player, who played for the Detroit Red Wings (National Hockey League) and the New England Whalers (World Hockey Association). In the NHL, he scored more goals (801), assists (1,049), and points (1,850) than any other player in ice hockey history. He played professional hockey until past the age of 50.

Hutton Leonard 1916– . English cricketer, born in Pudsey, West Yorkshire. He captained England in 23 test matches 1952–56 and was England's first professional captain. In 1938 at The Oval he scored 364 against Australia, a world record test score until beaten by Gary Sobers 1958.

CAREER HIGHLIGHTS:
Test Cricket
Runs: 6,971
Average: 55.51
Best: 364 v. Australia, 1938

Johnson Jack 1878–1968. US heavyweight boxer. He overcame severe racial prejudice to become the first black heavyweight champion of the world 1908 when he had to go to Australia to challenge Tommy Burns. The US authorities wanted Johnson 'dethroned' because of his color but could not find suitable challengers until 1915 when he lost the title dubiously to the giant Jess Willard.

CAREER HIGHLIGHTS
Fights: 107
Wins: 86
Draws: 11
Defeats: 10

Jones Robert Tyre 'Bobby' 1902–1971. US golfer. He was the game's greatest amateur player who never turned professional but won 13 major amateur and professional tournaments, including the Grand Slam of the amateur and professional opens of both the US and Britain in 1930.

Khan Imran 1952– . Pakistani cricketer. He played county cricket for Worcestershire and Sussex in the UK, and made his test debut for Pakistan 1971, subsequently playing for his country 75 times. In first class cricket, he scored over 16,000 runs and took over 1,200 wickets.

CAREER HIGHLIGHTS
Test Cricket:
Appearances: 75
Runs: 3,000
Average: 33.70
Best: 135 not out v. India 1986–87
Wickets: 341
Average: 22.04
Best: 8-58 v. Sri Lanka 1981–82

Khan Jahangir 1963– . Pakistani squash player, who won the world open championship a record six times 1981–85 and 1988.

CAREER HIGHLIGHTS
World Open champion: 1981-85, 1988
World Amateur champion: 1979, 1983, 1985
British Open champion: 1982-89

King Billie Jean (born Moffitt) 1943– . US lawn tennis player. She won a record 20 Wimbledon titles between 1961 and 1979 when she broke Elizabeth Ryan's record.

CAREER HIGHLIGHTS
Wimbledon
singles: 1966-68, 1972-73, 1975
doubles: 1961-62, 1965, 1967-68, 1970-73, 1979
mixed: 1967, 1971, 1973-74
US Open
singles: 1967, 1971-72, 1974
doubles: 1964, 1967, 1974, 1978, 1980
mixed: 1967, 1971, 1973, 1976
French Open
singles: 1972
doubles: 1972
mixed: 1967, 1970
Australian championships
singles: 1968
mixed: 1968.

Klammer Franz 1953– . Austrian skier, who won a record 35 World Cup downhill races 1974-1985. Olympic gold medallist 1976.

Korbut Olga 1955– . Soviet gymnast, who attracted world attention at the 1972 Olympic Games with her 'cheeky' floor routine, and won three gold medals.

CAREER HIGHLIGHTS
Olympic Games
Gold medals: 1972 Team, beam, floor exercise
1976 Team

Kristiansen Ingrid 1956– . Norwegian athlete, an outstanding long-distance runner at 5,000 m, 10,000 m, marathon, and cross-country. She has won all the world's leading marathons. In 1986 she knocked 45.68 seconds off the world 10,000 m record.

CAREER HIGHLIGHTS
World Cross Country Champion: 1988
London Marathon: 1984, 1985, 1987, 1988

Latynina Larissa Semyonovna 1935– . Soviet gymnast. Winner of more Olympic medals than any person in any sport. She won 18 between 1956-64, including nine gold. She won a total of 12 individual Olympic and world championship gold medals.

Leonard Sugar Ray 1956– . US boxer. In 1988 he became the first man to win world titles at five officially recognized weights. In 1976 he was Olympic light-welterweight champion and won his first professional title in 1979 when he beat Wilfred Benitez for the WBC welterweight title. He has since won titles at junior-middleweight (WBA version) 1981, middleweight (WBC) 1987, light-heavyweight (WBC) 1988, and super-middleweight (WBC) 1988. In 1989 he drew with Thomas Hearns.

Lewis Carl (Frederick Carleton) 1961– . US athlete. At the 1984 Olympic Games he equalled Jesse Owens' performance, winning gold medals in the 100 and 200 metres, sprint relay, and long jump. In the 1988 Olympics, he repeated his golds in the 100 metres and long jump, and won a silver in the 200 metres.

CAREER HIGHLIGHTS
Olympic Games
gold:
100 metres 1984, 1988 200 metres 1984
4x100 metres Relay 1984
Long Jump 1984, 1988
silver:

200 metres 1988
World Championships
gold:
100 metres 1983
4x100 metres Relay 1983, 1987
Long Jump 1983, 1987
silver:
100 metres 1987.

Lopez Nancy 1957– . US golfer, who turned professional 1977 and has won more than $2.5 million. She was the first woman to win $200,000 in a season, 1979, and has twice won the US LPGA title (1978, 1985). She has won over 35 tour events and was inducted into the Hall of Fame 1987.

Louis Joe. Assumed name of Joseph Louis Barrow 1914–1981. US boxer, nicknamed 'the Brown Bomber'. He was world heavyweight champion 1937–49 and made a record 25 successful defences (a record for any weight).

Marciano Rocco Francis Marchegiano 'Rocky' 1923–1969. US boxer, world heavyweight champion 1952–56. He retired after 49 professional fights, the only heavyweight champion to retire undefeated.

CAREER HIGHLIGHTS
Professional fights: 49
wins: 49
knockouts: 43
defeats: 0

Matthews Stanley 1915– . English footballer who played for Stoke City, Blackpool, and England. He played nearly 700 Football League games, and won 54 international caps. He was the first European Footballer of the Year 1956, and the first footballer to be knighted.

CAREER HIGHLIGHTS
Football League appearances: 698, goals: 71
International appearances: 54, goals: 11
FA Cup: 1953
Footballer of the Year: 1948, 1963
European Footballer of the Year: 1956.

Merckx Eddie 1945– . Belgian cyclist known as 'The Cannibal'. He won the Tour de France a joint record five times 1969-74.

CAREER HIGHLIGHTS
Tour de France: 1969-72, 1974
Tour of Italy: 1968, 1970, 1972-74

Tour of Spain: 1973
World Professional Champion: 1967, 1971, 1974
World Amateur champion: 1964.

Montana Joe 1956– . US American footballer. He appeared in three winning Super Bowls with the San Francisco 49ers 1982, 1985, and 1989, winning the Most Valuable Player award in the first two, and setting a record for passing yardage 1989.

Navratilova Martina 1956– . Czechoslovakian tennis player, who became a naturalized US citizen 1981. The most outstanding woman player of the 1980s, she has 51 Grand Slam victories, including 17 singles titles. She has won the Wimbledon singles title eight times, including six in succession 1982–87.

CAREER HIGHLIGHTS
Wimbledon
singles: 1978-79, 1982-87
doubles: 1976, 1979, 1981-84, 1986
mixed: 1985
US Open
singles: 1983-84, 1986-87
doubles: 1977-78, 1980, 1983-84, 1986-87
mixed: 1985, 1987
French Open
singles: 1982, 1984
doubles: 1975, 1982, 1984-88
mixed: 1974, 1985
Australian Open
singles: 1981, 1983, 1985
doubles: 1980, 1982-85, 1987-88.

Nicklaus Jack William 1940– . US golfer, nicknamed 'the Golden Bear'. He won a record 20 major titles, including 18 professional 'majors' 1962-86.

CAREER HIGHLIGHTS
US Amateur: 1959, 1961
US Open: 1962, 1967, 1972, 1980
British Open: 1966, 1970, 1978
US Masters: 1963, 1965-66, 1972, 1975, 1986
US PGA: 1963, 1971, 1973, 1975, 1980
US Ryder Cup team: 1969, 1971, 1973, 1975, 1977.

Norman Greg. Nickname 'the Great White Shark' 1955– . Australian golfer. After many wins in his home country, he enjoyed success on the European PGA Tour before joining the US Tour. He has won the world match-play title three times.

CAREER HIGHLIGHTS
British Open: 1986
World Match-play Championship: 1980, 1983, 1986
Dunlop Masters: 1981–82
Canadian Open: 1984

Owens (James Cleveland) 'Jesse' 1913–1980. US track and field athlete, who excelled in the sprints, hurdles, and the long jump. At the 1936 Olympics he won four gold medals.

Palmer Arnold (Daniel) 1929– . US golfer, who helped to popularize the game in the USA in the 1950s and 1960s. He won the Masters 1958, 1960, 1962, and 1964; the US Open 1960; and the British Open 1961 and 1962.

Pelé Adopted name of Edson Arantes do Nascimento 1940– . Brazilian footballer, a prolific goal scorer, often considered to be the best footballer of all time. He appeared in four World Cup competitions 1958–70 and won three winner's medals.

Piggott Lester 1935– . English jockey. He was regarded as a master tactician and adopted a unique high riding style. A champion jockey 11 times 1960–1982 he rode a record nine Derby winners.

Prost Alain 1955– . French motor racing driver. He won 32 races from 130 starts, and was world champion 1985–86.

Rhodes Wilfred 1877–1973. England cricketer. He was the game's most prolific wicket-taker, taking 4,187 wickets 1898–1930, and also scored 39,802 first class runs.

Richards Gordon 1905–1986. English jockey who was champion on the flat a record 26 times 1925–1953.

Robinson 'Sugar' Ray. Assumed name of Walker Smith 1920–1989. US boxer, world welterweight champion 1945–51, defending his title five times. He defeated Jake LaMotta 1951 to take the middleweight title. He lost the title six times and won it seven times. He had 202 fights, and fought until the age of 45.

CAREER HIGHLIGHTS
Total fights: 202
Wins: 175
Draws: 6

Defeats: 19
No Contests: 2

Roche Stephen 1959– . Irish cyclist. One of the outstanding riders on the continent in the 1980s, he was the first British winner of the Tour de France in 1987 and the first English-speaking winner of the Tour of Italy the same year, as well as the 1987 world professional road race champion.

Rodnina Irina 1949– . Soviet ice skater. From 1969–1980 she won 23 world, Olympic, and European gold medals in pairs competitions. Her partners were Alexei Ulanov and then Alexsandr Zaitsev, who became her husband 1975.

Sawchuk (Terrance Gordon) 'Terry' 1929–1970. Canadian ice hockey player, often regarded as the greatest goaltender of all time. He played for Detroit, Boston, Toronto, Los Angeles, and New York Rangers 1950–67, and holds the NHL record of 103 shut-outs (games in which he did not concede a goal).

Scudamore Peter 1958– . British National Hunt jockey. He was champion jockey 1982 (shared with John Francome), 1986, 1987, 1988, and 1989. In the 1988–89 season he became the third jockey to ride 1,000 National Hunt winners; in Feb 1989 he became the first man to ride 150 winners in a season.

Senna Ayrton 1960– . Brazilian motor racing driver. He had his first Grand Prix win in the 1985 Portuguese Grand Prix, has since surpassed Jim Clark's record for most pole positions, and in 1988 was world champion, winning a championship record eight races.

CAREER HIGHLIGHTS
World Champion: 1988
Grand Prix Wins:
1985: Portuguese, Belgian
1986: Spanish, Detroit
1987: Monaco, United States
1988: San Marino, Canadian, United States, British, German, Hungarian, Belgian, Japanese
1989: San Marino, Monaco, Mexico

Shoemaker William Lee 'Bill' 1931– . US jockey, who was the most successful of all time. He rode 8,621 winners from 38,853 mounts and his career earnings exceeded $10 million.

Sobers Garfield St Aubrun 'Gary' 1936– . West Indian test cricketer. One of the game's great all-rounders, he scored more than 8,000 test runs, took over 200 wickets, held more than 100 catches, and holds the record for the highest test innings, 365 not out.

CAREER HIGHLIGHTS
All First Class Cricket
Runs: 28,315
Average: 54.87
Best: 365 not out West Indies v. Pakistan, 1957-58
Wickets: 1,043
Average: 27.74
Best: 9-49 West Indies v. Kent, 1966
Test cricket
Runs: 8,032
Average: 57.78
Best: 365 not out v. Pakistan, 1957-58
Wickets: 235
Average: 34.03
Best: 6-73 v. Australia, 1968-69.

Spitz Mark Andrew 1950– . US swimmer. He won a record seven gold medals at the 1972 Olympic Games, all in world record times.

CAREER HIGHLIGHTS
Olympic medals:
Gold:
4 x 100 metres freestyle relay 1968, 1972
4 x 200 metres freestyle relay 1968, 1972
4 x 100 metres medley relay 1972
100 metres freestyle 1972
200 metres freestyle 1972
100 metres butterfly 1972
200 metres butterfly 1972
Silver:
100 metres butterfly 1968
Bronze:
100 metres freestyle 1968.

Stewart John Young 'Jackie' 1939– . Scottish motor racing driver. Until surpassed by Alain Prost (France) 1987, Stewart held the record for the most Formula One Grand Prix wins (27).

Thompson Francis Morgan 'Daley' 1958– . English athlete, who broke the world decathlon record four times, and won two Olympic titles, one world title, three European titles, and three Commonwealth titles.

Tyson Mike 1966– . US boxer, who became heavyweight champion of the world 1987. He won the WBC heavyweight title 1986 when he beat Trevor Berbick to become the youngest world heavyweight champion. He beat James 'Bonecrusher' Smith for the WBA title 1987 and later that year he became the first undisputed champion since 1978 when he beat Tony Tucker for the IBF title.

Wilander Mats 1964– . Swedish lawn tennis player. He won his first Grand Slam event 1982 when he beat Guillermo Vilas to win the French Open, and has since won eight Grand Slam titles. He has played a prominent role in Sweden's rise to the fore of men's tennis in the 1980s including Davis Cup successes.

CAREER HIGHLIGHTS
Wimbledon:
doubles: 1986
US Open:
singles: 1988
French Open:
singles: 1982, 1985, 1988
Australian Open:
singles: 1983–84, 1988

Women in Society

Over the past decade people have begun to realize that the world is often viewed and subsequently analysed through male eyes, and that this ignores the lives of half the world's population. The examination of women's position in society is now considered worthy of serious academic study, and many institutions of higher education run courses which cover this area. Indeed, in a period of financial restraint in educational spending in the UK, Women's Studies has been one of the few areas of growth in recent years in the humanities and social sciences. There is no fixed curriculum in Women's Studies, but it aims to develop alternative perspectives and methodologies grounded in women's own experiences.

This section contains *Biographies* of some notable women, and a *Chronology* of women's rights in the UK. Many of the women included in the biographical section have been referred to as feminists. Some would not have chosen to describe themselves in this way, and might even have been repelled by the label. However, they all recognized women's subordination and, in one sphere or another, sought to end it. Progress is at last being made, but contradictions still exist between the formal equality of the sexes which is now enshrined in the Equal Pay and the Sex Discrimination Acts and the inequalities between the sexes which remain, both in many state policies and in everyday life.

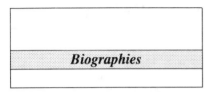

Biographies

Addams Jane 1860–1935. American sociologist and feminist. She founded and led one of the earliest community centres at Hull House, Chicago, in 1889 and was Vice-President of the National American Woman Suffrage Association from 1911 to 1914. In 1915 she led the Women's Peace Party and the first Women's Peace Congress. Her publications include *Newer Ideals of Peace* 1907 and *Twenty Years at Hull House* 1910. She was a co-winner of the Nobel Peace Prize 1931.

Anderson Elizabeth Garrett 1836–1917. First English woman doctor, born Garrett. She qualified in 1865 as a medical practitioner, despite prejudiced opposition, and established a dispensary for women in 1866, which survives as the Elizabeth Garrett Anderson Hospital (diagnostic). She was the sister of Millicent Fawcett and the first (and only) female member of the British Medical Association (1873–92). In 1908 she became mayor of her native Aldeburgh in Suffolk, England's first woman mayor.

Anthony Susan B 1820–1906. American pioneering feminist, who also worked for the anti-slavery and temperance movements. Her campaigns included demands for equality of pay for female teachers, the Married Women's Property Act and women's suffrage. In 1869 with Elizabeth Cady Stanton she founded the National Woman Suffrage Association. From 1868 to 1870 she edited and published a radical women's newspaper *The Revolution* and from 1881 to 1886 she worked on the *History of Woman Suffrage*. She was instrumental in setting up the International Council of Women and founded the International Woman Suffrage Alliance in 1904 in Berlin.

Beauvoir Simone de 1908–86. French socialist, feminist, and author, who taught philosophy at the Sorbonne 1931–43. Her book *The Second Sex* 1949 is a classic text which became a seminal work for many feminists. Her novel of post-war Paris, *Les Mandarins* 1954, has characters resembling Camus, Koestler, and Sartre (she was long associated with the last-named); and she also published autobiographical volumes.

Becker Lydia 1827–90. English botanist and campaigner for women's rights. Born in Manchester, she developed an interest in botany, gave lectures to girls' schools and corresponded with Darwin. Her first publication was *Botany for Novices* 1864. In 1865 she established the Manchester Ladies Literary Society as a forum for women to study scientific subjects. She campaigned for women's suffrage and in 1867 she co-founded and became secretary of the National Society for Women's Suffrage. In April 1868 she was the first woman to speak in public on women's rights when she addressed the British Association Congress with a paper entitled 'Some supposed differences in the minds of men and women in regard to educational necessities'. In 1870 she founded a monthly newsletter *The Women's Suffrage Journal* and edited it over the next 20 years. She organized a women-only demonstration in support of female suffrage in the Free Trade Hall in Manchester, and became secretary of the London Central Committee for Women's Suffrage and eventually a parliamentary candidate.

Behn Aphra 1640–89. English novelist and playwright, the first English woman to earn her living as a writer. Although celebrated in her day, she was often criticized for her sexual explicitness. She was also unusual in often presenting her novels and plays from a woman's point of view. She had the patronage of James I and was employed as a government spy in Holland in 1666. In 1688 her novel *Oronooko* the first attack on slavery in English literature was published. From 1670–1687 fifteen of her plays were produced to great acclaim. Her best play was *The Rover* which attacked forced and mercenary marriages.

Besant Annie 1847–1933. British socialist,

feminist, and activist. Separated from her clerical husband in 1873 because of her free-thinking views, she was associated with the radical atheist Charles Bradlaugh and the Fabians, and became a disciple of the mystic Madame Blavatsky in 1889. She thereafter preached theosophy and, as a supporter of Indian independence, became president of the Hindu National Congress in 1917.

Butler Josephine Elizabeth 1828–1906. British social reformer who agitated for the admission of women to higher education, helped to secure the Married Women's Property Act, and campaigned against Victorian attitudes towards single women and for the improvement of the lot of prostitutes. She carried on a campaign against the Contagious Diseases Acts of 1862–70, which made women in garrison towns liable to compulsory examination for venereal disease. As a result of Butler's campaigns, the acts were repealed in 1883.

Cady Stanton Elizabeth 1815–1902. American feminist who founded and led the first women's movement in the US and who worked for the abolition of slavery. She was the friend and political collaborator of Susan B Anthony, and together they founded the National Woman Suffrage Association in 1869, with Stanton as its first president. Also with Anthony she wrote and compiled the *History of Woman Suffrage* from 1881–86 and organized the International Council of Women in Washington DC. Her publications include: *Degradation of Disenfranchisement* and *Solitude of Self* 1892 both of which had enormous influence, and in 1885 and 1898 she published (in two parts) a feminist critique of the Bible: *The Woman's Bible*.

Davison Emily 1872–1913. English militant suffragette, who died while trying to stop the King's horse at the Derby at Epsom and was trampled by the horse. A teacher with degrees from Oxford and London universities, she joined the Women's Social and Political Union in 1906 and served several prison sentences for militant action such as stone throwing, setting fire to pillar boxes, and bombing Lloyd George's country house. Her coffin was carried

through London draped in the colours of the suffragette movement – purple, white, and green – and escorted by 2,000 uniformed suffragettes.

Fawcett Millicent 1847–1929. English suffragette, younger sister of Elizabeth Garrett Anderson. A non-militant, she rejected the violent acts of some of her contemporaries in the suffrage movement. She joined the first Women's Suffrage Committee in 1867 and emerged as the leader of the women's suffrage movement in 1890. She was president of the National Union of Women's Suffrage Societies from 1897-1918. She was also active in property reform and campaigned for the right of married women to own their own property. Her publications include *Political Economy for Beginners* 1870, *Women's Suffrage* 1912 and *Women's Victory and After*.

Firestone Shulamith 1945– . Canadian feminist writer, a founder member of Redstockings (a radical feminist organization) and also the New York Radical Feminists. Her book *The Dialectic of Sex* 1970, had a great influence on the thinking of feminists in the early 1970s. She was also one of the most influential early organizers of the Women's Liberation Movement in the US.

Friedan Betty 1921– . American liberal feminist, influential in the women's movement in the 1970s. Her book *The Feminine Mystique* 1963 was one of the earliest and most influential books for the women's movement both in the USA and in Britain. She founded the National Organization for Women (NOW) in 1966 and was its first president. She also founded the National Women's Political Caucus in 1971, and the first women's bank in 1973, and called the First International Feminist Congress in 1973. She was popularly nicknamed 'the mother of the new feminist movement'. Her later book *The Second Stage* 1981 seems to move towards a position of more freedom of choice for individual women rather than a concern for restrictions imposed upon women generally by society.

Greer Germaine 1939– . Australian feminist who gained overnight fame and notoriety with the publication of *The Female Eunuch* 1970. She became a familiar figure in the British media and as a *Sunday Times* columnist. Later works include *The Obstacle Race* 1979 - a study of contemporary women artists - and *Sex and Destiny: The Politics of Human Fertility* 1984. The most recent book appears to contradict the earlier ideas of sexual freedom which are expressed in *The Female Eunuch*.

Holtby Winifred 1898–1935. British novelist, poet, and journalist. An ardent advocate of women's freedom and racial equality, she is best known for her novel *South Riding* 1936, set in her native Yorkshire. Her other works include an analysis of women's position in contemporary society *Women and a Changing Civilization* 1934.

Kollontai Alexandra 1872–1952. Russian revolutionary, politician, diplomat, and writer. Enraged at the appalling conditions of factory workers in Russia, she devoted herself to improving conditions for the working class and, later, for working women. She studied economics in Zurich from 1898 and in 1905 published *On the Question of Class Struggle*. She was harassed by the police for her views and in 1914 she went into exile in Germany. On her return to Russia she joined the Bolsheviks and toured the US. She was the only female member of the first Bolshevik government as Commissar for Public Welfare. In 1918 she organized the first all-Russian Congress of Working and Peasant Women. A controversial figure in the government, she was sent abroad by Stalin, first as Trade Minister, then as ambassador to Sweden in 1943. She took part in the armistice negotiations ending the Soviet-Finnish War in 1944. She also campaigned for domestic reforms such as acceptance of free love, simplification of divorce laws and collective childcare. Her book *The Love of Worker Bees* 1923 aroused great controversy.

Millett Kate 1934– . American radical feminist lecturer, writer and sculptor, whose book *Sexual Politics* 1970 was a landmark in feminist thinking. She was one of the earliest and most influential theorists of the Women's Movement and was a founding member of the National Organization of Women (NOW). Later books include *Flying* 1974, *The Prostitution Papers* 1976 and *Sita* 1976.

Mitchell Juliet 1940– . British psychoanalyst and writer. She first came to public notice with an article in New Left Review (1966) entitled *The Longest Revolution*. It was one of the first attempts to combine socialism and feminism using Marxist theory to try to explain the reasons behind women's oppression. Of her more recent publications, *Women's Estate* 1971 and *Psychoanalysis and Feminism* 1974 have had great influence on feminist thinking.

Pankhurst Emmeline 1858–1928. British suffragette, born Goulden. Founder of the Women's Social and Political Union in 1903, she launched in 1906 the militant suffragette campaign, and was several times imprisoned and then released after hunger-strikes. In 1926 she turned her attention to politics and joined the Conservative Party. She became the prospective parliamentary candidate for the Whitechapel district of London. She was the mother of two prominent feminists, *Dame Christabel Pankhurst* (1880–1958), the political leader of the suffragette movement, and *Sylvia Pankhurst* (1882–1960), who suffered nine times under the 'Cat and Mouse Act', was a pacifist in World War I, and a staunch supporter of the Ethiopian cause against Italy.

Perkins Gilman Charlotte 1860–1935. American feminist socialist lecturer, poet, novelist and historian. She described herself as a humanist. *The Yellow Wallpaper* 1892 is a fictional account of her own breakdown. She is best known as the author of *Women and Economics*, which became a feminist classic, proposing the ending of the division between 'men's work' and 'women's work' by abolishing housework. She wrote many books over the period 1900 to 1923 and from 1909 to 1916 wrote and published a magazine *The Forerunner* in which her feminist Utopian novel *Herland* 1915 was serialized. She committed suicide on discovering that she was dying of breast cancer.

Rich Adrienne 1929– . American radical feminist poet and writer. In the 1960s her poetry was closely involved with the student and anti-war movements in the USA but since then she has concerned herself with women's issues. In 1974, when given the National Book Award, she declined to accept it as an individual but with Alice Walker and Audrey Rich accepted it on behalf of all women. In 1976 she published *Of Woman Born*, on motherhood as a personal experience rather than as a institution, and *On Lies, Secrets and Silence*.

Rowbotham Sheila 1943– . British socialist feminist, historian, lecturer and writer. She first taught in schools and then became involved with the Workers Educational Association. An active socialist since the early 1960s, she has contributed to several left-wing journals. Her pamphlet *Women's Liberation and the New Politics* 1970 laid down the fundamental approaches and demands of the emerging British women's movement. Other publications include: *Hidden from History* 1973; *Women's Consciousness, Man's World* 1973 and *Beyond the Fragments* 1979.

Steinem Gloria 1934– . American journalist and liberal feminist who emerged as a leading figure in the American new women's movement in the late 1960s. She was also involved in other radical protest campaigns against racism and the Vietnam War. She co-founded the *Women's Action Alliance* in 1970 and also *Ms* magazine. In 1983 a collection of her best-known articles was published as *Outrageous Acts and Everyday Rebellions*.

Walker Alice 1944– . American poet, novelist, critic, and essay writer. She was active in the civil rights movement in the US in the 1960s and as a black woman has written about the double burden for women of racist and sexist oppression. She is consulting editor of *Ms* magazine and has taught both Women's and Black Studies. She has published three volumes of poetry, two collections of short stories, and three novels; *The Color Purple* 1983 won a Pulitzer Prize and has been made into a film.

Wollstonecraft Mary 1759–97. British feminist whose controversial book *Vindication of the Rights of Women* 1792 demanded equal educational opportunities for women. She joined a group of radical intellectuals called the English Jacobins. She married William Godwin and died in giving birth to a daughter, Mary, who was later to become Mary Shelley, the author of *Frankenstein*.

Woolf Virginia 1882–1941. British novelist, philosopher and critic, born Stephen. Her first novel *The Voyage Out* 1915 explores the tensions experienced by women who want marriage and a career. In *Mrs Dalloway* 1922, she perfected her 'stream of consciousness' technique. Among her later books are *To the Lighthouse* 1927, *Orlando* 1928, and *The Years* 1928, which considers the importance of economic independence for women. With her husband, Leonard Sidney Woolf, she founded the Hogarth Press in 1917. She committed suicide by drowning herself.

1562	Statute of Artificers made it illegal to employ men or women in a trade before they had served seven years' apprenticeship. (It was never strictly enforced for women, as many guilds still allowed members to employ their wives and daughters in workshops.)
1753	Lord Hardwick's Marriage Act brought marriage under state control and created a firmer distinction between the married and unmarried.
1803	Abortion was made illegal.
1836	Marriage Act reform permitted civil weddings and enforced the official registration of births, deaths and marriages.
1839	Custody of Infants Act allowed mothers to have custody of their children under seven years old.
1840s	A series of factory acts limited the working day and occupations of women and children. Bastardy amendment put all the responsibility for the maintenance of an illegitimate child on to its mother.
1857	Marriage and Divorce Act enabled a man to obtain divorce if his wife had committed adultery. (Women were only eligible for divorce if their husband's adultery was combined with incest, sodomy, cruelty, etc.)
1857–82	Married Women's Property Acts allowed them to own possessions of various kinds in their own right for the first time.
1861	Abortion became a criminal offence even if performed as a life saving act or done by the woman herself.
1862–70	Contagious Diseases Acts introduced compulsory examination of suspected prostitutes for venereal disease.
1860s	Fathers could be named and required to pay maintenance for illegitimate children.
1864	Schools Enquiry Commission recommendations led to the establishment of high schools for girls.
1867	Second Reform Act enfranchised the majority of male householders. First women's suffrage committee was formed in Manchester.
1869	Women ratepayers were allowed to vote in municipal (local) elections.
1871	Newham College, Cambridge, was founded for women.
1872	Elizabeth Garrett Anderson Hospital for women opened in London.
1874	London School of Medicine for women was founded.
1878	Judicial separation of married couples became possible. Maintenance orders could be enforced in court.
1880	TUC adopted principle of equal pay for women.
1882	Married Women's Property Act meant that wives were given legal control over their own earned income.
1883	Contagious Diseases Acts were repealed.
1885	Age of consent was raised to 16.

1887 National Union of Women's Suffrage Societies became a nationwide group under Millicent Fawcett.

1903 Women's Social and Political Union was founded by Emmeline and Christabel Pankhurst.

1905–10 Militant campaigns split WSPU. Sylvia Pankhurst formed East London Women's Federation.

1918 Parliament (Qualification of Women) Act gave the vote to women householders over 30.

1923 Wives were given equal rights to sue for divorce on the grounds of adultery.

1925 Guardianship of Infants Act gave women equal rights to the guardianship of their children.

1928 The 'Flapper' Vote: all women over 21 were given the vote.

1937 Matrimonial Causes Act gave new grounds for divorce including desertion for three years and cruelty.

1946 Royal Commission on equal pay was formed.

1944 Butler Education Act introduced free secondary education for all.

1948 Cambridge University allowed women candidates to be awarded degrees.

1960 Legal aid became available for divorce cases.

1967 Abortion Law Reform Act made abortion legal under medical supervision and within certain criteria.

1969 Divorce reform was introduced which reduced the time a petitioner needed to wait before applying for a divorce.

1973 Matrimonial Causes Act provided legislation to enable financial provision to be granted on divorce.

1975 Sex Discrimination and Equal Pay Acts. National and Scottish Women's Aid Federations were formed.

1976 Domestic Violence and Matrimonial Proceedings Act. Sexual Offences (Amendment) Act attempted to limit a man's defence of consent in rape cases.

1977 Employed married women's option to stay partially out of the National Insurance system was phased out. Women qualified for their own pensions.

1980 Social Security Act allowed a married woman to claim Supplementary Benefit and Family Income Supplement if she was the main breadwinner.

1983 Government forced to amend the 1975 Equal Pay Act to conform to EEC directives.

1984 Matrimonial and Family Proceedings Act made it less likely for a woman to be granted maintenance on divorce. It also reduced the number of years a petitioner must wait before applying for a divorce to one year.

1986 Granting of invalid care allowance was successfully challenged in European Court of Justice. Sex Discrimination Act (Amendment) allowed women to retire at the same age as men, and lifted legal restrictions preventing women from working night shifts in manufacturing industries. Firms with less than five employees were no longer exempt from the Act.

The Arts

The earliest art, whether painting or drama, literature or music, probably had magical and religious functions. The development of Western art, however, unlike the art of many other cultures, has been accompanied by a growing body of philosophy and criticism. Aesthetic criteria introduced by the ancient Greeks still influence our perceptions and judgements of art, notably the belief that art should represent or reflect reality, and that it should give pleasure and exaltation.

Two currents of thought run through our ideas about art. In one, derived from Aristotle, art is concerned with *mimesis* ('imitation'), the representation of appearances, and gives pleasure through the accuracy and skill with which it depicts the real world. The other view, derived from Plato, holds that the artist is inspired by the Muses (or by God, the inner impulses, or the collective unconscious) to express that which is beyond appearances – inner feelings, eternal truths, or the essence of the age.

Theorists have answered the question 'what is art?' in a number of different ways, and critics have talked about 'good art' and 'bad art'. The term art has been used at various times to refer to all the processes and products of human skill, imagination, or invention – the art of government, or the art of logic, for example, as well as the art of poetry. For in a broad sense, all art is the opposite of nature: this meaning is embodied in the contrast between 'artificial' – that is, created by people – and 'natural'.

This part of the Pocket Encyclopedia contains sections on the Visual Arts, Architecture, Cinema, Photography, Literature, Theatre, and Music and Dance. Each section focusses on a particular art, but also forms part of an overview of the arts in general. The art of theatre, for example, may combine elements of literature, music, and dance. The work of an individual artist, however outstanding, also needs to be set in the context of his or her society: an artist's theme and style, or mode of depicting, relate both to an inner vision and to the world outside.

Visual Arts

In the visual arts of Western civilizations, painting and sculpture have been the dominant forms for many centuries. This has not always been the case in other cultures. Islamic art, for example, is one of ornament, for under the Muslim religion artists were forbidden to usurp the divine right of creation by portraying living creatures. In some cultures masks, tattoos, pottery, and metalwork have been the main forms of visual art. In the recent past technology has made new art forms possible, such as photography and cinema, and today electronic media have led to entirely new ways of creating and presenting visual images.

This section first gives an overview of the main styles and movements in Western art, in a historical sequence: *Ancient Art* looks at prehistoric art, the art of early civilizations, the art of ancient Egypt, and the art of early Aegean civilizations. Then *Classical Art* looks at the art of ancient Greece and Rome. Next, *Medieval Art* looks at early Christian and Byzantine art, the art of the Dark Ages, and the art of the Middle Ages. This is followed by *The Italian Renaissance*, the art of *The 15th and 16th Centuries* in Northern Europe, England, and Spain, *The 17th Century* in Europe, *The 18th Century* in Europe, *The 19th Century* in Europe, and *The 20th Century*. Finally, *Eastern Art* looks briefly at the arts of Islamic civilizations, of China, of India, and of Japan. Within the historical sections, outstanding individual artists and their works have been selected to represent their period or movement: a table of *Great Artists* provides a biographical summary. Architecture, and the modern arts of Cinema and Photography, are treated in separate sections.

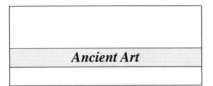

Ancient Art

prehistoric art 25,000–1000 BC. The history of the fine arts, painting and sculpture, begins about 21,000 BC in the Paleolithic, or Old Stone Age. Vivid, lifelike images of animals and humans have been found incised, painted or sculptured on the walls deep inside the caves where our ancestors sheltered, mostly in Spain and in south western France, but also in Portugal, Sicily, and Russia. The images of reindeer, mammoth, horses and bison are most common, varying from very small to almost lifesize. It is thought that they served as part of a 'magic' ritual to ensure a successful hunt. Paintings such as those at the cave of Lascaux in France show great skill in draughtsmanship, with vigorous and sweepingly graceful outlines. Stone Age people also used flint tools to carve small figurines in bone, horn, or stone. The most famous of these is the so-called Venus of Willendorf, a limestone statuette 4.5 in high, found in lower Austria and dating from about 21,000 BC. Her exaggeratedly bulbous form makes clear her magic significance as a fertility figure.

art of early civilizations 14,000–300 BC. Architecture became the new art form when people began to settle in communities as farmers rather than as hunters. They decorated their buildings with sculpture, imposing a sense of pattern and order on them, although Stonehenge in Britain 1800–1400 BC had not achieved this sophistication. In Europe, *Celtic art* ornamented tombs, crosses, metalwork and pottery with stylized animal and plant forms in swirling curvilinear patterns. Pottery had reached Europe from the Near East where it began as early as 5500 BC in Mesopotamia, where sign pictures also grew into cuneiform (wedge-shaped) writing. The Near and Middle East produced many highly developed urban civiliz-

ations, including the *Sumerian* 4000 BC, and the *Persian* 550 BC. In these cultures, sculptures and reliefs of people, gods, and animals decorated palaces, temples, and tombs telling stories or praising their gods and rulers. A fine example is the grand stairway of the *Persian royal palace*, Persepolis, from 518–516 BC. Outstanding examples of precious metalwork, glassware, and pottery also survive, of which there are splendid collections in the British Museum and the Louvre.

Egyptian art 3000–200 BC. The Great Sphinx at Giza 2680–2565 BC, a gigantic human-headed lion carved from an outcropping of natural rock, is the supreme example of Egyptian sculpture. 185 ft long and 63 ft high, it was meant to guard for eternity the god-king's pyramid tomb nearby. Most Egyptian art is funerary, largely consisting of sculptured relief panels painted in bright, lifelike colours covering the walls of tombs and temples. They depend on strong, simple outlines, the main aim being clarity: to picture in their idealized prime the dead, their servants and families, and the objects, animals, foods and activities they enjoyed so that they could be magically transported into the afterworld to be enjoyed forever. Human forms are recomposed almost diagrammatically to show the whole of a person, face and legs in profile, upper torso in front view, hips three-quarters and with the eye magnified. If anything needed further description a hieroglyphic label would be added. Statues, whether of wood or stone, were also generally painted. They retain a strong cubic sense of the block from which they were hewn, with the figures facing straight ahead, the arms in a single unit with the body. The serene vision of eternity found in all Egyptian art is epitomized in the beautiful portrait head of Queen Nefertiti in the Staatlich Museum, Berlin, dating from about 1360 BC.

art of Aegean civilizations 2800–100 BC. The *Minoan* and *Mycenean* civilizations flourished in the area of the Aegean Sea from about 2800 BC. Based on Crete, Minoan society was pleasure-loving and open, and its major monument, the new palace at Knossos 1700 BC, was decorated with cheerful frescoes of scenes from daily life, plants, birds and leaping fish and dolphins. Their pottery was painted in the same fresh, spontaneous style with plant and animal motifs curving to suit the form of the vases. In 1400 they were conquered by the Myceneans from the Peloponnese, whose art reflected its more warlike society. Instead of airy palaces, they constructed fortified citadels such as Mycenae itself, which was entered through the Lion Gate 1330, named for the remarkable monumental sculpture that adorns it. In the nearby Cyclades Islands a unique art form emerged about 2800: the small marble Cycladic figures much admired today, which represent the Great Mother Goddess in such streamlined simplicity that her face is simply an elongated oval with a triangular nose. Many of the ideas and art forms of these early sea-faring civilizations were to be adapted by the Greeks who came from Central Asia between 2000–1000 BC to establish their own splendid culture that was to dominate Western taste and thought for many centuries.

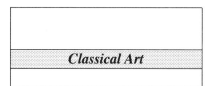

Classical Art

Greek art 1000–27 BC. Greek temples are almost sculptures in themselves, designed not to be entered but to be looked at. The sculptured reliefs which decorated them, such as the Elgin Marbles in the British Museum, which came from the Parthenon in Athens, show perfectly the Greek artistic ideal: the human form at its most beautiful.

The major periods of Greek art can be divided into the Archaic (late 8th century–480 BC), Classical (480–323 BC), and Hellenistic (323 –27 BC). No large-scale painting survives, although colour was very important, and even the white marble sculptures we admire today were originally brightly painted.

In the *Archaic* period the statues of naked standing men *kouroi* and draped females *korai* show an Egyptian influence in their rigid frontality. By about 500 BC the figure was allowed to relax its weight on to one leg and immediately seemed to come alive. The archaic smile which gave these early figures a certain cheerful sameness vanished in the *Classical* period when expressions assumed a dignified serenity. Further movement was introduced in new poses such as in Myron's bronze *Diskobolus/The Discus Thrower* 460–50 BC, and in the rhythmic Parthenon reliefs of men and horses supervised by Pheidias. Artists were no longer anonymous and among sculptors whose work is known are **Praxiteles**, **Scopas**, **Lysippus**, and **Polykleitos**, whose *Doryphoros/The Spear Carrier* 450–440 BC was of such harmony and poise that it set a standard for beautiful proportions which is still in use today. Praxiteles introduced the female nude into the sculptural repertory with the graceful *Aphrodite of Knidos* c. 350 BC. It was easier to express movement in bronze, hollow-cast by the lost wax method, but few bronze sculptures survive and many are known only through Roman copies in marble. The *Hellenistic* period, when the Greek Empire under Alexander the Great spread to Egypt and beyond Iraq, produced such sculptures as the *Winged Victory of Samothrace* with its dramatic drapery, the expressive *Dying Gaul* and the tortured *Laocoon*, which explored the effects of movement and of deeply-felt emotion.

Vase painting is the one form of Greek painting which has survived the centuries. Good, even great, artists worked as both potters and painters until the 5th century BC and the works they signed were exported throughout the Empire. Made in several standard shapes and sizes, the pottery served as functional containers for wine, water, and oil. The first decoration took the form of simple lines and circles, from which the *Geometric style* emerged near Athens in the 10th century BC. It consisted of precisely drawn patterns, the most characteristic being the key meander. Gradu-

213

ally the bands of decoration multiplied and the human figure, geometrically stylized, was added.

About 700 BC the potters of Corinth invented the *Black Figure* technique in which the unglazed red clay was painted in black with mythological scenes, gods and battles in a narrative frieze. About 530 BC Athenian potters reversed the process and developed the more sophisticated *Red Figure* pottery, which allowed for more detailed and elaborate painting of the figures in red against a black background. This grew increasingly naturalistic, with lively scenes of daily life. The finest examples date from the mid-6th century to mid-5th century BC at Athens. Later painters tried to follow major art trends and represent spatial depth, thus dissipating the unique quality of their fine linear technique.

The ancient Greeks excelled in carving gems and cameos, and in jewellery and metalwork. They also invented the pictorial mosaic and from the 5th century BC onwards floors were paved with coloured pebbles depicting mythological subjects. Later, specially cut cubes of stone and glass called *tesserae* were used, and Greek craftsmen working for the Romans reproduced famous paintings such as that of *Alexander at the Battle of Issus* from Pompeii, giving us some idea of these lost masterpieces.

Roman art 753 BC–410 AD. During the 8th century BC the Etruscans appeared as the first native Italian civilization, north and west of the river Tiber. Their art shows influences of archaic Greece and the Near East. Their coffins (*sarcophagi*), carved with reliefs and topped with portraits of the dead, reclining on one elbow as if at an eternal banquet, were to influence the later Romans and early Christians.

Under Julius Caesar's successor Augustus 27 BC–14 AD the Roman Empire was established. Art and architecture played an important role in unifying the European nations under Roman rule. The Romans greatly admired Greek art and became the first collectors, importing vast quantities of marbles and

bronzes, and even Greek craftsmen to make copies. Realistic portrait sculpture was an important original development by the Romans. A cult of heroes began and in public places official statues of generals, rulers and philosophers were erected. The portrait bust developed as a new art form from about 75 BC; these were serious, factual portraits of a rugged race of patriarchs to whose wisdom and authority their subject nations should reasonably submit.

Narrative relief sculpture also flourished in Rome, again linked to the need to commemorate publicly the glorious victories of their heroes. These appeared on monumental altars, triumphal arches and giant columns such as *Trajan's Column* 106–113 AD which records his historic battles like a strip cartoon, winding its way around the column for 656 ft. Strict realism in portraiture gave way to some Greek-style idealization in the propaganda statues of the emperors, befitting their semi-divine status. Gods and allegorical figures feature with Rome's heroes on such narrative relief sculptures as those on Augustus's giant altar to peace, the *Ara Pacis* 13–9 BC.

Very little *Roman painting* has survived, and much of what has is the volcanic eruption of Mount Vesuvius in 79 AD which buried the southern Italian seaside towns of Pompeii and Herculaneum under ash, thus preserving the lively and impressionistic wall paintings which decorated the holiday villas of an art-loving elite. Favourite motifs were illusionistic and still-life. A type of interior decoration known as *Grotesque*, rediscovered in Rome during the Renaissance, combined swirling plant motifs, strange animals and tiny fanciful scenes. Grotesque was much used in later decorative schemes whenever it was fashionable to quote the Classical period.

The art of *mosaic* was universally popular throughout the Roman Empire. It was introduced from Greece and used for floors as well as walls and vaults, in *trompe l'oeil* effects, geometric patterns and scenes from daily life and mythology.

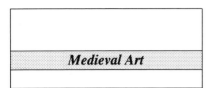

Medieval Art

early Christian and Byzantine art 330–1453 AD. In 313 the Emperor Constantine was converted to Christianity and made it one of the official religions of the Roman state. Churches were built, and artistic traditions adapted to the portrayal of the new Christian saints and symbols. Roman burial chests *(sarcophagi)* were adopted by the Christians and their imagery of pagan myths gradually changed into biblical themes.

Byzantine style developed in the East in Constantinople which in 330 became the headquarters of the Roman Empire. An Eastern Christian tradition was maintained there until 1453 when Constantinople was conquered by the Turks. The use of mosaic came to be associated with both Byzantine art and early Christian church decoration in the West. As Ravenna became the Western imperial capital in the 5th century, the ecclesiastical buildings there, built in the 5th and 6th centuries, are a glorious tribute to the art of mosaic, presenting powerful religious images on walls and vaults in brilliant, glittering colour. Byzantine art moved away from the natural portrayal of people and froze into stylization symbolizing the divine. Ornament flattened into intricate lacework patterns. Oriental, highly decorative and unchanging, the Byzantine style can be seen in the icons, often thought to be miracle-working, which have remained for centuries the main religious art of Greece and Russia.

art of the Dark Ages 252–900 AD. The 500 years between the fall of the Roman Empire and the establishment of Charlemagne's new Holy Roman Empire in 800 are known as the Dark Ages, and its art that of the *Migration Period*. Through a time of turmoil and invasion, with the northern 'barbarians' overrunning the old Mediterranean civilizations, the

Christian church maintained its stability and the interchange of artistic traditions fostered creativity.

The art of the migrant peoples consisted mainly of portable objects, articles of personal use or adornment. They excelled in metalwork and jewellery, often in gold with garnet or enamel inlays and ornamented with highly stylized, animal-based interlace patterns. This type of ornament was translated into manuscript illumination such as the decorated pages of the *Lindisfarne Gospel* in the British Museum which dates from the 7th century, or the 8th-century *Book of Kells* in Trinity College, Dublin. With Charlemagne's Christian Empire modelled on that of ancient Rome, a cultural renaissance ensued, drawing its inspiration from the late Classical artistic traditions of the early Christians. At Charlemagne's capital, Aachen, the human figure was reintroduced into art and continuous narrative was rediscovered in the *Tours Bibles* produced there. They in turn influenced the sculptured reliefs on the bronze doors at St Michael's Church, Hildesheim in Germany, dating from 1015, the first doors cast in one piece in the West since Roman times.

art of the Middle Ages 900–1400 AD. Under the unifying force of the Latin Church, a new civilization spread across Europe which during the 10th century produced a style in art called *Romanesque*, and in England, *Norman*. Chiefly evident in relief sculpture surrounding church portals, on capitals and corbels, it translated manuscript illuminations into stone, combining naturalistic elements from the antique Roman style with the fantastic, poetical, and pattern-loving Celtic and Germanic tradition. Imaginary beasts, monsters, saints and sinners mingle with humour and innocence in an enchanted world of biblical themes. Fine examples remain in Burgundy and south west France, extending down into Spain on the pilgrimage route to Santiago de Compostela.

Gothic during the late 12th and 13th centuries European cities began to raise great cathedrals, and the sculptural decoration became more monumental. The cathedrals of Chartres and Reims in France had such extensive sculptural programmes that many artists came from far afield to work and learn there. A new interest in the natural world is shown in such examples as the strikingly life-like founder figures of Naumberg Cathedral, East Germany, c. 1245, or in the naturalistic foliage on the capitals at Southwell in Nottinghamshire, England.

With the increased height of the cathedrals, stained glass windows became their new glory. Chartres, where an entire set of stained glass is preserved, awesomely illustrates the magical effect of coloured light seemingly suspended within its dark interior. Both windows and sculpture, by depicting the lives of the saints and texts from the bible, gave the faithful an encyclopedic view of the Christian history of the world.

Art patronage, although still mainly concerned with religious imagery, now burgeoned in the many small courts of Europe and under this influence art became more stylized, delicate and refined. Even the Virgin Mary was portrayed as an elegant young queen. In her most characteristic pose, holding the Christ child in her arms, her weight shifts gracefully on to one hip causing her body to form an S-curve and her drapery to fall into elegant folds. This figure stance, the 'Gothic sway', became a hallmark of the period. Court patronage produced exquisite small ivories, precious goldsmith's work, devotional books illustrated with miniatures, and tapestries which warmed cold castle walls, depicting romantic tales or the joys of springtime.

In Italy, the monumentality of the antique Roman past subdued the spread of northern Gothic ideas. A type of *Gothic Classicism* was developed by the sculptors Nicola and Giovanni **Pisano** (working 1258–1314), whose four great pulpits carved in relief (Siena, Pisa, Pistoia) show the influence of antique sarcophagi but also that of French Gothic in the dramatic expressiveness of their figures.

An innovative group of painters brought the art of *fresco painting*, always important in Italy, to a new height.

Giotto's cycle of the lives of Mary and Christ in the Arena Chapel, Padua c.1300 set a new standard for figural naturalism, seen as proto-Renaissance, and in the Town Hall of Siena Ambrogio **Lorenzetti** illustrated the effects of *Good and Bad Government* (1337) in panoramic townscapes and landscapes.

Panel painting, in jewel-like colours on a gold background, developed from Byzantine models, and the Sienese painter **Duccio**'s *Maestá* for the High Altar of Siena Cathedral (1308–11) achieved a peak of expressive power of line and colour. Simone **Martini** developed this into courtly refinement in both frescoes (for example Assisi, Siena) and panel paintings, and became a major influence on the *International Gothic* style which in the years around 1400 achieved the perfect mix of French courtliness and the Italian command of form, together with a delight in the observed details of nature. A magnificent example of this moment in art can be seen in the miniatures painted for the devotional book, the *Très Riches Heures du Duc de Berry*, by the Flemish **Limbourg** brothers in about 1415.

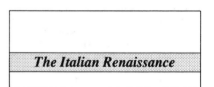

The Italian Renaissance

Florence the rebirth or 'Renaissance' of Classical art and learning began in Florence in the early 15th century. The self-made men of Florence, merchants and bankers, saw themselves as direct descendants of the great men of ancient Rome and, led by the Medici family, vied with each other in patronage of all the arts, building palaces and churches filled with sculptured and painted monuments to themselves. People, and the delightful world they lived in, were suddenly important.

The most far-reaching innovation of the period, which was one of continual discovery and rediscovery, was the invention of scientific *perspective* by Filippo **Brunelleschi** 1377–1446, the architect who later built the dome of Florence Cathedral. Perspective allowed artists to create an authentic three-dimensional space, correctly sized to the figures within their paintings. Pictorial illusionism was the game and anyone could play. **Masaccio** 1401–28 immediately seized on it for his frescoes in the Brancacci Chapel, Santa Maria del Carmine, in which the apostles look like Roman gods. The sculptor **Donatello** c.1386–1466 used perspective in his relief sculptures. His bronze statues like the youthful *David* 1430–32, the first free-standing nude since antiquity, or his equestrian statue of the mercenary General Gattamelata (Padua, 1443) look back to Classical prototypes but have the alert liveliness of all early Renaissance art. In his later work, such as his wood-carving of the aged Mary Magdalene 1445, he sought dramatic expression through distortion, even ugliness. His only real rival was the goldsmith and bronze sculptor Lorenzo **Ghiberti** 1378–1455, who only gradually adapted his graceful International Gothic style to Renaissance ideals in such works as the gilt-bronze Baptistery doors which Michelangelo called 'The Gates of Paradise'.

Paolo **Uccello**'s 1397–1475 decorative paintings reflect an obsessive interest in mathematical perspective.

Fra Angelico c.1400–55 used sweet colours and a delicately simple style to express his religious feeling. Andrea Del **Castagno**'s style was fiercely linear. The antithesis of his violent suffering figures are **Piero** della Francesca's strangely silent ones. Solidly rounded in pale light, immobile within perfect perspective spaces, they express an enigmatic timelessness. His mastery of geometry, proportion, form and colour is breathtakingly evident in his frescoes of *The Legend of the True Cross* in San Francesco in Arezzo 1452–66.

Many skilful sculptors produced public statues, grandiose tombs, Roman-style portrait busts and innumerable versions of the Madonna and Child. The Florentines enjoyed seeing themselves in religious paintings and they appear in crowd scenes in many magnifi-

cent frescoes in the churches of their city, such as those by Domenico del **Ghirlandaio**. He was the most popular painter in Florence in the latter part of the century, respected for his 'warts and all' honesty which is epitomized in his portrait of *An Old Man with a Child* c.1480 in the Louvre. His contemporaries included **Pollaiuolo**, whose interest centres on the nude in action, **Verrocchio**, famous for the equestrian statue of Bartolomeo Colleoni in Venice 1481–96, and **Botticelli** 1445–1510 whose poetic, gracefully linear paintings of Madonnas and mythological subjects such as *The Birth of Venus* 1482 show the Florentine ideal of female beauty. Almost every art work produced included some reference to antiquity, either in form or content.

Leonardo da Vinci 1452–1519. Through his genius, the art of the early 16th century became the *High Renaissance*, attaining a grandeur that appealed particularly to the popes, who now became the leading art patrons in their attempt to build the 'New Rome'. Leonardo's enquiring scientific mind led him to investigate every aspect of the natural world from anatomy to aerodynamics. His notebooks and drawings remain his finest legacy, but his experiments also revolutionized painting style. Instead of a white background, he used a dark one to allow the overlying colour a more three-dimensional existence. He invented 'aerial perspective' whereby the misty atmosphere (*sfumato*) blurs and changes the colours of the landscape as it dissolves into the distance. His principle of grouping figures within an imaginary pyramid, linked by their gestures and emotions, became a High Renaissance compositional rule. His *Madonna on the Rocks* (Louvre, Paris) exemplifies all these ideas.

Michelangelo Buonarroti 1475–1564. His giant talent dominated the High Renaissance, with no other artist able to escape his influence. He said of his stone carvings, such as the monumental *David* in Florence 1501–4 that he was simply revealing the figure hidden within the block. His massive figure style was translated into paint in the Sistine Chapel frescoes (Vatican, Rome) covering the ceiling with human figures, mostly nude, all grandly Classical, telling the Old Testament story from Genesis to the Deluge 1508–11 and finishing on the altar wall with a titanic *Last Judgement* 1541.

Raphael Santi 1483–1520. He quickly mastered the innovations of Leonardo and Michelangelo and in 1509 was commissioned to fresco the *Stanza della Segnature* in the Vatican, where his classicist *School of Athens* is his masterpiece. Immensely prolific and popular, he combined both sweetness and grandeur in his work.

Mannerism the next major art movement was heralded by Raphael's princial follower, Giulio **Romano**, who exaggerated Raphael's style into an individual one of his own. This flouted the 'rules' of Renaissance order and harmony by striving for idiosyncratic, sometimes alarming, effects. The Florentine **Andrea** del Sarto 1486–1531 and his assistants **Pontormo** and **Rosso** Fiorentino each pursued self-consciously mannered styles, as did Giorgio **Vasari**, who is chiefly remembered for his book *The Lives of the Most Excellent Architects, Painters and Sculptors* 1550 in which he himself coined the term 'Mannerist' and laid down the chronology of the history of art which is still in use today. Mannerism appealed particularly to courtly patrons and it became increasingly effete. The Medici, now Grand Dukes, employed such artists as the sculptor Benvenuto **Cellini**, as famous for his racy autobiography as for the gilt salt cellar he made for the King of France, Agnolo **Bronzino**, whose patrician portraits display a stony hauteur, and **Giovanni** da Bologna whose elegant small bronze statuettes were widely reproduced.

Venice the Venetian Renaissance was slow in coming because of the city's traditional links with the East. Two non-Venetians were influential: **Antonello** da Messina c. 1430–79, who in 1475 brought to Venice the new Flemish technique of oil painting, and Andrea **Mantegna** c. 1431–1506, an archaeologically-minded painter whose figures looked like antique sculptures. Giovanni **Bellini** c. 1430–

1516 specialized in devotional pictures of the Madonna, but his sensitive appreciation of light and colour introduced that sensual Venetian talent which later made **Titian** (Tiziano Vecelli) 1487–1576 the preferred painter of the Emperor Charles V and his son Philip II of Spain. His fellow-painter **Giorgione** died young, leaving only a few mysteriously poetic works. **Veronese** (c. 1528–88) and Jacopo **Tintoretto** 1518–94 worked on a much larger scale, Veronese excelling in sumptuous *trompe l'oeil* interior decorations and Tintoretto in dramatic religious paintings, spectacularly lit and composed with daring foreshortening. His paintings for the Venetian Scuola di San Rocco 1566–88 in their exciting exuberance foreshadow the next major movement, the *Baroque*.

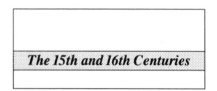

The 15th and 16th Centuries

Northern Europe took its artistic inspiration from Gothic sources, always more precious and less monumental than the Italians, but shared their insatiable interest in realistic portrayals of themselves and their world.

Netherlands one of the first examples of the new *humanism* is in the work of Claus **Sluter** c. 1380–1406. His mourning figures on the tomb of Philip the Bold, Duke of Burgundy, their faces hidden by the hoods of their robes, are poignantly mute but solidly real people.

In Flanders, where the patrons were wealthy merchants, Robert **Campin** 1378–1444 put his *Madonna and Child before a Firescreen* 1420–30 (National Gallery, London) into an ordinary living room and through its open window showed a Flemish town. Mary's halo is replaced by the circular firescreen behind her, an example of disguised symbolism, making the supernatural seem real.

Among Campin's followers, all marvellous

draughtsmen, was Jan **van Eyck** d.1441 whose strength lay in his detailed analysis of the beauty of the world around him. His personal recipe for oil painting, a stunning innovation, makes his colours glow like precious jewels. In his *Arnolfini Wedding* 1434 (National Gallery, London) the bride and groom appear in a domestic interior crammed with disguised symbols, in a kind of pictorial marriage certificate. Flemish realism reached Italy with the Portinari Altarpiece, an *Adoration of the Shepherds* by Hugo van der **Goes** d. 1481. Commissioned by the Medici agent in Bruges, it was sent to Florence where it had a considerable effect on Italian artists. The quietly contemplative portraits of Hans **Memlinc** d. 1481 sum up the achievement of 15th-century Netherlands painters.

Individual styles proliferated in the 16th century. Hieronymous **Bosch** c. 1450–1516 painted nightmare pictures filled with tiny human figures caught in a surrealist demonic world. Pieter **Bruegel** the Elder 1525/30–69 treated biblical subjects as contemporary events, sympathetically viewing a miserable humanity. In his paintings of the seasons 1565 he brilliantly evokes both winter's icy silence and the golden warmth of summer.

Germany the giant among German artists was Albrecht **Dürer** 1471–1528. His intellectual powers put him in line with the great Italian masters and their influence introduced a new solidity of form into his basically Gothic style. Particularly important as a graphic artist, he was widely influential through woodcuts and engravings. Mathias **Grünewald** c. 1460–1528, a tragic visionary, used colour symbolically in the Isenheim Altar in Colmar 1512–15, painted for hospital patients to see his Crucified Christ, covered with festering wounds, sharing their suffering. Lucas **Cranach** the Elder 1473–1538 painted self-conscious courtly nudes, and Albrecht **Altdorfer** c. 1489–1538 painted landscapes in which tiny human figures are dwarfed by nature's immensity.

Spain Philip II did not care for the work of **El Greco** 1541–1614, the painter who really established Spain as an artistic centre. Trained in Venice, and particularly influenced by Tintoretto, he developed his hallucinatory style in Toledo, where his patrons were ecclesiastics and the intelligentsia. In his *Burial of Count Orgaz* 1586 the flame-like figures and unearthly colours typically blend mystic vision and reality.

England Renaissance ideas arrived with the German Hans **Holbein** the Younger 1497–1543, by 1536 court painter to Henry VIII. His piercing portraits of the king and his wives, and his delicate portrait drawings, give a superb pictorial record of the Tudor court. The court of Elizabeth I comes to life for us through the art of the miniature. Nicholas **Hilliard** c. 1547–1619 developed an unparalleled technique, delicate, refined and often lyrically poetic as in his *Young Man Amid Roses* c. 1590, (Victoria and Albert Museum, London).

France Jean **Fouquet** c. 1420–81 painted miniatures as well as altarpieces in which Italian influences take tangible shape. Jean **Clouet** d. 1541 and his son François d. 1572 were court painters to King Francis I. Jean Clouet's portrait of the king splendidly expresses his concern with elegance and decoration, and François' half-nude portrait of Diane de Poitiers, *The Lady in Her Bath*, is a piece of refined eroticism. His style reflects Italian Mannerist ideas as developed by the so-called *School of Fontainebleau* founded by **Rosso** Fiorentino and **Primataccio** who came to decorate the royal hunting lodge in the 1530s. They devised a unique type of stucco decoration combining figures in high relief with decorative swags, cartouches and strapwork. These Mannerist motifs were copied all over northern Europe, where they were called 'Renaissance'.

The 17th Century

Italy in Rome, the Counter Reformation of the Catholic church against Protestantism launched an exciting, emotionally appealing new style, the *Baroque*. The sculptor-architect Gianlorenzo **Bernini** 1598–1680 was its principal exponent, revitalizing Rome with his exuberantly dramatic masterpieces. His *Ecstasy of St Teresa* at Santa Maria della Vittoria is a theatrical set-piece in which supernatural light pours from a hidden window to illuminate the rapturous saint whose body seems to shudder as an angel prepares to pierce her heart with the arrow of divine love.

Large-scale illusionistic fresco painting transformed ceilings into heavens, thronged with flying saints and angels. A spectacular example is **Pietro** da Cortona's colossal *Allegory of Divine Providence* 1629–37 in the Barberini Palace, glorifying the pope and his family. Hundreds of figures are drawn upwards towards God's golden light in which swarm bees, the Barberini family emblem.

Balancing this flamboyant artistic stream were the *Classicists*, who even in religious commissions looked back to the concepts of harmony and order of antiquity. Annibale **Carracci** 1560–1609 in the years around 1600 decorated Cardinal Farnese's gallery of antique sculpture in the Farnese Palace, turning the walls and ceiling into a *trompe l'oeil* classical picture gallery. He also initiated the landscape as a new category of art with his *Flight into Egypt* 1603, which has as its real subject an idealized vision of the classical Roman countryside, harmonious and calm.

Among Annibale's assistants who became famous in their own right were the consistently classicizing **Domenichino** 1581–1641 and Guido **Reni** 1575–1642 who often succumbed to popular taste with emotional paintings of repentant sinners rolling tearful eyes towards heaven.

The work of Michelangelo Merisi da **Caravaggio** 1573–1619 introduced something totally different and unique, a harsh realism in which ordinary folk with dirty feet appear as saints and apostles lit by a raking spotlight, as if God's piercing eye had picked them out from the surrounding blackness of sin. One of his most striking followers was Georges de **La Tour** 1593–1652, a French artist whose simplified figures assume a spiritual purity, modelled by God's light in the form of a single candle shining in the darkness.

France art was used to establish the splendour of Louis XIV's centralized authority and divine kingship. Although grandiose in the extreme, the decorative schemes, portraits and history paintings produced by the members of the new artists' Academy (formed 1648) were based on Classical rules, rigidly controlled by Charles **Lebrun** 1619–90, who was appointed First Painter to the King in 1662. He was the first director of the Academy and of the Gobelins Manufactory, which employed its members to produce the art, tapestries and furnishings for Louis's new Palace of Versailles.

The two major French artists of the century lived in Rome, escaping the constricting grip of the Academy. **Claude** Lorrain 1600–82 was the first painter to specialize entirely in landscapes, reducing the story-telling elements to small foreground figures. The romantic suggestiveness of the Classical past appealed to him, and he created an enchanting idyllic world, luminous and poetic. The intellectual Nicolas **Poussin** 1594–1665 composed his classical landscapes with mathematical precision, but his people remained important, noble and heroic. Not even his religious works escape the pervasive influence of antiquity. In his *Last Supper* 1647 (Edinburgh) Christ and the disciples lounge on couches as if at a Roman banquet.

Spain as in Rome, art in Spain aimed to excite Counter-Reformation zeal. José **Ribera** 1591–1652 carried a Caravaggesque style to brutal extremes to shock people into identifying with the sufferings inherent in Christian history. Francisco **Zurbarán** 1598–1664 expressed religious feeling in the opposite way, with solemn, silent monks and saints lost in a private world of meditation. Bartolomé Estebán **Murillo** 1617–82 painted sentimental Holy Families and sugar-sweet Madonnas fluently, cheerfully, and with a graceful feather touch and lovely colours.

Diego Rodriguez de Silva **Velazquez** 1599–1660 was the giant of Spanish painting, reflecting many aspects of the 17th-century Spanish world. By 1623 he was court painter to Philip IV in Madrid, where he was influenced by Philip's collection of 16th-century Venetian paintings. The most fascinating of his lifelike portraits of the Spanish court is *Las Meninas/ The Ladies-in-Waiting* 1655, a complex group portrait which includes Velazquez himself at his easel, and the king and queen as pale reflections in a mirror.

Netherlands Peter Paul **Rubens** 1577–1640 brought the sensual exuberance of the Italian Baroque to the Netherlands. A many-sided genius, artist, scholar and diplomat, he used his powerful pictorial imagination to create, with an army of assistants, innumerable religious and allegorical paintings for the churches and palaces of Catholic Europe. His largest commission was the cycle of 21 enormous canvases allegorizing the life of Marie de Medici, Queen of France (Louvre, Paris). His sheer delight in life can be seen in his magnificent colours, opulent nudes and expansive landscapes.

Rubens's Grand Baroque style did not suit the Protestant merchants of the new Dutch Republic, who wanted small paintings reflecting their own lives and interests. Among the artists who responded to this demand, the towering genius was **Rembrandt** van Rijn 1606–69, all of whose paintings hint at some inner drama. In his portraits and biblical scenes he saw light as a spiritual mystery which momentarily allows his characters to loom out of the surrounding shadows. His self-portraits (nearly 100 in number) touchingly trace the drama of his own passage through life and even the large group portrait, *The Night Watch* 1642 becomes a suspense story. A master draughtsman and printmaker, over 1,000 drawings survive.

The greatest of the straightforward portraitists was Frans **Hals** 1581/5–1666 whose free brush strokes caught fleeting moments brilliantly in such paintings as the so-called *Laughing Cavalier* 1624.

Genre pictures, scenes of daily life, merrymakers and peasants, often uncouth, comic or satirical, were the speciality of such painters as Jan **Steen** 1626–79 in whose anecdotal scenes of traditional festivals or slovenly households the pleasures of drink, gluttony and wantonness hold sway.

During the 1650s genre painters took a different view of their society. Instead of depicting boisterous low-life, painters like Pieter de **Hooch** 1629–84 chose scenes of domestic virtue, well-ordered households where families live in harmony in quiet sunlit rooms. Jan **Vermeer** 1632–75 was the greatest master of these scenes of peaceful prosperity, arranging domestic interiors as if they were abstract forms and enclosing his characters within an enamelled world of pearly light. *A Young Woman Standing at a Virginal* (National Gallery, London) is a superb example of the small group of paintings he produced, each one a masterpiece.

The Dutch specialities of seascape and landscape changed dramatically during the century, with the emphasis on low horizons and a great expanse of sky. Experts in this were Aelbert **Cuyp** 1620–91 who bathed his views in a golden light, and Jacob van **Ruisdael** 1638/9–1709, who painted in many moods, responding to the shifting patterns of light and shade in nature.

Still-life painting also burgeoned: fruit, flowers, fish, banquets, breakfasts, groaning boards of every kind, in which the artist displayed skill in painting inanimate objects, often with a hidden religious significance.

England Charles I had employed Rubens to paint the ceiling of the Banqueting House in

Whitehall 1629–30. Rubens's assistant Anthony **van Dyck** became court painter in 1632 and created magnificent portraits of the aristocracy, cool and elegant in shimmering silks. The German Peter **Lely** succeeded him under the Restoration to depict a society that exudes an air of well-fed decadence. By contrast, the English-born Samuel **Cooper** 1609–72, painter to the Parliamentarians and most famous for his portraits of Oliver Cromwell ('warts and all'), was a miniaturist whose serious, objective portraits raised the status of his art to that of oil painting.

The 18th Century

France the beginning of the 18th century saw the start of a frivolous new style in art, the *Rococo*. Jean-Antoine **Watteau** 1684–1721 devised for his aristocratic patrons the *Fête Gallante*, a type of painting in which amorous couples in poetic landscapes contemplate the transience of life and love.

The more overtly sensual work of François **Boucher** 1703–70, First Painter to Louis XV, included voluptuous scenes of naked gods and goddesses. Painting at the same time, but completely against the mainstream, was Jean-Baptiste-Siméon **Chardin** 1699–1779, whose still-lifes and genre scenes have a masterful dignity. Jean-Honoré **Fragonard** 1732–1806 continued with the Rococo theme under Louis XVI, light-heartedly reflecting the licentiousness of courtly life, but all this changed with the Revolution and in 1789 Neo-Classicism became the dominant style under the Republic. Its artistic dictator, Jacques-Louis **David** 1748–1825 in his *Death of Marat* turned a political murder into a classical tragedy. Later, under Napoleon's Empire, David painted heroic portraits and scenes celebrating its glory.

Italy Antonio **Canova** 1757–1822, the sculptor, also exalted Napoleon and his family in classicizing portraits, and the vogue for this style dominated most English and European sculpture right through the Victorian era. Rococo illusionistic fresco painting in Italy was the special province of Giovanni-Battista **Tiepolo** 1696–1770, a Venetian who decorated palaces and churches there and elsewhere in Europe. His painted ceilings became vast, airy regions whose delicate colour shadings made the sky seem endless.

The *vedutisti* (view-painters) produced souvenir views for the English gentlemen on the Grand Tour to complete their education with a first-hand sight of Renaissance and Classical art. In Venice, Francesco **Guardi** 1712–93 painted atmospheric visions of the floating city, pulsating with life. The views of (Giovanni) Antonio **Canaletto** 1697–1768, though faithfully observed, are static in comparison.

In Rome, Giovanni Battista **Piranesi** 1720–78 produced etchings inspired by his feeling for the poetry of ruins. His most original work, however, was a series which turned the ruins into images of terrifying imaginary prisons, fantasies of architectural madness.

Spain produced one artist of enormous talent and versatility at this time, Francisco de **Goya** y Lucientes 1746–1828, whose work expresses a wide range of feeling and emotion and explores a variety of themes. Court painter to Charles IV and later to Joseph Bonaparte under the French occupation of Spain, his portraits were acutely perceptive, his war scenes savagely dramatic, his religious paintings believable and his strange late fantasies powerfully imaginative. He is often seen as the source of 20th-century art.

England produced a memorable group of fine artists, each expressing the varied interests of the age. Joseph **Wright** of Derby 1734–97, scientifically-minded, painted such scenes as *Experiment with an Air Pump* 1768. George **Stubbs** 1724–1806 specialized in horse paintings, based on painstaking scientific investigation. Sir Joshua **Reynolds** 1723–92, first president of the Royal Academy (founded

1768) wanted to introduce the *European Grand Manner* into English painting with history paintings on exalted themes of heroism, but the demand was for portraits and his were confident but lacking in spontaneity, based more on theory than on inspiration.

Thomas **Gainsborough** 1727–88 was also a popular portraitist, although he would have preferred to paint landscapes and made much of them in the backgrounds of his pictures. William **Hogarth** 1697–1764 is best known through engravings of his satirical series of paintings such as *The Rake's Progress*.

Reacting against the academic theorizing of Reynolds, the poet William **Blake** 1757–1827 illustrated his writings with mystical visions and the imaginative Henry **Fuseli** 1741–1825 plundered the depths of his subconscious for grotesque and fantastic dream images in such paintings as *The Nightmare* 1782.

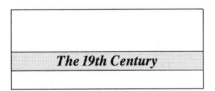

The 19th Century

The 19th century was the age of industrialization, when the newly powerful middle classes became patrons of art.

France vast historical, religious and mythological pictures were no longer greatly in demand and after the fall of Napoleon in 1814 French artists trained in the *Academic Grand Manner* had to seek new dramatic themes. They looked to the world around them, and Theodore **Géricault** 1791–1824 found his subject in the gruesome sufferings of the survivors of a recent shipwreck which he portrayed in his huge *Raft of the Medusa* 1816 (Louvre, Paris). His desire to express and evoke emotion put Géricault among the *Romantics* whose art sought to speak passionately to the heart, in contrast to the *Classicists* who appealed to the intellect. These two opposing approaches dominated much of the art of the century.

Eugène **Delacroix** 1798–1863 became the best-known Romantic painter. His *Massacre of Chios* 1824 (Louvre) shows Greeks enslaved by wild Turkish horsemen, a contemporary atrocity. Admired as a colourist, he used a technique of divided brushwork – adjacent brush marks of contrasting colour which the eye mixes as it scans – which anticipates the Impressionists. He learned this from seeing Constable's *Hay Wain* when it was exhibited in Paris in 1824.

By contrast, the brushwork is invisible in the enamelled paintings of Jean-Auguste-Dominique **Ingres** 1780–1867, the leading exponent of French Neo-Classicism. Drawing was the foundation of his style, emphasizing line and control at the expense of colour and expression.

Gustave **Courbet** 1819–77, reacting against both Classicists and Romantics, set out to establish a new *Realism*, based solely on direct observation of the things around him. His *Burial at Ornans* 1850 showed ordinary working people gathered round a village grave and shocked the Establishment art world with its 'vulgarity' and 'coarseness'. Another Realist was Honoré **Daumier** 1808–79 whose lithographs of the 1830s dissected Parisian society with a surgeon's scalpel.

Throughout Europe, 19th-century artists found their ideal subject matter in the landscape. In France, Jean-Baptiste-Camille **Corot** 1796–1875 made it acceptable by recomposing his open-air studies into a harmonious, classical whole, although a romantic mood pervades his later misty confections. Theodore **Rousseau** 1812–67 led a group of artists who in 1844 sought refuge from the Industrial Revolution in the woods of Barbizon near Paris. Their close observation of nature produced a new awareness of its changing moods. Jean-François **Millet** 1814–75 also settled at Barbizon but his romantic landscapes, such as *The Angelus* 1857–59 (Louvre), introduce idealized peasants who manage to commune with nature while toiling to wrest it from their daily bread.

Germany a different, more melancholy Romantic sensibility invaded the landscapes of a small group of painters working in Germany.

223

Seeking to express the mystery of God in nature and people's oneness with it, the evocative paintings of Caspar David **Friedrich** 1774–1840 usually include a small poetic figure contemplating distant mountain peaks or moonlit seashores.

England the two greatest artists of the century were landscapists: Joseph Mallord William **Turner** 1775–1851 and John **Constable** 1776–1837, both finding inspiration in the thriving English watercolour school. Turner was the master painter of English Romanticism. Not concerned with the human figure, it was always through nature itself that he could express human feeling, as in the poignant last voyage of the ship *The Fighting Temeraire* 1839 (Tate Gallery, London). His increasing obsession with light and its deep emotional significance turned his late pictures into misty abstract visions. Reputedly his dying words were 'The sun is God'.

Constable was also fascinated with the effects of light. He made innumerable painted sketches of the changing windy sky and in his *Hay Wain* 1821 used white marks like snowflakes to express the way light gives the landscape its freshness and sparkle. His technique of broken brush strokes gave great vibrancy and life to his colours and portended the developments of Impressionism.

Although primarily interested in romantic literary or biblical themes, the *Pre-Raphaelite* movement led by Dante Gabriel **Rossetti** in the 1840s and 1850s, took a detailed look at nature in their claim to a realistic vision, from which the medievalist designer-artist William **Morris** 1834–96 developed his stylized patterns of leaves and flowers for fabrics and wallpapers.

The opposition to the Pre-Raphaelites was led by two Establishment artists, Frederic, Lord **Leighton** 1830–96 and Sir Lawrence **Alma-Tadema** 1836–1912, whose equally romantic view pretended to Classicism by centring on pseudo genre scenes of daily life in ancient Greece and Rome. This pleased their educated patrons enough to earn knighthoods for them both.

Impressionism in the second half of the century in France took an innovative look at nature. A direct precursor was Edouard **Manet** 1832–83, who carried on Courbet's scientific spirit of realism, making the eye the sole judge of reality. Stylistically, he gave up modelling forms in volume to suggest them by juxtaposed colours and gradations of tones, and like Courbet the subject matter of his pictures was always modern life. His *Déjeuner sur l'herbe/Luncheon on the Grass* (Louvre) updated a Renaissance prototype to 1862.

The Impressionists delighted in depicting real life but the scenes and objects they painted became increasingly less important than the way they were affected by the ever-changing play of light. Evolving in the 1860s, the Impressionist group painted out of doors, capturing the immediacy and freshness of light on rippling water or on moving leaves. To catch these fleeting moments they broke up the forms they painted into fragments of pure colour laid side by side directly on the canvas, rather than mixing them on a palette. The members of the group were Alfred **Sisley** 1839–99, Camille **Pissarro** 1831–1903, Claude **Monet** 1840–1926 whose *Impression, Sunrise* of 1872 gave the movement its name, Pierre-Auguste **Renoir** 1841–1919, and Edgar **Degas** 1834–1917.

By the late 1870s they had each gone on to pursue individual interests, and the acceptance of a common purpose had had its day. Sisley and Pissarro continued painting landscapes, but Renoir was more interested in the female nude and Degas in 'snapshot' studies of dancers and jockeys. Monet remained obsessed with the optical effects of light on colour and carried his original fragmented technique to the final extreme in series of paintings such as those of the façade of Rouen Cathedral 1894 or his famous water lilies, showing the changing colour effects at different times of day. With these variations on a theme the actual subject did not matter at all, and in this he anticipated the abstract art of the 20th century.

Post-Impressionism other artists of the same generation who used the innovations of the Impressionists as a basis for developing their own styles are called the Post-Impressionists. They include Paul **Cézanne** 1839–1906 ,who infused something more permanent into their spontaneous vision by using geometrical shapes to form a solid scaffolding for his pictorial compositions, and Georges **Seurat** 1859–91, who achieved greater structure in his landscapes through the technique of *Pointillism* (also known as *Neo-Impressionism*) which turns the Impressionist's separate brush-strokes into minute points of pure colour. The eye then mixes these for itself. Green grass, for instance, is made up of closely packed points of blue and yellow. In this painstaking method any idea of spontaneity vanishes, and the effect is stable and serene.

Henri de **Toulouse-Lautrec** 1864–1901 portrayed the low-life of Parisian bars and music halls without sentiment or judgement. Like Degas, he recorded contemporary life in informal poses from odd angles and his bold, colourful posters show the influence of Japanese colour prints.

The great Dutch individualist Vincent **van Gogh** 1853–90 longed to give visible form to every emotion and used violent rhythmic brushwork and brilliant unnatural colours to express his inner passions, even in something as simple as a pot of sunflowers. Paul **Gauguin** 1848–1903 also went beyond the Impressionists' notion of reality, seeking a more direct experience of life in the magical rites of so-called primitive peoples in his colourful works from the South Seas.

Symbolism was a movement initiated by poets as a reaction to materialist values, and their 1886 Manifesto sought to re-establish the imagination in art. Their most admired painter was Gustave **Moreau** 1826–98 whose paintings of biblical and mythological subjects contain psychological overtones expressed through exotic settings, strange colours and eerie light. Odilon **Redon** 1840–1916 translated dreams into bizarre and striking visual images.

The Nabis (Hebrew 'prophet') were followers of Gauguin who used simple forms and flat colours as he did for emotional effect, in a new style called *synthetisme*. Among the Nabis, Pierre **Bonnard** 1867–1947 and Edouard **Vuillard** 1868–1940 were less concerned with mystical ideas and found that with contemporary domestic interiors they could develop their interest in sumptuously coloured and patterned surfaces. Their work was dubbed *intimisme*.

sculpture the work of the Parisian Auguste **Rodin** 1840–1917 shows an extraordinary technical facility and a deep understanding of the human form. A romantic realist who infused his forms with passion, such famous sculptures as *The Thinker* and *The Kiss* were originally designed for a never completed giant set of bronze doors, *The Gates of Hell*, a theme taken from Dante's *Divine Comedy*. The Musée Rodin in Paris houses many examples of his work and their preparatory drawings.

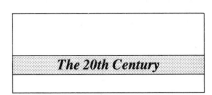

The 20th Century

The 20th century has been an age of '-isms' in art. Using their newly-won freedom, artists created such a bewildering variety of art that categorization became necessary. During the century the theory behind a work of art gradually became more important. The Post-Impressionist and Symbolist ideas of delving within the self to express the invisible were developed by Matisse, Picasso, and many other artists. Each successive movement in art shocked the public but, at the same time, many artists were producing individual works quite separate from these movements.

Pablo **Picasso** 1881–1973, the Spanish painter, was the artistic giant of the 20th century. His masterly draughtsmanship, visual intelligence, and immense originality made him the source of many revolutionary changes. His *Les Demoiselles d'Avignon* 1907 was inspired by Cézanne and by African art in its simplified forms and distortions of shape and colour. In addition to producing the first Cubist painting, Picasso was also regarded as a founder of Surrealism, but in the 1930s his work took on a more serious foreboding and anguished aspect, culminating in *Guernica* 1936, where all his expressive innovations are used to show the universal horror felt in the civilized world by Franco's bombing of a Basque town in the Spanish Civil War. He continued to paint into his 80s, having also become an original sculptor and potter. Picasso's overwhelming creativity has impressed his genius and original vision on the world.

Fauvism was a movement which began in France about 1905. The *Fauves* (French 'wild beasts') exaggerated reality, contorted shapes and heightened colours to show they were painting more than what they saw in nature. Henri **Matisse** 1869–1954, the leader of the movement, spent his life working on the basic expressionism of colour and form, greatly influencing 20th-century art and art theory. André **Derain** 1880–1954 developed further Gauguin's style of *cloisonnisme*, using large areas of solid colour. Maurice **de Vlaminck** 1876–1958 exaggerated Van Gogh's heavy outlines, and Georges **Rouault** 1871–1958 used heavy dark colours for his moral themes of sad Messiah-like clowns, prostitutes, and evil lawyers. Although the Fauve movement only lasted until 1908, it was the foundation of French *Expressionism*.

Cubism Together with Georges **Braque** 1882–1963 Picasso developed *Cubism* and introduced such techniques as collage, with cut-up photographs, printed texts, and objects included in the painting. Cubism avoided emotional and narrative expression to depict almost colourless shapes split up into a series of semi-geometric facets overlapping, interlocking and semi-transparent as though seen from different viewpoints. The aim was to show objects as they are known to be rather than as they happen to look at a particular moment. Cubism announced that a work of art exists in its own right rather than as a representation of the real world, and it attracted such artists as

Juan Gris, Albert Gleizes, Fernand Leger, Jean Metzinger, and Robert Delauney.

Futurism the Italian poet Filippo **Marinetti** 1876–1944 published the *Futurist Manifesto* in 1909 urging Italian artists to join him in Futurism. They eulogized the modern world and the 'beauty of speed and energy' in their works, trying to capture the dynamism of a speeding motor car or train by combining the shifting geometric planes of Cubism with vibrant colours. Gino Severini painted a topsy-turvy landscape as if seen from the moving window of a *Suburban Train Arriving at Paris* 1915 (Tate Gallery) and Giacomo **Balla** represented the abstract idea of speed by the moving object in such pictures as *Abstract Speed-wake of a Speeding Car* 1919 (Tate Gallery). Umberto *Boccioni*, a sculptor, froze his figures as if they were several frames of a film moving at once.

Vorticism was a similar movement in Britain, led by Percy **Wyndham Lewis** 1884–1957. It uses angular abstract shapes to excite the eye into the sensation of movement.

Expressionism Germany was the scene of two successive Expressionist groups. In 1905 a group of artists in Dresden started *Die Brücke* ('The Bridge'), developing Fauve ideas. Led by Ernst Ludwig **Kirchner** 1880–1938, they sought to charge everything with spiritual significance, using raw colours to express different emotions. The group broke up in 1913. In Munich *Der Blaue Reiter* ('The Blue Rider') group was set up in 1911 by Wassily *Kandinsky* 1866–1944 who painted the first *abstract* or *non-objective* painting. The English artist Roger *Fry* called Kandinsky's work 'pure visual music' when it was shown in London in 1913.

Suprematism Kasimir **Malevich** 1878–1935, working in Russia with Futurist ideas of dynamism and Cubist ideas of expressing more than the physical, juxtaposed simple geometrical shapes of solid colour to describe the supremacy of feeling in creative art, calling it Suprematism. From the first of these works in 1913, each one became simpler until there was only a white square on a black background and finally a white square on a white background, the ultimate in spiritual enlightenment. With the square indiscernable from the background, this is the first work where the idea is more important than the result.

Constructivism was a contemporary movement in Moscow which rejected the past and invented images for the new age. Naum **Gabo** 1890–1977 made scaffolding-like giant heads showing that what is beneath the surface of anything is more important than the surface. He and Vladimir **Tatlin** 1885–1953 described intangible time through three-dimensional progressions of stretched string, forcing the eye to travel along them and so 'through time'. They aimed to create art for the Revolution which, however, rejected them.

De Stijl Piet **Mondrian** 1872–1944, the Dutch painter, like Malevich, tried to express the 'truths of the Universe' through pure aesthetics. Using primary colours, black, white, and mid-grey, he painted parallel horizontal lines which intersected vertical ones. The perfection described by the parallel lines, the right-angle intersections, and the rectangles of pure colour mirrored the ultimate perfection of the universe. In 1917 he headed a group called De Stijl ('The Style') which included Theo **van Doesburg** 1883–1931. They believed in the concept of the 'designer', that all life, work, and leisure should be surrounded by art. Everything functional should be aesthetic as well.

Dada, so called for its infantile associations, was a movement born around 1915 out of the desire to shock, and to question established artistic rules and values. Much of it was impermanent, performance art which lasts only as long as it is performed, or made from the ephemeral waste products of society. In Germany Kurt **Schwitters** 1887–1948 and Max **Ernst** 1891–1976 created collages of disposable rubbish such as bus tickets and advertisements. Marcel **Duchamp** 1887–1968, who produced humorous pastiches of other artists, reduced the creative act to one of choice by putting everyday items like a bicycle wheel mounted on a kitchen stool on display and calling them 'ready-mades'.

Surrealism Dada was short-lived yet many

aspects survived into Surrealism. Max Ernst and Jean (Hans) **Arp** 1887–1966, both Dadaists, developed paintings which juxtaposed everyday objects and themes in bizarre, dream-like ways, as did the Italian Giorgio **de Chirico** 1887–1978. The writer André Breton (1896–1966) published the first *Surrealist Manifesto* in 1924, which based itself on Freud's new discovery of the subconscious and the importance of dreams in psychoanalysis. René **Magritte** 1898–1967 painted dream-world scenes filled with Jungian symbolism and humorous couplings of illusion and reality. Salvador **Dali** 1904– used photographic clarity to depict contorted landscapes and figures which seem both familiar and disconcerting.

The 1930s produced some remarkable individual talents, with France becoming less and less the centre of the art world. In Britain Paul **Nash** 1889–1946 and Graham **Sutherland** 1903–80 turned their landscape paintings into mysterious or poetically haunting scenes. Stanley **Spencer** 1891–1959 depicted religious and dream-like scenes under the disguise of everyday life. The Swiss Paul **Klee** 1879–1940 painted humorous semi-abstract pictures to call forth reactions from the subconscious. Marc **Chagall** 1881–1955 also delved into this realm using Russian Jewish images from his youth.

Abstract Expressionism many European artists moved to the USA in the years around World War II. New York became the centre of world art and Abstract Expressionism its first major movement. Influenced by Mondrian and other Europeans who settled there, American artists diverged into two groups: the *Gesture*, or *Action Painters*, and the *Colour Field Painters*. Jackson **Pollock** 1912–56 led the Gesture Painters. By putting his canvas on the floor and swirling paint on it he created a complex web of multicoloured trails which the spectator could retrace with his eyes, thereby reliving the artist's dynamic act of creation. The Colour Field Painter Mark **Rothko** 1903–70 filled large canvases with patches of solid colour, the contemplation of which offered the spectator a transcendental experience.

Pop Art because abstract art was not instantly understandable by all, it was thought to be only for the elite, and a group of younger artists launched Pop Art in 1956. Using popular imagery such as soup tins, comic-strips, or movie-star faces, it was a mischievous, cheerful art called by one of its British initiators, Richard Hamilton, 'low-cost, mass-produced, young and Big Business'. Allen Jones, Peter Blake, and David **Hockney** took part in the movement. In the USA artists including Andy **Warhol** 1930–87 with his repetitive images and Roy **Lichtenstein** 1923– with his re-arranged comic-strips seemed more interested in commenting on the materialistic values inherent in their borrowed imagery.

Op Art used abstraction to create optical illusions, confusing the spectator's eye with coloured lines and dots that apear to jump, blend, and waver. Bridget **Riley** 1931– has made these optical investigations a central part of her work.

three-dimensional art the desire to create movement in art also inspired sculptors like Jean **Tinguely** 1925– whose machine constructions are run by electricity, and Alexander **Calder** 1898–1976 who invented *mobiles*, flat shapes attached in interesting patterns to rods that hang from the ceiling and move gently in the air. Among the sculptors in more traditional materials, Constantin **Brancusi** 1876–1957 created smooth, reflective egg-like shapes suggesting aspects of birth and life; Henry **Moore** 1898–1986 made gradually more abstract and monumental forms by refining the shapes of his *Reclining Woman*; Jacob **Epstein** 1880–1959 emphasized expressive meaning through exaggerated human features and Alberto **Giacometti**'s 1901–66 distinctive stick men were an attempt to describe human mental and spiritual isolation.

contemporary trends there have been several movements since the 1960s, all of which resemble Dada in their antagonistic attitude to artistic ideas of the past.

Super Realism, successor to Pop Art, sought to imitate reality so precisely as to be uncanny, as in the sculptures of Duane Hanson, or paintings of Richard Estes.

Minimalism strove to express a narrow purity of vision through its concern for the physical materials used.

Conceptualism saw the idea as so important that the actual art object was no longer necessary.

Performance Art involved 'events', ephemeral in the extreme.

At the same time, some artists evolved new individual styles. The painter Francis **Bacon** 1910– contorts and mutilates his human figures to express the unpleasant emotions imposed on them by modern life. In the 1980s there was a swing back to figurative art, and the '-isms' gave way to the 'neo-' with such movements as *Neo-Expressionism* and *Neo-Geo(metric)* which acknowledge the art of the past and use freely visual images from the present, by dipping into the worldwide data bank of images created by modern communications. By adapting, combining, and revitalizing our vast store of images, today's artists can express the fragmentation which is characteristic of the present age.

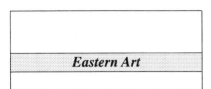

Eastern Art

Islamic art is one of ornament, for under the Muslim religion artists could not usurp the divine right of creation by portraying living creatures. Intricate, interlacing patterns based on geometry, Arabic calligraphy, and stylized plant motifs (including the swirling 'Arabesque') swarm over surfaces, structured by a rigid sense of symmetry. Lustreware pottery, ceramic tiles, and carpets were primary art forms. In Islamic Persia miniature painting illustrating literary or historical scenes, often in a lovingly detailed Paradise Garden setting, flourished during the Safavid period 1502–1736 and after 1526 under the Moghul Empire in India.

Chinese art manifested itself in pottery as early as 4000 BC, and its porcelains, and jade and ivory carvings, are major art forms. Painting was influenced by calligraphy; the ideographic script, which used the same brush, ink, and paper, called for the same dexterity, and produced the same spontaneous impression. Whether as hanging scrolls or handscrolls that unrolled to provide a continuous picture, paintings on silk and paper included calligraphy, often a poem. Traditional subjects were a bamboo branch, sprig of blossom, or snowy mountain landscape. Seen from a bird's-eye view, the space within a landscape was as meaningful as the subject.

Indian art influenced all of South-East Asia. From Buddha's death (48 BC) it centred on the religion which revered him as 'The Incarnation of the Truth'. Images of the Buddha followed a symbolic pattern: his plumpness signified well-being, his posture relaxation, his expression tranquillity. Hinduism also flourished and both Buddhist and Hindu temples were covered in high-relief sculpture. By the 13th century Hinduism became the major religion. The figures of its many exotic deities are rounded and sensuous, their poses based on religious dance movements. Eroticism enters with exuberantly amorous couples symbolizing the unity of the divine. Miniature painting, beginning in the 11th century, reached its peak under the Moghuls (16th–17th centuries).

Japanese art mastered all the Chinese and Buddhist traditions, adding its own interest in surface texture, bright colours, and dramatic compositions. Their most original contribution to world art was the *Ukiyo-e* colour print. Originating in genre paintings of 16th– to 17th century theatre scenes, actors, and bathhouse girls, it developed into the woodcut, and after 1740 the true colour print, while its subject matter expanded beyond the amusements of daily life to include flowers, birds, animals, and landscapes. Their brilliant combination of flat decorative colour and expressive pattern influenced 19th-century European art. Masters included **Utamaro** 1753–1806 and **Hokusai** 1760–1849. Distinguished artists also worked in miniature sculpture, producing tiny carved *netsuke* figures, widely collected in the West.

229

GREAT ARTISTS

Period	Artist
Classical	Myron 4th century BC Phidias c.500 BC Praxiteles 4th century BC Lysippus 4th century BC
Medieval	Pisano 1245–1314 Giotto c.1266–1337 Lorenzetti 1306?–45 Duccio c.1255/60–c.1318
Italian Renaissance	Masaccio 1401–28 Donatello c.1386–1466 Piero della Francesca 1410/20–92 Botticelli 1445–1510 Leonardo da Vinci 1452–1519 Michelangelo 1475–1564 Raphael 1483–1520
Mannerism	Vasari 1511–74 Bellini c.1430–1516 Mantegna c.1431–1506 Titian 1487–1576
15th and 16th centuries outside Italy	Van Eyck d.1441 Bosch c.1450–1516 Bruegel the Elder 1525/30–69 Dürer 1471–1528 El Greco 1541–1614 Holbein 1497–1543
17th century	Bernini 1598–1680 Carracci 1560–1609 Caravaggio 1573–1619 Claude Lorrain 1600–82 Poussin 1594–1665 Rubens 1577–1640 Rembrandt 1606–69 Steen 1626–79 Vermeer 1632–75 Van Dyck 1599–1641
18th century	Watteau 1684–1721 David 1748–1825 Canova 1757–1822 Tiepolo 1696–1770 Goya 1746–1828 Reynolds 1723–92 Gainsborough 1727–88 Hogarth 1697–1764
19th century	Delacroix 1798–1863 Ingres 1780–1867 Friedrich 1774–1840 Turner 1775–1851 Constable 1776–1837 Monet 1840–1926 Renoir 1841–1919 Cezanne 1839–1906 Van Gogh 1853–90 Rodin 1840–1917
20th century	Picasso 1881–1973 Matisse 1869–1954 Kandinsky 1866–1944 Mondrian 1872–1944 Duchamp 1887–1968 Magritte 1898–1967 Dali 1904– Klee 1879–1940 Pollock 1912–56 Rothko 1903–70 Hockney 1937– Moore 1898–1986 Brancusi 1876–1957 Epstein 1880–1959 Bacon 1910–

Architecture

Architecture is the art of building structures. The term covers the design of any structure for living or working in: houses, churches, temples, palaces, castles; and, as such, the style of building of any particular country at any period of history. Some theorists include under the term architecture only structures designed by a particular architect. Here, however, it includes so-called vernacular architecture: traditional buildings such as the cottages and farms of particular areas that have evolved slowly through the centuries but can claim no particular designer.

This section contains an overview of the ***History*** of Western architecture with a look at important styles in their historical context; ***Biographies*** of a selection of people who have made significant contributions to architecture, town planning, and landscape design; and definitions of ***Terms*** used in architecture.

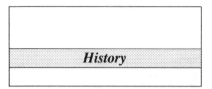

History

Ancient the earliest buildings were shelter structures, more or less permanent, which began to appear during the Bronze Age: circular bases constructed of dry-stone walling, with thatched roofs. All over Europe, the same societies began to erect megaliths for religious reasons we can only guess at; Stonehenge (c. 2000 BC) is a fairly late example. But it was in the Middle East, between 3000 and 1200 BC, that the first civilization arose, the Babylonian, and with it the first examples of what we should call architecture. Ur was a walled city dominated by a *ziggurat*, a huge structure topped by a temple. The civilization of ancient Egypt provided the *pyramids*, massive monuments of exact symmetry with decorative sculptures and wall painting and the first use of the decorated column and lintel to form colonnades. Examples include Karnak, Akhenaton, Abu Simbel, tombs of the Valley of the Kings, and the temple of Isis at Philea.

Classical with the Greeks, between about the 16th and the 2nd century BC, architecture as an art form really came into being. Their codification and use of the Classical orders – Doric, Ionic and Corinthian – provided a legacy which, refined and modified by the Romans, has influenced all subsequent Western architecture. The great example of Greek architecture is the Parthenon. The Romans were the first to use bricks and cement to produce the vault, arch and dome; they added the Tuscan and Composite orders to the Greek system. The emphasis in Roman architecture was on impressive public buildings (Colosseum), basilicas (Pantheon), triumphal arches and monuments (Trajan's Column) and aqueducts (Nîmes).

Byzantine in Byzantium a wholly Christian architecture was developing, from the 4th century onwards, with churches based on the Greek cross plan (Hagia Sophia, Istanbul; St Mark's, Venice); they used formalized, symbolic painted and mosaic decoration.

Romanesque the architecture of the Christianity of the West developed first as Romanesque, 8th to 12th century, marked by rounded arches, solid volumes and emphasis on perpendicular elements. In England, this was the period of Norman architecture (Durham Cathedral). Experiments in vaulting led towards the Gothic.

Gothic this architectural style developed in France in the 12th century and lasted until the 16th. It is marked out by the use of the rib vault, pointed arch and flying buttress, particularly in religious buildings; there is an emphasis on the vertical, with galleries and arcades replacing internal walls. It is divided into *Early Gothic* (Sens Cathedral), *High Gothic* (Chartres Cathedral) and *Late Gothic* or *Flamboyant*. In England the corresponding divisions are *Early English* (Salisbury Cathedral), *Decorated* (Wells Cathedral) and *Perpendicular* (King's College Chapel, Cambridge).

Islamic in Spain, from the 7th century onwards, the Moorish occupation was also having a profound influence on Christian architecture, introducing the dome and the pointed arch (later incorporated into Gothic). Examples of influential Islamic buildings are the Great Mosque, *Cordova*, and the Alhambra, Granada.

Renaissance the 15th and 16th centuries saw the rebirth of Classical architecture in the *Neo-Classical movement*, largely through the work of Vitruvius. Major Italian architects were Alberti, Brunelleschi, Bramante, Michelangelo, Raphael and Palladio; in England *Palladianism* was represented by Inigo Jones. A 16th-century offshoot was *Mannerism*, in which motifs were used in deliberate opposition to their original significance, that is, for their manner rather than their meaning.

Baroque the architecture of the 17th and 18th centuries was exuberantly extravagant, and seen at its best in large-scale public buildings in the work of Bernini, Borromini,

architecture

Gothic arch

mouldings

corbel   spandrel

spring of arch

capital

column

base

Tuscan
the orders of
classical architecture

Doric

Ionic

Corinthian

entablature

capital

shaft

base
Composite

classical temple

entablature pediment

cornice

tympanum

cornice

frieze

architrave   triglyph   metope

capital

abacus

shaft

column

233

Vanbrugh, Hawksmoor, and Wren. Its last stage is the *Rococo*, characterized by still greater extravagance, a new lightness in style, and the use of naturalistic motifs such as shells, flowers and trees.

Neo-Classical the 18th and 19th centuries saw a return to classical principles, for example in the large-scale rebuilding of London and Paris by Adam, Nash and Haussman.

Neo-Gothic the later 19th century saw a renewed enthusiasm for the Gothic style in the *Gothic revival*, particularly evident in churches and public buildings (*Houses of Parliament* by Sir Charles Barry).

Art Nouveau a new movement surfaced at the end of the 19th century, characterized by sinuous, flowing shapes, informal room plans and attention not only to architectural design but to every last detail of the interior. The style is best seen in England in the work of Charles Rennie Mackintosh (Glasgow Art School) and in Spain by that of Antonio Gaudi.

Modernism an increasing emphasis on rationalism and rejection of ornament led to Modernism, also known as *Functionalism* or *International Style*, which sought to exclude everything that did not have a purpose, and used the latest technological advances in glass, steel and concrete to full advantage. Major architects include Frank Lloyd Wright, Mies van der Rohe, Le Corbusier, and Alvar Aalto.

town planning with the planning of whole new cities such as in the 1950s Le Corbusier's Chandigarh in India and Brasilia in Brazil, town planning emerged as a discipline in its own right.

neo-vernacular by the 1970s a reversion from the modern movement's box-like structure and synthetic materials began to be felt in a renewed enthusiasm for *vernacular* architecture (traditional local styles), to be seen in the work of, for instance, the British firm Darbourne and Darke.

Post-Modernism in the 1980s a post-modernist movement has emerged, split into two camps: *high tech*, represented in Britain by architects such as Norman Foster, Richard Rogers and James Stirling (Hong Kong and Shanghai Bank, Lloyd's, Staatsgalerie Stuttgart respectively), and architects using elements from the architecture of previous times, whether consciously obeying the tenets of the Classical orders – *Neo-Classicism* yet again – like Quinlan Terry, or using such elements at whim, like Michael Graves.

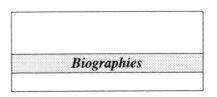

Biographies

Aalto Alvar 1898–1976. Finnish architect and designer. One of Finland's first modernists, he evolved an architectural style entirely his own, characterized by asymmetry, curved walls and contrast of natural materials. His work included the Hall of Residence, Massachusetts Institute of Technology, Cambridge, Massachusetts 1947–49; Finlandia Hall, Helsinki 1972. He also invented bent plywood furniture in 1932.

Abercrombie Sir Leslie Patrick 1879–1957. Pioneer of British town planning. He is best known for his work of replanning British cities after damage in World War II (such as the Greater London Plan, 1944) and for the New Towns policy.

Adam Robert 1728–92. Scottish architect and interior decorator, leader of the British Neo-Classical revival. In the interiors of Harewood House, Luton Hoo, Syon House, Osterley Park and others, he employed delicate stucco decoration with Neo-Classical motifs. With his brother, *James Adam* (1732–94), also an architect, he speculatively developed the Adelphi near Charing Cross, London, largely rebuilt in 1936.

Alberti Leon Battista 1404–72. Italian Renaissance architect and theorist, noted for his recognition of the principles of Classical architecture and their modification for Renaissance practice in *On Architecture* 1452/1485.

Barry Sir Charles 1795–1860. British architect of the Neo-Gothic Houses of Parliament at Westminster 1840–60.

Borromini Francesco 1599–1667. Italian Baroque architect. He worked under Bernini, later his rival, on St Peter's, Rome, and created the oval-shaped San Carlo alle Quatro Fontane, Rome.

Bramante Donato c. 1444–1514. Italian Renaissance architect and artist. Inspired by Classical designs, he was employed by Pope Julius II in rebuilding part of the Vatican and St Peter's.

Breuer Marcel 1902– . Hungarian-born architect and designer, who studied and taught at the Bauhaus. He is best known for his tubular steel chair, 1925, the first of its kind. He moved to England, then to the USA, where he was in partnership with Gropius 1937–40. His buildings show an affinity with natural materials; best known among them is the Bijenkorf, Rotterdam (with Elzas) 1953.

Brown Lancelot 1716–83. English gardener and architect, known as 'Capability Brown' because he said sites had 'capability'; his works include Blenheim Palace, Oxfordshire, with mounds, curved paths, and lakes, Highclere Hampshire; and Bowood Wiltshire.

Brunel Isambard Kingdom 1806–1959. British engineer and inventor (son of Sir Marc Brunel), who made major contributions in ship-building and bridge-construction. His work includes the Clifton Suspension Bridge over the river Severn at Bristol, and the Saltash Bridge over the river Tamar near Plymouth, and the ships *Great Western* 1838, the *Great Britain* 1845 and the *Great Eastern* 1858.

Brunelleschi Filippo 1377–1446. Italian Renaissance architect. One of the earliest and greatest Renaissance architects, a pioneer in the scientific use of perspective. He was responsible for the construction of the dome of Florence Cathedral (completed 1438), a feat deemed impossible by many of his comtemporaries.

Burlington Richard Boyle, 3rd Earl of, 1694–1753. British architect and architectural patron; one of the premier exponents of Palladianism in Britain. His buildings – best known

among them is Chiswick House in London 1725–29 – are characterized by absolute adherence to the Classical rules and are consequently somewhat dry and fastidious.

Casson Sir Hugh 1910– . British architect, director of architecture for the Festival of Britain 1948–51 and president of the Royal Academy of Arts from 1976.

Chambers Sir William 1726–96. British architect, popularizer of Chinese influence (Kew Gardens pagoda) and designer of Somerset House, London.

Cockerell Charles 1788–1863. British architect who built mainly in a Neo-Classical style derived from antiquity and from Wren. His best known surviving buildings are the Ashmolean Museum and Taylorian Institute in Oxford 1841–45.

Foster Norman 1935– . British architect of the high-tech school. His best known buildings are the Willis Faber office, Ipswich 1975, the Sainsbury Centre for the Visual Arts, Norwich 1978, and the Hong Kong and Shanghai Bank, Hong Kong 1986.

Fuller Richard Buckminster 1895–1983. American architect, inventor in 1947 of the lightweight geodesic dome, a half-sphere of triangular components independent of any buttress or vault.

Gaudi Antonio 1852–1926. Spanish architect, noted for his flamboyant style. He was influenced by Moorish and medieval architecture. His Church of the Holy Family, Barcelona, begun 1883, was still under construction when he died.

Geddes Sir Patrick 1854–1932. A pioneering British town planner, who established the current theory of town planning, in particular the importance of surveys and research work. His major work is *City Development* 1904.

Gibbs James 1682–1754. English Neo-Classical architect whose works include St Martin's-in-the-Fields, London 1722–26, Radcliffe Camera, Oxford 1737–49.

Gropius Walter Adolf 1883–1969. German-born American architect, founder-director of the Bauhaus school in Weimar 1919–28, and an advocate of team architecture and artistic standards in industrial production. From 1937 he lived in the USA, becoming professor of architecture at Harvard and designing the Harvard Graduate Centre 1949–50.

Haussmann Georges Eugène, Baron Haussmann 1809–91. French administrator, who replanned medieval Paris 1853–70, with wide boulevards and parks.

Hawksmoor Nicholas 1661–1736. English architect, assistant to Wren in London churches and St Paul's; joint architect with Vanbrugh of Castle Howard and Blenheim Palace. The original west towers of Westminster Abbey, long attributed to Wren, are his.

Howard Sir Ebenezer 1850–1928. British planner and founder of the ideal of the Garden City. His major work is *Tomorrow* 1898 (republished as *Garden Cities of Tomorrow* in 1902).

Jekyll Gertrude 1843–1932. British landscape gardener, who collaborated with Edwin Lutyens. She used natural construction materials, was sensitive to colour, as shown in her 'grey garden' of silver-leaved plants, and abandoned Victorian 'bedding-out' to draw on the tradition of the cottage garden.

Jencks Charles 1939– . American architectural theorist and furniture designer. He coined the term 'post-modern architecture' and wrote the influential book *The Language of Post-Modern Architecture*.

Johnson Philip Cortelyou 1906– . American architect, who invented the term international style. He began designing in the style of Mies van der Rohe (house at New Canaan, 1949) but became one of the early, and spectacular, exponents of Post-Modernism. His best known building is the giant AT&T building in New York, a pink skyscraper with a Chippendale cabinet top 1978.

Jones Inigo 1573–c. 1652. The first true English Renaissance architect, influenced by Palladio. His two visits to Italy gave him an unrivalled knowledge of Renaissance architecture in Italy. He designed the Queen's House, Greenwich 1616, and the Banqueting Hall, Whitehall 1619 and scenery for Jonson's masques.

Kahn Louis 1901–74. American architect, noted for his unusual 'service' towers surrounding the main working spaces of buildings such as Salk Laboratories, La Jolla, California.

Lasdun Sir Denys 1914– . British architect, whose works include the National Theatre on the South Bank. He was knighted in 1976.

Le Corbusier. Pseudonym of Charles Edouard Jeanneret 1887–1965. Swiss-born French architect, for whom the house was a habitable machine to be designed to functional criteria. His works include the Palace of the Nations, Geneva, Cité Radieuse, Marseille, and the town plan for Chandigarh, India.

Lethaby William Richard 1857–1931. English architect, and assistant to Richard Norman Shaw. He embraced the principles of William Morris and Philip Webb and had a great influence in the Arts and Crafts Movement, especially as first director of the Central School of Arts and Crafts (which he helped to found) from 1894.

Le Vau Louis 1612–70. French architect, who drafted the plan of Versailles, and built the Louvre and Tuileries.

Loos Adolf 1870–1933. Viennese architect. He rejected the ornamentation and curved lines of the Viennese Art Nouveau. His main importance is as a polemicist; his most famous and influential article was *Ornament and Crime*, published in 1908.

Lutyens Sir Edwin Landseer 1869–1944. British architect, whose works include the government buildings in New Delhi, Hampstead Garden Suburb, the Whitehall Cenotaph, London YWCA, and the British Embassy in Washington.

Mackintosh Charles Rennie 1868–1928. Scottish Art Nouveau architect, designer and painter, whose work includes the Glasgow School of Art 1896.

Mackmurdo Arthur H 1851–1942. English designer and architect. He founded the Century Guild in 1882, a group of architects, artists, and designers inspired by William Morris and John Ruskin. His book and textile designs are forerunners of Art Nouveau.

Mansart Jules-Hardouin 1646–1708. French

architect of the Palace of Versailles and the Grand Trianon, and designer of the Place de Vendôme and the Place des Victoires, Paris.

Michelangelo 1475–1564. Italian sculptor, painter, architect, and poet, Michelangelo di Lodovico Buonarroti Simoni. In addition to his work as an artist, Michelangelo was one of the greatest architects. His most important works are the façade for Brunelleschi's church of San Lorenzo in Rome 1514; the Biblioteca Laurenziana 1525–26; his designs for the Capitol 1539; and the completion of St Peter's in Rome 1546–64 (begun by Bramante).

Mies van der Rohe Ludwig 1886–1969. German-born American architect, director of the Bauhaus 1929–33. His works include the new Illinois Institute of Technology 1941, where he taught 1938–58, and the bronze and glass Seagram Building, New York 1956-59.

Morris William 1834–96. British poet, craftsman, and socialist. Although known principally for his furniture, wallpaper, church decorations and beautifully decorated books, he also had a considerable influence on a generation of architects, including William Lethaby and Philip Webb.

Nash John 1752–1835. British architect, who designed Regent's Park and its terraces, Regent Street (later rebuilt), and Marble Arch, intended as the entrance gate to Buckingham Palace.

Nervi Pier Luigi 1891–1979. Italian architect, who used soft steel mesh within concrete to give it flowing form. His best known works include the Turin exhibition hall 1949, and the UNESCO building in Paris 1952.

Niemeyer Oscar 1907– . Brazilian architect, joint designer of the United Nations headquarters in New York, and of many buildings in Brasilia.

Olbrich Joseph Maria 1867–1908. Viennese architect who worked under Otto Wagner and was opposed to the lush over-ornamentation of Art Nouveau. His most important buildings, however, remain Art Nouveau in spirit: the Vienna Secession 1897–78, the Hochzeitsturm 1907 and the Tietz department store, both in Dsseldorf.

Palladio Andrea 1508–80. Italian architect, who from 1540 designed country houses, such as the Villa Rotonda near Vicenza, for patrician families of the Venetian Republic and whose work had a profound influence on generations of Neo-Classical architects.

Paxton Sir Joseph 1801–65. British architect, garden superintendent to the Duke of Devonshire from 1826, and designer of the Great Exhibition building of 1851 (Crystal Palace), revolutionary in its structural use of glass and iron.

Pei I M 1917– . Chinese-born American modernist/high tech architect. His best known buildings include the John Hancock tower, Boston, the National Airlines terminal at Kennedy Airport, New York, and the extension to the National Gallery, Washington DC. Projects during the 1980s include renovations to the Louvre Museum, Paris, and new work for Canary Wharf, London dockland.

Piranesi Giovanni Battista 1720–78. Italian architect, most influential for his powerful etchings of Roman antiquities and as a theorist of architecture, advocating imaginative use of Roman models.

Repton Sir Humphrey 1752–1818. English landscape gardener, who coined the term 'landscape gardening'. He was a leading landscape gardener of the generation after Lancelot Brown, and worked for some years in partnership with John Nash. Repton was responsible for the landscaping of some 200 gardens and parks.

Richardson Harry Hobson 1838–86. American architect, who built a great deal in a Romanesque style derived from that of northern Spain. He had a strong influence on Louis Sullivan.

Rogers Richard 1933– . British architect whose works include the Pompidou Centre in Paris 1977 and the Lloyd's building in London 1986.

Ruskin John 1819–1900. British art and social critic, whose writings had a profound influence on architecture. His enthusiasm for medieval architecture helped establish the Neo-Gothic style, and his belief in the importance of the work of craftsmen helped pave the way for the Arts and Crafts Movement.

Saarinen Eero 1910–61. American architect, son of Eliel Saarinen; he was born in Finland, but taken to the USA in 1923 by his father. His works include the American Embassy in London, and Dulles Airport, Washington.

Saarinen Eliel 1873–1950. Finnish-American architect, founder of the Finnish Romantic school, of which Helsinki railway station is an example. He contributed to US skyscraper design by his work in Chicago.

Sant'Elia Antonio 1888–1916. Italian architect. Although he died (in World War I) too early to achieve much in the way of building, his drawings, conveying a Futurist vision of a metropolis with skyscrapers, traffic lanes and streamlined factories, were influential.

Schinkel Karl Friedrich 1781–1841. Prussian architect of the Neo-Classical style, recognized as the greatest German architect of the 19th century. Major works include the Old Museum, Berlin 1823–30, and the Charlottenhof and the Roman Bath 1826 and 1833 in the park of Potsdam.

Scott Sir George Gilbert 1811–78. British architect, largely responsible for the mid-19th-century Gothic revival in England; his restoration work in Ely Cathedral and Westminster Abbey had debatable results, but his Albert Memorial, Foreign Office, and St Pancras Station won contemporary and more recent praise.

Scott Sir Giles Gilbert 1880–1960. British architect, grandson of Sir George Scott, and designer of Liverpool Anglican Cathedral, Cambridge University Library, and Waterloo Bridge 1945.

Serlio Sebastiano 1475–1554. Italian painter, architect and architectural theorist. He was most important as the author of *L'Architettura* 1537–51, practical rules for the use of the Classical orders and spread the Neo-Classical style throughout Europe.

Shaw Richard Norman 1831–1912. British architect. His style was eclectic, using elements from vernacular and Georgian architecture rather than the Gothic and Tudor then popular. Major buildings include New Zealand Chambers, London 1872, Lowther Lodge, Kensington 1873 (now the Royal Geographical Society), Shaw's house, Hampstead 1875.

Smirke Robert 1780–1867. Leading Greek Revival architect in Britain; designer of the British Museum.

Soane Sir John 1753–1837. British architect, whose individual Neo-Classical style resulted in works curiously presaging modern taste. Little of his major work, the Bank of England, London, remains. Other buildings include his own house in Lincoln's Inn Fields, London, now the Soane Museum.

Spence Sir Basil 1907–76. British architect. He was professor of architecture at the Royal Academy 1961–68, and his controversial works include Coventry Cathedral, Sussex University, the British Embassy in Rome, the Home Office and Knightsbridge Barracks. He was knighted in 1960 and awarded an OM in 1962.

Stirling James 1926– . British architect. He designed the engineering building at Leicester University, and the Clore Gallery (the extension to house the Turner collection of the Tate Gallery), opened 1987.

Sullivan Louis Henry 1856–1924. American architect, influenced by Harry Richardson. He worked in Chicago and designed early skyscrapers such as the Wainwright Building, St Louis 1890 and the Guaranty Building, Buffalo 1894. He was influential in the anti-ornament movement. Frank Lloyd Wright was his pupil.

Summerson Sir John 1904– . English architectural scholar and critic, and curator of Sir John Soane's museum 1945–84. Influential books include *Georgian London* 1945, and *The Classical Language of Architecture* 1964.

Tange Kenzo 1913– . Japanese architect, whose works include the National Gymnasium, Tokyo, for the 1964 Olympics, and the city plan of Abuja, Nigeria (completed 1986).

Terry Quinlan 1937– . British Neo-Classical architect whose work includes many country houses, for example Merks Hall, Great Dunmow, Essex 1982, and the Richmond riverside project commissioned 1984.

Unwin Sir Raymond 1863–1940. Leading English town planner of the time, who put the Garden City ideals of Sir Ebenezer Howard into practice, overseeing Letchworth (begun 1903), Hampstead Garden Suburb (begun 1907) and Wythenshawe outside Manchester (begun 1927).

Venturi Robert 1925– . American architect and pioneer of Post-Modernism. His best known books are *Complexity and Contradiction in Architecture* 1967 and *Learning from Las Vegas* 1972. He was commissioned for London's National Gallery extension in 1986.

Vitruvius (Marcus Vitruvius Pollio) 1st century BC Roman architect, whose ten-volume interpretation of Roman architecture *De architectura* influenced Alberti, Palladio, and many others.

Voysey Charles Francis Annesley 1857–1941. British architect and designer. His fame as an architect rests on his country houses, which are characteristically asymmetrical with massive buttresses, long sloping roofs and rough-cast walls; he designed all furniture and interior details with a cosy sentimentality.

Wagner Otto 1841–1918. Viennese architect who at first designed in the Art Nouveau style, for example Vienna Stadtbahn 1894–97, but later rejected ornament in favour of rationalism, as in his Post Office Savings Bank, Vienna 1904–6. He influenced younger Viennese architects.

Waterhouse Alfred 1830–1905. English architect. He was a leading exponent of Victorian Neo-Gothic using, typically, multi-coloured tiles and bricks. His best known work is the Natural History Museum in London 1868.

Webb Philip 1831–1915. English architect. He designed almost exclusively houses, including the Red House for William Morris, and was one of the leading figures, with Richard Norman Shaw and C F A Voysey, in the revival of domestic English architecture in 19th century. Houses include Joldwyns, Surrey 1873, Clouds, East Knoyle, Wiltshire 1880, and Standen, East Grinstead 1891–94.

Wilkins William 1778–1839. English architect who pioneered the Greek Revival in England with his design for Downing College, Cambridge. He is best known for the unsuccessful National Gallery, which ruined his reputation.

Wren Sir Christopher 1632–1723. English architect. Professor of astronomy at Oxford from 1660, he was asked to plan the rebuilding of the city after the Great Fire of London of 1666. His plan was not adopted but his individual buildings include St Paul's Cathedral (1675–1710), and other City churches (St Michael's, Cornhill, St Bride's, Fleet Street, St Mary-le-Bow, Cheapside), the Sheldonian Theatre and Ashmolean Museum at Oxford, and part of Hampton Court Palace.

Wright Frank Lloyd 1869–1959. American architect whose freedom from convention and rule was influential worldwide, for example his own home Taliesin West, Wisconsin 1938, and the Guggenheim Museum, New York 1959.

Wyatt James 1747–1813. English architect, contemporary of the Adam brothers, who designed in the Neo-Gothic style. His over-enthusiastic 'restorations' of medieval cathedrals earned him the nickname 'Wyatt the Destroyer'.

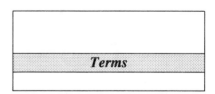

Terms

arch a curved structure consisting of several wedge-shaped stones or other hard blocks which are supported by their mutual pressure. The term is also applied to any curved structure which is an arch in form only.

Art Deco a style, in art and architecture, originating in France in 1925, and continuing through the 1930s, using rather heavy, geometric simplification of form, for example Radio City Music Hall, New York.

Arts and Crafts a social movement based in design and architecture, founded by William

Morris in the latter half of the 19th century and supported by Pugin and Ruskin, stressing the importance of manual processes and largely anti-machine in spirit.

atrium an inner, open courtyard.

Baroque term used to describe the ornate European art and architecture of the 17th and 18th centuries, and used broadly to characterize the historical period.

basilica a type of Roman public building, consisting of a hall with side aisles divided off by rows of columns, which was adopted by Christians for early churches.

Bauhaus a school founded in 1919 by the architect Walter Gropius at Weimar in an attempt to fuse all the arts and crafts in a unified whole. Moved to Dessau under political pressure in 1925, it was closed by the Nazis in 1933. Associated with the Bauhaus were Klee, Kandinsky and Ludwig Mies van der Rohe. The tradition never died, and in 1972 the Bauhaus Archive was installed in new premises in W Berlin.

buttress a reinforcement, in brick or masonry, built against a wall to give it strength. A *flying buttress* is an arc transmitting the force of the wall to be supported to an outer buttress, common in Gothic architecture.

Byzantine term used to describe the style of religious art and architecture of Byzantium and the Eastern Orthodox Christian church from the 4th century, characterized by the use of formalized, symbolic painted and mosaic decorations.

cantilever a horizontal beam fixed at one end to a rigid support and free to move at the other end. This type of structure is used widely in building; in cantilever bridges, where the projecting arms are built inwards from the piers to meet in the centre of the span, and in cantilever cranes where a straight steel truss rests on a central support.

caryatid a building support or pillar, in the shape of a woman; a male figure is a *telamon* or *atlas*.

church a Christian place of worship. A typical Latin cross plan church is illustrated but the main elements are found in all churches.

Chicago school a style of unornamented skyscrapers developed in Chicago in the late 19th century by, among others, Louis Sullivan.

cladding a thin layer of external covering, for example, tiles, wood, stone, concrete.

Classical architecture the architecture of ancient Greece and Rome. This provided a legacy which has influenced all subsequent Western architecture.

cloister a convent or monastery, and more particularly a covered walk within these, often opening on to a courtyard.

colonnade a row of columns supporting arches or an entablature.

De Stijl name of Dutch avant-garde art periodical founded by Theo van Doesburg and Piet Mondrian, which gave its name to a group of abstractionist artists and architects, including Gerrit Rietveld.

dome (cupola) a roof or vault built on a circular base, or on a pendentive if the base is of any other shape. A dome can be round or pointed, in a variety of forms.

garden city a self-sufficient community, designed to combine the advantages of town and country living, proposed in 1899 by Sir Ebenezer Howard 1850–1928, founder of the association which established Letchworth in Hertfordshire.

gargoyle a spout projecting from the roof gutter of a building with the purpose of directing water away from the wall. The term is usually applied to the ornamental forms found in Gothic architecture; these were carved in stone and took the shape of fantastic animals, angels, or human heads.

golden section a proportion, possibly derived from Euclid, in which the third term is the sum of the first and second; that is A:B = B:(A+B), believed since the ancient Greeks to be particularly pleasing.

Gothic term used to describe 12th- to 16th-century European architecture, characterized by the use of the rib vault, pointed arch, and flying buttress.

ha-ha a sunken boundary wall permitting an unobstructed view beyond a garden; a device much used by Capability Brown.

types of masonry

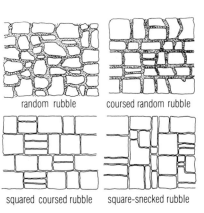

smooth   cylopean   random rubble   coursed random rubble

diamond-pointed   vermiculated   squared coursed rubble   square-snecked rubble

masonry the art of building with stone.

mezzanine an architectural term derived from the diminutive of the Italian word for middle; it is a storey with a lower ceiling placed between two higher storeys, usually between the ground and first floors of a building.

minaret a slender turret or tower attached to an Islamic mosque. It has one or more balconies, from which the *muezzin* calls the people to prayer five times a day.

module in construction, a part which governs the form of the rest; for example Japanese room sizes are traditionally governed by multiples of standard tatami floor mats; modern prefabricated buildings are mass-produced in a similar way.

obelisk a tall, tapering column of stone; much used in ancient Egyptian as well as Roman architecture.

pantheon originally a temple for worshipping all the gods, such as that in ancient Rome, rebuilt by Hadrian and still used as a church; now, as the Panthéon, Paris, a building where famous people are buried.

peristyle a range of columns surrounding a building or open courtyard.

piano nobile the main floor of a house, containing the main reception rooms.

portico a porch with pediment and columns.

Renaissance in architecture, term used to describe the period from about 1420 to 1550 in Italy, characterized by a renewed interest in Classical (particularly Roman) principles of design. In the other arts the term is also used more broadly to refer to this historical period throughout Europe.

Rococo term used to describe an 18th-century European style of art and architecture, characterized by elaborate ornamentation and the use of naturalistic motifs.

Romanesque term used to describe Western Christian architecture of the 8th to 12th centuries, marked by rounded arches, solid volumes, and emphasis on perpendicular elements. In England the style was called *Norman*.

skyscraper a type of tall building first developed in 1868 in New York, USA, where land prices were high and the geology adapted to such methods of construction; today techniques have been evolved which also make them possible on London's clay and in earthquake areas. The world's highest is in Chicago.

town planning the design of buildings or groups of buildings in a physical and social context, concentrating on the relationship between various buildings and their environment, as well as on their uses.

vault an arched ceiling or roof built mainly of stone or bricks.

241

vernacular the domestic or peasant building tradition of different localities, not designed by trained architects; for example thatched cottages in England, stone in Scotland, adobe huts in Mexico, wooden buildings in the Nordic countries.

Wiener Werkstätte a group of Viennese craftsmen and designers established in 1903 by Joseph Hoffman and Moser under the influence of William Morris's Arts and Crafts Movement.

Cinema

Cinema is a modern art. It borrows from the other arts, such as music, drama, and literature, but, unlike them, is entirely dependent for its origins on technological developments. Since the earliest picture shows by the Lumière brothers in 1895, cinema has changed enormously. Indeed, considering its relatively short life, it has developed at a rate unparalleled in any other art form. The last few decades in particular have seen a fundamental change in the style of films, reflected in a shift away from the idea of studio control and star supremacy prevalent in the days of silent films and the Hollywood of the 1930s and 1940s to the idea of film as a form of artistic expression, the creation of an individual director (or, more rarely, producer). But whatever its form, cinema has, throughout its history, reflected and recorded contemporary social attitudes and changes in taste and lifestyle. It has also – in its ability to amuse, excite, anger, move and disturb – often sought to influence these attitudes and changes. Whether providing a reflection of reality, or an escape from it, a pure entertainment, or a unique and personal artistic creation, the appeal of cinema is universal.

This section provides an overview of the wide-ranging appeal and varied nature of cinema. It contains *Biographies* of a selection of some of the many people who, in different ways, have made a significant and unique contribution to cinema; a list of *Academy Award Winners* in the principal categories of best film, director, actor and actress; and a *Chronology* of film, marking important dates and events that are generally considered to be landmarks in the development of film as a technique as well as an art.

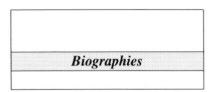

Biographies

Allen Woody. Pseudonym of American comedian, writer, film director, and clarinettist Allen Stewart Konisberg 1935– . A versatile comedian-philosopher, Allen is best known for his cynical, witty, often self-deprecating parody and special brand of off-beat humour. His films include *Play It Again Sam* 1972, *Annie Hall* 1977 – (for which he won three Academy Awards), and *Hannah and Her Sisters* 1986 – all of which he also directed.

Antonioni Michelangelo 1912– . Italian film director, famous for his subtle analysis of neuroses and personal relationships of the leisured classes. His work includes *L'Avventura* 1960, *Blow Up* 1967 and *The Passenger* 1975.

Attenborough Sir Richard 1923– . British actor, film producer, and director. An influential figure in the British cinema, he was outstanding in the film roles of Pinkie in *Brighton Rock* 1947 and the murder suspect Christie in *10 Rillington Place* 1970; films directed include *Oh! What a Lovely War* 1968, *A Bridge Too Far* 1976, dealing with Arnhem, and *Gandhi* 1982, which won six Academy Awards. He was knighted in 1976.

Balcon Sir Michael 1896–1977. British film producer, responsible for the 'Ealing Comedies' of the 1940s and early 1950s, *Kind Hearts and Coronets* 1949, and *The Lavender Hill Mob* 1951.

Bardot Brigitte 1934– . French film actress, whose appeal as a 'sex kitten' did much to popularize French cinema internationally. Her films include *And God Created Woman* 1950.

Barrault Jean-Louis 1910– . French actor and director of the Théâtre de France/Odéon 1959–68. He showed his gifts as a mime artist in the films *Les Enfants du Paradis* 1944, and *La Ronde* 1950, both now classics.

Bergman Ingmar 1918– . Swedish film producer and director. Regarded by many as one of the greatest film artists, his work deals with complex moral, psychological and metaphysical problems and is often heavily tinged with pessimism. His work include *Wild Strawberries* 1957, *The Seventh Seal* 1957, *Persona* 1966, *Cries and Whispers* 1972, *The Serpent's Egg* 1978, *Autumn Sonata* 1978, and *Fanny and Alexander* 1982.

Bergman Ingrid 1917–82. Swedish actress, whose films include *Casablanca* 1943 and *For Whom the Bell Tolls* 1943. By leaving her husband for film producer Roberto Rossellini, whom she married in 1950, she broke an unofficial moral code of Hollywood 'star' behaviour and was ostracized for many years. She was re-admitted to make *Anastasia* 1956, for which she won an Academy Award. Her later films include *Murder on the Orient Express* 1974.

Berkeley Busby 1895–1976. American film director, who used female dancers to create large-scale pattern effects in ingeniously extravagant sets, for example *Gold Diggers of 1933* in 1933.

Bertolucci Bernardo 1940– . Italian director, regarded as one of the most talented of the younger generation of Italian film directors. His work combines political and historical satire with an elegant visual appeal. His films include *The Spider's Stratagem* 1970, *The Conformist* 1970, *Novecento/1900* 1976, but he is probably best known for his controversial *Last Tango in Paris* 1972.

Bogarde Dirk. Stage name of Dutch-born British actor Derek van den Bogaerde 1921– . After initial success in popular British films, he has gone on to acquire an international reputation for more complex roles in films such as *Death in Venice* 1971.

Boulting John 1913–85 and Roy 1913– . British twin-brother director-producer team that was particularly influential in the years following World War II. Their films include *Brighton Rock* 1947. *Lucky Jim* 1957, and *I'm All Right Jack* 1959.

Bow Clara 1905–65. American silent film actress, known as the 'It' girl from the sex appeal of her appearance in *It* 1927.

Boyer Charles 1899–1977. French film actor, who made his name in Hollywood in the 1930s as the 'great lover' in films such as *Mayerling* 1937 and *The Garden of Allah* 1936.

Brando Marlon 1931– . American actor whose naturalistic style of acting and casual mumbling speech earned him a place as one of the most distinctive actors of all time. His films include *A Streetcar Named Desire* 1951, *Julius Caesar* 1953, *On the Waterfront* 1954, *The Godfather* 1972.

Buñuel Luis 1900–83. Spanish surrealist film director, famous for his controversial and often anti-clerical films, for example *L'Age d'Or* The Golden Age 1930 and *The Discreet Charm of the Bourgeoisie* 1972.

Caine Michael. Stage name of British actor Maurice Micklewhite 1933- . Noted for his dry, laconic Cockney style. His films include *The Ipcress File* 1965, *Alfie* 1966, *The Eagle Has Landed* 1976, and *Mona Lisa* 1986.

Capra Frank 1897– . American film director. His films, which often have sentimental, idealistic heroes, include *It Happened One Night* 1934, *Mr Deeds Goes to Town* 1936, and *You Can't Take It With You* 1938.

Carné Marcel 1909– . French film director, his work is noted for its atmosphere and subtle characterization. His films include *Le Jour se lève* Daybreak 1939 and *Les Enfants du Paradis* 1944.

Cassavetes John 1929– . American actor and film director, who appeared in many films, including *The Dirty Dozen* 1967 and *Rosemary's Baby* 1968. He has also directed experimental, apparently improvised films, including *Shadows* 1960 and *The Killing of a Chinese Bookie* 1980.

Chaplin Sir Charles Spencer ('Charlie') 1889–1977. British actor and film director. One of the outstanding figures of the early cinema, he began his career in silent films such as *The Tramp* 1915, *The Gold Rush* 1925, *Modern Times* 1936, then progressed to films with sound, *The Great Dictator* 1940. Despite his many other films, he is probably still best remembered as a comical bowler-hatted figure with baggy trousers and moustache. He was knighted in 1975.

Cimino Michael 1943– . American film director, who established his reputation with *The Deer Hunter* 1978 (which won five Academy Awards). His other films include *Heaven's Gate* 1980 and *The Year of The Dragon* 1986.

Clair René. Pseudonym of French film director René Lucien Chomette 1898–1981. His *Sous les Toits de Paris* Under the Roofs of Paris 1930 was one of the first French sound films.

Colman Ronald 1891–1958. British actor who specialized in the role of the romantic hero in Hollywood during the 1920s and 1930s. His films include *A Tale of Two Cities* 1936, *Lost Horizon*, *The Prisoner of Zenda* 1937, and *A Double Life* 1948 (for which he received an Academy Award).

Cooper Gary 1901–62. American actor who came to epitomize the sincere Yankee in films such as *Mr Deeds Goes to Town* 1936 and *Sergeant York* (for which he won an Academy Award in 1941).

Coppola Francis Ford 1939– . Director and screenwriter, in 1972 he directed *The Godfather*, one of the biggest money-makers of all time. Other successes include *The Godfather Part II* (which, like the original, won several Academy Awards) and *Apocalypse Now* 1979.

Crawford Joan 1908–77. American film actress, noted for her strongly dramatic roles, as in *Mildred Pierce* 1945 (for which she won an Academy Award).

Crosby Harry Lillis (Bing) 1904–77. American dance-band singer of the 1920s, who went on to popularize the image of the relaxed crooner in the 1930s and 1940s, with songs such as 'Pennies from Heaven' and 'White Christmas' (featured in films with those titles). He also made a series of 'road' film comedies with Dorothy Lamour and Bob Hope, for example *Road to Singapore* 1940.

Davis Bette 1908– . American actress, who made her name playing strong-willed, independent women in the 1930s and 1940s.

Later films included *Dangerous* 1935 and *Jezebel* 1938 (both winning her Academy Awards), and *Whatever Happened to Baby Jane?* 1962.

De Mille Cecil B(lount) 1884–1959. American film director, who specialized in biblical epics, for example *The Ten Commandments* 1956.

De Niro Robert 1943– . American actor, best known for his sensitive portrayal of strong and often complex characters. His films include *Mean Streets* 1973, *Taxi Driver* 1976, *The Deer Hunter* 1978, also *The Godfather Part II* 1974, and *Raging Bull* 1979 for both of which he won Academy Awards.

De Sica Vittorio 1902–74. Italian actor and director. His film *Bicycle Thieves* remains a classic example of post-war Italian Neo-Realism (a movement characterized by a 'naturalistic' style of film-making).

Dean James. Stage name of American actor James Byron 1931–55. Killed in a road accident when only his first film *East of Eden* 1955, had been shown, he posthumously became a cult figure with *Rebel Without a Cause* 1955 and *Giant* 1956.

Dietrich Marlene. Stage name of the German-American actress Magdalene von Losch 1904– . She first won fame by her appearance with Emil Jannings in *The Blue Angel* 1930, and went on to Hollywood where her husky voice and 'smouldering' image made her a superstar for 30 years.

Disney 'Walt' (Walter Elias) 1901–66. American film-maker whose name has become almost a by-word for family entertainment. He is best remembered as the inventor of the famous children's cartoon characters Mickey Mouse, Donald Duck, Bambi, and so on.

Eastwood Clint 1930– . American film actor, who started the vogue for 'spaghetti westerns' in films such as *A Fistful of Dollars* 1964.

Eisenstein Sergei Mikhailovich 1898–1948. Soviet film director who pioneered the use of montage (a technique of deliberately juxtaposing shots in such a way as to create a particular meaning) as a means of propaganda, as in *Battleship Potemkin* 1925.

Fairbanks Douglas 1883–1939. American actor, famous for his swashbuckling style, whose silent films include *The Three Musketeers* 1915. He and Mary Pickford, whom he married in 1920, were idolized as 'the world's sweethearts'.

Fairbanks Douglas, Junior 1909– . American actor, son of Douglas Fairbanks, who excelled in similar roles, for example *The Prisoner of Zenda* 1937.

Fassbinder Rainer Werner 1946–82. German film director, noted for his enormous productivity (over 30 films) and stylized films about love, hate, and prejudice, such as *Fear Eats the Soul* 1974.

Fellini Federico 1920– . Italian film director, noted for his strongly subjective poetic imagery. His films include *La Strada* 1954, *La Dolce Vita* 1960, and *8 1/2* 1963.

Fields W(illiam) C(laude) 1879–1946. American actor and screenwriter. One of the most original comedians to appear in films, his distinctive speech and professed anti-establishment attitudes gained him enormous popularity in films such as *The Bank Dick* 1940 and *Never Give a Sucker an Even Break* 1941. He has remained a cult figure over 40 years after his death.

Flaherty Robert 1884–1951. American pioneer documentary film director. His most famous film is *Nanook of the North* 1920.

Flynn Errol 1909–59. Australian actor, noted for his dashing, swashbuckling roles. His films include *Captain Blood* 1935 and *The Master of Ballantrae* 1953.

Fonda Henry 1905–82. American film actor whose engaging sincerity made him ideal in the role of the American pioneer and honourable man. His films include *Grapes of Wrath* 1940.

Fonda Jane 1937– . American actress, daughter of Henry Fonda, and active in left-wing politics; she won Academy Awards for her performances in *Klute* 1971 and *Coming Home* 1979.

Ford John 1895–1973. Irish-American film director. Active from the silent days, he was one of the original creators of the 'western'.

His *Stagecoach* 1939 is generally regarded as a masterpiece of the genre.

Gable Clark 1901–60. American actor celebrated for his romantic roles, and nicknamed the 'king of Hollywood'. His most famous role was as Rhett Butler in *Gone With the Wind* 1939.

Gance Abel 1889– . French director, whose *Napoléon* 1927, recently re-released to wide critical acclaim, is generally regarded as a masterpiece.

Garbo Greta. Stage name of Swedish actress Greta Lovisa Gustafsson 1905– . One of the first silent Hollywood stars, she went on to become a legend. Her films include *Anna Christie* 1930, *Mata Hari* 1931, *Anna Karenina* 1935, and *Ninotchka* 1939.

Garland Judy. Stage name of American singer and actress Frances Gumm 1922–69. She is best remembered for her childhood role of Dorothy in *The Wizard of Oz* 1939, featuring the song 'Over the Rainbow'.

Godard Jean-Luc 1930– . French film director, known for his highly innovative use of cutting and visual juxtapositions. His films include *A Bout du Souffle* 1959.

Goldwyn Samuel 1882–1974. American film producer. One of the leading figures in the Hollywood power struggles of the 1920s and 1930s, he was famed for his 'Goldwynisms', such as 'Anyone who visits a psychiatrist should have his head examined.'

Grant Cary. Stage name of Anglo-American actor Archibald Leach 1904–86. His screen personality as the witty, casual, debonair man made him a favourite for more than three decades. His films include *The Philadelphia Story* 1940 and *Notorious* 1946.

Grierson John 1898–1972. Scottish film producer who pioneered the documentary film in Britain. His films include *Drifters* 1929 and *Night Mail* 1936.

Griffith D(avid) W(ark) 1875–1948. American film director and one of the most influential figures in the development of the cinema as an art. Pioneer of the techniques of flashback, close-up and longshot, his masterpiece as director was *Birth of a Nation* 1915.

Guinness Sir Alec 1914– . Celebrated British character actor who has excelled in dramatic portrayals. His performance in *Bridge on the River Kwai* 1957 earned him an Academy Award. He was knighted in 1959.

Harlow Jean. Stage name of American film actress Harlean Carpentier 1911–37. A toughly frank sex symbol of the 1930s, she was the first 'platinum blonde'. Her films include *Hell's Angels* 1930 and *Saratoga* 1937.

Hawks Howard 1896–1977. American director and producer of a wide range of films with popular appeal, including *The Big Sleep* 1946.

Head Edith 1900–81. American costume designer for a thousand films, who won eight Academy Awards, for films including *The Heiress* 1949 and *The Sting* 1973.

Hepburn Katharine 1909– . American actress whose gangly grace and husky voice brought stardom in films from *Morning Glory* 1933, to *Guess Who's Coming to Dinner* 1967, and *The Lion in Winter* 1968, for all of which she received Academy Awards.

Hitchcock Sir Alfred 1899–1980. British-American film director. Noted for creating suspense in his mystery films, his camera-work, and his hallmark of making 'walk-on' appearances in his own films, which include *The Thirty-Nine Steps* 1935, *Strangers on a Train* 1951, *Psycho* 1960, and *The Birds* 1963.

Hoffman Dustin 1937– . American actor who popularized the role of the anti-hero in the 1960s and 1970s. His films include *The Graduate* 1967, *Midnight Cowboy* 1969, and *Kramer vs Kramer* 1979, for which he won an Academy Award.

Howard Leslie. Stage name of British film actor Leslie Stainer 1893–1943. He specialized in the romantically idealistic, sensitive hero. His films include *The Scarlet Pimpernel* 1935, and *Gone With the Wind* 1939.

Howard Trevor Wallace 1916– . British film actor best known for his role in *Brief Encounter* 1945.

Ivory James 1928– . American director best known for his collaboration with Indian producer Ismael Merchant. Merchant-Ivory productions include *Shakespeare Wallah* 1965,

The Europeans 1979, *Heat and Dust* and *Room with a View* 1986.

Jolson Al. Stage name of Russian-born American singer Asa Yoelson 1886–1950. He was a star of early sound films, for example *The Jazz Singer* 1927.

Karloff Boris. Stage name of British actor William Henry Pratt 1887–1969, Best known for his appearances in horror films such as *The Mummy* 1932, his portrayals of the Frankenstein monster have become classics.

Kaye Danny. Stage name of American film comedian Daniel Kominski 1913–87. His films include *The Secret Life of Walter Mitty* 1946. In 1954 he was given a special Academy Award for his 'unique talents, his service to the industry and the American people'.

Keaton Buster. Stage name of American comedian Joseph Frank Keaton 1896–1966. One of the great silent-film comedians, his films include *The General* 1926.

Korda Sir Alexander 1893–1956. Hungarian-born British film producer and director, a dominant figure during the 1930s and 1940s. His films include *The Private Life of Henry VIII* 1933, *The Third Man* 1950, and *Richard III* 1956.

Kubrick Stanley 1928– . American-born British film director, producer, and screenwriter. After initial success in Hollywood, he moved to Britain in 1961 where he made films such as *Dr Strangelove* 1964. His *2001: A Space Odyssey* 1968 has acquired the status of a classic among science fiction films.

Kurosawa Akira 1910– . Japanese director whose films, including *Throne of Blood* 1957, *Kagemusha*, and *Ran* are characterized by their magnificent epic quality and visual splendour. He is one of the few Japanese directors to gain international acclaim.

Lang Fritz 1890–1976. Austrian film director with a distinctive style of film-making. His works are heavily tinged with pessimism and include *Metropolis* 1925 and *The Big Heat* 1953.

Laughton Charles 1899–1962. Anglo-American character actor, who specialized in larger-than-life roles such as the king in *The Private Life of Henry VIII* 1933 (for which he won an Academy Award).

Laurel and Hardy Stan Laurel 1890-1965 and Oliver Hardy 1892-1957. American film comedians (Laurel was English-born). The most successful comedy team in the history of the screen, their unique partnership survived the transition from silent films to sound, and delighted audiences for decades. Their films were revived as a worldwide cult in the 1970s and include *Way Out West* 1937 and *A Chump at Oxford* 1940.

Lean Sir David 1908– . British film director who specializes in atmospheric films. His work includes *The Bridge on the River Kwai* 1957, *Lawrence of Arabia* 1962 (for which he won Academy Awards) and *A Passage to India* 1985.

Losey Joseph 1909–84. Influential American director, who also worked in the UK, and whose films include *The Servant* 1963 and *The Go-Between* 1971.

Lubitsch Ernst 1892–1947. German-American film director, known for his stylish comedies, for example *Ninotchka* 1939, starring Greta Garbo.

Lucas George 1944– . American director and producer. He is best known for his collaboration with Steven Spielberg on *Star Wars* 1977, *The Empire Strikes Back* 1980, and *Return of the Jedi* 1983.

Lumière Auguste 1862–1954 and Louis 1864–1948. French brothers, pioneers of the colour photograph and the commercial cinema.

Merchant Ismael 1936. Indian producer, who collaborated with James Ivory on films including *Shakespeare Wallah* 1965, *The Europeans* 1979, *Heat and Dust* 1983, and *Room with a View* 1986.

Mills Sir John 1908– . British actor-director, who established his reputation in stiff-upper-lip wartime roles, as in *In Which We Serve* 1942. Later films include *Ryan's Daughter* 1971 (for which he received an Academy Award). He was Knighted in 1976.

Monroe Marilyn. Stage name of American actress Norma Jean Mortenson 1926–62, who has become a screen legend since her death.

Her films include *The Seven Year Itch* 1955 and *Some Like It Hot* 1959.

Murnau Pseudonym of the German film director Friedrich Wilhelm Plumpe 1889–1931, one of the greatest directors of the classic period of silent films. His films include *Nosferatu* 1922.

Newman Paul 1925– . American actor and director. Hollywood's leading male star of the 1960s and 1970s, he has a series of creditable performances to his name in films such as *The Hustler* 1962 and *The Color of Money* 1986 (for which he won an Academy Award).

Olivier Laurence Kerr, Baron Olivier 1907– . English actor and director. Although predominantly a stage actor, his acting and direction of filmed versions of Shakespeare's plays have received outstanding critical acclaim, for example *Henry V* 1944, *Hamlet* 1948 (both of which earned him Academy Awards), and *Richard III* 1955.

Ozu Yasujiro 1903–63. Japanese film director who has gained popularity in the West in recent years. His films include *Tokyo Story* 1953.

Pasolini Pier Paolo 1922–75. Italian film director, one of the most influential figures of the post-war years. His films include *The Gospel According to St Matthew* 1904 and *The Decameron* 1970.

Polanski Roman 1933– . French-born director. He suffered a traumatic childhood in Nazi-occupied Poland and later, his wife, actress Sharon Tate, was the victim of a particularly brutal murder. His tragic personal life is reflected in a fascination with horror and violence in his work. His films include *Repulsion* 1965, *Cul de Sac* 1966, *Rosemary's Baby* 1968, and *Tess* 1979.

Powell Michael 1905– . English director, best known for his collaboration with screenwriter Emeric Pressburger. Their work, often criticized for over-extravagance, shows an extraordinary imagination and originality. Films include *Black Narcissus* 1947 and *A Matter of Life and Death* 1946.

Puttnam David Terence 1941– . British film producer largely influential in reviving the British film industry internationally. Notable successes include *Chariots of Fire* 1981 and *The Killing Fields* 1984.

Ray Satyajit 1921– . Indian film director, noted for his trilogy of life in his native Bengal: *Pather Panchali/Unvanquished* and *The World of Apu* 1955–59.

Reed Sir Carol 1906–76. British film producer and director, an influential figure in the British film industry of the 1940s. His work includes *The Third Man* 1950.

Renoir Jean 1894–1979. French film director, noted for his sensitive and subtle portrayal of social realism and his use of powerful visual imagery. His films include *La Grande Illusion/Grand Illusion* 1937 and *Regle du Jour/The Rules of the Game* 1939. In 1975 he received an honorary Academy Award for his life's work.

Resnais Alain 1922– . French director whose work is characterized by a preoccupation with memory and non-conventional concepts of time. His distinctive techniques are much admired, and his *L'Année Dernière à Marienbad/Last Year at Marienbad* 1961 is generally regarded as a masterpiece.

Roeg Nicolas 1928– . British film director. His work is noted for its stylish visual appeal and imaginative, often off-beat, treatment of subjects. His films include *Walkabout* 1971, *Don't Look Now* 1973, and *Castaway* 1986.

Russell Ken 1927– . British director. A flamboyant film-maker, he is often criticized for self-indulgence in his work, which is full of vitality, imagination and extravagance. His films include *Women in Love* 1969, *The Music Lovers* 1971, *Altered States* 1979, and *Gothic* 1986.

Scorsese Martin 1942– . American director whose films concentrate heavily on complex characterization and the theme of alienation. His work includes *Mean Streets* 1973, *Taxi Driver* 1976, *Raging Bull* 1979, and *The Color of Money* 1986.

Selznick David O(liver) 1902–65. American film producer. His independent company Selznick International was responsible for many influential films of the 1930s and 1940s, including *Gone With the Wind* 1939.

Spielberg Steven 1947– . American director, whose hugely successful films, including *Close Encounters of the Third Kind* 1977, *Raiders of the Lost Ark* 1983, and *ET* 1985 have given popular cinema a new 'respectable' appeal.

Stewart James 1908– . American actor who specialized in the role of the gangly, stubbornly honest, ordinary American, for example *Mr Smith Goes to Washington* 1939.

Streep Meryl 1951– . American actress noted for her strong character roles. Her films include *The Deer Hunter* 1978, *Kramer vs Kramer* 1979, and *Out of Africa* 1986.

Tarkovsky Andrei 1932–86. Russian film director whose work is characterized by unorthodox cinematic techniques and visual beauty. His films include the science fiction epic *Solaris* 1972, *Mirror* 1975, and *The Sacrifice* 1986.

Tati Jacques. Stage name of French actor and film director Jacques Tatischeff 1908–82. A brilliant comic mime artist, he is best remembered for *Monsieur Hulot's Holiday* 1953.

Taylor Elizabeth 1932– . English-born American actress, one of the most popular screen personalities of all time. Her films include *Butterfield 8* 1960 (for which she won an Academy Award) and *Cleopatra* 1963.

Temple Shirley 1928– . American actress, most successful child star of the 1930s. Her films include *Bright Eyes* 1934, in which she sang 'Good Ship Lollipop' and for which she received an Academy Award.

Truffaut Francois 1932–84. French director who won international acclaim with *Jules et Jim* 1961 and *Day for Night* 1973 (for which he won an Academy Award). His work was largely influenced by Hitchcock.

Valentino Rudolf 1895–1926. Italian film actor, the archetypal romantic lover of the Hollywood silent films, for example *The Sheik* 1922 and *Blood and Sand* 1922.

Visconti Luchino 1906–76. Italian film director who pioneered the naturalistic style of film-making, that was later to be associated with De Sica. His films include *Ossessione/ Obsession* 1942, *Il gattopardo/The Leopard* 1963, and *Death in Venice* 1971.

Wajda Andrzej 1926– . Polish director. One of the major figures in post-war European cinema, his work includes the cult film *Ashes and Diamonds* 1953 and *Man of Marble* 1977.

Warhol Andy 1927–87. American filmmaker and pop artist, whose plotless experimental avant-garde films, though ridiculed by some, were an important part of the cultural scene of the 1960s and 1970s. His work includes *Sleep* 1963, *Flesh* 1968, and *Trash* 1980.

Wayne John. Stage name of American actor Marion Morrison 1907–79, nicknamed 'duke', from the name of a dog he once owned, Wayne was the archetypal 'western' star. His films include *Stagecoach* 1939 and *True Grit* 1969 (for which he won an Academy Award).

Weir Peter 1938– . Australian director. His works are characterized by their atmospheric quality and often contains a strong spiritual element. They include *Picture at Hanging Rock* 1975, *Witnesss* 1985, *and Mosquito Coast* 1986.

Welles Orson 1915–86. American writer, actor, director. Experimentalist and controversial life-force of the cinema whose first Hollywood film *Citizen Kane* 1941 is still regarded by many critics as the best film ever made.

Wilder Billy 1906– . Austrian-American film director, noted for such sophisticated comedies as *Some Like it Hot* 1959 and *The Apartment* 1960.

ACADEMY AWARD WINNERS ('OSCARS')

Annual cinema awards have been given from 1927 onwards by the American Academy of Motion Pictures, nicknamed 'Oscars' (1931), allegedly because a new secretary exclaimed (of the bronze statuette presented to winners) 'That's like my uncle Oscar!'

Year	*Award*	
1972	*Best Picture:*	*The Godfather*
	Best Director:	Bob Fosse *Cabaret*
	Best Actor:	Marlon Brando *The Godfather*
	Best Actress:	Liza Minnelli *Cabaret*
1973	*Best Picture:*	*The Sting*
	Best Director:	George Roy Hill *The Sting*
	Best Actor:	Jack Lemmon *Save the Tiger*
	Best Actress:	Glenda Jackson *A Touch of Class*
1974	*Best Picture:*	*The Godfather II*
	Best Director:	Francis Ford Coppola *The Godfather II*
	Best Actor:	Art Carney *Harry and Tonto*
	Best Actress:	Ellen Burstyn *Alice Doesn't Live Here Anymore*
1975	*Best Picture:*	*One Flew Over the Cuckoo's Nest*
	Best Director:	Milos Forman *One Flew Over the Cuckoo's Nest*
	Best Actor:	Jack Nicholson *One Flew Over the Cuckoo's Nest*
1976	*Best Picture:*	*Rocky*
	Best Director:	John G Avildsen *Rocky*
	Best Actor:	Peter Finch *Network*
	Best Actress:	Faye Dunaway *Network*
1977	*Best Picture:*	*Annie Hall*
	Best Director:	Woody Allen *Annie Hall*
	Best Actor:	Richard Dreyfuss *The Goodbye Girl*
	Best Actress:	Diane Keaton *Annie Hall*
1978	*Best Picture:*	*The Deer Hunter*
	Best Director:	Michael Cimino *The Deer Hunter*
	Best Actor:	Jon Voight *Coming Home*
	Best Actress:	Jane Fonda *Coming Home*
1979	*Best Picture:*	*Kramer vs Kramer*
	Best Director:	Robert Beaton *Kramer vs Kramer*
	Best Actor:	Dustin Hoffman *Kramer vs Kramer*
	Best Actress:	Sally Field *Norma Rae*

1980   *Best Picture:*   Ordinary People
              Best Director: Robert Redford *Ordinary People*
              Best Actor: Robert de Niro *Raging Bull*
              Best Actress: Sissy Spacek *Coalminer's Daughter*

1981   *Best Picture:*   *Chariots of Fire*
              Best Director: Warren Beatty *Reds*
              Best Actor: Henry Fonda *On Golden Pond*
              Best Actress: Katharine Hepburn *On Golden Pond*

1982   *Best Picture:*   *Gandhi*
              Best Director: Richard Attenborough *Gandhi*
              Best Actor: Ben Kingsley *Gandhi*
              Best Actress: Mery Streep *Sophie's Choice*

1983   *Best Picture:*   *Terms of Endearment*
              Best Director: James L Brooks *Terms of Endearment*
              Best Actor: Robert Duvall *Tender Mercies*
              Best Actress: Shirley MacLaine *Terms of Endearment*

1984   *Best Picture:*   *Amadeus*
              Best Director: Milos Forman *Amadeus*
              Best Actor: F Murray Abraham *Amadeus*
              Best Actress: Sally Field *Places in the Heart*

1985   *Best Picture:*   *Out of Africa*
              Best Director: Sidney Pollack *Out of Africa*
              Best Actor: William Hurt *Kiss of the Spider Woman*
              Best Actress: Geraldine Page *The Trip to Bountiful*

1986   *Best Picture:*   *Platoon*
              Best Director: Oliver Stone *Platoon*
              Best Actor: Paul Newman *The Color of Money*
              Best Actress: Marlee Matlin *Children of A Lesser God*

1987   *Best Picture:*   *The Last Emperor*
              Best Director: Bernardo Bertolucci *The Last Emperor*
              Best Actor: Michael Douglas *Wall Street*
              Best Actress: Cher *Moonstruck*

1988   *Best Picture:*   Rain Man
              Best Director: Barry Levinson *Rain Man*
              Best Actor: Dustin Hoffman *Rain Man*
              Best Actress: Jodie Foster *The Accused*

1826–34	Various machines invented to show moving images: the stroboscope, zoetrope, and thaumatrope.
1872	Eadweard Muybridge demonstrated movement of horses' legs using 24 cameras.
1877	Invention of Praxinoscope; developed as a projector of successive images on screen in 1879 in France.
1878–95	Marey, a French physiologist, developed various forms of camera for recording human and animal movements.
1887	Augustin le Prince produced the first series of images on a perforated film; Thomas Edison, having developed the phonograph, took the first steps in developing a motion-picture recording and reproducing device to accompany recorded sound.
1888	William Friese-Green showed the first celluloid film and patented a movie camera.
1889	Edison invented 35mm film.
1890–94	Edison, using perforated film, developed his Kinetograph camera and Kinetoscope individual viewer; developed commercially in New York, London and Paris.
1895	The Lumière brothers, Auguste (1862–1954) and Louis (1864–1948) projected, to a paying audience, a film of a train arriving at a station. Some of the audience fled in terror.
1896	Pathe introduced the Berliner gramophone, using discs in synchronization with film. Lack of amplification, however, made the performances ineffective.
1899	Edison tried to improve amplification by using banks of phonographs.
1900	Attempts to synchronize film and disc were made by Gaumont in France and Goldschmidt in Germany, leading later to the American Vitaphone system.
1902	Georges Méliès (1861–1938) made *Le Voyage dans la Lune/A Trip to the Moon*.
1903	The first 'western' was made in the USA: *The Great Train Robbery* by Edwin S Porter.
1906	The earliest colour film (Kinemacolor) was patented in Britain by George Albert Smith.
1908–11	In France, Emile Cohl experimented with film animation.
1910	With the dominating influence of the Hollywood Studios, film actors and actresses began to be recognized as international stars.
1912	In Britain, Eugene Lauste designed experimental 'sound on film' systems.
1914–18	Full newsreel coverage of World War I
1915	*The Birth of a Nation*, D W Griffith's epic on the American Civil War, was released in the USA.
1917	35mm was officially adopted as the standard format for motion picture film by the Society of Motion Picture Engineers of America.

1918–19	A sound system called Tri-Ergon was developed in Germany which led to sound being recorded on film photographically. The photography of sound was developed by Lee De Forrest in his Phonofilm system.
1923	First sound film (as Phonofilm) demonstrated
1926	*Don Juan*, a silent film with a synchronized music score was released.
1927	The first major sound film, *The Jazz Singer*, consisting of some songs and a few moments of dialogue, by Warners, New York. The first Academy Awards (Oscars) were given.
1928	Walt Disney released his first Mickey Mouse cartoon, *Steamboat Willie*. The first all-talking film *Lights of New York*.
1930	*The Big Trail*, a western filmed and shown in 70mm rather than the standard 35mm format, was released. 70mm is still used, but usually only for big budget epics such as *Lawrence of Arabia*.
1932	Technicolor (three-colour) process was used for a Walt Disney cartoon film.
1935	*Becky Sharp*, the first film in three-colour Technicolor (a process now abandoned), was released.
1937	Walt Disney released the first feature length (82 minutes) cartoon, *Snow White and the Seven Dwarfs*.
1939	*Gone With the Wind*, regarded as one of Hollywood's greatest achievments, was released.
1952	Cinerama, a wide-screen presentation utilizing 3 cameras and 3 projectors, was introduced in New York.
1953	Commercial 3-D (three-dimensional) cinema and wide screen Cinemascope were launched in the USA. Cinemascope used a single camera and projector to produce a widescreen effect by using an anamorphic lens. The cameras were clumsy and the audiences disliked wearing the obligatory glasses. The new widescreen cinema was accompanied by the introduction of Stereographic sound which eventually became standard.
1959	The first film in 'Smell-O-Vision', *The Scent of Mystery*, was released. The process did not catch on.
1970	Most major films were released in Dolby Stereo.
1976-77	Most films became available on video for viewing at home.
1982	3-D made a comeback. Some of the films released using the process, such as *Jaws 3* and *Friday the Thirteenth Part Three*, were commercial successes but the revival was short lived.

Photography

Photography is a process for producing images on sensitized materials by various forms of radiant energy: for example, visible light, ultra-violet, infra-red, or X-rays; radioactive radiation; or an electron beam. Alhazen (965–1038), Arab scientist and mathematician, described the principles of the lens and camera obscura (a tiny hole in the wall of a darkened room which can produce an inverted image of the scene outside) and the theory of human vision in the early 11th century, but modern photography began in the 19th century.

This section contains *Biographies* of a selection of people who have made important contributions to the technical and artistic development of photography, definitions of technical *Terms*, and a *Chronology* of the history of photography.

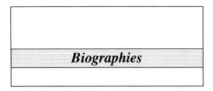

Biographies

Adams Ansel 1902–84. American photographer, particularly known for his superbly-printed images of dramatic landscapes and organic forms of the American West. He was associated with the Zone System of exposure estimation.

Atget Eugene 1857–1927. French photographer. He took up photography at the age of 40, and for 30 years documented urban Paris, leaving a huge body of work.

Avedon Richard 1923– . American photographer. A successful fashion photographer with *Harper's Bazaar* magazine in New York in the mid 1940s, he has become one of the highest-paid commercial photographers.

Beaton Cecil 1904–80. British portrait and fashion photographer, designer, illustrator, diarist and noted conversationalist.

Brandt Bill 1905–83. British photographer, who produced a large body of richly-printed and romantic black and white studies of people, London and nudes. He also published many photographic books.

Brassäi. Pseudonym of Gyula Halesz 1899–1986. French photographer of Hungarian origin. From the early 1930s on he documented, mainly by flash, the nightlife of Paris, before turning to more abstract work.

Cameron Julia Margaret 1815–79. British photographer. She made lively, portraits of the Victorian intelligentsia using a large camera, five-minute exposures and wet plates.

Cartier-Bresson Henri 1908– . French photographer. Considered the greatest of photographic artists. His documentary work was achieved using a small format camera. He was noted for his ability to structure the image and to capture the decisive moment.

Daguerre Louis Jacques Mande 1787–1851. French pioneer of photography. Together with Niépce, he is credited with the invention of photography (though others were reaching the same point simultaneously). His method of producing daguerreotypes 1835,a one-off image process, was patented in 1839, to be superseded ten years later by Fox Talbot's negative/positive process.

Evans Walker 1903–75. American photographer, best known for his documentary photographs of changing America during the 1930s and 1940s.

Fenton Roger 1819–69. British photographer. The world's first war photographer, he went to the Crimea in 1855; he also founded the Royal Photographic Society in London.

Herschel Sir John 1792–1871. English scientist and astronomer who discovered and used hypo (sodium thiosulphate) as a print fixer, the word 'photography' from Greek *photos* ('light') and *graphos* ('drawing') and the terms 'negative' and 'positive'.

Hill and Adamson David Octavius Hill 1802–70 and Robert R Adamson 1821–48. Scots photographers who, working together, turned out 2,500 calotypes (mostly portraits) in five years from 1843.

Hine Lewis 1874–1940. American sociologist. He recorded in photographs child labour conditions in US factories at the beginning of this century, his work leading to a change in the law.

Kertesz Andre 1894–1986. American photographer. A master of the 35mm format camera, he recorded his immediate environment in places such as Paris and New York with wit and style.

Lartigue Jacques-Henri 1894–1986. French photographer. He began taking extraordinary and humorous photographs of his family at the age of seven, and went on to make autochrome colour prints of beautiful women.

Moholy-Nagy Laszlo 1895–1946. American photographer. Through his illuminating theories and practical experiments he had enormous influence on the photography of this century.

Muybridge Eadweard 1830–1904. British photographer. He made a series of animal locomotion photographs in the US in the 1870s which proved that, at speed, animals often do not touch the ground. He then explored motion in birds and humans.

Penn Irving 1917– . American fashion, advertising, portrait, editorial and fine art photographer. He has been associated with *Vogue* magazine in the US throughout his long career.

Steichen Edward 1897–1973. American photographer, best known for his innovative fashion, portrait and documentary work.

Steiglitz Alfred 1864–1946. American photographer. After forming the Photo Secession group in 1903, he began the magazine *Camera Work*. Through exhibitions at his gallery '291' in New York he established photography as an art form.

Strand Paul 1890–1976. American photographer, who used large format cameras for his strong, clear, close-up photographs of natural objects.

Talbot William Henry Fox 1800–77. British pioneer of photography. He made photograms several years before Daguerre's invention was announced and invented the Calotype process, the first negative/positive method. *The Pencil of Nature* 1844 by Fox Talbot was the first book of photographs published.

Uelsmann Jerry 1934– . American photographer, noted for his dream-like images, which he creates by synthesizing many elements into one with great technical skill.

Weston Edward 1886–1958. American photographer. A founder-member of the F64 group, he is noted for technical mastery in his Californian landscapes and nude studies.

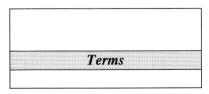

Terms

aperture an opening through which light passing through the lens to strike the film can

be controlled by shutter speed and iris diaphragm, set mechanically or electronically at various diameters.

ASA a numbering system for rating the speed of films, devised by the American Standards Association. It has now been superseded by **ISO**, the International Standards Organisation.

autochrome a single-plate additive colour process devised by the Lumière brothers in 1903. It was the first commercially available process, in use from 1907 to 1935.

calotype a paper-based photograph using a wax paper negative, the first example of the negative/positive process invented by Fox Talbot around 1834.

camera obscura a darkened box with a tiny hole for projecting the inverted image of the scene outside on a screen inside.

Cibachrome a process of printing directly from transparencies introduced in 1963, now marketed by Ilford UK Ltd. Distinguished by rich, saturated colours, it can be home-processed and is one of the most permanent processes.

daguerreotype a one-off photographic image taken by using mercury vapour and iodine sensitized silvered plates; discovered by Daguerre in 1835.

exposure meter a device for measuring light to indicate correct duration of exposure. Reflected light meters average readings reflected from the subject; incident meters measure light falling on the subject.

'f' stops a series of numbers on the lens barrel designating the size of the variable aperture; altering them also changes the appearance of the image.

hypo a term for sodium thiosulphate, discovered in 1819 by Sir John Herschel and used as a fixative for photographic images from 1837.

negative/positive a reverse image, which when printed is again reversed, restoring the original scene. Invented by Fox Talbot around 1834.

orthochromatic film or paper of decreased sensitivity, which can be processed with a red safe-light. Blue objects appear lighter and red ones darker because of increased blue sensitivity.

panchromatic highly sensitive black and white film made to render all visible spectral colours in correct grey tones. It is always developed in total darkness.

Polaroid an American corporation set up by Dr Edwin Land in 1947 when he invented film which yields instant finished prints. Colour Polaroid cameras were introduced in 1963.

SLR camera a single lens reflex camera, in which the image is seen in the taking lens. This type of camera is the most widely used today, and usually comes in 35 mm format.

telephoto lens a lens of longer focal length than normal, taking a very narrow view, and giving a large image through a combination of telescopic and ordinary photographic lenses.

thaumatrope a disc with two different pictures at opposite ends of its surface which combine into one when rapidly rotated because of the persistence of visual impressions.

35 mm a width of film, the most popular format for the modern camera. The 35 mm camera falls into two categories, the SLR and the rangefinder.

TLR camera a twin lens reflex camera, which has a viewing lens mounted above and parallel to the taking lens, of the same angle of view and focal length.

wide-angle lens a lens of shorter focal length than normal, increasing spatial depth between objects taking in a wider angle of view.

zoetrope an optical toy with a series of pictures on the inner surface of a cylinder. When rotated and viewed through a slit, it gives the impression of continuous motion.

zoom lens a lens which by variation of focal length allows speedy transition from long-shots to close-ups.

Zone System a system of exposure estimation which groups infinite tonal gradations into ten zones, zone 0 being black and zone 10 white. An 'f' stop change in exposure is required from zone to zone.

1515	Leonardo da Vinci described the camera obscura.
1750	The painter Canaletto used a camera obscura as an aid to his painting in Venice.
1790	Thomas Wedgewood in England made photograms – placing objects on leather, sensitized using silver nitrate.
1826	Nicephore Niépce 1765–1833, a French doctor, produced the world's first photograph from nature on pewter plates with a camera obscura and an eight-hour exposure.
1835	Niépce and L J M Daguerre produced the first daguerreotype camera photograph.
1839	Daguerre was awarded an annuity by the French government and his process given to the world.
1841	Fox Talbot's calotype process was patented – the first multi-copy method of photography using a negative/positive process, sensitized with silver iodide.
1843	Hill and Adamson began to use calotypes for portraits in Edinburgh.
1844	Fox Talbot published the first photographic book, *The Pencil of Nature*.
1851	Fox Talbot used a one-thousandth of a second exposure to demonstrate high-speed photography.
1855	Roger Fenton made documentary photographs of the Crimean War from a specially constructed caravan with portable darkroom.
1859	Under the pseudonym Nadar, Gaspard-Felix Tournachan 1820–1910, French writer, caricature amd photographer, made photographs underground in Paris using battery-powered arc lights.
1860	Queen Victoria was photographed by Mayall. Abraham Lincoln was photographed by Matthew Brady for political campaigning.
1861	The single lens reflex plate camera was patented by Thomas Sutton.
1862	Nadar took aerial photographs over Paris.
1870	Julia Margaret Cameron used long lenses for her distinctive portraits.
1878	In the US Eadweard Muybridge analysed the movements of animals through sequential photographs, using a series of cameras.
1880	A silver bromide emulsion was fixed with hypo. Photographs were first reproduced in newspapers in New York using the half-tone engraving process. The first twin-lens reflex camera was produced in London.
1889	Eastman Company in the US produced the Kodak No. 1 camera and roll film, facilitating universal, hand-held snapshots.
1902	In Germany Deckel invented a prototype leaf shutter and Zeiss introduced the Tessar lens.
1904	The autochrome colour process was patented by the Lumière brothers.
1905	Alfred Steiglitz opened the gallery '291' in New York promoting photography. Lewis Hine used photography to expose the exploitation of children in American factories, causing protective laws to be passed.
1907	The autochrome process began to be factory-produced.
1914	Oskar Barnack designed a prototype Leica camera for Leitz in Germany.

1924   Leitz launched the first 35 mm camera, the Leica, delayed because of World War I. It became very popular with photo-journalists because it was quiet, small, dependable and had a range of lenses and accessories.

1929   Rolleiflex produced a twin-lens reflex camera in Germany.

1935   In the US, Mannes and Godowsky invented Kodachrome transparency film, which has great sharpness and rich colour quality. Electronic flash was invented in the US. Social documentary photography received wide attention through the photographs of Dorothea Lange, Margaret Bourke-White, Arthur Rothstein, Walker Evans, and others taken for the US government's Farm Security Administration of the plight of the poor tenant farmers in the mid-West.

1936   *Life* magazine, noted for photo-journalism, was first published in the US.

1938   *Picture Post* magazine was introduced in the UK.

1940   Multigrade enlarging paper by Ilford was made available in the UK.

1945   The Zone System of exposure estimation was explained in the book *Exposure Record* by Ansel Adams.

1947   Polaroid black and white instant process film was invented by Dr Edwin Land, who set up the Polaroid corporation in Boston, Massachusetts. The principles of holography were demonstrated in England by Dennis Gabor.

1955   Kodak introduced Tri-X, a black and white 200 ASA film.

1959   The zoom lens was invented in Germany by Voigtlander.

1960   Laser was invented in the US, making holography possible. Polacolor, a self-processing colour film, was introduced by Polaroid, using a 60–second colour film and dye diffusion technique.

1963   Cibachrome, paper and chemicals for printing directly from transparencies, was made available by Ciba-Geigy of Switzerland. One of the most permanent processes, it is marketed by Ilford in the UK.

1969   Photographs were taken on the moon by US astronauts.

1972   SX70 system, a single lens reflex camera with instant prints, was produced by Polaroid.

1980   Ansel Adams sold an original print *Moonrise:Hernandez* for $45,000, a record price, in the US. Voyager 1 sent photographs of Saturn back to earth across space.

1985   Minolta Corporation in Japan introduced the world's first body-integral autofocus single lens reflex camera.

Literature

The great body of world literature consists of words set apart in some way from ordinary everyday communication. In the ancient oral traditions, before stories and poems were written down, literature had a mainly public function – mythic and religious. As literary works came to be preserved in writing, and then, eventually, printed, their role tended to become more private, as a vehicle for the exploration and expression of emotion and of the human situation. Aesthetic criteria came increasingly to the fore; the English poet and critic Coleridge defined prose as words in their best order, and poetry as the 'best' words in the best order. The distinction between verse and prose is not always clear cut, but in practice poetry tends to be metrically formal (making it easier to memorize), whereas prose corresponds more closely to the patterns of ordinary speech. Poetry therefore had an early advantage over prose in the days before printing, which it has not relinquished until comparatively recently. Over the centuries poetry has taken on a wide range of forms, from the lengthy narrative such as the epic to the lyric, expressing personal emotion in songlike form; from the ballad, and the 14-line sonnet, to the extreme conciseness of the 17-syllable Japanese haiku. Prose came into its own in the West as a vehicle for imaginative literature with the rise of the modern novel in the 18th century.

This section consists of an overview of various *Literary Genres* and types of literature; biographical notes on a selection of the world's *Great Writers*; lists of recent winners of *Literary Prizes*; and a *Chronology* highlighting major developments and leading writers in world literature from ancient to modern times. Throughout this section the emphasis is on non-dramatic literature; plays and playwrights are treated separately in the Theatre section. Language, and the languages of the world, the material of literature – including grammar and usage – are covered in a separate section.

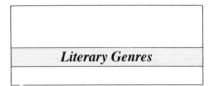

Literary Genres

allegory the description or illustration of one thing in terms of another; a work of poetry or prose in the form of an extended metaphor or parable which makes use of symbolic fictional characters, as in the allegorical romantic epic *The Faerie Queene* 1590–96 by Edmund Spenser in homage to Queen Elizabeth I. Allegory is often used for moral purposes, as in John Bunyan's *Pilgrim's Progress* 1678. Medieval allegory often used animals as characters; this tradition survives today in such works as *Animal Farm* 1945 by George Orwell.

biography an account of a person's life. When it is written by that person, it is an *autobiography*. Biography can be simply a factual narrative, but it was also firmly established as a literary form in the 18th century in England with *Lives of the English Poets* 1779–81 by Samuel Johnson and Samuel Boswell's biography of Johnson 1791.

children's literature in the sense of works specifically written for children is relatively recent; the earliest known illustrated children's book in English is *Goody Two Shoes* 1765, possibly written by Oliver Goldsmith. *Fairy tales* were originally part of a vast range of oral literature, credited only to the writer who first recorded them, such as Charles Perrault. During the 19th century several writers including Hans Christian Andersen wrote original stories in the fairytale genre; others, such as the Grimm brothers, collected (and sometimes adapted) existing stories. Early children's stories were always written with a moral purpose; this was particularly true in the 19th century, apart from the unique case of Lewis Carroll's *Alice* books. The late 19th century was the great era of children's literature in the UK, with Lewis Carroll, Beatrix Potter, Charles Kingsley, and J M Barrie. It was also the

golden age of illustrated children's books, with such artists as Kate Greenaway. Among the great 20th-century children's writers in English have been Kenneth Grahame (*The Wind in the Willows* 1908) and A A Milne (*Winnie the Pooh* 1926). *Adventure stories* have often appealed to children even when written for adults – examples include *Robinson Crusoe* by Daniel Defoe, and the satirical *Gulliver's Travels* by Jonathan Swift. *Books about animals* today occupy a position which seems to be both for adults and children – *Watership Down* by Richard Adams is an example.

detective fiction novels or short stories in which a mystery is solved mainly by the action of a professional or amateur dective. Where the mystery to be solved concerns the commission of a crime, the work is called *crime fiction*. The earliest work of detective fiction as understood today was *Murders in The Rue Morgue* 1841 by Edgar Allen Poe, and his detective Dupin became the model for those who detected by deduction from a series of clues. The most popular deductive sleuth was Sherlock Holmes in the stories by Sir Arthur Conan Doyle. The height of the genre was the 'golden age': the period from the 1920s to the 1940s, when the most famous writers were women – Agatha Christie, Margery Allingham, Dorothy L Sayers. Types of detective fiction include the *police procedural*, where the mystery is solved by detailed police work, as in the work of Swedish writers Maj Sjowall and Per Wahloo; the *inverted novel*, where the identity of the criminal is known from the beginning, only the method or the motive remaining to be discovered, as in *Malice Aforethought* by Francis Iles; the *hard-boiled school* of private investigators begun by Raymond Chandler and Dashiell Hammett, which became known for its social realism and explicit violence. More recently, the form and traditions of the genre are used as a framework within which to explore other concerns, as in *Innocent Blood* and *A Taste For Death* by P D James, *The Name of the Rose* by Umberto Eco, and the works of many women writers who explore feminist ideas, for example Barbara Wilson with *Murder in the Collective* . As with most genres, crime fiction has produced its oddities: *Murder in Pastiche* by Marion Mainwaring is written in the styles of nine famous writers; Agatha Christie, Georgette Heyer and Ellis Peters have all written detective novels with historical settings; *Murder Off Miami* by Dennis Wheatley was a dossier containing real clues such as photographs, ticket stubs, and hairpins for the reader to solve the mystery. The solution was in a closed envelope at the back of the book.

epic a narrative poem or cycle of poems dealing with some great action, often the founding of a nation or the forging of national unity, and often using religious or cosmological themes. In the Western tradition, the crucial works are the *Iliad* and *Odyssey* attributed to Homer, works probably intended to be chanted in sections at feasts. Greek and later criticism, which considered the Homeric epic the highest form of poetry, produced a genre of *secondary epic*, notably the *Aeneid* of Virgil, Tasso's *Jerusalem Delivered* and Milton's *Paradise Lost*, which attempt to emulate Homer, often for a patron or a political cause. The term epic is also applied to narrative poems of other traditions in Europe: the Anglo-Saxon *Beowulf* and the Finnish *Kalevala*; in India the *Ramayana* and *Mahabharata*; the Babylonian *Gilgamesh*; all of these had evolved in different societies to suit similar social needs and used similar literary techniques.

essay a short prose work which deals in a personal and often meditative way with a particular subject. The term was first used in French, for Montaigne's *Essais* 1580–95, and the form became popular in the 18th century with the development of periodicals such as the *Tatler* and *Spectator* in England. In the 19th century the essay was often used as a vehicle for literary criticism. The term essay is less used today, although its form and approach survive, particularly in newspapers and magazines as 'opinion pieces'.

fantasy non-realistic fiction. Much of the world's fictional literature could be called fantasy, but as a contemporary genre fantasy

started to thrive in the late 1960s after the success of Tolkien's *Lord of the Rings* 1954–55. Earlier works by such writers as Lord Dunsany, Hope Mirrlees and E R Eddison which are not classifiable in fantasy subgenres such as science fiction, horror, or the ghost story could be called fantasy. Dominant themes, drawn from the stock of world literature, used by Tolkien and his imitators, are those of the quest for a cure for evil and the reconciliation of the demands of the fantasy world and the more domestic claims of the ordinary world. Much fantasy is pseudo-medieval in subject matter and tone, following the spirit rather than the substance of Tolkien; but another strong influence has been the work of Mervyn Peake – *Titus Groan* 1946, *Gormenghast* 1950, and *Titus Alone* 1959 – in its grotesquerie and passion. Important works since Tolkien are Ursula Le Guin's *Earthsea Trilogy* and Stephen Donaldson's *Thomas Covenant*. Important works in the more urban tradition of Peake are John Crowley's *Little Big*, Michael Moorcock's *Gloriana* and Gene Wolfe's *Free, Life Free*. Much of the matter of such books overlaps with that of *magic realist* writers like Gabriel Garcìa Márquez and Angela Carter.

fiction a general term for any work or type of work whose content is completely or largely invented; the opposite of fact. In the 20th century the term is usually used to refer to imaginative works of narrative prose (such as the novel or the short story), and contrasted with *non-fiction* such as history, biography, or works on practical subjects, and with *poetry*. This usage reflects the dominance in contemporary Western literature of the novel as a vehicle for imaginative literature: strictly speaking, poems can also be fictional (as opposed to factual). Genres such as the *historical novel* often combine a fictional plot with real events; *biography* may also be 'fictionalized' through the use of imagined conversations or events.

free verse poetry without metrical form. At the beginning of the 20th century, under the very different influences of Whitman and Mallarmé, many poets became convinced that the

19th century had done most of what could be done with regular metrical forms and rejected regular metre in much the same spirit as Milton had rhyme, preferring irregular metres which made it possible to express thought clearly and without distortion. This was true of T S Eliot and the Imagists; it was also true of poets who, like the Russians Essnin and Mayakovsky, placed emphasis on public performance. Poets including Robert Graves and the later Auden have criticized free verse on the ground that it lacks the difficulty of true accomplishment, but their own metrics would have been considered loose much of the time by earlier critics. The freeness of free verse is largely relative.

historical novel a fictional prose narrative set in the past. Literature set in the historic past has always abounded, but Sir Walter Scott began the modern tradition by setting imaginative romances of love, impersonation, and betrayal in a past based on known fact; his use of historical accuracy, and that of European imitators such as Manzoni, gave rise to the genre. Some historical novels of the 19th century were overtly nationalistic, but most were merely novels set in the past to heighten melodrama while providing an informative framework; the genre was used by Victor Hugo and Charles Dickens, among many others. In the 20th century the historical novel also became concerned with exploring psychological states and the question of the difference in the mentality of the past. Successful examples of this are Robert Graves' novels about the Roman Emperor Claudius *I, Claudius* and *Claudius the God* and Margaret Yourcenar's *Memoirs of Hadrian*. The less serious possibilities of the historical novel were exploited by writers including Jeffery Farnol, Stanley Weyman, and Rafael Sabatini in the early 20th century as *historical romance*; Dorothy Dunnett and George MacDonald Fraser revived the historical romance with some success in the late 1960s. The historical novel acquired subgenres – the stylized *Regency novel* of Georgette Heyer and her imitators; the *Napoleonic War sea story*, notably those of C S Forester and Patrick O'Brien. These forms

have developed their own conventions, particularly when imitating a massively popular ancestor – this has happened in large degree to the *western*, many of which use gestures from Owen Wister's classic *The Virginian*, and to the *novel of the American South* in the period of the Civil War in the wake of Margaret Mitchell's *Gone With the Wind*. Perhaps the most popular sub-genre of the historical novel in the late 20th century has been sequences of *novels about families*, often industrialists of the early 19th century.

horror a modern genre of fiction, devoted primarily to scaring the reader, but often also aiming at a catharsis of common fears through their exaggeration into the bizarre and grotesque. Horror is derived from the Gothic novel, which dealt in shock effects, as well as from folk tales and ghost stories throughout the ages. Dominant figures in the horror tradition are Mary Shelley (*Frankenstein* 1818), Bram Stoker, and H P Lovecraft and, among contemporary writers, Stephen King and Clive Barker. Horror writing tends to use motifs such as vampirism, the eruption of ancient evil, and monstrous transformation, which often derive from folk traditions, as well as more modern concerns such as psychopathology.

literary criticism the establishment of principles governing literary composition, and the assessment of literary works. The earliest systematic literary criticism was the *Poetics* of Aristotle; a later Greek critic was the author of the treatise *On the Sublime*, usually attributed to Longinus. Horace and Quintilian were influential Latin critics. The Italian Renaissance introduced humanist criticism, and the revival of classical scholarship exalted the authority of Aristotle and Horace. Like literature itself, European criticism then applied Neo-Classical, Romantic, and modern approaches. Contemporary criticism often applies insights to literary works from structuralism, semiotics, feminism, Marxism, and psychoanalysis, whereas earlier criticism tended to deal with moral or political ideas, or with a literary work as a formal object independent of its creator.

novel an extended fictional prose narrative,

often including some sense of the psychological development of the central characters and of their relationship with a broader world. There were works that could be called novels in ancient Greece and Rome, and a similar tradition existed in Japan as early as the 11th century, but the modern novel took its name and inspiration from the Italian *novella*, a kind of short tale which became popular in the 13th century. Boccaccio and other 14th- and 15th-century Italian writers were widely translated and influenced the development of the European novel; Cervantes in Spain (*Don Quixote* 1605) was also influential through translations into French and English. By the 18th century the works of Fielding (*Tom Jones* 1749), Richardson, Sterne, and Smollett had firmly established the tradition of the novel in England. By the 19th century the novel had become the main form of narrative fiction in Europe and the USA, for both writers and readers, and had begun to be divided into subgenres such as the *novel of manners* or domestic novel, the *historical novel*, and the *Gothic romance*.

oral literature stories which are or have been transmitted in spoken form, such as public recitation, rather than through writing or printing. Most preliterate societies seem to have had a tradition of oral literature, including short 'folk tales', legends, proverbs, and riddles as well as longer narrative works; and most of the ancient epics – such as the Greek *Odyssey* and the Mesopotamian *Gilgamesh* – seem to have been composed and added to over many centuries before they were committed to writing. Some ancient stories from oral traditions have only been written down as literary works relatively recently, such as the Finnish *Kalevala* (1822); many *fairy tales*, such as those collected in Germany in the early 19th century by the Grimm brothers, also come into this category. The extent to which this sort of *folk literature* has been consciously embellished and altered, particularly in Europe in the 19th century for nationalistic purposes, is controversial.

poetry the imaginative expression of emotion or thought, often in metrical form, and often in figurative language. Poetry has traditionally been distinguished from *prose* (ordinary written language), especially with the term *verse* or rhythmical arrangement of words, although the distinction is not always clear cut. Poetry is often divided into *lyric*, or song-like poetry (sonnet, ode, elegy, pastoral), and *narrative*, or story-telling poetry (ballad, lay, epic). Poetic form has also been used as a vehicle for satire (by Pope, for example), parody, and expositions of philosophical, religious, and practical subjects.

romance in medieval times the term was used for tales of love and adventure, in verse or prose, which became popular in France about 1200 and spread throughout Europe. There were *Arthurian romances* about the legendary King Arthur and his knights, and romances based on the adventures of Charlemagne and on classical themes. The term gradually came to mean any fiction remote from the conditions and concerns of everyday life. In this sense, romance is a broad term which can include or overlap with such genres as the *historical novel* or *fantasy*. In the 20th century the term *romantic novel* is often used disparagingly, to imply a contrast with a realistic novel.

satire a work, in poetry or prose, which uses wit, humour, or irony, often through allegory or extended metaphor, to ridicule human pretensions or expose social evils. The Roman poets Juvenal and Horace wrote *Satires*, and the form became particularly popular in Europe in the 17th and 18th centuries, used by Voltaire in France and by Pope and Swift in England. Satire is related to *parody* in its intention to mock, but satire tends to be more subtle and to mock an attitude or a belief, whereas parody mocks a particular work such as a poem by imitating its style, often with purely comic intent rather than to make a moral point. Both satire and parody, to be effective, require a knowledge of the original attitude, person, or work that is being mocked (although much satire, such as *Gulliver's Travels* by Swift, can also be enjoyed simply on a literal level, as an adventure story).

science fiction is sometimes known as *SF*, allowing the alternative versions *science fantasy* and *speculative fiction*. The genre often takes its ideas and concerns from current ideas in science and social science (or at second or later hands from earlier works in the genre) and aims to shake up standard perceptions of reality. SF works are often set in the near or far future and deal with such matters as travel through space or time, robots, aliens, utopias and dystopias (often satiric), and psychic powers. The genre is sometimes held to have had its roots in the works of Mary Shelley, notably *Frankenstein* 1818; important early practitioners were Jules Verne and H G Wells. In the 20th century the American pulp magazine tradition of SF produced writers such as Arthur C Clarke, Isaac Asimov, Robert Heinlein and Frank Herbert; a consensus of 'pure storytelling' and traditional values was disrupted by writers associated with the British magazine *New Worlds* – Brian W Aldiss, Michael Moorcock, J G Ballard – and by younger American writers – Joanna Russ, Ursula le Guin, Thomas Disch, Gene Wolfe – who used the form for serious literary purposes and for political and sexual radicalism. Thriving SF traditions, only partly influenced by, and not influencing, the Anglo-American one, exist in France, Germany, and Eastern Europe.

short story a short work of prose fiction, which in general either sets up and resolves a single narrative point or sets up and leaves hanging a mood or an atmosphere. Various lengths of short narrative fiction were used before, and as alternatives to, the novel, and many writers of the 19th century wrote occasional short stories, but the form achieved real significance in the hands of Chekhov, Kipling, de Maupassant and Katherine Mansfield. In the 20th century the short story is also often used for genre pieces such as detective fiction and science fiction.

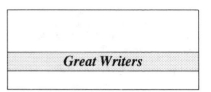

Great Writers

Abu Nuwās Hasan ibn Hāni 762–c. 815. Arab poet. His work was based on old forms, but the new freedom with which he used them, his eroticism, and his ironic humour, have contributed to his reputation as perhaps the greatest of Arab poets.

Austen Jane 1775–1817. English novelist, noted for her domestic novels of manners. All her novels are set within the confines of middle-class English provincial society, and show her skill at drawing characters and situations with delicate irony. Her first attempt was the burlesque *Love and Friendship* written in 1790; her mature works are *Sense and Sensibility* 1811 (like its successors, published anonymously), *Pride and Prejudice* 1813, *Mansfield Park* 1814, *Emma* 1816, *Persuasion* 1818, and *Northanger Abbey* 1818, a skit on the Gothic novel. The same spirit pervades her *Letters*, especially to her sister Cassandra.

Balzac Honoré de 1799–1850. French novelist. His first success, *Les Chouans* 1829, was inspired by Sir Walter Scott, but his major work was the monumental series *La Comédie humaine* (planned as 143 volumes, of which only 80 were completed), which portrayed vice and folly in contemporary French society. It includes *Eugénie Grandet* 1833, dealing with avarice; *Le Père Goriot* 1834, doting fatherly love; *Cousine Bette* 1846, jealousy; and *Cousin Pons* 1847, greed.

Bashō. Pseudonym of Japanese poet Matsuo Munefusa 1644–94. The master of the haiku, a 17–syllable poetic form with lines of 5, 7, and 5 syllables, which he infused with subtle allusiveness and made the accepted form of poetic expression in Japan. His most famous work is *Oku-no-hosomichi/The Narrow Road to the Deep North* 1694, an account of a visit to northern Japan, which consists of haikus interspersed with prose passages.

Baudelaire Charles Pierre 1821–67. French poet, whose work combined rhythmical and musical perfection with a morbid romanticism and eroticism, often using oriental imagery (he had been sent to India as a young man because of his dissipation), and finding beauty in decadence and evil. His first book of verse, *Les Fleurs du mal/Flowers of Evil* 1857, caused a scandal, and was condemned by the censor as endangering public morals, but was enormously influential, paving the way for Rimbaud, Verlaine, and the symbolist school.

Blake William 1757–1827. British mystical poet and artist. His works, for which he engraved both text and illustrations himself, embody his own mystic mythology, and include *Songs of Innocence* 1789, *The Marriage of Heaven and Hell* 1793, *Songs of Experience* 1794, and *Milton* 1804 (his most famous lines, set to music as 'Jerusalem', are taken from the preface). He also produced illustrations for *Paradise Lost, The Book of Job*, and Dante's *Divine Comedy*.

Boccaccio Giovanni 1313–75. Italian writer, best remembered for his *Decameron* 1348–53, containing 100 tales as told by ten young people seeking refuge from the plague in the country. Its bawdiness and exuberance as well as narrative skill and characterization made the work enormously popular and influential, inspiring Chaucer, Shakespeare, Dryden, and Keats among many others.

Brontë family of English writers, including the three sisters *Charlotte* 1816–55, *Emily Jane* 1818–48 and *Anne* 1820–49, and their brother *Patrick Branwell* 1817–48, who were brought up in isolation at Haworth rectory (now a museum) in Yorkshire. In 1846 the sisters published a volume of poems under the pseudonyms Currer (Charlotte), Ellis (Emily) and Acton (Anne) Bell. In 1847 (using the same names), they published the novels *Jane Eyre* (by Charlotte), *Wuthering Heights* (by Emily), and *Agnes Grey*, Anne's much weaker work. During 1848–49 Branwell, Emily, and Anne all died of tuberculosis. Charlotte subsequently published *Shirley* 1849, in which the

heroine resembles Emily, and *Villette* 1853.

Burns Robert 1759–96. Scottish poet, born at Alloway near Ayr, notable for his use of the Scots dialect at a time when it was not considered 'suitable' for literature. His fame rests equally on his poems, published in *Poems, Chiefly in the Scottish Dialect* 1786, including 'Holy Willie's Prayer', 'Tam o'Shanter', 'The Jolly Beggars', and 'To a Mouse', and his songs, of which he contributed some 300 to Johnson's *Scots Musical Museum* 1787–1803, and Thomson's *Scottish Airs with Poetry* 1793–1811, sometimes wholly original, sometimes adaptations of traditional works.

Byron George Gordon, 6th Baron Byron 1788–1824. English poet, who became the symbol of Romanticism and political liberalism throughout Europe in the 19th century. He published his first volume *Hours of Idleness* 1807, and attacked its harsh critics in *English Bards and Scotch Reviewers* 1809. He gained fame with the first two cantos of *Childe Harold* 1812, romantically describing his tours in Portugal, Spain and the Balkans (third canto 1816, fourth 1818). This was followed by *The Prisoner of Chillon 1816*, showing the influence of Shelley, *Beppo* 1818, *Mazeppa* 1819, and his masterpiece *Don Juan* 1819–24. He dabbled in Italian revolutionary politics, and sailed for Greece in 1823 to further the Greek struggle for independence, but died of fever at Missolonghi.

Camoëns or **Camões**, Luís Vaz de 1524–80. Portuguese poet. A soldier and adventurer, he was shipwrecked in 1558, but the manuscript of his poem, the *Lusiads*, was saved with him. It was published in 1572, telling of the voyages of the Portuguese explorer Vasco da Gama and incorporating much Portuguese history, and is considered the country's national epic. His posthumously published lyric poetry is also now valued.

Cervantes *(Saavedra)* Miguel de 1547–1616. Spanish novelist, playwright, and poet. He wrote several plays, and his pastoral romance *Galatea* was published in 1585. His masterpiece *Don Quixote*, telling of a knight errant out of his time, and of his servant Sancho Panza, appeared in 1605 and immediately achieved great success; within a few years it had been translated into English and French, and it was an important influence on the development of the European novel. He also wrote *Novelas Exemplares* 1613, a collection of short poems, the *Viage del Parnaso* 1614, a burlesque poem, and a sequel to *Don Quixote* 1615, considered even better than the first in construction and characterization.

Chaucer Geoffrey c. 1340–1400. The greatest and most influential English poet of the Middle Ages. He held various official appointments, such as controller of London customs, and was sent on missions to Italy (where he may have met Boccaccio and Petrarch), France, and Flanders. His early work showed formal French influence, as in his adaptation of the French allegorical poem on courtly love the *Romaunt of the Rose*; more mature works reflected the influence of Italian realism, as in his long narrative poem *Troilus and Criseyde*, adapted from Boccaccio. In his masterpiece, *The Canterbury Tales* c. 1387, a collection of tales told by a group of pilgrims on their way to the shrine of Thomas Becket, he showed his own genius for metre and characterization. The popularity of his work assured the dominance of the southern English dialect in literature.

Dante Alighieri 1265–1321. Italian poet, soldier and politician. A Florentine, he fell in love with Beatrice (Portinari) in 1274, a love which survived her marriage to another and her death in 1290, which Dante described in *La Vita Nuova* c. 1295. His *Divina Commedia* c. 1307–21, an imaginary journey through Hell, Purgatory and Paradise, under the guidance of Virgil, representing Reason, and Beatrice, representing Faith, is generally considered the greatest poem of the Middle Ages.

Defoe Daniel c. 1660–1731. English novelist and journalist, best remembered for his adventure novel *Robinson Crusoe* 1719. A master of realistic narrative, he was also the author of the pirate story *Captain Singleton* 1720, the picaresque novel *Moll Flanders* 1722, and much political satire.

Dickens Charles 1812–70. English novelist, noted for his memorable characters (such as Mr Micawber and Uriah Heep), and for his portrayals of the social evils of Victorian England. As a child of 12 he worked briefly in a blacking factory (as did the hero of *David Copperfield* 1849). He wrote *Sketches by Boz* for the *Morning Chronicle*. The publication of the first number of the *Pickwick Papers* 1836 made him famous. This was followed by *Oliver Twist* 1838, *Nicholas Nickleby* 1839, *Barnaby Rudge* 1840, and *The Old Curiosity Shop* 1841, all in weekly parts. A visit to the USA in 1842 was reflected in *American Notes* and *Martin Chuzzlewit* 1843. *A Christmas Carol*, also 1843, was the first of his Christmas books. Later novels were *Dombey and Son* 1848, *Bleak House* 1853, *Hard Times* 1854, *Little Dorrit* 1857, *A Tale of Two Cities* 1859, a historical novel indebted to Carlyle's *French Revolution*; *Great Expectations* 1861, *Our Mutual Friend* 1864, and *Edwin Drood*, influenced by Wilkie Collins's mystery stories but left unfinished at his death.

Donne John 1572–1631. British metaphysical poet, so called because of his use of subtle imagery and figurative language. His appointment as private secretary to Sir Thomas Egerton was ended by his secret marriage to Ann More (died 1617), niece of Egerton's wife, subject of many of his love poems. Originally a Roman Catholic, he took orders in the Anglican Church in 1615, and as Dean of St Paul's 1621–31 was noted for his sermons. His poetry was not collected for publication until after his death, and was long out of favour, but he is now recognized as one of the greatest English poets. Many of his sonnets are popularly known by their first lines, such as 'No man is an island' and 'Death, be not proud'.

Dostoevsky Fyodor Mihailovich 1821–81. Russian novelist. His first novel, *Poor Folk*, appeared in 1846. In 1849 he was arrested as a socialist revolutionary, and was sent to the penal settlement at Omsk for four years. Pardoned in 1859, he published the humorous *Village of Stepanchikovo*, *The House of the Dead* 1861, recalling his prison experiences, and *The Insulted and the Injured* 1862. He lived abroad for a period, but returned to Russia in 1871. *Crime and Punishment* 1866, *The Idiot* 1868, and the great work of his last years, *The Brothers Karamazov* 1880, all show his genius for psychological analysis of character and creating narrative tension.

Eliot George. Pseudonym of English novelist Mary Ann Evans 1819–80. From 1851 she worked in London on the *Westminster Review*, and from 1854 she lived with philosopher and critic George Henry Lewes (1817–78). She published *Amos Barton*, the first of the *Scenes of Clerical Life*, in 1857 under the name of George Eliot. She portrayed rural Victorian society, particularly its intellectual hypocrisy, with realism and irony in *The Mill on the Floss* 1860, *Silas Marner* 1861, and *Middlemarch* 1872, her masterpiece.

Eliot T(homas) S(tearns) 1888–1965. American-born poet, critic, and dramatist, British subject 1927. Settling in London in 1915, he expressed the disillusionment of the generation affected by World War I in his first volume, *Prufrock and other Observations* 1917. He established his central position in modern poetry with his bleak vision *The Waste Land* 1922. *Ash Wednesday* 1930 reflected his emergence in 1927 as an Anglo-Catholic, as did the poetic drama *Murder in the Cathedral* 1935, dealing with Becket. *The Cocktail Party* 1949 attempted a revival of contemporary verse drama. His collection *Old Possum's Book of Practical Cats* 1939 was used for the musical *Cats* 1981. He was also an influential literary critic, helping, for example, to re-assess the importance of Donne.

Fielding Henry 1707–54. English novelist, whose individual genius at narrative influenced the form and technique of the novel and helped to make it the most popular form of literature in England. *Joseph Andrews* 1742 began as a parody of Samuel Richardson's sentimental *Pamela*, but became a success in its own right. His masterpiece is *Tom Jones* 1749, which he described as a 'comic epic in prose'.

Firdawsî Mansûr Abu'l-Qâsim c. 935–c. 1020. Persian poet, generally considered the greatest epic poet of Persia. His *Shahnama/ The Book of Kings* relates the history of Persia in 60,000 verses, and includes the legend of Sohrab and Rustum, in which the father unknowingly kills his son in battle.

Flaubert Gustave 1821–80. French novelist, one of the greatest of the 19th century. His masterpiece, noted for its psychological realism, is *Madame Bovary* 1857, the story of a country doctor's wife who commits suicide after a series of unhappy love affairs. Other works include *Sentimental Education* 1869, *Three Tales* 1877, and *Dictionary of Trite Ideas*, a collection of clichés and stock phrases amassed throughout his life.

Goethe Johann Wolfgang von 1749–1832. German poet, novelist, dramatist, philosopher and statesman, generally considered the founder of modern German literature. At first inspired by the works of Shakespeare, he wrote the play *Götz von Berlichingen* 1773. He became the leader of the romantic and emotional *Sturm und Drang* ('storm and stress') movement with the autobiographical novel *The Sorrows of the Young Werther* 1774. His masterpiece is the poetic play *Faust* 1808, completed in a second part in 1831. A visit to Italy 1786–88 inspired the classical dramas *Iphigenie auf Tauris* 1787 and *Tasso* 1790. Also memorable are the *Wilhelm Meister* novels 1796–1829, and his lyrics, many of which were set to music.

Hâfiz Shams al-Din Muhammad c. 1326–90. Persian poet, generally considered the greatest lyric poet of Persia. Born in Shiraz, he taught in a Dervish college there. His *Diwan*, a collection of short odes, contains some extolling the pleasures of life and others satirizing his fellow Dervishes.

Hardy Thomas 1840–1928. English poet and novelist. In his novels, set in the imaginary county of 'Wessex' in SW England, human loves and hates are played out against a harshly indifferent force of nature which he believed to govern the world. His novels include *Far from the Madding Crowd* 1874, *The Return of the Native* 1878, *The Mayor of Casterbridge* 1886, *The Woodlanders* 1887, and *Tess of the*

D'Urbervilles 1891, which caused an outcry because the heroine was a woman seduced. Even greater antagonism was roused by *Jude the Obscure* 1895, which reinforced his decision to confine himself to verse. He also wrote remarkable love lyrics, especially those linked with his dead first wife Emma Gifford, and a blank verse panorama of the Napoleonic Wars, *The Dynasts* 1904–8.

Heine Heinrich 1797–1856. German revolutionary and romantic poet. His *Reisebilder*, which announced his revolutionary sympathies, appeared in 1826, and the *Buch der Lieder/Book of Songs* in 1827. From 1831 he lived mainly in Paris, as a correspondent for German newspapers. Schubert and Schumann set many of his songs to music.

Homer c. 800 BC. Legendary Greek epic poet, according to tradition a blind minstrel and the author of the *Iliad* and the *Odyssey*. The *Iliad* tells of the siege of Troy, and the *Odyssey* of the adventures of Ulysses returning from it. Although there is controversy about the origin of the poems (they are now generally believed to stem from a number of bards of ancient oral tradition), they are landmarks which had an enormous influence on all of subsequent Western literature.

Horace (Quintus Horatius Flaccus) 65–8BC. Roman poet. Son of a freedman, he fought under Brutus at Philippi and lost his estate, but was introduced by Virgil to Maecenas in c. 38, who gave him a small property in the Sabine hills, and recommended him to the patronage of Augustus. He published in 35–30 *Satires* on contemporary society, and in his *Odes* and *Epistles* dealt with both political and personal themes with unrivalled economy and grace of language. He also wrote an influential critical work, *Ars poetica*.

Iqbāl Sir Muhammad 1873–1938. Islamic poet and thinker, generally considered the greatest modern Islamic poet. His literary works, in Urdu and Persian, were mostly verse in the classical style, suitable for public recitation. His most celebrated work is the Persian *Asrā-e khūdī/Secrets of the Self* 1915, in which he put forward a theory of the self which was

the opposite of the traditional abnegation of Islam. He sought through his writings to arouse Muslims to take their place in the modern world, and was an influence on the movement which led to the creation of Pakistan.

James Henry 1843–1916. Anglo-American novelist, whose main theme is the impact of European culture upon the American soul. Novels include *Roderick Hudson* 1876, *The American* 1877, *The Portrait of a Lady* 1881, *Washington Square* 1881, *The Bostonians* 1886, *The Wings of a Dove* 1902, *The Ambassadors* 1903, and *The Golden Bowl* 1904. The supernatural tale *The Turn of the Screw* 1898 was used for an opera by Benjamin Britten. After 1875 he lived in Europe, becoming a naturalized British subject in 1915. His style, always subtle, became increasingly complex.

Joyce James Augustin Aloysius 1882–1941. Irish writer, born in Dublin, who revolutionized the form of the English novel with his 'stream of consciousness' technique. His works include *Dubliners* 1914 (short stories), *Portrait of the Artist as a Young Man* 1916 (semiautobiographical), and *Ulysses* 1922, which records the events of a single Dublin day, mingling direct narrative with the unspoken and unconscious reactions of the characters. The book, banned at first for obscenity in England and the USA, was enormously influential. *Finnegan's Wake* 1939 continued Joyce's experiments with language, attempting a synthesis of all existence.

Kālidāsa ?c. 5th century AD. Indian epic poet and dramatist, who according to tradition served at the court of King Vikramaditya at Ujjain. His works, in Sanskrit, include the classic drama *Sakuntala*, the love story of King Dushyanta for the nymph Sakuntala.

Keats John 1795–1821. English poet, a leading figure in the Romantic movement. He published *Poems* 1817, and *Endymion* 1818. In 1819 he wrote the richly imaginative *The Eve of St Agnes*, the *Odes* (including odes *To Autumn*, *On a Grecian Urn*, and *To a Nightingale*), and in this year he fell hopelessly in love with Fanny Brawne. In 1820 he published his last volume of poetry; stricken with tuberculosis, he went to Italy hoping for a cure, but died in Rome. Valuable insight into his own feelings is provided by his *Letters*, published in 1848.

Lawrence D(avid) H(erbert) 1885–1930. British novelist and poet, who in his work expressed his belief in emotion and the sexual impulse as creative and true to human nature. Son of a Nottinghamshire miner, he achieved fame with the semi-autobiographical *Sons and Lovers* 1913. In 1914 he married Frieda von Richthofen, with whom he had run away in 1912, and who was the model for Ursula Brangwen in *The Rainbow* 1915, and its sequel *Women in Love* 1921. His travels in search of health (he suffered from tuberculosis, from which he eventually died near Nice) prompted books such as *Mornings in Mexico* 1927. Most famous of his novels is *Lady Chatterley's Lover* 1928, banned as obscene in the UK until 1960. He also excelled in the short story, such as 'The Woman Who Rode Away'.

Li Bo 701–762. Chinese poet. He wrote in traditional forms, but his exuberance, the boldness of his imagination, and the intensity of his feeling have won him recognition as perhaps the greatest of all Chinese poets. Although he was mostly concerned with higher themes, he is also noted for his celebration of the joys of drinking.

Mann Thomas 1875–1955. German novelist, particularly concerned with the theme of the artist's relation to society. His first novel, *Buddenbrooks* 1900, dealt with an old Hanseatic family in his native Lübeck, and *The Magic Mountain* 1924 led to a Nobel prize in 1929. Forced abroad by the Nazi regime, he became a US citizen in 1940. Later works were *Dr Faustus* 1947 and *Confessions of Felix Krull* 1954. Most famous of his short stories was 'Death in Venice' 1913.

Milton John 1608–74. English Puritan poet. His early poems include the pastoral *L'Allegro* and *Il Penseroso* of 1632, the masque *Comus* 1633, and the elegy for a dead friend *Lycidas* 1637. His middle years were devoted to the Puritan cause, writing pamphlets, including one advocating divorce, and another

(*Areopagitica*) freedom of the press. From 1649 he was (Latin) secretary to the Council of State, his assistants (as his sight failed) including Marvell. The masterpieces of his old age are his epic poems on biblical themes, *Paradise Lost* 1667, *Paradise Regained* 1677, and the classic drama *Samson Agonistes*, also 1677. His majestic use of language has been compared with that of Virgil.

Montaigne Michel Eyquem de 1533–92. French writer, noted for his creation of the essay form. A lawyer, he became mayor of Bordeaux 1581–85, publishing his *Essais* from 1580. They deal with all aspects of life from an urbanely sceptical viewpoint, and through the translation of John Florio in 1603 influenced Shakespeare and other English writers.

Murasaki Shikibu 978–c. 1015 pseudonym of an unknown Japanese woman writer. Her masterpiece of romantic prose fiction, the *Tale of Genji*, written about 1015, is one of the great works of Japanese literature, and has been described as the world's first novel.

Petrarch (Italian *Petrarca*), Francesco 1304–74. Italian poet, a friend of Boccaccio, and a devotee of the classical tradition, who has been called the father of modern poetry. His *Il Canzoniere* were sonnets in praise of his idealized love 'Laura', whom he first saw in 1327 (a married woman, she refused to become his mistress) and who died of plague 1348. His 14-line sonnets, in a form which was given the name Petrarchan, were influential for centuries.

Pope Alexander 1688–1744. English poet and satirist, noted for his biting wit, which he expressed in the form of heroic couplets. His *Essay on Criticism* 1711 pilloried literary figures of the age, and his mock-heroic poem *Rape of the Lock* 1712 established his reputation. He translated the *Iliad* 1715–20 and the *Odyssey* 1725–26, and also wrote the much-quoted philosophical *Essay on Man* 1733–34 and *Moral Essays* 1731–35. Many of his lines have attained almost the status of proverbs, such as 'A little knowledge is a dangerous thing'.

Proust Marcel 1871–1922. French novelist. An invalid from childhood, he retired after the death of his father (1904) and mother (1905) to the quiet of a cork-lined room in his Paris flat to write his mammoth autobiographical series of novels *À la Recherche du Temps Perdu/ Remembrance of Things Past* 1913–27.

Rabelais François c. 1494–1553. French Renaissance humanist and satirist, best remembered for *Pantagruel* 1532–33 and *Gargantua* 1534, satiric allegories laced with coarse humour which tell of the adventures of the giant Gargantua and his son Pantagruel.

Shakespeare William 1564–1616. English dramatist and poet, generally considered the greatest English playwright. His works are central to English literature as well as theatre. Early plays, written c. 1589–93, were the tragedy *Titus Andronicus*; the comedies *The Comedy of Errors, The Taming of the Shrew*, and *Two Gentlemen of Verona*; the three parts of *Henry VI*; and *Richard III*. About 1593 he came under the patronage of the Earl of Southampton, to whom he dedicated his long poems *Venus and Adonis* 1593 and *Lucrece* 1594; he also wrote for him the comedy *Love's Labour's Lost*, satirizing Raleigh's circle, and seems to have dedicated to him his sonnets written c. 1593–96, in which the mysterious 'Dark Lady' appears. From 1594 Shakespeare was a member of the chamberlain's (later the king's) company of players, and had no rival as a dramatist, with the lyric plays *Romeo and Juliet, Midsummer Night's Dream*, and *Richard II* 1594–95, followed by *King John* and *The Merchant of Venice* in 1596. The Falstaff plays of 1597–99: *Henry IV* (parts I and II), *Henry V*, and *The Merry Wives of Windsor* (said to have been written at the request of Elizabeth I), brought his fame to its height. About the same time he wrote *Julius Caesar* 1599. The period ended with the lyrically witty *Much Ado about Nothing, As You Like It*, and *Twelfth Night* c. 1598–1601. With *Hamlet* 1601, a 'darker' period seems to begin, reflected also in the comedies *Troilus and Cressida, All's Well that Ends Well*, and *Measure for Measure* c. 1601–4. *Othello, Macbeth*, and *King Lear* followed 1604–6, together with *Timon of Athens* in which pessimism reaches its depths.

Antony and Cleopatra and *Coriolanus* 1607–8 have a more balanced acceptance of life. Shakespeare was only part author of *Pericles*, but like the other plays of c. 1608–11, *Cymbeline, The Winter's Tale*, and *The Tempest*, it has a sunset glow about it. During 1613 he collaborated with Fletcher in *Henry VIII* and probably in *Two Noble Kinsmen*. The collected edition of his plays (the First Folio) was published in 1623 by his fellow-actors, Heminge and Condell.

Shelley Percy Bysshe 1792–1822. English poet, a leading figure in the Romantic movement. His collaboration in the pamphlet *The Necessity of Atheism* in 1811 caused his expulsion from Oxford. In London he fell in love with 16–year-old Harriet Westbrook, whom he married in 1811, but they were soon estranged. Political freedom was the theme of his revolutionary poem *Queen Mab* 1813. In 1814 he left England with Mary Wollstonecraft Godwin, whom he married in 1816 and who became known as the writer Mary Shelley, author of *Frankenstein* 1818. By 1818 they were living in Italy, where he produced the tragedy *The Cenci* 1819, the lyric drama *Prometheus Unbound* 1820, and *Adonais* 1821, on the death of Keats, as well as his most famous short lyrics, 'Ode to the West Wind', 'The Cloud', and 'To a Skylark'. He was drowned while sailing near Spezia.

Soyinka Wole 1934– . Nigerian writer, who was a political prisoner in Nigeria 1967–69 (prison memoirs *The Man Died* 1972). His works include the play *The Lion and the Jewel* 1963, and *Aké, The Years of Childhood,* an autobiography.

Spenser Edmund 1552–99. English poet, best remembered for his allegorical poem *The Faerie Queene* 1590–96, in homage to Queen Elizabeth, of which only six of the planned 12 books were published. His other works include *The Shepheard's Calendar* 1579, the *Epithalamion* 1595, and love sonnets. He has been called the 'poet's poet' for his versification, richness of language, and fertile imagery.

Sterne Laurence 1713–68. Irish writer, best remembered for his unique comic masterpiece

The Life and Opinions of Tristram Shandy, Gent. 1760–67, an eccentrically whimsical and bawdy work which foreshadowed many of the techniques and literary devices of 20th-century novelists, including Joyce. He also wrote the popular *Sentimental Journey through France and Italy* 1768.

Swift Jonathan 1667–1745. Irish poet and satirist, best known for his *Gulliver's Travels* 1726, a satire on people and political institutions which has also appealed to generations of children and adults as an adventure story. He also wrote *A Tale of a Tub* 1697, and many poems and political pamphlets.

Tagore (Sir) Rabindranath 1861–1941. Indian writer in Bengali. One of the most influential Indian authors of the 20th century, he translated into English his own verse *Gitanjali* ('song offerings') 1912 and his verse play *Chitra*, which brought him world fame.

Tolstoy Leo Nikolaievich 1828–1910. Russian novelist. His masterpieces are *War and Peace* 1864, an epic novel dealing with the Napoleonic Wars, and *Anna Karenina* 1877. He preached his own version of ascetic Christianity in his didactic later books *What is Religion?* and *The Kreutzer Sonata* and his novel *Resurrection* 1900, which influenced Gandhi.

Turgenev Ivan Sergeievich 1818–83. Russian writer, noted for his poetic realism, his pessimism, and his skill at characterization, particularly of women. Major works include the play *A Month in the Country* 1849, and the novels *A Nest of Gentlefolk* 1858, *Fathers and Sons* 1862, and *Virgin Soil* 1877. His series of *A Sportsman's Sketches* 1852 strongly criticized serfdom. He lived abroad from 1856.

Villon François 1431–85. French poet, noted for his satiric humour, pathos, and lyric power in works which used the *argot* (slang) of the time. Very little of his work survives, but his best known poem is the *Ballade des dames du*

temps jadis containing the line 'Ou sont les nièges d'antan?'('Where are the snows of yesteryear?').

Virgil (Publius Vergilius Maro) 70–19 BC. Roman poet. Born near Mantua, he was of the small farmer class whose life he celebrated in his pastoral *Eclogues* 37 BC, and *Georgics* or 'Art of Husbandry' 30 BC. His epic poem, the *Aeneid*, in 12 books, glorified the dynasty of his patron Augustus. By the 3rd century his works were used for divination, and he was popularly thought a magician. He was one of the most influential Roman writers, partly because his apparent forecast of the birth of Christ in the fourth eclogue led to his acceptance as an 'honorary Christian' by the medieval church.

Wordsworth William 1770–1850. English poet, a leading figure in the Romantic movement. In 1797 he settled with his sister Dorothy in Somerset to be near Coleridge, collaborating with him in *Lyrical Ballads* 1798 (which included 'Tintern Abbey') and attempting to avoid poetic diction and 'give the charm of novelty to things of every day'. From 1799 he lived in the Lake District. Outstanding among later works were the *Poems* 1807 (including 'Intimations of Immortality'), and *The Prelude* (written by 1805, published 1850), which was written to form part of the great autobiographical work *The Recluse*, never completed.

Yeats William Butler 1865–1939. Irish poet and playwright, a leader of the Celtic revival, and a founder of the Abbey Theatre in Dublin . His early poetry was romantically lyrical, as in 'The Lake Isle of Innisfree', and he drew on Irish legend for his poetic plays *The Countess Cathleen* 1892 and *The Land of Heart's Desire* 1894. His later works were sharper and had a mystical aspect; his mystical beliefs were expressed in his prose work *A Vision* 1925 and 1937. His later books of poetry include *The Wild Swans at Coole* 1919 and *The Winding Stair* 1933.

Booker Prize for Fiction (British)

1969	P H Newby *Something to Answer For*
1970	Bernice Rubens *The Elected Member*
1971	V S Naipaul *In a Free State*
1972	John Berger *G*
1973	J G Farrell *The Siege of Krishnapur*
1974	Nadine Gordimer *The Conservationist; Stanley Middleton Holiday*
1975	Ruth Prawer Jhabvala *Heat and Dust*
1976	David Storey *Saville*
1977	Paul Scott *Staying On*
1978	Iris Murdoch *The Sea, The Sea*
1979	Penelope Fitzgerald *Offshore*
1980	William Golding *Rites of Passage*
1981	Salman Rushdie *Midnight's Children*
1982	Thomas Keneally *Schindler's Ark*
1983	J M Coetzee *Life and Times of Michael K*
1984	Anita Brookner *Hotel du Lac*
1985	Keri Hulme *The Bone People*
1986	Kingsley Amis *The Old Devils*
1987	Penelope Lively *Moon Tiger*
1988	Peter Carey *Oscar and Lucinda*

Nobel Prize for Literature (International)

1970	Alexander Solzhenitsyn (Russian)
1971	Pablo Neruda (Chilean)
1972	Heinrich Böll (West German)
1973	Patrick White (Australian)
1974	Eyvind Johnson, Harry Edmund Martinson (both Swedish)
1975	Eugenio Montale (Italian)
1976	Saul Bellow (American)
1977	Vincente Aleixandra (Spanish)
1978	Isaac Bashevis Singer (American)
1979	Odysseus Elytis (Greek)
1980	Czeslaw Milosz (Polish-American)
1981	Elias Canetti (Bulgarian-British)
1982	Gabriel García Márquez (Columbian-Mexican)
1983	William Golding (British)
1984	Jaroslav Seifert (Czechoslovakian)
1985	Claude Simon (French)
1986	Wole Soyinka (Nigerian)
1987	Joseph Brodsky (Soviet)
1988	Naguib Mahfouz (Egyptian)

Prix Goncourt for fiction (French)

1970	Michel Tournier *Le Roi des aulnes*
1971	Jacques Laurent *Les Bêtises*
1972	Jean Carrière *L'Épervier de Maheux*
1973	Jacques Chessex *L'Ogre*
1974	Pascal Lainé *La Dentellière*
1975	Emile Ajar *La Vie devant soi*
1976	Patrick Grainville *Les Flamboyants*
1977	Didier Decoin *John L'Enfer*
1978	Patrick Modiano *Rue des boutiques obscures*
1979	Antonine Maillet *Pelagie-la-Charrette*
1980	Yves Navarre *Le Jardin d'acclimation*
1981	Lucien Bodard *Anne Marie*
1982	Dominique Fernandez *Dans la Main de l'ange*
1983	Frederick Tristan *Les Égares*
1984	Marguerite Duras *L'Amant*
1985	Yann Queffelec *Les Noces barbares*
1986	Michel Host *Valet de Nuit*
1987	Tahir Ben Jelloun *La Nuit Sacrée*

Pulitzer Prize for fiction (American)

1970	Jean Stafford *Collected Stories*
1972	Wallace Stegner *Angle of Repose*
1973	Eudora Welty *The Optimist's Daughter*
1975	Michael Shaara *The Killer Angels*
1976	Saul Bellow *Humboldt's Gift*
1978	James Alan McPherson *Elbow Room*
1979	John Cheever *The Stories of John Cheever*
1980	Norman Mailer *The Executioner's Song*
1981	John Kennedy Toole *A Confederacy of Dunces*
1982	John Updike *Rabbit is Rich*
1983	Alice Walker *The Color Purple*
1984	William Kennedy *Ironweed*
1985	Alison Lurie *Foreign Affairs*
1986	Larry McMurtry *Lonesome Dove*
1987	Peter Taylor *A Summer to Memphis*
1988	Toni Morrison *Beloved*

c. 1500 BC	*Vedas*, Hindu scriptures, written in Sanskrit.
12th century	*I Ching/Book of Changes*, Chinese work on divination, attributed to Wen Wang.
8th century	Homer, Greek epic poet, reputed to be the author of the *Iliad* and *Odyssey*.
c. 650	*Epic of Gilgamesh* written down, Mesopotamian epic poem (the story itself is at least 1,500 years older).
c. 612	Sappho, Greek lyric female poet, was born.
518	Pindar, writer of odes, was born.
5th century	The *Pentateuch* (five books of Moses) of the Jewish *Bible* (Old Testament) reached its final form. Other parts of the Bible (Psalms and Proverbs) were much older.
c. 400	The *Upanishads*, prose and verse commentaries on the *Vedas* (Hindu scriptures).
c. 310	Theocritus, Greek pastoral poet, was born.
c. 300	The *Mahabharata* and *Ramayana*, Hindu epic poems.
106	Cicero, Roman orator and prose writer, was born.
70	Virgil, Roman poet, author of the *Aeneid*, was born.
65	Horace, Roman poet, was born.
43	Ovid, Roman poet, was born.
60 AD	Juvenal, Roman satirist, was born.
1st century	The Gospels of the Christian New Testament were written.
5th century	Kālidāsa, Indian poet, regarded as the greatest writer in classical Sanskrit, was writing.
c. 450	Germanic invasion of England, from which the development of English as an independent language is dated.
7th century	the *Quran* or *Koran*, the Islamic scriptures, was written.
618–906	Tang Dynasty in China, the great period of Chinese poetry. Book printing was invented in China.
c. 670–80	Caedmon, the earliest English Christian poet, was writing.
699	Li Bo, Chinese poet, was born.
713	Du Fu, Chinese poet, was born.
750–1050	'Golden Age' of classical Arabic literature.
c. 750	*Beowulf*, the only surviving Old English Heroic epic; *Wanderer* and *Seafarer*, Old English elegaic poems; 'Golden Age' of Chinese poetry.
762	Abu Nuwās, Arab poet, was born.
c. 800	*Meng Shu*, a collection of edifying Chinese anecdotes for children, was introduced into Japan. One of the earliest known examples of children's literature, it was influential until the 19th century.
890	*Anglo-Saxon Chronicle* begun, recording historic events until 1140.
c. 890	*Cantilène de Ste Eulalie*, earliest known French poem.
c. 900	*Arabian Nights* begun.
c. 955	Firdawsî, Persian poet, was writing.

c. 1015	*The Tale of Genji* by Murasaki Shikibu, romantic novel, one of the greatest Japanese prose works.
c. 1066	Omar Khayyam, Persian poet and scientist, was writing.
1066	Norman Conquest of England. Over the next 100 years Old English developed into Middle English. The French ruling classes had an increasing effect on the language and literature.
c. 1110	Rise of Troubadour poetry in France and Provençe.
1140	Chrétien of Troyes, French court poet, author of Arthurian romances, was born.
c. 1150	Rise of Middle English lyric poetry.
12th century	Rise and development of Icelandic sagas.
c. 1200	*Niebelungenlied*, German epic poem; *Ancrene Riwle/Rule for Anchoresses*, Middle English devotional prose.
c. 1225	*Roman de la Rose/Romance of the Rose* by Guillaume de Lorris, influential French allegorical poem on courtly love, later adapted by Chaucer.
1304	Petrarch, Italian poet, was born.
1307–21	Dante Alighieri, greatest Italian poet, wrote his *Divina Commedia/Divine Comedy*.
1340	Geoffrey Chaucer, greatest late medieval English poet, was born. Works include *The Canterbury Tales* 1387, and *Troilus and Criseyde* c. 1388.
1348–53	Boccaccio, Italian poet, wrote his *Decameron*.
c. 1362	Hâfiz, Persian poet, was born.
c. 1362–98	William Langland wrote his *Piers Plowman*, didactic allegorical poem.
c. 1400	*Gawain and the Green Knight*, anonymous English Arthurian romance, was written.
1431	François Villon, French poet, was born.
1470	Sir Thomas Malory wrote his *Le Morte d'Arthur*, a cycle of Arthurian legends.
1477	William Caxton established the first printing press in England.
1494	François Rabelais, French satirist, was born.
1524	Luis Vaz de Camoëns, Portuguese epic poet, was born.
1532	Ludovico Ariosto, Italian poet, wrote his romantic epic *Orlando Furioso*.
c. 1560	Hsu Wei wrote his *Ching P'ing Mei*, first Chinese classic novel.
1572	John Donne, first of the major English 'metaphysical' poets, was born.
1575	Torquato Tasso, Italian poet, wrote his *Gerusalemme Liberata/Jerusalem Liberated*, romantic epic.
1590–96	Edmund Spenser, English poet, wrote his *Faerie Queene*, allegorical romantic epic.
1590–1600	William Shakespeare wrote his sonnets.
1605	Miguel de Cervantes, Spanish novelist, published the first part of his novel *Don Quixote*.

1611	Authorized Version of the Bible was published in English.
1631	John Dryden, English poet and dramatist, was born.
1667	John Milton, English poet, wrote his *Paradise Lost*, an epic on the Fall of Man.
1668	*Oroonoko* was written by English novelist Aphra Behn.
1670	Andrew Marvell, English poet, was writing.
c. 1675	Poems by Bashō (pen-name of Matsuo Munefusa) brought the Japanese haiku form into popularity.
1648	*The Pilgrim's Progress* by John Bunyan, English writer.
1688	Alexander Pope, English poet and satirist, was born.
1719	*Robinson Crusoe* by Daniel Defoe, English novelist.
1720	Novels were first serialized in English newspapers.
1728	*Gulliver's Travels* by Jonathan Swift, Irish author and satirist.
1741	*Pamela* by Samuel Richardson, English novelist, one of the founders of the modern novel.
1748	John Cleland, English writer, published *Memoirs of a Woman of Pleasure*, better known as *Fanny Hill*.
1749	Johann Wolfgang von Goethe, German poet, dramatist, novelist, and philosopher, was born; *Tom Jones* by Henry Fielding, English novelist.
1750	Thomas Gray, English poet, wrote 'Elegy in a Country Churchyard'.
1755	*Dictionary of the English Language* by Samuel Johnson, English author and lexicographer.
1757	William Blake, English poet and artist, was born.
1759	Robert Burns, Scottish poet, was born; Voltaire, French author and satirist, wrote *Candide*.
1760	Cao Xuequin's *The Dream of the Red Chamber*, the most famous Chinese novel; volumes 1-2 of *Tristram Shandy*, comic novel by Laurence Sterne, English novelist.
1765	*Goody Two-Shoes*, one of the earliest illustrated children's books in England, possibly by the poet Oliver Goldsmith.
1775	*Sturm und Drang* ('Storm and Stress') movement, the beginning of Romanticism, expanded in Germany.
1776	Edward Gibbon, English historian, began to publish his *The Decline and Fall of the Roman Empire*.
1778	William Hazlitt, English essayist, was born.
1788	Lord Byron, English Romantic poet, was born.
1791	*Life of Samuel Johnson* by James Boswell.
1792	Percy Bysshe Shelley, English Romantic poet, was born.
1795	John Keats, English Romantic poet, and Thomas Carlyle, Scottish writer and historian, were born.

1797	Heinrich Heine, German Romantic poet, was born.
1798	William Wordsworth and Samuel Taylor Coleridge published their *Lyrical Ballads*, the first major work of the Romantic period in England; Adam Mickiewicz, Polish poet, was born.
1799	Aleksandr Pushkin, Russian poet, was born.
1803	Ralph Waldo Emerson, US poet, was born.
1809	Alfred Tennyson, English poet, Edgar Allan Poe, US writer of horror fantasy, and Nikolai Gogol, Russian novelist and short story writer, were all born.
1810	Alfred de Musset, French poet, was born.
1813	*Pride and Prejudice* by Jane Austen, English novelist.
1815	Mikhail Lermontov, Russian poet, was born.
1818	Ivan Turgenev, Russian novelist, was born; *Frankenstein*, philosophical horror novel, by Mary Shelley, English novelist.
1819	*Ivanhoe*, historical novel, by Walter Scott, Scottish novelist.
1822	*Kalevala* published, Finnish legends collected from oral tradition.
1827	Honoré de Balzac began his *Comédie humaine/Human Comedy*, a series of novels and stories.
1830	*Le Rouge et le noir/The Red and the Black* by Stendhal, French novelist.
1842	Stéphane Mallarmé, French Symbolist poet, was born.
1844	Gerard Manley Hopkins, English poet, and Paul Verlaine, French poet, were born.
1847	Charlotte Brontë, English novelist, published *Jane Eyre*, her sister Emily Brontë published *Wuthering Heights*, and William Thackeray, English novelist, published *Vanity Fair*.
1850	*David Copperfield* by Charles Dickens, English novelist. *The Scarlet Letter*, by Nathaniel Hawthorne, US novelist.
1851	*Moby Dick* by Herman Melville, US novelist.
1854	Arthur Rimbaud, French Symbolist poet, was born.
1855	*Leaves of Grass*, by Walt Whitman, US poet.
1856	*Madame Bovary* by Gustave Flaubert, French novelist.
1857	*Les Fleurs du mal/Flowers of Evil* by Charles Baudelaire, French poet; *Barchester Towers* by Anthony Trollope, English novelist.
1858	*The Song of Hiawatha* by Henry Wadsworth Longfellow, US poet.
1861	Rabindranath Tagore, Indian philosopher and poet, was born.
1862	*Les Misérables* by Victor Hugo, French writer.
1864	*War and Peace* by Leo Tolstoy, Russian novelist.
1865	William Butler Yeats, Irish poet, was born; *Alice's Adventures in Wonderland* by Lewis Carroll, English mathematician and author.
1866	*Crime and Punishment* by Fyodor Dostoievsky, Russian novelist.

1868	Maxim Gorky, Russian author, was born; *The Moonstone*, first English detective novel, by Wilkie Collins, English novelist.
1869	*The Ring and the Book* by Robert Browning, English poet.
1871	*Middlemarch* by George Eliot, English novelist.
1873	Muhammad Iqbal, Urdu poet, was born.
1875	Thomas Mann, German novelist, and Rainer Maria Rilke, German poet, were born.
1876	*Tom Sawyer* by Mark Twain, US novelist.
1881	*The Portrait of a Lady* and *Washington Square* by Henry James, US novelist.
1885	*Germinal* by Émile Zola, French novelist.
1887	*A Study in Scarlet*, the first Sherlock Holmes story, by Arthur Conan Doyle, English detective story writer.
1891	*Tess of the D'Urbervilles* by Thomas Hardy, English novelist and poet; Osip Mandelshtam, Russian poet, was born.
1895	*The Time Machine* by H G Wells, English novelist and science fiction writer.
1899	Jorge Luis Borges, Argentinian short story writer, was born.
1900	*Lord Jim* by Joseph Conrad, Polish-born English novelist.
1901	*Kim* by Rudyard Kipling, English novelist, short story writer, and poet.
1908	*The Wind in the Willows* by Kenneth Grahame, English author.
1910	Arnold Bennett, English novelist, published the first of his Clayhanger series of novels.
1913	*Sons and Lovers* by D H Lawrence, English novelist; Marcel Proust, French novelist, published the first part of his *À la récherche du temps perdu/Remembrance of Things Past*.
1917	English writer P G Wodehouse published *The Man with Two Left Feet*, his first work featuring Jeeves and Bertie Wooster.
1917–18	Wilfred Owen, English poet, wrote his war poetry.
1918	Aleksandr Blok, Russian Symbolist poet, wrote 'The Twelve', a poem greeting the Russian revolution.
1920	*Bliss* by Katherine Mansfield, New Zealand short story writer.
1922	*The Waste Land* by T S Eliot, Anglo-US poet; *Ulysses* by James Joyce, Irish novelist; Andrei Bely, Russian Symbolist novelist and poet, published the definitive version of his novel *Petersburg*.
1924	*A Passage to India*, by E M Forster, English novelist.
1925	Posthumous publication of *The Trial*, by Franz Kafka, Czech novelist.
1926	*The Murder of Roger Ackroyd* by Agatha Christie, English detective story writer.
1927	*Steppenwolf* by Herman Hesse, German writer; *To the Lighthouse* by Virginia Woolf, English writer.
1928	*Mariana Pinada* by Federico García Lorca, Spanish poet and playwright.

1929   *A Farewell to Arms* by Ernest Hemingway, US novelist.

1932   *Brave New World* by Aldous Huxley, English novelist.

1934   *Tender is the Night* by F Scott Fitzgerald, US novelist; *Tropic of Cancer* by Henry Miller, US novelist; Wole Soyinka, Nigerian author, was born.

1937   *La Nausée/Nausea* by Jean-Paul Sartre, French novelist and philosopher.

1938   *Brighton Rock* by Graham Greene, English novelist.

1939   *The Grapes of Wrath* by John Steinbeck, US novelist.

1942   *L'Étranger/The Outsider* by Albert Camus, French novelist.

1945   *Animal Farm* by George Orwell, English author; *Brideshead Revisited* by Evelyn Waugh, English novelist.

1948   *The Age of Anxiety* by W H Auden, English poet; *The Naked and the Dead* by Norman Mailer, US novelist.

1950   The *70 Cantos* by Ezra Pound, US poet.

1951   *The Catcher in the Rye* by J D Salinger, US novelist.

1953   Ian Fleming, English novelist, published *Casino Royale*, first 'James Bond' novel.

1954   *Lord of the Flies* by William Golding, English novelist, *Lord of the Rings* by J R R Tolkien, English writer and scholar; *Lucky Jim* by Kingsley Amis, English novelist; *Bonjour Tristesse/Hello Sadness* by Françoise Sagan, French novelist; posthumous publication of *Under Milk Wood* by Dylan Thomas, Welsh poet.

1955   *Lolita* by Vladimir Nabokov, Russian-US novelist.

1956   *The Outsider* by Colin Wilson, English novelist; *Anglo Saxon Attitudes* by Angus Wilson, English novelist.

1957   *Voss* by Patrick White, Australian novelist; *On the Road* by Jack Kerouac, US novelist.

1958   *Doctor Zhivago* by Boris Pasternak, Russian poet and novelist; *Breakfast at Tiffany's* by Truman Capote, US novelist.

1959   *Die Blechtrommel/The Tin Drum* by Günter Grass, German novelist.

1960   *The Loneliness of the Long Distance Runner* by Alan Sillitoe, English novelist.

1961   *A Severed Head* by Iris Murdoch, English novelist.

1962   *One Day in the Life of Ivan Denisovich* by Alexander Solzhenitsyn, Russian novelist.

1963   *The Collector* by John Fowles, English novelist; *The Spy Who Came In From the Cold* by John Le Carré, English novelist.

1964   *Herzog* by Saul Bellow, US novelist; *The Whitsun Weddings* by Philip Larkin, English poet.

1965   *For The Union Dead* by Robert Lowell, US poet

1966   Paul Scott, English novelist, began his 'Raj Quartet' series of novels.

1967   *Cien años de soledad/One Hundred Years of Solitude* by Gabriel García Márquez, Colombian novelist.

1968   *Couples* by John Updike, US novelist.

1969   *Portnoy's Complaint* by Philip Roth, US novelist; *Slaughterhouse Five* by Kurt Vonnegut, US novelist.

1973   Roland Barthes, French critic, published *Le Plaisir du texte/The Pleasure of the Text.*

1975   *The History Man* by Malcolm Bradbury, English novelist.

1979   Dorris Lessing, British novelist, began the *Canopus in Argus* series of novels.

1980   *Earthly Powers* by Anthony Burgess, British novelist.

1982   *Monsignor Quixote* by Graham Greene, British novelist.

1983   *The Color Purple* by Alice Walker, US novelist; *Name of the Rose* by Umberto Eco, Italian novelist and critic.

1984   *The Unbearable Lightness of Being* by Milan Kundera, Czech novelist.

1985   Mario Vargas Llosa, Peruvian novelist published *Historia de Mayta/The Real Life of Alejandro Mayta.*

1987   *The Wrench* by Primo Levi, Italian writer.

1988   *Satanic Verses* by Salman Rushdie, British writer. The book (whose title refers to verses deleted from the Koran) offended many Muslims with alleged blasphemy.

Theatre

Theatre, as distinct from literature, is a living art. Shakespeare's *Hamlet*, for example, taken as a work of literature, has been the subject of a huge body of literary criticism. As a piece of drama, however, it is open to infinite interpretation, for no two performances – even by the same actor – can ever be the same. Furthermore, *Hamlet* is generally regarded as 'good' literature, but a performance with poor direction and poor acting can turn it into 'bad' theatre. As a result theatre, perhaps even more than literature, is subject to the tastes and fashions of its day – both in content and presentation. This section is therefore intended to provide an introduction to the theatre today, to the events and people that have formed it and, in considering dramatic works, to those which are still most frequently performed. For the term 'theatre' encompasses three separate and yet interdependent areas: in its most literal sense, it is the place where the drama unfolds, whether it is the mobile carts of medieval times or highly mechanized theatre complexes such as the Barbican Centre in London; it is also the world of actors, directors, designers and indeed theatre-goers themselves; and, finally, it is the drama or 'piece of theatre', whether *Hamlet* or a pantomime. Theatre in this context covers any live entertainment performed by actors, with the exception of opera and dance, which are treated in separate sections.

This section contains an introduction to various *Theatrical Genres*, types of drama and important movements, giving a brief definition and history for each; *Biographies* of important figures in the theatre; and a *Chronology* of theatrical events which puts theatrical developments since ancient times in their historical perspective. Since it is impossible to measure the achievement of Ibsen, for example, as a playwright, against the skills of Gielgud as an actor, or indeed to compare Gielgud's performance as Macbeth with that of Kean a hundred years earlier, the biographical section should not be regarded as a 'top 50'. Rather, it is a selection of some people of the theatre who, in their different ways, have all played a major role in its development.

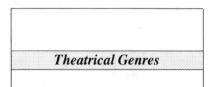

Theatrical Genres

Absurd, Theatre of the term applied to the works of a group of playwrights in the 1950s, including Beckett, Ionesco, Genet and Pinter. They expressed through drama the belief that in a godless universe human existence has no meaning or purpose and therefore all communication breaks down. This concern was shown in the form as well as the content of their plays, so that logical construction and argument gives way to irrational and illogical speech and to its ultimate conclusion, silence, as in Beckett's play *Breath* 1970.

burlesque in the 17th and 18th centuries, a form of satirical comedy parodying a particular play or dramatic genre. For example, Gay's *The Beggar's Opera* 1728 is a burlesque of 18th-century opera, and Sheridan's *The Critic* 1777 satirizes the sentimentality in the drama of this time. In the US the term burlesque was used for a sex and comedy show invented by Michael Bennett Leavitt in 1866 consisting of a variety of acts including acrobats, chorus and comedy numbers. During the 1920s the striptease was introduced to counteract the growing popularity of the cinema, and Gypsy Rose Lee became its most famous artiste. Burlesque was banned in New York in 1942.

circus (Latin 'circle') originally, in Roman times, an arena for chariot races and gladiatorial combats. In modern times, it is an entertainment, often held in a large tent or 'big top', involving performing animals, acrobats and clowns. In 1897 the American Phineas Taylor Barnum created the 'Greatest Show on Earth' which included a circus, menagerie and 'freaks', all transported in 100 rail cars.

comedy in the simplest terms, a drama with a happy ending, as opposed to tragedy. Since much comedy relies on topical allusion and taste many comedies, successful during their

time, have subsequently been forgotten. The comic tradition was established by Aristophanes, Menander, and the Roman writers Terence and Plautus. In medieval times, the Vices and Devil of the Morality plays developed into the stock comic characters of the Renaissance *Comedy of Humours* with such notable villains as Jonson's Mosca in *Volpone*. The timeless comedies of Shakespeare and Molière were followed in England during the 17th century by the witty *Comedy of Manners* of Restoration writers such as Etherege, Wycherley and Congreve. Their often coarse but always vital comedies became toned down in the later Restoration dramas of Sheridan and Goldsmith. A fashion for sentimental comedies dominated most of the 19th century and left little that is remembered today until its close brought the realistic tradition of Shaw and the elegant social comedies of Wilde. The polished comedies of Coward and Rattigan from the 1920s to 1940s were eclipsed during the late 1950s and 1960s by a trend towards satire and a more cynical humour as seen in the works of Joe Orton and Peter Nichols. From the 1970s the 'black comedies' of Alan Ayckbourn have dominated the English stage.

commedia dell'arte popular form of Italian improvised drama in the 16th and 17th centuries. It was performed by specially trained troupes of actors with their own stock characters and situations. It exerted considerable influence on writers such as Molière and on the English genres Pantomime, Harlequinade, and the Punch and Judy show. It laid the foundation for a tradition of mime, particularly in France, which has continued with the contemporary mime of Jean-Louis Barrault and Marcel Marceau.

Cruelty, Theatre of a theory advanced by Antonin Artaud in his book *Le Théâtre et son double* 1938 and adopted by a number of writers and directors including Peter Brook. It aims to shock the audience into an awareness of basic, primitive human nature, through the release of feelings usually repressed by conventional behaviour.

farce a broad form of comedy involving

stereotyped characters in complex, often improbable situations frequently revolving around extra-marital relationships, hence the term 'bedroom farce'. Originating from the physical knockabout comedy of Greek satyr plays and the broad humour developed from medieval religious drama, the farce was developed and perfected during the 19th century by Labiche and Feydeau in France, and Pinero in England. In modern times two notable English series have been the Aldwych farces of Ben Travers in the 1920s and 1930s and the Whitehall farces produced by Brian Rix during the 1950s and 1960s.

Kabuki popular form of Japanese drama incorporating music, dance and acting, developed during the 17th century from the more aristocratic 'No' tradition. Plays are long, episodic, and based mainly on legendary themes, although content is secondary to the display of elaborate costumes, staging and virtuoso ability of the actors, who are all male.

masque a spectacular and essentially aristocratic entertainment with a fairy or mythological theme in which music, dance, and extravagant costumes and scenic design were more important than plot. It reached its height of popularity at the English court between 1600 and 1640, with the collaboration of Ben Jonson as writer and Inigo Jones as stage designer. The masque had great influence on the development of ballet and opera, and the elaborate frame in which it was performed developed into the proscenium arch.

melodrama although today often used as a derogatory term, it was first applied to plays accompanied by music, which became popular throughout Europe during the 19th century. The early melodramas used extravagant theatrical effects for artificially heightening the violent emotions and actions, and were frequently played against a Gothic background of mountains or ruined castles. Beginning with the early work of Goethe and Schiller, it was popularized in France by Pixérécourt and first introduced to England in an unauthorized translation by Thomas Holcroft as *A Tale of Mystery* in 1802.

mime in modern usage, a term for acting in which gestures, movements and facial expression replace dialogue. In ancient Greece mime was a crude, realistic comedy with speech and exaggerated gesture. It is essential to the stage actor's repertory of expression, and plays an important role in ballet. It has also developed as a form of theatre in its own right, particularly in France, where Marcel Marceau and Jean-Louis Barrault have continued the traditions established in the 19th century by Deburau and back to the practices of the commedia dell'arte in Italy.

Morality plays late medieval drama, derived from the Mystery plays, which aimed to instruct. The dramas were allegories of human life in which the Virtues and Vices were personified, the latter often to comic effect. *Everyman* is the most famous example which survives today. The Morality plays had an important influence on the course of Elizabethan drama and the Jonsonian Comedy of Humours.

music hall light entertainment consisting of a 'variety' of songs and comic turns which reached its heyday during the early 20th century. It arose from tavern entertainment; special music halls were built and soon Empires and Hippodromes were established in most English towns. Famous music hall performers have included Albert Chevalier, Marie Lloyd, Harry Lauder and George Formby. Many had their special character 'trademark' such as Vesta Tilley's immaculate masculine outfit as Burlington Bertie. With the onset of radio and television, music hall declined but has had something of a revival in the informal entertainment of the pub – the place of its origin. The American equivalent is known as 'Vaudeville'.

musical comedy a popular form of theatre combining a story with elements of song and dance often performed by a chorus. Derived from light opera, the first examples were staged by George Edwardes at the Gaiety Theatre in London from 1892. Typical of the 1920s were *The Student Prince* 1924 and *The Desert Song* 1926 by Sigmund Romberg, but the genre reached a more sophisticated expression in America during the 1930s and 40s with the work of George Gershwin, Cole Porter, Irving Berlin and Jerome Kern, and in England with Noel Coward and the more romantic Ivor Novello. The word 'comedy' was dropped and the era of the 'musical' arrived with Rodgers and Hammerstein's *Oklahoma!* in 1943, bringing with it a more integrated combination of plot and music, as in Lerner and Loewe's *My Fair Lady* 1956 and Bernstein's *West Side Story* 1957. Sandy Wilson's *The Boy Friend* 1953 revived the British musical, and was followed by hits such as Bart's *Oliver* 1960, *Oh What a Lovely War!* 1963 produced by Joan Littlewood and Charles Chiltern, and finally the hugely successful Lloyd Webber musicals including *Jesus Christ Superstar* 1970, *Cats* 1981, and *The Phantom of the Opera* 1986.

Mystery (or Miracle) plays medieval religious dramas based on stories from the Old and New Testaments which were performed around the time of church festivals, reaching their height in Europe during the 15th and 16th centuries. A whole cycle running from the Creation to the Last Judgement was performed in separate scenes on mobile wagons by various town guilds. Four English cycles survive, Coventry, Wakefield (or Townley), Chester, and York. Versions are still performed, notably the York cycle at York. The German equivalent, the *Mysterienspiel* , survives today as the *Passion Play*. It is essentially concerned with the Crucifixion of Christ and the most famous takes place every ten years at Oberammergau.

No (or Noh) stylized, classical drama of Japan; an aristocratic form as opposed to the popular Kabuki, developed from the 14th century by Kwanami and his son. The plays are based on mythical themes which are expressed through music, chant and dance. There is no scenery but costumes and masks are elaborate.

pageant originally the wagon on which medieval plays were performed; the term was later applied to the moving, spectacular procession of songs, dances and tableaux which became fashionable during the 1920s and which

exists today in forms such as the Lord Mayor's Show in London. Related to the pageant is the open-air entertainment *Son et Lumière*, in which the history of a place is performed in a series of episodes accompanied by sound, and lighting effects projected on to the site of a castle, for example.

pantomime in the English theatre, a traditional Christmas entertainment descended from the harlequin spectacles of the 18th century and burlesque of the 19th century, which gave rise to the tradition of the principal boy being played by an actress and the dame by an actor. The role of the harlequin diminished altogether as themes developed on folktales such as *The Sleeping Beauty* and *Cinderella*, and with the introduction of additional material such as popular songs, topical comedy and audience participation. The term 'pantomime' was also applied to Roman dumbshow performed by a masked actor, to 18th-century ballets with mythical themes, and, in 19th-century France, to the wordless Pierrot plays from which modern 'mime' developed.

puppet theatre a form of drama acted by puppets usually manipulated by unseen operators. There are many types of puppet; probably the best known in England are finger or glove puppets, of which the most famous is Punch, who has developed from the Pulcinella of the commedia dell'arte. By the 16th and 17th centuries refined versions of the travelling puppet shows became popular with the aristocracy and puppets were extensively used as vehicles for caricature and satire until the 19th century. There has been a revival of interest in the 20th century, partly stimulated by the influence of the Joruri tradition in Japan with its large, intricate puppets and by leading exponents such as Obraztsov and his Moscow Puppet Theatre, and most recently by Fluck and Law, whose satirical 'Spitting Image' puppets, caricaturing famous people, have appeared on television.

revue a stage presentation involving short satirical and topical items in the form of song, sketches and monologues. The first revue seems to have been *Under the Clock* 1893 by

Hicks and Brookfield. Until the 1920s revues were spectacular entertainments, but the 'intimate revue' (such as *Sweet and Low* 1943) became increasingly popular under Cochran, who employed writers such as Noel Coward. During the 1960s the satirical revue took off with the Cambridge Footlights' production *Beyond the Fringe*, firmly establishing the revue tradition among the young and at 'fringe' theatrical events. Another offshoot is the 'continuous revue' blending comedy and nudity, started at the Windmill Theatre in London and running 'continuously' (hence its name) from the 1930s until 1964.

tragedy very generally, a play dealing with a serious theme, usually one in which a character falls to disaster either as a result of personal failings or circumstances beyond his or her control. The Greek view of tragedy, as defined by Aristotle and expressed by the great tragedians Aeschylus, Euripides, and Sophocles, provided the subject matter for later tragic dramas, but it was the Roman Seneca (whose works were intended to be read rather than acted) who influenced the Elizabethan tragedy of Marlowe and Shakespeare. French classical tragedy developed under the influence of both Seneca and an interpretation of Aristotle which gave rise to the theory of unities of time, place and action, as observed by Racine, one of its greatest exponents. In Germany the tragedies of Goethe and Schiller led to the exaggerated melodrama, which replaced pure tragedy. In the 18th century unsuccessful attempts were made to 'domesticate' tragedy. In the 20th century tragedies in the narrow Greek sense of dealing with exalted personages in an elevated manner have virtually died out. Tragedy has been replaced by dramas with 'tragic' implications or overtones, as in the work of Ibsen, Pinter and Osborne, for example, or by the hybrid tragi-comedy.

tragi-comedy a drama which contains elements of tragedy and comedy; for example, Shakespeare's 'reconciliation' plays such as *The Winter's Tale*, which reaches a tragic climax but then lightens to a happy conclusion. A tragi-comedy is the usual form for plays in the tradition of the Theatre of the Absurd, such as *En attendant Godot/Waiting for Godot* 1953 by Beckett and *Rosencrantz and Guildenstern are Dead* 1967 by Stoppard.

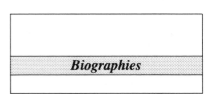

Biographies

Aeschylus c 525–456 BC. Greek dramatist. He wrote some 90 plays, of which seven survive, including *The Suppliant Women* c 490 BC and the trilogy *Oresteia* 458 BC, dealing with the curse on the house of Agamemnon. He is widely regarded as the founder of European tragedy.

Anouilh Jean 1910– . French playwright, whose plays dramatize his concerns with the contrasts between innocence and experience, poverty in a world of riches, and the role of memory. His plays include *Antigone* 1942 *L'Invitation au château/Ring Round the Moon*, 1947, *Colombe* 1950, and *Becket* 1959, about Thomas à Becket and Henry II.

Aristophanes c 448–380 BC. Greek comic dramatist, who satirized contemporary issues such as the new learning of Socrates in *The Clouds* 423 BC and the power of women in *Lysistrata* 411 BC. The chorus plays a prominent role, frequently giving the play its title, as in *The Birds* 414 BC, *The Wasps* 422 BC, and *The Frogs* 405 BC.

Ayckbourn Alan 1939– . British dramatist, and director of the Theatre-in-the-Round, Scarborough, from 1959. His prolific output, characterized by his acute ear for comic dialogue, includes the trilogy *The Norman Conquests* 1974, *Woman in Mind* 1986 and *A Small Family Business* 1987.

Beaumarchais Pierre Augustin Caron de 1732–99. French dramatist. His two best known comedies, *The Barber of Seville* 1775 and *The Marriage of Figaro* 1784, ridiculing the aristocracy, inspired operas of those titles by

Rossini and Mozart.

Beckett Samuel 1906– . Irish novelist and dramatist, who wrote in French and English. His most famous play, *En attendant Godot/ Waiting for Godot* 1952, in which two tramps wait endlessly for the enigmatic 'Godot', is possibly the best known example of Theatre of the Absurd, portraying the 'absurdity' of the human condition in an irrational universe. This predicament is explored to further extremes in *Fin de Partie/End game* 1957 and *Happy Days* 1961.

Bernhardt Sarah. Stage name of French actress Rosine Bernard 1845–1923. Particularly noted for her golden voice, she dominated the stage of her day, frequently performing at the Comédie-Française. Her most famous roles were as Cordelia in *King Lear*, Racine's *Phè-dre*, Doña Sol in Hugo's *Hernani* and in the male roles of *Hamlet* and of Napoleon's son in Rostand's *L'Aiglon*.

Brecht Bertolt 1898–1956. German, Marxist writer, whose 'alienation' theory, requiring the audience and actors to adopt a critical detach-ment from the drama, is the antithesis of the nomal 'suspension of disbelief' in the theatre. His work includes *The Threepenny Opera* 1928 (an adaptation of Gay's *The Beggar's Opera*) with music by Kurt Weill, *Galileo* 1938, *Mother Courage* 1941 and *The Caucasian Chalk Circle* 1949. From 1949 he established in East Ger-many the Berliner Ensemble, a theatre group.

Chekhov Anton Pavlovich 1860–1904. Rus-sian dramatist. His play *The Seagull* 1896 was a failure at first, but succeeded when revived by Stanislavsky for the Moscow Arts Theatre in 1898, for which Chekhov also wrote *Uncle Vanya* 1899, and his two masterpieces *The Three Sisters* 1901 and *The Cherry Orchard* 1904. The latter illustrate Chekhov's sense of atmosphere and internal development of character.

Congreve William 1670–1729. English dra-matist, the greatest exponent of Restoration Comedy, whose plays are noted for the ele-gance of their construction and prose style. He had immediate success with *The Old Bachelor* 1693, followed by *The Double Dealer* 1694, and

Love for Love 1695. His most famous play, *The Way of the World* 1700, with its delightful heroine Millamant, was not well received at the time.

Corneille Pierre 1606–84. French dramatist, regarded as the founder of French classical drama. His most famous play *Le Cid* 1637, a tragi-comedy and landmark in French drama, was attacked by critics for its form, but it enjoyed huge public success. A series of classi-cal tragedies followed, *Horace* 1639, *Cinna* 1640, *Polyeucte* 1643, and a comedy, *Le Men-teur* 1643. After the failure of *Pertharite* 1652, his fame began to diminish in favour of Racine.

Coward Sir Noël 1899–1973. English actor, director, dramatist and composer. He is best remembered for his sophisticated comedies, *The Vortex* 1924, *Hay Fever* 1925, *Private Lives* 1930, with Gertrude Lawrence, and *Blithe Spirit* 1941. He appeared in a number of first productions of his plays.

Craig Edward Gordon 1872–1966. British director and designer, the son of actress Ellen Terry. His first stage production was Purcell's *Dido and Aeneas* 1900, and he subsequently staged productions throughout Europe includ-ing Ibsen's *The Vikings* 1903, in which his mother appeared. His innovations and theo-ries on stage design and lighting effects, expounded in *On the Art of the Theatre* 1911, have had a huge influence on stage production in Europe and the USA.

Eliot T(homas) S(tearns) 1888–1965. Poet and dramatist, born in the USA and a British subject from 1927. He initiated a revival of poetic drama with *Murder in the Cathedral* 1935, about the murder of Thomas à Becket, which was followed by *The Family Reunion* 1939 with its classical overtones. In his later plays, *The Cocktail Party* 1949 and *The Con-fidential Clerk* 1953, he assumed the form of a drawing-room comedy and turned to a plainer verse style. The Lloyd Webber musical *Cats* 1981 used his verse.

Euripides c 484–407 BC. Greek dramatist. His influence on later drama was probably more important than that of either of the other two great tragedians, Aeschylus and Sophocles. A realist, concerned with individual passions and social issues rather than higher principles, he wrote the tragedies *Bacchae* 405, *Electra* 413, *Trojan Women* 415 and *Medea* 431, and the tragi-comedies *Iphigenia in Tauris* 413 and *Alcestis* 438.

Farquhar George 1678–1707. Late Restoration dramatist, born in Ireland. His most famous plays, *The Recruiting Officer* 1706 and *The Beaux' Stratagem* 1707, are in the tradition of the Restoration Comedy of Manners.

Garrick David 1717–79. British actor and theatre manager. He was responsible for changing the acting style of his time by replacing the traditional declamatory delivery with a naturalness of manner. He is noted for his performances as Richard III, Hamlet and Lear. In 1747 he became manager of the Drury Lane Theatre in London, and was responsible for a number of significant theatrical conventions, including concealed stage lighting and banishing spectators from the stage.

Goethe Johann Wolfgang von 1749–1832. German poet, dramatist, and man-of-letters. His first play, *Götz von Berlichingen* 1773, inspired by the work of Shakespeare, became the cornerstone of the romantic 'Sturm und Drang' movement. A stay in Italy, 1786–88, inspired the classical dramas *Iphigenie auf Tauris* 1787 and *Torquato Tasso* 1789. His masterpiece, the poetic play *Faust*, was published in two parts 1808 and 1832. Its length and sheer scale present enormous staging difficulties, producers have often resorted to using *Urfaust*, an earlier draft.

Gielgud Sir John 1904– . British actor and producer. A great-nephew of the actress Ellen Terry, he made his début at the Old Vic in 1921, attracted notice as Romeo in 1924, and created his most famous role as Hamlet in 1929. Although he is probably best known as a Shakespearean actor, his numerous stage appearances include performances in plays by Chekhov and Sheridan, and in works by the modern playwrights Alan Bennett, Peter Shaffer, and David Storey.

Granville-Barker Harley 1877–1946. British theatre director and author. Although he

wrote plays including *The Madras House* 1910 and *Waste* 1907, his major contribution to the development of British theatre was as director-manager with J. E. Vedrenne at the Royal Court Theatre from 1904–18, directing plays by Shaw, Yeats, Ibsen, Galsworthy, and Masefield. From 1927–47 he wrote the scholarly series *Prefaces to Shakespeare*, which long influenced the staging of Shakespeare.

Hall Sir Peter (Reginald Frederick) 1930– . British theatre director. From 1960–68 he directed the Royal Shakespeare Theatre at Stratford, and developed the Royal Shakespeare Company at the time when the Aldwych became its London base. He was director of the National Theatre from 1973 and also artistic director at Glyndebourne from 1984.

Ibsen Henrik 1828–1906. Norwegian dramatist whose work, characterized by its poetic realism, revolutionized the course of European drama. The two verse-dramas, *Love's Comedy* 1862 and *Peer Gynt* 1867, were followed by his masterly series of realistic social dramas: *Pillars of Society* 1877, *A Doll's House* 1879, *Ghosts* 1881, *An Enemy of the People* 1882, *The Wild Duck* 1884, *Rosmersholm* 1886, *The Lady from the Sea* 1888 and *Hedda Gabler* 1890. His later plays include *Little Eyolf* 1894 and *When We Dead Awaken* 1899.

Ionesco Eugène 1912– . Romanian-born French dramatist, a leading exponent of the Theatre of the Absurd movement. Most of his plays are in one act and express his concern with the futility of language as a means of communication, as in *La Cantatrice chauve/ The Bald Prima Donna* 1950, *La Leçon/The Lesson* 1951 and *Les Chaises/The Chairs* 1951. His full-length plays include *Rhinocéros* 1958 and *Le Roi se meurt/Exit the King* 1961.

Irving Sir Henry. Stage name of English actor-manager John Brodribb 1838–1905. From 1871 he established himself as the leading actor of the late 19th century, chiefly at the Lyceum Theatre in London, where he became manager from 1878. He staged a series of successful Shakespearean productions there, including *Romeo and Juliet* 1882, with himself and Ellen Terry playing the leading roles. In

1895 he was the first actor to be knighted.

Jonson Ben 1572–1637. English dramatist. His first success, *Every Man in His Humour* 1598, established the English Comedy of Humours in which each character embodies a 'humour' or vice such as greed, lust or avarice. His first tragedy *Sejanus* 1603 included Burbage and Shakespeare in the cast, but it is for his classic comedies that he is most famous: *Volpone, or The Fox* 1606, *The Alchemist* 1610, and *Bartholomew Fair* 1614. He collaborated with Inigo Jones on numerous court masques between 1605 and 1612.

Lessing Gotthold Ephraim 1729–81. German dramatist and critic. His play *Miss Sara Sampson* 1755 was the first tragedy of ordinary German life and his next play *Minna von Barnhelm* 1767, the first bourgeois comedy.

Lorca Frederico García 1898–1936. Spanish poet and dramatist, whose works are now receiving a considerable revival 50 years after his death in the Spanish Civil War. His best works are the three powerful and intense tragedies: *Bodas de sangre/Blood Wedding* 1933, a savage story of feuding families, *Yerma* 1934, and possibly his finest, *La Casa de Bernarda Alba/The House of Bernarda Alba* 1936, first produced professionally in London in 1986 with Glenda Jackson as the tyrannical mother heading a household of sisters.

Marlowe Christopher 1564–93. English poet and dramatist, a powerful influence on Shakespeare and the course of Elizabethan drama. In 1587–88 he wrote the flamboyant verse drama *Tamburlaine the Great*, which was followed by *The Tragical History of Doctor Faustus* c 1589, *The Jew of Malta* c 1590, a grim comedy standing mid-way between the medieval Morality play and Jonson's Comedy of Humours, and the historical drama *Edward II* c 1591–2. He was murdered, allegedly in a pub brawl, but probably for political reasons.

Miller Arthur 1915– . American playwright. His plays, deeply concerned with family relationships and contemporary American values, include *All My Sons* 1947, a condemnation of war profiteering, *Death of a Salesman* 1949, *The Crucible* 1953, about witch-hunting

in Salem in the 17th century, and *After the Fall* 1964, in which the character of Maggie is allegedly based on the actress Marilyn Monroe, to whom he was married 1956–61.

Molière pseudonym of Jean-Baptiste Poquelin 1622–73. Actor and greatest French comic dramatist, who founded and acted in the Illustre-Théâtre in Paris from 1643. He established his reputation with *Les Précieuses ridicules* 1658. This was followed by his great satiric masterpieces, which include *L'Ecole des femmes* 1662, *Le Tartuffe* 1664, banned until 1667 for attacking the hypocrisy of the clergy, *Le Misanthrope* 1666, *Le Médecin malgré lui* 1666, *L'Avare* 1668, *Le Bourgeois gentilhomme* 1670, and *Le Malade imaginaire* 1673.

Olivier Laurence Kerr, Baron Olivier 1907– . British actor and producer. He established his reputation at the Old Vic, particularly in *Hamlet* 1937. His other major stage roles include Henry V, Richard III and Archie Rice in Osborne's *The Entertainer*, which were all filmed. He was director of the Chichester Festival Theatre 1961–65 and first director of the National Theatre Company 1962–73.

O'Neill Eugene Gladstone 1888–1953. American dramatist. His first full-length play, *Beyond the Horizon* 1920, won a Pulitzer Prize. His best plays are characterized by a down-to-earth quality even when he is experimenting with expressionism, symbolism, or stream of consciousness, and include *The Emperor Jones* 1921, *Desire under the Elms* 1924, *Mourning Becomes Electra* 1931 (a version of Aeschylus' *Oresteia*) and *The Iceman Cometh* 1939. He was awarded a Nobel Prize in 1936.

Pinero Sir Arthur Wing 1855–1934. British dramatist, a leading exponent of the 'well-made' play, enjoying a huge success in his time with his farces *The Magistrate* 1885, *Dandy Dick* 1887, and *The Cabinet Minister* 1890. A departure to more substantial social drama came with *The Second Mrs Tanqueray* 1893, a 'problem play', and the comedies *Trelawny of the 'Wells'* 1898 and *The Gay Lord Quex* 1899.

Pinter Harold 1930– . English dramatist. Many of his plays are tragi-comedies on the theme of the breakdown of communication, broadly in the tradition of the Theatre of the Absurd. His notable stage plays include *The Birthday Party* 1958, *The Caretaker* 1960, *The Homecoming* 1965 and a series of one act plays, *The Lover* 1963, *Silence* and *Landscape* 1969 and *No Man's Land* 1975.

Pirandello Luigi 1867–1936. Italian novelist and dramatist. His early plays were adaptations of his short stories showing the futility of human endeavour and the impossibility of defining reality. Central to these concerns are his best known play, *Sei personaggi in cerca d'autore/Six Characters in Search of an Author* 1921, and *Enrico Quarto/Henry IV* 1922.

Racine Jean 1639–99. French dramatist, and greatest exponent of the classical tragedy. Most of his plays have a woman in the title role, as in *Andromaque* 1667, *Iphigénie* 1674, and *Phèdre* 1677. After the failure of *Phèdre*, he gave up writing for the theatre, but was persuaded by Mme de Maintenon to write two religious dramas, *Esther* 1689 and *Athalie* 1691, which achieved posthumous success.

Reinhardt Max. Stage name of American-Austrian theatrical producer Max Goldmann 1873–1943. He excelled in lavish spectacles, such as *Oedipus Rex* in Berlin 1910 and *The Miracle* with Lady Diana Cooper at Olympia, London, in 1911, which are remembered for his control of huge crowds on stage, and use of new techniques of lighting and stage devices. He also directed small-scale intimate dramas in Berlin theatres and founded the Salzburg Festival in 1920. From 1933 he worked in the USA.

Sartre Jean-Paul 1905–80. French writer and philosopher. A founder of Existentialism, he expressed its tenets in his dramas *Les Mouches/The Flies* 1942, a retelling of the Orestes myth, and *Huis-clos/In Camera* (also called *No Exit*) 1944, in which three characters are confined in a hell of their own making. In 1951 his most ambitious, but less theatrically successful, play *Le Diable et le Bon Dieu* was written followed by *Les Séquestrés d'Altona/The Condemned of Altona* 1959.

Schiller Johann Christoph Friedrich von 1759–1805. German Romantic poet and playwright. He was a friend of Goethe and a leading exponent of the 'Sturm und Drang' movement. His first play *Die Räuber/The Robbers* 1781 was an immediate success, particularly with the young. His later works include the historical trilogy *Wallenstein* 1798–99, and *Maria Stuart* 1800, *Die Jungfrau von Orleans/The Maid of Orleans* 1801, and *Wilhelm Tell* 1804.

Shaffer Peter (Levin) 1926– . English dramatist, whose first play *Five Finger Exercise* 1958 was successfully produced in London and New York. His other plays include the epic *The Royal Hunt of the Sun* 1964, about the Spanish conquest of the Incas, *Black Comedy* 1965, the powerful psychological drama *Equus* 1973, and *Amadeus* 1979 about Salieri and Mozart.

Shakespeare William 1564–1616. English playwright and poet, the greatest English dramatist. By 1589 he was an established actor and playwright in London and from 1594 was a member of the Chamberlain's (later the King's) company of players. His work first appeared as a collected body in the First Folio, published in 1623 by Heninge and Condell, but it is difficult to date individual plays with precision. Very roughly, they divide into the following periods: c 1590–1600 the history plays and comedies, including *Henry IV* (parts I and II), *Henry V*, *Richard III*, *A Midsummer Night's Dream* and *As You Like It*, c 1601–1607 the great tragedies and darker comedies, including *Hamlet*, *Othello*, *Macbeth*, *King Lear*, *Measure for Measure* and *Troilus and Cressida*, c 1608–1612 the mature 'romance' or 'reconciliation' plays, including *The Tempest* and *The Winter's Tale*. For the first 200 years after his death, Shakespeare's plays were frequently performed in cut or revised form (Nahum Tate's *King Lear* was given a happy ending), and it was not until the 19th century, with the critical assessments of Coleridge and Hazlitt, that the original texts were restored. Since then the plays have been consistently performed throughout the world, and have exerted an immeasurable influence on the history of the theatre.

Shaw George Bernard 1856–1950. Irish dramatist and critic. A prolific writer, he allied himself with a new and essentially political and polemical movement in the theatre, aiming in his work to engage the intellect rather than the emotions of his audience. His plays include *Mrs Warren's Profession* (1893, but banned until 1902 because it dealt with prostitution), *Arms and the Man* 1894 (about war), *Candida* 1903, the epic *Man and Superman* 1903, *Major Barbara* 1905, *Pygmalion* 1913 (adapted as the musical *My Fair Lady*), *Heartbreak House* 1917, and *St Joan* 1924.

Sheridan Richard Brinsley 1751–1816. Anglo-Irish dramatist and theatre manager. He was manager of the Drury Lane Theatre from 1776, rebuilt it in 1794, and continued until 1809 when it was destroyed by fire. He is best remembered for his two social dramas, *The Rivals* 1775, with the comic Mrs Malaprop, and *The School for Scandal* 1777 – masterpieces of the Comedy of Manners.

Sophocles 496–406 BC. Greek dramatist. He wrote over 100 plays, of which seven tragedies and a satyr play survive, including *Ajax* c 450 BC, *Antigone* c 441, *Oedipus Rex* c 425, *Electra* 409 and *Oedipus at Colonus* 406. His dramas are subtle studies of the interaction between character and circumstance or fate. He introduced a third actor to the stage and reduced the chorus to a lyrical device emphasising changes of mood rather than directly affecting the action.

Stanislavsky Konstantin Sergeivich 1863–1938. Russian actor, director and teacher of acting. He founded the Moscow Art Theatre in 1918 and achieved his greatest success as a director with his productions of Chekhov and Gorky. He was the originator of 'method' acting, which he described in *My Life in Art* 1924 and other works, and which had great influence on acting techniques in Europe and the USA. He rejected the declamatory style of acting in favour of an approach concentrating on the psychological development of character.

Strindberg August 1849–1912. Swedish dramatist and novelist, who wrote over 50 plays in a variety of styles including historical plays, symbolic dramas (the two-part *The Dance of Death* 1901) and 'chamber plays' such as *The Ghost (or Spook) Sonata* 1907. His two best known plays, *The Father* 1887 and *Miss Julie* 1888, are both powerful studies of human frailty and hostility between the sexes.

Synge J(ohn) M(illington) 1871–1909. Irish playwright, a leading figure in the Irish dramatic revival of the early 20th century. His six plays show a poetic ear for the speech patterns of the Aran Islands and West Ireland where they are set, and are classics of Irish drama. They include *In Shadow of the Glen* 1903, *Riders to the Sea* 1904, and his masterpiece, *The Playboy of the Western World* 1907, which caused riots at the Abbey Theatre, Dublin, when first performed.

Vega Carpio Lope Felix de 1562–1635. Spanish Renaissance playwright, enormously influential on the course of Spanish drama and writers such as Molière. He wrote over 1,500 plays, most of which are tragi-comedies. He set out his views on drama in *Arte nuevo de hacer comedias/The New Art of Writing Plays* c 1609, while reaffirming the classical form. Possibly his best known play is *Fuenteovejuna* 1614, acclaimed in this century as the first proletarian drama.

Webster John 1580–1634. English dramatist, who ranks after Shakespeare as the greatest tragedian of his time and the one whose plays are most frequently revived today. His two great plays *The White Devil* c 1612 and *The Duchess of Malfi* 1614 are dark, violent tragedies obsessed with death and decay, and infused with poetic brilliance.

Wilde Oscar 1854–1900. Irish writer. In the theatre he is best known for his elegant, stylish comedies with witty dialogue, such as *Lady Windermere's Fan* 1892, *A Woman of No Importance* 1893, *An Ideal Husband* 1895, and his most consistently successful play, *The Importance of Being Earnest* 1895.

Williams Tennessee 1914–83. Pseudonym of American playwright Thomas Lanier Williams. He excelled in creating the atmosphere of life in the Deep South in *The Glass Menagerie* 1945, *A Streetcar Named Desire* 1947, and *Cat on a Hot Tin Roof* 1955.

c 3200 BC	Beginnings of Egyptian religious drama, essentially ritualistic.
c 600	Choral performances (dithyrambs) in honour of Dionysus form beginnings of Greek tragedy, according to Aristotle.
c 534	First festival of tragedy held at Athens and won by Thespis.
500–300	Great age of Greek drama which included tragedy, comedy and satyr plays (grotesque farce).
468	Sophocles' first victory at Athens festival. His use of a third actor altered the course of the tragic form.
458	Aeschylus' *Oresteia* first performed.
c 425–388	Comedies of Aristophanes including *The Birds* 414, *Lysistrata* 411 and *The Frogs* 405. In tragedy the importance of the chorus diminished under Euripedes, author of *The Bacchae* 405.
c 350	Menander's 'New Comedy' of social manners developed.
c 330	Aristotle's *Poetics* analysed the nature of tragedy. Theatre of Dionysus in Athens built.
c 240 BC- *200 AD*	Emergence of Roman drama, adapted from Greek originals under Plautus, Terence and Seneca. All were to have great influence on Elizabethan writers.
c 375 AD	Kâlidâsa's *Sakuntalâ* marked the height of Sanskrit drama in India.
c 970	Earliest example of Christian liturgical drama, written by Ethelwold, Bishop of Winchester
1210	Priests were forbidden to appear on public stage. This led to secularization of drama in the vernacular.
c 1250–1500	European Mystery (or Miracle) plays flourished, first in the churches, later in market places, and performed in England by town guilds.
c 1375	No (or Noh) drama developed in Japan.
c 1495	*Everyman*, the best known of all the Morality plays, first performed.
1500–1600	Italian commedia dell'arte troupes performed popular, improvised comedies; they were to have a large influence on Molière and on English Harlequinade and Pantomime.
c 1551	Nicholas Udall's *Ralph Roister Doister* written, the first English comedy.
c 1576	First English playhouse, 'The Theatre', built by James Burbage in Shoreditch, London.
1587	Marlowe's *Tamburlaine the Great* marked an important advance in the use of blank verse and the beginning of the great age of Elizabethan and Jacobean drama in England.
c 1589	Kyd's *Spanish Tragedy* - the first of the 'revenge' tragedies.
1594	Lord Chamberlain's Men formed; a theatre company to which Shakespeare was attached as actor/writer from 1595.

1599 The Globe Theatre built on Bankside, Southwark, London.

c 1590–1612 Shakespeare's greatest plays, including *Hamlet* and *King Lear*, were written.

1604 Inigo Jones designed *The Masque of Blackness* for James I, written by Ben Jonson. Masques were the height of fashion at the English court around this time.

1613 The Globe Theatre burned down (rebuilt 1614; demolished 1644).

1614 Lope de Vega's *Fuenteovejuna/The Sheep Wall* marked Spanish renaissance in drama.

1637 Corneille's *Le Cid* established classical tragedy in France.

1642 Act of Parliament closed all English theatres.

1660 With the restoration of Charles II to the English throne, dramatic performances recommenced. The first professional actress appeared as Desdemona in Shakespeare's *Othello*.

1664 Molière's *Tartuffe* was banned for three years by religious factions.

1667 Racine's first success, *Andromaque*

1680 Comédie-Française formed by Louis XIV.

1700 Congreve, the greatest exponent of Restoration comedy, wrote *The Way of the World*.

1716 First known American theatre built at Williamsburg.

1728 Gay's *The Beggar's Opera* first performed.

1737 Stage Licensing Act required all plays to be licensed and approved by the Lord Chamberlain before performance.

1747 Garrick became manager of Drury Lane Theatre, London.

1767–8 In Germany, Lessing's *Minna von Barnhelm* and publication of *Hamburgische Dramaturgie*.

1773 In England, Goldsmith's *She Stoops to Conquer* and Sheridan's *The Rivals* 1775 established the 'comedy of manners'. Goethe's *Götz von Berlichingen* is the first 'Sturm und Drang' play (literally storm and stress); this German Romantic movement, depicting extravagant emotions, was influential throughout Europe at this time and led to the rise of English melodrama.

1775 Sarah Siddons, English tragedy actress, made her début at the Drury Lane Theatre.

1781 Schiller's *Die Raüber/The Robbers*

1784 Beaumarchais' *Le Mariage de Figaro*, (written 1778) finally performed after difficulties with censorship because of its alleged revolutionary tendencies.

1802 Holcroft's *A Tale of Mystery* marked the rise of melodrama in England.

1814 Edmund Kean's London début as Shylock in Shakespeare's *The Merchant of Venice*.

1815 Gas lighting installed at Covent Garden.

1830 Hugo's *Hernani* caused riots in Paris. His work marked the beginning of a new Romantic drama, changing the course of French theatre.

1836	Gogol's *The Government Inspector*, a social satire, initially passes the Russian censors.
1838	The début of the French tragic actress, Rachel, at the Comédie-Française
1843	The Theatres Act further strengthened the powers of the Lord Chamberlain to censor plays.
1869	Sarah Bernhardt's first success, in *Le Passant* in Paris.
1878	Henry Irving became actor-manager of the Lyceum with Ellen Terry as leading lady.
1879	Ibsen's *A Doll's House* - an example of Ibsen's hugely influential plays, which marked the beginning of realism in European theatre.
1888	Strindberg's *Miss Julie*.
1893	Shaw wrote *Mrs Warren's Profession* (banned until 1902 because it deals with prostitution). Shaw's works bring the new realistic drama to Britain and introduce social and political issues as subjects for the theatre.
1895	Wilde's *The Importance of Being Earnest*.
1896	The first performance of Chekhov's *The Seagull* failed.
1899	Abbey Theatre, Dublin, founded by W.B. Yeats and Lady Gregory, marked the beginning of an Irish dramatic revival.
1904	Chekhov's *The Cherry Orchard*.Founding of Royal Academy of Dramatic Art (RADA) to train young actors, by Beerbohm Tree in London.
1904–7	Granville Barker and J.E. Vedrenne were managers of the Royal Court Theatre and directed works by Shaw, Yeats, Ibsen, Galsworthy.
1919	Theatre Guild founded in US to perform less commercial new plays.
1923	Shaw's *St Joan*. O'Casey's first play, *The Shadow of a Gunman*.
1925	Coward's *Hay Fever*. Travers' *A Cuckoo in the Nest*, the first of the Aldwych farces.
1928	Brecht's *Die Dreigroschenoper/The Threepenny Opera* with score by Kurt Weill. In USA Jerome Kern's *Show Boat* with Paul Robeson, one example of the success of musical comedies. Others by Cole Porter, Irving Berlin, George Gershwin became popular.
1930	Gielgud's first performance as Hamlet.
1935	T.S. Eliot's *Murder in the Cathedral*.
1943	The first of the 'musicals', *Oklahoma!* opened.
1947	First Edinburgh Festival with fringe theatre events. Tennessee Williams's *A Streetcar Named Desire*.
1953	Arthur Miller's *The Crucible* opened during the period of 'witch-hunting' of communists in US under McCarthy. *Waiting for Godot* by Beckett exemplified the Theatre of the Absurd.
1956	English Stage Company formed at the Royal Court Theatre to provide a platform for new dramatists. Osborne's *Look Back in Anger* included in its first season.

1957	Bernstein's *West Side Story* opened in New York.
1960	Pinter's *The Caretaker*.
1961	Royal Shakespeare Company formed under directorship of Peter Hall, based at Stratford and the Aldwych, London.
1963–4	National Theatre Company formed at the Old Vic under the directorship of Sir Laurence Olivier.
1965	Edward Bond's *Saved* initially banned by the Lord Chamberlain.
1967	Stoppard's *Rosencrantz and Guildenstern are Dead*. Success in USA of *Hair* - first of the 'rock' musicals.
1968	Abolition of theatre censorship in UK.
1970	Peter Brook's production of *A Midsummer Night's Dream*.
1976	National Theatre opened a new theatre complex on the South Bank, London.
1980	Howard Brenton's *The Romans in Britain* led to a private prosecution of the director for obscenity.
1982	Royal Shakespeare Company opened the Barbican Centre, London.
1982–3	Trevor Nunn's production *Nicholas Nickleby* won Tony award, marking its success in UK and USA.
1986	*The Phantom of the Opera* opened in London, the latest in a series of successful Lloyd Webber musicals.
1987	The Theatre Museum opened in Covent Garden, London. Planning permission granted for the building of a replica of The Globe Theatre by Sam Wanamaker on the original site.
1988	Agatha Christie's *The Mousetrap* entered its 36th year, the longest running play in the world.
1989	Remains of the Rose Theatre, where Shakespeare's plays were first performed, were discovered at Southwark, London.

Music and Dance

This section looks at the forms, styles, terms and people important in Western music and dance. The music of other cultures is often based on scale divisions different from ours and could not be discussed here without using complex terminology. Despite its long history and substantial artistic achievements, the significance of non-western music was not properly recognized in the West until Debussy listened to a Japanese gamelan orchestra at the Paris Exposition of 1889. The sounds he heard affected his own music, which in turn influenced the ideas of younger composers. Messiaen was similarly stimulated by hearing a Balinese gamelan orchestra at another Paris exposition, in 1931. Contemporary composers have not waited for the unfamiliar to arrive in the West, but have travelled to find it. Messiaen's pupils Boulez and Stockhausen made extensive trips to Indonesia and Japan; Benjamin Britten also went to Bali. David Fanshawe has spent time in Africa and Tonga. Philip Glass studied with the Indian sitarist Ravi Shankar, while a fellow graduate of the Juilliard School, Steve Reich, visited Ghana to study African drumming. This is a time of exciting cross-fertilization between cultures. Zubin Mehta, born in India, is now conductor of the New York Philharmonic, and a Japanese conductor, Seiji Ozawa, is music director in Boston; the compositions of a New Yorker, John Cage, arouse great enthusiasm in Tokyo. Music is moving, perhaps, towards a universal language.

This section contains biographies and a table of *Great Composers* in the classical tradition, a table of major *Operas* and their first performances, sections on *Jazz* and *Popular Music*, definitions of important *Musical Terms*, and a chronology of *Milestones in Musical History*. This is followed by a table of major works in *The Ballet Repertory* and a *Chronology* of milestones in the history of dance.

GREAT COMPOSERS

Giovanni Palestrina	c.1525–1594	Italian	motets, masses
Claudio Monteverdi	1567–1643	Italian	operas, vocal music
Henry Purcell	1659–1695	English	vocal music, operas
Antonio Vivaldi	1678–1741	Italian	concertos, chamber music
Georg Frideric Handel	1685–1759	German	oratorios, operas, orchestral music
Johann Sebastian Bach	1685–1750	German	keyboard, choral music, concertos
Joseph Haydn	1732–1809	Austrian	symphonies, oratorios, chamber music
Wolfgang Amadeus Mozart	1756–1791	Austrian	symphonies, operas, chamber music
Ludwig van Beethoven	1770–1827	German	symphonies, chamber music, opera
Carl Maria von Weber	1786–1826	German	operas, concertos
Gioacchino Rossini	1792–1868	Italian	operas
Franz Schubert	1797–1828	Austrian	songs, symphonies,chamber music
Hector Berlioz	1803–1869	French	operas, symphonies
Felix Mendelssohn	1809–1847	German	symphonies, concertos
Frederik Chopin	1810–1849	Polish	piano music
Robert Schumann	1810–1856	German	piano, vocal music, concertos
Franz Liszt	1811–1886	Hungarian	piano, orchestral music
Richard Wagner	1813–1883	German	operas
Giuseppe Verdi	1813–1901	Italian	operas
César Franck	1822–1890	Belgian	symphony, organ works
Bedrich Smetana	1824–1884	Czech	symphonies, operas
Anton Bruckner	1824–1896	Austrian	symphonies
Johann Strauss II	1825–1899	Austrian	waltzes, operettas
Johannes Brahms	1833–1897	German	symphonies, concertos
Camille Saint-Saëns	1835–1921	French	symphonies, concertos operas
Modest Mussorgsky	1839–1881	Russian	operas, orchestral music
Peter Ilyich Tchaikovsky	1840–1893	Russian	ballet music, symphonies
Antonin Dvořák	1841–1904	Czech	symphonies, operas
Edvard Grieg	1843–1907	Norwegian	concertos, orchestra music
Nikolai Rimsky-Korsakov	1844–1908	Russian	operas, orchestral music
Leos Janáček	1854–1928	Czech	operas, chamber music
Edward Elgar	1857–1934	English	orchestral music
Giacomo Puccini	1858–1924	Italian	operas
Gustav Mahler	1860–1911	Czech	symphonies
Claude Debussy	1862–1918	French	operas, orchestral music
Richard Strauss	1864–1949	German	operas, orchestral music
Carl Nielsen	1865–1931	Danish	symphonies
Jean Sibelius	1865–1957	Finnish	symphonies, orchestral music
Sergei Rachmaninov	1873–1943	Russian	symphonies, concertos
Arnold Schoenberg	1874–1951	Austrian	operas, orchestral and chamber music
Maurice Ravel	1875–1937	French	piano, chamber music
Béla Bartók	1881–1945	Hungarian	operas, concertos
Igor Stravinsky	1882–1971	Russian	ballets, operas
Anton Webern	1883–1945	Austrian	chamber, vocal music
Alban Berg	1885–1935	Austrian	operas, chamber music
Sergei Prokofiev	1891–1953	Russian	symphonies, ballets
George Gershwin	1898–1937	American	musicals, operas
Dmitri Shostakovich	1906–1975	Russian	piano music
Olivier Messiaen	1908–	French	piano, organ, orchestral music
Benjamin Britten	1913–1976	English	vocal music, opera
Karlheinz Stockhausen	1928–	German	electronic, vocal music

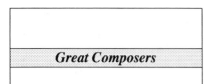

Great Composers

Bach Johann Sebastian 1685–1750. Born in Eisenach, Germany, he worked in Weimar and Leipzig. A master of contrapuntal technique, his music marks the culmination of the Baroque polyphonic style. His huge output includes orchestral works such as the six *Brandenburg Concertos* 1721, organ works, more than 200 cantatas and large-scale choral works such as the *St Matthew Passion* 1729 and the Mass in B Minor 1733.

Bartók Béla 1881–1945. Born in Sinnicolaul Mare, Hungary. With Zoltan Kodaly, he made an extensive study of the folk music of Hungary, Slovakia and Rumania, which led him to develop a new musical language making tonal use of the 12 notes of the chromatic scale. His works include six string quartets 1908–39, the opera *Bluebeard's Castle* 1911 and the *Concerto for Orchestra* 1943. He spent the last five years of his life in the USA.

Beethoven Ludwig van 1770–1827. Born in Bonn, he settled in Vienna in 1792. From the age of 30 he was troubled with increasing deafness. In a career which spanned the decline of Classicism and the growth of Romanticism, his mastery of musical expression in every genre made him the dominant influence in 19th-century music. His orchestral works, which include nine symphonies, five piano concertos and one violin concerto, are probably the most frequently performed in the repertoire. His 32 piano sonatas, 16 string quartets and other chamber music also remain popular.

Berg Alban 1885–1935. Born and lived in Vienna. Like Webern, he studied with Schoenberg and used the latter's serial technique, though there are tonal and Romantic elements in his music. His best-known works are the operas *Wozzeck* 1925 and *Lulu* 1937 and violin concerto 1935.

Berlioz Hector 1803–69. Born in Côte-St André, near Grenoble. He was the only great French Romantic composer. Much of his music has a theatrical quality and was inspired by contemporary drama and literature. His mastery of thematic development, and in particular the idea of using a recurring 'fixed idea' *(idée fixe)*, is evident in works such as the *Symphonie Fantastique* 1830 and *Harold in Italy* 1834. Ahead of his time in his innovative use of orchestral colouring and contrasts, he was barely acknowledged in France during his life, though he did receive the Légion d'Honneur for his *Grand Messe des Morts* 1837.

Brahms Johannes 1833–97. Born in Hamburg, he moved to Vienna in 1863. Using traditional classical forms, he expanded their scope, thus bridging the gap between Classicism and Romanticism in German music. His four symphonies, two piano concertos and violin concerto, all written after he had reached his forties, are part of the Romantic repertoire. He also wrote piano and chamber works, songs and the non-liturgical *German Requiem* 1857–68.

Britten Benjamin 1913–76. Born in Lowestoft, Suffolk. After a short period in the USA 1939–42, he spent the rest of his life in Aldeburgh where, with the tenor Peter Pears, he founded the annual music festival. He wrote some instrumental works but his main achievement lies in his vocal and, in particular, his operatic works. His first opera *Peter Grimes* 1945 was followed by chamber operas such as *Albert Herring* 1947 and several other large-scale operas such as *Billy Budd* 1951. He wrote the *War Requiem* for the consecration of Coventry Cathedral in 1962.

Bruckner Anton 1824–96. Born in Ansfelden, Austria, he settled in Vienna in his forties. A Classic-Romantic in his use of form, he shows Wagnerian influence in the solemnity and expansiveness of his work. His nine symphonies, in particular the Fourth 1881 and Seventh 1884, have now won universal acclaim. A deeply religious man, he also wrote three masses and a *Te Deum* 1881–84.

Chopin Frédéric 1810–49. Born in Selazowa Wola, Poland, of half French, half Polish parentage, he lived in Paris from 1831. A virtuoso performer, he composed almost entirely for the piano, producing a new repertory for the instrument including 27 études, 25 preludes, three sonatas and two concertos. Influenced by the Italian opera composer Bellini, and the by Irish composer Field, his music displays and innovative keyboard technique an rhythm (especially his use of rubato) and strong nationalistic flavour in its passion and use of folk music. The year before his death, from consumption, he gave concerts in England and Scotland.

Debussy Claude 1862–1918. Born in St Germain-en-Laye, France, he spent most of his life in Paris. Influenced by both Impressionist painters and Symbolist poets, his work moved from the naturalistic (his early tone poem *Prélude à l'Aprè-midi d'un Faune* 1894) to the more purely abstract *La Mer* 1905 and the ballet *Jeux* 1912). He developed an original, delicate language using a scale of whole tones and innovative harmonies and achieved a new range of timbres and rhythms for both piano and orchestra. He completed one opera, *Pelléas et Mélisande* 1902, based on a play by Maeterlinck.

Dvořák Antonin 1841–1904. Born in Nelahozeves, Czechoslovakia. He spent much of his life in Prague, but visited England eight times and was head of the National Conservatory in New York 1892–95. He was an important nationalist composer, and his direct, fresh style is best exemplified in his orchestral and chamber works, including nine symphonies, the two *Slavonic Dances* 1878–86, the cello concerto and some notable string quartets.

Elgar Edward 1857–1934. Born in Broadheath, near Worcester, England, he lived in Malvern and then Hereford. Working in obscurity for many years, he first gained national recognition with the *Enigma Variations* 1899, followed by the oratorio *The Dream of Gerontius* 1900, the *Cockaigne* overture 1901 and the *Pomp and Circumstance Marches* 1901–07. Later came the two symphonies 1908 and

1911, and the cello concerto 1919. The combination of tenderness and nobility in his music makes him widely admired in Britain, but he is still little appreciated worldwide.

Franck César 1822–90. Born in Liège, he left Belgium in 1844 and spent the rest of his life in Paris. Influential as an organist, teacher and composer. There are elements of the Romantic and mystical in his work. His organ works, particularly the *Pièce heroique* 1878 and *Three Chorales* 1890, are widely admired, as are the *Symphonic Variations* 1885 and the symphony of 1889.

Gershwin George 1898–1937. Born in New York. A jazz pianist and composer of popular songs, mostly with lyrics by his brother Ira, his *Rhapsody in Blue* 1924 brought notice from more intellectual audiences. His other principal works include a piano concerto, the tone poem *An American in Paris* 1928, and the opera *Porgy and Bess* 1935.

Grieg Edvard 1843–1907. Born in Bergen, Norway, he was determinedly Norwegian in his musical inspiration. Much of his best music is small scale, namely his songs, dances and piano works. Among orchestral works are the Piano Concerto 1869, one of the most popular in the concert repertoire, and the incidental music for Ibsen's *Peer Gynt* 1876.

Handel George Frideric 1685–1759. Born in Halle, Germany, he spent most of his life in England. He came to dominate English musical life with his efforts to convert audiences to Italian opera and his subsequent elecation of the oratorio to a more important musical form, culminating in the *Messiah* 1742, written in three weeks. He also wrote several instrumental works, including the orchestral suites *The Water Music* 1715 and *Music for the Royal Fireworks* 1749.

Haydn Joseph 1732–1809. Born in Rohrau, near Bratislava, he spent much of his life as kapellmeister to the Austrian Esterházy family, but visited London twice. A teacher of both Mozart and Beethoven, he was a major exponent of the classical sonata form in his numerous chamber and orchestral works (he wrote over 100 symphonies). He also wrote much choral music, the best-known including the oratorios *The Creation* 1798 and *The Seasons* 1801.

Janáček Leŏs 1854–1928. Born in Hukvaldy, Czechoslovakia, he lived much of his life in Brno. Essentially a theatrical composer, he had his first success with the opera *Jenufa*. His other operas, including *Katya Kabanova* 1921 and *The Cunning Little Vixen* 1924, and his choral music, especially the *Glagolitic Mass* 1927, all show his individual use of rhythm, tonality and form.

Liszt Franz 1811–86. Born in Raiding, Hungary, he lived for periods in Paris, Weimar and then Rome, where he turned to a religious life and became known as the Abbé Liszt. Highly regarded as a brilliant pianist, he produced some 400 original compositions and 900 transcriptions for piano, as well as inventing a new orchestral form in his *Symphonic Poem*. A champion of his contemporaries, especially Wagner, he promoted 'The Music of the Future', breaking new ground with his use of chromaticism.

Mahler Gustav 1860–1911. Born in Kaliště, Czechoslovakis, he worked as a conductor throughout his life, notably with the Vienna Opera and the New York Philharmonic. His massive, richly textured symphonies, the moving *Das Lied Von der Erde/Song of the Earth* and his song cycles display a synthesis of Romanticism and new uses of chromatic harmonies and musical forms. His work has gained in popularity with modern audiences after several decades of neglect.

Mendelssohn Felix 1809–47. Born in Hamburg, he travelled extensively, often to Britain, before settling in Düsseldorf and then Leipzig. Using Classical forms he was nevertheless an early Romantic in the subjective quality he brought to his work. The overture and incidental music to *A Midsummer Night's Dream* 1827/43, the *Fingal's Cave* overture 1832, the violin concerto 1845 and the *Italian* 1833 and *Scottish* 1842 Symphonies have always been popular works in the concert repertoire.

Messiaen Oliver 1908– . Born in Avignon, France, he has spent most of his life in Paris, where he was appointed organist at La Trinité church in 1931. A devout christian, he considers that his music has two predominant elements: religious faith and colour. An innovator both with tone and rhythm, his teaching influenced contemporary composers including Boulez and Stockhausen. Among his better-known works are the *Quatuor pour la fin du temps* 1941, the large-scale *Turangalila Symphony* 1949, and several organ pieces.

Monteverdi Claudio 1567–1643. Born in Cremona, Italy, he lived in Mantua and Venice, where he was director of music at St Mark's. The greatest 17th-century Italian composer and an exponent of monody and recitative as opposed to polyphony, he holds an important place in European music. His operas *Orfeo* 1607 and *The Coronation of Poppea* 1642 are two early masterpieces in the form. He also wrote many madrigals, motets and much sacred music, notably the *Vespers* 1610, a six-part mass.

Mozart Wolfgang Amadeus 1756–91. Born in Salzburg, Austria. A child prodigy, he travelled extensively in his early youth, settling in Vienna from the age of 25, where he died a pauper. Strongly influenced by Haydn, his music marks the height of the Classical age in its purity of melody and form. His large output includes operas such as *The Marriage of Figaro* 1786, *Don Giovanni* 1787, *The Magic Flute* 1791, nearly 50 symphonies, chamber and keyboard music. His last work was his *Requiem.*

Mussorgsky Modest 1839–81. Born in Karevo in Pskov, Russia. After an early career in the army, he became a civil servant, but his life was cut short by alcoholism. A member of the nationalist group, the Five, he was influenced by both folk music and literature, and was largely self-taught. His best-known compositions include *A Night on the Bare Mountain* 1867, *Pictures at an Exhibition* 1874 and the opera *Boris Godunov* 1874, one version of which was 'revised' by Rimsky-Korsakov.

Nielsen Carl 1865–1931. Born in Norre-Lyndelse, Denmark's greatest composer. His works show an openness to new musical ideas and a reaction against Romanticism. He is best known for his six symphonies, but his compositions also include the Clarinet Concerto 1928, chamber and piano works, and two operas *Saul and David* 1902 and *Maskarade* 1906.

Palestrina Giovanni Pierluigi da c. 1525–94. Born in Palestrina, near Rome, he worked for most of his life in Rome in the service of the church. He wrote much secular and sacred choral music, his religious work gaining him a reputation as the master of polyphonic vocal music. Apart from motets and madrigals, his greatest achievement is considered to be his 105 masses, which include the outstanding *Missa Papae Marcelli.*

Prokofiev Sergei 1891–1953. Born in Sontsovka, Russia, he travelled widely as a pianist and lived in Paris for a while, before returning to Russia in 1932. He was essentially a classicist in his use of form, but his extensive and varied output demonstrates great lyricism, humour and craftsmanship. The range of his work is displayed in compositions such as the *Classical Symphony* 1918, the operas *Love for Three Oranges* 1921 and *War and Peace* 1946, the ballets *Romeo and Juliet* 1938 and *Cinderella* 1945, and the children's classic *Peter and the Wolf* 1936.

Puccini Giacomo 1858–1924. Born in Lucca, Italy, one of the most popular opera composers. His reputation was firmly established with *Manon Lescaut* 1893. This, and other favourites such as *La Bohème* 1896, *Tosca* 1900, *Madame Butterfly* 1904, and the unfinished *Turandot* 1926, all show his strong gift for melody and dramatic effect.

Purcell Henry 1659–95 born in London, he was composer to the Chapel Royal and, from 1679, organist at Westminster Abbey. His versatility, creative genius and ability to express extremes of joy and sadness, have given him a reputation as the greatest English composer. Some of the best-known of his 500 compositions are *Dido and Aeneas* 1689, *King Arthur* 1691, *The Fairy Queen* 1692, *The Indian Queen* 1692, and *Ode on St Cecilia's Day* 1692.

Rachmaninov Sergei 1873–1943. Born in Semyonovo, he left Russia in 1917 to travel as a concert pianist in the West, and later settled in California. A great advocate of melodic invention, he wrote some fine music for piano, including the Second and Third 1901 and 1909 concertos and *Rhapsody on a Theme of Paganini* 1934. His 79 songs make him the creator of the Russian Lied; also popular are the Second Symphony 1908 and *The Bells* 1913.

Ravel Maurice 1875–1937. Born in Ciboure, near St Jean de Luz, France. He was a pupil of Fauré, and his compositions show a personal synthesis of influences from Classicism to Impressionism. Particularly admired for his brilliant piano works and his use of orchestral colour, well-known examples include the *Rhapsodie espagnole 1908, Daphnis et Chloë 1912, La Valse 1920, Bolero 1928,* and the two piano concertos 1931/32.

Rimsky-Korsakov Nikolai 1844–1908. Born in Tikhvin, Russian. Initially a naval officer, he wrote part of his First Symphony 1865 at sea. The most prolific of the nationalist group The Five, he is most admired for his colourful orchestration as in *Capriccio espagnol* 1887 and *Scheherezade* 1888. His 15 operas include the posthumously performed *The Golden Cockerel* 1909.

Rossini Gioacchino 1792–1868. Born in Pesaro, Italy. Influenced by Mozart, Rossini quickly emerged as an opera composer, popular for his sense of melody and humour. He wrote 36 operas betwen 1810 and 1829, including *The Barber of Seville* 1816 (which took him just 13 days), and *La Cenerentola* 1817. After *William Tell* 1829, he wrote nothing until the *Stabat Mater* 1842, *Petite Messe solonelle* 1864 and pieces later assembled by Respighi as the ballet *La boutique fantasque* 1919.

Saint-Saëns Camille 1835–1921. Born in Paris. A prolific composer in all genres, much influenced by Liszt, he is best remembered for the symphonic poem *Danse macabre* 1874, the succesful opera *Samson and Delilah* 1877, the Third Symphony 1886, and concertos for piano, violin and cello. He is also noted for his musical joke, the *Carnival of the Animals* 1886.

Schoenberg Arnold 1874–1951. Born in Vienna, he settled in the USA in 1934. An influential and revolutionary composer in his use of the 12–note system, his experimentation with atonality and the serial technique of composition continued throughout his life. Notable works are the string sextet *Verklärte Nacht* 1899, the music drama *Die Gluckliche Hand* 1908–1913, the song cycle *Pierrot Lunaire* 1912, in which *Sprechgesange* (German 'speech-song') is used, and his incomplete opera *Moses and Aaron* 1930.

Schubert Franz 1797–1828 born in Vienna. Heir to Haydn and Mozart, he was an early Romantic whose greatest contribution was his many songs or *Lieder*, which combine the expression of strong emotions with pure melody. The huge output of his brief life also includes nine symphonies, piano and chamber music, such as the *Trout Quintet* 1819, and seven masses.

Schumann Robert 1810–1856 born in Zwickau, near Dresden, Germany. Important to the Romantic movement, both as a prolific composer and able critic, he suffered increasingly from depression, finally attempting suicide and dying in an asylum two years later. His many *Lieder*, four song cycles, and piano works best display his talent for creativity and expression, but he also wrote chamber, choral, and orchestral music, including the four symphonies 1841–53, the Piano Concerto 1845, and the Cello Concerto 1860.

Shostakovich Dmitri 1906–75 born in St Petersburg, Russia. Often considered the 'composer-laureate of the Soviet state', he nevertheless had a turbulent relationship with officialdom, which is reflected in his music. Retaining tonality, he wrote 15 symphonies, several of which are programmatic in their depiction of political events. His other works include string quartets, operas and piano works.

Sibelius Jean 1865–1957 born in Hämeenlinna, Finland. From the age of 32 he was supported as a composer by the state, though he stopped composing in his sixties. Mainly respected as a major symphonist in Scandinavia, Britain and the USA, he displayed a strong personal style from the outset. His works include strongly nationalistic symphonic poems such as *En Saga* 1893, *Finlandia* 1900, *Tapiola* 1926, and the popular Violin Concerto 1904.

Smetana Bedřich 1824–84 born in Litomyšl, Czechoslovakia. An important national figure, he founded a school of music in Prague and became director of the national theatre in 1866, the year that his hugely successful comic opera *The Bartered Bride* was premiered. Despite becoming deaf in 1874, he continued to compose, producing works such as the cycle of six symbolic poems *My Country* 1874–79, but eventually ended his life in an asylum.

Stockhausen Karlheinz 1928– born in Mödrach, near Cologne, Germany. The most influential avant-garde composer of the second half of the 20th century, he has continued to explore new musical sounds and compositional techniques since the 1950s, using electronic music in particular. His major works include *Klavierstücke* 1952–85, *Momente* 1961–64, revised 1972, *Mikrophonie I* 1964 and *Mikrophonie II* 1965. In recent years he has concentrated on a cycle of seven musical ceremonies, starting with *Donnerstag aus Licht* 1977–80.

Strauss Johann II 1825–99. Born in Vienna, he is the member of the famous music-making family whose works are still most performed. These include *The Blue Danube* 1867, *Tales from the Vienna Woods* 1868, *Wine, Women and Song* 1869, *Vienna Blood* 1973, *Roses from the South* 1880, *Voices of Spring* 1883, and the operetta *Die Fledermaus* 1874.

Strauss Richard 1864–1949. Born in Munich, Germany. A prominent conductor, he was influenced by the German heritage but had a strongly personal style, particularly in his use of bold, colourful orchestration. He first established his reputation with tone poems such as *Don Juan* 1889, *Till Eulenspiegel's Merry Pranks* 1895, and *Also sprach Zarathustra* 1896. He then moved on to operatic success with *Salome* 1905, and *Elektra* 1909, both of which have elements of polytonality, followed by a reversion to a more traditional style with *Der Rosenkavalier* 1911.

Stravinsky Igor 1882–1971. Born at Ora-nienbaum, near St Petersburg, Russia, he lived in Paris from 1920 before moving to the USA and becoming naturalized in 1945. He was a major 20th-century figure. He first reached prominence with the ballets *The Firebird* 1910 and *Petrushka* 1911, but his early masterpiece was the controversial *The Rite of Spring* 1913 with its unconventional use of rhythms and harmonies. His versatility is evident in the varied nature of his works: the Neo-Classicism of his ballet *Pulcinella* 1920, the choral-orchestral *Symphony of Psalms* 1930, and his later use of serial techniques in works such as the *Canticum Sacrum* 1955 and the ballet *Agon* 1953–57.

Tchaikovsky Peter Ilyich 1840–93. Born in Votkinsk, he was the first Russian composer to establish a reputation with Western audiences. His strong sense of melody, personal expression and brilliant orchestration are clear throughout his large output; this includes six symphonies, three piano concertos, a violin concerto, symphonic poems, the ballets *Swan Lake* 1877, *The Sleeping Beauty* 1890, and *Nutcracker* 1892, and the opera *Eugene Onegin* 1879.

Verdi Giuseppe 1813–1901. Born in Le Ron-cole, Parma. The great Italian opera composer of the Romantic period, he brought his native operatic style to new heights of dramatic expression, working to perfect and develop his technique throughout his life. His operas range from his early success with *Nabucco* 1842 to *Falstaff* 1893, and include *Rigoletto* 1851, *Il Trovatore* 1853, *La Traviata* 1853 and *Aida* 1871. He also wrote a magnificent *Requiem* in 1884.

Vivaldi Antonio 1678–1741. Born in Venice, Italy, he spent much of his life there as a teacher but died in poverty in Vienna. A prolific composer, he is noted for instrumental works works – over 400 concertos, 23 sym-phonies and 75 sonatas – and his development of the solo concerto is especially significant. His music, which also includes over 40 operas and much sacred music, was largely neglected until the 1930s.

Wagner Richard 1813–83. Born in Leipzig, Germany, he led a turbulent life in Europe, falling in and out of favour with the German authorities, until he settled there to work on his national theatre at Bayreuth, eventually com-pleted in 1876. His vision of opera as a 'music drama', or total art form, caused wide contro-versy, as did his development of new operatic forms and his use of recurring Leitmotivs. He worked ceaselessly to achieve his aims, pro-ducing operas such as *Lohengrin* 1846–48, *Tristan and Isolde* 1865 and the massive four-opera work *The Ring of the Nibelung* 1876. His last work was *Parsifal* 1882.

Weber Carl Maria von 1786–1826. Born in Eutin, Germany. Often considered the first Romantic composer, he was also the founder of German national opera with *Der Freischütz* 1821. Of his several operas, only *Euryanthe* 1823 is entirely sung. He also wrote piano music such as *Invitation to the Dance* 1819, and *Konzerstück* 1821. He died in London after launching his opera *Oberon* 1826.

Webern Anton 1883–1945. Born in Vienna, Austria. He studied with Schoenberg, adop-ting atonality and then 12–note composition, but used it more rigorously in delicate, highly crafted short forms. Works such as his Sym-phony 1928 have been very influential.

MAJOR OPERAS AND THEIR FIRST PERFORMANCES

Date	Opera	Composer	Librettist	Place
1607	Orfeo	Monteverdi	Striggio	Mantua
1642	The Coronation of Poppea	Monteverdi	Busenello	Venice
1689	Dido and Aeneas	Purcell	Tate	London
1724	Julius Caesar in Egypt	Handel	Haym	London
1762	Orpheus and Eurydice	Gluck	Calzabigi	Vienna
1786	The Marriage of Figaro	Mozart	Da Ponte	Vienna
1787	Don Giovanni	Mozart	Da Ponte	Prague
1790	Così fan tutte	Mozart	Da Ponte	Vienna
1791	The Magic Flute	Mozart	Schikaneder	Vienna
1805	Fidelio	Beethoven	Sonnleithner	Vienna
1816	The Barber of Seville	Rossini	Sterbini	Rome
1821	Der Freischütz	Weber	Kind	Berlin
1831	Norma	Bellini	Romani	Milan
1835	Lucia di Lammermoor	Donizetti	Cammarano	Naples
1836	Les Huguenots	Meyerbeer	Scribe	Paris
1842	Russlan and Ludmilla	Glinka	Shirkov/Bakhturin	St Petersburg
1850	Lohengrin	Wagner	Wagner	Weimar
1851	Rigoletto	Verdi	Piave	Venice
1853	Il Trovatore	Verdi	Cammarano	Rome
1853	La Traviata	Verdi	Piave	Venice
1859	Faust	Gounod	Barbier/Carré	Paris
1865	Tristan and Isolde	Wagner	Wagner	Munich
1866	The Bartered Bride	Smetana	Sabina	Prague
1868	Die Meistersinger von Nürnberg	Wagner	Wagner	Munich
1871	Aida	Verdi	Ghislanzoni	Cairo
1874	Boris Godunov	Mussorgsky	Mussorgsky	St Petersburg
1874	Die Fledermaus	Johann Strauss II	Haffner/Genée	Vienna
1875	Carmen	Bizet	Meilhac/Halévy	Paris
1876	The Ring of the Nibelung	Wagner	Wagner	Bayreuth
1879	Eugene Onegin	Tchaikovsky	Tchaikovsky/Shilovsky	Moscow
1881	The Tales of Hoffman	Offenbach	Barbier	Paris
1882	Parsifal	Wagner	Wagner	Bayreuth
1885	The Mikado	Sullivan	Gilbert	London
1887	Otello	Verdi	Boito	Milan
1890	Cavalleria Rusticana	Mascagni	Menasci/Targioni-Tozzetti	Rome
1890	Prince Igor	Borodin	Borodin	St Petersburg
1892	Pagliacci	Leoncavallo	Leoncavallo	Milan
1892	Werther	Massenet	Blau/Milliet/Hartmann	Vienna
1896	La Bohème	Puccini	Giacosa/Illica	Turin
1900	Tosca	Puccini	Giacosa/Illica	Rome
1902	Pelléas et Mélisande	Debussy	Maeterlinck	Paris
1904	Jenůfa	Janáček	Janáček	Brno
1904	Madame Butterfly	Puccini	Giacosa/Illica	Milan
1905	Salome	Richard Strauss	Wilde/Lachmann	Dresden
1909	The Golden Cockerel	Rimsky-Korsakov	Byelsky	Moscow
1911	Der Rosenkavalier	Richard Strauss	Hofmannsthal	Dresden
1918	Duke Bluebeard's Castle	Bartók	Balázs	Budapest
1925	Wozzeck	Berg	Berg	Berlin
1935	Porgy and Bess	Gershwin	Ira Gershwin/Heyward	Boston
1937	Lulu	Berg	Berg	Zürich
1945	Peter Grimes	Britten	Slater	London
1946	War and Peace	Prokofiev	Prokofiev/Mendelson	Leningrad
1951	The Rake's Progress	Stravinsky	Auden/Kallman	Venice
1978	Paradise Lost	Penderecki	Fry	Chicago
1986	The Mask of Orpheus	Birtwistle	Zinovieff	London

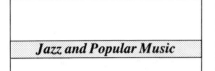

Jazz and Popular Music

Armstrong Louis ('Satchmo') 1900–1971. US jazz trumpet player and singer, born in New Orleans. His Chicago recordings in the 1920s with the Hot Five and Hot Seven made him known for his warm and pure trumpet tone, his improvisation and gravelly voice.

Beach Boys, the US pop group formed 1961. They began as exponents of vocal-harmony surf music with Chuck Berry guitar riffs (hits include 'Surfin' USA' 1963, 'Help Me, Rhonda' 1965) but the compositions, arrangements, and production by Brian Wilson (1942–) became highly complex under the influence of psychedelic rock, peaking with 'Good Vibrations' 1966.

Beatles, the English pop group 1960–70. The members, all born in Liverpool, were John Lennon (1940–80, rhythm guitar, vocals), Paul McCartney (1942– , bass, vocals), George Harrison (1943– , lead guitar, vocals), and Ringo Starr (formerly Richard Starkey, 1940– , drums). Using songs written by Lennon and McCartney, they brought the Mersey beat to prominence with worldwide hits including 'She Loves You' 1963, 'I Want To Hold Your Hand' 1963, and 'Can't Buy Me Love' 1964.

Berry Chuck (Charles Edward) 1931– . US rock-and-roll singer, prolific songwriter, and guitarist. His characteristic guitar riffs became staples of rock music, and his humorous story-telling lyrics were also influential. He had a string of hits in the 1950s beginning with *Maybellene* 1955.

bhangra a type of pop music evolved in the UK in the late 1970s from traditional Punjabi music, combining electronic instruments and ethnic drums.

blues 12-bar folk song in which, typically, the second line of the three-line verse is a repetition of the first, with variations, so giving the singer

time to improvise the third line. It originated among American blacks in the rural South in the late 19th century, and the words are often melancholy. Blues guitar and vocal styles have influenced jazz and, particularly, pop music.

1920s–30s The *rural* or *delta blues* was usually performed solo with guitar or harmonica, for example by Robert Johnson (1911–38) and Bukka White (1906–77), but the earliest recorded style, *classic blues*, by musicians such as W C Handy (1873–1958) and Bessie Smith (1894–1937), was sung with a small band.

1940s–50s Urban blues, using electric amplification, emerged in the cities of the North, especially Chicago. As exemplified by Howlin' Wolf (real name Chester Burnett, 1910–76), Muddy Waters (real name McKinley Morganfield, 1915–83), and John Lee Hooker (1917–), urban blues became *rhythm and blues*.

1960s The jazz-influenced guitar style of B B King (1925–) inspired many musicians of the *British blues boom*, including Eric Clapton (1945–).

1980s The 'blues *noir*' of Robert Cray (1953–) found a wide audience.

boogie-woogie a form of jazz played on the piano, using a repeated motif in the left hand. It was common in the USA from around 1900 to the 1940s. Notable boogie-woogie players included Pinetop Smith (1904–29), Meade 'Lux' Lewis (1905–64), and Jimmy Yancey (1898–1951).

Bowie David. Stage name of David Jones 1947– . British pop singer and songwriter, born in Brixton, London. He became a glitter-rock star with the album *The Rise and Fall of Ziggy Stardust and the Spiders from Mars* 1972, and collaborated in the mid-1970s with the electronic virtuoso Brian Eno (1948–) and Iggy Pop. He has also acted in plays and films, including Nicolas Roeg's *The Man Who Fell to Earth* 1976.

Byrds, the US pioneering folk-rock group 1964–73. Remembered for their 12-string guitar sound and the hits 'Mr Tambourine Man' 1965 (a version of Bob Dylan's song) and 'Eight Miles High' 1966, they moved towards country rock in the late 1960s.

calypso a type of West Indian satirical ballad with a syncopated beat.

Charles Ray 1930– . US singer, songwriter, and pianist, whose first hits were 'I've Got A Woman' 1955, 'What'd I Say' 1959, and 'Georgia on My Mind' 1960. He has recorded gospel, blues, rock, soul, country, and rhythm and blues.

Clapton Eric 1945– . English blues and rock guitarist, singer, and composer, member of the groups Yardbirds and Cream in the 1960s. One of the pioneers of heavy rock and an influence on younger musicians, he later adopted a more subdued style.

Coleman Ornette 1930– . US alto saxophonist and composer. In the late 1950s he rejected the established structural principles of jazz for free avant-garde improvisation. He has worked with small and large groups, ethnic musicians of different traditions, and symphony orchestras.

Coltrane John (William) 1926–1967. US jazz saxophonist who first became known in 1955 with the Miles Davis quintet. He was a powerful and individual artist whose performances were noted for experimentation, and whose quartet was highly regarded for its innovations in melody and harmony.

country and western the popular music of the white US South and Southwest, evolved from the folk music of the English, Irish, and Scottish settlers with a strong blues influence. Characteristic instruments are slide guitar, mandolin, and fiddle. Lyrics typically extol family values and traditional sex roles. Country music encompasses a variety of regional styles, and ranges from mournful ballads to fast and intricate dance music.

1920s Jimmie Rodgers (1897–33) wrote a series of 'Blue Yodel' songs that made him the first country-music recording star.

1930s Nashville, Tennessee, became a centre for the country-music industry, with the Grand Ole Opry a showcase for performers. The Carter Family arranged and recorded hundreds of traditional songs. Hollywood invented the singing cowboy.

1940s Hank Williams (1923–53) emerged as the most influential singer and songwriter; *western swing* spread from Texas.

1950s The *honky-tonk* sound; Kentucky *bluegrass*; ballad singers included Jim Reeves (1923–64) and Patsy Cline (1932–63).

1960s The Bakersfield, California, school dominated by Buck Owens (1929–) and Merle Haggard (1937–) contrasted with lush Nashville productions of singers such as George Jones (1931–) and Tammy Wynette (1942–).

1970s Dolly Parton (1946–) and Emmylou Harris (1947–); the Austin, Texas, *outlaws* Willie Nelson (1933–) and Waylon Jennings (1937–); *country rock* pioneered by Gram Parsons (1946–73).

1980s Neotraditionalist *new country* represented by Dwight Yoakam (1957–) and Nanci Griffith (1954–).

Davis Miles (Dewey Jr) 1926– . US jazz trumpeter, composer, and band leader. He recorded bebop with Charlie Parker 1945, pioneered cool jazz in the 1950s and jazz-rock fusion from the late 1960s. His influential albums include *Birth of the Cool* 1949, *Sketches of Spain* 1959, and *Bitches' Brew* 1970.

Dixieland jazz jazz style which originated in New Orleans in the early 20th century.

Dylan Bob. Adopted name of Robert Allen Zimmerman 1941– . US singer and songwriter, whose work in the 1960s, first in the folk-music tradition and from 1965 in an individualistic rock style, was influential on later pop music.

Ellington 'Duke' (Edward Kennedy) 1899–1974. US pianist, who had an outstanding career as a composer and arranger of jazz. He wrote numerous pieces for his own jazz orchestra, and became one of the most important figures in jazz over a 55-year span. Compositions include 'Mood Indigo', 'Sophisticated Lady', 'Solitude', and 'Black and Tan Fantasy'.

Fitzgerald Ella 1918– . US jazz singer, recognized as one of the greatest voices of jazz, both in solo work and with big bands. She is noted for her interpretations of Gershwin and Cole Porter songs.

funk a style of dance music of black American origin, relying on heavy percussion in polyrhythmic patterns. Leading exponents include James Brown (1928–) and George Clinton (1940–).

Getz Stan(ley) 1927– . US tenor saxophonist of the 1950s 'cool jazz' school. He was the first US musician to be closely identified with the Latin American *bossa nova* sound.

Gillespie Dizzy. Stage name of John Birks Gillespie 1917– . US jazz trumpeter, together with Charlie Parker the chief creator and exponent of the bebop style.

Goodman 'Benny' (Benjamin David) 1909–1986. US clarinetist, nicknamed 'the King of Swing' for the new jazz idiom he introduced. Leader of his own band from 1934, he is remembered for numbers such as 'Blue Skies' and 'King Porter Stomp'.

gospel music a type of song developed in the 1920s in the black Baptist churches of the US South from spirituals, which were 18th and 19th century hymns joined to the old African pentatonic (five-note) scale. Outstanding among the early gospel singers was Mahalia Jackson (1911–72), but from the 1930s to the mid-1950s male harmony groups predominated, among them the Dixie Hummingbirds, the Swan Silvertones, and the Five Blind Boys of Mississippi.

Hawkins Coleman (Randolph) 1904–1969. US virtuoso tenor saxophonist. He was until 1934 a soloist in the swing band led by Fletcher Henderson (1898–1952), and was an influential figure in bringing the jazz saxophone to prominence as a solo instrument.

heavy metal a style of rock characterized by loudness, sex-and-violence imagery, and guitar solos. It developed out of the hard rock of the late 1960s and early 1970s (Led Zeppelin, Deep Purple). Bands include Motörhead, Def Leppard, and AC/DC. The term comes from *The Naked Lunch* by US author William Burroughs.

Hendrix Jimi (James Marshall) 1942–1970. US rock guitarist, songwriter, and singer, legendary for his virtuoso experimental technique and flamboyance.

hip-hop a style of popular music originating in New York in the early 1980s. It uses scratching (a percussive effect obtained by manually rotating a vinyl record) and heavily accented electronic drums behind a rap vocal. The term 'hip-hop' also comprises break dancing and graffiti.

Holiday Billie. Stage name of Eleanor Gough McKay 1915–1959. US jazz singer, also known as 'Lady Day'. She made her debut in Harlem clubs and became famous for her emotionally charged delivery and idiosyncratic phrasing; she brought a blues feel to performances with swing bands. Songs she made her own include 'Strange Fruit' and 'I Cover the Waterfront'.

Holly Buddy. Stage name of Charles Hardin Holley 1936–1959. US rock-and-roll singer, guitarist, and songwriter, born in Lubbock, Texas. He had a distinctive, hiccuping vocal style and was an early experimenter with recording techniques. Many of his hits with his band, the Crickets, such as 'That'll Be the Day' 1957, 'Peggy Sue' 1957, and 'Maybe Baby' 1958, have become classics. He was killed in a plane crash.

house music a type of dance music of the 1980s originating in the inner-city clubs of Chicago, USA, combining funk with European high-tech pop, using dub, digital sampling, and cross-fading. *Acid house* has minimal vocal and melody, instead surrounding the mechanically emphasized 4/4 beat with found noises, stripped-down synthesizer riffs, and a wandering bass line.

Jackson Michael 1958– . US rock singer and songwriter, noted for his meticulously choreographed performances. He had his first solo hit in 1971 but his worldwide popularity reached a peak with the albums *Thriller* 1982 and *Bad* 1987.

jazz polyphonic, syncopated music characterized by improvisation, which developed in the USA at the turn of this century out of black American and other indigenous popular music.

1880–1900 Originated chiefly in New Orleans from ragtime.

1920s Centre of jazz moved to Chicago (Louis Armstrong, Bix Beiderbecke) and St Louis.

1930s The *swing* bands used call-and-response arrangements with improvised solos (Paul Whiteman, Benny Goodman).

1940s Swing grew into the *big band* era (Glenn Miller, Duke Ellington); rise of *West Coast* jazz (Stan Kenton) and rhythmically complex, highly improvisational *bebop* (Charlie Parker, Dizzy Gillespie, Thelonius Monk).

1950s Jazz had ceased to be dance music; *cool jazz* (Stan Getz, Miles Davis, Modern Jazz Quartet) developed in reaction to the insistent, 'hot' bebop and *hard bop*.

1960s Free-form or *free jazz* (Ornette Coleman, John Coltrane).

1970s Jazz rock (US group Weather Report, formed 1970; British guitarist John McLaughlin, 1942–); jazz funk (US saxophonist Grover Washington Jr, 1943–); more eclectic free jazz (US pianist Keith Jarrett, 1945–).

1980s Resurgence of tradition (US trumpeter Wynton Marsalis, 1962– ; British saxophonist Courtney Pine, 1965–) and avant-garde (US chamber-music Kronos Quartet, formed 1978; anarchic British group Loose Tubes, formed 1983).

Marley Bob (Robert Nesta) 1945–1980. Jamaican reggae singer, a Rastafarian whose songs, many of which were topical and political, popularized reggae in the UK and the USA in the 1970s. One of his best-known songs is 'No Woman No Cry'; his albums include *Natty Dread* 1975 and *Exodus* 1977.

merengue a type of Latin American dance music with a lively 2/4 beat. Accordion and saxophone are prominent instruments, with ethnic percussion. It originated in the Dominican Republic and became popular in New York in the 1980s.

Mingus Charles 1922–1979. US bass player and composer. He was influential for his experimentation with atonality and dissonant effects, opening the way for the new style of free collective jazz improvisation of the 1960s.

Morton Jelly Roll. Stage name of Ferdinand Joseph La Menthe 1885–1941. US jazz pianist, singer, and composer. Influenced by Scott Joplin, he played a major part in the development of jazz from ragtime to swing by means of improvisation and imposing his own personality on the music. His band from 1926 was called the Red Hot Peppers.

New Age a type of instrumental pop music of the 1980s, often semi-acoustic or electronic; less insistent than rock.

New Wave in pop music, a style that evolved parallel to punk in the second half of the 1970s. It shared the urban aggressive spirit but was musically and lyrically more sophisticated; examples are the early work of Elvis Costello in the UK and Talking Heads in the USA.

Parker 'Charlie', 'Bird', 'Yardbird' (Charles Christopher) 1920–1955. US alto saxophonist and jazz composer, associated with the trumpeter Dizzy Gillespie in developing the bebop style. His mastery of improvisation influenced performers on all jazz instruments.

pop music short for popular music, an umbrella term for all modern music not classifiable as jazz or classical. Pop became distinct from folk music with the advent of sound-recording techniques, and incorporated blues, country and western, and music hall; electronic amplification and other technological innovations have played a large part in the creation of new styles. The traditional format is a song of roughly three minutes with verse, chorus, and middle eight bars.

1910s The singer Al Jolson was one of the first recording stars. Ragtime was still popular.

1920s In the USA Paul Whiteman and his orchestra, and the country singer Jimmie Rodgers (1897–1933); in the UK the singer Al Bowlly (1899–1941, born in Mozambique).

1930s The crooner Bing Crosby, vocal groups such as the Andrews Sisters, and swing bands.

1940s Rhythm and blues evolved in the US while Frank Sinatra was a teen idol and Glenn Miller played dance music; the UK preferred singers such as Vera Lynn.

1950s In the USA *doo-wop* (a vocal group style based on a cappella street-corner singing), *rockabilly* and the rise of *rock and roll*. British pop records were often cover versions of US originals.

1960s The Beatles and *Mersey beat* transcended UK borders, followed by the Rolling Stones; in the USA *surf music* (group harmony vocals or fast, loud, guitar-based instrumentals), *Motown*, *folk rock* (the Byrds), Bob Dylan; *psychedelic rock* evolved from 1966 (Pink Floyd).

1970s First *glitter rock* (David Bowie), *heavy metal*, and *disco* (dance music with a very emphatic, mechanical beat); in the UK also *pub rock* (a return to basics, focusing on live performance). From 1976 *punk*; the US term *New Wave* encompassed bands not entirely within the punk idiom (Talking Heads, Elvis Costello).

1980s Punk continued as *hardcore* or mutated into *gothic*; dance music developed regional US variants: *hip-hop* (New York), *go-go* (Washington DC), and *house* (Chicago). Live audiences grew, leading to anthemic *stadium rock* (U2, Bruce Springsteen) and increasingly elaborate stage performances (Michael Jackson, Prince). An interest in worldwide *roots music* sparked new fusions.

Presley Elvis (Aaron) 1935–1977. US singer and guitarist, born in Tupelo, Mississippi, the most influential performer of the rock-and-roll era. With his recordings for Sun Records in Memphis, Tennessee, 1954–55 and early hits such as 'Heartbreak Hotel' 1956, 'Hound Dog' 1956, and 'Love Me Tender' 1956, he created an individual vocal style, influenced by Southern blues, gospel music, country music, and rhythm and blues.

psychedelic rock or *acid rock*, a type of pop music, with advanced electronic equipment for both light and sound, which began about 1966. The free-form improvisations and light shows of the hippie years had by the 1980s become stadium performances with lasers and other special effects.

ragtime syncopated music ('ragged time') in two-four rhythm, usually played on piano. It developed among black American musicians in the late 19th century; it was influenced by folk tradition, minstrel shows, and marching bands, and later merged into jazz. Scott Joplin was a leading writer of ragtime pieces, called rags.

raï Algerian type of pop music developed in the 1970s from the Bedouin song form *melhoun*, using synthesizers and electronic drums.

rap music a rapid, rhythmic chant over a prerecorded backing track. Rap emerged in New York in 1979 as part of the hip-hop culture, although the usually macho, swaggering lyrics have roots in the Afro-American tradition of ritual boasts and insults. 'The Message' by Grandmaster Flash and the Furious Five 1982 expanded the content, and women rappers (Salt 'n' Pepa, the Cookie Crew, and others) have countered the sexism.

Reed Lou 1942– . US rock singer, songwriter, and former member (1965–70) of the seminal New York garage band *the Velvet Underground*. His solo work deals largely with urban alienation and angst, and includes the albums *Berlin* 1973, *Street Hassle* 1978, and *New York* 1989.

reggae the predominant form of West Indian popular music of the 1970s and 1980s, characterized by a heavily accented onbeat. The lyrics often refer to Rastafarianism. Musicians include Bob Marley (1945–81), Lee 'Scratch' Perry (1940–) (performer and producer), and the group Black Uhuru (1974–).

rhythm and blues (R & B) a term covering all black US popular music of the 1940s–60s: it replaced the tag 'race music'. The music drew on swing and jump-jazz rhythms and blues vocals and was a progenitor of rock and roll. It diversified into soul, funk, and other styles. Singers include Bo Diddley (1928–), who wrote many classic numbers, Jackie Wilson (1934–84), and Etta James (c. 1938–).

rock and roll a type of pop music born of a fusion of rhythm and blues and country and western, and based on electric guitar and drums. In the mid-1950s, with the advent of Elvis Presley, it became the heartbeat of Western teenage rebellion. It found perhaps its purest form in late-1950s *rockabilly*; the blanket term 'rock' later came to comprise a multitude of styles.

Rolling Stones, the British band formed 1962, notorious as the 'bad boys' of rock. Original members were Mick Jagger (1943–), Keith Richards (1943–), Brian Jones (1942–69), Bill Wyman (1936–), Charlie Watts (1941–), and the pianist Ian Stewart (1938–85). In the 1970s they became a rock-and-roll institution and by the late 1980s Jagger and Richards were working separately.

roots music term originally denoting reggae, later encompassing any music indigenous to a particular culture; also called *world music*.

Examples are W African *mbalax*, E African *soukous*, S African *mbaqanga*, French Antillean *zouk*, Javanese gamelan, Latin American salsa, Cajun music, and European folk music.

salsa a Latin big-band dance music popularized by Puerto Ricans in New York in the 1980s and by, among others, the Panamanian singer Rubén Blades (1948–).

Sinatra Frank (Francis Albert) 1915– . US singer and film actor. He achieved fame with the Tommy Dorsey band with songs such as 'Night and Day' and 'You'd Be So Nice To Come Home To'. After a slump in his career, he established himself as an actor. *From Here to Eternity* 1953 won him an Academy Award. His later songs include 'My Way'.

skiffle a style of British popular music, introduced by the singer and banjo player Lonnie Donegan (1931–) in 1956, using improvised percussion instruments such as tea chests and washboards.

soca Latin Caribbean music, a mixture of *so*ul and *ca*lypso.

soul music style of rhythm and blues, influenced by gospel music, and sung by, among others, Sam Cooke, Aretha Franklin (1942–), and Al Green (1946–).

Springsteen Bruce 1949– . US rock singer, songwriter, and guitarist, born in New Jersey. His music combines traditional rock melodies and reflective lyrics of working-class life on albums such as *Born to Run* 1975, *Born in the USA* 1984 and in concerts with the E Street Band.

steel band type of musical ensemble popular in the West Indies, especially Trinidad, consisting mostly of percussion instruments made from oil drums.

Supremes, the US vocal group, pioneers of the Motown sound, formed 1959 in Detroit, from 1962 a trio comprising, initially, Diana Ross (1944–), Mary Wilson (1944–), and Florence Ballard (1943–76). The most successful female group of the 1960s, they had a string of pop hits beginning with 'Where Did Our Love Go?' 1964 and 'Baby Love' 1964. Diana Ross left the group 1969.

swing music jazz style popular in the 1930s–40s, with a simple harmonic base of varying tempo from the rhythm section (percussion, guitar, piano), and superimposed solo melodic line, for example from trumpet, clarinet, or saxophone. Exponents included Benny Goodman, Duke Ellington, and Glenn Miller.

syncopation the deliberate upsetting of rhythm by shifting the accent to a beat that is normally unaccented.

Turner Tina (born Annie Mae Bullock) 1938– . US rhythm-and-blues singer who recorded 1960–76 with her husband as *Ike and Tina Turner*, notably *River Deep, Mountain High* 1966 produced by Phil Spector. Tina Turner had success in the 1980s as a solo performer, as on *Private Dancer* 1984.

U2 Irish rock group formed 1978 by singer Bono Vox (1960–), guitarist Dave 'The Edge' Evans (1961–), bassist Adam Clayton (1960–), and drummer Larry Mullen (1961–). Radical Christians, they play socially concerned stadium rock, and their albums include *The Unforgettable Fire* 1984 and *The Joshua Tree* 1987.

zydeco style of dance music originating in Louisiana, USA, similar to Cajun but more heavily influenced by blues and West Indian music.

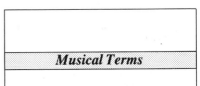

Musical Terms

acoustics the science of sound; the term is often used to refer to the sonic characteristics of a concert hall.

aleatory music music produced by chance procedures, such as by throwing dice (Latin *alea*) or using computers. Pioneered by the American composer John Cage in the 1950s.

alto (Italian 'high') 1) low-register female voice also called *contralto* ; 2) an unusually high adult male voice, also known as a counter tenor; 3) (French) viola.

anthem a short, usually elaborate, religious

choral composition, sometimes accompanied by the organ.

aria (Italian 'air') solo vocal piece in opera or oratorio, often in three sections, the third repeating the first, after a contrasting central section.

atonality music which avoids the use of a key centre or tonic and in which the 12 notes of the octave are used impartially. It was foreshadowed in the 19th century in the later works of Liszt but not widely adopted until the music of Schoenberg and his followers in the 20th century.

avant-garde (French 'vanguard') in music, compositions ahead of their time; the term usually refers to the work of Boulez, Stockhausen and others produced after World War II.

bagatelle (French 'trifle') a short character piece, often for piano.

ballade a term used by Chopin, Brahms, Liszt and Grieg, among others, for a dramatic instrumental piece, possibly inspired by the literary equivalent.

baritone lower-range male voice midway between bass and tenor.

baroque descriptive of the period in music between 1600 and 1750 and of the style associated with its major composers, Vivaldi, Bach, and Handel.

bass 1) lowest range of male voice; 2) lower regions of musical pitch.

bel canto (Italian 'beautiful song') term which usually refers to the 18th-century Italian style of singing with great emphasis on perfect technique and beautiful tone which reached its peak in the operas of Rossini, Donizetti and Bellini.

big band description of jazz sound created in the late 1930s and 1940s by bands of 15 or more players, such as those of Duke Ellington, Benny Goodman, when there is more than one instrument to some of the parts.

cadenza usually a bravura passage for the soloist in a concerto.

canon a form for a number of 'voices' or parts in which each enters successively, at fixed time intervals, in exact imitation of each other. The parts may then end together or continue their repetition as in a round.

cantata an extended sacred or secular choral work, sometimes with solo voices, and usually with orchestral accompaniment.

capriccio (Italian 'caprice') a short, lively instrumental piece, often humorous or whimsical in character.

chamber music music written for a small instrumental group, such as a string quartet, in which each part is played by a single instrument.

chorale a traditional hymn tune of the German Protestant Church.

chromatic a scale proceeding by semitones. All 12 notes in the octave are used rather than the seven notes of the diatonic scale.

classical term generally used to refer to the period when emphasis was on form and balanced proportions of music rather than the expression of emotion. The Classical age reached its height in the 18th century, for example, in the music of Haydn and Mozart.

clef the symbol used to indicate the pitch of the lines of the staff in musical notation.

coda (Italian 'tail') a concluding section of a movement added to indicate finality.

coloratura a rapid ornamental vocal passage with runs, trills, etc. A *coloratura soprano* has a light, high voice suited to such music.

concerto a composition, usually in three movements, for solo instrument (or instruments) and orchestra.

concrete music music created by reworking natural sounds on record or tape, in particular that of Pierre Schaeffer in 1948.

continuo short for *basso continuo,* the bass line on which a keyboard player, often accompanied by a bass stringed instrument, built up a harmonic accompaniment in much 17th-century music.

contralto another name for the female alto voice.

counterpoint the simultaneous combination of two or more independent melodic lines to form a harmonious whole.

diatonic a diatonic scale consists of the seven notes of any major or minor key.

dodecaphonic a term applied to the 12-note

system of composition.

dominant the fifth degree of the scale, for example G in C major.

electronic music music produced since the 1950s in which composers such as Stockhausen and Boulez work with electronically assembled or arranged sounds.

etude (French 'study') a musical exercise designed to develop technique.

film music music specially written to accompany films, either live, as with early silent films, or for the soundtrack.

form the shape or structure of a piece of music.

fugue (Latin 'flight') a complicated contrapuntal form for a number of parts or 'voices' which enter successively in imitation of each other.

gamelan a type of Indonesian orchestra, mainly using tuned metal percussion instruments, the music of which has influenced Western composers.

glissando a rapid uninterrupted scale produced by sliding the finger across the keys or strings.

Gregorian chant plainsong choral chants associated with Pope Gregory the Great 590–604, which became standard in the Roman Catholic Church.

harmony any simultaneous combination of sounds, but particularly the succession and relationship of chords.

harmonics the series of sounds of different pitches generated naturally by the vibration of a pipe or string when a note is played. This gives tone colour or timbre to an instrument.

impromptu a short piano piece that suggests spontaneity.

intermezzo a short orchestral interlude often used between the acts of an opera to denote the passage of time.

interval the pitch difference between two notes, usually measured in terms of the diatonic scale.

key 1) the diatonic scale around which a piece of music is written, that is, a passage in C major will mainly use the notes of the C major scale; 2) the lever activated by a keyboard player.

leitmotiv (German 'leading motive') a recurring theme or motive used to indicate a character or idea - a technique used especially by Wagner in his operas.

libretto (Italian 'little book') the text of an opera or other dramatic vocal work, or the scenario of a ballet.

lied (German 'song') a genre particularly associated with the Romantic songs of Schubert, Schumann, Brahms and Wolf.

madrigal a secular composition for several voices, which reached its height in Italy in the 16th century and became popular in Elizabethan England.

Mass in music, the setting of the invariable parts of the Mass, that is *Kyrie, Gloria, Credo, Sanctus* with *Benedictus*, and *Agnus Dei*, such as Bach's Mass in B Minor.

melody a sequence of notes forming a theme or tune.

minimalism the music of contemporary American composers such as Steve Reich, Philip Glass, and Terry Riley in which the repetition of short figures is used extensively.

minnesingers German poet-musicians of courtly love in the 12th and 13th centuries.

meistersingers amateur musicians in Germany who organized themselves into guilds.

mezzo-soprano female voice halfway between soprano and contralto.

minuet European courtly dance of the 17th century, later used with the trio as the third movement in a classical symphony.

modulation movement from one key to another in harmony.

monody declamation by accompanied solo voice, used particularly at the turn of the 16th and 17th centuries.

motet a form of sacred, polyphonic music for unaccompanied voices which originated in the 13th century.

movement a section of a large work, such as a symphony, which is often complete in itself.

nationalism in music, a movement which became evident in the 19th century when composers (such as Smetana and Grieg) showed particular concern for the folk material of their country, the local instruments and, above all, the national spirit and its expression in music.

nocturne a lyrical, dreamy piano piece introduced by John Field and adopted by Chopin.

opera an extended, dramatic work where all, or most, of the text is sung, with instrumental accompaniment.

operetta a light opera, which may use spoken dialogue.

opus (Latin 'work') a term, used with a figure, to indicate the numbering of a composer's works, usually in chronological order.

oratorio a setting for solo voices, chorus and orchestra, of a religious or contemplative text, performed in a church or concert hall.

orchestration the scoring of a composition for orchestra.

overture an orchestral introduction to an opera or ballet. A *concert overture*, such as Mendelssohn's *Fingal's Cave,* is a piece designed purely for the concert hall.

pizzicato (Italian 'pinched') strings plucked, not bowed.

plainsong ancient chant of the Christian Church first fixed by Ambrose, Bishop of Milan, and then by Pope Gregory in the 6th century.

polyphony music combining two or more 'voices', each with an individual melody.

polytonality the simultaneous use of more than one key. A combination of two keys is bitonality.

prelude a composition intended as the preface to further music, or as a mood-setting introduction to a stage work, as in Wagner's *Lohengrin*; as used by Chopin, a short piano work.

programme music music that tells a story, depicts a scene or painting, or illustrates a literary or philosophical idea, such as Beethoven's *Pastoral Symphony* .

punk a style of rock music popular in the late 1970s, such as the Sex Pistols.

recitative speech-like declamation of narrative episodes in opera.

requiem the Mass for the Dead in the Roman Catholic Church. Notable settings include those by Mozart and Berlioz.

rhapsody an instrumental fantasia, often based on folk melodies, such as Lizst's *Hungarian Rhapsodies* .

rock opera popular form of modern opera using rock and jazz elements, such as *Jesus Christ Superstar* .

romanticism in music, a term which generally refers to a preoccupation with the expression of emotion and with nature and history as a source of inspiration. Often linked with nationalistic feelings, the Romantic movement reached its height in the 19th century, such as Schumann, Wagner.

rondo a form of instrumental music where the principal subject is repeated several times. Rondo form is often used for the last movement of a sonata or concerto.

rubato from *tempo rubato* (Italian 'robbed time') a slight flexibility in the tempo for extra expressive effect, usually in keyboard music.

scale progression of notes which varies according to the musical system being used, for example, the seven notes of the diatonic scale, the 12 notes of the chromatic scale. Major and minor scales derive from the Ionian and Aeolian modes respectively, two of the 12 modes or scales of ancient music.

scherzo (Italian 'joke') a lively piece, usually in rapid triple time, often the third movement of a symphony or sonata.

serenade a piece for chamber orchestra or wind instruments in several movements, originally intended for evening entertainment, such as Mozart's *Eine Kleine Nachtmusik* .

serialism another name for the twelve-note system of composition.

sinfonietta an orchestral work which is of a shorter, lighter, nature than a symphony.

sonata a work, usually in three or four related movements, for solo piano, or an instrument with piano accompaniment.

sonata form or first movement form, used extensively in the classical period in chamber and symphonic music, consisted of the exposition, development and recapitulation of two main themes.

soprano the highest range of female voice.

suite formerly a grouping of old dance forms, the term has more recently been used to describe a set of instrumental pieces, sometimes assembled from a stage work, such as Tchaikovsky's *Nutcracker Suite* .

symphonic poem a term originated by Liszt for his 13 one-movement orchestral works which interpret a story from literature or history, and used by many other composers. Richard Strauss preferred the title *tone poem*.

symphony an extended orchestral work usually in four related movements, though the term has come to be used more loosely.

syncopation the deliberate upsetting of rhythm by shifting the accent to a beat that is normally unaccented.

tempo (Italian 'time') the speed at which a piece of music is played.

theme the basic melody or musical figure from which a piece of music is developed.

tenor the highest range of adult male voice.

timbre the tone colour of an instrument.

toccata a display piece for keyboard instru-ment, particularly the organ.

tonality music which is centred on a single key, in contrast to *atonality* and *polytonality*.

tone poem another name for *symphonic poem* as used by Richard Strauss.

tonic the first degree or key note of the scale, for example C in C major.

twelve-note system a system of composition in which the 12 notes of the chromatic scale are arranged in a particular order, called 'series' or 'note-row'. The entire work consists of restatements of the series in any of its forma-tions. Schoenberg and Webern were the most important and influential composers to use this technique.

variations a series of different developments of one self-contained theme, such as *Variations on the St Anthony Chorale* by Brahms.

vibrato a slight but rapid fluctuation of pitch, in voice or instrument.

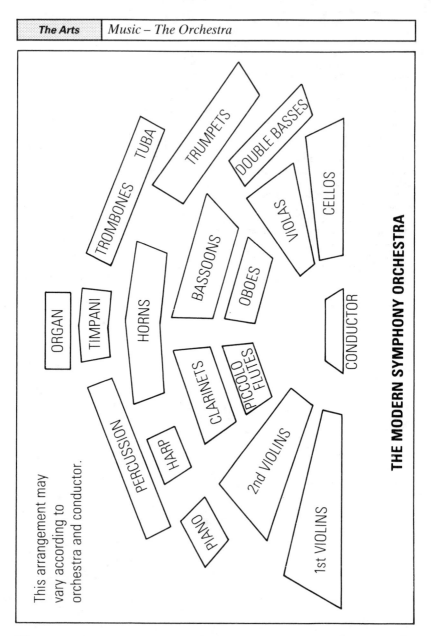

This arrangement may vary according to orchestra and conductor.

THE MODERN SYMPHONY ORCHESTRA

PITCH AND COMPASS OF VOICE AND INSTRUMENT

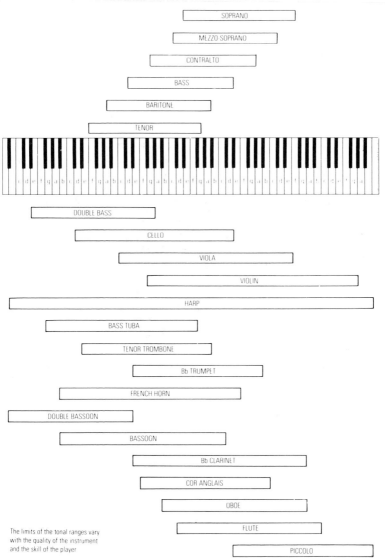

The limits of the tonal ranges vary
with the quality of the instrument
and the skill of the player.

590AD   St Gregory the Great was elected Pope. His enlightened leadership inspired church music to new heights, initiating Gregorian Chant.

1026   The Italian monk Guido d'Arezzo completed his treatise *Micrologus*. He founded modern notation and tonic so-fa.

1207   Walther von der Vogelweide, Tannhauser and Wolfram von Eschenbach competed in a song contest at Wartburg Castle, as the age of the Minnesingers or German poet-musicians approached its height.

1240   The earliest known canon, *Sumer is Icumen In,* was composed around this year.

1280   *Carmina burana,* a collection of students' songs, was compiled in Benediktbuern, Bavaria.

1288   France's greatest troubadour, Adam de la Halle, died in Naples.

1320   *Ars nova,* a tract by Philippe de Vitry, gave its name to a new, more graceful era in music.

1364   Music's first large-scale masterpiece, the *Notre Dame Mass* of Guillaume de Machaut, was performed in Rheims at the coronation of Charles V of France.

1453   John Dunstable, England's first important composer, died in London.

1473   The earliest known printed music, the *Collectorium super Magnificat* by Johannes Gerson, was published in Esslingen, near Stuttgart.

1521   Josquin des Prez, the leading musician of his time, died in Condé-sur-Escaut, Burgundy.

1564   The violin was designed and manufactured by Andrea Amati in Cremona.

1575   Thomas Tallis and William Byrd jointly published their *Cantiones sacrae,* a collection of 34 motets.

1576   Hans Sachs, the most famous of mastersingers, died in Nuremberg.

1597   The first opera, *La Dafne* by Jacopo Peri, was staged privately at the Corsi Palazzo in Florence.

1610   Monteverdi's *Vespers* was published in Venice.

1637   The world's first opera house opened in Venice.

1644   Antonio Stradivarius was born. More than 600 of his violins, made in Cremona, survived into the 20th century.

1672   The violinist John Banister pioneered public concerts in London.

1709   Bartolemmeo Cristofori built the first piano in Florence.

1721   Bach completed his six *Brandenburg Concertos.*

1722   Jean-Philippe Rameau's book *Traité de l'harmonie* founded modern harmonic theory.

1725   Vivaldi's *The Four Seasons* was published in Amsterdam.

1732   Covent Garden Theatre opened in London. It was later destroyed twice, in 1808 and 1856, by fire, but rebuilt.

1742	Handel's *Messiah* received its world première in Dublin.
1757	Johann Stamitz died in Mannheim, where he had founded the world's first virtuoso orchestra.
1761	Haydn took up liveried service as vice Kapellmeister with the aristocratic Esterháy family, to whom he was connected until his death in 1809.
1788	Mozart completed his last three symphonies, nos 39-41, in six weeks.
1795	The composer and inventor Thomas Wright introduced metronome markings.
1798	The *Allgemeine Musikalische Zeitung,* which became an influential journal of music criticism, was first published in Leipzig.
1805	Beethoven's *Eroica Symphony* vastly expanded the horizons of orchestral music.
1815	Schubert's output for this year included two symphonies, two masses, 20 waltzes and 145 songs.
1821	Weber's opera *Der Freischutz* heralded the start of the Romantic era.
1828	The limits of instrumental virtuosity were redefined by Paganini's Vienna debut.
1830	Berlioz's dazzlingly avant-garde and programmatic *Symphonie Fantastique* startled Paris concertgoers. The work did not reach Britain or the USA for 36 years.
1831	Grand opera was inaugurated with *Robert le Diable* by Meyerbeer.
1851	Jenny Lind, the singer managed by P T Barnum, earned $176,675 from nine months' concerts in the USA.
1842	The Vienna Philharmonic Orchestra gave its first concerts.
1854	In Weimar, Liszt conducted the premières of his first symphonic poems.
1855	Like most orchestras around this date, the New York Philharmonic for the first time sat down while playing (cellists were already seated).
1865	Wagner's opera *Tristan and Isolde* scaled new heights of expressiveness using unprecedented chromaticism. Schubert's *Unfinished Symphony* (1822) was premièred in Vienna.
1875	The first of a series of collaborations between Arthur Sullivan and the librettist W S Gilbert, *Trial by Jury,* was given its première.
1876	Wagner's *The Ring of the Nibelung* was produced in Bayreuth. Brahms' *First Symphony* was performed in Karlsruhe.
1877	Edison invented the cylindrical tin-foil phonograph, but few showed interest.
1883	The Metropolitan Opera House opened in New York with a production of Gounod's *Faust.*
1885	Liszt composed *Bagatelle without Tonality* (his *Faust Symphony* of 1857 opened with a twelve-note row).
1894	Debussy's *Prélude à l'Après-midi d'un Faune* anticipated 20th century composition with its use of the whole-tone scale.
1895	Henry Wood conducted the first Promenade Concert at the Queen's Hall in London. The 'Proms' moved to the Royal Albert Hall in 1941.

1899   Scott Joplin's *Maple Leaf Rag* was published in Sedalia, Missouri.

1902   Caruso recorded ten arias in a hotel room in Milan, the success of which established the popularity of the phonograph. By the time of his death in 1921 he had earned $2,000,000 from sales of his recordings.

1908   Saint-Saëns became the first leading composer to write a film score, for *L'Assassinat du Duc de Guise.*

1911   Irving Berlin had his first big success as a songwriter with *Alexander's Ragtime Band.*

1912   Schoenberg's atonal *Pierrot Lunaire,* for reciter and chamber ensemble, foreshadowed many similar small-scale quasi-theatrical works.

1913   Stravinsky's ballet *The Rite of Spring* precipitated a riot at its première in Paris.

1919   Schoenberg, who was experimenting with serial technique, set up the Society for Private Musical Performances in Vienna, which lasted until 1921.

1922   Alessandro Moreschi, last of the castrati, died in Rome.

1925   Louis Armstrong made his first records with the Hot Five. Duke Ellington's Washingtonians also started recording.

1927   Jerome Kern's *Showboat*, with libretto by Oscar Hammerstein II, laid the foundations of the modern American musical.

1937   The NBC Symphony Orchestra began its 17-year association with Arturo Toscanini, one of the greatest conductors in the history of music.

1938   Prokofiev's score for Eisenstein's *Alexander Nevsky* raised film music to new levels. Big band music became popular.

1939   Elisabeth Lutyens was one of the first English composers to use 12-note composition in her *Chamber Concerto no.1* for nine instruments.

1940   Walt Disney's *Fantasia* introduced classical music, conducted by Leopold Stokowski, to a worldwide audience of filmgoers.

1942   In Chicago, John Cage conducted the premiere of his *Imaginary Landscape no 3*, scored for marimbula, gongs, tin cans, buzzers, plucked coil, electric oscillator, and generator.

1945   Bebop jazz was initiated. The jazz greats Charlie Parker and Dizzy Gillespie first recorded together.

1952   The BBC Symphony Orchestra was founded in London under Sir Adrian Boult.

1954   Stockhausen's *Electronic Studies* for magnetic tape were broadcast in Cologne. Edgard Varèse's *Déserts*, the first work to combine instruments and pre-recorded magnetic tape, was performed in Paris. Elvis Presley made his first rock-and-roll recordings.

1955   Boulez's *Le Marteau sans Maître,* for contralto and chamber ensemble, was performed in Baden-Baden. Its formidable serial technique and exotic orchestration was acclaimed by the avant-garde. The Miles Davis Quintet with John Coltrane united two of the most important innovators in jazz.

1956   The first annual Warsaw Autumn festival of contemporary music was held. This became particularly important for the promotion of Polish composers such as Lutoslawksi and Penderecki.

1957   Leonard Bernsein's *West Side Story* was premiered in New York. A computer, programmed at the University of Illinois by Lejaren Hiller and Leonard Isaacson, composed the *Illiac Suite* for string quartet.

1963   Shostakovich's opera *Lady Macbeth of Mezensk*, earlier banned and condemned in *Pravda* 1936, was produced in a revised version as *Katerina Ismailova*.

1965   Robert Moog invented a synthesizer that considerably widened the scope of electronic music. The film soundtrack of *The Sound of Music*, with music by Rodgers and lyrics by Hammerstein, was released, and stayed in the music charts for the next two years. Bob Dylan used electric instrumentation on *Highway 61 Revisited*.

1967   The Beatles' album *Sgt Pepper's Lonely Hearts Club Band*, which took over 500 hours to record, was released. The first Velvet Underground album was released. Psychedelic rock spread from San Francisco, and hard rock developed in the UK and the USA.

1969   Peter Maxwell Davies' theatre piece *Eight Songs for a Mad King* for vocalist and six instruments, was premiered in London by the Pierrot Players, later to become the Fires of London ensemble under Davies' direction.

1976   Philip Glass' opera *Einstein on the Beach* using the repetitive techniques of minimalism, was given its first performance in Paris. Punk rock arrived with the Sex Pistols' 'Anarchy in the UK'.

1977   The Institute for Research and Coordination of Acoustics and Music (IRCAM) was founded in Paris under the direction of Pierre Boulez, for visiting composers to make use of advanced electronic equipment.

1983   Messiaen's only opera, *Saint François d'Assise*, was given its first performance in Paris. Lutoslawski's Third Symphony was premiered to worldwide acclaim by the Chicago Symphony Orchestra under Sir Georg Solti. Compact discs launched in the West.

1986   Paul Simon's *Graceland* popularized world music.

DATE	BALLET	COMPOSER	CHOREOGRAPHER	PLACE
1670	Le Bourgeois Gentilhomme	Lully	Beauchamp	Chambord
1735	Les Indes Galantes	Rameau	Blondy	Paris
1761	Don Juan	Gluck	Angiolini	Vienna
1778	Les Petits Riens	Mozart	Noverre	Paris
1801	The Creatures of Prommetheus	Beethoven	Viganò	Vienna
1828	La Fille Mal Gardée	Hérold	Aumer	Paris
1832	La Sylphide	Schneitzhoeffer	F. Taglioni	Paris
1841	Giselle	Adam	Coralli/Perrot	Paris
1842	Napoli	Gade/Paulli/Helsted/Lumbye	Bournonville	Copenhagen
1844	La Esmeralda	Pugni	Perrot	London
1869	Don Quixote	Minkus	M Petipa	Moscow
1870	Coppélia	Delibes	Saint-Léon	Paris
1876	Sylvia	Delibes	Mérante	Paris
1877	La Bayadère	Minkus	M Petipa	St Petersburg
1877	Swan Lake	Tchaikovsky	Reisinger	Moscow
1882	Namouna	Lalo	L Petipa	Paris
1890	The Sleeping Beauty	Tchaikovsky	M Petipa	St Petersburg
1892	Nutcracker	Tchaikovsky	M Petipa/Ivanov	St Petersburg
1898	Raymonda	Glazunov	M Petipa	St Petersburg
1905	The Dying Swan	Saint-Saëns	Fokine	St Petersburg
1907	Les Sylphides	Chopin	Fokine	St Petersburg
1910	Carnival	Schumann	Fokine	St Petersburg
1910	The Firebird	Stravinsky	Fokine	Paris
1911	Petrushka	Stravinsky	Fokine	Paris
1911	Le Spectre de la Rose	Weber	Fokine	Monte Carlo
1912	L'Après-midi d'un Faune	Debussy	Nijinsky	Paris
1912	Daphnis et Chloë	Ravel	Fokine	Paris
1913	Jeux	Debussy	Nijinsky	Paris
1913	Le Sacre du Printemps	Stravinsky	Nijinsky	Paris
1915	El Amor Brujo	Falla	Imperio	Madrid
1917	Parade	Satie	Massine	Paris
1919	La Boutique Fantasque	Rossini/Respighi	Massine	London
1919	The Three-Cornered Hat	Falla	Massini	London
1923	La Creation du Monde	Milhaud	Börlin	Paris
1923	Les Noces	Stravinsky	Nijinska	Paris
1924	Les Biches	Poulenc	Nijinska	Monte Carlo
1927	The Red Poppy	Glière	Lashchilin/Tikhomirov	Moscow
1928	Apollon Musagète	Stravinsky	Balanchine	Paris
1928	Le Baiser de la Fée	Tchaikovsky	Nijinska	Paris
1928	Bolero	Ravel	Nijinska	Paris
1929	The Prodigal Son	Prokofiev	Balanchine	Paris
1929	La Valse	Ravel	Nijinska	Monte Carlo
1931	Bacchus and Ariane	Roussel	Lifar	Paris
1931	Façade	Walton	Ashton	London
1931	Job	Vaughan Williams	de Valois	London
1937	Checkmate	Bliss	de Valois	Paris
1937	Les Patineurs	Meyerbeer/Lambert	Ashton	London
1938	Billy the Kid	Copland	Loring	Chicago
1938	Gaîté Parisienne	Offenbach/Rosenthal	Massine	Monte Carlo
1938	Romeo and Juliet	Prokofiev	Psota	Brno, Moravia

DATE	BALLET	COMPOSER	CHOEOGRAPHER	PLACE
1942	Gayaneh	Khachaturian	Anisimova	Molotov-Perm
1942	The Miraculous Mandarin	Bartók	Milloss	Milan
1942	Rodeo	Copland	de Mille	New York
1944	Appalachian Spring	Copland	Graham	Washington
1944	Fancy Free	Bernstein	Robbins	New York
1945	Cinderella	Prokofiev	Zakharov	Moscow
1949	Carmen	Bizet	Petit	London
1951	Pineapple Poll	Sullivan/Mackerras	Cranko	London
1956	Spartacus	Khachaturian	Jacobson	Leningrad
1957	Agon	Stravinsky	Balanchine	New York
1959	Episodes	Webern	Balanchine	New York
1962	A Midsummer Night's Dream	Mendelssohn	Balanchine	New York
1962	Pierrot Lunaire	Schoenberg	Tetley	New York
1964	The Dream	Mendelssohn/Lanchbery	Ashton	London
1965	Lied von der Erde	Mahler	MacMillan	Stuttgart
1967	Anastasia	Martinu	MacMillan	New York
1968	Enigma Variations	Elgar	Ashton	London
1969	The Taming of the Shrew	Stolze/Scarlatti	Cranko	Stuttgart
1972	Duo Concertante	Stravinsky	Balanchine	New York
1974	Elite Syncopations	Joplin, etc	MacMillan	London
1976	A Month in the Country	Chopin/Lanchbery	Ashton	London
1978	Mayerling	Liszt/Lamchbery	MacMillan	London
1978	Symphony of Psalms	Stravinsky	Kylian	Scheveningen, The Netherlands
1980	Gloria	Poulenc	MacMillan	London
1980	Rhapsody	Rachmaninov	Ashton	London

1000 BC	King David danced 'with all his might' before the ark of the Covenant in Jerusalem - one of the earliest instances of ritual dance.
405 BC	*Bacchae* by Euripides was staged in Athens. The play demanded a considerable amount of dancing.
142 BC	Consul Scipio Aemilianus Africanus closed the burgeoning dance schools of Rome in a drive against hedonism.
774 AD	Pope Zacharias forbade dancing.
1050	The *Ruodlieb*, a poem written by a monk at Tegernsee, Bavaria, contained the first European reference to dancing in couples.
1313	Rabbi Hacén ben Salomo of Zaragoza, in Aragon, like many other Jews in medieval times, was the local dancing master.
1489	A rudimentary allegorical ballet was performed in honour of the marriage of the Duke of Milan, at Tortona, Italy.
1581	In Paris, the first modern-style unified ballet, the *Ballet Comique de la Reine*, was staged at the court of Catherine de Medici.
1588	Dance and ballet's first basic text, *L'Orchésographie*, by the priest Jehan Tabouret, was printed in Langres, near Dijon.
1651	In London, John Playford published *The English Dancing Master*. The 18th edition (1728) described 900 country dances.
1661	Louis XIV founded L'Académie Royale de Danse in Paris.
1670	The first classic ballet, *Le Bourgeois Gentilhomme* was produced in Chambord, France.
1681	In Paris, women appeared in ballet for the first time in the opera-ballet *Le Triomphe de L'amour*.
1734	The dancer Marie Sallé streamlined the traditional costume, and Marie Camargo shortened her skirts.
1760	The great dancer and choreographer Jean-Georges Noverre published in Lyon *Lettres sur la Danse et sur les Ballets*, one of the most influential of all ballet books.
1778	Noverre and Mozart collaborated on *Les Petits Riens* in Paris. The cast included the celebrated Auguste Vestris.
1812	The waltz arrived in England. The couples, wrote Byron, were 'like two cock-chafers spitted on the same bodkin'.
1820	Carlo Blasis, teacher and choreographer, published his *Traité élémentaire théoretique et pratique de l'arte de la danse* in Milan which, together with his later works of dance theory, codified techniques for future generations of dancers.
1821	The first known picture of a ballerina *sur les pointes*, the French Fanny Bias by F. Waldeck, dates from this year.
1832	The first performance of *La Sylphide* at the Paris Opéra opened the Romantic era of ballet and established the central significance of the ballerina. Marie Taglioni, the producer's daughter, who took the title role, wore the new-style diaphanous dress.

1841 Ballet's Romantic masterpiece *Giselle* with Carolotta Grisi in the leading role, was produced in Paris.

1844 The polka reached London.

1866 *The Black Crook*, the ballet-extravaganza from which American vaudeville and musical comedy developed, began its run of 474 performances in New York.

1870 *Coppélia*, 19th century ballet's comic masterpiece, was presented in Paris.

1877 *Swan Lake* was premiered in Moscow, but failed through poor production and choreography. The Petipa-Ivanov version, in which Pierina Legnani performed her famous 32 *fouettés*, established the work in 1895.

1897 Anna Pavlova made her debut in St Petersburg with the Imperial Russian Ballet.

1905 Isadora Duncan appeared in Russia, making an immense impression with her 'anti-ballet' innovations derived from Greek dance.

1906 Vaslav Nijinsky made his debut in St Petersburg.

1909 The first Paris season given by Diaghilev's troupe of Russian dancers, later to become known as the Ballets Russes, marked the beginning of one of the most exciting periods in Western ballet.

1913 The première of Stravinsky's *The Rite of Spring* provoked a scandal in Paris.

1914 The foxtrot was introduced in England.

1926 Martha Graham, one of the most innovative figures in modern ballet, gave her first recital in New York. In England, students from the Rambert School of Ballet, opened by Marie Rambert in 1920, gave their first public performance in *A Tragedy of Fashion*, the first ballet to be choreographed by Frederick Ashton.

1928 The first performance of George Balanchine's *Apollon Musagète* in Paris, by the Ballets Russes, marked the birth of Neoclassicism in ballet.

1931 Ninette de Valois' Vic-Wells ballet gave its first performance in London. In 1956 the company became the Royal Ballet.

1933 The Hollywood musical achieved artistic independence through Busby Berkeley's kaleidoscopic choreography in *Forty-Second Street* and Dave Gould's airborne finale in *Flying down to Rio*, in which Fred Astaire and Ginger Rogers appeared together for the first time.

1940 The Dance Notation Bureau was established in New York for recording ballets and dances.

1948 The New York City Ballet was founded with George Balanchine as principal choreographer. The immensely popular film *The Red Shoes* appeared, choreographed by Massine and Robert Helpman and starring Moira Shearer.

1950 The Festival Ballet, later to become the London Festival Ballet, was created by Alicia Markova and Anton Dolin who had first danced together with the Ballets Russes in 1929.

1952 Gene Kelly starred and danced in the film *Singin' in the Rain*.

1953 The US experimental choreographer Merce Cunningham, who often worked with the composer John Cage, formed his own troupe.

325

1954   Bill Haley's *Rock Around the Clock* heralded the age of rock and roll.

1956   The Bolshoi Ballet opened its first season in the West at Covent Garden in London, with Galina Ulanova dancing in *Romeo and Juliet*, startling audiences with its dramatic style.

1957   Jerome Robbins choreographed Leonard Bernstein's *West Side Story*, demonstrating his outstanding ability to work in both popular and classical forms.

1960   The progressive French choreographer Maurice Béjart became director of the Brussels-based *Ballet du XXième Siècle* company.

1961   Rudolf Nureyev defected while dancing with the Kirov Ballet in Paris. He was to have a profound influence on male dancing in the West. The South African choreographer John Cranke became director of the Stuttgart Ballet for which he was to produce several major ballets.

1962   Glen Tetley's ballet *Pierrot Lunaire*, in which he was one of the three dancers, was premiered in New York. In the same year he joined the Nederlands Dans Theater.

1965   US choreographer Twyla Tharp produced her first works.

1966   The School of Contemporary Dance was founded in London, from which Robin Howard and the choreographer Robert Cohan created the London Contemporary Dance Theatre, later to become an internationally renowned company. The Choreographer Norman Morrice joined the Ballet Rambert and the company began to concentrate on contemporary works.

1968   Arthur Mitchell, the first black dancer to join the New York City Ballet, founded the Dance Theatre of Harlem.

1974   Mikhail Baryshnikov defected while dancing with a Bolshoi Ballet group in Toronto.

1978   The Release of Robert Stigwood's film *Saturday Night Fever* popularized disco dancing worldwide.

1980   Natalia Makarova, who had defected in 1979, staged the first full-length revival of Petipa's *La Bayadère* in the West with the American Ballet Theatre in New York.

1981   Wayne Sleep, previously principal dancer with the Royal Ballet, starred as lead dancer in Andrew Lloyd-Webber's musical *Cats*, choreographed by Gillian Lynne.

1983   The release of the film *Flashdance* reflected the current cult of break dancing.

1984   The avant-garde group Michael Clark and Company made its debut in London.

1989   Sylvie Guillem became principal guest artist at the Royal Opera House, Covent Garden, London.

Science and Technology

Activities such as healing, star-watching, engineering, and warfare have been practised in many societies since ancient times, often with success. The European scientific revolution between about 1650 and 1800, however, propelled all these activities into an accelerating rate of progress, largely through its replacement of medieval speculative philosophy with a novel combination of observation, experimentation and rationality. The continued success of that revolution, and its economic value, is shown by the worldwide spread of applied science. It is clear also that the phenomenon is double-edged, as exemplified by the way the earth has armed itself with nuclear weapons while at the same time ridding itself of the smallpox virus.

The method of scientific research includes an interaction between tradition, experimentation and observation, and deduction. The subject area called Philosophy of Science investigates the nature of this complex interaction, in particular the extent of its ability to gain access to the truth about the material world. Traditionally, pure science and especially physics has been the main area of study for philosophers. Today, serious questions concerning the proper use of science and the role of science education are restructuring this field of study.

This part of the Pocket Encyclopedia contains sections on Astronomy, Computing, Earth Sciences, Life Sciences, Medicine, Physics, Chemistry, Mathematics, and Technology. Each section focusses on a particular topic, but also forms part of an overview of science and technology in general. Galileo, for example, was central not only to astronomy but also to mathematics and physics. Scientists tend to be remembered for their spectacular discoveries and technologists for inventions, but, in addition, the common theme running through all of the sciences is the aim to produce reliable explanations of, and laws about, the material world, and, through technology, to apply science for practical purposes.

Astronomy

Astronomy – 'the science of the stars' – deals with celestial bodies such as our earth, its moon, the sun, the other planets and members of our solar system, and stars and other bodies in all of space. It is concerned with their positions and motions; with their sizes, masses, temperatures and physical conditions; with their origins and fates; and, ultimately, with the origin, evolution and fate of the entire Universe.

Astronomy is the oldest science – there are observational records from Babylonia, China and Ancient Egypt. Through the Greeks and Ptolemy of Alexandria, to the flowering of European astronomy with Copernicus, Brahe, Kepler and Galileo, right to the powerful radio-telescopes and deep-space probes of today, astronomy deals with the ultimate questions in science. Its vast distances and time spans, and concepts such as bent space and black holes, defy the mind's grasp. How big is the Universe? When did it, and presumably time, begin? How do newer discoveries, such as pulsars, fit into our interpretations of the astronomical data?

An important new development is radio astronomy, the study of radio waves emitted naturally by objects in space. In 1931 Karl Jansky first detected radio waves from the centre of our galaxy. Since World War II astronomers have mapped the spiral structure of our galaxy from the radio waves given out by interstellar gas, and have detected many individual radio sources within our galaxy and beyond. Radio astronomers have also detected weak background radiation thought to be from the Big Bang explosion that marked the birth of the Universe.

This section contains a historical overview or *Chronology*, from the very first scientific observations of the sky to the most up-to-date 'close encounters' with comets; a *Journey to the Stars*, working outwards from our earth; a review of *Celestial Bodies*, from small to big; a digest of important *Places and Organizations* in astronomy; a list of key *Terms*; *Biographies* of great astronomers, and details of *Space Research*.

2300 BC	Chinese astronomers made their earliest observations.
2000 BC	Babylonian priests made their first observational records.
1900 BC	Stonehenge was constructed: first phase.
365 BC	The Chinese observed the satellites of Jupiter with the naked eye.
3rd cent BC	Aristarchus argued that the sun is the centre of the solar system.
2nd cent AD	Ptolemy's complicated earth-centred system was promulgated, which dominated the astronomy of the Middle Ages.
1543 AD	Copernicus revived the ideas of Aristarchus in *De Revolutionibus*.
1608	Lippershey invented the telescope, which was first used by Galileo in 1609.
1609	Kepler's first two laws of planetary motion were published (the third appeared in 1619).
1632	Leiden established the world's first official observatory.
1633	Galileo's theories were condemned by the Inquisition.
1675	The Royal Greenwich Observatory was founded in England.
1687	Newton's *Principia* was published, including his 'law of universal gravitation'.
1718	Halley predicted the return of the comet named after him, observed in 1758: it was last seen in 1986.
1781	Herschel discovered Uranus and recognized stellar systems beyond our galaxy.
1796	Laplace elaborated his theory of the origin of the solar system.
1801	Piazzi discovered the first asteroid, Ceres.
1814	Fraunhofer first studied absorption lines in the solar spectrum.
1846	Neptune was identified by Galle, following predictions by Adams and Leverrier.
1859	Kirchhoff explained dark lines in the sun's spectrum.
1887	The earliest photographic star charts were produced.
1889	E E Barnard took the first photographs of the Milky Way.
1890	The first photograph of the spectrum was taken.
1908	Fragment of comet fell at Tungusta, Siberia.
1920	Eddington began the study of interstellar matter.
1923	Hubble proved that the galaxies are systems independent of the Milky Way, and by 1930 had confirmed the concept of an expanding universe.
1930	The planet Pluto was discovered by Clyde Tombaugh at the Lowell Observatory, Arizona, USA.
1931	Jansky founded radioastronomy.
1945	Radar contact with the moon was established by Z Bay of Hungary and the US Army Signal Corps Laboratory.
1948	The 200-inch Hale reflector telescope was installed at Mount Palomar, California, USA.
1955	The Jodrell Bank telescope 'dish' in England was completed.

1957	The first Sputnik satellite (USSR) opened the age of space observation.
1962	The first X-ray source was discovered in Scorpio.
1963	The first quasar was discovered.
1967	The first pulsar was discovered by Jocelyn Bell.
1969	The first manned moon landing was made by US astronauts.
1976	A 236-inch reflector telescope was installed at Mount Semirodniki (USSR).
1977	Uranus was discovered to have rings.
1977	The spacecraft Voyager 1 and 2 were launched, passing Jupiter and Saturn 1979–81.
1978	The spacecraft Pioneer Venus 1 and 2 reached Venus.
1978	A satellite of Pluto, Charon, was discovered by James Christie of the US Naval Observatory.
1979	The UK infrared telescope (UKIRT) was established on Hawaii.
1985	Halley's comet returned.
1986	Voyager 2 reached Uranus and discovered ten new moons.
1987	Bright supernova visible to the naked eye for the first since 1604.
1989	Voyager 2 reaches Neptune.

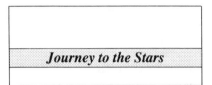

Journey to the Stars

earth the planet on which we live: it is the third planet outward from the sun, lying with its satellite, the moon, between Venus and Mars. Its orbit round the sun is an ellipse of which one focus is formed by the sun. The mean distance of earth from the sun is c. 149,597,870 km/92,955,800 mi. The plane of its orbit is called the ecliptic, and it is inclined to the earth's equatorial plane at an angle of 23.4°; this inclination is responsible for the phenomena of the seasons. The earth, moving at an average speed of 30 km/18.5 mi a second, makes a complete circuit in the solar year, 365 days 5 h 49 min 46 s. It has also a daily movement, rotating about its own axis in 23 h 56 min 4.1 s, which is responsible for day and night. By using atomic clocks it has been possible to prove that the earth's rate of rotation is slowing down.

The earth is an oblate spheroid or, taking into account an 18–metre rise at the N Pole and a 26–metre depression at the S Pole, 'pear-shaped'. The equatorial diameter is 12,756 km/7926.5 mi and the polar diameter is 12,713 km/7900 mi; the earth's equatorial circumference is 40,076 km/24,902 mi and its polar circumference is 40,009 km/24,860 mi.

moon the natural satellite of the earth, 3,476 km/2,160 mi in diameter, with a mass 1/81 that of the earth. Its average distance from earth is 384,400 km/238,850 mi, and it orbits earth every 27.32 days (the *sidereal month*). The moon spins on its axis so that it keeps one side permanently turned towards the earth. The moon is illuminated by sunlight, and goes through a cycle of phases from New (invisible) via First Quarter (half moon) to Full and back again to New, every 29.53 days (the *synodic month*, also known as a *lunation*).

The moon has no air or water. On its sunlit side

temperatures reach 130° C, but during the two-week lunar night the surface temperature drops to −170° C. Its composition is rocky, with a surface heavily scarred by meteorite impacts that have formed craters up to 240 km/150 mi across. The youngest craters are surrounded by bright rays of ejected rock. The largest scars have been filled by dark lava to produce the lowland plains known as seas or *maria*. These dark patches form the familiar 'man-in-the-moon' pattern. Rocks brought back by Apollo astronauts show the moon is 4,600 million years old, the same age as the earth. Unlike the earth, most of the moon's surface features were formed within the first 1,000 million years of its history when it was subjected to heavy bombardment by meteorites.

The origin of the moon is open to debate. Theories suggest that it split from the earth; that it was a separate body captured by earth's gravity; or that it formed in orbit around the earth. The latest idea suggests that the moon was formed from debris thrown off when a body the size of Mars struck the earth early in the earth's history.

sun the star at the centre of the solar system, around which the earth and other planets orbit. Its diameter is 1,392,000 km/865,000 mi, and it lies 149,597,870 km/92,955,800 mi from earth. The sun is composed of about 70% hydrogen and 30% helium by mass, with other elements making up less than 1%. The temperature at its centre is probably 15 million °C. Like all stars, the sun generates energy by nuclear fusion reactions that turn hydrogen into helium at its centre. The sun is about 4,700 million years old, nearly halfway through its total predicted lifetime of 10,000 million years.

It spins on its axis every 25 days near its equator, but more slowly towards the poles. Its rotation can be followed by watching the passage of dark sunspots across its disk. Sometimes bright eruptions called flares occur near sunspots. Above the sun's photosphere lies a layer of thinner gas called the chromosphere, visible only in special instruments or at eclipses. Tongues of gas called prominences

MAJOR SPACE PROGRAMMES

Name	Launch Date	Number of flights	Main achievements
Ariane (European)	1979-	continues	Launch rocket for satellites based in Korou, French Guiana; operated commercially by Arianespace
Apollo (USA)	1968-72	7	Saturn rockets as launchers; Neil Armstrong first person on moon; collected rocks and dust; 6 moon landings in all
Gemini (USA)	1965-66	10	Edward White first US space walker; first space docking
Giotto (European)	1985-86	1	Flew within 600 km of Halley's comet nucleus
Mercury (USA)	1961-63	6	Alan Shepherd first US spaceman; John Glenn first American in orbit
Pioneer (USA)	1958-78	continues	Probed the outer planets; Pioneer 10 first to leave solar system
Salyut (USSR)	1971-82	7	Scientific research, observation aboard orbiting space station
Skylab (USA)	1973	4	Scientific research aboard converted Saturn V upper stage
Soyuz (USSR)	1967-	continues	Ferries cosmonauts to Salyut space stations
Space Shuttle (USA)	1981-	continues	First reusable manned spacecraft; research, observation and experimentation
Spacelab (European)	1985-	continues	Workspace and equipment module for Space Shuttle's cargo bay
Sputnik (USSR)	1957-61	10	Sputnik 1 first artificial satellite; Sputnik 2 took first creature (dog, Laika) into space
Voskhod (USSR)	1964-65	2	First multi-person crew (3 men); Alexi Leonov first space walker
Vostok (USSR)	1961-63	6	Yuri Gagarin first spaceman; Valentina Tereshkova first spacewoman
Voyager (USA)	1977-79	2	Deep-space probes, ultimately leaving solar system

extend from the chromosphere into the corona, a halo of hot gas surrounding the sun. Gas boiling from the corona streams outwards through the solar system, forming solar wind. Activity on the sun, including sunspots, flares and prominences, waxes and wanes during the *solar cycle* every 11 years or so.

solar system the sun and all the other bodies in orbit around it: the nine planets, their moons, asteroids and comets. The solar system is thought to have formed from a cloud of gas and dust in space 4,600 million years ago. The sun contains 99% of the mass of the solar system. The edge of the solar system is not clearly defined; it is marked only by the limit of the sun's gravitational influence, which extends about 1.5 light years, almost halfway to the nearest star.

Milky Way the faint band of light crossing the sky, consisting of countless stars in the plane of our galaxy, too distant to be seen individually by the naked eye. The name Milky Way is sometimes also used for our galaxy. The densest parts lie in the constellation Sagittarius, towards the centre. In places, the Milky Way is interrupted by lanes of dark dust which obscure light from the stars beyond, such as the Coalsack Nebula in Crux (the Southern Cross) and the Cygnus Rift.

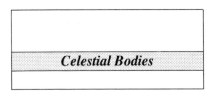

Celestial Bodies

celestial body 'of the sky'; an object which is seen outside the earth and its atmosphere, ranging from tiny fragments of rock a few centimetres across to giant stars hundreds of times the size of our sun. The term is not usually used for artificial objects such as rockets and space probes.

meteor a flash of light in the sky, popularly known as a *shooting star*, caused by a particle of dust burning up in the atmosphere. Most meteors are smaller than grains of sand. They enter the atmosphere at speeds up to 70 km/45 mi per sec and burn up by friction at a height of around 100 km/60 mi. On any clear night, several *sporadic* meteors can be seen each hour. But several times each year the earth encounters swarms of dust shed by comets, which give rise to a *meteor shower*. The meteors in a shower seem to radiate from one particular point in the sky, after which the shower is named, e.g. the Perseid meteor shower of August appears to radiate from the constellation Perseus. A particularly brilliant meteor is termed a *fireball*.

meteorite a piece of rock or metal from space that reaches the surface of the earth, moon or other body. Meteorites are thought to be fragments from asteroids, although some may be pieces from the heads of comets. Over 5,000 meteorites are estimated to hit the earth each year. Most fall in the sea or in remote areas and are never recovered. Most meteorites are stony in composition, although some are made of iron and a few have a mixed rock-iron composition. The largest known meteorite is iron, weighing 60 tonnes, which lies where it fell in prehistoric times at Grootfontein, Namibia. Meteorites are slowed down by the earth's atmosphere, but if they are moving fast enough they can form a crater on impact.

satellite any small body that orbits a larger one, either natural or artificial. Natural satellites are called moons. The first *artificial satellite,* Sputnik 1, was launched into orbit around the earth by the USSR in 1957. Artificial satellites are used for scientific purposes, communications, weather forecasting, and military purposes. At any time there are several thousand artificial satellites orbiting the earth, including active satellites, satellites that have ended their working lives, and discarded sections of rockets. The largest artificial satellites can be seen by the naked eye. Artificial satellites eventually re-enter the earth's atmosphere. Usually they burn up by friction, but sometimes debris falls to the earth's surface, as with Skylab.

asteroid any of many thousands of small

bodies, composed of rocks and iron, that orbit the sun. They are also known as minor planets. Most asteroids lie in a belt between the orbits of Mars and Jupiter, though some are on orbits that bring them close to the earth, and some, such as the Apollo asteroids, even cross the earth's orbit. Asteroids are thought to be fragments left over from the formation of the solar system. As many as 100,000 may exist, but their total mass is only a few hundredths the mass of the moon. The largest is Ceres, 1,000 km/621 mi in diameter. The brightest as seen from earth is Vesta, which has a light-coloured surface.

comet a small, icy body orbiting the sun on a highly elliptical path. A comet consists of a central nucleus a few kilometres across, often likened to a dirty snowball because it consists mostly of ice mixed with dust. As the comet approaches the sun the nucleus heats up, releasing gas and dust which form a tenuous *coma* up to 100,000 km/60,000 mi across, around the nucleus. Gas and dust stream away from the coma to form the comet's tail, which may extend for millions of kilometres.

Comets are believed to have been formed at the birth of the solar system. Billions of them now reside in the *Oort cloud* beyond the planets. The gravitational effect of passing stars pushes some towards the sun, when they become visible from earth. Most comets swing around the sun and return to distant space, not to be seen again for thousands or millions of years. But some have their orbits altered by the gravitational pull of the planets so that they reappear every 200 years or less. These are termed *periodic comets*. Of the 800 or so comets whose orbits have been calculated, about 1 in 5 is periodic; the only one visible to the naked eye is Halley's comet. That with the shortest known period is Encke's comet, which orbits the sun every 3.3 years. A dozen or more comets are discovered every year, some by amateur astronomers.

moon in astronomy, any small body that orbits a planet. That which orbits Earth is known as the Moon. Mercury and Venus are the only planets in our solar system that do not

have moons.

planet a body in orbit around a star. Planets do not give out light of their own, but reflect the light of the central star. Planets can be made of rock, metal or gas. There are nine planets in the solar system, orbiting the sun. The inner four, called the *terrestrial planets*, are small and rocky, and include our planet Earth. The outer planets are large balls of liquid and gas; the largest is Jupiter, which contains more than twice as much mass as all the other solar-system planets combined. There is no good evidence for any planets beyond Pluto. Other stars almost certainly have planets, but they would be too faint to see from earth.

nebula a cloud of gas and dust in space. Nebulae are the birthplaces of stars. One is the Orion nebula, visible to the naked eye below the 'belt' of Orion. It is an *emission nebula*, glowing brightly because its gas is energized by stars that have formed within it. In another type of bright nebula, a *reflection nebula*, light from stars is reflected off grains of dust in the nebula, as surrounds the stars of the Pleiades cluster. A *dark nebula* appears as a dark patch silhouetted on a lighter background, such as the Coalsack Nebula in Crux (the Southern Cross) and the Horsehead Nebula in Orion. Some nebulae are produced by gas thrown off from dying stars.

neutron star a very small, dense star composed mostly of atomic particles called neutrons. These stars are thought to form when massive stars explode as supernovae at the ends of their lives. In the explosion, the protons and electrons of the star's atoms merge to make neutrons. A neutron star may have the mass of our sun, or more, compressed into a globe only 20 km/12 mi in diameter. Being so small, neutron stars can spin very quickly. The rapidly 'flashing' radio stars called pulsars are believed to be neutron stars. A neutron star cannot have a mass of more than about three suns, or its gravity will be so strong that it shrinks even further to become a black hole.

pulsar a celestial source that emits pulses of energy at very regular intervals, ranging from a few seconds to small fractions of a second.

Pulsars were discovered in 1967 at the Mullard Radio Astronomy Observatory, Cambridge, England, by a team under Antony Hewish. Over 300 radio pulsars are now known in our galaxy, although a million may exist. They are thought to be rapidly rotating neutron stars, which flash at radio and other wavelengths like a lighthouse as they spin. Two pulsars, the one in Crab Nebula and one in the constellation Vela, give out flashes of visible light. Pulsars gradually slow down as they get older, and eventually the flashes fade. *X-ray pulsars* are a related class of object caused by hot gas falling on to a spinning neutron star in a binary system.

star a luminous globe of gas, producing its own heat and light by nuclear reactions. Our own sun is an average star. Stars consist mostly of hydrogen and helium gas. They are born from large clouds of gas in space. Surface temperatures range from above 30,000 °C down to 2,000 °C, and the corresponding colours from blue-white to red. The brightest stars have masses 100 times that of the sun, and emit as much light as millions of suns. They live for less than a million years before exploding as supernovae. An example is the peculiar star Eta Carinae, visible in the southern hemisphere. The faintest stars are the red dwarfs, less than one-thousandth the brightness of the sun. The smallest mass possible for a star is about 8% that of the sun (80 times the mass of the planet Jupiter), otherwise nuclear reactions do not take place. Objects with less than this critical mass shine only dimly, and are termed *brown dwarfs*. There is no clear distinction between a small brown dwarf and a large planet.

For most of a star's life, energy is produced by the fusion of hydrogen into helium at its centre. Towards the end of its life, a star like the sun swells up into a red giant, before losing its outer layers as a planetary nebula, and finally shrinking to become a white dwarf.

galaxy a congregation of millions or billions of stars, held together by gravity. There are two main shapes. *Spiral* galaxies are flattened in shape, with a central bulge of old stars surrounded by a disk of younger stars, arranged in spiral arms like a catherine wheel. Barred spirals are a class of spiral galaxies that have a straight bar of stars across their centre, from the ends of which the spiral arms emerge. The arms of spiral galaxies contain gas and dust from which new stars are still forming. *Elliptical* galaxies contain old stars and very little gas. They include the most massive galaxies known, containing a million million stars. Some elliptical galaxies are thought to be merged spiral galaxies. Most galaxies occur in clusters, containing anything from a few to thousands of members. Although the Universe is expanding, individual clusters do not expand: rather, the space between clusters expands.

Our own galaxy, the Milky Way, is a spiral type about 100,000 light years in diameter, containing at least 100,000 million stars. It is a member of a small cluster, the Local Group. Our sun lies in one of its spiral arms, about 25,000 light years from the centre.

radio galaxy a galaxy that is a strong source of radio waves. All galaxies, including our own, emit some radio waves, but radio galaxies are up to a million times more powerful. In many cases the strongest radio emission comes not from the visible galaxy but from two clouds, invisible in an optical telescope, that can extend for millions of light years either side of the galaxy. This double structure at radio wavelengths is also shown by some quasars, suggesting a close relationship between the two types of object. In both cases, the source of energy is thought to be a massive black hole at the centre. Some radio galaxies are thought to result from two galaxies in collision, or which have recently merged.

quasar an object that appears star-like but which lies far off in the Universe, named for its *quasi-stellar* appearance. Light from quasars shows large redshifts, which places them far off in the universe, the most distant lying 10,000 million light years or more away. Although quasars are small, with diameters of less than a light year, they give out as much energy as hundreds of galaxies. Quasars are thought to be the brilliant centres of distant galaxies, caused by stars and gas falling towards an immense black hole at the galaxy's centre. Some quasars emit radio waves, which is how they were first identified in 1963, but most are radio-quiet. About 3,000 are now known. They are important in studies of the early history of the Universe.

black hole a hypothetical object whose gravity would be so great that nothing could escape from it, not even light. Anything that fell into a black hole would not be seen again. Black holes are thought to form when massive stars, much heavier than our sun, shrink at the ends of their lives. A black hole can grow by sucking in more matter, including other stars, from the space around it. Matter that falls into a black hole is squeezed to infinite density at the centre of the hole. Black holes can be detected because gas falling towards them becomes so hot that it emits x-rays. Satellites above the earth's atmosphere have detected x-rays from a number of objects in our galaxy that might be black holes. Massive black holes containing the mass of millions of stars are thought to lie at the centres of quasars. Microscopic black holes may have been formed in the chaotic conditions of the Big Bang. The English physicist Stephen Hawking has shown that such tiny black holes could 'evaporate' and explode in a flash of energy.

Universe all of space and its contents. The Universe is mostly empty space, dotted with galaxies for as far as telescopes can see. The most distant detected galaxies and quasars lie 10,000 million light years or more away. The Universe is thought to be between 10,000 million and 20,000 million years old, and to have originated in a immense explosion called the Big Bang. The space between the galaxies is expanding. Whether or not the expansion will continue depends on the average density of matter in the Universe. If the density is above a critical value, then gravity will eventually slow the expansion and reverse it. However, observations suggest that there is not enough matter in the Universe to halt the expansion, which will continue forever.

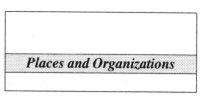

Places and Organizations

Arecibo the site in Puerto Rico of the world's largest single radio-telescope dish, 305 m/1,000 ft in diameter. Suspended between towers in a hollow in the hills, it uses the rotation of the earth to scan the sky. It is operated by the US's Cornell University.

Baikonour The name given in the USSR to the rocket launching site at Tyuratam.

Cape Canaveral promontory on the Atlantic coast of Florida, USA, 367 km/228 mi N of Miami. It was known 1963–73 as Cape Kennedy. The John F. Kennedy Space Center, from which all US manned space flights have been launched, is here.

Edwards Air Force Base military USAF centre in California, situated on a dry lake bed, with extensive runways and advanced facilities. Often used as a landing site by the Space Shuttle.

European Space Agency (ESA) an organization of European nations to engage in space research and technology for peaceful purposes. ESA was founded in 1975 by Belgium, Denmark, France, West Germany, Ireland, Italy, Netherlands, Spain, Sweden, Switzerland and the United Kingdom, with headquarters in Paris. ESA has developed various scientific and communications satellites, the Giotto space probe, the Ariane rocket and has built Spacelab for the USA. ESA plans to build its own space station, Columbus, for attachment to the US space station, and is working on its own shuttle project, Hermes.

Intelsat International Telecommunications Satellite Organization, established in 1964 to operate a worldwide system of communications satellites. More than a hundred countries are members of Intelsat, with headquarters in Washington DC, USA. Intelsat satellites are stationed in geostationary orbit over the Atlantic, Pacific and Indian Oceans. The first Intelsat satellite was *Early Bird*, launched in 1965.

Jodrell Bank site in Cheshire, England, of the Nuffield Radio Astronomy Laboratories of the University of Manchester. Its largest instrument is the 76 m/250 ft radio dish, completed in 1957 and modified in 1970. A 38 m × 25 m/125 ft × 83 ft elliptical radio dish was introduced in 1964, capable of working at shorter wavelengths. These radio telescopes are used in conjunction with five smaller dishes to produce detailed maps of radio sources.

Kennedy Space Center the NASA installation at Cape Canaveral, Florida. Headquarters of the Center are on Merritt Island. Apollo spacecraft and the Space Shuttle have been launched from here. The Center is dominated by the Vehicle Assembly Building, 160 m/525 ft tall, used for assembly of Saturn rockets and Space Shuttles.

Kourou second-largest town of French Guiana, NW of Cayenne. It is the site of the Guiana Space Centre engaged in work for the European Space Agency. Situated near the equator, it is an ideal site for launches of satellites into geostationary orbit.

NASA National Aeronautics and Space Administration. The US government agency, founded in 1958, for non-military spaceflight and aeronautical research. Its headquarters are in Washington DC and its major installation is at Cape Canaveral.

observatory a site or facility for observation of natural phenomena, especially astronomical. The earliest recorded observatory was at Alexandria, built by Ptolemy Soter, c 300 BC. The erection of observatories was revived in W Asia c 1000 AD, and extended to Europe. That built on Hven Island, Denmark, in 1576, for Tycho Brahe, was elaborate, but survived only to 1597. It was followed by those at Paris 1667, Greenwich 1675, and Kew 1769. Among the most famous modern observatories are the Hale at Mount Palomar, California; Kitt Peak in Arizona; La Palma in the Canary Islands; and Mount Semirodniki in the Caucasus, which have the most powerful optical telescopes covering the sky from the northern

hemisphere. Famous radio astronomy observatories include Jodrell Bank, the Mullard at Cambridge, England, Arecibo in Puerto Rico, Effelsberg in W Germany, and Parkes in Australia. Until recently the skies of the southern hemisphere were comparatively neglected, but in the 1970s important optical telescopes were established at Cerro Tololo, Chile; La Silla, Chile; and Siding Spring, Australia. Observatories can now also be set up in orbit, above the earth's atmosphere, as satellites, in space stations, and in the Space Shuttle.

Palomar Mount the location of an observatory, 80 km/50 mi NE of San Diego, California, having a 5 m/200 in diameter reflector. When dedicated in 1948 it was the largest optical telescope in the world.

Parkes the site in New South Wales, Australia, of the Australian National Radio Astronomy Observatory, featuring a radio telescope of 64 m/210 ft aperture, run by the Commonwealth Scientific and Industrial Research Organization (CSIRO).

Plesetsk a rocket-launching site in the Soviet Union, 170 km/105 mi S of Archangel. From here the USSR has launched unmanned satellites since 1966, many of them for military purposes.

Royal Greenwich Observatory the national astronomical observatory of the UK, founded in 1675 at Greenwich, E London, by King Charles II to provide navigational information for seamen. The eminence of the Observatory's work meant that, in 1884, Greenwich Time and the Greenwich Meridian were adopted as international standards of reference. After World War II the Observatory was moved to Herstmonceux Castle in Sussex, and plans to move to Cambridge in 1990. The Observatory also operates telescopes on La Palma in the Canary Islands, including the 4.2 m/165 in William Herschel Telescope commissioned in 1987.

Tyuratam the main space launching site in the USSR, NE of the Aral Sea. It is the Soviet equivalent of the USA's Cape Canaveral, but much larger. The Soviets refer to it as Baikonour, which is a town some distance away. The first earth satellites were launched from here. All Soviet manned space flights, and all Soviet space probes, have been launched from Tyuratam.

Yerkes Observatory astronomical centre in Wisconsin, USA. Founded by George Hale in 1897, it houses the world's largest optical refracting optical telescope, with a lens of diameter 102 cm/40 in.

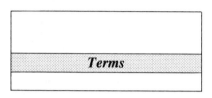

Terms

astronomical unit the average distance of the earth from the sun. 149,597,870 km/92,955,800 mi.

Big Bang the hypothetical event which marked the origin of the Universe as we know it. At the time of the Big Bang, the entire Universe and all space and matter were squeezed into a hot, super-dense state. The Big Bang explosion threw this material outwards, producing the expanding Universe. The cause of the Big Bang is unknown; observations of the current rate of expansion of the Universe suggest that it took place between 10,000 million and 20,000 million years ago.

constellation in astronomy, one of the 88 areas into which the sky is divided for the purposes of identifying and naming objects. The first constellations were simple star patterns in which early civilizations visualized gods, sacred beasts and mythical heroes. The constellations in general use today have been modified and extended from a list of 48 known to the ancient Greeks, who inherited some from the Babylonians. The modern list of 88 constellations was officially adopted by the International Astronomical Union in 1930.

eclipse the event when one astronomical body passes into the shadow of another. A *solar eclipse* occurs when the moon passes in front of the sun as seen from earth, and covers it partially or totally. A solar eclipse can happen only during a new moon. During a total elipse

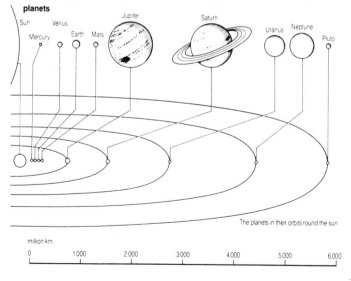

planets

Sun
Mercury   Venus   Earth   Mars   Jupiter   Saturn   Uranus   Neptune   Pluto

The planets in their orbits round the sun

million km

0   1,000   2,000   3,000   4,000   5,000   6,000

the sun's corona can be seen. A total solar eclipse can last just over 7.5 minutes, although partial eclipse will be visible from Cornwall on 11 Aug 1999. When the moon is at its farthest from earth it does not completely cover the face of the sun, leaving a ring of sunlight visible. This is an *annular eclipse* (from the Latin word *annulus*, ring). Between two and five solar eclipses occur each year.

A *lunar eclipse* occurs when the moon passes into the shadow of the earth, so that the moon's surface becomes dim until emerging from the shadow. Lunar eclipses may be partial or full, and they can happen only at full moon. Total lunar eclipses last for up to 100 minutes; the maximum number each year is three.

light year a measure of distance (not time) – the distance travelled by a beam of light in one year, 9.461×10^{12} km/5.88 million million mi.

magnitude measure of the brightness of a star or other celestial object. Faint objects have larger magnitudes, sixth magnitude being the faintest visible to the naked eye under good conditions. The brightest objects have negative (minus) magnitudes, such as Sirius, the brightest star in the night sky, which is magnitude -1.46. A difference of five magnitudes is equal to a brightness difference of 100 times; each magnitude step is equal on this geometric scale to a brightness difference of 2.512 times. *Apparent magnitude* is the brightness that an object appears from earth. *Absolute magnitude* is measured at the standard distance of 10 parsecs (32.6 light years) from the star. The apparent magnitude of the sun is -26.8, but its absolute magnitude is only $+4.8$.

orbit the path of one body in space around another, such as the orbit of the earth around the sun, or the moon around the earth. When the two bodies are similar in mass, as in a double star, both bodies move around their common centre of mass. The movement of objects in orbit follows Kepler's laws, which apply to artificial satellites as well as to natural bodies. As stated by the laws, the orbit of one body around another is an ellipse. The ellipse can be highly elongated, as in the case of comet orbits around the sun, or it may be almost circular, as in planets and some artificial satellites. The closest point of a planet's orbit to the sun is called *perihelion*; the most distant point is *aphelion*. (For a body orbiting the earth, the closest and furthest points of the orbit are called *perigee* and *apogee*.)

parsec in astronomy, a unit of distance measurement applied to stars and galaxies. One parsec is equal to 3.2616 light years. It is the distance at which a star would have a parallax of one second of arc using as base line the earth's orbital radius around the sun.

radio astronomy the study of radio waves emitted naturally by objects in space. Radio emission comes from hot gas (*thermal radiation*), electrons spiralling in magnetic fields (*synchroton radiation*), and specific wavelengths (*lines*) emitted by atoms and molecules in space, such as the 21cm line emitted by hydrogen gas. Among the radio sources in our galaxy are the remains of supernova explosions, such as the Crab Nebula, and pulsars. Strong sources beyond our galaxy include radio galaxies and quasars. Their existence far off in the Universe demonstrates how the Universe has been evolved with time. Radio astronomers have also detected weak *background radiation* thought to be from the Big Bang explosion that marked the birth of the Universe.

radio telescope an instrument for detecting radio waves from the Universe. Radio telescopes usually consist of a metal bowl, which collects and focuses radio waves like a concave mirror collects and focuses light waves. Other radio telescopes are shaped like long troughs, while some consist of simple rod-shaped aerials. Radio telescopes are much larger than optical telescopes, because the wavelengths they detect are much longer than the wavelength of light. Even a large dish such as that at Jodrell Bank can see the radio sky less clearly than a small optical telescope sees the visible sky. The largest single radio astronomy dish is 305 m/1,000 ft across, at Arecibo, Puerto Rico.

redshift in astronomy, the lengthening of the wavelengths of light from an object, as a result of the object's motion away from us. It is an example of the Doppler effect. Lengthening the wavelengths causes them to move or shift towards the red end of the spectrum, hence the name. The amount of redshift can be measured by the displacement of lines in an object's spectrum. By measuring the amount of redshift in light from stars and galaxies, astronomers can tell how quickly these objects are moving away from us. The redshift in light from galaxies is evidence for the expanding Universe. A strong gravitational field can also produce a redshift in light; this is termed *gravitational redshift*.

solar wind a stream of atomic particles, mostly protons and electrons, from the sun's corona flowing outwards through the solar system at speeds from 300 km/200 mi to 1,000 km/600 mi per second. The fastest streams come from 'holes' in the sun's corona that lie over areas where there is no surface activity. The solar wind pushes the gas of comets' tails away from the sun, and 'gusts' in the solar wind cause geomagnetic disturbances and aurorae on earth.

telescope a device for collecting and focusing light and other forms of electromagnetic radiation (see also radio telescope). A telescope produces a magnified image, which makes the object seem nearer, and it shows fainter objects than can be seen by the eye alone. A telescope with a large *aperture*, or opening, can see finer detail and fainter objects than one with a small aperture.
There are two main types of optical telescope: the *refracting telescope*, which uses lenses, and the *reflecting telescope*, which uses mirrors. A third type, the *catadioptric telescope*, with a combination of lenses and mirrors, is becoming increasingly popular. The largest refracting telescope in the world has an aperture of 102 cm/40 in at Yerkes Observatory, Wisconsin, USA.
The largest reflector, with a 6 m/236 in mirror, is at Zelenchukskaya, USSR. Telescopes with larger apertures are planned, but they will be composed of numerous smaller mirrors. The first such *multiple-mirror telescope* was installed on Mount Hopkins, Arizona, in 1979. It con-sists of six mirrors of 1.8 m/72 in aperture, which perform like a single 4.5 m/176 in mirror. Large telescopes can now be placed in orbit, above the distorting effects of the earth's atmosphere. Telescopes in space have been used to study infrared, ultraviolet and X-rays that do not penetrate the atmosphere, but which carry much information about the births, lives and deaths of stars and galaxies. The 2.4 m/95 in Space Telescope, due for launch in 1988, will see the sky more clearly than any telescope on earth.

unidentified flying object (UFO) any light or object seen in the sky whose immediate identity is not apparent. The term *flying saucer* was coined after a 1947 sighting by Kenneth Arnold. On investigation, the vast majority of UFOs turn out to be natural or artificial objects, most notably bright stars and planets, meteors, aircraft and satellites. Despite unsubstantiated claims, there is no evidence that UFOs are alien spacecraft, and few scientists believe that UFOs represent anything genuinely unknown.

zodiac name given by the ancient Greeks to that zone of the heavens containing the paths of the sun, moon and the five planets then known. It was about 1° in width, and the stars contained in it were grouped into 12 signs each 3° in extent, viz. Aries, Taurus, Gemini, Cancer, Leo, Virgo, Libra, Scorpio, Sagittarius, Capricorn, Aquarius, Pisces. The modern constellations do not cover the same areas of sky as the zodiacal signs of the same name.

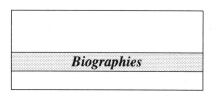

Biographies

Aristarchus of Samos 310-264 BC Greek astronomer, famed as being the first to maintain that the earth revolves round the sun.
Brahe Tycho 1546–1601. Danish astronomer who made the observations from which

Johannes Kepler proved that planets orbit the sun in ellipses. His observations of the comet of 1577 showed that it moved on an orbit among the planets, overthrowing the Greek view that comets were in the earth's atmosphere.

Copernicus Nicolaus 1473–1543. Polish astronomer. For 30 years he worked on the hypothesis that the motion of the earth was responsible for the apparent movements of the heavenly bodies, but his great work *De Revolutionibus Orbium Coelestium* was not published until the year of his death. In this work he postulated that the sun is the centre of our system, and he thus became a prime founder of modern astronomy.

Flamsteed John 1646–1719. First Astronomer Royal of England. Born near Derby, he was appointed astronomer to Charles II in 1675, and began systematic observations of the positions of the stars, moon and planets at Greenwich in the following year. His observations were posthumously published in 1725.

Galileo Galilei 1564–1642. Italian mathematician, astronomer, and physicist, born at Pisa. He developed the telescope and was the first to see the four main satellites of Jupiter, mountains and craters on the moon, and Venus's appearance going through 'phases' as would be expected if it were orbiting the sun. His observations and arguments were an unwelcome refutation of the ideas of Aristotle currently taught at the (church-run) universities, especially because they made plausible for the first time the sun-centred theory of Copernicus.

Hale George Ellery 1868–1938. US astronomer, who made pioneer studies of the sun and founded three major observatories. Born in Chicago, he invented the spectroheliograph in 1889, a device for photographing the sun at particular wavelengths. In 1897 he founded the Yerkes Observatory in Wisconsin, with a 102 cm/40 in refracting telescope, the largest refractor ever built. In 1904 he moved to Mount Wilson, California, where he discovered that sunspots are cooler areas on the sun, associated with strong magnetic fields. In 1917 he established a 2.5 m/100 in reflector on

Mount Wilson. This was the world's largest telescope until superseded in 1948 by the 5 m/200 in reflector on Mount Palomar, which was also planned by Hale before he died.

Halley Edmund 1656–1742. English astronomer. Born in London, he became friendly with Sir Isaac Newton, whose *Principia* he financed. He is remembered as having observed Halley's Comet in 1682 and for accurately predicting (in 1704) that it would reappear in 1758. He was Astronomer Royal from 1720.

Herschel Sir William 1738–1822. British astronomer. In 1781 he discovered Uranus, and later several of its satellites. During his appointment as astronomer to George III from 1782 he discovered the motion of the double stars round one another, and recorded it in his *Motion of the Solar System in Space* 1783. He constructed a 1.2 m/4 ft telescope, of 12 m/40 ft focal length, at Slough, in 1789, and discovered infra-red solar rays in 1800. He was helped in his observations by his sister *Caroline Lucretia Herschel* (1750–1848), who discovered eight comets. His son *Sir John Frederick William Herschel* (1792–1871) was also an astronomer and established an observatory near Capetown in 1834, where he discovered thousands of close double stars, clusters and nebulae, reported in 1847.

Hoyle Sir Fred 1915– . British astronomer, carried out pioneering work on the evolution of stars and the formation of the chemical elements. His work on the evolution of stars was published in *Frontiers of Astronomy* 1955. In 1957, with Geoffrey and Margaret Burbridge and William Fowler, he showed that chemical elements heavier than hydrogen and helium are built up by nuclear reactions inside stars. He has created controversy by suggesting, with Chandra Wickramasinghe, that life originates in the gas clouds of space and is delivered to the earth and planets by passing comets (*Lifecloud* 1978).

Hubble Edwin Powell 1889–1953. American astronomer, discovered the existence of other galaxies outside our own, classified them according to their shape, and discovered the expansion of the Universe. In 1925 he introduced the classification of galaxies as spirals, barred spiral and ellipticals. In 1929 he announced *Hubble's law*, i.e. that the galaxies are moving apart at a rate that increases with their distance, an observation that can be explained by the expanding Universe.

Kepler Johannes 1571–1630. German mathematician and astronomer, proved that the planets orbit the sun in ellipses, and discovered the three laws of planetary motion that bears his name. Born in Württemberg, he became assistant to Tycho Brahe in 1600 and succeeded him as Imperial Mathematician in 1601. His analysis of Tycho's observations of the planets led him to discover *Kepler's laws*, the first two of which he published in *Astronomia Nova* 1609 and the third in *Harmonices Mundi* 1619.

Lemaître Georges Edouard 1894–1966. Belgian cosmologist who put forward the Big Bang theory for the origin of the Universe. In 1927, Lemaître predicted that the entire Universe was expanding, which Hubble confirmed, and suggested that the expansion had been started by an initial explosion, the Big Bang, a theory that is now generally accepted.

Lovell Sir Bernard 1913–   . British astronomer. During World War II he worked at the Telecommunications Research establishment (1939–45), and in 1951 became professor of radio astronomy at the University of Manchester and director of Jodrell Bank Experimental Station (now Nuffield Radio Astronomy Laboratories). His books include *Radio Astronomy* 1951 and *The Exploration of Outer Space* 1961.

Oort Jan Hendrik 1900–   . Dutch astronomer, who in 1927 calculated the mass and size of our galaxy, and the sun's distance from its centre, from the observed movements of stars around the galaxy's centre. In 1944 Oort's student Hendrik van de Hulst calculated that hydrogen in space would emit radio waves at 21 cm wavelength, and in the 1950s Oort's team mapped the spiral structure of our galaxy from the radio waves given out by interstellar hydrogen. In 1950 Oort proposed that comets exist in a vast swarm, now called the **Oort Cloud**, at the edge of the solar system.

Ptolemy (Claudius Ptolemaeus) c 100–178 AD. Astronomer and geographer. A native of Egypt, he carried out observations in Alexandria, and published a Geography which was a standard source of information until the 16th century. His greatest work was known as the *Almagest*, in which he developed the theory of Aristotle that the earth is the centre of the Universe, with the sun, moon and stars revolving around it. Not until 1543 was the *Ptolemaic system* superseded by the theory of Copernicus.

Ryle Sir Martin 1918–84. British radio-astronomer, Astronomer-Royal 1972–82. At the Mullard Radio Astronomy Observatory, Cambridge, he developed the technique of sky-mapping using 'aperture synthesis', combining smaller 'dishes' to give the characteristics of one large one. His work on the distribution of radio sources in the Universe brought confirmation of the 'Big Bang theory'.

Whipple Fred Lawrence 1906–   . US astronomer, director of the Smithsonian Astrophysical Observatory 1955–73, predicted in 1949 that the nucleus of a comet is like a dirty snowball, confirmed in 1986 by space probe studies of Halley's Comet.

1903	Tsiolkovsky published the first practical paper on astronautics.
1926	Goddard launched the first liquid fuel rocket.
1937–45	Werner von Braun developed the V2 rocket.
1957	Sputnik 1 (Russian 'fellow-traveller': USSR), the first space satellite, orbited earth at a height of 229–898 km/142–558 mi in 96.2 min on 4 Oct; Sputnik 2 (USSR), was launched 3 Nov carrying a live dog 'Laika' (died on board 10 Nov).
1958	Explorer 1 (USA), the first US satellite, 31 Jan discovered Van Allen radiation belts.
1960	Tiros 1 (USA), the first weather satellite, was launched 1 Apr.
1961	Vostok 1 (USSR), first manned spaceship (Yuri Gagarin), was recovered on 12 Apr after a single orbit at a height of 175–142 km/109–88 mi in 89.1 min.
1962	Friendship 7 (USA); John Glenn was the first American in orbit round the earth on 20 Feb; Telstar (USA), a communications satellite, sent the first live television transmission between USA and Europe.
1963	Vostok 6 (USSR); Valentina Tereshkova was the first woman in space 16–19 Jun.
1966	Venera 3 (USSR), space probe, launched Nov 1965, crash-landed on Venus 1 Mar, the first man-made object to reach another planet.
1967	Soyuz 1 (USSR); Vladimir Komarov was the first man to be killed in space research when his ship crash-landed on earth on 24 Apr.
1969	Apollo-Saturn 11 (USA) was launched 16–24 Jul; Neil Armstrong was the first man to walk on the moon.
1970	Luna 17 (USSR) was launched 10 Nov; its unmanned lunar vehicle, *Lunokhod*, took photos and made soil analyses on the moon.
1971	Salyut 1 (USSR), the first orbital space station, was established 19 Apr; it was visited by the Soyuz 11 manned spacecraft.
1971–2	Mariner 9 (USA) was the first space probe to orbit another planet, when it circled Mars.
1972	Pioneer 10 (USA), earth's first starship, was launched 3 Mar; it reached Jupiter 1973; in 1983 it made its first passage of the asteroid belt, reached Neptune, and passed on into the first voyage beyond the solar system. Apollo 17 (USA) was launched Dec.
1973	Skylab 2 (USA), the first US orbital space station, was established.
1975	Apollo 18 (USA), 15–24 Jul, made a joint flight with Soyuz 19 (USSR), in a link-up in space.
1976	Viking 1 (USA), unmanned spacecraft, launched 20 Aug 1975; reached Mars, the spacecraft lander touching down on 20 Jul; Viking 2 (USA) was launched 9 Sept 1975, its lander touching down on Mars 3 Sept 1976.
1977	Voyager 1 (USA), launched 5 Sept, and Voyager 2 (USA), launched 20 Aug, both unmanned spacecraft, reached Jupiter Jan/Jul 1979, Uranus 1986, and Neptune 1989.
1978	Pioneer Venus 1 (USA) was launched 20 May and Pioneer Venus 2 (USA) on 20 Aug; both reached Venus Dec.

1979	Ariane (European Space Agency satellite launcher) was launched.
1981	Space Shuttle (USA), first re-usable manned spacecraft, was launched 12 Apr.
1982	Venera 13 and 14 (USSR) landed on Venus; soil samples indicated that the surface is similar to Earth's volcanic rock.
1985	Two Vega probes (USSR) released balloons for the first time into the atmosphere of another planet (Venus).
1986	Space Shuttle (USA) exploded shortly after launch killing all seven crew members. The space probe *Giotto* showed Halley's comet to be one of the darkest objects ever detected in the solar system, with an irregular nucleus 14.5 km/9 mi $\times$ 3km/2 mi. Voyager 2 reached Uranus and found it to have six more moons than was previously thought, making 12 known moons in all.
1988	US Shuttle programme resumed with launch of *Discovery*. Soviet Shuttle *Buran* launched. Soviets Musa Manarov and Vladimir Titov set space endurance record after spending 365 days 59 minutes in space.
1989	Unmanned spacecraft launched by the space shuttle *Atlantis* which will photograph Venus at close distance in 1990; it will detect any feature larger than a football pitch, and map 90% of the surface. US Magellen mission to Venus launched. Voyager 2 reached Neptune.

Computing

Computing, or computer studies, is the science of the design and application of machines that can handle and manipulate data, which are generically known as computers. The term computer is derived from the verb 'compute', which means to reckon or calculate, and the first of these machines were built specifically to perform calculations for gun-firing and navigation tables. The early machines were all mechanically operated but modern computers are all electronic and are used mainly for commercial applications such as word processing, handling payrolls and bank balances, controlling industrial robots, and monitoring the functioning of cars, space vehicles and medical equipment. Current research is concerned with developing computers that can handle data faster and more 'intelligently' than before.

The five parts of this section comprise an overview of *How Computers Work,* describing the basic components and functioning of an electronic computer and highlighting the four main types of modern computer; a more detailed description of the *Main Parts of a Computer* as used with a typical business machine; a definition of some *Basic Computer Terms* that include various technical words relating to the electronics of computing; a *Table of Programming Languages* that compares the nature and uses of eight common types of coding used to instruct a computer what to do with the data supplied; and a *Chronology of Computing* that starts with the development of the first machines capable of handling complex mathematical calculations and leads to the creation of supercomputers.

How Computers Work

Background the earliest computing device was the abacus used by the ancient Greeks and Romans and still in use in the East today. There are mechanical devices using sliding scales, similar to the slide-rule, which date back almost two millennia, for performing various kinds of calculation, usually as an aid to navigation. In 1642, the French philosopher-mathematician Blaise Pascal built a mechanical adding machine, and in 1671, German philosopher-mathematician Gottfried Leibniz built a machine to perform multiplication. In 1835, British mathematician Charles Babbage designed the first mechanical computer, the analytical engine. The work of another British mathematician Alan Turing, in the 1930s, marked the next major milestone. He developed the mathematical theory of computation and, in particular, showed how a machine could be conceived which could perform any computation (the so-called Turing Machine). The digital computer is the direct descendant of these ideas. In the 1940s, American mathematician John von Neumann developed the basic design for today's electronic computers. Finally, with the development of the transistor in 1952 and the subsequent microelectronics revolution, the Computer Age was started.

Basic system a computer is a collection of various components. At the heart is the CPU (central processing unit), which performs all the computations. This is supported by memory which holds the current program and data, and 'logic arrays' which help move information around the system. A main power supply is needed and, in the case of a mini- or mainframe computer, a cooling system. The computer's 'device driver' circuits control the peripheral devices, or add-ons, which can be attached.

These will normally be keyboards and VDU (visual display unit) screens for user input and output, disc drive units for mass memory storage, and printers for printed output.

A computer can only carry out tasks as commanded by the programmer, who translates instructions written in everyday language into a program that is a coded form matching the electronic coding within the computer's internal machinery. The program and data to be manipulated – text, figures, images, or sounds - are input into the computer which then processes the data and outputs the results. The results can be printed out or displayed on a VDU, or stored in a memory unit for subsequent manipulation. Whatever the task, a computer can function in only one of four ways: input/output operations, arithmetical operations (addition, subtraction, multiplication, and division), logic and comparison operations (for example, is the value of A equal to, less than, or greater than B), and movement of data to, from, and within the central memory of the machine. The programmer's role is to devise a set of instructions, an *algorithm*, that utilizes these four functions in a combination appropriate to the job in question.

Types there are four 'sizes' corresponding roughly to their memory capacity and processing speed. *Microcomputers* are the smallest and the most common and are used in small businesses, at home and in schools. They are usually single-user machines and are often referred to as home computers. *Minicomputers*, also known as personal computers, are generally larger and will be found in medium-sized businesses and university departments. They may support from a dozen to 30 or so users at once. *Mainframes*, which can often service several hundreds of users all at once are found in large organizations such as national companies and government departments. *Supercomputers* are the most powerful of all. There are very few in the world and are mostly used for special highly complex scientific tasks, such as analysing the results of nuclear physics experiments and weather forecasting.

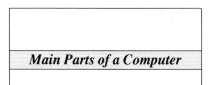

Main Parts of a Computer

CPU (central processing unit) is the part of the computer that reads the program, fetches data, performs operations on the data in accordance with the program, and outputs its results. It is composed of five main elements: the *ALU* (arithmetic and logic unit), which contains the basic operations (its 'instruction set') and applies them to data; a *program counter* to keep track of the program being executed; a number of *registers* for storing intermediate results and data awaiting processing; (normally) an *electronic clock* which emits regular pulses that co-ordinate the CPU's activities; a *control unit* for organizing the processing.

graphics tablet in computing, also known as a bit pad, this is an input device consisting of a pressure-sensitive tablet on which marks can be made with a stylus. The position of any mark is automatically identified and communicated to a computer for interpretation. A graphics tablet is often used with a form overlaid for users to tick boxes in positions that each relate to specific registers in the computer, but some recent development in handwriting recognition may increase its versatility in the future.

joystick in computing, an input device, similar to a joystick used to control the flight of an aircraft, which signals to a computer the direction and extent of displacement of a handheld lever. Often used to control the movement of a *cursor* (marker) on a VDU (computer screen), joysticks are most popular for moving predetermined specific shapes, or icons (such as space invader characters) in computer games. They allow fast and direct input.

keyboard in computing, an input device resembling a typewriter keyboard, which sends signals to a computer indicating which keys have been depressed. There are many variations on the layout of keys and the labelling of keys for different purposes. Extra numeric keys may be added, as can special-purpose function keys, such as LOAD, SAVE, PRINT, whose effect can be defined by programs in the computer.

light pen in computing, an input device resembling an ordinary pen, used to indicate or mark locations on a computer screen. At its tip, the pen has a photoreceptor which emits signals as light from the screen passes beneath it. From the timing of this signal and a grid-like representation of the screen in the computer's memory, a computer program can calculate the position of the light pen. With certain computer aided design (CAD) programs, the light pen can be used to instruct the computer to change the shape, size, position and colours of sections of a screen image.

memory in computing, any device, collection of devices or components in a computer system used to store data and programs either permanently or temporarily. There are two main types: internal memory and external memory. *Internal memory* is either read-only (stored in ROM, PROM and EPROM chips) or it is read/write (stored in RAM chips). Read-only memory stores information that must be constantly available or accessed very quickly, and that is unlikely to need to be changed. It is non-volatile, that is, it is not lost when the computer is switched off. Read/write memory is volatile; it stores programs and data temporarily only while the computer is switched on. *External memory* is permanent, non-volatile memory employing storage devices which include magnetic discs (such as floppy discs, hard discs), magnetic tape (e.g. tape streamers, cassettes), laser discs including CD-ROM (compact discs) and bubble memories. By rapidly swapping blocks of information in and out of internal memory from external memory, the limited size of a computer's memory may artificially be increased. To the user, this virtual memory, as it is called, gives the impression of a very large internal memory. All computer memory stores information in binary code (using the binary number system). Memory capacity is measured in K (kilobyte).

modem (*MO*dulator-*DEM*odulator) an electronic device for converting digital (discrete) signals from a computer into analogue (continuous) signals on a telecommunications network and vice versa.

mouse in computing, an input device, used to control a pointer on a computer screen. Moving the mouse across a desk-top produces corresponding movement in the pointer. A mouse normally has one or more controlling buttons on its 'head' to instruct the computer in a specific way when the pointer is superimposed on a menu option on the screen, and its connecting wire is its 'tail'.

plotter an output device that draws pictures under computer control. Flatbed plotters move a pen up and down across a flat drawing surface while roller plotters roll the drawing paper past the pen as it moves from side to side.

printed circuit board (*PCB*) an electrical circuit created by laying (printing) 'tracks' of a conductor such as copper onto one or both sides of an insulating board. Components such as integrated circuits (chips), resistors and capacitors can be soldered onto the surface of the board (surface-mounted) or, more commonly, attached by inserting their connecting pins or wires into holes drilled in the board.

printer in computing, an output device for producing printed copy of textual, numeric and graphical data. Types include the *daisywheel*, which produces good quality text but no graphics; the *dot matrix*, which creates character patterns from a matrix of small dots, producing text and graphics, but of indifferent quality; and the *laser printer*, which reproduces high quality text and graphics.

touch screen an input device allowing the user to communicate with the computer by pointing a finger at a display screen. Typically, the screen detects the finger either through a sensitive membrane or when the finger interrupts a grid of light beams crossing the screen surface. Software in the device then calculates

the centre-point of the finger and communicates the co-ordinates (grid reference) to the computer.

VDU (visual display unit) an electronic output device for displaying the data processed by a computer on a screen. The oldest and the most popular type is the *cathode ray tube* (*CRT*), which uses essentially the same technology as a television screen. Plasma display technology is similar to that of domestic fluorescent light tubes; points of luminous gas are created, under the computer's control, from which images can be constructed. *Liquid crystal display* (*LCD*) relies on a property of certain substances to change the polarity of light and to realign their molecules in the presence of an electric field. The electrodes that govern the process are shaped into segments of

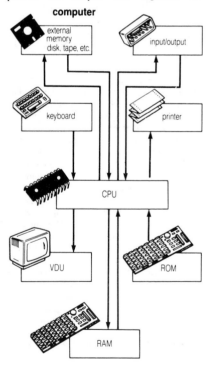

350

characters and numbers from which a computer-controlled display is made up.

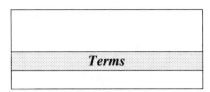

address in a computer memory, a number indicating a specific location. At each address, a single piece of data can be stored. For microcomputers, this normally amounts to one byte (enough to represent a single character such as a letter or number). The maximum capacity of a computer memory depends on how many memory addresses it can have. This is normally measured in units of 1,024 bytes (known as kilobytes, or Kb or K).

assembly code computer programming language closely related to the internal codes of the machine itself. It consists chiefly of a set of short mnemonics which are translated, by a program called an assembler, into machine code for the computer's CPU (central processing unit) to follow directly. In assembly language for example, JMP means 'jump' and LDA is 'load accumulator'. Used by programmers who need to write very fast or efficient programs.

binary number system or code a system of numbers to base two using combinations of the two digits 1 and 0. The value of any position in a binary number increases by powers of 2 (doubles) with each move from right to left (1, 2, 4, 8, 16, etc). For example, 1011 in the binary number system means $(1 \times 8) + (0 \times 4) + (1 \times 2) + (1 \times 1)$, which adds up to 11 in the everyday, decimal system (which uses successive powers of 10). Binary numbers play a key role in modern digital computers where they form the basis of the internal coding of information, the values of bits (short for 'binary digits') being represented as on/off (1 and 0) states of switches and high/low voltages in circuits.

BINARY NUMBER SYSTEM

binary (base 2)	octal (base 8)	decimal (base 10)	hexadecimal (base 16)
0	0	0	0
1	1	1	1
10	2	2	2
11	3	3	3
100	4	4	4
110	5	5	5
110	6	6	6
111	7	7	7
1000	10	8	8
1001	11	9	9
1010	12	10	A
1011	13	11	B
1100	14	12	C
1101	15	13	D
1110	16	14	E
1111	17	15	F
10000	20	16	10
1111111	377	255	FF
11111010001	3721	2001	7D1

bit a binary digit or place in a binary number.

byte in computing, a sequence or string of usually eight bits (binary digits) constituting a unit of memory or a character (a letter, number or symbol). Strictly it is a subdivision of a 'word' (the number of bits of information that a computer can process in a single operation, perhaps 32 bits in a minicomputer and 64 in a mainframe). A byte is a subdivision of this and is the number of bits needed to represent a single character (eight bits in extended ASCII, the American Standard Code for Information Interchange). Also now refers to a single memory location; computer memory size is measured in thousands of bytes (kilobytes or Kb) or millions of bytes (megabytes or Mb).

database in computing, a structured, centralized collection of data, organized to allow access by several or many different user programs. The data is held in files and arranged into hierarchies, networks, or relations – the three main types of database structure. For

351

example, a telephone directory stored as a database might allow all the people whose names start with the letter B to be selected by one program, and all those living in London by another. A database management system (DBMS) program ensures that the integrity of the data is maintained by controlling the degree of access of the application programs using the data. Databases are normally used by large organizations with mainframes or minicomputers. A collection of databases is known as a databank.

digital in electronics and computing, a term meaning 'coded as numbers'. A digital computer operates on symbols which are internally coded as binary numbers. A *digital display* shows discrete values as numbers (as opposed to an analogue signal such as the continuous sweep of a pointer on a dial). *Digital recording* is a technique whereby the pressure of sound waves is sampled more than 30000 times a second and the values recorded as numbers which, during playback, are re-converted to sound waves. This gives very high quality reproduction. *Digital data transmission* uses a similar technique, converting all signals (whether pictures, sounds or words) into numeric (normally binary) codes before transmission and then re-converting them on receipt. This virtually eliminates any distortion or degradation of the signal during transmission, storage or processing. *Digital electronics* is the technology which underlies the techniques described above.

fifth generation computer an anticipated new type of computer based on emerging microelectronic technologies. The basis will be very fast computing machinery, with many processors working in parallel. These will be possible because of very large-scale integration (VSLI) which can put many more circuits onto a silicon chip. Such computers will run advanced 'intelligent' programs. The other four generations are usually said to be:

First Generation (1943–1959): based on valves and wire circuits

Second Generation (1959–1964): based on transistors and printed circuits

Third Generation (1964–72): first machines to use integrated circuits

Fourth Generation (from 1972): based on large scale integration (LSI) of circuits.

The Fifth-generation Project is a 10–year research programme begun in Japan in 1982 to develop the new type of computer systems. It has been a spur for several other national and international programmes including *ESPRIT* in Europe and *Alvey* in the UK.

machine code in computing, a binary (two-state) code in which computer programs are expressed as a prerequisite to being executed by the computer. Once, all computer programs had to be written in machine code. Later, assembler (or assembly code) and, finally, high-level programming languages were developed which are easier for people to use and can automatically be translated into machine code prior to execution.

microprocessor a computer's central processing unit (CPU) contained on a single integrated circuit. The appearance of the first microprocessors in 1971 heralded the introduction of the microcomputer, a small, cheap computer built around a microprocessor. The pocket calculator is also a product of microprocessor technology.

operating system (*OS*) in computing, a program that controls the routine operations of a computer; it is sometimes called DOS (disc operating system) when the program is on disc. The operating system looks after the computer's filing system and handles the input and output of data and programs between the processor unit, external memory devices (such as disc drives) and input and output devices such as keyboard and visual display unit (VDU). Many makes of computer have their own operating system, but some are accepted standards. These include CP/M (by Digital Research) and MSDOS (by Microsoft) for microcomputers; and Unix (by Bell Laboratories) for minicomputers.

RISC acronym for Reduced Instruction Set Chip. A kind of computer processor on a single silicon chip offering speed and size improvements over current chips. Computers based on

RISC chips have just become commercially available and considerably outperform their predecessors.

robot any computer-controlled machine that can be taught or programmed to do work. Records of mechanical people and animals having been built go back more than 2000 years, bolstered by the fabulous creations of popular myth. However, it is only since the advent of the computer that the true robot has emerged. The most common types are mechanical 'arms'. Fixed to the floor or a workbench, they perform functions such as paint spraying or assembling parts in factories.

silicon chip popular term for an integrated circuit with microscopically small components on a piece of silicon crystal only a few millimetres square. This tiny circuit, often with upwards of a million components, is mounted in a rectangular plastic package with metal pins down the long sides so that they can be connected to printed circuit boards for inclusion in electronic devices such as computers, calculators, televisions, car dashboards and domestic appliances.

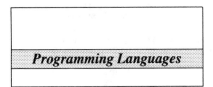

Programming Languages

programming language in computing, a special notation in which instructions for controlling a computer are written. Programming languages are designed to be easy for users to write and read but must be capable of being mechanically translated (by a compiler or interpreter) into the machine code that the computer can execute. The table overleaf shows eight different ways of instructing a computer to find the total of the numbers 1 to 10 each using a different language.

programming in computing, the activity of writing statements in a programming language for the control of a computer. Applications programming is for 'end user' programs, such as word-processing packages. Systems programming is for operating systems and the like, which are concerned more with the internal workings of the computer.

There are several programming styles. *Procedural programming*, in which programs are written as lists of instructions which the computer obeys in sequence, is by far the most popular. It is the 'natural' style, closely matching the computer's own sequential operation. Procedural programming languages, such as BASIC and COBOL, all support three basic constructs: sequence (executing statements in the list in strict order); iteration (looping through parts of the list); selection (jumping to different parts of the list when different conditions are met). *Declarative programming*, such as in the programming language Prolog, does not describe how to solve a problem, but rather describes the logical structure of the problem. Running such a program is more like proving an assertion than following a procedure. *Functional programming* is a style based largely on the definition of functions. There are very few functional programming languages, Hope and ML being the most widely used, though many more conventional languages (for example C) make extensive use of functions. *Object oriented programming*, the most recently developed style, involves viewing a program as a collection of objects which behave in certain ways when they are passed certain 'messages', for example an object might be defined to represent a table of figures which will be displayed on screen when a 'display' message is received.

Today most programming is done at a computer terminal using special-purpose program-editing software, rather like word processing. In the past, the process was more laborious, with programs having to be coded as holes punched into cards or paper tape.

PROGRAMMING LANGUAGES

Language	Main Uses	Description	Examples
assembler	Jobs needing speed and good control of the machine	fast and efficient but very hard to debug once written	``` LD B,AH SUB A SUMJ: ADD A,(B) DEC B JR NZ,SUMJ JP [display routine] ```
BASIC	in education and at home	easy to learn but lacks many of the features of other languages	``` 10 SUM = 0 20 FOR J = 1 TO 10 30 SUM = SUM + J 40 NEXT J 50 PRINT SUM ```
C	systems programming	fast and efficient; has now largely replaced assembler for such jobs	``` sum = 0; for (j=1; j=10; j++) sum = sum +j; printf("%d/n", sum); ```
COBOL	business programming	oriented strongly to commercial work; used almost exclusively for it	``` SET SUM TO 0. PERFORM SUM-J VARYING J FROM 1 BY 1 UNTIL J = 10. DISPLAY SUM. SUM=J. COMPUTE SUM=SUM+J. ```
Fortran	scientific programming	at first, lacking in features of other languages; since 1977 has been much improved	``` SUM = 0 DO 10 J = 1, 10 WRITE (1,100) SUM 10 SUM = SUM + J 100 FORMAT (1X, 16) ```
Lisp	artificial intelligence systems and research programming	a list processing language with many functional features. The code can look obscure	``` (SETQ SUM 0) (REPEAT ((UNTIL GREATERP J 10)) (PRINT SUM)) (SETQ SUM (PLUS SUM J)) (SETQ J (ADD1 J))) ```
Pascal	education, business, systems and scientific programming	a good all-rounder; easy to learn, with a set of features	``` sum : = 0; for j : = 1 to 10 do sum : = sum + j; writeln(sum); ```
Prolog	artificial intelligence systems and research programming	the first logic programming language and the only one in common use	``` sum—j(11, SUM) :- write (SUM),nl. sum—j(J, SUM) :- SUM1 is SUM + J, J1 is J + 1, sum—j(J1, SUM1). [call using sum—j (1, 0).] ```

1614	John Napier invented logarithms.
1625	William Oughtred (1575–1660) invented the slide rule.
1623	Wilhelm Schickard (1592–1635) invented the first mechanical calculating machine.
1645	Blaise Pascal produced a calculator.
1672–74	Leibniz built his first calculator, the Stepped Reckoner.
1801	Joseph-Marie Jacquard developed an automatic loom controlled by punched cards.
1820	First mass-produced calculator (the Arithmometer, by Charles Thomas de Colmar 1785–1870).
1822	Charles Babbage's first model for the Difference Engine.
1830s	Babbage created the first design for the Analytical Engine.
1890	Herman Hollerith developed the punched card ruler for the USA census.
1936	Alan Turing published the mathematical theory of computing.
1938	Konrad Zuse constructed the first binary calculator, using Boolean algebra.
1943	'Colossus' electronic code-breaker developed at Bletchley Park, England; Harvard University Mark I or Automatic Sequence-Controlled Calculator (partly financed by IBM): the first program-controlled calculator.
1945	ENIAC (Electronic Numerator, Integrator, Analyser and Computer) completed at the University of Pennsylvania.
1948	Manchester University (England) Mark I, completed: first stored-program computer.
1951	Ferranti Mark I: the first commercially produced computer; 'Whirlwind', the first real-time computer, built for the USA air defence system; investigation of transistor.
1952	EDVAC (Electronic Discrete Variable Computer) completed at the Institute for Advanced Study, Princeton, USA (by von Neumann and others).
1953	Magnetic core memory developed.
1957	FORTRAN, the first high-level computer language, developed by IBM.
1958	The first integrated circuit.
1963	The first minicomputer built by Digital Equipment (DEC): the PDP-8; the first electronic calculator (Bell Punch Company).
1964	IBM System/360: the first compatible family of computers.
1965	The first supercomputer: the Control Data CD6600.
1970	The first microprocessor: the Intel 4004.
1974	CLIP-4, the first computer with a parallel architecture.
1975	The first personal computer: Altair 8800.
1981	The Xerox Start system, the first WIMP system (Windows, Icons, Menus and Pointing devices).
1985	The Inmos T414 Transputer: the first 'off the shelf' ◊RISC microprocessor for building parallel computers.
1988	First optical microchip, which uses light instead of electricity, developed.
1989	Wafer-scale (the size of a beer-mat) silicon memory chips, able to store 200 million characters, launched.

Earth Sciences

Earth Sciences has emerged in recent years as an enlightened synthesis of several traditional disciplines such as geology, meteorology, oceanography, geophysics and geochemistry. Its importance is increasingly being recognized in that, like its biological counterpart ecology, the scientific study of our planet's structure and its past will hold the key to how we affect its future. Humans are in an ever-increasing position of power over global aspects of nature, and in order to ensure our future we must learn to preserve and conserve the earth and use its resources in a sustainable way. The mining and extraction of metals and minerals and gems, the prediction of weather and earthquakes, the pollution of the atmosphere and the 'greenhouse effect', and the gigantic forces that shaped the world we live in, all fall within the scope of Earth Sciences.

This section contains a look back at *Ice Ages*, and a digest of the exciting recently-developed concepts of continental drift and plate tectonics – *The Changing Earth*. There are explanations of *Geological Terms*, the workings of *Atmosphere and Weather*, and *Mapping Earth's Surface*. In addition there are definitions of *Geological Features*, plus a brief look at our planet's *Mineral Wealth*. Complementary material, from the viewpoint of human wants, can be found in the section on Resources under the general heading Society.

Ice Ages

sheet spread over N Europe, reaching Ireland and the Atlantic, leaving its remains as far south as Switzerland. Formerly there were thought to have been only three or four such periods, but recent research has shown about 20 major incidences. For example, ocean-bed cores record the absence or presence in their various layers of such cold-loving small marine animals as radiolaria, which indicate a fall in

geological time chart

Millions of years ago	Epoch	Period	Era	Eon
0.01 1.8	Holocene Pleistocene	Quaternary	Cenezoic	Phanerozoic
5 25 38 55 65	Pliocene Miocene Oligocene Eocene Palaeocene	Tertiary		
144 213 248		Cretaceous Jurassic Triassic	Mesozoic	
286 360 408 438 505 590		Permian Carboniferous Devonian Silurian Ordovician Cambrian	Palaeozoic	
2500		Proterozioic	Precambrian	
4600		Archaean		

Ice Age any period of glaciation occurring in the earth's history but most commonly in the Pleistocene period, immediately preceding historic times. However, other ice ages have occurred throughout geological time. Between ice ages came interglacials, when temperatures rose, ice melted and sea levels rose. Europe and America underwent glacial conditions similar to those of the polar regions today. On the North American continent the glaciers reached as far south as the Great Lakes and the ice

ocean temperature at regular intervals.

The occurrence of an ice age is governed by a combination of factors (the Milankovitch hypothesis): (1) the earth's change of attitude in relation to the sun, that is, the way it tilts in a 41,000 year cycle and at the same time wobbles on its axis in a 22,000–year cycle, making the time of its closest approach to the sun come at different seasons; and (2) the 92,000–year cycle of eccentricity in its orbit round the sun, changing from an elliptical to a near circular orbit, the severest period of an ice age coinciding with the approach to circularity. According to calculations, the ice reached a maximum in the present cycle 6000 years ago. There is a possibility that the ice age is not yet over. It will probably reach another maximum in 60,000 years.

MAJOR ICE AGES

Name (European/US)	date (years ago)
Pleistocene:	
Riss and Wurm/Wisconsin	80,000–10,000
Mindel/Illinoian	550,000–400,000
Gunz/Kansan	900,000–700,000
Danube/Nebraskan	1.7–1.3 million
Permo-Carboniferous	330–250 million
Ordovician	440–430 million
Verangian	615–570 million
Sturtian	820–770 million
Gnejso	940–880 million
Huronian	2,700–1,800 million

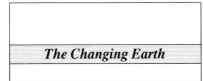

The Changing Earth

crust the outermost part of the structure of the earth, consisting of two distinct parts. The *oceanic* crust is on average about 10 km/6.2 mi thick and is fairly even in composition. Beneath a surface sediment lies a layer of basalt, then a layer of gabbro. The composition of the whole oceanic crust shows a high proportion of *si*licon and *ma*gnesium and is given the name *sima* by geologists.

In contrast the *continental* crust is extremely complex. It varies in thickness between about 40 and 70 km/25 and 44 mi, being deeper beneath mountain ranges. It consists of a great many rock types, including a surface layer of sedimentary and volcanic rocks overlying a zone of metamorphic rocks built on a thick layer of granodiorite. *Si*licon and *al*uminium

dominate the composition and the term *sial* is given to continental crustal material. Because of the movements of plate tectonics, the ocean crust is nowhere older than about 200 million years. However parts of the continental crust are more than ten times that age.

mantle the section of the earth's structure between the crust and the core. It is separated from the former by the Mohorovičić discontinuity, and from the latter by the Gutenberg discontinuity. Mantle material is thought to consist of silicates such as olivine and spinel. The patterns of seismic waves passing through it show its lower layers to be solid. However from 75 km to 250 km/45 to 155 mi in depth is a zone through which seismic waves pass more slowly (the 'low velocity zone'). The inference is that materials in this zone are close to their melting points and they are partly molten. The low velocity zone is probably the asthenosphere, on which ride the solid mantle and the crust above it, constituting the rigid plates of the lithosphere.

core the innermost part of the structure of the earth. It is divided into an inner core, the upper boundary of which is 1600 km/940 mi from the centre, and an outer core, 1820 km/1060 mi thick. Both parts are thought to be made of nickel and iron, with the inner core being solid and the outer core being liquid. The temperature may be 3,000°C. These hypotheses are based on seismology (the observation of the paths of earthquake and other vibrational waves through the earth), and calculations of the earth's density.

plate tectonics the concept in earth sciences that attributes continental drift and seafloor spreading to the continual formation and destruction of huge curved 'plates' making up the crust, the outermost layer of the earth. Convection currents within the earth's mantle produce upwellings of new material along lines at the earth's surface. These lines are the oceanic ridges. The new material forms plates at the surface and these move away from the oceanic ridges. When two plates meet, one rises over the other and the lower is absorbed back into the mantle. These 'subduction zones' occur in ocean trenches. The continents take little part in the generation and destruction of plate material, being made of a lighter substance, and they are carried passively here and there on the moving plates. The concept was first formulated in the mid-1960s, as a modification of Alfred Wegener's early ideas of continental drift, and has gained widespread acceptance amongst earth scientists.

seafloor spreading the growth of the ocean crust outwards (sideways) from oceanic ridges. It was first detected by British geophysicists Vine and Matthews in 1963, when they noted that the floor of the Atlantic ocean was made of rocks that were arranged in strips, each strip being magnetized either normally or reversely (due to changes in the earth's polarity when the North Pole becomes the South Pole and vice versa, termed magnetic reversal). These strips were parallel to one another and to the oceanic ridge. The inference was that each strip was formed at some stage in geological time when the magnetic field was polarized in a certain way. Confirmation came when sediments were discovered to be deeper further away from the oceanic ridge, because they had been in existence longer and had more time to accumulate. Nowadays the concept of seafloor spreading has been incorporated into plate tectonics.

ocean ridge the seabed topographic feature that indicates the presence of a constructive plate margin, where the giant curved plates that make up the earth's surface are formed. Such a ridge can rise many thousands of metres above the surrounding abyssal plain. Such ridges usually have rift valleys along their crests, indicating where the flanks are being pulled apart by the growth of the lithospheric plates beneath. The crests, being made of new rocks, are usually quite free of sediment, while increasing depths of sediment are found with increasing distances down the flanks.

ocean trench the seabed topographic feature that indicates the presence of a destructive plate margin, where the giant curved plates that make up the earth's surface are destroyed. The under-riding (subduction) of one plate beneath an adjacent one means that the bed of

the ocean is dragged downwards. Oceanic trenches are found around the edge of the Pacific Ocean and the north-east Indian Ocean, with minor ones in the Caribbean and near the Falkland Islands. They represent the deepest parts of the ocean floor, the deepest being the Marianas Trench with a depth of 11,022 m/36,160 ft.

rift valley a valley formed by the subsidence of a block of the earth's crust between two or more parallel faults. Rift valleys are usually steep-sided and form where the crust is being pulled apart, as at oceanic ridges, or in the Great Rift Valley that runs roughly north–south in East Africa.

continental drift theory in geology first

continental drift

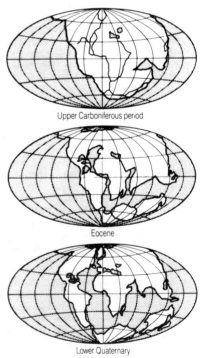

Upper Carboniferous period

Eocene

Lower Quaternary

proposed by Alfred Wegener (German meteorologist and geophysicist 1880–1930) that the earth consisted some 200 million years ago of a single large continent, which he called ***Pangaea,*** and which subsequently broke apart to form the continents as we know them today. The theory of plate tectonics has provided a convincing explanation of how such vast movement may have occurred.

seismology the study of earthquakes and how their shock waves travel through the earth. By examining the global pattern of waves produced by an earthquake, seismologists can deduce the nature of the materials through which they have passed. This leads to an understanding of the earth's internal structure. On a smaller scale artificial earthquake

waves, generated by explosions or mechanical vibrators, can be used to search for subsurface features in, for example, oil or mineral exploration.

tremor a small-intensity earthquake.

earthquake a shaking or convulsion of the earth's surface, the scientific study of which is called seismology. Earthquakes result from a build-up of stresses within rocks until strained to fracturing point. Most occur along faults (fractures or breaks) in the earth's strata. These tectonic earthquakes are the greatest and most wide-spread in their effects. The great majority are under the sea. The magnitude of an earthquake is measured on the Richter scale. The point at which an earth-

earthquake belts

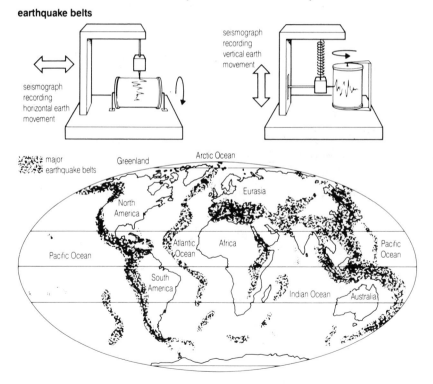

quake originates is the *seismic focus*. The point on earth's surface directly above this is the *epicentre* . The possibility of prediction is being investigated by measurement of underground pressure waves and the study of such phenomena as the change of gases in the crust, the level of water in wells and the behaviour of animals. The possibility of earthquake prevention is remote.

epicentre the point on the earth's surface immediately above the focus of an earthquake. Most damage usually takes place at an earthquake's epicentre. It is also used to refer to a point directly above or below a nuclear explosion ('ground zero').

tidal wave a misleading name for a tsunami.

tsunami a giant wave generated by an undersea earthquake or other disturbance. In the open ocean it may take the form of several successive waves, travelling at tens of kilometres per hour but with an amplitude of only a metre or so, hence usually unnoticed by ships at sea. In the coastal shallows, however, the tsunami slows down and increases in height, producing a towering wave tens of metres high that can sweep far inland with great loss of life and property. Before each wave there may be a sudden unexpected withdrawal of water from the coast. Tsunami is a Japanese word meaning 'harbour wave'. A common term for the phenomenon is, misleadingly, a 'tidal wave'.

Mercalli scale the scale used to measure the *intensity* of an earthquake. (It differs from the Richter scale in that the latter measures *magnitude*.) Intensity is a subjective value, based on observed phenomena, and varies from place to place with the same earthquake. It was named after the Italian seismologist Giuseppe Mercalli (1850–1914).

Richter scale a scale of the *magnitude* of an earthquake. (Magnitude differs from the intensity which is measured by the Mercalli scale.) The magnitude is a function of the total amount of energy released, and each point on the Richter scale represents a ten-fold increase in energy over the previous point. The scale is named after its originator, the American seismologist Charles Richter (1900–85).

MERCALLI SCALE

Intensity value	Desription
I	only detected by instrument
II	felt by people resting
III	felt indoors; hanging objects swing; feels like passing traffic
IV	feels like passing heavy traffic; standing cars rock; windows, dishes and doors rattle; wooden frames creak
V	felt outdoors; sleepers woken; liquids spill; doors swing
VI	felt by everybody; people stagger; windows break; trees and bushes rustle; weak plaster cracks
VII	difficult to stand upright; noticed by vehicle drivers; plaster, loose bricks, tiles and chimneys fall; bells ring
VIII	car steering affected; some collapse of masonry; chimney stacks and towers fall; branches break from trees; cracks in wet ground
IX	general panic; serious damage to buildings; underground pipes break; cracks and subsidence in ground
X	most buildings destroyed; landslides; water thrown out of canals
XI	rails bent; underground pipes totally destroyed
XII	damage nearly total; rocks displaced; objects thrown into air

RICHTER SCALE

Magnitude value	Relative amount of energy released	Notable examples
1		
2		
3		
4	1	Carlisle, 1979 (a significant one for Britain)
5	30	San Francisco
6	100	San Fernando, 1971
7	30,000	Chimbote
8	1,000,000	Tangsham, 1976
		San Francisco, 1906
		Lisbon, 1755 Alaska, 1964

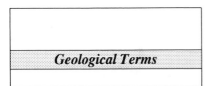

Geological Terms

geology the science of the earth, its origin, composition, structure, and history. It is divided into several branches: mineralogy deals with the minerals of the earth: petrology deals with rocks; stratigraphy deals with the deposition of successive beds of sedimentary rocks; palaeontology deals with fossils; and tectonics deals with the deformation and movement of the earth's crust.

involves the investigation of sedimentary structures to determine ancient geographies and environments, and the study of fossils for identifying and dating particular beds.

tectonics the study of the movements of the rocks. On a small scale, tectonics involves the formation of folds and faults. On the large scale it deals with the movements of vast regions of the earth's surface (plate tectonics).

uniformitarianism the principle that 'the present is the key to the past'. In other words, the processes that can be seen operating at the earth's surface today are the same as those that have operated throughout geological time. For example, desert sandstone rocks containing sand-dune formations formed in the past under conditions similar to those operating in pres-

THE MAJOR BRANCHES

'Hard rock' geology	petrology - igneous and metamorphic rocks
	mineralogy - minerals
	geochemistry - matter
	geophysics - energy
'Soft rock' geology	petrology - sedimentary rocks
	palaeontology - fossils
	stratigraphy - dating and sequence of beds (strata)
	sedimentology - deposition of sediments
Structural geology	the structures of rock
Geormorphology	landscapes, their formation and destruction

petrology the study of rocks, their mineral composition and their origins.

stratigraphy the sequence of formation of layers or beds (strata) in sedimentary rocks, and the conditions under which they formed. It

ent-day deserts. The principle was formulated by pioneer geologist James Hutton.

igneous rock a rock formed from cooling magma or lava, and solidifying from a molten state. Igneous rocks are classified according to

363

their feldspar character, grain size, texture and chemical composition.

portation). There are two forms - chemical and physical. Chemical erosion involves the altera

IGNEOUS ROCKS

Particle size

Oxygen content	Coarse (plutonic)	Medium	Fine (volcanic)
less than 45%	peridotite		
(ultrabasic)	kimberlite		
45-52%	gabbro	dolerite	basalt
(basic)			
52-66%	diorite		andesite
(intermediate)	seyenite		trachyte
more than 66%	granite		chyolite
(acid)			

metamorphic rock a rock altered in structure and composition by pressure and heat although it does not melt (in which case it would be an igneous rock).

tion of the mineral component of the rock, by means of rainwater or the substances dissolved in it, and its subsequent movement. The decay of granite by the conversion of its feldspar

METAMORPHIC ROCKS

Main primary material (before metamorphisis)

typical depth and temperature of formation		shale with several minerals	sandstone with only quartz	limestone with only calcite
15 km	300°C	slate	quartzite	marble
20 km	400°C	schist		
25 km	500°C	gneiss		
30 km	600°C	hornfels	quartzite	marble

sedimentary rock a rock formed by the accumulation and cementation of particles, usually in water and under gravity.

bed in geology, the unitary 'building block' of sedimentary rock. A bed consists of a simple layer of rock, often separated above and below from other beds by well defined partings called bedding planes. It can be from a millimetre to many metres thick, and can extend over any area. Also used to indicate the floor beneath a body of water (lake bed) and a layer formed by a fall of particles (lava bed).

erosion the processes whereby the rocks and soil of the earth's surface are loosened, worn away and transported (the often confused term, weathering, does not involve trans-

minerals into china clay by carbonic acid in rainwater, and the dissolving of limestone in caves and potholes, are examples. Physical erosion involves the breakdown and transportation of exposed rocks by physical forces. The shattering of cliff-faces in mountainous areas by the expansion of frost in the rock cracks, and the movement of boulders in an avalanche, are examples. In practice the two work together. Water, consisting of sea waves and currents, rivers and rain; ice, in the form of glaciers, frost and melting snow; and wind, hurling sand fragments against exposed rocks and moving dunes along, are the most potent forces of erosion.

intrusion a mass of igneous rock that has

formed by 'injection' of molten rock into existing cracks beneath the surface of the earth, as distinct from a volcanic rock mass which has erupted from the surface.

lava the molten material exuded from a volcano which cools to form extrusive igneous rock. Lava differs from its parent magma in that the fluid 'fractionates' on its way to the surface of the earth, that is, certain heavy or high-temperature minerals settle out and the constituent gases form bubbles and boil away into the atmosphere. A lava high in silica is very stiff and does not flow far, while low-silica lava can flow for long distances.

or sand, or consolidated into a hard mass as an igneous, sedimentary or metamorphic rock.

strata (singular: stratum) layers or beds of sediment or sedimentary rocks, usually well defined and separated from each other by bedding planes. Strata form horizontally under gravity, but large-scale crust movements may tilt, crack, twist or even invert them. After being buried beneath other rocks, erosion or earthquakes or the processes of mountain-building may expose them at the surface. Their study is termed stratigraphy.

weathering the process by which exposed rocks are broken down by the action of rain,

WEATHERING

Physical weathering	*temperature changes* - weaking rocks by expansion and contraction
	frost - wedging rocks apart by the expansion of water on freezing
	rain - making loose slopes unstable
	wind - wearing away rocks by sandblasting, and moving sand dunes along
	unloading - the loosening of rock layers by release of pressure after the erosion and removal of those layers above
Chemical weathering	*carbonation* - the breakdown of calcite by reaction with carbonic acid in rainwater
	hydrolysis - the breakdown of feldspar into china clay by reaction with carbonic acid in rainwater
	oxidation - the breakdown of iron-rich minerals due to rusting
	hydration - the expansion of certain minerals due to the uptake of water
Gravity	*soil creep* - the slow downslope movement of surface material
	landslide - the raid downward movement of solid material
	avalanche - scouring by ice, snow, and accumulated debris
Rivers	*abrasion* - wearing away stream beds and banks by trundling boulders along
	corrosion - the wear on the boulders themselves as they are carried along
Glaciers	deepening of valleys by the weight of ice
	scouring of rock surfaces by embedded rocky debris
Sea	*hydraulic effect* - expansion of air pockets in rocks and cliffs by constant hammering by waves
	abrasion and corrosion - see **Rivers**

magma molten material beneath the earth's surface from which igneous rocks are formed. This may not be the same as lava extruded at the surface, since as magma rises to form lava it may distill off some its gaseous components, and some of its solids may crystallize before eruption.

rock the constituent of the earth's crust, either in its unconsolidated form as clay, mud,

frost, wind and the other elements of the weather. Two types of weathering are recognized. The first is *physical* weathering. This involves such effects as frost wedging, in which water trapped in a rock crack expands on freezing and splits the rock. The second type is *chemical* weathering. The carbon dioxide in the atmosphere combines with the rain water to produce weak carbonic acid, which may react with certain minerals in the rocks and break them down. The two types of weathering usually go hand-in-hand. Indeed, in some cases it is still not clear which type is involved. For example, 'onion-skin' weathering that produces rounded inselbergs in arid regions, such as Ayers Rock in central Australia, may be caused by the daily physical expansion and contraction of the surface rock layers in the heat of the sun. Or it may be caused by the chemical reaction of the minerals just beneath the surface with the infrequent rains.

Atmosphere and Weather

meteorology the scientific observation and study of the phenomena of weather and climate. At meteorological stations readings are taken of the more important factors determining weather conditions. Atmospheric pressure is measured by a mercury barometer, temperature by a screened thermometer, and humidity by a hydrometer, which expresses relative humidity as a percentage of the maximum. Winds are categorized by the Beaufort Scale, and the Beaufort weather code signifies every weather condition by suitable initials, with capitals denoting intensity. Cloud observations gauge how many tenths of sky are covered by each type, and rainfall is collected by a funnel and measured each 12 hours. Specially equipped weather ships maintained by several nations, including Britain, at a number of ocean stations, report on weather conditions and advise air traffic. They carry radar and twice daily make balloon soundings of wind, temperatures and humidity. Increasing costs have reduced their number, and there is growing reliance on reports from satellites which signal back a wide range of information, and on a broader basis, but offering some practical difficulties of interpretation. All these data are

reported to, and collated by, central agencies, such as the Meteorological Office, London, and US Weather Bureau, Washington. They are then pooled on an international basis. Computers have enabled a promising start to be made in the stupendous task of using physical laws to calculate the future trend and to give long-range weather forecasts.

weather the day-to-day variations of meteorological and climatic conditions at a particular place.

climate weather conditions at a particular place over a period of time. Climate encompasses all the meteorological elements and the factors that influence them. The primary factors that determine the variations of climate over the surface of the earth are (a)the effect of latitude and the tilt of the earth's axis to the plane of the orbit about the sun (66.5°); (b)the difference between land and sea; (c) contours of the ground; and (d) location of the area in relation to ocean currents. Climate types were first classified by Vladimir Köppen in 1918. The complexity of the distribution of land and sea, and the consequent complexity of the general circulation of the atmosphere, makes the distribution of the climate extremely complicated. Centred on the equator is a belt of tropical rain-forest which may be either constantly wet or monsoonal, that is, seasonal with wet and dry seasons in each year. Bordering each side of this is a belt of savannah, with lighter rainfall and less dense vegetation. After this usually comes a transition through steppe (semi-arid) to desert (arid), with a further transition through steppe to Mediterranean climate with dry summer, followed by the moist temperate climate of middle latitudes. Next comes a zone of cold climate with moist winter, but where the desert extends into middle latitudes the zones of Mediterranean and moist temperate climates are missing, and the transition is from desert to a cold climate with moist winter. In the extreme E of Asia a cold climate with dry winters extends from about 7° N to 3° N. The polar caps have tundra and ice-cap climates, with little or no precipitation. Catastrophic variations to climate may be caused by the impact of another planetary body, or clouds resulting from volcanic activity.

isobar a line drawn on maps and weather charts linking all places with the same atmospheric pressure (usually measured in millibars) at a given time. When used in weather forecasting, the distance between the isobars is an indication of the barometric gradient. Where they are close together cyclonic weather is indicated, bringing strong winds and a depression, and where far apart anticyclonic bringing fine weather and lighter winds. The pressures indicated on the meteorological charts have generally been corrected to sea-level.

isotherm a line on a map linking all places having the same temperature at a given time.

cyclone an area of low atmospheric pressure. Cyclones are formed by the mixture of cold, dry polar air with warm, moist equatorial air. These masses of air meet in temperate latitudes; the warm air rises over the cold, resulting in rain. Winds blow in towards the centre in an anti-clockwise direction in the northern hemisphere, clockwise in the southern hemisphere; the systems are characterized by variable weather, and are common over the British Isles. They bring rain or snow, winds up to gale force, low cloud, and sometimes fog. Tropical cyclones are a great danger to shipping (the tornado is a rapidly moving cyclone). In middle high latitudes low-pressure systems are referred to as depressions or lows; the term cyclone is avoided.

anticyclone an area of high atmospheric pressure are caused by descending air, which becomes warm and dry. Winds radiate from a calm centre, taking a clockwise direction in the northern hemisphere, and an anticlockwise direction in the southern hemisphere. Anticyclones are associated with clear weather and distinguished by the absence of rain and violent winds. In summer they bring hot, sunny days and in winter they bring fine, frosty spells, although fog and low cloud are not uncommon.

depression in meteorology, a cyclonic area or 'low' – a region of low atmospheric pressure.

In the midlatitudes (such as the UK) they are usually associated with wet, windy, unsettled weather.

front in meteorology, the interface between two air masses of different temperature or humidity. Fronts are usually found when warm air from one region of the earth's surface meets cold air from another. Warm air, being lighter, tends to rise above the cold; its moisture is carried upwards and usually falls as rain or snow - hence the changeable weather conditions at fronts. Fronts are rarely stationary but move with the air masses. A warm front brings warm air into an area occupied by cold air; a cold front does the reverse.

current the flow of a body of water or air moving in a definite direction. Oceanic currents may be: *drift currents*, broad and slow-moving; *stream currents*, narrow and swift-moving, e.g. Gulf Stream and Kuroshio/Japan Current; *upwelling currents* which bring cold, nutrient-rich water from the ocean bottom to provide food for plankton, which in turn supports fish and sea birds, such as Gulf of Guinea Current and the Peru (Humboldt) Current. Once in ten years or so, the latter, which runs from the Antarctic up the W coast of South America, turns warm, with heavy rain and rough seas, and has disastrous results (as in 1982–3) for the Peruvian anchovy industry and wildlife.

Coriolis effect named after its discoverer, French mathematician Gaspard Coriolis 1792–1843, it results from the deflective force of the earth's W-to-E rotation. Winds and ocean currents are deflected to the right in the N and to the left in the S hemisphere. It has to be allowed for in launching guided missiles, but has negligible effect on the clockwise or anticlockwise direction of water running out of a bath.

weather areas divisions of the sea areas around Great Britain for the purpose of weather forecasting for shipping, particularly to indicate where strong and gale-force winds are expected.

atmosphere the mixture of gases which surrounds the earth, prevented from escaping

weather areas

atmosphere

The earth's atmosphere

height in km

atmospheric pressure as fraction of pressure at sea level

atmospheric temperature

above about 200km temperature of atmosphere reaches 1500°C during daytime.

regions of atmosphere classified by temperature:

-100°C   0°C + 100°C

meteorological phenomena

ionosphere: regions which reflect radio waves

Appleton F₁ layer

short waves (nightime)

Appleton F₂ layer

short waves (daytime)

Space shuttle

$\frac{1}{10\ 000\ 000\ 000}$

aurorae

Heaviside-Kennelly (E) Layer

medium waves

Thermosphere

Mesopause

$\frac{1}{1\ 000\ 000}$

D Layer

Mesosphere

meteors

long waves

$\frac{1}{1000}$

Stratopause

weather balloons

Stratosphere

ozone layer

Tropopause

Concorde

weather

$\frac{1}{10}$

Troposphere

Everest: 8.8km

sea level

scale change

369

by the pull of the earth's gravity. As we go higher in the atmosphere, a small and smaller fraction of it is 'resting' above us, so atmospheric pressure decreases. In its lowest layer, the ***troposphere***, the atmospheric pressure consists of nitrogen (78%) and oxygen (21%), both in molecular form (two atoms bound together). The other 1% is largely argon, but there are very small quantities of other gases, as well as water vapour. The troposphere is heated by the earth, which is warmed by infra-red and visible radiation from the sun. Warm air rises in the troposphere, cooling as it does so. This is the primary cause of rain and most other weather phenomena.

cloud water vapour condensed into minute water particles which float in masses in the atmosphere. Like fogs or mists, from which clouds are distinguished by the height at which they occur above the ground, they are formed by the cooling of air charged with water vapour which condenses on tiny dust particles. Clouds are usually classified according to the height at which they occur and their shape.

fog cloud that collects at the surface of the earth, composed of water vapour which has condensed on particles of dust in the atmosphere. Cloud and fog are both caused by the air temperature falling below dew point. The thickness of fog is dependent on the number of water particles it contains. Usually, fog is formed by the meeting of two currents of air, one cooler than the other, or by warm air flowing over a cold surface. Sea fogs commonly occur where warm and cold currents meet, and the air above them mixes. Fog frequently forms on calm nights over the land, as the land surface cools more rapidly than the air immediately above it. Officially, fog refers to a condition when visibility is reduced to 1 km/0.62 mi or less, and mist or haze to that giving a visibility of 1–2 kilometres. A mist is produced by condensed water particles, and a haze by smoke or dust.

smog a natural fog containing impurities (unburned carbon and sulphur dioxide) from domestic fires, industrial furnaces and certain power stations, and internal combustion

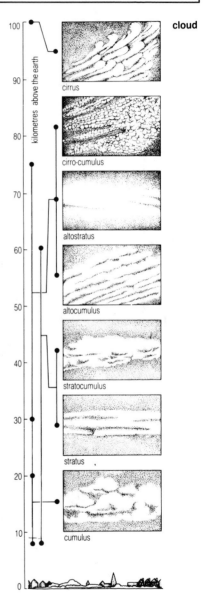

cloud

cirrus

cirro-cumulus

altostratus

altocumulus

stratocumulus

stratus

cumulus

engines (petrol or diesel). The use of smoke-less fuels, the treatment of effluent and penalties for excessive smoke from poorly maintained and operated vehicles can be extremely effective in cutting down smog. It can cause substantial illness and loss of life, particularly among chronic bronchitics, and damage to wildlife.

precipitation the meteorological term for water that falls to earth from the atmosphere. As such it covers rain, snow, sleet, hail, dew and hoar frost.

rain precipitation in the form of separate drops of water that fall to the earth's surface from clouds. The drops are formed by the accumulation of droplets that condense from water vapour in the air. The condensation is

(with records of over 400 mm). It is caused by the circulation of moisture in strong convection currents, usually within cumulonimbus-type cloud. Water droplets freeze as they are carried upwards. Further layers of ice are deposited around this nucleus as the circulation continues, until they become too heavy to be supported by the currents and they fall as a hailstorm.

frost condition of the weather when the air temperature is below freezing 0°C/32°F. Water in the atmosphere then freezes and crystallizes on the ground or exposed objects. As cold air is heavier than warm, *ground frosts* are more common than *hoar frost*, which is formed by the condensation of water particles in the same way as dew collects.

BEAUFORT SCALE

Number	Description	Features	Air speed mi per hr	m per sec
0	calm	smoke rises vertically; water smooth	less than 1	less than 0.3
1	light air	smoke shows wind direction; water ruffled	1-3	0.3-1.5
2	slight breeze	leaves rustle; wind felt on face	4-7	1.6-3.3
3	gentle breeze	loose paper blows around	8-12	3.4-5.4
4	moderate breeze	branches sway	13-18	5.5-7.9
5	fresh breeze	small trees sway, leaves blown off	19-24	8.0-10.7
6	strong breeze	whistling in telephone wire; sea spray from waves	25-31	10.8-13.8
7	moderate gale	large trees sway	32-38	13.9-17.1
8	fresh gale	twigs break from trees	39-46	17.2-20.7
9	strong gale	branches break from trees	47-54	20.8-24.4
10	whole gale	trees uprooted, weak buildings collapse	55-63	14.5-28.4
11	storm	widesread damage	64-72	28.5-32.6
12	hurricane	widespread structural damage	Above 73	Above 32.7

usually brought about by cooling, either when the air rises over a mountain range or when, being a warm air mass, it rises above a cooler air mass.

hail precipitation in the form of pellets of ice, typically of a few millimetres' diameter

snow flaked particles caused by the condensation in air of excess water vapour below freezing point. Light reflecting in the crystals, which have a basic hexagonal (six-sided) geometry, gives snow a white appearance.

dew moisture that collects on the ground

371

during clear, calm nights, particularly after a warm day. As temperature falls during the night the air and the water vapour in it become chilled. Condensation takes place on the cooled surfaces of grass, leaves, etc. When the moisture begins to form, the surrounding air is said to have reached its dew-point. If the temperature falls below freezing point during the night, the dew will freeze, or if the temperature is low and the dew-point is below freezing point, the water vapour condenses directly into ice; in both cases hoar frost is formed.

wind a lateral movement of the earth's atmosphere. Although modified by features such as land and water, there is a basic world-wide system. A belt of low pressure (the doldrums) lies along the equator. The Trade Winds blow towards this from the Horse Latitudes (high pressure areas 3° N and 3° S of the equator), blowing from the NE in the northern hemisphere, and from the SE in the southern. The *Westerlies* (also from the Horse Latitudes) blow from the SW north of the equator and from the NW to the south. Cold winds blow outwards from high-pressure areas at the poles. More local effects result from the land heating and cooling faster than the adjacent sea, producing onshore winds in the daytime and offshore winds at night.

Beaufort scale system of recording wind velocity, devised in 1806 by Admiral Sir Francis Beaufort (1774–1857), who became hydrographer to the Royal Navy in 1829. It is a numerical scale ranging from 0 to 17, calm being indicated by 0 and a hurricane by 12; 13–17 indicate degrees of hurricane force. In 1874 it received international recognition; it was modified in 1926. Measurements are made at 10 m above ground level.

tornado an extremely violent revolving storm, caused by a rising column of warm air propelled by strong wind. The diameter of the tornado may be a few hundred metres or less, but it rises to a great height, and is marked by swirling funnel-shaped clouds. Tornadoes moving at speeds of up to 400 kph/250 mph are common in the Mississippi basin and cause

great destruction. The most severe tornadoes are always accompanied by thunderstorms.

tornado

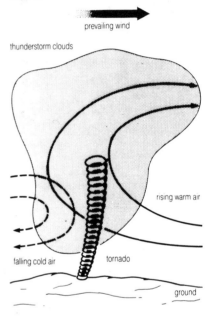

prevailing wind

thunderstorm clouds

rising warm air

falling cold air   tornado

ground

typhoon a violent revolving storm occurring chiefly in autumn along the eastern seaboard of Asia between the Philippines and Japan. Typhoon is the local term for hurricane.

hurricane a revolving storm in tropical regions. A hurricane begins between 1° and 2° N or S of the equator and moves westwards. A central calm area, called the eye, is surrounded by inwardly spiralling winds of up to 320 kph/200 mph. A hurricane is accompanied by lighting and torrential rain and can cause extensive damage and loss of life along the western shores of tropical oceans. In meteorology a hurricane is a wind of force 12 or more on the Beaufort scale.

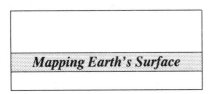

Mapping Earth's Surface

map a diagrammatic representation, for example, of part of the earth's surface or the distribution of the stars. Modern maps are made using aerial photography; a series of overlapping stereoscopic photographs are taken which can then be used to prepare a three-dimensional image. Laser beams, microwaves, and infra-red equipment are also used for land surveying, and satellite pictures make a valuable contribution when large areas are under survey.

projection in cartography, the means of depicting the spherical surface of the earth on a flat piece of paper. The theory is that, if a light were placed at the centre of a transparent earth, the surface features could be thrown as shadows on a piece of paper placed close to the surface. This paper may be flat and placed on a pole (azimuthal or zenithal), or may be rolled cylindrically around the equator (cylindrical), or may be in the form of a tall cone resting on the equator (conical). The resulting maps differ from one another, distorting either area or direction, and each is suitable for a particular purpose. For example, projections distorting area the least are used for distribution maps, and those with least distortion of direction are used for navigation charts. The Flemish map-maker Gerhard Kremer 1512–94 devised *Mercator's projection* in which the parallels and meridians on maps are drawn uniformly at 9°. The true area of countries is increasingly distorted the farther N and S they are from the Equator.

poles The geographic N and S points of penetration of the earth's surface by the axis about which it rotates. The magnetic poles are the points towards which a freely suspended magnetic needle will point, and they vary continually; in 1985 the magnetic North Pole was some 350 km/218 mi NW of Resolute Bay in Canada's Northwest Territories. It moves northwards c.10 km/6 mi each year, although it can vary in a day by about 80 km/50 mi from its average position. It is relocated every decade in order to update navigational charts. Periodic changes within the earth's core cause a reversal of the magnetic poles (the last occasion was 700,000 years ago), and it is calculated that in about 1200 years' time the N magnetic pole will become the S magnetic pole. Many animals, including migrating birds and fish, are thought to orientate themselves partly using the earth's magnetic field.

latitude and longitude *latitude* is the angular distance of any point from the equator, measured N or S along the earth's curved surface, equalling the angle between the respective horizontal planes. It is measured in degrees, minutes, and seconds, each minute equalling one sea-mile (1.85 km) in length. *Longitude* is the angle between the terrestrial meridian drawn from the pole, through a place, and a standard meridian now taken at Greenwich, England. All determinations of longitude are based on the earth turning through 36° in 24 hours, or the sun reaching 1° W each hour. At the equator one degree of longitude measures about 112 km/70 mi.

nautical mile a unit of distance used in navigation. It equals the average length of one minute of arc on a great circle of the earth. In the United Kingdom it was formerly defined as 6080 feet. The International Nautical Mile is now defined as 1852 m.

Arctic Circle an arbitrary line drawn round the North Pole at 66°33' N. The region N of this line experiences at least one night during the northern summer when the sun never sets ('midnight sun'), and at least one day during the northern winter when the sun never rises. The Arctic Ocean, which occupies much of the Arctic Circle, is frozen to great depths in winter; there is no land beneath it, as there is under the South Pole's Antarctic ice cap.

Antarctic Circle an imaginary line that runs round the South Pole at latitude 66°33' S. The region south of this line experiences at least

map projection

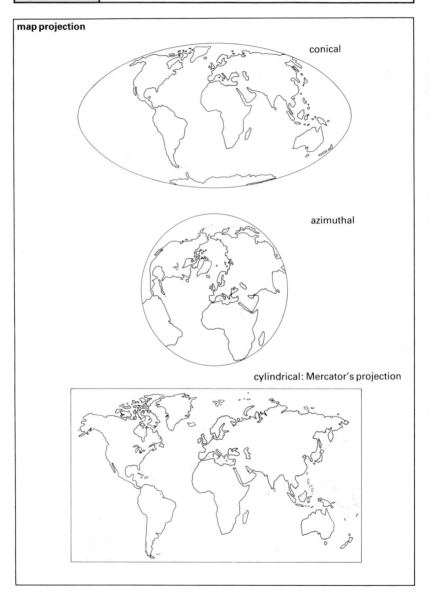

conical

azimuthal

cylindrical: Mercator's projection

one night during the southern summer during which the sun never sets, and at least one day during the southern winter during which the sun never rises. The line encompasses the continent of Antarctica and the Antarctic Ocean.

equator the *terrestrial equator* is the great circle whose plane is perpendicular to the earth's axis (the line joining the poles). Its length is 40,076 km/24,901.8 mi, divided into 360° of longitude. The *celestial equator* or Equinoctial is the circle in which the plane of the terrestrial equator intersects the celestial sphere.

tropics the tropics of Cancer and Capricorn, defined by the parallels of latitude 23° 28' N and S of the equator, are the limits of the area of earth's surface in which the sun is directly overhead for at least one day each year.

great circle a plane cutting through a sphere, and passing through the centre point of the sphere, cuts the surface along a great circle. Thus, on the earth, all meridians of longitude are half great circles; of the parallels of latitude, only the equator is a great circle. The shortest route between two points on the earth's surface is along the arc of a great circle, and these are used extensively in air routes (although on maps, due to vagaries of their projection, they are not straight lines).

meridian a great circle drawn on the earth's surface passing through both poles, and thus through all places with the same longitude. Terrestrial longitudes are usually measured from the Greenwich Meridian.

International Date Line A modification of the 180th meridian which marks the difference in time between E and W. The date is put forward a day when crossing the line going W, and back a day when going E. Much of this line runs through the mid Pacific Ocean, with local deviations around land to avoid having two dates at the same time in an island or nation. The IDL was chosen at the International Meridian Conference in 1884.

Geological Features

archipelago a group of islands, or an area of sea containing a group of islands. The islands of an archipelago are often volcanic in origin, formed either when a hot spot within the earth's mantle produces a chain of volcanoes on the surface, such as the Hawaiian Archipelago, or at a destructive plate margin where the subduction (under-riding) of one plate beneath another produces an arc-shaped island group, such as the Aleutian Archipelago. Alternatively an archipelago may be caused by a rise in sea level flooding a hilly landscape, leaving hills as islands.

caldera in geology, a very large basin-shaped crater. Calderas are found at the tops of volcanoes, where the original peak has collapsed into an empty chamber beneath. The basin, many times larger than the original volcanic vent, may be flooded, producing a crater lake, or the flat floor may contain a number of small volcanic cones, showing where the volcanic activity continued after the collapse.

canyon a deep narrow hollow running through mountains.Canyons are cut by river action, usually in areas of low rainfall, where the river receives water from outside the area.

crater a bowl-shaped topographic feature, usually round and with steep sides. Craters are formed by explosive events such as the eruption of a volcano or by the impact of a meteorite. A caldera is a much larger feature.

delta a triangular tract of land at a river's mouth, formed by deposited silt or sediment. Familiar examples of large deltas are those of the Mississippi, Ganges and Brahmaputra, Rhône, Po, Danube, and Nile; the shape of the last-named is like the Greek letter Δ, and thus gave rise to the name.

desert area without sufficient vegetation to

support human life. Scientifically this term includes the ice areas of the polar regions, although a desert is generally thought of as restricted to the earth's warmer zones particularly at the latitudes of the tropics. The tropical desert belts are caused by the descent of dry air that has already risen and dropped its water at the equator.

Deserts constitute almost a third of the earth's land surface and may have existed from time immemorial, or be created by changes in climate, or by the human-aided process of desertification, including over-grazing, destruction of timber shelter belts, and the overpopulation which leads to exhaustion of the soil by too intensive cultivation without restoration of fertility.

dune a bank or hill of wind-drifted sand. Loose sand is blown and bounced along by the wind, up the windward side of a dune. The sand particles then fall to rest on the lee side, while more are blown up from the windward. In this way a dune moves gradually downwind. Dunes are seen in sandy deserts and along beaches.

fault in geology, a crack in a rock along which the two sides have evidently moved, due to differing strains in the adjacent rock bodies. Displacement of rock masses horizontally or vertically along a fault may be microscopic, or they may be massive causing major earthquakes.

glacier a mass of ice which originates in mountains in the snowfields above the snow-line, where the annual snowfall exceeds the annual melting and drainage. Under the weight of the layers above, the snow compacts to ice, and under pressure the ice can move plastically (glacier flow). It moves slowly down a valley or depression, and is constantly replenished from its source.

hot spot in geology, a hypothetical region of high thermal activity in the earth's mantle. It is believed to be the origin of many chains of

ocean islands, such as Polynesia (including Hawaii) and the Galapagos. A volcano forms on the ocean crust immediately above the hot spot, is carried away by plate tectonic movement, and becomes extinct. A new volcano forms beside it, above the hot spot. The result is an active volcano and a chain of increasingly old and eroded volcanic stumps stretching away in the direction of plate movement.

lake body of still water lying in depressed ground without direct communication with the sea. Lakes are common in glaciated mountain regions, along the course of gently declining rivers, and in low land near the sea. The main classifications are by origin as follows: *glacial lakes* such as in the Alps; *barrier lakes* formed by landslides, valley glaciers, etc.; *crater lakes*; *tectonic lakes* occurring in natural features.

mesa a flat-topped mountain with steep cliff sides, particularly those found in the desert areas of the USA and Mexico.

mountain a large-scale topographic feature where the earth's surface rises to great heights with steep sides and a narrow top (summit). Height is either relative (in relation to the local surroundings) or absolute (usually taken as height above sea level). The distinction between high hills and low mountains is vague and depends on local topography, generally occurring at around 1000 m/3300 ft. The tallest land mountain is Mount Everest, in the Himalaya range, at 8848 m/29,028 ft above sea level.

peninsula a tongue of land surrounded on three sides by water but still attached to a larger landmass. The state of Florida, USA, is a classic example.

river a body of water, larger than a stream, that flows downwards along a particular course. It originates at a point called its source, and enters the sea or a lake at its mouth. Along its length it may be joined by smaller rivers called tributaries, all these together forming the river system.

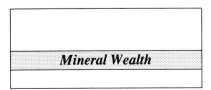

Mineral Wealth

mineralogy the study of minerals. The classification of minerals is chiefly based on their chemical constitution, *viz.* metallic, ionic, and molecular. In addition, their crystallographic and physical characters, their mode of formation and occurrence form part of the study. In the case of minerals of economic importance a knowledge of mining and metallurgy is also needed.

Mohs scale a scale useful in mineral identification because any mineral will scratch any other mineral lower on the scale than itself, and similarly it will be scratched by any other mineral higher on the scale.

MOHS SCALE

Number	Defining mineral	Other substances compared
1	talc	
2	gypsum	2½ fingernail
3	calcite	3½ copper coin
4	fluorite	
5	apatite	5½ steel blade
6	orthoclase	5¾ glass
7	quartz	7 steel file
8	topaz	
9	corundum	
10	diamond	

The scale is not regular; diamond, at number 10, the hardest natural substance, is 90 times harder in absolute terms than corundum, number 9.

gem a mineral precious by virtue of its composition, hardness and rarity, cut and polished for ornamental use, or engraved. Of 120 minerals known to have been used as gemstones, only about 25 are in common use in jewellery; of these, the diamond, emerald, ruby, and sapphire are classified as precious, and the topaz, amethyst, opal, aquamarine, etc., as semi-precious.

diamond a precious gem stone, the hardest natural substance known (10 on Mohs scale). Composed of carbon and with a chemical formula C, it crystallizes in the cubic system; other common crystals are octahedra and dodecahedra. Rough diamonds are dull or greasy before being cut, and only some 20% are suitable as gems. Industrial diamonds are used for cutting (for example the tungsten carbide tools used in steel mills are themselves cut with diamond tools), grinding, polishing. Diamonds act as perfectly transparent windows, and do not absorb infrared radiation, hence their use aboard NASA space-probes to Venus in 1978.

emerald green variety of the mineral beryl, $Be_3Al_2Si_6O_{18}$.

ruby the red transparent gem variety of the mineral corundum, Al_2O_3, crystallizing in the hexagonal system; it is without true cleavage. They have been produced artificially and are widely used in lasers.

sapphire the blue transparent gem variety of the mineral corundum, Al_2O_3.

topaz a mineral, fluosilicate of aluminium, $Al_2SiO_4(FOH)_2$. It is usually yellow, or pink if it has been heated, and is used in making jewellery.

amethyst a variety of quartz, SiO_2, coloured violet by the presence of small quantities of manganese, and used as a semi-precious stone.

opal a non-crystalline form of silica, occurring in stalactites in volcanic rocks. The common opal is opaque, milk-white, yellow, red, blue, or green, and lustrous. The precious opal is colourless, having innumerable cracks from which emanate brilliant colours produced by minute crystals of cristobalite.

aquamarine a blue variety of the mineral beryl $Be_3Al_2Si_6O_{18}$.

Life Sciences

Life Sciences has emerged in recent years as an enlightened synthesis of several traditional disciplines including biology, zoology, and botany, and newer, more specialized areas of study such as biophysics and sociobiology. The scientific study of the living world as a whole has led to many new ideas and discoveries, as well as to an emphasis on ecology, the study of living organisms in their natural environment. This approach reflects our growing awareness that we, as humans, are one small part of the living world, and that we have ever-increasing power to conserve or destroy, or even create, life as we choose.

This section begins with an overview of the *Main Branches* of the life sciences, and then looks at different topics in turn: *Evolutionary Biology* deals with theories of the origins of life; *Reproduction and the Life Cycle* looks at the processes by which life continues on earth; *Ecology and Resources* looks at the relationships between life and the environment as a whole and at positive ways in which conservation can be practised; *Order in the Living World* deals with the classification of different forms of life; *The Microscopic World* looks at the smallest elements of life. These are followed by overviews of *Animals* and *Plants*, *Biographies* of people who have made important contributions to the life sciences, and a look at *The New Synthesis* of classical genetics and the new science of molecular biology, including key terms.

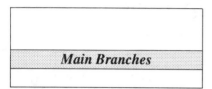

Main Branches

biology the science of life. The word was first used by the German physician Treviranus in 1802, and was popularized by Lamarck. Strictly speaking, biology includes all the life sciences, for example, anatomy and physiology, cytology, zoology and botany, ecology, genetics, biochemistry and biophysics, animal behaviour, embryology, and plant breeding. Although medical students such as Hippocrates, in the fifth century BC, made the first accurate biological observations, describing medicinally useful plants and their properties, attempts at a scientific physiology were bound to fail in the absence of scientific instruments, a tradition of experiment, and a body of organized knowledge with its own terminology. Only with the Renaissance did free enquiry come into its own. The 16th century saw the production of encyclopaedias of natural history, such as that of Gesner (1516–65), and the beginnings of modern anatomy, notably at Padua under Versalius (1514–64), who was succeeded by Fabricius. William Harvey, a student at the latter, laid the foundation of modern physiology by his work on the circulation of the blood – the first time any basic function of the body had been scientifically explained. Linnaeus introduced a binomial system of classification. During the 19th century, attempts to understand the origins of the great diversity of life forms gave rise to several theories of biological evolution, culminating in Darwin's theory of evolution by natural selection. The ensuing debates over the processes of evolution then stimulated an interest in the new fields of embryology and genetics towards the end of the century. More recently still, the application of the principles of chemistry to organic substances led to developments in biochemistry and molecular biology.

agriculture cultivation of land by humans, developed in Egypt at least 17,000 years ago. Its modernization began in 18th-century Britain, and its mechanization in 19th-century USA. Following World War II, there was an explosive growth in agricultural chemicals – herbicides, insecticides, fungicides, fertilizers; in the 1960s there was development of high-yielding species for special conditions, especially in the *green revolution* in the Third World, and in the industrialized countries cattle and poultry production on 'production lines' and battery systems; in the 1970s there was a movement towards more sophisticated natural methods and a reversion to *organic farming* without chemical sprays and fertilizers; in the 1980s hybridization by genetic engineering methods was developed, and pest control by the use of chemicals plus pheromones.

bioengineering the application of engineering to biology and medicine. Common applications include the design and use of artificial limbs, joints and organs, including hip joints and heart valves.

biophysics the application of physical laws to the properties of living organisms. Examples include using the principles of mechanics to calculate the strength of bones and muscles, and thermodynamics to study plant and animal energetics.

botany the study of plants. It is subdivided into a number of smaller studies, such as the identification and classification of plants (termed taxonomy), their external formation (plant morphology), their internal arrangement (plant anatomy), their microscopic examination (histology), their life history (plant physiology), and their distribution over the earth's surface in relation to their surroundings (plant ecology). Palaeobotany concerns the study of fossil plants, while economic botany deals with the utility of plants. Horticulture, agriculture, and forestry are specialized branches of botany. The most ancient botanical record is carved on the walls of the temple at Karnak, about 1500 BC. The first Greek Herbal was drawn up about 350 BC by

Diocles of Carystus. Botanical information was collected into the works of Theophrastus of Eresus (380–287 BC), a pupil of Aristotle, who founded the technical plant nomenclature. Cesalpino in the 16th century sketched out a system of classification based on flowers, fruits, and seeds, while Jung (1587–1658) used flowers only as his criterion. John Ray (1627–1705) arranged plants systematically, based on his findings on fruit, leaf and flower, and described about 18,600 plants. Swedish Carl von Linné or Linnaeus (1707–78), who founded systematics, included in his classification all known plants and animals, and giving each a binomial descriptive label. Banks, Solander, Brown, Bauer, and others travelled throughout the world studying plants, and found that all could be fitted into a systematic classification based on Linnaeus' work. Linnaeus was also the first to recognize the sexual nature of flowers, this work being followed up later by Sprengel, Amici, Robert Brown, and Charles Darwin. Later work revealed the detailed cellular structure of plant tissues, and the exact nature of photosynthesis. Sachs (1832–97) defined the function of chlorophyll, and the significance of plant stomata. In the period since World War II much has been achieved towards the clarification of cell function, repair and growth by the hybridization of plant cells: the combination of the nucleus of one cell with the protoplasm of another.

embryology the study of the changes undergone by living matter in its early life history, from fertilization to birth or hatching.

ethology the comparative study of animal behaviour in its natural setting, pioneered during the 1930s by K Lorenz and K von Frisch who, along with N Tinbergen, received the Nobel prize in 1973. Ethology is concerned with the causal mechanisms (both the stimuli that elicit behaviour and the physiological mechanisms controlling it), as well as the development of behaviour, its function and evolutionary history. Ethologists believe that the significance of an animal's behaviour can only be understood in its natural context, and emphasized the importance of field studies and

an evolutionary perspective. A recent development within ethology is sociobiology.

histology study of the microscopic structure of the tissues of organisms.

horticulture the art of growing flowers, fruit and vegetables. Courses in horticulture usually include outdoor gardening, propagation, and hothouse care.

physiology that branch of biology that deals with the functioning of living animals.

sociobiology the application of population genetics to the evolution of behaviour. It builds on W D Hamilton's concept of inclusive fitness to emphasize that the evolutionary function of behaviour is to allow an organism to contribute as many of its own alleles as it can to future generations (an idea encapsulated in Dawkins' notion of the 'selfish gene'). Contrary to some popular interpretations, it does not assume that all behaviour is genetically determined. The use of game theory is an important aspect of sociobiology.

zoology the branch of biology concerned with the study of animals. It includes description of present-day animals, the evolution of animal forms, anatomy, physiology, embryology, and geographical distribution.

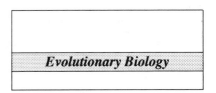

Evolutionary Biology

evolution a slow process of change from one form to another, as in the evolution of the universe from its formation in the Big Bang to its present state, or in the evolution of life on earth. With respect to the living world, the idea of continuous evolution can be traced as far back as Lucretius in the first century BC, but it did not gain wide acceptance until 19th century following the work of Sir Charles Lyell, J B Lamarck, Charles Darwin and T H Huxley. Darwin assigned the major role in evolutionary change to natural selection acting on genetic variation, which is ultimately produced by spontaneous changes (mutations) in the genetic material of organisms. *Natural selection* occurs because those individuals that are better adapted to their particular environments reproduce more effectively, thus contributing more genes to future generations. Darwin's theory was later combined with Mendel's discoveries in genetics, to give the modern theory of evolution, often called neo-Darwinism. Although neither the general concept of evolution nor the importance of natural selection is doubted by biologists, there remains dispute over other possible processes involved in evolutionary change. Besides natural selection and sexual selection, chance may play an important role in deciding which genes become characteristic of a population, a phenomenon sometimes referred to as 'genetic drift'. In addition, it is now clear that evolutionary change does not always occur at a constant rate, but that the process sometimes shows long periods of relative stability interspersed with periods of rapid change. This has led to new theories, such as punctuated equilibrium model.

extinction in biology, the complete disappearance of a species. In the past extinctions generally occurred because species were unable to adapt quickly enough to a changing environment. Today, most extinctions are due to human activity. Some species, such as the dodo of Mauritius, the moas of New Zealand and the passenger pigeon of North America have been exterminated by hunting. Others become extinct when their habitat is destroyed. Mass extinctions are episodes during which whole groups of species have become extinct, the best known being that of the dinosaurs, other large reptiles and various marine invertebrates some 65 million years ago. Another mass extinction occurred about 10,000 years ago when many giant species of mammals died out. This is known as the 'Pleistocene overkill' because their disappearance was probably hastened by the hunting activities of prehistoric humans.

homologous in biology, an organ or struc-

ture possessed by members of different taxonomic groups (species, genera, families, orders) which, although now different in form or usage, originally derived from the same structure in a common ancestor. The wing of a bat, the arm of a monkey and the flipper of a seal are homologous, because they all derive from the forelimb of an ancestral mammal. The wing of a bird and the wing of an insect are not homologous, even though they are both used for flying, because they are not derived from the same structure.

natural selection the process whereby gene frequencies in a population change due to certain organisms producing more descendants than others, because they are better able to survive and reproduce. Natural selection results in the genetic constitution of the population, and ultimately the species, being altered in favour of the particular genes that successful individuals bear. The accumulated effect of natural selection is to produce adaptations such as the thick coat of a polar bear or the spade-like forelimbs of a mole. It was recognized by Darwin as the main process driving evolution.

nature the living world, including plants, animals, fungi, and all microorganisms.

neo-Darwinism the modern theory of evolution, built up during the 1930s by integrating Darwin's theory of evolution through natural selection with the theory of genetic inheritance founded on the work of Gregor Mendel.

human species, origins of evolution of modern humans from ancestral primates. The African apes (gorilla and chimpanzees) are shown by anatomical and molecular comparisons to be our closest living relatives. The date of the split between the human and African ape lines is not known from fossil finds, but molecular clock studies put it at five million years ago or more. There are no ape or *hominid* (of the human group) fossils from this period. The oldest known hominid remains date from 3.5 million years ago, from Ethiopia and Tanzania. They show hominids were already walking upright at this time. There is disagreement over the status of these creatures, known as *Australopithecus afarensis*. Some believe they were our direct ancestors, other that they were an off-shoot of the line that led to modern humans. The first stone tools date from about a million years later, probably made by the hominid *Homo habilis*, who had a slightly larger body and brain than *A. afarensis*. Other *Australopithecus* hominids among them *A. robustus* and *A. gracilis*, lived in Africa at the same time as *H. habilis*, but these are not generally considered to be our ancestors. Over 1.5 million years ago a new hominid species, *H. erectus*, with a much larger brain, appeared in Africa. It is not clear if *H. Habilis* evolved from *A. afarensis*, but it is generally believed that *H. erectus* evolved from *H. habilis* The erectus people were probably the first to use fire, and the first to move out of Africa. Their remains are found as far afield as China, Spain, and southern Britain. Modern humans, *H. sapiens sapiens*, and the Neanderthals *H. sapiens neanderthalensis*, are probably descended from *H. erectus*. Neanderthals were large-brained but heavily-built, probably adapted to the cold conditions of the ice ages. They lived in Europe and the Middle East, and died out about 40,000 years ago, leaving *H. sapiens sapiens* as the only remaining species of the hominid group.

phylogeny the historical sequence of changes that occurs in a given species during the course of evolution.

punctuated equilibrium model an evolutionary theory which claims that periods of rapid change alternate with periods of relative stability (stasis), and that the appearance of new lineages is a separate process from the gradual evolution of adaptive changes within a species. The idea was developed in 1972 by Niles Eldridge and Steven J Gould to explain discontinuities in the fossil record. The pattern of stasis and more rapid change is now widely accepted, but the second part of the theory remains unsubstantiated.

saltation the idea that an abrupt genetic change can occur in an individual, which then gives rise to a new species. The idea has now been largely discredited.

speciation the emergence of a new species

during evolutionary history. One cause of speciation is the geographical separation of populations of the parent species, followed by their reproductive isolation, so that they no longer produce viable offspring if they interbreed. Other less common causes of speciation are assortative mating, and the appearance of polyploidy.

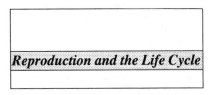

Reproduction and the Life Cycle

life the ability to grow, stay in 'working order', reproduce, and respond to such stimuli as light, heat and sound. It is thought that life began about 4,000 million years ago, the earliest fossil evidence being thread-like chains of cells discovered in 1980 in deposits in the northwest of Australia, that have been dated as 3,500 million years old.

It seems probable that the original atmosphere of earth consisted of carbon dioxide, nitrogen and water and that complex organic molecules such as amino acids were created when the atmosphere was bombarded by ultra-violet radiation or by atmospheric lightning. Experiments in the laboratory have attempted to replicate these conditions and have successfully shown that amino acids and purine and pyrimidine bases (which make up DNA) and other vital molecules can be created in this way. The earliest forms of cellular life were very probably bacteria-like and from these developed the network of plant and animal life of today.

life cycle in biology, the sequence of different stages through which members of a given species pass. Most vertebrates have a simple life cycle consisting of the production of sex cells or gametes, fertilization and a period of development as an embryo, followed by a period of juvenile growth after hatching or birth, with a concluding phase of sexual reproduction which terminates at death. Invertebrate life cycles are generally more complex and may involve major reconstitution of the individual's appearance (metamorphosis) and completely different styles of life. Thus, dragonflies live an aquatic life as larvae and an aerial life during the adult phase. In many other invertebrates and protozoa there are several different stages in the life cycle, and in parasites these often occur in different host organisms. Plants have a special type of life cycle with two distinct phases, known as an alternation of generations.

reproduction the process by which a living organism produces other organisms similar to itself. Reproduction may be asexual or sexual.

sexual reproduction a reproductive process which requires the union, or fertilization, of the gametes (except in fungi). These are generally produced by two different individuals, although self-fertilization can occur in hermaphrodites. Most organisms other than bacteria and cyanobacteria show some sort of sexual process. Except in some lower organisms, the gametes are of two distinct types, called eggs and sperm. The organisms producing the eggs are called females, and those producing the sperm, males.

asexual reproduction a biological term applied to reproductive processes which are not sexual and so which do not involve fusion of gametes. They include binary fission, in which the parent organism splits into two or more 'daughter' organisms, or budding, in which a new organism is formed initially as an outgrowth of the parent organism. The asexual production of spores, as in ferns and mosses, is another common process, and many plants reporduce asexually by means of runners, rhizomes, bulbs and corms.

alternation of generations the typical lifecycle of terrestrial plants and some seaweeds, in which there are two distinct forms occurring alternately. One is diploid and produces haploid spores by meiosis; this is called the sporophyte (spore-producer). The other is haploid and produces gametes (sex cells); this is called the gametophyte (gamete-producer).

The gametes fuse to form a diploid zygote which develops into a new sporophyte, and so the sporophyte and gametophyte alternate. In mosses, the familiar green moss plant is gametophyte, while the long-stalked spore capsules growing from it are sporophyte. In ferns the familiar plant is the sporophyte and the gametophyte, which grows separately from it, is very small and inconspicuous. All higher plants are sporophytes, and the gametophyte is not seen because it completes its life within the body of the sporophyte. The lifecycles of certain animals (for example, jellyfish) are sometimes said to show alternation of generations, but this is rarely as regular and clearly-defined as in plants.

sporophyte the diploid spore-producing generation in the life cycle of a plant that undergoes alternation of generations.

gametophyte the haploid generation in the lifecycle of a plant that produces gametes.

parthenogenesis the development of an ovum (egg) without any genetic contribution from a male. In most cases, there is no fertilization at all, but in a few the stimulus of being fertilized by a sperm is needed to initiate development, although the male's chromosomes are not absorbed into the nucleus of the ovum. Parthenogenesis is the normal means of reproduction in some plants (for example, dandelions) and animals (for example, certain fish and rotifers). Certain sexually reproducing species, such as aphids, show parthenogenesis at some stage in their life cycle, and it can be artificially induced in many animals (for example, rabbits) by cooling, pricking or applying acid to an egg.

gamete a cell generated for sexual reproduction. In most organisms, the gametes are haploid, that is they contain half the number of chromosomes of the parent, due to reduction division or meiosis. In higher organisms, gametes are of two distinct types, large immobile ones known as eggs or egg-cells and small ones known as sperm. In some lower organisms the gametes are all the same, or they may belong to different mating strains but have no obvious differences in size or appearance.

pollen the grains formed by seed plants that contain the male gametes. In angiosperms pollen is produced within anthers, and in most gymnosperms it is produced in male cones. A pollen grain is typically yellow and, when mature, has a hard outer wall. Since pollen grains are extremely resistant to decay, much important information on the vegetation of earlier times can be gained from the study of fossil pollen. The study of pollen grains is known as palynology.

sperm strictly speaking, the male gamete of animals, but the name is also sometimes applied to the motile male gametes, or antherozoids, of lower plants. In most animals, the sperm are motile, and are propelled by a long flagellum, but in some (for example, crabs and lobsters) they are non-motile. Each sperm cell looks rather like a tadpole, with a head capsule containing a nucleus, a middle portion containing mitochondria (which provide energy) and the long tail or flagellum behind.

ovum the female gamete (sex-cell) before fertilization. In animals, it is called an egg, and is produced in the ovaries. In plants, where it is also known as an egg-cell or oosphere, the ovum is produced in an ovule. The ovum is non-motile. It must be fertilized by a male gamete before it can develop further, except in cases of parthenogenesis.

fertilization in sexual reproduction, the union of two gametes (sex cells, often called egg and sperm) to produce a zygote, which combines the genetic material contributed by each parent. In terrestrial insects, mammals, reptiles and birds, fertilization occurs within the female's body; in the majority of fish and amphibians, and most aquatic invertebrates, it occurs externally, when both sexes release their gametes freely into the water. In most fungi, gametes are not released, but the hyphae of the two parents grow towards each other and fuse to achieve fertilization. In higher plants, pollination precedes fertilization. In self-fertilization the male and female gametes come from the same plant; in cross-fertilization they come from different plants. Self-fertilization occurs rarely in her-maphrodite animals.

zygote the name given to an ovum (egg) after fertilization, but before it undergoes cleavage at the start of its development.

egg in animals, the ovum, or female gamete (reproductive cell). After fertilization by a sperm cell, it begins to divide to form an embryo. Eggs may be deposited by the female (ovipary) or they may develop within her body (vivipary and ovovivipary). In the oviparous reptiles and birds, the egg is protected by a shell, and well supplied with nutrients in the form of yolk. In plants, the ovum is called an egg-cell.

seed the reproductive structure of higher plants (angiosperms and gymnosperms). It develops from a fertilized ovule and consists of an embryo and a food store, surrounded and protected by an outer seed coat, called the testa. The food store is contained either in a specialized nutritive tissue, the endosperm, or in the cotyledons of the embryo itself. In angiosperms the seed is enclosed within a fruit, whereas in gymnosperms it is usually naked and unprotected, once shed from the female cone. Following germination the seed develops into a new plant but there may be a delay in germination to ensure growth occurs under favourable conditions.

spore a small reproductive or resting body, usually consisting of just one cell. Unlike a gamete, it does not need to fuse with another cell in order to develop into a new organism. Spores are produced by the lower plants, most fungi, some bacteria, and certain protozoa. They are generally light and easily dispersed by wind movements. Plant spores are haploid and are produced by the sporophyte, following meiosis.

embryo early development stage of animals and plants following fertilization of an ovum (egg cell), or parthenogenetic activation of an ovum. In animals the embryo exists either within an egg (where it is nourished by food contained in the yolk), or in mammals, in the uterus of the mother.

metamorphosis a period during the life cycle of many invertebrates, most amphibians and some fish, during which the individual's body changes from one form to another through a major reconstitution of its tissues. Thus, adult frogs are produced by metamorphosis from tadpoles, while butterflies are produced from caterpillars following metamorphosis within a pupa.

larva the young of an animal, in species where the young has a different appearance and way of life from the adult. Larvae are typical of the invertebrates, and some (for example, shrimps) have two or more distinct larval stages. (However, some invertebrates hatch as tiny replicas of their parents, while in others the young differ only slightly, for example, the nymphs of certain insects.) Among vertebrates, it is only the amphibians and some fish that have a larval stage. The process whereby the larva changes into an adult is known as metamorphosis.

pupa the non-feeding, largely immobile stage of some insect life cycles, in which larval tissues are broken down and adult tissues and structures are formed. In most insects it is exarate, with the appendages (legs, antennae, wings) visible outside the pupal case, but in butterflies and moths it is obtect, with the appendages developing inside the pupal case.

ageing in common usage, the period of deterioration of the physical condition of a living organism that leads to death; but in biological terms, the entire life-process, beginning at the moment when as egg is fertilized and starts to develop into a new individual, and continuing to its eventual death. Three current theories attempt to account for ageing. The first suggests that the process is genetically determined, to remove individuals that can no longer reproduce by causing their death. The second suggests that it is due to the accumulation of mistakes during the replication of DNA at cell division. The third suggests that it is actively induced by pieces of DNA which move between cells, or cancer-causing viruses; these may become abundant in old cells and induce them to produce unwanted proteins or interfere with the control functions of their DNA.

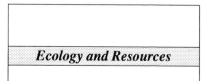

Ecology and Resources

ecology the study of the relationship between an organism and the environment in which it lives, including other living organisms and the non-living surroundings. The term was first introduced by the biologist Ernst Haeckel in 1866. Ecology may be concerned with individual organisms (for example, behavioural ecology, foraging strategies), with populations or species (for example, population dynamics) or with entire communities (for example, competition between species for access to resources, or predator-prey relationships). Applied ecology is concerned with the management and conservation of habitats and the consequences and control of pollution.

conservation in the life sciences, care for, and protection of, the biosphere. Since the 1950s it has been increasingly realized that the earth, together with its atmosphere, animal and plant life, and mineral and agricultural resources, form an interdependent whole which is in danger of irreversible depletion and eventual destruction unless positive measures are taken to conserve a balance. Action by governments has been supplemented by private agencies, such as the World Wildlife Fund. In attempts to save particular species or habitats, a distinction is often made between *preservation*, that is maintaining the pristine state of nature exactly as it was or might have been, and *conservation*, the management of natural resources in such a way as to allow any of its excess production to be controlled, or to be used for commercial purposes, including integration of the requirements of the local human population with those of the animals, plants or the habitat being conserved.

endangered species a plant or animal species whose numbers are so few that it is at risk of becoming extinct. Thus, there are only about 50 Javan rhino alive today and, unless active steps are taken to promote this species' survival, it will probably be extinct within a few decades. Officially designated endangered species are listed by IUCN.

CITES *Convention on International Trade in Endangered Species.* An international agreement signed by 81 countries under the auspices of the IUCN to regulate the trade in endangered species of animals and plants. Because it was first signed in 1973 at Washington DC, it is sometimes known as the *Washington Convention.*

Organizations

Countryside Commission an official conservation body, created for England and Wales under the Countryside Act 1968.

International Union for the Conservation of Nature (IUCN) an organization established by the United Nations to promote the conservation of wildlife and habitats in the national policies of member states.

Nature Conservancy Council (NCC) a UK government agency established in 1973 to oversee nature conservation. It is responsible for designating and managing National Nature Reserves and other conservation areas (for example, Sites of Special Scientific Interest, SSSIs) and for the enforcement of legislation that protects wildlife and habitats.

World Wildlife Fund an international organization established in 1961 to raise funds for conservation by public appeal. Its headquarters are at Gland, Switzerland, but many countries have their own autonomous branches. Projects include conservation of particular species (for example, the tiger and giant panda) or special areas (for example, the Simen Mountains, Ethiopia).

Feeding relationships

trophic level in ecology, the position occupied by a species (or group of species) in a food chain. The main levels are primary producers (for example, plants), primary consumers (for example, herbivores), secondary consumers (for example, carnivores), and decomposers.

autotroph any living organism which synthesizes organic substances from inorganic molecules using light or chemical energy. All green plants and many planktonic organisms are autotrophs, using sunlight to convert carbon dioxide and water into sugars by photosynthesis. A few bacteria use chemical energy; for example, some bacteria use the chemical energy of sulphur compounds to synthesize organic substance. Materials synthesized and stored by autotrophs provide the energy sources of all other organisms: they are the *primary producers* in all food chains.

heterotroph any living organism that obtains its energy from organic substances which have been produced by other organisms. All animals and fungi are heterotrophs, and they include herbivores (which feed on autotrophs), carnivores (which feed on other heterotrophs), and saprotrophs (which feed on dead animal and plant material).

herbivore an animal which feeds on green plant material. In a broader sense, any animal that lives by eating plants or their products, including seeds, fruit and nectar, as well as photosynthetic organisms in the plankton. Herbivorous animals are more numerous than other types because their food is the most abundant. They form a vital link in the food chain between plants and carnivores.

carnivore an animal which eats other animals. Sometimes confined to animals that eat the flesh of vertebrate prey, but often used more broadly, to include animals that eat any other animals, even microscopic ones. Carrion eaters may or may not be included. Additionally, the name carnivore is sometimes used to refer to members of the mammalian group Carnivora, which includes cats, dogs, bears, badgers, and weasels.

omnivore an animal which feeds on both plant and animal material. Omnivores have digestive adaptations intermediate between those of herbivores and carnivores, with relatively unspecialized digestive systems and gut micro-organisms which can digest a variety of foodstuffs.

food chain or food web the sequence of organisms through which energy and other nutrients are successively transferred in an ecological system. The main components of the sequence are the autotrophs or *primary producers*, principally plants and photosynthetic microorganisms, the herbivores that feed on them, the carnivores that feed on the herbivores, and the decomposers that break down the dead bodies and waste products of all three groups, ready for recycling. Many organisms, however, feed at several different levels (for example, omnivores such as bears and badgers, feed on both fruit and meat), so that the relationships often form a complex web rather than a simple chain.

parasite a creature depending on another for the necessities of life, for example, lice, fleas, the acarus that causes scabies, tapeworms, and the microscopic organisms that cause syphilis and malaria. Plants, too, may be parasitic.

host an organism that is parasitized by another. In commensalism, the partner that does not benefit may also be called the host.

epiphyte a plant which grows on another plant or object above the surface of the ground, and which has no roots in the soil. An epiphyte does not parasitize the plant it grows on, but merely uses it for support.

saprophyte an obsolete term for a saprotroph. It reflected the mistaken belief that fungi and bacteria, the principal saprotrophs, were plants, hence the ending *-phyte* (Greek: plant).

commensalism a relationship between two species whereby one (the commensal) benefits from the association, while the other neither benefits nor suffers. For example, certain species of millipede and silverfish inhabit the nests of army ants and live by scavenging on the refuse of their hosts, but without affecting the ants.

symbiosis closely interdependent relationship between two different species of animals or plants for their mutual benefit ('mutualism'). For example, trichonympha live in the stomach of wood termites digesting the wood (for its own food) and converting it to carbohydrate for the host who would otherwise be unable to digest wood. Another example is the lichen (a symbiotic relationship between a fungus and an alga). In a broader (less correct) sense, symbiosis may also refer to commensal relationships (whereby one species lives with a host without conferring either benefit or harm on the host: for example, house mice living in human habitations) and parasitism (whereby one species lives in or on a host species at the host's expense: for example, the flea).

Terms

biological control the control of pests such as insects and fungi through biological means, rather than the use of chemicals. This can include breeding resistant crop strains (for example, wheat varieties resistant to the fungi that cause 'rust'), inducing infertility in the pest (for example, by sterilizing male insects, or spraying with a juvenile hormone that prevents insect larvae maturing into adults), breeding viruses that attack the pest species, or introducing the pest's natural predator (for example, the release of a cactus-eating moth caterpillar to control the spread of prickly pear cactus in Australia). Biological control is preferable to chemical control of pests because it tends to be naturally self-regulating for example, the predators of a pest will die off when there are few pests left to eat), and it does not involve using pesticides that affect human health. However living systems are so complex that it is difficult to predict all the consequences of introducing a biological controlling agent.

biomass the gross weight of organisms present in a given area. It may be specified for one particular species (for example, earthworm biomass), for a category of species (for example, herbivore biomass) or for all species (total biomass).

biosphere or *ecosphere* that region of the earth's surface (land and water), and the atmosphere above it, which can be occupied by living organisms.

carbon cycle the sequence by which carbon circulates and is recycled through the natural world. The carbon element from carbon dioxide in the atmosphere is taken up, during the process of photosynthesis, the oxygen component being released back into the atmosphere. Photosynthesis is carried out by plants and by organisms such as diatoms and dinoflagellates in the oceanic plankton. The carbon they accumulate is later released back into circulation through the decomposition of decaying plant matter, the consumption of plant matter or plankton by herbivores, or the burning of fuels such as coal (fossilized plants). Today, the carbon cycle is being altered by the increased consumption of fossil fuels, and burning of large tracts of tropical forests, as a result of which levels of carbon dioxide are building up in the atmosphere and contributing to the greenhouse effect.

carrying capacity in ecology, the maximum number of animals of a given species that a particular area can support. When the carrying capacity is exceeded, there is insufficient food (or other resources) for all members of the population. The population may then be reduced by emigration, reproductive failure, or death through starvation.

environment in ecology, the sum of conditions affecting a particular organism, including physical surroundings, climate and influences of other living organisms. In common usage, 'the environment' often means the total global environment, without reference to any particular organism. In genetics, the external influences that affect an organism's development, and thus its phenotype.

eutrophication the over-enrichment of lake waters, primarily by nitrate fertilizers washed from soil by rain, and phosphates from detergents in municipal sewage. These encourage the growth of algae to the extent of eliminating oxygen, thereby making the water uninhabitable for fish and other animal life.

fertility an organism's ability to reproduce. Individuals become infertile (unable to reproduce) when they cannot generate gametes (eggs or sperm) or when their gametes cannot yield a viable embryo after fertilization.

greenhouse effect the atmosphere, like the glass of a greenhouse, lets much of the sun's visible and near ultraviolet radiation through it to warm the earth's surface. The warm earth re-radiates electromagnetic radiation but of a far lower frequency (for infrared) to which the atmosphere, like glass, is not as transparent. This 'trapping' or 'greenhouse' effect contributes to raising the earth's temperature. Activities of people, such as burning fossil fuels, which increase the carbon dioxide (a good infrared absorber) in the atmosphere are tending to promote the greenhouse effect; conceivably the earth's temperature could rise enough for polar ice to melt, raising the sea level dangerously.

habitat in ecology, the localized environment in which an organism lives. Habitats are often described by the dominant plant type or physical feature, thus an oak-wood habitat or rocky seashore habitat.

indicator species a plant or animal whose presence or absence in an area indicates certain environmental conditions. For example, some lichens sensitive to sulpur dioxide in the air, and absence of these species indicates stmospheric pollution. Many plants show a preference for either alkaline or acid soil conditions, while certain plants, mostly trees, require aluminium, and are only found in soils where it is present.

nature reserve area set aside to preserve its original scenic formation or vegetation, and often to provide a sanctuary and breeding ground for rare birds or animals. The National Parks Act, 1949, gave powers to designate such areas in Britain, to be placed in the charge of the Nature Conservancy Council established 1973.

niche in ecology, the 'place' occupied by a species in its habitat, including its food requirements, the time of day at which it feeds, the parts of the habitat it uses (for example, trees or open grassland). Ecological theory holds that two species cannot occupy exactly the same niche and coexist; they will be in direct competition and one will eventually give way to the other.

nitrogen cycle in ecology, the process whereby nitrogen is passed through the ecosystem. Nitrogen in the form of inorganic compounds (such as nitrates) in the soil is absorbed by plants and turned into organic compounds (such as proteins) in plant tissue. A proportion of this nitrogen is consumed by herbivores and used for their own biological processes, with some of this in turn being passed on to the carnivores. The nitrogen is finally returned to the soil, either as excreta or when the organisms die, to be returned to inorganic form by bacterial decomposers. Although this atmosphere contains a great deal of free nitrogen, this cannot be used by most organisms. However, certain bacteria and cyanobacteria are capable of nitrogen fixation, that is they can extract nitrogen directly from the atmosphere and convert it to compounds such as nitrates which other organisms can use. Some nitrogen-fixing bacteria live in a mutualistic association with leguminous plants (peas and beans) or other plants (for example, alder) where they form characteristic nodules on the roots. The presence of such plants greatly increases the nitrate content, and hence the fertility of the soil.

nitrogen fixation the process in which nitrogen in the atmosphere is converted into nitrogenous compounds either by lightning, or by the action of microorganisms, such as cyanobacteria and bacteria.

pesticide a chemical such as DDT which is used to destroy pests (usually insects).

pollution the harmful effect on the environment of the by-products of any human activity, principally industrial and agricultural processes, for example, noise, smoke, gases, chemical effluents in seas and rivers, indestructible pesticides, sewage and household waste. Natural disasters such as volcanic eruptions may also cause pollution through ash ejected into the atmosphere and deposited on the land surface. Natural dispersal and breakdown counters pollution to a degree, but it rapidly escalates to danger level. Complete control would involve increases in production costs for the industries concerned, but failure to implement adequate controls results in damage to the environment, and an increase in the incidence of cancer, and other diseases. It could also eventually lead to areas that have become

heavily polluted being uninhabitable.

recycling the reclamation of potentially useful material from household and industrial waste, thus reducing pollution, saving expenditure on scarce raw materials, and slowing down the depletion of non-renewable resources.

sewage disposal the disposal of human excreta and other water-borne waste products from houses, factories, streets. It is conveyed through sewers and treated before being discharged into rivers or the sea. Sewage works are the responsibility of local authorities. The sludge may be spread over fields attached to the works, or it may be processed and sold as a fertilizer. In places near the coast, raw sewage may be dumped into the sea. The use of raw sewage as a fertilizer, (as long practised in China) has the drawback that disease-causing microorganisms may survive in the soil and be taken into the body by consumption of subsequent crops.

standing crop in ecology, the total number of individuals of a given species alive in a particular area at any moment. It is sometimes measured as the weight (or biomass) of a given species.

succession in ecology, the change that occurs in the structure and composition of the vegetation in a given area from the time it is first colonized, or after it has been disturbed (for example, by fire, flood, or clearance). If allowed to proceed undisturbed, succession leads naturally to a climax community (for example, oak forest or *savannah* grassland) that is determined by the climate and soil characteristics of the area.

sustained yield cropping in wildlife conservation the removal of surplus individuals from a population of organisms such that the population maintains a constant size. This usually requires selective removal of animals of all ages and both sexes to ensure a balanced population structure. Excessive cropping of young females, for example, may lead to fewer births in following years, and a fall in population size. The appropriate cropping frequencies can be determined from an analysis of a life table.

water cycle in ecology, the natural circulation of water through the biosphere. Water is lost from the earth's surface to the atmosphere either by evaporation from the surface of lakes, rivers and oceans or through the transpiration of plants. This atmospheric water forms clouds which, under the appropriate conditions, condense to deposit moisture on the land and sea as rain or snow.

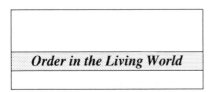

Order in the Living World

taxonomy an alternative name for the science of biological classification.

classification the arrangement of organisms into a hierarchy of groups, on the basis of their similarities in biochemical, anatomical or physiological characters. Species are assumed to share characters because they acquire them from a common ancestor. (Care is taken to exclude shared characteristics known to be due to convergent evolution.) Such a classification is thus thought to mirror the evolutionary relationships between organisms. The basic grouping is a species, several of which may constitute a genus, which in turn are grouped into families, and so on up through orders, classes, phyla (or, in plants, divisions) to kingdoms.

binomial system of nomenclature the system in which all organisms are identified by a two-part Latinized name. Devised by the biologist Linnaeus, it is also known as the Linnean System. The first name identifies the genus, the second the species within that genus. Usually the names are descriptive. Thus, the name of the dog, *Canis familiaris*, *means the 'familiar species of the dog genus'*, *Canis being Latin for 'dog'. Each species is defined by an officially designated* **type specimen** housed at a particular museum. The rules for naming organisms in this way are specified in a number of International Codes of Taxonomic Nomenclature administered by two International Commissions on Nomenclature, one zoological and one botanical.

phylum a division of animals or plants which contains several classes.

genus a set of species that share a large number of characteristics in common. Thus, all doglike species (including dogs, wolves and jackals) belong to the genus *Canis*. Species of the same genus are thought to be descended from a common ancestor species. Related genera are grouped into families.

species in biology, a distinguishable group of organisms, which resemble each other or consist of a few distinctive types (as in polymorphism), and which can all interbreed (actually or potentially) to produce fertile offspring. Species are the lowest level in the system of biological classification. Examples include lions, Douglas fir, cabbage white butterflies and sperm whales. All living human beings belong to the same species because they can all interbreed, even though they may differ considerably in such features as skin colour, height, head shape, and so on.

Related species are grouped together in a genus. Within a species there are usually two or more separate populations, which may become distinctive enough, in time, to be designated sub-species or varieties, and could eventually give rise to new species, through speciation.

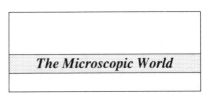

The Microscopic World

cell in biology, a discrete, membrane-bound portion of living matter – the unit of physical life. Bacteria, amoebae, and certain other microorganisms consist of single cells. Plants and animals are composed entirely of cells of various kinds. The body of a mammal (including that of the human species) originates from an organism consisting of a single-cell – an ovum or egg-cell generated by the female and fertilized by fusion with a spermatozoon or seed-cell generated by the male. The fertilized ovum (embryo) is a microscopic body chiefly consisting of protoplasm, or clear jelly, the simplest form of living substance. The protoplasmic part of the cell is called the cytoplasm. It is enclosed in a membranous wall and contains a small spherical body called a nucleus – an essential part of most cells, without which they cannot reproduce. The only cells of the body which have no nucleus are the red blood cells. The nucleus of the embryo contains a denser spot called the nucleolus, but many kinds of cells do not.

The composition of the protoplasm varies, but its breakdown products when the cell dies are mostly proteins. It contains also carbohydrates, fats, and the lipoids lecithin and cholesterin, besides inorganic salts such as the phosphates and chlorides of potash, soda, and lime. The cell wall in most animal cells is not a definite membrane, but the shape of the cell is maintained by surface tension or chemical action.

Cells reproduce by division, a complicated process which starts in the nucleus. The function of the cell is to convert energy from one form into another, for example, food and oxygen into chemical energy. Sexual reproduction is performed by the union of two special kinds of cells. When the human ovum is fertilized by fusion with a spermatozoon, the new cell contains the chromosomes from both – 48. The sex of the new individual is determined by the distribution of the special sex chromosomes. The ordinary cells of the female body have two X chromosomes; the cells of the male body have an X and a Y chromosome – two different types. The mature ovum contains one X chromosome and the mature spermatozoon contains either an X or a Y chromosome.

If on fertilization two X chromosomes meet, the result is a female; if an X and a Y meet, the result is a male. All men thus inherit from their fathers one Y chromosome which gives their male characteristics: some (perhaps one in 300) inherit two, which give added height, greater emotional instability, inability to bear frustration, and great aggressiveness. These men are often criminally violent, and possession of the Y-factor, immediately detectable under the microscope, has (as in France and Australia 1968) been successfully pleaded in mitigation in murder cases.

Ionization arising from gamma or X-radiation can damage chromosomes, and in the case of reproduction chromosomes this may lead to disruption of the chromosomes and potential degradation of the offspring.

In 1976 the barrier between the plant and animal kingdoms was broken by the achievement in the laboratory (in UK, USA and Hungary), of the fusion of a plant and animal cell to form a hybrid, e.g. red blood cell from a hen and a yeast cell, using polyethylene glycol as a fusing agent. There has as yet been no development beyond a single cell.

cytology the study of cells, especially in relation to their functions. Major advances have been made possible in this field by the development of electron microscopes.

Terms

archaebacteria a name given to three groups of bacteria whose DNA differs significantly from that of other bacteria (called the 'eubacteria'). All are strict anaerobes, that is, they are killed by oxygen. This is a primitive condition, and shows that the archaebacteria are related to the earliest life forms, which appeared about 4,000 million years ago, when there was little oxygen in the earth's atmosphere. The methanogens represent one group of archaebacteria.

bacillus a group of rod-like bacteria that occur everywhere in the soil and air, and are responsible for diseases such as anthrax as well as causing food spoilage.

bacteria microscopic unicellular organisms with prokaryotic cells. They are now classified biochemically, but their varying shapes provide a rough classification, for example, *cocci* are round or oval, *rods* are cylindrical, and *spirillae* are spiral. They reproduce by binary fission, and since this may occur approximately every 20 minutes, a single bacterium is potentially capable of producing 16 million copies of itself in a day. Bacteria mutate readily, a characteristic which accounts both for the rapid emergence of strains which are resistant to antibiotics. Unlike viruses, bacteria do not necessarily need contact with a live cell to become active. Bacteria are generally thought of as harmful, and certain types do cause disease. However, many other types perform useful functions in the healthy human body, break down waste products or improve soil fertility. Bacteria are essential in many food and industrial processes, for example, making butter, cheese and yoghurt, as well as curing tobacco, tanning leather, and sewage disposal. Bacteria cannot normally survive temperatures above 10°C/21°F, but those in deep sea hot vents in the eastern Pacific are believed to withstand temperatures of 35°C/66°F.

bacteriophage a virus that attacks bacteria.

diatom class of microscopic unicellular algae (marine or freshwater), class Bacillariophyceae, which as fossils constitute diatomaceous earth (diatomite) used in the rubber and plastics industries, and as living creatures are a constituent of plankton.

eukaryote one of the two classes into which all living organisms (except viruses) are divided. The cells of eukaryotes possess a clearly defined nucleus, bounded by a membrane, within which DNA is formed into distinct chromosomes. Their cells contain mitochondria, chloroplasts and other organelles which are lacking in the cells of the alternative class, the prokaryotes. All organisms other than bacteria and cyanobacteria are eukaryotic.

microbe in biology, a microscopic organism, a germ, bacillus, micro-organism, or bacterium, which has life and the ability to multiply.

procaryote one of the two classes of living cell, that in which there is no definite nucleus, as in bacteria and blue-green algae.

protozoa a group of single-celled eukaryotic organisms without rigid cell walls. Some, such as amoeba, ingest other cells, but most are saprotrophs or parasites. A few of the euglenoids contain chlorophyll and are photosynthetic. The group is polyphyletic, that is, it contains organisms which have different evolutionary origins.

slime mould an extraordinary organism that shows some features of fungi and some of protozoa. Slime moulds are not closely related to any other group, although they are often classed, for convenience, with the fungi. They fall into two main types, the *cellular slime moulds* and the *plasmodial slime moulds*. The former go through a phase of living as single cells, that look very like amoebae, and feed by engulfing the bacteria found in rotting wood, dung or damp soil. When a food supply is exhausted, up to 100,000 of these amoebae form into a colony which looks like a single slug-like animal and migrates to a fresh source of bacteria. It then takes on the aspect of a fungus, and forms long-stalked fruiting bodies which release spores. These germinate to release amoebae, which repeat the life cycle. The plasmodial slime moulds are similar in many ways, but have a more complex lifestyle involving sexual reproduction. They form a slimy mass of protoplasm with no internal cell walls, that slowly spreads over the bark or fallen branches of trees.

virus an infectious particle consisting of a 'core' of nucleic acids (DNA or RNA) enclosed in a protein 'shell'. Viruses are acellular, and outside the cell of another organism they remain completely inert, being able to function and reproduce only if they can force their way into a living cell so as to be able to use the cell's system to replicate themselves. In doing so, they may disrupt or alter the host cell's own DNA. The healthy human body reacts to such an invasion by producing an antiviral protein, interferon, which prevents the infection spreading to adjacent cells. Viruses are responsible for causing diseases like canine distemper, chickenpox, common cold, herpes, influenza, measles, rabies, smallpox, yellow fever and many plant diseases. Recent evidence implicates viruses in the development of some forms of cancer. *Retroviruses* are of special interest because they have an RNA genome, and can produce DNA from this RNA, a process which apparently contravenes the central dogma. *Viroids*, discovered in 1971 are even smaller than viruses, a single strand of nucleic acid with no protein coat. They cause stunting in plants and some rare diseases in animals, including humans.

yeast a mass of minute circular or oval vegetable cells about .000085 m/^{1}/$_{3000}$ in in diameter, each of which is a complete plant capable under suitable conditions of reproducing new cells by budding.

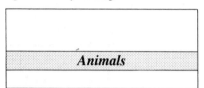

Animals

animal one of the two 'kingdoms' of living things, the science of which is zoology, the other being the vegetable kingdom or plants, the science of which is botany.

Animals and plants are fundamentally similar in microscopical structure, being composed of a substance, protoplasm, and the tissues in the more elaborately organized examples of the two kingdoms alike consist primarily of minute particles of protoplasm known as cells. But the overall structure of all the familiar animals and plants is so different that there is no difficulty in distinguishing one from the other. There is also the important physiological difference that animals are capable of living and developing only by the nutritive assimilations of the protoplasmic tissues of other living organisms, plant or animal. Animals are dependent on plants, and must have succeeded them in the evolution of living things. But these differences, both anatomical and physiological, between the more complex and familiar animals and plants break down in the simplest, most primitive forms of animals, the Protozoa, which are so distinct from other animals that

they are given the rank of a sub-kingdom, the rest being assigned to the sub-kingdom Metazoa. Owing to the dying out of formerly existing links, the Metazoa can be classified into a number of primary, definable groups, each of which is known as a phylum, meaning a stock or line of descent; and the classification, or taxonomy, of animals is based on the resemblances such as exist between a whale and a shark and which have been acquired as adaptations to a similar mode of life.

animal classification there are over ten million species of animal in the world. Animals can be readily divided into those with a backbone, the *vertebrates*, and those without, the *invertebrates*. Invertebrates represent some 95% of all animals; they vastly outnumber vertebrates in terms of species also, and they show a greater variety of forms. Classification of the animal kingdom is into phyla (from the Greek word for 'race'). Each phylum is then subdivided into classes, orders, families, genera, and species. The class Mammalia, to which humans belong, numbers less than 5,000 species, and of these, nearly half are rodents and about a quarter are bats. An example of the class Mammalia is the tiger, which belongs to the order Carnivora, family Felidae, is grouped with the lion, leopard, and jaguar in the genus *Panthera*, and is distingushed as a species by the addition of the species name, *Panthera tigris*.

Main Animal Types
amphibian a class of vertebrates (Greek 'double life') which generally spends a gill-breathing larval ('tadpole') stage in fresh water, before becoming an air-breathing adult living on land, returning to the water to breed. Amphibians cannot maintain a temperature much different to their surroundings. They include salamanders, newts, frogs, toads and the tropical worm-like caecilians.

annelid worm segmented worm of the phylum Annelida, which includes earthworms, leeches and marine worms such as lugworms and ragworms. There is a distinct head and the soft body is divided into a number of similar segments shut off from one another by internal partitions. There are no jointed legs or other appendages.

arthropod invertebrate animal with jointed legs and a segmented body with a horny or chitinous casing, the latter being shed periodically and replaced as the animal grows. This definition includes arachnids such as spiders and mites, as well as crustaceans, millipedes, centipedes and insects. They were all formerly placed in the same phylum, Arthropoda, but it is now believed that some groups had a separate origin.

bird warm-blooded, vertebrate animal clothed in feathers, and with its forelimbs transformed into wings. Birds are egg-laying, and feathers and scales originate as epidermal appendages. Except in brain development, they are structurally as highly organized as mammals. Their behaviour is largely instinctive. Yet their body temperature is much than that of mammals, and both physically and mentally they have become highly specialized.

centipede arthropod of the class Chilopoda, having a distinct head, single pair of antennae, and numerous similar segments each bearing a single pair of jointed limbs. Mostly nocturnal and predatory, centipedes have strong 'jaws' with poison fangs to kill insects and worms. Some tropical species reach 30 cm/1 ft, with a bite dangerous to humans.

crustacean one of the class of arthropods that includes crabs, lobsters, shrimps, woodlice, barnacles and many less familiar forms. The external skeleton is made of protein and chitin hardened with lime. Each segment bears a pair of appendages which may be modified as antennae, for feeding, swimming, walking or grasping. Most breathe with gills. There are 30,000+ species, varying from 0.025 cm/0.001 in to 3 m/10 ft across. Most are marine and they are very important in the food-chains of the sea.

echinoderm marine invertebrate which has a basic body structure divided into five sectors. The phylum Echinodermata ('spiny-skinned') includes the starfish, brittlestars, sea-lilies, sea urchins and sea-cucumbers. The skeleton is external, made of a series of limy plates, and they generally move using tube-feet – small water-filled sacs which can be protruded or pulled back to the body.

fish aquatic vertebrate that breathes using gills. There are three main groups, not very closely related: the jawless fishes (lamprey, hagfish); the sharks and rays; and the bony fishes. In the latter, the majority of living fishes (about 20,000 species), the skeleton is bone, movement is controlled by mobile fins, and the body is usually covered with scales. The gills are covered by a single flap. Many have a swim bladder which the fish uses to adjust its buoyancy. Most lay eggs, sometimes in vast numbers.

flatworm invertebrate of the phylum Platyhelminthes. Some are free-living, but many are parasitic – the tapeworms and flukes. The body is simple and bilaterally symmetrical. The gut has a mouth but no anus or, in tapeworms, is absent. Many are hermaphrodite (male and female), with complex sex organs, the parasitic forms producing large numbers of eggs.

insect arthropod of the class Insecta whose body is divided into head, thorax and abdomen. The head bears one pair of antennae. The thorax bears three pairs of legs, and usually two pairs of wings. More than a million species are known; many more are discovered each year. Size varies from 0.02 cm/0.007 in to 35 cm/1.5 ft. The skeleton is external and made of chitin. The more 'primitive' species (such as cockroaches, bugs) change appearance gradually from hatching to adult. In more 'advanced' species (such as butterflies, flies, beetles) the larva which emerges from the egg is very different from the adult, and between the two is a 'resting' and reorganizing stage, the pupa.

invertebrate any animal without a backbone. More than two million species are known, as against 41,000 species of vertebrates.

jellyfish marine animal of the phylum Cnidaria, with an umbrella-shaped body of semitransparent gelatinous substance fringed

animal classification

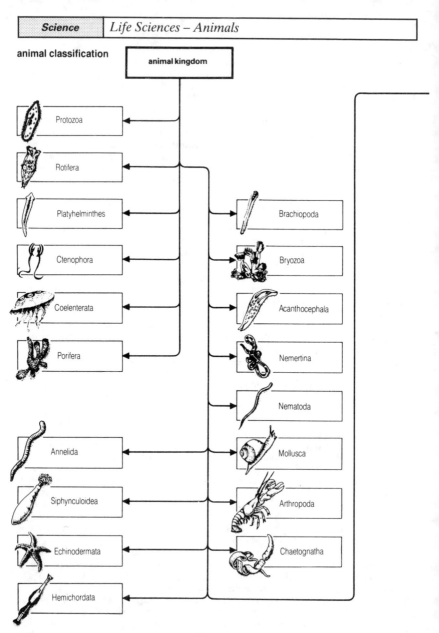

animal kingdom

Protozoa

Rotifera

Platyhelminthes

Ctenophora

Coelenterata

Porifera

Annelida

Siphynculoidea

Echinodermata

Hemichordata

Brachiopoda

Bryozoa

Acanthocephala

Nemertina

Nematoda

Mollusca

Arthropoda

Chaetognatha

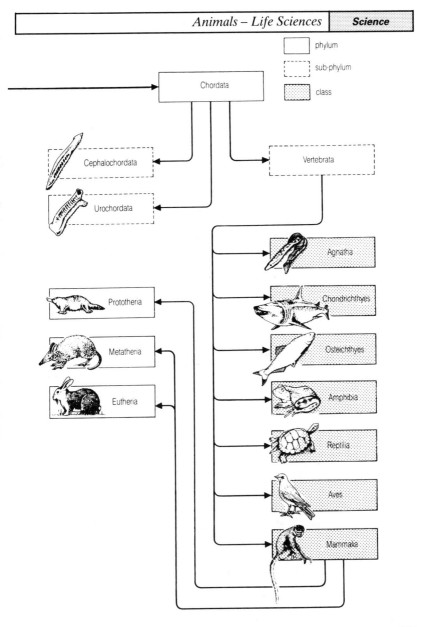

legend:
- phylum
- sub-phylum
- class

Chordata

Cephalochordata

Urochordata

Vertebrata

Agnatha

Chondrichthyes

Osteichthyes

Amphibia

Reptilia

Aves

Mammalia

Prototheria

Metatheria

Eutheria

by stinging tentacles. Jellyfish feed on small animals paralysed by these stings. Most move freely, but some are attached by stalks to rocks or seaweed.

mammal vertebrate which suckles its young and has fur or hair, lungs and four-chambered heart. It maintains a constant body temperature in varied surroundings. Most mammals give birth to live young, but the platypus and echidna lay eggs. There are over 4,000 species, adapted to almost every conceivable way of life. The smallest shrew is only 2 gm/0.07 oz, the largest whale up to 200 tonnes.

millipede arthropod of the class Diplopoda, having a distinct head with a pair of short clubbed antennae, and numerous similar segments with two pairs of legs on each. Millipedes live in damp dark places, feeding mainly on rotting vegetation, and some produce a poisonous secretion in defence.

mollusc soft bodied, limbless, and cold-blooded invertebrate, some being marine, although some molluscs inhabit fresh water and a few are terrestrial. Molluscs include shellfish, snails, slugs, and cuttlefish. There is no internal skeleton, but most species have a hard shell covering the body. In some cases, for example the cuttle and squid, the shell is internal. There is a fold of skin, the mantle, which covers the whole body or the back only, and secretes the calcareous substance forming the shell. The lower ventral surface forms the locomotory organ, or foot.

nematode worm unsegmented worm, pointed at both ends, and with a tough smooth outer skin, of the phylum Aschelminthes. Nematodes include some soil and water forms, but a large number are parasites, such as the roundworms and pinworms that live in animals, or the eelworms that attack plant roots. Nematodes are one of the most numerous types of animal.

reptile egg-laying scaly-skinned vertebrate which breathes using lungs and is 'cold-blooded' – needing an outside source of heat to achieve a high body temperature. The main types are tortoises, turtles, crocodiles and alligators, snakes and lizards. The metabolism

is slow, and in some cases (some large snakes) intervals between meals may be months.

rotifer tiny invertebrate, also called 'wheel animalcule' of the Phylum Aschelminthes. Mainly freshwater, some marine, rotifers have a ring of cilia which carries food to the mouth, and also provides propulsion. Smallest of multicellular animals, few reach 0.05 cm/0.02 in.

scorpion arthropod of the class Arachnida, related to spiders. Common in the tropics and sub-tropics, scorpions have a head and crab-like pincers, eight legs, a segmented body, and a long tail ending in a poisonous sting, rarely fatal to humans. Some species reach 15 cm/6 in. They mate after a courtship dance, produce live young, and hunt chiefly at night.

sea anemone invertebrate sea-dwelling animal of the class Cnidaria with a tube-like body attached by the base to a rock or shell. The other end has an open 'mouth' surrounded by stinging tentacles, which capture crustaceans and other small organisms. Sea anemones occur in many beautiful colours, especially in tropical waters.

sea urchin echinoderm, related to starfish, in which the body is globular, heart- or shield-shaped, enclosed by a box armour of limy plates. The spines on the skin may assist in locomotion, or be modified for grasping, as well as giving protection. Urchins graze using five movable teeth surrounding the mouth.

spider arthropod of the class Arachnida, with a cephalothorax (combined 'head-chest'), separated from the abdomen by a narrow waist. There are eight legs, and up to eight eyes. Below the abdomen are the spinnerets from which silk is spun to make the web, although some species stalk their prey. Their fangs inject substances to subdue and digest their prey, the juices of which are then sucked in by the spider.

sponge very simple animal of the phylum Porifera, usually marine. A sponge has a hollow body, its cavity lined by cells bearing flagellae, whose whip-like movements keep water circulating, bringing a stream of food particles. The body walls are strengthened with protein (as in the bath-sponge) or little spikes.

starfish echinoderm with arms radiating from a central body. Usually there are five arms, but some species have more. Starfish are predators, some species using their suckered tube-feet to pull open the shells of bivalve molluscs, then pushing their stomach inside out to surround and digest the animal inside.

vertebrae any animal with a backbone. Vertebrates include mammals, birds, reptiles, amphibians and fishes; in all over 41,000 species.

worm general name for any softbodied, elongated invertebrate. There are many groups of worms, zoologically unrelated, including annelids (such as earthworms), flatworms (such as flukes), and nematodes (roundworms), as well as the marine ribbon-worms (Nemertea).

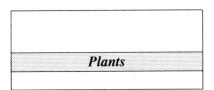

Plants

plant an organism that carries out photosynthesis, has cellulose cell walls and complex eukaryotc cells and is immobile. However, a few parasitic plants have lost the ability to photosynthesize, but are still considered as plants. Some authorities would also include the single-celled algae, such as *Chlamydomanas* with the plants, although these can move around. On the other hand, some classification schemes exclude all algae, even seaweeds, from the plant kingdom, and put them with the protists. Many of the lower plants (the algae and bryophytes) consist of a simple body or thallus upon which the organs of reproduction are borne. Simplest of all are the threadlike algae, for example, *Spirogyra*, which consist of a chain of cells. The seaweeds (algae) and mosses and liverworts (bryophytes) represent a further development, with their simple, multicellular bodies that have specially modified areas in which the reproductive organs are

carried. Higher in the morphological scale are the ferns, clubmosses and horsetails (pteridophytes). Ferns produce leaf-like fronds bearing sporangia on their under-surface in which the spores are carried. The spores are freed and germinate to produce small independent bodies carrying the sexual organs; thus the fern, like other pteridophytes, and some seaweeds, has two quite separate generations in its life cycle. The pteridophytes have special supportive water-conducting tissues, which identify them as vascular plants. This group includes all seed plants, that is the gymnosperms (conifers, yews, cycads and ginkgo) and the angiosperms (flowering plants). The seed plants are the largest group, and structurally the most complex. They are usually divided into three parts, root, stem and leaves. Stems grow above or below ground. Their cellular structure is designed to carry water and salts from the roots to the leaves in the xylem, and sugars from the leaves to the roots in the phloem. The leaves manufacture the food of the plant by means of photosynthesis, which occurs in the chloroplasts which they contain. Flowers and cones are modified leaves arranged in groups and enclosing the reproductive organs from which the fruits and seeds result. Plants are autotrophs, that is they make their own food, and are the primary producers in all terrestrial food chains, so that all animal life on land is directly or indirectly dependent on them. As crop plants and animal feed they also supply most human food. They play a vital part in the carbon cycle, removing carbon dioxide from the atmosphere and generating oxygen. The study of plants is known as botany.

plant classification the taxonomy or classification of plants. Originally the plant kingdom included bacteria, diatoms, dinoflagellates, fungi and slime moulds, but these are not now thought of as plants. The unicellular algae, such as *Chlamydomonas*, are often now put with the protists instead of the plants, and some classification schemes even classify the multicellular algae (seaweeds and freshwater weeds) in a new kingdom, the Protoctista,

plant classification

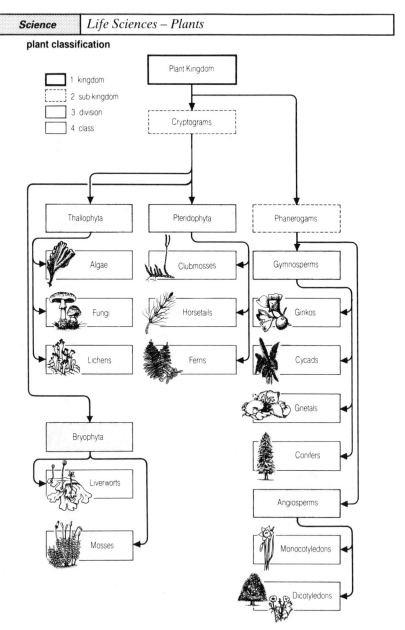

Legend:
1 kingdom
2 sub-kingdom
3 division
4 class

Plant Kingdom

Cryptograms

Thallophyta — Algae, Fungi, Lichens

Pteridophyta — Clubmosses, Horsetails, Ferns

Phanerogams — Gymnosperms, Angiosperms

Gymnosperms — Ginkos, Cycads, Gnetals, Conifers

Bryophyta — Liverworts, Mosses

Angiosperms — Monocotyledons, Dicotyledons

along with the protists. The groups that are always classified as plants are the bryophytes (mosses and liverworts), pteridophytes (ferns, horsetails and clubmosses) gymnosperms (conifers, yews, cycads and ginkgos) and angiospersms (flowering plants). The angiospersms are split into the monocotyledons (for example, orchids, grasses, lilies) and the dicotyledons (for example, oak, buttercup, geranium and daisy).

The basis of plant classification was established by Linnaeus. Among the angiosperms, it is largely based on the number and arrangement of the flower parts.

photosynthesis the process by which green plants and photosynthetic bacteria and cyanobacteria utilize light energy from the sun to produce food molecules (carbohydrates) from carbon dioxide and water. There are two distinct stages within the process. During the *light reaction* sunlight is used to split water (H_2O) into oxygen (O_2), protons (hydrogen ions, H^+) and electrons. Oxygen is given off as a by-product during the light reaction. The protons and electrons are then used to convert carbon dioxide (CO_2) into carbohydrates (CH_2O) – the *dark reaction* for which sunlight is not required. Photosynthesis is dependent on the ability of chlorophyll to capture the energy of sunlight and use it to split water molecules. Other pigments, such as carotenoids, are also involved in capturing light energy and passing it on to chlorophyll. Photosynthesis by cyanobacteria was responsible for the appearance of oxygen in the earth's atmosphere 2,500 million years ago, and photosynthesis by plants maintains the oxygen level today.

chlorophyll the green pigment present in the majority of plants which is responsible for the absorption of light energy during the light reaction of photosynthesis. It absorbs the red and blue-violet parts of sunlight but reflects the green, thus giving the characteristic colour to most plants. Chlorophyll is found within the chloroplasts, which are present in large numbers especially in the leaves. Cyanobacteria and other photosynthetic bacteria also have chlorophyll, though of a slightly different type. Chlorophyll is similar in structure to haemoglobin, but with magnesium instead of iron as the reactive part of the molecule.

Main Plant Types

alga simple plant which contains chlorophyll and photosynthesizes, but without true leaves, stems and roots. Most algae are aquatic, commonly called seaweeds, and reproduce usually by spores. Included in the group are minute single-celled organisms such as the freshwater *Chlamydomonas*, simple multicellular forms such as the filamentous *Spirogyra*, and also the larger and more complex wracks, kelps and other seaweeds.

angiosperm flowering plant in which the seeds are enclosed within an ovary, which ripens to a fruit. Angiosperms are divided into monocotyledons and dicotyledons, and include the vast majority of flowers, herbs, grasses, bushes and trees (except conifers).

clubmoss plant of the class Lycopodiales, allied to ferns and horsetails. A larger spore-bearing generation, with leaves and stems with conducting vessels ('veins'), alternates with a small underground sexual generation. Important and numerous about 300 millions years ago, when many grew to tree size, the surviving 100 or so species are all small. The common clubmoss or stag's-horn moss *Lycopodium clavatum* is found on upland heaths.

conifer plant of the class Coniferales, in the gymnosperm group. These are trees or shrubs, often pyramidal in form, with leaves that are 'needles' or scale-like. The 'flowers' are the male and female cones, and pollen is distributed by the wind. The seeds develop in the female cones. Conifers include pines, firs, yews, monkey-puzzles, and larches. Most are evergreen.

cycad primitive flowering plant superficially resembling a fern or palm, but belonging, like conifers, to the gymnosperm group. Cycads also have cones, some being 60 cm/2 ft long. Cycads are known from 200 million years ago, the 80 or so living species in tropical regions being only a small remnant of the group. Some species yield 'sago' from the stem.

dicotyledon angiosperm with two cotyledons (seed-leaves), forming the majority of flowering plants. They generally have broad leaves with net-like veins. Dicotyledons may be small plants such as daisies and buttercups; shrubs; or trees such as oak and beech.

fern plant of the class Filicales, related to horsetails and clubmosses. Ferns are spore-bearing, not flowering, plants, and most are perennial herbs spreading by low-growing roots. The leaves, known as fronds, vary widely in size and shape. Some taller types, tree-ferns, grow in the tropics. There are over 7,000 species, including bracken, an agricultural weed.

ginkgo maidenhair tree *Ginkgo biloba*, is the only surviving representative of the class Ginkgoales of the gymnosperm group. Ginkgos were characteristic of Mesozoic landscapes. *G. biloba* still grows wild in China. The two-lobed leaves are characteristic. It reaches 30 m/100 ft and drops its leaves in winter.

gnetal plant of the small specialized class Gnetales of the gymnosperm group, which includes *Welwitschia mirabilis*, a woody desert plant of southwest Africa, and the shrub *Ephedra*, from which the drug ephedrine is derived.

gymnosperm flowering plant whose seeds are 'naked', that is, not borne within a true fruit as they are in angiosperms. Most gymnosperms have cones. There are four main groups of gymnosperms – conifers, cycads, ginkgos, and gnetals.

horsetail plant of the class Equisetales, related to ferns and clubmosses. There are about 25 living species, bearing their spores on cones at the stem tip. The upright stems are ribbed, and often have spaced whorls of branches. Today they are of modest size, but hundreds, of millions of years ago giant tree-like forms existed.

lichen organism of dual composition, a close association of a fungus and an alga. The alga contributes food material from photosynthesis, the fungus makes the bulk of the body. Lichens can withstand considerable drought. Some, such as 'reindeer moss', have

food value, others are used for dyes, such as litmus, or in medicine.

liverwort plant of the class Hepaticae, allied to mosses. Usually small, liverworts live in damp places and the main sexual generation consists of a 'thallus', which may be flat, green and lobed, like a small leaf, or 'leafy' and moss-like. The spore-bearing generation is smaller, typically 'parasitic' on the thallus, and throws up a capsule from which spores are spread.

monocotyledon angiosperm with a single cotyledon (seed-leaf). Monocotyledons usually have narrow leaves with parallel veins and smooth edges, and hollow or soft stems. Their flower parts are arranged in threes. Most are small plants such as orchids, grasses and lilies, but some, such as palms, are trees.

moss plant of the class Musci, allied to liverworts. Mosses have stems and leaves, but no true roots. The main plant is the sexual generation, the spore-bearing generation growing on it and producing characteristic stalked capsules. Most mosses flourish best in damp conditions.

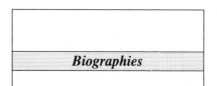

Biographies

Audubon John James 1785–1851. American naturalist, hunter and wildlife artist. In 1827 he published the first parts of his *Birds of North America*, with a remarkable series of colour plates. Later he produced a similar work on American quadrupeds. The National Audubon Society (originating 1886) has branches throughout the US and Canada for the study and protection of birds.

Banks Sir Joseph 1743–1820. British naturalist and explorer. He accompanied Captain Cook round the world 1768–71, played a leading part in the development of New South Wales, was a principal founder of the Botanical Gardens at Kew, London, introduced new plants into various parts of the world, and was President of the Royal Society from 1778.

Cuvier Georges, baron 1769–1832. French comparative anatomist. In 1798 he produced his *Tableau élémentaire de l'histoire naturelle des animaux*, in which his scheme of classification is outlined. Cuvier was the first to relate the structure of fossil animals to that of their living allies. His great work, *Le Règne animal*, embodies a systematic survey of the animal kingdom.

Darwin Charles Robert 1809–1882. British scientist; founder of the modern theory of evolution, and discoverer of the principle of natural selection. As naturalist of the surveying voyage of HMS *Beagle* 1831–6, he made many observations, especially in South America and the nearby Galapagos Islands. In 1859 he published *On the Origin of Species by Means of Natural Selection* which set out the huge amounts of evidence he had collected to show that evolution had occurred, and explained the principles of natural selection and sexual selection. The book aroused bitter controversy because it did not agree with the literal sense of the Book of Genesis. Darwin himself played little part in the debates, but his *Descent of Man* 1871 added fuel to the theological discussion. Darwin then devoted himself chiefly to botanical studies till his death.

Frisch Karl von 1886–1982. German zoologist, founder with Lorenz of ethology, the study of animal behaviour in the natural environment. Specializing in bees, he discovered how they communicate the location of sources of nectar by 'dances'.

Haeckel Ernst Heinrich 1834–1919. German scientist and philosopher. A supporter of Darwin, he worked for more than 50 years on his own 'recapitulation' theory (that embryonic stages represent past stages in the organism's evolution). Although the theory has been superseded, it stimulated much research in embryology.

Hooke Robert 1635–1703. British experimental physicist and inventor, who furthered the sciences of mechanics and microscopy.

Huxley Thomas Henry 1825–1895. British scientist, humanist, and agnostic thinker. Following the publication of Darwin's *On the Origin of Species* in 1859, he won fame as 'Darwin's bulldog', and for many years was the most prominent and popular champion of evolution.

Lamarck Jean Baptiste de 1744–1829. French naturalist. He studied medicine and meteorology before turning to botany. His greatest works were his *Philosophie Zoologique* 1809 and the *Histoire naturelle des animaux sans vertèbres* 1815–22. He proposed a theory of evolution based on the now discredited idea that acquired characteristics are inherited.

Leeuwenhoek Anthony van 1632–1723. Dutch anatomist and pioneer microscopist. With the simple (single-lens) microscopes he constructed he was able to observe cells and microorganisms for the first time, and he investigated a great many different subjects, including the structure of the red blood cells, the sperm cells of animals, and yeasts.

Linnaeus Carolus 1707–78. Swedish naturalist and physician, born Carl Linné, but more commonly known by the Latinized version of his name. He travelled extensively in Europe, collecting hundreds of new species, and wrote 14 botanical works, including *Systema Naturae* which contained his system for classifying plants into groups depending on the number of stamens in their flowers. He also devised a system for naming plants and animals, using one Latin (or Latinized) word to represent the genus and a second to distinguish the species. These binominal systems represented the first comprehensive method of identifying and classifying plants.

Lorenz Konrad 1903– . Austrian ethologist. Director of the Max Planck Institute for the Physiology of Behaviour in Bavaria 1961–73, he is known for his studies of animal behaviour.

Mendel Gregor 1822–1884. Austrian monk, abbot of the Augustinian abbey at Bræunn from 1868 and founder of genetics. By experiments with generations of peas in the monastery garden he developed a theory of particulate inheritance, involving dominant and recessive characters. He published his results 1865–9, but his work remained unrecognized until the early 20th century.

Ray John 1627–1705. British naturalist who devised a classification system accounting for nearly 18,000 plant species. It was the first to divide flowering plants into monocotyledons and dicotyledons, with additional divisions made on the basis of leaf and flower characters and fruit types.

Thoreau Henry David 1817–62. US author and naturalist, whose book *Walden, or Life in the Woods* 1854 and many other works showed a close observation of nature from what would now be called an ecological standpoint.

Tinbergen Nikolaas 1907– . Dutch zoologist, specializing in the study of instinctive behaviour. He has had considerable influence in establishing the relatively new science of ethology.

Vries Hugo de 1848–1935. Dutch botanist, who conducted important research on osmosis in plant cells and was a pioneer in the study of plant evolution. His work led to the rediscovery of Mendel's Laws and the formulation of the theory of mutation.

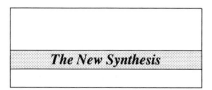

The New Synthesis

genetics the study of inheritance and of genes, which are the units of inheritance. The founder of genetics was Gregor Mendel. From his experiments with plants such as peas he realized that inheritance takes place by means of discrete 'particles', which later came to be called genes. Before Mendel, it had been assumed that the characteristics of the two parents were blended during inheritance, but Mendel showed that the genes remained intact although their combinations change. In the century since Mendel genetics has advanced greatly, first by means of breeding experiments

and light-microscope observations (classical genetics), later by means of biochemical and electron-microscope studies (molecular genetics). An important advance was the elucidation of the structure of DNA by Watson and Crick, and the subsequent cracking of the genetic code. These discoveries opened up the possibility of deliberately manipulating genes, or genetic engineering.

molecular biology the study of the molecular basis of life, including the biochemistry of molecules such as DNA, RNA, and proteins, and the structure and function of the various parts of living cells.

biosynthesis the synthesis of organic compounds from simple inorganic ones by living cells. One important biosynthetic reaction is the conversion of carbon dioxide and water to glucose by plants, during photosynthesis. Other biosynthetic reactions produce cell constituents including proteins and fats. Biosynthesis requires energy, and in photosynthesis this is obtained from sunlight, but in most biosynthetic reactions it is supplied by ATP. The term is also used in connection with biotechnology processes.

biotechnology the industrial use of living organisms to produce food, drugs, or other products. Modern processes include fermentation to produce methane and alcohol for fuel from sugar or waste food products; the use of bacteria to remove heavy metals from polluted areas; and the production of protein from oil residues. The most recent advances in biotechnology involve genetic engineering, in which single-celled organisms with modified DNA are used to produce useful substances such as insulin.

genetic engineering the natural course of heredity is interfered with by any breeding programme, but true genetic engineering is direct manipulation of genetic material by biochemical techniques. This is often achieved by introduction of new DNA, ordinarily by means of an infecting virus. This transplantation of genes is used to increase our knowledge of cell function and reproduction, but it can also achieve practical ends, for example, plants grown for food could be given the ability to fix nitrogen, found in some bacteria, and so reduce the need for expensive fertilizers, or simple bacteria may be enabled to produce rare drugs. However, there is a risk that when transplanting genes between different types of bacteria (*Escherichia coli*, which lives in the human intestine, is often used) new and harmful bacteria might be produced, which, on escape from the laboratory, might start an uncontrollable epidemic. One solution, apart from strict safety precautions, is to render the bacteria genetically unable to exist outside the laboratory.

Key Terms

allele an alternative form of a given gene. Thus, blue and brown eyes are determined by different alleles of the gene for eye colour.

base pair the linkage of two base (purine or pyrimidine) molecules in DNA. One base of each pair lies on one of the two strands of the DNA double helix, and one on the other strand, so the base pairs link the two strands, rather like the rungs of a ladder. In DNA, there are four bases: adenine and guanine (purines) and cytosine and thymine (pyrimidines). Adenine always pairs with thymine and cytosine with guanine. Because the pairs are so specific, DNA can replicate itself precisely, by separating the two strands of the helix and forming new strands using the original ones as templates. This is the basis of heredity. When RNA is formed from DNA, base pairs are again used to copy the genetic message, but in RNA another base, uracil, substitutes for thymine.

chromosome a structure in a cell nucleus responsible for the transmission of hereditary characteristics.

clone a group of genetically identical plants or animals. In nature, they are produced by certain types of asexual reproduction, for example, the plantlets that grow from a strawberry runner are genetically identical to the parent individual. By contrast, higher animals and plants normally reproduce sexually, as a result of which their offspring inherit only half of each parent's genes. Interest in generating clones of higher plants and animals has centred on the economic value of perpetuating particularly successful varieties or breeds.

diploid having two sets of chromosomes in each cell. In sexually reproducing species, one set is derived from each parent, the gametes, or sex cells, of each parent being haploid (having only one set of chromosomes) due to meiosis.

DNA deoxyribonucleic acid; a complex two-stranded molecule that contains, in chemically coded form, all the information needed to build, control and maintain a living organism. DNA is a double-stranded nucleic acid that forms the basis of genetic inheritance in all organisms, except for a few viruses that depend on RNA. In eukaryotic organisms, it is organized into chromosomes and contained in the cell nucleus.

By specifying protein sequences, DNA can build a whole organism. All aspects of the functioning of an organism depend on enzymes, and enzymes are proteins also, so DNA controls the rates of protein production also. DNA is 'translated' into protein by means of messenger RNA.

dominance in genetics, the concept that certain characteristics are dominant, that is, they mask the expression of other characteristics, known as recessives. For example if a person has one allele (gene variant) for blue eyes and one for brown eyes, the brown colour will predominate.

enzyme biological catalyst able to convert one chemical to another quickly, without being destroyed itself, for example, those in yeast, used in making bread and alcohol, and those within the human body which digest food, such as pepsin in the stomach. Bulk production of enzymes from bacteria, and increasingly the re-use of pure enzymes bonded to glass, and other materials, underpins the manufacture of, for example, detergents, and low-cost processed cheese. In medicine enzymes may be used to correct disorders of the body's metabolism.

Frankenstein law in the USA, the ruling by the Supreme Court 1980 that new forms of life created in the laboratory may be patented.

gene a unit of inherited material, situated on a strand of nucleic acid (DNA or RNA). In higher organisms, genes are located on the chromosomes. The term 'gene' was first used in 1909 by the Danish geneticist Wilhelm Johannsen to refer to the inherited factor that consistently affects a particular character in an individual that bears it, for example, the gene for eye colour. Also termed a Mendelian gene, after Gregor Mendel, it may have several variants or alleles, each of which specifies a particular form of that character, for example, the alleles for blue eyes or brown eyes. Some alleles show dominance, that is they mask the effect of others, known as recessive alleles.

In the 1940s, it was established that a gene could be identified with a particular length of DNA, which coded for a complete protein molecule, leading to the 'one-gene-one-enzyme' principle. Later it was realized that proteins might be made up of several polypeptide chains, each with a separate gene, so this principle was modified to 'one-gene-one-polypeptide'. However, the fundamental idea remains the same, that genes produce their visible effects simply by coding for proteins; they control the structure of those proteins via the genetic code, as well as the amounts produced and the timing of production. Genes undergo mutation and recombination to produce the variation on which natural selection operates.

genetic code the way in which instructions for building proteins, the basic structural molecules of living matter, are 'written' in the genetic material DNA. This relationship between the sequence of bases, the sub-units in a DNA molecule, and the sequence of amino acids, the sub-units of a protein molecule, is the basis of heredity. The code employs codons of three bases each; it is the same in almost all organisms, except for a few minor differences recently discovered in some bacteria.

genotype the particular set of alleles (variants of genes) possessed by a given organism. The term is usually used in conjunction with phenotype, which is the product of the genotype and all environmental effects.

haploid having one set of chromosomes in each cell. Most higher organisms are diploid, that is they have two sets, but moss plants and many seaweeds are haploid, as are female honey bees (because they develop from eggs that have not been fertilized). *Polyploid* means having more than twice the basic (haploid) number of chromosomes.

heredity the transmission of traits from parent to offspring.

heterozygous having two different alleles of the gene for a given trait. In homozygous organisms, by contrast, both chromosomes carry the same allele. An individual organism will generally be heterozygous for some genes but homozygous for others.

homozygous having two identical alleles of the gene for a given trait. Homozygous individuals always breed true, that is they produce offspring that resemble them in appearance, when bred with a genetically similar individual. Recessive alleles are only expressed in the homozygous condition.

hybrid the offspring from a cross between individuals of two different species, or two inbred lines within a species. In most cases, hybrids between species are infertile and unable to reproduce sexually. In plants, however, doubling of the chromosomes (polyploidy) can restore the fertility of such hybrids. Hybrids between different genera are extremely rare; an example is the leylandii cypress which, like many hybrids shows exceptional vigour, or heterosis. In the wild, a 'hybrid zone' may occur where the ranges of two related species meet.

linkage the association between two or more genes, which tend to be inherited together because they are on the same chromosome. The closer together they are on the chromosome, the less likely they are to be separated by crossing-over (one of the processes of recombination) and they are then described as being 'tightly linked'.

meiosis type of sexual reproduction in which a cell nucleus divides into parts, each containing half of the total number of chromosomes of the original. Two of these unite to form a new and different cell.

mitosis type of asexual reproduction in which the genetic information is reproduced exactly in the new cells, rather than by being split and recombined, as in meiosis.

mutation a change in a particular gene that produces a new variation in a given character of an organism which is thereafter incorporated into the genetic material (DNA) of that organism. This type of change is one of the bases of evolutionary theory. Mutational changes may be spontaneous, or induced, for example by radiation, and may involve the deletion, addition, duplication or inversion of base pairs making up a given segment of DNA. It has been estimated that a given gene will undergo mutation about once in every ten million generations.

peptide a molecule comprising two or more amino acids joined by peptide bonds. A peptide is, generally speaking a much smaller molecule than a protein, but there is no clear dividing line between them. The term peptide is applied to the breakdown products of proteins, to the precursors of proteins, and to hormones such as vasopressin and oxytocin (nine amino acids each). The term 'polypeptide' is used interchangeably with 'peptide' although it generally implies a longer-chain molecule.

phenotype in genetics, the traits actually displayed by an organism. The phenotype is not a direct reflection of the genotype because some alleles are masked by the presence of other dominant alleles. Furthermore, the phenotype is modified by the effects of the environment (for example, poor food stunting growth).

protein a long chain molecule made up of amino acids, joined together by peptide bonds. Proteins are essential to all living organisms. As enzymes they regulate all aspects of metabolism. Structural proteins such as keratin and collagen make up the skin, claws, bones, tendons and ligaments, while muscle proteins produce movement, haemoglobin transports oxygen, and membrane proteins regulate the movement of substances into and out of cells.

For humans, protein is an essential part of the diet.

recessivity in a diploid organism, a recessive allele is one that can only produce a detectable effect on the phenotype of the organism bearing it when both chromosomes carry it, that is, when the same allele has been inherited from both parents, and the individual is homozygous for it. In heterozygous individuals, its effects will be masked by a dominant allele.

replication the production of copies of the genetic material, DNA; it occurs during cell division (mitosis and meiosis).

RNA *ribonucleic acid*. A nucleic acid involved in the construction of proteins from DNA, the genetic material. It is usually single-stranded, unlike DNA, and consists of a large number of nucleotides strung together, each of which comprises the sugar ribose and one of four bases (uracil, cytosine, adenine or guanine). RNA is copied from DNA by the formation of base pairs, with uracil taking the place of thymine. RNA occurs in three major forms, each with a different function in the synthesis of protein molecules. *Messenger RNA* (mRNA) acts as the template for protein synthesis. Each codon (a set of three bases) on the RNA molecule is matched up with the corresponding amino acid, in accordance with the genetic code. This process (translation) takes place in the ribosomes, which are made up of proteins and *ribosomal RNA* (rRNA). *Transfer RNA* (tRNA) is responsible for combining with specific amino acids, and then matching up a special 'anticodon' sequence of its own with a codon or the mRNA. This is how the genetic code is translated.

Although RNA is normally associated only with the process of protein synthesis, it may be the hereditary material itself in some viruses.

sex linkage the tendency for certain characters to occur exclusively, or predominantly, in one sex only. Human examples include red-green colour blindness and haemophilia, both found predominantly in males. In both cases, these characters are recessive and are determined by genes on the X chromosome: since females possess two X chromosomes, any such recessive allele on one of them is likely to be masked by the corresponding allele on the other. In males (who have only one X chromosome paired with an inert Y chromosome) any gene on the X chromosome will automatically be expressed. Colour blindness and haemophilia can appear in females, but only if they are homozygous for these traits, due to inbreeding, for example.

transcription in living cells, the process by which the information for the synthesis of a protein is transferred from the DNA strand on which it is carried to the messenger RNA strand involved in the actual synthesis. It occurs by the formation of base pairs between the DNA molecule and the nucleotides that make up the new RNA strand.

translation in living cells, the process by which proteins are synthesized. During translation, the information coded as a sequence of nucleotides in messenger RNA is transformed into a sequence of amino acids in a peptide chain. The process involves the 'translation' of the genetic code.

Medicine

Medicine and its ever-increasing array of allied sciences, such as pathology (study of cellular disease processes) and epidemiology (study of disease patterns in communities and regions), still have as their focus the prevention, diagnosis, alleviation and cure of disease, both physical and mental. A *medicine* is also any substance used in the treatment of disease. The basis of medicine is anatomy, or the structure and form of the body, and physiology, or the study of the body's functions.

In the West, medicine increasingly relies on new drugs and sophisticated surgical techniques, while diagnosis of disease is more and more by 'non-invasive' procedures such as Computerized Axial Tomography (CAT) scanning. The time and cost of Western-type medical training makes it inaccessible to many parts of the Third World; where health care of this kind is provided, it is often by auxiliary medical helpers trained in hygiene and the administration of a limited number of standard drugs for the prevalent diseases of a particular region. ***Complementary*** or ***alternative medicine*** encompasses forms of diagnosis and treatment which stress the use of more natural herbal drugs, and techniques which until recently have been unfamiliar in Western medicine, such as acupuncture, homoeopathy, naturopathy, massage, and osteopathy.

The following pages provide an overview of medical science, including a world survey of major ***Diseases and Disorders***, explanations of significant ***Medical Terms***, a guide to major ***Drug Types***, and a ***Chronology*** of events in the history of medicine. Psychology is covered in a separate section under the general heading Society.

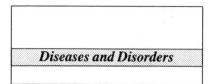

Diseases and Disorders

AIDS abbreviation for *acquired immune deficiency syndrome*, the newest and gravest of sexually transmitted diseases (STDs). It is caused by the human immunodeficiency virus (HIV), now known to be a retrovirus, a comlex organism first identified in 1983. A 1989 UK government survey estimates that 1.6% of all British males aged around 30 will die of AIDS-related diseases.

anaemia a condition caused by a shortage of haemoglobin, the oxygen-carrying component of the blood. It arises either from abnormal loss or defective production of haemoglobin.

angina or *angina pectoris*. Severe pain in the chest due to impaired blood supply to the heart muscle because a coronary artery is narrowed (atheroma). The pain is a crushing one across the chest and may extend down the arm, rather than appearing to come from the heart.

arteriosclerosis hardening of the arteries, a thickening and loss of elasticity of their walls. It is associated with smoking, ageing, and a diet high in saturated fats.

arthritis inflammation of the joints. More common in women, *rheumatoid arthritis* is an autoimmune disease in the small joints of the hands and feet, causing a greater or lesser degree of deformity and painfully restricted movement. It is alleviated by drugs and surgery may be performed to correct deformity. *Osteoarthritis* appears in later life and tends to affect larger joints, such as the hip and knee, so that artificial joints may be used to restore mobility. The disease seems to be inluenced by heredity and may be triggered by a viirus infection.

asthma difficulty in breathing out due to spasm of the bronchi (air passages) in the lungs. Attacks may be provoked by allergy, infection, stress, or emotional upset. Treatment is with bronchodilators to relax the bronchial muscles and thereby ease the breathing.

atherosclerosis thickening and hardening of the walls of blood vessels, associated with *atheroma* (furring of the interior of the artery by deposits, mainly of cholesterol within its walls).

bilharzia or *schistosoma* disease causing anaemia, inflammation, formation of scar tissue, diarrhoea, dysentery, enlargement of the spleen and liver, and cirrhosis of the liver. It is contracted by bathing in water contaminated with human sewage.

bronchitis inflammation of the bronchi (air passages) of the lungs, usually caused initially by a viral infection, such as a cold or flu. It is aggravated by atmospheric pollutants.

cancer a group of diseases characterized by abnormal proliferation of cells. Regardless of where the cancer arises, its cells are usually degenerate, capable only of reproducing themselves (tumour formation) so as to outnumber the surrounding healthy cells. Also, malignant cells tend to spread from their site of origin by the process known as metastasis. Triggering agents include chemical carcinogens, for example asbestos dust and cigarettte smoking; viruses; radiation; diet and possibly psychological stress. Treatment includes surgery, radiotherapy, and chemotherapy using cytoxic drugs which slow or halt cell division. In 1987, monoclonal antibodies were discovered; these molecules are genetically geared to react with specific cells.

cerebral haemorrhage the bursting of a blood vessel in the brain, caused by factors such as high blood pressure combined with hardening of the arteries, or chronic poisoning with lead or alcohol; it is popularly known as a *stroke*. It may cause death, or damage parts of the brain and lead to paralysis or mental impairment. The effects are usually long-term.

cholera intestinal infection caused by a bacterium *Vibrio cholerae*, and characterized by violent diarrhoea. Transmitted by contaminated water or food, it is still prevalent in tropical regions.

coronary artery disease condition in which the fatty deposits of atherosclerosis form in, and therefore narrow, the coronary arteries which

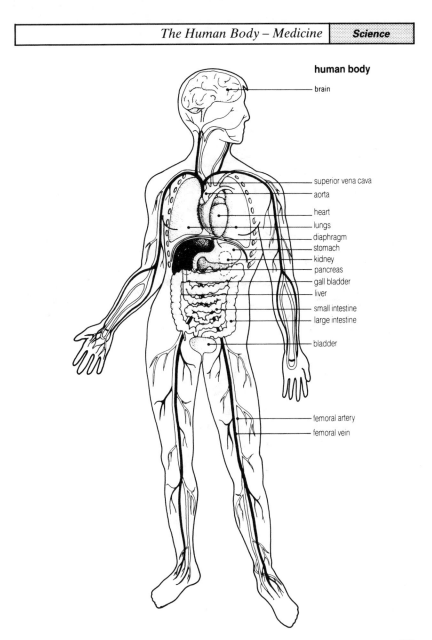

human body

- brain
- superior vena cava
- aorta
- heart
- lungs
- diaphragm
- stomach
- kidney
- pancreas
- gall bladder
- liver
- small intestine
- large intestine
- bladder
- femoral artery
- femoral vein

Key
1. cranium (skull)
2. mandible
3. clavicle
4. scapula
5. sternum
6. rib cage
7. humerus
8. vertebra
9. ulna
10. radius
11. pelvis
12. coccyx
13. metacarpals
14. phalanges
15. femur
16. patella
17. fibula
18. tibia
19. metatarsals
20. phalanges
21. superficial (upper) layer of muscles

supply the heart muscle. It can lead to angina, heart attacks, and damage to the heart muscle. It is a common cause of death in developed countries, especially among older men.

dementia mental deterioration as a result of physical changes in the brain. It may be due to degenerative change, circulatory disease, infection, injury, or chronic poisoning. *Alzheimer's disease* is the commonest form of dementia, estimated to afflict 5--10% of the aged population. It is a disease of mental process rather than physical function, characterized by memory loss and progressive intellectual impairment. The cause is unknown, although a link with high levels of alluminium in drinking water was discovered in 1989. There is as yet no treatment.

diabetes a disease *diabetes mellitus* in which a deficiency in the islets of the pancreas prevents the body producing the hormone insulin, so that it cannot use sugars properly. In adults it may be controlled by diet and/or insulin; in children it usually needs daily insulin injection. It can lead to blindness, and untreated, causes death in coma.

dysentery infection of the large intestine usually due to amoebae or bacillae micro-organisms causing abdominal cramps and diarrhoea. It is spread by infected water and foods, and remains common in some tropical areas.

epilepsy a group of disorders characterized by the occurrence of seizures. *Symptomatic epilepsy* is that arising from a known cause, such as a tumour or blood clot on the brain, head injury, or high fever. *Idiopathic epilepsy*, which is much more common, is a condition which develops without known cause.

filariasis collective term for several diseases, prevalent in tropical areas, caused by roundworm (nematode) parasites.

hepatitis inflammatory disease of the liver, usually caused by a virus. Hepatitis B is a long-term viral disease, causing jaundice and linked with cancer, but preventable by vaccine. It is carried by the blood and other body fluids. Other causes include systematic lupus erythematosus (connective tissue disease) or amoebic dysentery.

hypertension abnormally high blood pressure. It increases the risk of severe illness including kidney disease, stroke, and heart attack.

leishmaniasis parasitic disease caused by microscopic protozoans (*Leishmania*) and transmitted by sandflies. It may cause either localized infection or dangerous fever. It is prevalent in NE Africa and S Asia.

leprosy a chronic disease caused by a bacterium which is closely related to that of tuberculosis. The infection attacks skin and nerves.

leukaemia any one of a group of cancer-like diseases of the blood cells, with widespread involvement of the bone marrow. Cure and control by radiotherapy or drugs is more successful in younger patients.

malaria infectious parasitic disease transmitted by mosquitoes, marked by periodic fever and an enlarged spleen, which affects some 200 million people a year. When a female mosquito of the *Anopheles* genus bites a human with malaria, it takes in with the human blood the malaria parasite *Plasmodium*. This matures within the insect, and is then transferred when the mosquito bites a new victim. Iniside the body the parasite settles first in the liver, then multiplis to attack the red blood cells, when the symptoms of malaria become evident. Treatment is by antimalarial drugs.

multiple sclerosis (MS) an incurable chronic disease of the central nervous system, occurring in young or middle adulthood. It is characterized by degeneration of the myelin sheath which surrounds nerves in the brain and spinal cord. Its cause is unknown.

obesity condition of being overweight (generally, 20% or more above the desirable weight for your sex and height).

pneumonia inflammation of the lungs due to bacterial or viral infection. It is characterized by a build-up of fluid in the alveoli, the clustered air sacs (at the end of the air passages) where oxygen exchange takes place.

stroke a sudden episode involving the blood supply to the brain. It may also be termed a cerebrovascular accident (CVA) or apoplexy.

trypanosomiasis collection of debilitating long-term diseases caused by infestation with the microscopic single-celled *Trypanosoma*. They include sleeping sickness (nagana) in Africa, transmitted by the bites of tsetse flies, and Chagas' disease in the Americas, spread by assassin-bugs.

typhoid fever infectious disease caused by the bacterium *Salmonella typhi*, and usually contracted through contaminated food or fluids. It is characterized by fever, and damage to internal organs, mainly the spleen and intestine. Treatment is with antibiotics.

venereal disease (VD) a disease mainly transmitted by sexual contact, although commonly, the term is used specifically for gonorrhea and syphilis, both occurring worldwide, and chanchroid and lymphogranuloma venerum, seen mostly in the tropics.

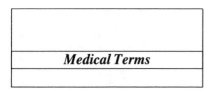

Medical Terms

abortion the ending of a pregnancy before the fetus is developed sufficiently to survive outside the womb. Abortion may be accidental (miscarriage) or deliberate (termination of pregnancy).

allergy special sensitivity of the body which makes it react, with an exaggerated response of the natural immune defence mechanism, to the introduction of an otherwise harmless foreign substance termed an allergen.

anaesthetic a drug which produces loss of sensation or consciousness; the resulting state is *anaesthesia*, in which the patient is insensitive to stimuli. Anaesthesia may also happen as a result of nerve disorder. Anaesthetics given, include general (inducing overall unconsciousness) and local, and also acupuncture and hypnosis. *Epidural anaesthesia* (injection into the space around the membranes covering the spinal cord) is used in childbirth,

and for major abdominal operations; the patient remains conscious, and there is reduced risk of complications, with quicker recovery.

analgesia relief of pain, the sensation which is felt when electrical stimuli travel along a nerve pathway, from peripheral nerve fibres to the brain via the spinal cord.

antibody a protein produced by the blood in response to the presence of invading substances, or antigens, including the proteins carried on the surface of bacteria and viruses. Antibody production is just one aspect of immunity in vertebrates.

antigen any substance which causes production of antibodies. Common antigens include the proteins carried on the surface of bacteria, viruses, and pollen grains. The proteins of incompatible blood groups or tissues also act as antigens, which has to be taken into account in medical procedures such as blood transfusion and organ transplants.

arteriography a method of examining the interior of an artery by injecting into it a radio-opaque solution which is visible on an x-ray photograph. Used for the heart's coronary arteries (coronary arteriogram), for example.

autoimmunity a situation where the body's immune responses are mobilized not against 'foreign' matter, such as invading germs, but against the body itself. So-called autoimmune diseases include myasthenia gravis, pernicious anaemia, rheumatoid arthritis, and lupus erythematosus.

biopsy removal of a tissue sample from the body for diagnostic examination.

blood group the classification of blood types according to antigenic activity. Red blood cells of one individual may carry molecules on their surface which act as antigens in another individual whose red blood cells lack these molecules. The two main antigens are designated A and B. These give rise to four blood groups: having A only (A), having B only (B), having both (AB), and having neither (O). Each of these groups may or may not contain the rhesus factor. Correct typing of blood groups is vital in transfusion since incompatible types of donor and recipient blood will result in blood clotting, with possible death of the recipient.

blood pressure the pressure of the blood in the arteries and veins of the circulatory system, due to the muscular activity of the heart.

blood test a laboratory evaluation of a blood sample. There are numerous blood tests, from simple typing to establish its group (in case a transfusion is needed) to sophisticated biochemical assays of substances, such as hormones, present in the blood only in minute quantities.

Caesarean section a surgical operation to deliver a baby by way of an incision in the mother's abdominal wall. It may be recommended for almost any obstetric complication implying a threat to mother or baby.

carrier anyone who harbours an infectious organism or disease-related genes without ill effects, but who can, however, pass the infection to others.

CAT scan or *CT scan* (*c*omputerized *a*xial *t*omography) a sophisticated method of diagnostic imaging. Quick and non-invasive, CT scanning is an important aid to diagnosis, pinpointing disease without the need for exploratory surgery.

cauterization the use of special instruments to burn or fuse small areas of body tissue with a minimum bleeding. Tiny blood vessels are cauterized to minimize blood loss during surgery.

cervical smear removal of a small sample of tissue from the cervix to screen for changes implying a likelihood of cancer. The procedure is also known as the 'Pap' test after its originator, George Papanicolau.

chemotherapy medical treatment with chemicals. It usually refers to the treatment of cancer with drugs.

dialysis a process in which the blood is passed through a filtration system in order to cleanse it of waste products. Dialysis is usually performed to compensate for failing kidneys. It may be life-saving in some types of poisoning.

dilatation and curettage (D and C) a common gynaecological procedure in which the cervix (neck of the womb) is widened or dilated, giving access so that the lining of the womb can be scraped away (curettage). It may be carried out to terminate a pregnancy, treat an incomplete miscarriage, or discover the cause of heavy menstrual bleeding.

electrocardiogram (ECG) a recording of the electrical changes in the heart muscle, detected by electrodes attached to the chest. Electrocardiography is invaluable in the diagnosis of heart disease.

electroencephalogram (EEG) a record of the electrical discharges of the brain, detected by electrodes attached to the scalp. The pattern of electrical activity revealed by electroencephalography is diagnostic in some brain disorders, especially epilepsy.

endoscope an optical instrument for looking inside the body, without the need for surgery. A modern endoscope consists of a bundle of optical fibres, some of which carry light to illuminate the target, while the rest are used for viewing. It can be inserted in the body to view, say, the stomach. Advanced endoscopes are fitted with scalpel devices so that they can be used for minor operations internally.

immunity the protection which animals have against the effects of foreign organisms and toxins on their body functions. Some white blood cells (polymorphs and macrophages) engulf bacteria and other invading organisms, while others (natural killer cells) destroy body cells that have become infected. The T-lymphocytes are responsible for binding to specific invading organisms and killing them, or rendering them harmless. The B-lymphocytes produce antibodies that are specific to particular micro-organisms. Against viruses, there is an additional form of defence, based on interferons, which prevent them from replicating in the host's cells.

mammography an X-ray procedure used to detect breast cancer at an early stage.

physiotherapy treatment of injury and disease by physical means such as electrical stimulation, exercise, heat, manipulation, and massage.

psychotherapy treatment approaches for mental problems which involve talking rather than surgery or drugs. Examples of such approaches include behaviour therapy, cognitive therapy, and psychoanalysis.

radiotherapy the treatment of disease by radiation from X-ray machines or radioactive sources. Radiation reduces the activity of dividing cells, so is useful in treating cancer tissue and some diseases of the skin, and may be used in combination with drugs and surgery.

scanning the non-invasive examination of body organs to detect abnormalities of structure or function. Detectable waves, for example ultrasound, magnetic, or X-rays, are passed through the part to be scanned. Their absorption pattern is recorded, analysed by computer, and displayed pictorially on a screen.

screening testing large numbers of apparently healthy people to detect early signs of disease.

surgery originally the removal of diseased parts or foreign substances from the body. The surgeon now uses not only the scalpel and electric cautery, but beamed high-energy ultrasonic waves, binocular magnifiers for microsurgery, and the intense light energy of the laser. The many specialized fields include *cardiac* (heart), *orthopaedic* (bones), *opthalmic* (eye), and *neuro-* (brain and nerves).

ultrasound a diagnostic imaging technique which works on exactly the same principle as sonar, a ship's echo-sounding equipment. High frequency sound waves transmitted through the body are absorbed and reflected to differing degrees by different body tissues, and the returning echoes are used to formulate a picture of a particular structure, such as an image of the unborn baby in the womb.

vaccine modified preparation of viruses, or bacteria, which is introduced into the body either orally or by a hypodermic syringe to induce the general reaction which produces immunity.

X-rays rays with a short wavelength that pass through most body tissues. Dense tissues such as bone prevent their passage and show up as white areas on x-ray photographs.

Drug Types

analgesic drug reducing sensitivity to pain, for example cocaine for local application; opium and its derivatives morphine and heroin; aspirin and paracetamol; certain barbiturates. Dangers of addiction may arise.

antacid a substance that neutralizes stomach acid. It may be taken between meals to relieve symptoms of hyperacidity, such as pain, bloating, nausea, and 'heartburn'. Excessive or prolonged need for antacids should be investigated medically.

antibiotic a drug which kills or inhibits the growth of bacteria and fungi. It is derived from living organisms such as fungi or other bacteria, which distinguishes it from other antibacterials.

anticoagulant a substance which suppresses the formation of blood clots. Common anticoagulants are heparin, produced by the liver and lungs, and derivatives of coumarin. Anticoagulants are used medically, in treating heart attacks, for example. They are also produced by blood-feeding animals such as mosquitoes, leeches, and vampire bats, to keep the victim's blood flowing.

anticonvulsant a drug used to prevent epileptic seizures (convulsions or fits).

antidepressant a drug used to relieve symptoms in depressive illness. The two most important groups are the tricyclic antidepressants (TCADs) and the monoamine oxidase inhibitors (MAOIs), which act by altering chemicals available to the central nervous system. Both may produce serious side effects.

anti-emetic a substance that counteracts nausea or vomiting.

antifungal a drug that acts against fungal infection, such as ringworm and athlete's foot.

antihypertensive therapy to control high blood pressure. The first step is usually a change in diet to reduce salt and, if necessary, caloric intake. If further measures are required, drugs such as beta-blockers and diuretics may be prescribed.

anti-inflammatory a substance that reduces swelling in soft tissues.

antipsychotic a drug used to treat the symptoms of severe mental disorder, also known as a *neuroleptic*.

antipyretic a drug, such as aspirin, used to reduce fever.

antiviral a drug that acts against viruses, usually preventing them from multiplying. Most virus infections are not susceptible to antibiotics. Antivirals have been difficult drugs to develop, and do not necessarily cure the diseases.

barbiturate a hypnosedative drug, commonly called 'sleeping pills'. Tolerance develops quickly in the user so that increasingly large doses are required to induce sleep. Its action persists for hours or days, causing confused, aggressive behaviour or disorientation. Highly addictive, most barbiturates are no longer prescribed, and are listed as controlled substances in the UK. Short-acting barbiturates are sometimes used to induce general anaesthesia.

beta-blocker a drug that blocks impulses which stimulate certain nerve endings (beta receptors) serving the heart muscles. This reduces the heart rate and the force of contraction. This, in turn, reduces the amount of oxygen (and therefore the blood supply) required by the heart. They are banned from use in competitive sport.

bronchodilator a drug that relieves obstruction of the airways by causing the bronchi and bronchioles to relax and widen. It is useful in the treatment of asthma.

contraceptive drug, device or technique that interferes with reproduction. Some types of pill prevent the ripening and release of an egg cell (ovum) or prevent the sperm fertilizing the egg; barrier methods, such as the condom or diaphragm, stop the sperm reaching the egg; intrauterine devices (IUDs) halt the implantation of the embryo in the wall of the womb.

corticosteroid any of several hormones secreted by the adrenal cortex; also synthetic forms with similar properties. Corticosteroids have anti-inflammatory and immunosuppressive effects and may be used to treat a number of conditions including rheumatoid arthritis, severe allergies, asthma, some skin diseases, and some cancers. Side-effects can be serious, including weight gain and thinning of the skin and bones. Therapy must be withdrawn very gradually.

cytotoxic drug that kills or damages cells. Although used specifically to kill the cells of a malignant tumour, or as an immunosuppressive following organ transplantation, it may damage healthy cells as well. Side effects include nausea, vomiting, hair loss, and bone marrow damage.

diuretic drug that rids the body of excess fluid by increasing the output of urine by the kidneys. It may be used in the treatment of heart disease, high blood pressure, kidney and liver disease, and some endocrine disorders.

hypnotic substance (such as barbiturate, benzodiazepine, alcohol) which depresses brain function, inducing sleep. Prolonged use may lead to tolerance and habituation; larger doses are required, and physical or psychological addiction occurs.

hypoglycaemic drug that lowers the level of glucose in the blood. Diabetics who do not require insulin can control their blood sugar level by diet and hypoglycaemic tablets.

immunosuppressive drug that suppresses the body's normal immune responses to infection or foreign tissue. It is used in the treatment of auto-immune disease, as part of chemotherapy for leukaemias, lymphomas, and other cancers, and to help prevent rejection following organ transplantion.

sedative drug (minor tranquillizer) with a calming effect. It will induce sleep in larger doses.

sleeping pill a hypnotic, which may be anxiolytic (anxiety reducing) in smaller doses. They can cause dependence and should not be taken for long periods.

steroid in biology, a type of lipid (fat), derived from sterols, with a complex molecular structure consisting of four carbon rings. Steroids include the sex hormones, such as testosterone, the corticosteroid hormones produced by the adrenal gland, and cholesterol.

c. 400 BC   Hippocrates recognized disease had natural causes.

c. 200 AD   Galen, the authority of the Middle Ages, consolidated the work of the Alexandrian doctors.

1543   Andreas Versalius gave the first accurate account of the human body.

1628   William Harvey discovered the circulation of the blood.

1768   John Hunter began the foundation of experimental and surgical pathology.

1785   Digitalis used to treat heart disease; the active ingredient was isolated 1904.

1798   Edward Jenner published his work on vaccination.

1877   Sir Patrick Manson, Scottish parasitologist, worked on animal carriers of infectious diseases.

1882   Robert Koch isolated the tuberculosis bacillus.

1884   Edwin Klebs, German pathologist, isolated the diptheria bacillus.

1885   Louis Pasteur produced the rabies vaccine.

1890   Joseph Lister demonstrated antiseptic surgery.

1897   Martinus Beijerinck, Dutch botanist, discovered viruses.

1899   German doctor, Felix Hoffman, developed aspirin; Sigmund Freud founded psychiatry.

1910   Paul Ehrlich synthesized the first specific bacterial agent, salvarsan (cure for syphilis).

1922   Insulin was first used to treat diabetes.

1928   Sir Alexander Fleming discovered the antibiotic penicillin.

1930s   Electro-convulsive therapy (ECT) was developed.

1932   Gerhard Domagk, German bacteriologist and pathologist, began work on the sulphonamide drugs, a kind of antibiotic.

1940s   Lithium treatment for depression was developed.

1950   Proof of a link between cigarette smoking and lung cancer was established.

1950s   Major development of antidepressant drugs and beta blockers for heart disease; Medawar's work on the immune system.

1950–75   Manipulation of the molecules of synthetic chemicals, the main source of new drugs.

1953   Vaccine for polio developed by Jonas Salk.

1960s   Heart transplant surgery began with the work of Christiaan Barnard; new generation of minor tranquillizers called benzodiazepenes developed.

1971   Viroids, disease causing organisms even smaller than viruses, isolated outside the living body.

1975   Nuclear medicine, for example positron emission tomography (Hounsfield), came into practical use.

1978   Birth of the first 'test-tube baby', Louise Brown, on 25 Jul in England.

1980s   AIDS (Acquired Immune Deficiency Syndrome) first recognized in the USA; recognition of the discovery of the transposable gene by Barbara McClintock, US geneticist.

1980   Smallpox eradicated by the World Health Organization.

1984   Vaccine for leprosy developed; discovery of the Human Immuno-deficiency Virus (HIV) responsible for AIDS, at the Institut Pasteur in Paris and in the USA.

1987   World's longest surviving heart transplant patient died in France, 18 years after his operation.

1989   Patient with Parkinson's disease first treated by graft of fetal brain tissue.

Physics

Physics (sometimes called 'natural philosophy') is a branch of science which is concerned with the ultimate laws which govern the structure of the universe and forms of matter and energy and their interactions. For convenience physics is often divided into branches such as nuclear physics, solid and liquid state physics, electricity, electronics and magnetism, optics, acoustics, heat and thermodynamics.

This section contains an overview of physics. First, *Atomic Physics* deals with the study of matter. Famous physicists, their inventions and discoveries are highlighted in *Biographies*. Brief definitions of *Terms* explain the scientific principles and concepts of various everyday words. Finally, *Landmarks* in physics highlights both the breadth of the subject and its close links with other scientific disciplines.

Atomic Physics

atom the minute separate entity which makes up all matter, and is the tiniest quantity of an element to retain the chemical properties of the element. Atoms range in size from 10^{-10} (1/10,000,000,000) of a metre to 4×10^{-10}. This means that they are so small that an atom of tungsten magnified 2,600,000 times (by a field ion microscope), appears as a bright spot not much larger than a pin's head. On this minute scale physicists cannot 'see' in a direct visual sense, but rely on methods such as interpretation of the diffraction pattern produced by electrons 'fired' through a thin specimen of a substance in an electron microscope.

Atoms consist of a very small **nucleus**, one ten-thousandth the size of the atom. The traditional model has particles of negative electricity called **electrons** moving round the nucleus in orbits which form concentric 'shells'. However, **quantum mechanics**, which looks at particles as 'waves', supplies a newer concept of the atom in which the nucleus is surrounded by 'clouds' of electrons which assume dumb-bell, cloverleaf, or other shapes. The outermost of these clouds, according to their shape and density, allow the prediction of what chemical reactions are possible and how molecules combine.

The simplest atom (hydrogen) has only one electron; the most complex naturally occurring (uranium) has 92. The nucleus is made up of particles (**protons** and **neutrons**) bound together by the strong nuclear force. Protons have a electrical charge and are the same in number as the orbiting electrons, which have an equal but negative charge, so that the two types of particle counterbalance each other. Neutrons are so called because they have no electrical charge. The number of protons is the chief factor in deciding the kind of atom being dealt with, since the atomic number of an element is simply

the number of protons in the nucleus of one atom. By adding or taking away protons and electrons, it is possible to fulfil the alchemist's dream, for example to transmute mercury (80 protons) into gold (79 protons), but the cost would be far in excess of the gold produced.

Protons and neutrons (together called **nucleons**) are composed of yet smaller sub-particles, **quarks**; electrons, however, are indivisible. In general terms, the so-called elementary particles are quarks and **leptons** (light particles), such as electrons and neutrinos. Quarks have proved difficult to isolate, and may even be, by their very nature, impossible to isolate. Particles may change from one form to another, and their behaviour is not exactly predictable. Physicists (with some exceptions, notably Einstein) accept that it is impossible, even in

hydrogen

atom

helium

carbon

proton   ○
neutron   ◉
electron ●

uranium nucleus

uranium nucleus
amidst its
orbiting electrons

principle, to fully predict the future behaviour of the particles (for example, simultaneous values of their position and momentum).

particle physics in 1895 J J Thomson discovered that all atoms contain identical, negatively charged particles (*electrons*) which could easily be freed. By 1913 Rutherford had shown that electrons surround a very small, positively-charged nucleus, thus, the nucleus of a hydrogen atom consists of a single positively charged particle, a *proton* (identified by Chadwick in 1932). Nuclei do not split apart easily; usually they need to be bombarded by particles such as protons, raised to very high kinetic energies by particle accelerators, first built around 1930.

1932 saw the discovery of a particle, predicted by Dirac, with the mass of an electron, but an equal and opposite charge – the *positron*. This was the first example of an *antiparticle*; it is now believed that almost all particles have corresponding antiparticles. The following year, Pauli argued that a hitherto unsuspected particle must accompany electrons in beta-emission; this so-called *electron-neutrino* interacts with other particles only rarely, so neutrino radiation is extremely penetrating.

particles and fundamental forces by the mid-1930s four fundamental kinds of force had emerged. The *electromagnetic force* acts between particles with electric charge, and was thought to be related to the exchange between the particles of *photons*, packets of electromagnetic radiation. The *strong force* (holding quarks together to form protons and neutrons, and binding them together inside the nucleus) is transmitted by the exchange of particles called *gluons* between quarks and antiquarks. Theoretical work on the *weak force* (responsible for beta radioactivity of the sun) began with Fermi in the 1930s; current theory suggests the exchange during weak interactions of *W* and *Z particles* with masses some 100 times that of the proton. The existence of W and Z particles was confirmed 1983 at CERN (Conseil Européen pour la Recherche Nucléaire, Geneva). The fourth fundamental force, *gravity*, is experienced by all particles; the projected go-between particles have been dubbed *gravitons*.

leptons, hadrons, and quarks the electron

and electron-neutrinos are examples of *leptons*, particles with half-integral spin which 'feel' the weak, but not the strong force. There are known to be two more electron-like leptons plus their neutrinos: the *muon* (found by Anderson in cosmic radiation in 1937), and the *Tauon* a surprise discovery of the 1970s. *Hadrons* (particles which 'feel' the strong force) started to turn up in bewildering profusion in experiments in the 1950s and 60s. They are classified into *mesons*, with whole-number or zero spins, and *baryons*, with half-integral spins. It was shown in the early 1960s that if hadrons of the same spin are represented as points on suitable charts, simple patterns are formed. This symmetry enabled a hitherto unknown particle, the *omega-minus*, to be predicted from a gap in one of the patterns; it duly turned up in experiments. In 1964 Gell-Mann and Zweig suggested that all hadrons were built from just three types or *flavours* of a new particle with half-integral spin and charge of magnitude either 1/3 or 2/3 that of an electron, which Gell-Mann christened the *quark*. Mesons are quark-antiquark pairs (spins either add to 1 or cancel to zero) and baryons are quark triplets. To account for new mesons such as the *psi* the number of quark flavours had risen to six by 1985. In the quark theory, the only truly elementary particles are leptons and quarks. The different types of leptons and quark composites are therefore known as *fundamental* or *subatomic particles*.

accelerator a device to bring charged particles (such as protons) up to high kinetic energies, at which they have uses in industry, medicine and in pure physics: when high energy particles collide with other particles the products formed give insights into the fundamental forces of nature. To give particles the energies needed requires many successive applications of a high voltage to electrodes placed in the path of the particles. To save space particles can be confined to a circular track using a magnetic field. The first *accelerator* to work on this principle was the *cyclotron* built in the early 1930s. The Super Proton Synchrotron at CERN, Geneva, which came into operation in 1976, has an unravelled

particle: major fundamental (subatomic) particles

Name	Symbol	Category	Mass (electron = 1)	Charge	Spin	Parity
electron	e	lepton	1	−1	1/2	
graviton	g	quantum	0	0	2	
K meson (kaon)	K	meson	998	−1,0,+1	0	−1
lambda particle	Λ	baryon	2231	0	1/2	+1
muon	μ	lepton	211	−1	1/2	
neutrino	ν	lepton	0	0	1/2	
neutron	n	baryon	1880	0	1/2	+1
omega particle	Ω	baryon	3345	−1	3/2	+1
photon	α	quantum	0	0	1	−1
pion	π	meson	280	−1,0,+1	0	−1
proton	p	baryon	1876	+1	1/2	+1
sigma particle	Σ	baryon	2380	−1,0,+1	1/2	+1
xi particle	Ξ	baryon	2644	−1,0	1/2	+1

More than one charge in the Charge column indicates that there is more than one particle of that type, which differ in charge (there may also be slight differences in mass). Certain particles with a single charge have antiparticles of opposite charge. Thus the positron resembles the electron in every respect except that its charge is +1; similarly, the antiproton has a charge of −1.
Lambda, omega, sigma, and xi particles are known collectively as hyperons.
Baryons and mesons togther make up the type termed hadrons.

length of some 2.2 km/1.4 mi; the Large Electron Proton Machine (LEP) which began operations in 1989 is 30 km/18.6 mi long.

atomic number the number of electrons, or the positive charge on the nucleus of an atom. The 105 elements are numbered one (hydrogen) to 105 (hahnium) in the Periodic Table.

atomic weight the weight of one atom of an element on a scale where the weight of an oxygen atom is 16.

isotope one of two or more atoms which have the same atomic number, but which contain a different number of neutrons. They may be stable or radioactive, natural or synthetic.

molecule the smallest particle of any substance that can exist in a free state yet still exhibit all the chemical properties of the substance. Molecules are composed of a number of atoms ranging from two atoms in a hydrogen molecule to many thousands of atoms in the molecules of complex organic substances. The composition of the molecule is determined by the nature of the bonds, probably electric forces, which hold the atoms together. According to the molecular or kinetic theory of matter, molecules are in a state of constant motion, the extent of which depends on their temperature, and they exert forces on one another.

radioactivity the spontaneous emission of radiation from the nuclei of atoms of certain substances, termed *radioactive*. Radiation is of three main types: *alpha* (fast-moving helium nuclei); *beta* (fast-moving electrons); and *gamma* (high-energy highly penetrating protons). Beta and gamma radiation are both damaging to body tissues, but are especially dangerous if a radioactive substance is ingested or inhaled.

uncertainty principle a principle established by Heisenberg, giving a theoretical limit to the precision with which an atomic particle's momentum and position can be measured simultaneously: the more accurately one is determined the more uncertainty there is in the other. The uncertainty arises because, according to *quantum mechanics*, it is meaningless to speak of a particle's position, momentum, and so on, except as a result of measurements, but these measurements involve an interaction (such as a photon of light bouncing off the particle under scrutiny), which disturbs the particle, though the disturbance is noticeable only at an atomic scale. The principle implies that one cannot, even in theory, predict the moment-to-moment behaviour of such a system.

helped to set up CERN at Geneva. His son, *Aage Bohr* (1922–), also a physicist, shared a

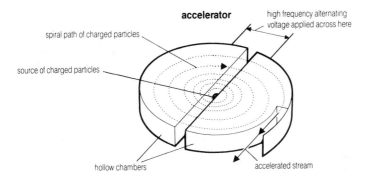

accelerator

high frequency alternating voltage applied across here

spiral path of charged particles

source of charged particles

hollow chambers

accelerated stream

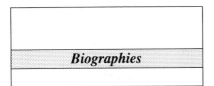

Biographies

Angström Anders Jonas 1814–1874. Swedish physicist, who did notable work in spectroscopy and solar physics. After him is named the *Angström unit*, used to express the wavelength of electro-magnetic radiations (light, radiant heat, X-rays). One Angström or Angström unit is one ten-millionth of a millimetre.

Black Joseph 1728–99. Scottish physicist and chemist who in 1754 discovered carbon dioxide (which he called fixed air). In physics, by his investigations (1761) of latent heat and specific heat, he laid the foundation for the work of his pupil, James Watt.

Blackett Patrick Maynard Stuart, Baron Blackett 1897–1974. British physicist. He was awarded a Nobel prize in 1948 for work in cosmic radiation and his perfection of the Wilson 'cloud-chamber'.

Bohr Niels Henrik David 1885–1962. Danish physicist. Nobel prizewinner 1922. In 1952 he

Nobel prize in 1975 for work on the theory of the atomic nucleus.

Born Max 1882–1970. British physicist, of German origin, who received a Nobel prize in 1954 for fundamental work on quantum mechanics, which explains the properties of atoms and molecules.

Boyle Robert 1627–91. British scientist. He published the seminal *The Skeptical Chymist* 1661; enunciated *Boyle's law*, stating that the product of the pressure and volume of a gas remain constant as long as the temperature remains constant (1662); was one of the founders of the Royal Society.

Cavendish Henry 1731–1810. British physicist. A grandson of the 2nd duke of Devonshire, he devoted his life to scientific pursuits, living in rigorous seclusion at Clapham Common. He discovered the composition of nitric acid and the composition of water. The Cavendish experiment was a device of his to discover the mass and density of the earth.

Chadwick Sir James 1891–1974. British physicist. He studied at Cambridge under Rutherford, and in 1932 discovered the particle in an atomic nucleus which became known as the neutron, because it has no electric charge. In 1935 he was awarded a Nobel prize, and in

1940 was one of the British scientists reporting on the atom bomb.

Cockcroft Sir John Douglas 1897–1967. British physicist. Born at Todmorden, W Yorkshire, he held an engineering appointment with Metropolitan-Vickers, and took up research work under Rutherford at the Cavendish Laboratory, Cambridge. He succeeded (with Irish physicist Ernest Thomas Sinton Walton 1903–   ) in splitting the nucleus of the atom for the first time in 1932, and in 1951 they were jointly awarded a Nobel prize.

Curie Marie (born Marya Sklodovska) 1867–1934. Polish chemist, wife of physicist *Pierre Curie* (1859–1906) from 1895. They were awarded the Nobel Prize for Physics (with Becquerel) in 1903 for their work on radioactivity, and in 1911 Marie received the Nobel Prize for Chemistry for her discovery of the elements polonium and radium. She died a victim of the radiation emitted by the chemicals with which she worked. Her daughter and son-in-law, *Irène Joliot-Curie* (1896–1956), and *Frédéric Joliot* (1900–59), received a Nobel prize for chemistry in 1935 for their creation of artificial radioactivity.

de Broglie Louis, 7th duc de Broglie 1892–. French theoretical physicist. In 1929 he was awarded a Nobel prize, having written much from 1924 on quantum theory and having accounted for certain properties of atomic particles in terms of waves, thus laying the foundations of wave mechanics.

Dirac Paul Adrien Maurice 1902–84. British physicist who worked out a version of quantum mechanics consistent with Einstein's special theory of relativity. The existence of the positron, an antiparticle of the electron, was one of its predictions.

Doppler Christian Johann 1803–53. Austrian physicist. He became professor of experimental physics at Vienna, and described the *Doppler effect*, which states that in the same way as the pitch of a sound alters if the body from which it proceeds is moving relatively to a fixed observer, so the light from a moving star varies in colour.

Einstein Albert 1879–1955. German-Swiss physicist who formulated the *theories of relativity* and did important work in radiation physics and thermodynamics. Born at Ulm, in Württemberg, in a Jewish family, he lived with his parents in Munich and then in Italy. In 1913 he took up a specially created post as director of the Kaiser Wilhelm Institute for Physics, Berlin. He received the Nobel Prize for Physics in 1921. After being deprived of his post at Berlin by the Nazis, he emigrated in 1933, to the USA and became professor of mathematics and a permanent member of the Institute for Advanced Study at Princeton, New Jersey. In 1905 he had published his first theory – the *special theory of relativity* – and in 1915 issued his general theory of relativity. His latest conception of the basic laws governing the universe was outlined in his unified field theory made public in 1953.

Fermi Enrico 1901–54. Italian-American physicist who proved the existence of new radioactive elements produced by bombardment with neutrons and discovered nuclear reactions produced by slow neutrons. Born in Rome, he was professor of theoretical physics there from 1926 to 1938, when he settled in the USA. The same year he was awarded a Nobel prize for his discoveries.

Foucault Jean Bernard Léon 1819–68. French physicist who, in 1851, produced the pendulum (named after him) which demonstrates the rotation of the earth on its axis, and was the inventor of the gyroscope.

Frisch Otto 1904–79. Austrian physicist who coined the term 'nuclear fission'. A refugee from Nazi Germany, he worked from 1943 at Los Alamos, then at Cambridge.

Gabor Dennis 1900–79. Hungarian-British physicist, who was awarded a Nobel prize in 1971 for his invention, in 1947, of *holography* (creating three-dimensional images by the use of lasers).

Galileo Galilei 1564–1642. Italian mathematician, astronomer, and physicist, who revolutionized the scientific thinking of his time. In mechanics, Galileo argued convincingly that freely-falling bodies, heavy or light, had the same, constant acceleration (though the story of his dropping cannon balls from the Leaning Tower is probably apocryphal), and that a body moving on a perfectly smooth horizontal surface would neither speed up nor slow down.

Gell-Mann Murray 1929– . American physicist who was awarded a Nobel prize for his work on elementary particles. In 1964 he formulated the theory of the 'quark' as the fundamental constituent of all matter and smallest particle in the universe.

Hahn Otto 1879–1968. West German physical chemist who discovered nuclear fission. With Strassmann 1938 he discovered that uranium nuclei split when bombarded with neutrons, which led to the development of the atom bomb (first used in 1945).

Heaviside Oliver 1850–1925. British physicist whose theoretical work had important implications for radio transmission. His studies of electricity published in *Electrical Papers* 1892 had considerable influence on long-distance telephony. In 1902 he predicted the existence of an ionized layer of air in the upper atmosphere which was verified by Kennelly and was later known as the Kennelly-Heaviside layer (now called the *E layer*). Deflection from it makes possible the transmission of radio signals round the world, which would otherwise be lost in outer space.

Heisenberg Werner Carl 1901–76. German physicist who was an originator of quantum mechanics and the formulator of the uncertainty (indeterminacy) principle that is central to atomic physics.

Helmholtz Hermann Ludwig Ferdinand von 1821–94. German scientist, renowned for his work in thermodynamics. In 1847 he published an epoch-making treatise on the conservation of energy. In his *Doctrine of the Sensations of Tone* 1862 gave a complete study of sound.

Hertz Heinrich 1821–94. German physicist who continued the work of Maxwell in studying electromagnetic waves, preparing the way for radio communication, and showed that their behaviour resembled that of light and heat waves. The unit of frequency, the hertz (Hz), is named after him.

Joule James Prescott 1818–89. British physicist whose work on the relations between electrical, mechanical, and chemical effects led to the discovery of the first law of thermodynamics (the conservation of energy). He determined the mechanical equivalent of heat (*Joule's equivalent*), and the SI unit of energy, the joule, is named after him.

Kelvin William Thomson, 1st Baron Kelvin 1824–1907. British physicist who pioneered the absolute scale of temperature. His work on the conservation of energy 1851 led to the second law of thermodynamics. Popularly known for his contributions to telegraphy, he developed stranded cables and sensitive receivers, greatly improving transatlantic communications.

Maxwell James Clerk 1831–79. British physicist. His short life was rich in contributions to every branch of physical science, particularly on gases, optics and colour sensation, electricity and magnetism. His theoretical work in the last sphere prepared the way for wireless telegraphy and telephony.

Michelson Albert Abraham 1852–1931. German-born American physicist who became the first American scientist to win a Nobel prize 1907. He invented the Michelson interferometer, made precise measurement of the speed of light, and from 1892 was professor at Chicago. In conjunction with Edward Morley he performed in 1887 the *Michelson-Morley experiment* to detect the motion of the earth through the postulated ether. The failure of the experiment proved the non-existence of the ether (a medium believed to be necessary for the propagation of light) and led Einstein to his theory of relativity.

Newton Sir Isaac 1642–1727. British natural philosopher and mathematician who laid the foundation of physics as a modern discipline. During 1665–6 he formulated the binomial theorem and the differential and integral calculus, dealing with the mathematics of infinitely large numbers and minute changes, and began to investigate the phenomenon of universal gravitation. He was elected Fellow of the Royal Society in 1672, and in 1685 his *universal law of gravitation* was completely expounded as follows: 'Every particle of matter in the universe attracts every other particle with a force whose direction is that of the line joining the two, and whose magnitude is directly as the product of the masses, and inversely as the square of their distance from each other.' His greatest work, *Philosophiae Naturalis Principia Mathematica*, was published in three volumes 1686–7, with the aid of British physicist Edmund Halley (1656–1742). The newton, the unit of force that is now part of the SI system (that is the force required to accelerate a mass of one kilogram by one metre per second) is named after him (unit symbol N).

Ohm Georg Simon 1787–1854. German physicist who promulgated what is known as *Ohm's law*. Ohm's law states that the steady current in a metallic circuit is directly proportional to the constant total electromotive force in the circuit. If a current I flows between two points in a conductor across which the potential difference (voltage) is E, then E/I is a constant (which is known as the resistance between the two points).

Pauli Wolfgang 1900–58. Austrian-American physicist, a Nobel prizewinner 1945 for his work on atomic structure. He originated *Pauli's exclusion principle*, that in a given system no two electrons, protons, neutrons or other particles of half-intergrated spin can be characterized by the same set of quantum numbers. He also predicted the existence of neutrinos.

Planck Max 1858–1947. German physicist who framed the quantum theory 1900. He was awarded the Nobel Prize for Physics in 1918, and became a Fellow of the Royal Society in 1926.

Raman Sir Venkata 1888–1970. Indian physicist who in 1928 discovered what became known as the *Raman effect*: the scattering of monochromatic light when passed through a transparent substance. He was awarded a Nobel prize in 1930 and in 1948 became director of the Raman Research Institute and national research professor of physics.

Rutherford Ernest 1871–1937. New Zealand physicist. A pioneer of modern atomic science, his main researches were in the field of radioactivity, and he was the first to recognize the nuclear nature of the atom. He was awarded a Nobel prize in 1908.

Sakharov Andrei Dmitrievich 1921– . Soviet physicist who is known both as 'the father of the Russian H-bomb' and as an outspoken civil rights campaigner. He protested against Soviet nuclear tests and was a founder of the Soviet Human Rights Committee.

Shockley William 1910– . American physicist who worked with American physicists John Bardeen (1908–) and Walter Houser Brattain (1902–) on the invention of the transistor, that heralded the microelectronics revolution. He was jointly awarded a Nobel prize with them in 1956.

Thomson Sir George Paget 1892–1975. British physicist, son of Sir Joseph Thomson, whose work on interference phenomena in the scattering of electrons by crystals helped to confirm the wave-like nature of particles. He shared a Nobel prize with American physicist Clinton Joseph Davisson (1881–1958) in 1937.

Thomson Sir Joseph John 1856–1940. British physicist who discovered the electron. Educated at Manchester and Cambridge, where he became Cavendish professor of experimental physics 1884–1918, he organized the Cavendish research laboratory which became a world-famous centre of atomic research. His work inaugurated the electrical theory of the atom, and his elucidation of positive rays and their application to an analysis of neon led to the discovery of isotopes, which are different atomic forms of the same chemical element. He was awarded a Nobel prize in 1906.

Volta Alessandro 1745–1827. Italian physicist who pioneered electrical science. Born at Como, he was a professor there and at Pavia. He invented the voltaic pile (the first battery), the electrophorus (an early electrostatic generator) and an electroscope (a device for detecting electric charge). The volt is named after him.

Wheatstone Sir Charles 1802–75. British physicist and inventor. His inventions included the concertina, harmonica, and stereoscope, and he took out the first British patent for the electric telegraph in 1837, with British physicist William Fothergill Cooke (1806–1879). He measured the speed of electric discharge in conductors, and also devised the *Wheatstone bridge* (a special electrical network for measuring resistance).

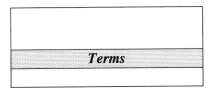

Terms

absolute zero the lowest temperature which could possibly exist, equivalent to −273.1°C when molecules would have no energy. Near this temperature the physical properties of materials change substantially, for example some metals lose their electrical resistance (superconductivity).

absorption has several meanings in science. It most commonly describes the taking up of one substance by another, such as liquid into a solid (like ink into blotting-paper) or a gas into a liquid (like ammonia into water). With pure single substances, the result of such absorption is a uniform solution. In optics, absorption is the phenomenon by which a substance retains radiation of particular wavelengths; for example, a piece of blue glass absorbs all visible light except the wavelengths in the blue part of the spectrum. In nuclear physics, the capture by elements such as boron of neutrons produced by fission in a reactor is also called absorption.

adsorption the taking up of a gas or liquid by the surface of a solid (as activated charcoal, for example, adsorbs gases). It is a phenomenon involving molecular attraction at the surface and should be distinguished from *absorption*.

anode the electrode towards which negative particles (***anions***) move within a device, such as the cells of a battery, electrolytic cells, diodes.

boiling point for any given liquid, the temperature at which the application of heat raises the temperature of the liquid no further, but converts it to vapour. The boiling point of water under normal pressure is 100°C or 212°F. The lower the pressure, the lower the boiling point and vice versa.

capacitance the ratio of the electric charge on a body to the resultant change of potential. A ***capacitor*** has a capacitance of one farad when a charge of one coulomb changes its potential by one volt. The farad is an impractically large unit and capacitors normally used in electronic circuits are of the order of millionths of a farad (microfarads) or less.

cathode the electrode towards which positive particles (***cations***) move within a device, such as the cells of a battery, electrolytic cells, diodes.

electric cell

a lead-acid cell

external circuit

flow of electrons

lead electrode

lead dioxide electrode

electrolyte (dilute sulphuric acid)

cell (electric) an apparatus in which chemical energy is converted into electrical energy; the popular name is 'battery', but this should be reserved for a collection of cells in one unit. Electric cells can be divided into: ***primary***, which produce electrical energy by chemical action and require replenishing after this action is complete; and ***secondary***, or ***accumulators***, which are so constituted that the action is reversible, and the original condition can be restored by an electric current. The first battery was made by Volta in 1800.

chain reaction in nuclear physics, a fission reaction which is maintained because neutrons released by the splitting of some atomic nuclei themselves go on to split others, releasing even more neutrons, and so on. Such a reaction can be controlled (as in a nuclear reactor) by using moderators to absorb excess neutrons. Uncontrolled, a chain reaction produces a nuclear explosion (as in an atom bomb).

colour quality or wavelength of light emitted or reflected from an object. Visible white light consists of electro-magnetic radiation of various wavelengths, and if a beam is refracted through a prism, it can be spread out into a spectrum, in which the various colours correspond to the different wavelengths. From high to low wavelengths the colours are red, orange, yellow, green, blue, indigo, violet. When a surface is illuminated, some parts of the white light are absorbed, depending on the molecular structure of the material and the dyes applied to it. A surface that looks red will have absorbed the light from the blue end of the spectrum, but have a high reflection of light from the red, long-wave end. Colours vary in brightness, in hue, and in saturation, that is the extent to which they are mixed with white.

cryogenics science of very low temperatures (approaching absolute zero), including the liquefaction of gases such as nitrogen, helium, hydrogen; and exploitation of special properties produced at these low temperatures, such as the disappearance of electrical resistance (superconductivity).

density measure of the compactness of a substance; its mass per unit volume, measured in kilograms per cubic metre. *Relative density* is the ratio of the density of a substance to that of water at °C.

diffraction the interference phenomena observed at the edges of opaque objects, or discontinuities between different media in the path of a wave train. The phenomena give rise to slight spreading of light into light and dark bands at the shadow of a straight edge. The *diffraction grating* is a device for separating a wave train such as a beam of incident light into its component frequencies (white light results in a spectrum). Sound waves can also be diffracted by a suitable array of solid objects.

diffusion term used in physical chemistry to describe at least three processes: the spontaneous mixing of gases or liquids (classed together as *fluids* in scientific usage) when brought into contact without mechanical mixing or stirring; the spontaneous passage of fluids through membranes; and the spontaneous passage of dissolved materials both through the material in which they are dissolved and also through membranes.

Doppler effect change in the observed frequency of waves due to relative motion between wave source and observer. It is responsible for the perceived change in pitch of an ambulance siren as it approaches and then recedes, and, on a somewhat grander scale, for the shift, towards the red end of the spectrum, of light from distant stars.

dynamics the branch of mechanics that deals with the mathematical and physical study of the behaviour of bodies under the action of forces which produce changes of motion in them.

electric charge the property of some bodies which causes them to exert forces on each other. Two bodies both with positive or negative charges repel each other, while opposite or 'unlike' charged bodies attract each other, since each is in the *electric field* of the other. In atoms, electrons possess a negative charge, and protons an equal positive charge, the unit of charge being the *coulomb* (C). Atoms have no overall charge but can sometimes gain electrons to become negative *ions* or lose them to become positive ions. So-called *static electricity*, seen in such phenomena as the charging of nylon shirts when they are pulled on or off, is in fact the rubbing-on or rubbing-off of electrons from the surface atoms. A flow of charge (such as electrons through a copper wire) constitutes an *electric current*; the flow of current is measured in *amperes*.

electric current the rate of flow of electric charge. Measured in amperes (coulombs per

electromagnetic waves

wavelength in metres	uses	usual source

frequency in metres

second).

electrode a conductor by means of which a current passes into or out of a substance, such as the electrodes of an electrolytic cell, an electric furnace, a discharge tube, or a radio valve. Conducting elements separated by an insulating material as in a capacitor (a store of electric charge), are also called electrodes.

electromagnetic field a region of space in which a particle with an electric charge experiences a force. If it does so only when moving, it is in a pure *magnetic field*, if it does so when stationary, it is in an *electric field*. Both can be present simultaneously, as with electromagnets.

electromagnetic waves oscillating electric and magnetic fields travelling together through space at a speed of nearly 300 million metres per second. The (limitless) range of possible frequencies of electromagnetic waves which can be thought of as making up the *electromagnetic spectrum* include radio waves, infrared radiation, visible light, ultraviolet radiation, and X-rays and gamma rays. Dividing 300 million by the frequency (number of cycles per second, or hertz) gives the wavelength of the waves in metres.

electronics the design and application of devices which amplify and switch electrically, without moving parts. The first device was the *thermionic valve* (using electrons moving in a vacuum) on the basis of which electronics developed during the first half of the 20th century to the stage of producing radio, radar, black and white television, and the earliest true computers. *Solid-state* technology, that of the transistor (invented 1949) and multi-transistor circuits in the form of silicon chips, has almost entirely superseded the valve, for reasons of cheapness, compactness, reliability, and low power consumption.

electrostatics the study of electric charges from stationary sources (not currents), for example amber, and lightning.

energy the capacity for doing work. *Potential energy* (PE) is energy deriving from position: thus a stretched spring has elastic PE; an object raised to a height above the earth's surface, or the water in an elevated reservoir, has gravitational PE; a lump of coal and a tank of petrol, together with the oxygen needed for their combustion, have chemical PE (due to relative positions of atoms). Other sorts of PE include *electrical* and *nuclear*. Moving bodies possess *kinetic energy* (KE).

Energy can be converted from one form to another, but the total quantity stays the same (in accordance with the conservation laws that govern many natural phenomena). For example, as an apple falls it loses gravitational PE but gains KE.

entropy in thermodynamics (the study of heat as related to other forms of energy), a parameter representing the state of disorder of a system at the atomic, ionic or molecular level; the greater the disorder, the higher the entropy. Thus the fast-moving disordered molecules of water vapour have higher entropy than those of more ordered liquid water, which in turn have more entropy than the molecules in solid crystalline ice. At absolute zero, the lowest possible temperature ($-273°C/0$ K), when all molecular motion ceases and order is assumed to be complete, entropy is zero.

force that which tends to change the state of rest or the uniform motion of a body in a straight line. It is measured by the rate of change of momentum of the body on which it acts, that is, the mass of the body multiplied by its acceleration $f=ma$.

forces the four fundamental interactions believed to be at work in the physical universe. *Gravity*, which keeps the planets in orbit around the sun, acts between all atomic particles with mass. *Electromagnetic forces*, which stop solids from falling apart, act between all atomic particles with electric charge. In addition to these long-range forces, there are two very short-range forces: the *weak*, responsible for the reactions which fuel the sun, and for the emission of beta particles from certain nuclei; and the *strong*, which binds together the protons and neutrons in the nucleus of atoms. By 1971 a theory was developed which suggested that the weak and electromagnetic forces were linked; experimental support came from observation at CERN in the 1980s. Physicists are now working on theories to unify all four forces.

frequency the number of cycles of a vibration occurring per unit of time. The unit of frequency is the hertz (Hz); 1 Hz = 1 cycle per second, 1 KHz (kilohertz) = 1,000 Hz, 1 MHz (megahertz) = 1,000,000 Hz. Human beings can hear sounds from objects vibrating in the range 20 Hz to 15,000 Hz. Ultrasonic frequencies are above that range.

gravity the force of attraction between an object and the earth because of their masses. According to Newton's law of gravitation, for an object of mass m at a distance d from the centre of the earth of mass M, the force of gravity F equals GmM/d_2, where G is the gravitational constant. According to Newton's second law of motion, F also equals mg, where g is the acceleration due to gravity. Therefore $g = d_2$ and is independent of the mass of the object; at the earth's surface it equals 9.086 m s^{-2} (metres per second per second). In other words, all objects fall to earth with the same acceleration, a fact proved by Galileo's apocryphal experiment of dropping objects off the Leaning Tower of Pisa.

heat a form of energy which, when added to or removed from an object, usually causes a rise or fall in its temperature. Heat always flows from a region of higher temperature to one of lower temperature. Its effect may be simply to raise the temperature, to cause expansion, to melt a solid, to vaporize a liquid, or to increase the pressure of a gas. The *specific heat* of a substance is the ratio of the quantity of heat required to raise the temperature of a given mass of the substance through a given range of temperature, to the heat required to raise the temperature of an equal mass of water through the same range.
There are three ways by which heat may be transferred from one place to another:
convection transmission through a fluid (liquid or gas) by currents, for example when the air in a room is warmed by a fire or radiator, or water is heated in a domestic hot-water system;
conduction heat passing from one part of a

medium to neighbouring parts with no visible motion of the medium accompanying the transfer of heat, as when the whole length of a metal rod is heated when one end is held in a fire;
radiation heat transfer by infrared rays. Radiant heat is of the same nature as light. It can pass through a vacuum, travels at the same speed as light, can be reflected and refracted, and does not affect the medium through which it passes.

heat capacity the quantity of heat required to raise the temperature of a substance by one degree. The *specific heat capacity* of a substance is the heat capacity per unit of mass, measured in joules per kilogramme per kelvin (J kg^{-1} K^{-1}).

humidity the quantity of water vapour in a given volume of the atmosphere (*absolute humidity*), or the ratio of the amount of water vapour in the atmosphere to the saturation value at the same temperature (*relative humidity*); at dew-point the latter is 100%. Relative humidity is measured by various types of *hygrometer*.

inductance that property of an electronic circuit or circuit component which when carrying a current is characterized by the formation of a magnetic field and the storage of magnetic energy. It is also a measure of the capability of a circuit or circuit component to store magnetic energy when carrying a current.

kinetics a branch of dynamics dealing with the action of forces producing or changing the motion of a body, as distinguished from *kinematics*, which deals with motion without reference to force or mass.

latent heat heat which changes the state (for example from solid to liquid) of a substance without changing its temperature.

lens a piece of transparent material (such as glass) with two polished surfaces – one concave or convex, and the other plane, concave or convex – to modify rays of light according to the type of lens they traverse. A *convex lens* converges the light and a *concave lens* diverges it. Lenses are essential to spectacles, microscopes, telescopes, cameras, and almost all optical instruments. *Compound lenses* for special purposes are built up from two or more lenses made of glass (or other suitable material) of different refractive index.

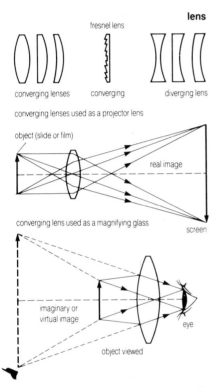

lens

converging lenses   converging   diverging lens

fresnel lens

converging lenses used as a projector lens

object (slide or film)

real image

converging lens used as a magnifying glass

screen

imaginary or virtual image

object viewed

eye

The image formed by a single lens suffers from several defects or aberrations, notably spherical aberration in which a straight line becomes a curved image, and chromatic aberration in which an image in white light tends to have coloured edges. Aberrations are corrected by the use of compound lenses.

light electromagnetic radiation in the visible range, that is, from about 400 nanometers in the extreme violet to about 770 nanometers in the extreme red. Light is considered to exhibit both particle and wave properties and the fundamental particle or quantum of light is called the *photon*. The speed of light (and of all electromagnetic radiation) in a vacuum is approximately 300 million metres per second or 186,000 miles per second, and is a universal constant denoted by c. This is allegedly the fastest speed in nature, but in 1971 a jet from the galaxy 3C 273 was calculated as travelling at three times this speed, which should be impossible.

magnetism that branch of physics dealing with the properties of *magnets* and *magnetic fields*. Magnetic fields are produced by moving charged particles: in electromagnets electrons flow through a coil of wire connected to a battery; in magnets spinning electrons within the atoms generate the field. Only certain ferromagnetic materials can be made into magnets; this is because forces act between adjacent atoms so that large groups, forming regions or domains, produce fields which reinforce.

Substances differ in degree and kind in their ability to be magnetized (*permeability*). Those substances, like iron, which have very high permeabilities, are said to be *ferromagnetic*. Apart from its universal application to dynamos, electric motors, switch-gear, and so forth, magnetism has become of considerable importance in modern science, including particle accelerators for nuclear research, memory stores for computers, tape recorders, cryogenics (low temperature physics), and investigations of matter and space.

Experiments have confirmed that homing pigeons and other animals rely on their perception of earth's magnetic field for their sense of direction, and by 1979 it was suggested that humans to some extent share this sense.

mass the quantity of matter in a body. The British unit of mass is the pound, that is the quantity of matter in a standard platinum cylinder preserved at the standards office at the Board of Trade; in the SI system, now under adoption in Britain, the base unit of mass is the kilogram. Mass determines the acceleration produced in a body by a given force working upon it, the acceleration being inversely proportional to the mass of the body. The mass also determines the force exerted on a body by the gravitational attraction of the earth, although this attraction varies slightly from place to place. At a given place, however, equal masses experience equal gravitational forces, which are known as the weights of the bodies. Masses may, therefore, be compared

magnetism

lines of magnetic force in the area
surrounding a bar magnet

by comparing the weights of bodies at the same place, as in a balance.

mechanics the branch of applied mathematics dealing with the motions of bodies and the forces causing them, and also with the forces acting on bodies in equilibrium. It is usually divided into *dynamics* and *statics*. *Quantum mechanics* is the system based on the quantum theory which has superseded Newtonian mechanics in the interpretation of physical phenomena on the atomic scale.

modulation in radio, the intermittent change of frequency, amplitude, and so on, of a radio carrier wave, in accordance with the audio-frequency speaking voice, music, or other signal being transmitted.

momentum of a body, is the product of its mass and its linear velocity; *angular momentum* (of a body in rotational motion) is the product of its moment (turning effect) of inertia and its angular velocity. The momentum of a body does not change unless it is acted on by an external force. The law of conservation of momentum is one of the fundamental concepts

of classical physics. It states that the total momentum of all bodies in a closed system is constant and unaffected by processes occurring within the system.

Newton's laws of motion the three laws that form the basis of Newtonian mechanics. They are:
(1) unless acted upon by a net force, a body at rest stays at rest and a moving body continues moving at the same speed in the same straight line;
(2) a net force applied to a body gives it a rate of change of momentum proportional to the force and in the direction of the force;
(3) when a body A exerts a force on a body B, B exerts an equal and opposite force on A, that is to every action there is an equal and opposite reaction.

optics the scientific study of light and vision, for example shadows cast by opaque objects, images formed in mirrors, and lenses, microscopes, telescopes, and cameras. Light rays are for all practical purposes straight lines, although Einstein has demonstrated that they may be 'bent' by a gravitational field. On striking a surface they are reflected or refracted with some attendant absorption of energy, and the study of these facts is the subject matter of *geometrical optics*.

osmosis the movement of solvent (liquid) through a semipermeable membrane separating solutions of different concentrations. The solvent passes from the dilute solution to the concentrated solution until the two concentrations are equal. Applying external pressure to the solution on the more concentrated side arrests osmosis, and is a measure of the osmotic pressure of the solution. Many cell membranes behave as semi-permeable membranes, and osmosis is an important mechanism in the transport of fluids in living organisms, for example in the transport of water from the roots up the stems of plants. Fish have protective mechanisms to counteract osmosis, which would otherwise cause fluid transport between the body of the animal and the surrounding water (outwards in saltwater fish, inwards in freshwater ones).

433

photon the smallest 'package', 'particle' or quantum of energy in which light, or any other form of electromagnetic radiation, is emitted.

power the rate of doing work or consuming energy; measured in watts or other units of work per unit time.

quantum theory the theory that many quantities, such as energy, cannot have continuous range of values but only a smaller number of discrete (particular) ones, because they are packaged in 'quanta of energy'.

radiation the emission of radiant energy as particles, waves, sound, and so on.

light or sound waves, when they hit a surface. The *law of reflection* states that the angle of incidence (the angle between the ray and a perpendicular line drawn to the surface) is equal to the angle of reflection (the angle between the reflected ray and a perpendicular to the surface). Thus, rays are reflected at the same angle at which they strike.

refraction the bending of light when it passes from one medium to another, such as from air to glass. Since light travels more slowly in glass than in air, the light bends towards the normal, that is perpendicular, in going from air to glass, but away from the normal when going from glass to air.

reflection

approaching or incident ray

angle of incidence
angle of reflection

normal (at right angles to surface)

reflected ray

mirror

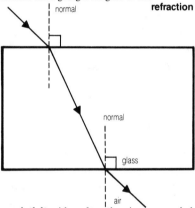

refraction

normal

normal

glass

air

relativity either of two theories propounded by Einstein concerning the nature of space and time, and with far-reaching implications in physics.

The *special theory of relativity* 1905 was devised to simplify the theory of electromagnetism. Starting with the premises that (1) the laws of nature are the same for all observers in unaccelerated motion; and (2) the speed of light is independent of the motion of its source, Einstein showed, for example, that the time interval between two events was longer for an observer in whose frame of reference the events occur in different places than for the observer for whom they occur at the same place. Such 'time dilation' has been confirmed

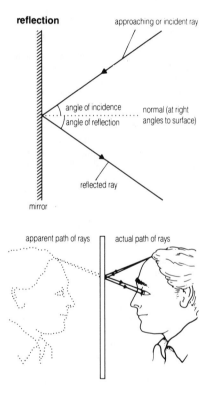

apparent path of rays

actual path of rays

reflection the deflection of waves, such as

by experiment and gives a degree of academic respectability to the notion of (forward) time-travel. Einstein's ideas were shown by the German mathematician Hermann Minkowski (1864–1909) to imply that time was in many respects like an extra dimension to space, so physicists now talk of four-dimensional 'space–time'. Einstein showed that for consistency with premises (1) and (2) the principles of dynamics as established by Newton needed modification; the most celebrated new result being the equation $E = mc^2$ which expresses an equivalence between mass (m) and energy (E), c being the speed of light in vacuum.

The *general theory of relativity* 1915 involved a new twist to the concept of space–time; its geometrical properties were to be conceived as modified locally by the presence of a body with mass. A planet's orbit around the sun (as observed in three-dimensional space) arises from its natural trajectory in modified space–time; there is no need to invoke, as Newton did, a force of gravity coming from the sun and acting on the planet. Although since modified in detail, general relativity remains central to modern astrophysics and cosmology; it predicts, for example, the possibility of black holes (small stellar objects collapsing under extreme gravitational force such that light cannot escape from them).

resistance that property of a substance which restricts the flow of electricity through it, associated with the conversion of electrical energy to heat; also the magnitude of this property. A *resistor* is an element whose principal characteristic is resistance, which depends on many factors which may include any or all of the following: the nature of the material, its temperature, dimensions, and thermal properties; degree of impurity; the nature and state of illumination of the surface; and the frequency and magnitude of the current. The practical unit of resistance is the *ohm*.

sound a physiological sensation received by the ear, originating in a vibration (pressure variation in the air), which communicates itself to the air, and travels in every direction, spreading out as an expanding sphere. All sound waves in air travel with a speed which depends on the temperature of the atmosphere; under ordinary conditions this is about 340 m/1,120 ft per second. The pitch of the sound depends on the number of vibrations imposed on the air per second, but the speed is unaffected. The loudness of a sound is dependent primarily on the extent (amplitude) of the to and fro vibration of the air. The lowest note audible to a human being has a frequency of about 26 Hz (vibrations per second), and the highest one of about 18,000 Hz; the lower limit of this range varies little with the person's age, but the upper range falls steadily from adolescence onwards.

spectrum an arrangement in order of magnitude of radiated frequencies of electromagnetic waves, or of the energies of atomic particles. The visible spectrum was first studied by Newton who showed in 1672 that a band of white light (sunlight) passing through a glass prism could be broken into a band of coloured light.

statics the branch of mechanics concerned with the behaviour of bodies at rest and forces in equilibrium, and distinguished from *dynamics*.

thermodynamics the branch of physics dealing with the transfer of heat into other forms of energy, on which is based the study of the efficient working of engines, such as the steam and internal combustion. The three laws of thermodynamics are:

(1) energy can be neither created nor destroyed: heat and mechanical work being mutually convertible;

(2) it is impossible for an unaided self-acting machine to convey heat from one body to another at a higher temperature;

(3) it is impossible by any procedure, no matter how idealized, to reduce any system to the absolute zero of temperature (0 K/−273°C) in a finite number of operations. Put into mathematical form these have widespread applications in physics and chemistry.

transformer a device in which by electromagnetic induction an alternating or intermittent current of one voltage is transformed

435

to another voltage, without change of frequency. A transformer has two coils, a primary for the input, and a secondary for the output, wound on a common iron core. The ratio of the primary to the secondary voltages (and currents) is directly (and inversely) proportional to the number of turns in the primary and secondary coils. It is widely used in electrical apparatus of all kinds and in particular in power transmission where high voltages and low currents are utilized.

ultrasound physical vibrations in matter occurring at frequencies above 20,000 Hz (cycles per second), the approximate limit of human hearing. Propagation of ultrasound in air or other gas is very poor and nearly all practical applications are in liquids or solids. The earliest practical application was to detect submarines during World War I but recently the field of ultrasonics has greatly expanded. The lower frequencies of 20,000–80,000 Hz are mainly used for cleaning in industry and in hospitals. Higher frequencies have been used in the form of pulses to produce echoes as a means of measuring the depth of the sea, to detect flaws in metal, and to show the condition of the foetus and the brain in medicine. High power ultrasound has been used with focusing arrangements to destroy tissue at a depth in the body, and extremely high frequencies of 1,000 MHz (megahertz) or more are used in ultrasonic microscopes.

viscosity the internal friction or resistance to relative motion of the parts of a fluid. Fluids like pitch, treacle, and heavy oils are highly viscous; a perfect fluid would be non-viscous.

wave a pulse or pattern of disturbances which travels through a medium by means of the forces between the particles of the medium. Waves transport energy and show the properties of reflection, refraction, diffraction, and interference. *Sound waves* are longitudinal, that is the particles of the medium (such as air) vibrate to and fro parallel to the direction in which the wave is travelling. *Seismic waves* in the earth's crust include both longitudinal and transverse (at right angles to the direction of propagation) components. *Electromagnetic waves* (such as light) have many of the properties of an ordinary wave, but no medium is needed; the 'disturbance' takes the form of alternating electric and magnetic fields.

work a measure of the result of transferring energy from one system to another to cause an object to move. Thus work W is equal to the product of the force F used and the distance d moved by the object ($W=F \times d$). For example, the work done when a force of 10 newtons moves an object 5 metres against some sort of resistance is 50 newton-metres ($= 50$ joules). Work should not be confused with *energy* (the capacity to do work, which is also mentioned in joules) or *power* (the rate of doing work, measured in watts).

c. 400 BC	The first 'atomic' theory was put forward by Democritus.
c. 250 BC	Archimedes' principle of buoyancy was established.
1600 AD	Magnetism was described by English physician William Gilbert (1544–1603).
c. 1610	The principle of falling bodies descending to earth at the same speed was established by Galileo.
1642	The principles of hydraulics were put forward by French mathematician, physicist, and philosopher Blaise Pascal (1623–1662).
1643	The mercury barometer was invented by Italian physicist Evangelista Torricelli (1608–47).
1656	The pendulum clock was invented by Dutch physicist and astronomer Christiaan Huygens (1629–95).
1662	Boyle's law concerning gas was established by Boyle.
c. 1665	Newton put forward the law of gravity, stating that the earth exerts a constant force on falling bodies.
1677	The simple microscope was invented by Dutch microscopist Antoni van Leeuwenhoek (1632–1723).
1690	The wave theory of light was propounded by Huygens.
1704	The corpuscular theory of light was put forward by Newton.
1714	The mercury thermometer was invented by German physicist Daniel Fahrenheit.
1771	The link between nerve action and electricity was discovered by Italian anatomist and physiologist Luigi Galvani (1737–98).
c. 1787	Charles' law relating the pressure, volume, and temperature of a gas was established by French physical chemist Jacques Charles (1746–1823).
1795	The metric system was adopted in France.
1800	Volta invented the Voltaic cell.
1801	Interference of light was discovered by British physicist Thomas Young (1773–1829).
1808	The 'modern' atomic theory was propounded by British physicist and chemist John Dalton (1766–1844).
1811	Avogadro's hypothesis relating volumes and numbers of molecules of gases was proposed by Italian physicist and chemist Amedeo Avogadro (1776–1856).
1814	Fraunhofer lines in the solar spectrum were mapped by Fraunhofer.
1815	Refraction of light was explained by French physicist Augustin Fresnel (1788–1827).
1819	Electromagnetism was discovered by Danish physicist Hans Oersted (1777–1851).
1821	The dynamo principle was described by British physicist and chemist Michael Faraday (1791–1867); the thermocouple was discovered by German physicist Thomas Seebeck (1770–1831).
1822	The laws of electrodynamics were established by French physicist and mathematician André Ampère (1775–1836).
1824	Thermodynamics as a branch of physics was proposed by French physicist Sadi Carnot (1796–1832).
1827	Ohm's law of electrical resistance was established by Ohm; Brownian motion resulting from molecular vibrations was observed by British botanist Robert Brown (1773–1858).
1829	The law of gaseous diffusion was established by Scottish chemist Thomas Graham (1805–69).
1831	Electromagnetic induction was discovered by Faraday.
1842	The principle of conservation of energy was observed by German physician and physicist Julius von Mayer (1814–78).

c.1847	The mechanical equivalent of heat was described by Joule.
1859	Spectrographic analysis was made by German chemist Robert Bunsen (1811–99) and German physicist Gustav Kirchhoff (1824–87).
1873	Light was conceived as electromagnetic radiation by Maxwell.
1877	A theory of sound as vibrations in an elastic medium was propounded by British physicist John Rayleigh (1842–1919).
1880	Piezoelectricity was discovered by Pierre Curie.
1887	The existence of radio waves was predicted by Hertz.
1895	X-rays were discovered by German physicist Wilhelm Röntgen (1845–1923).
1896	The discovery of radioactivity was made by French physicist Antoine Becquerel (1852–1908).
1897	The electron was discovered by J J Thomson.
1899	Rutherford discovered alpha and beta rays.
1900	Quantum theory was propounded by Planck; the discovery of gamma rays was made by French physicist Paul-Ulrich Villard (1860–1934).
1902	Heaviside discovered the ionosphere.
1904	The theory of radioactivity was put forward by Rutherford and British chemist Frederick Soddy (1877–1966).
1905	Einstein propounded his *special theory of relativity*.
1911	The discovery of the atomic nucleus was made by Rutherford.
1913	The Geiger counter was invented by German physicist Hans Geiger and Walther Müller.
1915	Einstein put forward his *general theory of relativity*; X-ray crystallography was discovered by William and Lawrence Bragg.
1916	Mass spectrography was discovered by British physicist William Aston (1877–1945).
1922	The orbiting electron atomic theory was propounded by Bohr.
1924	Appleton made his study of the Heaviside layer.
1927	The uncertainty principle of atomic physics was established by German physicist Werner Heisenberg (1901–76).
1928	Wave mechanics was introduced by Schrödinger.
1931	The cyclotron was developed by American physicist Ernest Lawrence (1901–58).
1932	The discovery of the neutron was made by Chadwick; the electron microscope was developed by Soviet-American physicist Vladimir Zworykin (1889–1982).
1933	The positron, the antiparticle of the electron, was discovered by Millikan.
1934	Artificial radioactivity was developed by Frédéric and Irène Joliot-Curie.
1939	Nnuclear fission was discovered by Hahn and German chemist Fritz Strassman (1902–).
1942	The first controlled nuclear chain reaction was achieved by Fermi.
1956	The neutrino, a fundamental particle, was discovered.
1960	The Mössbauer effect of atom emissions was discovered by German physicist Rudolf Mössbauer (1929–); the first maser was developed by American physicist Theodore Maiman (1927–).
1963	Maiman developed the first laser (*l*ight *a*mplification by *s*timulated *e*mission of *r*adiation).
1983	Existence of W and Z particles confirmed at CERN, validating the link between the weak and electromagnetic forces.
1986	First high-temperature superconductor, which conducts electricity without resistance at a temperature of 35K, discovered.

Chemistry

Chemistry is the scientific study of the elements – the way they interact with one another under certain conditions, the properties of the compounds they form, and how, on the one hand, they are the building blocks of all matter, and on the other, are made up of atoms. Nowadays, many aspects of chemistry are closely associated with other scientific disciplines such as atomic physics, astronomy, biology, and mineralogy.

An initial overview of *Key Concepts* presents the three states of matter, atoms and molecules, chemical formulae, and the various branches of chemistry. This is followed by *Inorganic Chemistry*, which is concerned with the elements and all their compounds except those of carbon; a representation of the *Periodic Table of Elements*, which attempts to establish a formal framework from which the properties of elements can be largely determined; and *Organic Chemistry*, which is concerned specifically with the compounds of carbon. Many of the inventors, discoverers, and philosophers associated with the study of chemistry are introduced in the *Biographies*. Finally, the *Chronology* traces the development of the subject from the alchemists, who tried to turn base metals into gold, to the present-day artificial creation of new elements.

Key Concepts

All matter can exist in three states: gas, liquid, or solid. It is composed of minute particles termed *molecules*, and may be further divided into *atoms*. Molecules which contain atoms of one kind only are known as *elements*, while those which contain atoms of different kinds are called *compounds*. The separation of compounds into simpler substances is *analysis*, and the building up of compounds from their components is *synthesis*. When substances are brought together without changing their molecular structure they are said to be *mixtures*. Chemical compounds are produced by a chemical action which alters the arrangement of the atoms in the molecule. Heat, light, vibration, catalyst, radiation or pressure, as well as moisture (for ionization), may be necessary to produce a chemical change.

To facilitate the expression of chemical composition, symbols are used to denote the elements. The symbol is usually the first letter or letters of the English or Latinized name of the element, for example: C, carbon; Ca, calcium; Fe, iron (ferrum). These symbols represent one atom of the element; molecules containing more than one atom are denoted by a subscript figure, as in water, H_2O. In some substances a group of atoms acts as a single atom, and these are enclosed in brackets in the symbol, as in $(NH_2)_2SO_4$, ammonium sulphate. The symbolical representation of a molecule is known as a *formula*. A figure placed before a formula represents the number of molecules of one substance present in another, as in $2H_2O$, two molecules of water. Chemical reactions are expressed by means of equations, as in:

$$NaCl + H_2SO_4 = NaHSO_4 + HCl$$

This equation states the fact that sodium chloride (NaCl) on being treated with sulphuric acid (H_2SO_4) is converted into sodium bisulphate(NaHSO_4) and hydrogen chloride (HCl).

Elements are divided into two classes: metals, having lustre, and being conductors of heat and electricity, and non-metals, which usually lack these properties. The *Periodic System*, established by Mendeleyev in 1869, classified elements according to their atomic weights, that is the least weight of the element present in a molecular weight of any of its compounds. Those elements which resemble each other in general properties were found to bear a relation to one another by weight, and these were placed in groups or families. Certain anomalies in this system were removed by classifying the elements according to their atomic number. The latter is the equivalent of the charge on the nucleus of the atom.

Inorganic chemistry deals with the description, properties, reactions, and preparation of the elements and their compounds, with the exception of carbon compounds. *Organic chemistry* is that branch of chemistry which deals with carbon compounds. *Physical chemistry* is concerned with the particular changes which materials may undergo in special circumstances. Physical changes are changes of state only, the properties of the material remaining unaltered. This branch studies in particular the movement of molecules, and the effects of temperature and pressure, especially with regard to gases and liquids.

Inorganic Chemistry

Inorganic chemistry is a major branch of chemistry dealing with the elements and their compounds, except the more complex carbon compounds which are considered in *Organic* *chemistry.* Many types of inorganic com-

COMPOSITION OF THE HUMAN BODY BY WEIGHT

Class	Chemical/element or substance	% body weight
As pure	Oxygen	65
elements	Carbon	18
or as	Hydrogen	10
minerals,	Nitrogen	3
salts, and	Calcium	2
so on	Phosphorus	1.1
	Inorganic molecules	1
	Potassium	0.35
	Sulphur	0.25
	Sodium	0.15
	Chlorine	0.15
	Magnesium, Iron, Manganese, Copper, Iodine, Cobalt, Zinc	Traces
As water	Water	60-80
and solid	Total solid material	20-40
matter		
As organic	Protein	15-20
molecules	Lipid	3-20
	Carbohydrate	1-15
	Small organic molecules	0-1

pounds exist, the oldest known being acids, bases, and salts. *Acids* usually have a sour taste, change blue vegetable colours (for example litmus) to red, and react with alkalis to form salts. *Alkalis* restore the colours of indicators changed by acids, and react with acids to form salts. All acids contain hydrogen. Acids containing one, two, or three atoms of replaceable hydrogen are called mono-, di-, or tri-basic, respectively. *Salts* are formed by the replacement of the acidic hydrogen by a metal or radical (a group of atoms). If only part of the hydrogen is replaced, an acid salt is formed. A basic salt is usually a compound of a normal salt (in which all the acidic hydrogen is replaced) with excess of base.

Another important group of compounds is the oxides, in which oxygen is combined with another element. Oxides are classified into: (1) *acidic* oxides, forming acids with water; (2)

basic oxides, forming bases (containing the hydroxyl group OH) with water; (3) neutral oxides; and (4) peroxides (containing more oxygen than the normal oxide). Acidic and basic oxides combine to form salts.

Other groups are the compounds of metals with halogens (fluorine, chlorine, bromine, and iodine), called halides (fluorides, chlorides, and so on), and with sulphur (sulphides).

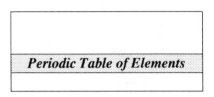

Periodic Table of Elements

The Periodic Table of the elements is a classification of the elements following the statement by Mendeleyev in 1869, that 'the properties of elements are in periodic dependence upon their atomic weight'. There are striking similarities in the chemical properties of the elements in each of the main vertical groups, and a graduation of properties along the horizontal periods. These are dependent on the electronic and nuclear structure of atoms of the elements. The table has been used to predict the existence of as yet unknown transuranic elements.

element one of the 105 known substances, of which 92 occur naturally, which consist of atoms having the same number of protons in their nuclei. Hydrogen and helium were produced in the 'Big Bang'; of the rest, those up to number 56 (iron) are produced by nuclear fusion within the stars, but the more massive, such as lead, uranium, and so on, are produced when an old star explodes and its gravitational energy as it collapses squashes nuclei together. The transuranium elements are artificially made by bombarding uranium with various atomic particles.

element

1	atomic number
Hydrogen	name
H	symbol
1.00794	atomic weight

1 Hydrogen **H** 1.00794								
3 Lithium **Li** 6.941	4 Beryllium **Be** 9.01218							
11 Sodium **Na** 22.98977	12 Magnesium **Mg** 24.305							
19 Potassium **K** 39.098	20 Calcium **Ca** 40.08	21 Scandium **Sc** 44.9559	22 Titanium **Ti** 47.90	23 Vanadium **V** 50.9414	24 Chromium **Cr** 51.996	25 Manganese **Mn** 54.9380	26 Iron **Fe** 55.847	27 Cobalt **Co** 58.9332
37 Rubidium **Rb** 85.4678	38 Strontium **Sr** 87.62	39 Yttrium **Y** 88.9059	40 Zirconium **Zr** 91.22	41 Niobium **Nb** 92.9064	42 Molybdenum **Mo** 95.94	43 Technetium **Tc** 97.9072	44 Ruthenium **Ru** 101.07	45 Rhodium **Rh** 102.9055
55 Caesium **Cs** 132.9054	56 Barium **Ba** 137.34		72 Hafnium **Hf** 178.49	73 Tantalum **Ta** 180.9479	74 Tungsten **W** 183.85	75 Rhenium **Re** 186.207	76 Osmium **Os** 190.2	77 Iridium **Ir** 192.22
87 Francium **Fr** 223.0197	88 Radium **Ra** 226.0254		104 Unnilquadium **Unq** 216.109	105 Unnilpentium **Unp** 262.114	106 Unnilhexium **Unh** 263.120	107 Unniseptium **Uns** 262		

57 Lanthanum **La** 138.9055	58 Cerium **Ce** 140.12	59 Praeseodymium **Pr** 140.9077	60 Neodymium **Nd** 144.24	61 Promethium **Pm** 144.9128	62 Samarium **Sm** 150.36

89 Actinium **Ac** 227.0278	90 Thorium **Th** 232.0381	91 Protactinium **Pa** 231.0359	92 Uranium **U** 238.029	93 Neptunium **Np** 237.0482	94 Plutonium **Pu** 244.0642

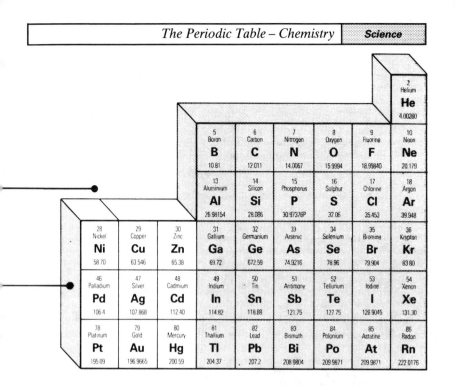

| 28 Nickel **Ni** 58.70 | 29 Copper **Cu** 63.546 | 30 Zinc **Zn** 65.38 | 31 Gallium **Ga** 69.72 | 32 Germanium **Ge** 672.59 | 33 Arsenic **As** 74.9216 | 34 Selenium **Se** 78.96 | 35 Bromine **Br** 79.904 | 36 Krypton **Kr** 83.80 |

Additional element groups shown:

| 2 Helium **He** 4.00260 |

| 5 Boron **B** 10.81 | 6 Carbon **C** 12.011 | 7 Nitrogen **N** 14.0067 | 8 Oxygen **O** 15.9994 | 9 Fluorine **F** 18.99840 | 10 Neon **Ne** 20.179 |

| 13 Aluminium **Al** 26.98154 | 14 Silicon **Si** 28.086 | 15 Phosphorus **P** 30.97376P | 16 Sulphur **S** 32.06 | 17 Chlorine **Cl** 35.453 | 18 Argon **Ar** 39.948 |

| 46 Palladium **Pd** 106.4 | 47 Silver **Ag** 107.868 | 48 Cadmium **Cd** 112.40 | 49 Indium **In** 114.82 | 50 Tin **Sn** 118.69 | 51 Antimony **Sb** 121.75 | 52 Tellurium **Te** 127.75 | 53 Iodine **I** 126.9045 | 54 Xenon **Xe** 131.30 |

| 78 Platinum **Pt** 195.09 | 79 Gold **Au** 196.9665 | 80 Mercury **Hg** 200.59 | 81 Thallium **Tl** 204.37 | 82 Lead **Pb** 207.2 | 83 Bismuth **Bi** 208.9804 | 84 Polonium **Po** 209.9871 | 85 Astatine **At** 209.9871 | 86 Radon **Rn** 222.0176 |

| 63 Europium **Eu** 151.96 | 64 Gadolinium **Gd** 157.25 | 65 Terbium **Tb** 158.9254 | 66 Dysprosium **Dy** 162.50 | 67 Holmium **Ho** 164.9304 | 68 Erbium **Er** 167.26 | 69 Thulium **Tm** 168.9342 | 70 Ytterbium **Yb** 173.04 | 71 Lutetium **Lu** 174.97 |

| 95 Americium **Am** 243.0614 | 96 Curium **Cm** 247.0703 | 97 Berkelium **Bk** 247.0703 | 98 Californium **Cf** 251.0786 | 99 Einsteinium **Es** 252.0828 | 100 Fermium **Fm** 257.0951 | 101 Mendelvium **Md** 258.0986 | 102 Nobelium **No** 259.1009 | 103 Lawrencium **Lr** 260.1054 |

COMPOSITION OF THE ATMOSPHERE

Air is primarily a mixture of nitrogen, oxygen, and carbon dioxide, but with minute traces of other gases

Gas	Symbol	% Volume	Role
Nitrogen	N	78.08	Cycled through human activities and through the action of micro-organisms on animal and plant waste
Oxygen	O_2	20.94	Cycled mainly through the respiration of animals and plants and through the action of photosynthesis
Carbon dioxide	CO_2	0.03	Cycled through respiration and photosynthesis in exchange reactions with oxygen. It is also a product of burning fossil fuels
Argon	Ar	0.093	
Neon	Ne	0.0018	
Helium	He	0.0005	Chemically inert and with only a few industrial uses
Krypton	Kr	Trace	
Xenon	Xe	Trace	
Ozone	O_3	0.00006	A product of oxygen molecules split into single atoms by the sun's radiation and unaltered oxygen molecules
Hydrogen	H_2	0.00005	Unimportant

Organic Chemistry

Organic chemistry is the chemistry of carbon compounds, particularly the more complex carbon compounds. Many of these are made only by living organisms (for example proteins, carbohydrates), and it was once believed organic compounds could not be made by any other means. This was disproved when Wöhler synthesized urea, but the name 'organic' (that is 'living') chemistry has remained in use. Many organic compounds are derived from oil, which represents the chemical remains of millions of microscopic marine organisms. The basis of organic chemistry is the ability of carbon to form long chains of atoms, branching chains, rings, and other complex structures. In a typical organic compound, each carbon atom forms a bond with each of its neighbouring carbon atoms in the chain or ring, and two more with hydrogen atoms (carbon has a valency of four). Other atoms that may be involved in organic molecules include oxygen and nitrogen. Compounds containing carbon and hydrogen are known as hydrocarbons; those containing carbon, hydrogen and oxygen are cbarbohydrates. Organic chemistry is largely the chemistry of a great variety of homologous series, in which the molecular formulae, when arranged in ascending order, form an arithmetical progression, for example the *alkanes*, methane CH_4, ethane C_2H_6, propane C_3H_8, butane C_4H_{10}, and so on. The physical properties undergo a gradual change from one member to the next.

Life is carbon-based because of the capacity of carbon atoms to form an almost infinite variety of molecules. Compounds made up of carbon chains are known as **aliphatic**, while those based on rings are **cyclic**.

In inorganic chemistry a specific formula usually represents one substance only, but in organic chemistry it is exceptional for a molecular formula to represent only one substance. Substances having the same molecular formula are called *isomers*, and the relationship is known as *isomerism*. Where substances

COMMON ORGANIC MOLECULE GROUPINGS

Formula	Name	Atomic bonding
CH_3	Methyl	H—C— with H above and H below
CH_2CH_3	Ethyl	—C—C—H structure
CC	Double bond	C=C
CHO	Aldehyde	—C double bond O
CH_2OH	Alcohol	—C—OH
CO	Ketone	C=O
COOH	Acid	—C with O and OH
CH_2NH_2	Amine	—C—N structure
C_6H_6	Benzene ring	benzene ring structure

have the same molecular formula, but differ in their structural formulae, they are called *strucural isomers*, for example chloropropane C_3H_7Cl can have the Cl atom attached to any of the C atoms, giving 1–, 2– or 3– chloropropane. *Spatial isomers*, or *stereo-isomers*, have the same molecular formula, and also the same structural formula, the difference lying in their spatial dispositions. The study of spatial isomers is known as *stereochemistry*.

Hydrocarbons form one of the most prolific of the many organic types; fuel oils are largely made up of hydrocarbons. The most fundamental of organic chemical reactions are oxidation, reduction, hydrolysis, condensation, polymerization, and molecular rearrangement. In living organisms, such changes are often brought about with the help of catalysts called enzymes. This branch of chemistry is generally referred to as *biochemistry*.

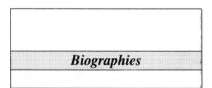

Biographies

Arrhenius Svante August 1859–1927. Swedish scientist, the founder of physical chemistry. Born near Uppsala, he became a professor at Stockholm in 1895, and made a special study of electrolysis. He received the Nobel Prize for Chemistry.

Baekeland Leo Hendrik 1863–1944. American chemist. Born in Ghent, he went to the USA in 1889, and undertook research on photographic materials, inventing Velox paper. His subsequent researches covered the fields of plastics, electro-chemistry, organic chemistry, and electrical insulation. He invented an early type of plastic known as Bakelite.

Bergius Friedrich Karl Rudolph 1884–1949. German research chemist, who received the Nobel Prize for Chemistry in 1931. He invented processes for converting coal into oil, and wood into sugar.

Berzelius Jöns Jakob 1779–1848. Swedish chemist who specialized in the determination of atomic and molecular weights. He invented the system of chemical symbols now in use, discovered several elements and did valuable work on catalysts.

Crookes Sir William 1832–1919. British scientist whose many chemical and physical discoveries included the metal thallium 1861, the radiometer 1875, and Crooke's high vacuum tube used in X-ray techniques.

Curie Marie (born Marya Sklodovska) 1867–1934. Polish chemist, wife of physicist *Pierre Curie* (1859–1906) from 1895. They were awarded the Nobel Prize for Physics (with French physicist Antoine Henri Becquerel) in 1903 for their work on radioactivity, and in 1911 Marie received the Nobel Prize for Chemistry for her discovery of polonium and radium. She died a victim of the radiation emitted by the chemicals with which she worked. Her daughter and son-in-law, *Irène Joliot-Curie* (1896–1956), and *Frédéric Joliot* (1900–59), received a Nobel Prize for Chemistry in 1935 for their creation of artificial radioactivity.

Dalton John 1776–1844. British chemist remembered for his tentative formulation of the atomic theory of chemical composition in *Absorption of Gases* 1805, elaborated in his *New System of Chemical Philosophy* 1808.

Davy Sir Humphry 1778–1829. British chemist. While a laboratory superintendent at Bristol, he discovered the respiratory effects of 'laughing gas' (nitrous oxide) in 1799, and in 1802 became professor at the Royal Institution, London. There he discovered, by electrolysis, the metals sodium, potassium, calcium, magnesium, strontium, and barium. He invented the 'safety lamp' for use in mines where methane was present, in effect enabling the miners to work in previously unsafe conditions.

Faraday Michael 1791–1867. British chemist. He became a laboratory assistant to Sir Humphry Davy at the Royal Institution in 1813, and in 1827 succeeded him as professor of chemistry there. In 1812 he began researches into electricity, and made his first electric

battery. In 1821 he began experimenting on electromagnetism, and ten years later discovered the induction of electric currents and made the first dynamo. Many more discoveries in electricity followed. In 1845 he began a second great period of research in which he discovered what he announced as the magnetization of light.

Fischer Hans 1881–1945. German chemist, who received the Nobel Prize for Chemistry in 1930 for his discovery of haemoglobin in blood.

Gay-Lussac Joseph Louis 1778–1850. French physicist and chemist. Born near Limoges, he became professor of physics at Paris in 1808. In 1804 he made balloon ascents to study the weather. He investigated the physical properties of gases and discovered new methods of producing sulphuric and oxalic acids.

Haber Fritz 1868–1934. German chemist, whose conversion of atmospheric nitrogen to ammonia opened the way for the synthetic fertilizer industry. His study of the combustion of hydrocarbons led to the commercial 'cracking' or fractionating of natural oil into its components, for example diesel, petrol, and paraffin. In electrochemistry he was the first to demonstrate that oxidation and reduction take place at the electrodes; from this he developed a general electrochemical theory. In World War I he worked on poison gas and devised gas masks; he was was awarded a Nobel prize in 1918.

Henry William 1774–1836. British chemist. In 1803 he formulated *Henry's law*: when a gas is dissolved in a liquid at a given temperature, the amount (that is the mass) which dissolves is in direct proportion to the gas pressure.

Kekulé Friedrich August 1829–96. German chemist, whose theory (1858) of molecular structure revolutionized organic chemistry. He is most famous for proposing two resonant (coexisting alternative) forms of the benzene ring.

Lavoisier Antoine Laurent 1743–94. French chemist, sometimes called the founder of modern chemistry. He proved that combustion needed only a part of 'air' which he called oxygen. He thereby destroyed the theory of phlogiston (an imaginary 'fire element' released during combustion). With Laplace he showed that water was a compound of oxygen and hydrogen. In this way he established the modern basic rules of chemical combination.

Liebig Justus, Baron von Liebig 1803–73. German chemist, and a major contributor to agricultural chemistry. He introduced the theory of radicals, and discovered chloroform.

Mendeleyev Dmitri Ivanovich 1834–1907. Russian chemist, framer of the Periodic Law which states that the chemical properties of the elements are periodic functions of their atomic weights.

Müller Paul 1899–1965. Swiss chemist, awarded a Nobel prize in 1948 for his discovery of the first synthetic contact insecticide, DDT, in 1939.

Nobel Alfred Bernhard 1833–96. Swedish chemist, inventor of dynamite in 1867. He bequeathed the fortune gained from explosives to found the Nobel prizes.

Pauling Linus Carl 1901– . American chemist, noted for his fundamental work on the nature of the chemical bond, and on the discovery of the helical structure of many proteins. He was awarded the Nobel Prize for Chemistry in 1954. An outspoken opponent of nuclear testing, he received the Nobel Peace Prize in 1962.

Priestley Joseph 1733–1804. British chemist. He discovered oxygen in about 1774 (two yearsw after German chemist Karl Scheele).

Ramsay Sir William 1852–1916. British chemist who, together with physicist Lord Rayleigh, discovered argon in 1894. In 1895 Ramsay manufactured helium, and in 1898 identified neon, krypton, and xenon. With Frederick Soddy he noted the transmutation of radium into helium in 1903, which led to the discovery of the density and atomic weight of radium. He received a Nobel prize in 1904.

Rutherford Ernest 1871–1937. New Zealand physicist. A pioneer of modern atomic science, his main researches were in the field of radioactivity, and he was the first to recognize the nuclear nature of the atom. He was awarded a Nobel prize in 1908.

Soddy Frederick 1877–1956. British physical chemist. After working for Rutherford and Ramsay, he was professor of chemistry at Aberdeen 1914–19 and at Oxford 1919–36. A pioneer of research into atomic disintegration – he coined the term 'isotopes' – he wrote a classic work on radioactivity (*Chemistry of the Radio-Elements* 1912–14), and was awarded a Nobel prize in 1921.

Sutherland Earl Wilbur 1915–74. American physiologist, discoverer of a chemical 'messenger' made by a special enzyme in the wall of cells. Many hormones operate by means of this messenger. He was awarded a Nobel prize in 1971.

Taube Henry 1915– . American chemist, who established the basis of modern inorganic chemistry by his study of the loss or gain of electrons by atoms during chemical reactions. He was awarded a Nobel prize in 1983.

Urey Harold Clayton 1893–1981. American chemist. In 1932 he isolated heavy water and discovered deuterium, receiving a Nobel prize in 1934. He was director of the War Research Atomic Bomb Project, Columbia, 1940–45..

Van 't Hoff Jacobus Henricus 1852–1911. Dutch physical chemist. He explained the 'asymmetric' carbon atom occurring in optically active compounds. His greatest work – the concept of chemical affinity as the maximum work obtainable from a reaction – was shown with measurements of osmotic and gas pressures, and reversible electric batteries. He was the first Nobel prize recipient in 1901.

Werner Alfred 1866–1919. Swiss chemist. He was awarded a Nobel prize in 1913 for his work on valency theory, which explains the chemical properties of an element in terms of the number of electrons orbiting the nucleus of its constituent atoms.

Wöhler Friedrich 1800–82. German chemist who synthesized the first organic compound (urea) from an inorganic compound (ammonium cyanate): it had previously been thought impossible to convert. He also isolated the elements aluminium, beryllium, yttrium, and titanium.

1 AD	Gold, silver, copper, lead, iron, tin, and mercury were known.
200	Solution, filtration, and distillation were known.
1100	Alcohol was first distilled.
1242	Gunpowder introduced to Europe from the Far East.
1540	First known scientific observation and experiment carried out. Sulphuric acid was described.
1604	Italian mathematician, astronomer and physicist Galileo invented the thermometer.
1620	Scientific method of reasoning expounded by English philosopher Francis Bacon in his *Novum Organum*.
1649	Carbon, sulphur, antimony, and arsenic were known.
1650	Leyden University in the Netherlands set up the first chemistry laboratory.
1660	Law concerning effect of pressure on gas was established by English chemist Robert Boyle (*Boyle's law*); definition of the element.
1662	The Royal Society was formed.
1695	Nehemiah Grew discovered magnesium.
1702	Dutch chemist Wilhelm Homberg discovered boron.
1742	Centigrade scale invented.
1746	Lead chamber process developed for manufacturing sulphuric acid; German chemist Andreas Marggraf discovered zinc.
1749	Phosphorus was known.
1750	Swedish chemist Axel Cronstedt discovered cobalt and nickel.
1756	Scottish chemist and physicist Joseph Black discovered carbon dioxide.
1769	German chemist Karl Scheele discovered oxygen.
1774	Scheele discovered chlorine; Gahn discovered manganese; Lavoisier demonstrated his *law of conservation of mass*.
1777	Lavoisier explained burning; sulphur was known to be an element.
1779	Dutch scientist Jan Ingenhousz demonstrated photosynthesis.
1781	English scientist Henry Cavendish showed water to be a compound.
1789	German chemist Martin Klaproth discovered zirconium.
1792	Italian physicist Alessandro Volta demonstrated the electrochemical series.
1791	Gregor discovered titanium.
1793	German chemist Hieronymous Richter demonstrated the *law of equivalent proportions*.
1797	French chemist Louis Vacquelin discovered chromium.
1799	Twenty-seven elements were known.
1800	Volta designed his electric battery.
1801	English chemist John Dalton demonstrated his *law of partial pressures*.
1803	English chemist John Dalton expounded his atomic theory.
1807	Sodium and potassium were first prepared by Davy.
1808	Gay-Lussac announced his *law of volumes*.
1811	Publication of Italian physicist Amedeo Avogadro's hypothesis on the relationship of volumes of gases and numbers of molecules to temperature and pressure.
1813	French chemist Bonard Courtois discovered iodine.
1815	Davy invented the safety lamp.
1817	Berzelius discovered selenium.
1818	Berzelius' atomic symbols were elaborated.
1819	French physicists Pierre-Louis Dulong and Alexis-Thérèse Petit's *law of atomic heats* was demonstrated.

1825	Danish physicist Hans Christian Oersted prepared aluminium.
1826	French chemist Antoine-Jerôme Balard prepared bromine. Matches were invented.
1828	The first organic compounds, alcohol and urea, were synthesized.
1834	Faraday expounded the *laws of electrolysis*.
1836	Acetylene was discovered.
1840	Liebig expounded the carbon and nitrogen cycles.
1846	Scottish chemist Thomas Graham's *law of diffusion* was expounded.
1849	Fifty-seven elements were known.
1850	Ammonia was first made from coal-gas.
1853	German chemist Robert Bunsen invented his burner.
1858	Italian chemist Stanislao Cannizzaro's method of atomic weights was expounded.
1859	Bunsen's flame tests.
1861	Lamy discovered tellurium.
1862	Haemoglobin was crystallized.
1866	Nobel invented dynamite.
1868	The first plastic substance - celluloid - was made.
1869	Mendeleyev expounded his Periodic Table.
1879	Saccharin was discovered.
1886	French chemist Ferdinand Moissan isolated fluorine.
1894	Ramsay and Rayleigh discovered inert gases.
1896	Radioactivity was discovered.
1897	The electron was discovered by English physicist Sir Joseph Thomson.
1898	The Curies discovered radium.
1899-1902	Debierne and Giesel discovered actinium.
1905	Einstein's *theory of relativity* was announced.
1912	Vitamins were discovered by British biochemist Gowland Hopkins; British physicist Lawrence Bragg demonstrated that crystals have a regular arrangement of atoms.
1919	Artificial disintegration of atoms by Rutherford.
1920	Rutherford found the proton.
1927	English chemist Neil Sidgwick's *theory of valency* was announced.
1928	Vitamin C was crystallized.
1929	Penicillin was discovered.
1932	Deuterium (heavy water) was discovered. English physicist James Chadwick found the neutron.
1933	English chemist Walter Haworth synthesized Vitamin C.
1939	German-American physicist Hans Bethe explained the source of solar energy.
1942	Plutonium was first synthesized.
1945	The atomic bomb was exploded.
1953	Hydrogen was converted to helium.
1954	Einsteinium and fermium were synthesized.
1982	Element 109, unnilennium, synthesized.

Mathematics

Mathematics is the science of spatial and numerical relations. The subject is divided into pure mathematics, which includes, as its main divisions, geometry, arithmetic, and algebra, the calculus, and trigonometry; and applied mathematics, which deals with mechanics, the mathematical theories of astronomy, electricity, optics, and thermodynamics. In recent years mathematics has been aided by the computer, a powerful new tool which can create and manipulate mathematical 'models', and everyday arithmetic has been made simpler by the general availability of the electronic pocket calculator.

This section explains, in *Mathematical Terms*, the fundamental concepts, theories, and principles of the subject; in *Geometry and Trigonometry*, the mathematics of the measurement, properties, and relationships of points, lines, angles, surfaces, and angles; and in *Biographies*, the work of important mathematicians. *Mathematical Symbols and Formulae* are presented as a chart at the end of the section.

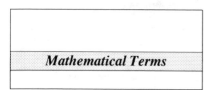

Mathematical Terms

abacus method of calculating with a handful of counters on a flat surface, used by the Greeks and Romans, and possibly by the builders of Stonehenge. Later types of abacus include those with beads on wires, still used in China. The method has principles in common with the electronic calculator.

algebra method of solving mathematical problems by the use of symbols (letters and signs) when figures are inadequate (the numbers involved may be very large or not known exactly). More advanced algebra is used to work out general problems, for example the equations derived by American physicist Albert Einstein (1879–1955) from his general theory of relativity, and the method of algebraic reasoning first devised by British mathematician George Boole (1815–64) and used in working out the construction of computers.

Arabic numerals the signs 0 1 2 3 4 5 6 7 8 9, which were in use among the Arabs before being adapted by the peoples of Europe during the Middle Ages in place of Roman numerals. They appear to have originated in India, and reached Europe by way of Spain.

arithmetic branch of mathematics that concerns all questions involving numbers, as in counting, measuring, or weighing. Simple arithmetic already existed in prehistoric times. The basic operation of arithmetic is counting. Most arithmetical questions could be answered by counting alone, though with great labour and expenditure of time. Formal calculations allow the same result to be achieved more quickly. The fundamental operations are addition and subtraction, and multiplication and division. Fractions arise naturally in the process of measurement. Decimals are a form of fractions. Powers, that is repeated multiplica-

tion of the same number, are represented by an index, for example 2^5 = '2 to the 5th' = $2 \times 2 \times 2 \times 2 \times 2$. Roots are the reverse of powers. For example, 2 is the 5th root of 32, because $2 \times 2 \times 2 \times 2 \times 2 = 32$. Logarithms form a convenient means of carrying out complicated fundamental arithmetic operations. The essential feature of modern arithmetic is the *place-value* system. The decimal numeral system employs ten numerals (0 1 2 3 4 5 6 7 8 9). In a decimal number, each position has a value ten times that of the position to its immediate right, for example in the number 23 the numeral 3 represents the number 3, but moved one place to the left it would equal three tens. Modern computers operate in base-two, using only two numerals (0 1), known as a binary system. In binary, each position has a value twice as great as the position to its immediate right, so that for example binary 111 is equal to 7 in the decimal system, and 1111 is equal to 15. *modular arithmetic* deals with events recurring in regular cycles, and is used in describing the functioning of petrol engines, electrical generators, and so on. For example in the modulo-twelve system, the answer to a question as to what time it will be in five hours if it is now ten o'clock, can be expressed $10 + 5 = 3$ (that is, $15 - 12$).

base in mathematics, the number of different symbols in a particular number system. Thus our usual (decimal) counting system of numbers has the base 10. In the binary number system, which has only the numbers 1 and 0, the base is 2. A base is also a number which, when raised to a particular power (that is, when multiplied by itself a particular number of times as in $10^2 = 10 \times 10 = 100$), has a logarithm equal to the power i.e., logarithm of 100 to the base 10 is 2.

binomial in algebra, an expression consisting of two terms, such as $a + b$, $a - b$. The *binomial theorem*, discovered by English mathematician and physicist Sir Isaac Newton (1642–1727) and first published in 1676, is a formula whereby any power of a binomial quantity may be found without performing the progressive multiplications.

calculus branch of mathematics that permits the manipulation of continuously varying quantities, applicable to practical problems involving such matters as changing speeds, problems of flight, varying stresses in the framework of a bridge, electrical circuits with varying currents and voltages, and so on. The term is the Latin word for pebble, used in calculations on the abacus. *Integral calculus* deals with the method of summation or adding together the effects of continuously varying quantities. *Differential calculus* deals in a similar way with rates of change. Many of its applications arose from the study of speed. Each of these branches of calculus deals with small quantities which during manipulation are made smaller and smaller, hence both comprise the *infinitesimal calculus*. Differential equations represent complex rates of change and integrals are their empirical solutions. If no known mathematical processes are available, integration can be performed graphically or by a machine, increasingly by computers.

coefficient the number part in front of an algebraic term, signifying multiplication. For example, in the expression $4x^2 + 2xy - x$, the coefficient of x^2 is 4 (because $4x^2$ means $4 \times x^2$), that of xy is 2 and that of x is -1 (because $-1 \times x = -x$). In some algebraic expressions, coefficients are represented by letters called constants, that stand for numbers, for example, in the equation $ax^2 + bx + c = 0$, a, b and c are constants.

complement in set theory within mathematics, the set consisting of the elements within the universal set that are not contained in the designated set. For example, if the universal set is the set of all positive whole numbers and the designated set S is the set of all even numbers, then the complement of S (denoted S') is the set of all odd numbers. In geometry, the complement of an angle is the number of degrees needed to make it a right angle (90°). For example, the complement of 60° is 30° or 60° and 30° are complementary angles. In number theory, the complement of a number is obtained by subtracting it from its base. For example, the complement of 7 in numbers to

base ten (the everyday way of counting) is 3.

constant in mathematics, a fixed quantity or one that does not change its value in relation to variables. For example, in the algebraic expression $y^2 = 5x - 3$, the numbers 5 and 3 are constants; so too are a and b in the general equation $ax + b = 0$. In physics, certain quantities are regarded as universal constants that never vary, for example, the speed of light in vacuum, represented by the letter c.

cybernetics science concerned with how systems organize, regulate and reproduce themselves, and also how they evolve and learn. It was founded and named by Norbert Wiener (1894–1964), an American mathematician. The name is derived from the Greek 'steersman'. In the laboratory inanimate objects are created that behave like living systems. Uses range from the creation of electronic artificial limbs to the running of the fully automated factory where decision-making machines operate at up to managerial level.

decimal number a number expressed to the base ten, the number system in ordinary use. Counting is in units (10^0), tens (10^1), hundreds (10^2), thousands (10^3), and so on. Decimal fractions have powers of ten as their denominators, for example, $3/10$, $4/100$, $5/1000$, and so on but are represented by a decimal point followed by the numerator of the fraction preceded if necessary by zeros. For example, the above fractions as decimals are 0.3, 0.04, and 0.005. The use of decimals greatly simplifies addition and multiplication of fractions, though not all fractions can be expressed exactly as a decimal fractions.

differentiation in mathematics, a procedure for finding the rate of change of one variable quantity relative to another. Together, differentation and integration of functions make up calculus.

exponential in mathematics, a function in which the variable quantity is an exponent, that is, an index or power to which another number or expression is raised. For example, $f(x) = ax$ is an exponential function in which a is typically a number, say 5, and x is the exponent (.1, 0.5, -10, and so on). Such functions are always positive and their values get closer and closer to 0 with increasingly negative values of x. The term 'exponential function' usually refers to $f(x) = ex$, the basis of natural or Naperian logarithms and definitive of many natural phenomena of growth and decay (such as the radioactive decay of various isotopes). In this expression e is an irrational number equal to 2.7283... *Exponential growth* is a form of increase in numbers in which the rate of growth is slow at first but then rises sharply. It applies, for example, to uncontrolled population growth. A graph of population number against time produces a curve that is characteristically rather flat at first but then shoots almost directly upwards.

factorial of a number is the product of all the whole numbers (integers) inclusive between 1 and the number itself. A factorial is indicated by the symbol !. For example, $6! = 1 \times 2 \times 3 \times 4 \times 5 \times 6 = 720$. Zero factorial, $0!$, is defined as 1.

fraction in mathematics, a number that indicates one or more equal parts of a whole (from Latin *fractio* meaning to break), probably arising from the need to break one object into several pieces to share it fairly among several people. The usual way of denoting this is to place below a horizontal line the number of equal parts into which the unit is divided (denominator), and above the line the number of these parts comprising the fraction (numerator); thus $2/3$ or $3/4$. Such fractions are called *vulgar* or *simple fractions*. A *proper fraction* is one in which the numerator is less than the denominator. A combination such as $5/0$ is not regarded as a fraction however (an object cannot be divided into zero equal parts), and mathematically any number divided by 0 is equal to infinity. An *improper fraction* is one in which the numerator is larger than the denominator, for example, $3/2$. An improper fraction can therefore be expressed as a mixed number, for example, $1\frac{1}{2}$. A *decimal fraction* is one in which the fraction is expressed by figures written to the right of the units figure (which may be 0) after a dot or point (the decimal point), for example 0.04, which is $4/100$.

function in mathematics, a procedure that defines a relationship between quantities, usually variables. For example, in the algebraic expression $y = 4x^3 + 2$, the variable y is a function of the variable x, generally written as $f(x)$. Commonly used in applied mathematics, physics and science generally: for example, the formula $t + 2\pi(l/g)^{1/2}$ shows that for a simple pendulum the time of swing t is a function of its length l and of no other variable quantity (π and g, the acceleration due to gravity, are constants).

geometry branch of mathematics concerned with the properties of space, usually in terms of plane (two-dimensional) and solid (three-dimensional) figures. It probably originated in Egypt, in land measurements necessitated by the periodic inundations of the River Nile, and was soon extended into surveying and navigation. Early geometers were Thales, Pythagoras and Euclid. Analytical methods were introduced and developed by Descartes in the 17th century.

index in mathematics, a number that indicates a function, as in the terms x^2, y^5, and 4^7; the indices are 2, 5, and 7, and indicate respectively $x \times x$; $y \times y \times y \times y \times y$, $4 \times 4 \times 4 \times 4 \times 4 \times 4 \times 4$. Such terms are multiplied by adding the indices, for example, $x^2 \times x^5 = x^7$; and divided by subtracting the indices, for example, $y^5 \div y^3 = y^2$. Any number with the index 0 is equal to 1 for example, $x^0 = 1$ and $99^0 = 1$. Also known as power or exponent. From the latin 'sign, indicator'; plural indices.

integer a positive or negative number. Fractions, such as $1/2$ and 0.35, are known as nonintegral numbers.

interest in finance, a sum of money paid to an investor in return for the loan, usually expressed as percentage per annum. *Simple interest* is interest calculated as a straight percentage of the amount invested. Thus, a sum of £100 invested at 10 per cent simple interest for five years earns £10 a year, giving a total of £50 interest (and at the end of the period the investor receives a total of £150). In *compound interest*, the interest earned over a period of time (for example, per annum) is added to the investment, so that at the end of the next period interest is paid on that total. It is thus a way of paying interest on the accumulated interest. The same sum of £100 invested for five years at 10 per cent compound interest earns a total of £61.05 interest (with £161.05 returned at the end of the period). Generally, for a sum S invested at x per cent simple interest for y years, the total amount returned is $S + xyS/100$. If it is invested at x per cent compound interest for y years, the total amount returned is $S[(100 + x)/100]y$.

logarithm mathematical function that makes the multiplication and division of large numbers simpler by substituting respectively the operations of addition and subtraction. The principle of logarithms is also the basis of the slide rule. With the general availability of the electronic pocket calculator, the need for logarithms has reduced. More formally, a logarithm (or log) is the exponent or index of a number to a specified base. For example, the log of 10 to the base 10 is 1; the log of 100 to the base 10 is 2, because $10^2 = 10 \times 10 = 100$. To multiply 100 by 100 (that is, $10^2 \times 10^2$), the indices are added, giving 10^4. Thus 10^4 or $\log 10^4 = 10,000$. For more difficult calculations, tables of logarithms and antilogarithms are available (usually to the base 10) which show conversions of numbers into logarithms, and vice versa. For example, to multiply $6,560 \times 980$, one looks up the logarithms of the numbers – 3.8169 and 2.9912 – adds them together (6.8081), then looks up the antilog of this to get the answer (6,428,000).

mathematics the science of spatial and numerical relationships. Many activities in business and commerce make extensive use of mathematics, including accountancy, banking and insurance. Higher mathematics has a powerful new tool in the high-speed electronic computer, which can create and manipulate mathematical 'models' of various systems in science, technology and commerce. Modern methods of teaching arithmetic are sometimes referred to as 'new maths'.

maximum and minimum in mathematics, of a curve representing a function in co-ordinate geometry, where slope changes from positive to negative after reaching a turning point (maximum), or from negative to positive after reaching a turning point (minimum). A tangent to the curve at a maximum or minimum has zero gradient. Maxima and minima can be found by differentiating the function for the curve and setting the differential to zero (the value of the slope at the turning point). For example, differentiating the function for the parabola $y = 2x^2 - 8x$ gives $dy/dx = 4x - 8$. Setting this equal to zero gives $x = 2$, so that $y = -8$ (found by substituting $x = 2$ into the parabola equation). Thus the function has a minimum at the point $(2, -8)$.

mean in mathematics, a specific related term intermediate between the first and last terms of a progression. The simple *arithmetic mean* is the average value of the quantities, that is, the sum of the quantities divided by their number. The *weighted mean* takes into account the frequency of the terms that are summed; it is calculated by multiplying each term by the number of times it occurs, summing the results and dividing this total by the total number of occurences. The *geometric mean* is the corresponding root of the product of the quantities.

number a symbol used in counting or measuring. In mathematics, there are various kinds of numbers. The ordinary numerals, 0, 1, 2, 3, 4, 5, 6, 7, 8, 9, give a counting system which, to the base ten, continues 10, 11, 12, 13, and so on. These are whole decimal numbers (also called cardinals or integers), with fractions represented as $1/4$, $1/2$, $3/4$ and so on, or as decimal fractions (0.25, 0.5, 0.75 and so on). They are also rational numbers. Numbers that cannot be represented as fractions and require symbols, such as $\sqrt{2}$, π and e are irrational: they can be expressed numerically only as the (inexact) approximations 1.414, 3.142 and 2.728 (to three places of decimals) respectively. Number systems can also be devised with bases other than 10. For example, numbers to base two (binary numbers) using only the 0 and 1, produce a series which starts 0, 1, 10, 11, 100, 101, 110, 111. They are commonly used in digital computers to represent the two-state 'in' or 'off' pulses of electricity.

percentage a way of representing a number as a fraction of 100. Thus 45 per cent (or 45%) equals $^{45}/_{100}$, and 45% of 20 is $20 \times {}^{45}/_{100} = 9$. In general, if a quantity x changes to y, the percentage change is $100(x - y)/x$. Thus, if the number of people in a room changes from 40 to 50, the percentage increase is $(100 \times 10)/40 = 25\%$. To express a fraction as a percentage, its denominator must first be converted to 100, for example, $^1/_8 = 12.5/100 = 12.5\%$. The use of percentages often makes it easier to compare fractions that do not have a common denominator.

permutation in mathematics, specified arrangement of a group of objects. In general, the number of permutations of a items taken b at a time is given by $a!/(a - b)!$, where the symbol ! stands for factorial (the product of all the integers (whole numbers) up to and including the number). For example, the number of permutations of four letters taken from any group of six different letters is $6!/2! = (1 \times 2 \times 3 \times 4 \times 5 \times 6)/(1 \times 2) = 360$. The theoretical number of four-letter 'words' that can be made from an alphabet of 26 letters is $26!/22! = 358,800$.

power in mathematics, also called an index or exponent, is written as a superior small numeral. A number or symbol raised to the power 2 is said to be squared (for example, 3^2, x^2) and something raised to the power three is said to be cubed (for example, 2^3, y^3).

probability the likelihood or chance that something will happen, often expressed as 'odds' or, in mathematics, numerically as a fraction. In tossing an unbiased coin the chance that it will land heads is the same as the chance that it will land tails, that is, 1 to 1 or 'evens'; mathematically this probability is expressed as $^1/_2$ or 0.5. The odds against any chosen number coming up on the roll of an unbiased dice are 6 to 1; the probability is $^1/_6$ or 0.1666... If two dice are rolled there are $6 \times 6 = 36$ different possible combinations. The chance that a double (two numbers the same) will come up is only one of these combinations; thus the

456

probability is $^1/_{36}$ or 0.02777... In general, the probability that n particular events will happen out of a total of m possible events is n/m. A certainty has a probability of 1; an impossibility has a probability of 0.

progression sequence of numbers each formed by a specific relationship to its predecessor: an arithmetical progression has numbers which increase or decrease by a common sum or difference (for example 2, 4, 6, 8); a geometric progression has numbers each bearing a fixed ratio to its predecessor (for example 3, 6, 12, 24), and harmonic progression is a sequence with numbers whose reciprocals are in arithmetical progression, for example 1, $^1/_2$, $^1/_3$, $^1/_4$.

quadratic equation in mathematics a polynomial equation of second degree (that is, an equation containing as its highest power the square of a single unknown variable, such as x^2). The general formula of such equations is $ax^2 + bx + c = 0$, in which a, b, and c are constants and only the coefficient a cannot equal 0. A quadratic equation may have as its solution values of x, two identical values of x, or no real values of x, (that is, the solutions are complex numbers), depending on the value of $b^2 - 4ac$.

reciprocal in mathematics, of a quantity, that quantity divided into 1. Thus the reciprocal of 2 is $^1/_2$ (= 0.5); of 150 is $^1/_{150}$ (= 0.00666666...); of x^2 is $1/x^2$ or x^{-2}.

Roman numerals an old number system using different symbols from today's Arabic numerals (the ordinary numbers 1, 2, 3, 4, 5, and so on). The seven key symbols in Roman numerals as represented today (originally they were a little different) are I (= 1), V (= 5), X (= 10), L (= 50), C (= 100), D (= 500) and M (= 1,000). There is no zero.

scalar quantity in mathematics, any quantity that has magnitude but no direction.

set in mathematics, any collection of defined things, usually denoted by a capital letter and indicated by curly brackets (braces). For example $L = \{\text{LETTERS OF THE ALPHABET}\}$ represents the set that consists of all the letters of the alphabet. The symbol stands for 'is a member of'; thus pL means that p belongs to the set consisting of all letters, and 4/L means that 4 does not belong to the set consisting of all letters.

simultaneous equations in mathematics, two or more algebraic equations that contain two or more unknown quantities and are simultaneously true. In the simplest case, that of two linear equations with two unknown variables, for example (i) $x + 3y = 6$ and (ii) $3y - 2x = 4$, the solution will be those unique values of x and y that are valid for both equations. One method of solution is first to eliminate one of the variables, whether by substitution, for example, in this case substituting for x in equation (ii) the value $6 - 3y$ obtained by rearranging equation (i); or by multiplying equation (i) by 2 (to give $2x + 6y = 12$) and adding this new equation to equation (ii) to give $9y = 16$, which is easily solved.

slide rule a mathematical instrument having pairs of sliding scales, used for rapid calculations, including multiplication, division, and the extraction of square roots, based on logarithms. Formerly popular with draughtsmen and engineers, it has been largely superseded by the electronic calculator.

square root in mathematics, of a number, another number which when squared (multiplied by itself) equals the given number. For example, the square root of 25 (written $\sqrt{25}$) is 5, because 5 x 5 = 25; the square root of 152.2756 is 12.34. As an index, a square root is represented by $^1/_2$; for example, $16^{1/2} = 4$. Strictly speaking, 16 (and all other numbers greater than zero) has two square roots: +4 and −4, because $(-4)^2$ also equals 16. Thus the square root of 16 is written +4. Negative numbers (less than 0) do not have square roots that are real numbers. Their roots are represented by complex numbers, in which the square root of −1 is given the symbol i (that is, $i^2 = -1$). Thus the square root of −4 is + 2i.

statistics the branch of mathematics concerned with the collection and interpretation of data. For meaningful interpretations, there should be a large amount of data to analyse. For example, faced with the task of determin-

ing the mean (average) age of the children in a school, an exact mean could be obtained by averaging the ages of every pupil in the school. A statistically acceptable answer might be obtained by calculating the average based on the ages of a representative sample, consisting say of a random tenth of the pupils from each class. Probability is the branch of statistics dealing with predictions of events. The science has many applications in government, business, industry, and commerce.

topology the branch of geometry which deals with those properties of a figure which remain unchanged even when the figure is transformed, that is bent, stretched, and so on, as for example when a square painted on a rubber sheet is deformed by distorting the sheet. A famous topological problem (studied extensively by the Norwegian mathematician Oystein Ore 1899–   ) is to provide a proof that only three colours are needed in producing a map, to give adjoining areas different colours. Topology has scientific applications, as in the study of turbulence in flowing fluids.

trigonometry branch of mathematics which solves problems relating to plane and spherical triangles. Its principles are based on the fixed proportions of angles and sides in a right-angled triangle, the simplest of which are the sine, cosine, and tangent (so-called trigonometrical ratios). Using trigonometry it is possible to calculate the lengths of the sides and the sizes of the angles of a triangle as long as one angle and one side are known. It is of practical importance in navigation and surveying and in topics such as simple harmonic motion in physics.

Venn diagram in mathematics, a diagram representing a set or sets and the logical relationships between them. Sets are drawn as circles. An area of overlap between two circles (sets) contains elements that are common to both sets, and thus represents a third set. Circles that do not overlap represent sets with no elements in common (disjoint sets). The method is named after the British logician John Venn (1834–1923).

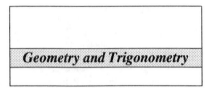

Geometry and Trigonometry

abscissa in co-ordinate geometry the horizontal or *x* co-ordinate, that is, the distance of a point from the vertical or *y*-axis. For example, a point with the co-ordinates (3,4) has an abscissa of 3.

alternate angles one of a pair of angles that lie on opposite sides of a transversal (a line cutting two other lines). If the two other lines are parallel, the alternate angles are equal.

altitude in geometry, the perpendicular distance from a vertex (corner) of a triangle to the base (the side opposite the vertex). In ordinary terms, the altitude is the height of the triangle.

angle in geometry, the inclination between a pair of lines. Angles are measured in degrees or radians. An angle of 90° (90 degrees) is a right angle. Angles of less than 90° are called *acute angles*; angles of more than 90° but less than 180° are *obtuse angles*. A *reflex angle* is an angle of more than 180° but less than 360°. Angles are measured using a protractor.

arc in geometry, a section of a curve. A circle has two kinds of arcs. An arc that is less than a semi-circle is called a *minor arc*; an arc that is greater than a semi-circle is a *major arc*.

area in geometry, the size of a surface, measured in square units (such as cm² or km²). The area *A* of a square is the length of side *l* squared: $A = l \times l = l^2$. For a rectangle, the area is given by $A = l \times b$ where *b* is the breadth (the shorter side). The area of a triangle is half the length of the base *l* times the perpendicular height *h* (altitude): $A = \frac{1}{2}l \times h$; of a parallelogram (a quadrilateral with one pair of sides equal and parallel) is the length times the height (the perpendicular distance between the longer pair of sides): $A = l \times h$; of a circle is π times the square of the radius, *r*: $A = \pi r^2$. The areas of more complex shapes can often be found by dividing them into simpler shapes whose areas can be calculated or estimated.

chord in geometry, a straight line joining any two points on a curve. In a circle, the chord that passes through the centre of the circle (the longest chord) is the diameter. In an ellipse (a regular oval), the longest and shortest chords are called the major and minor axes.

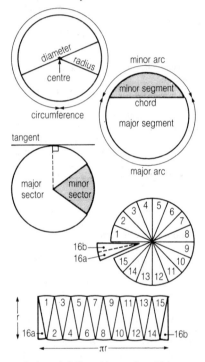

circle path followed by a point which moves so as to keep a constant distance, the ***radius***, from a fixed point, the ***centre***. The longest distance from one side of a circle to the other, called the ***diameter***, is thus twice the radius. The ratio of the distance all the way round the circle – the ***circumference*** – to the diameter is an irrational number called ***pi*** (π), roughly equal to 3.14159. A circle of diameter *d* has a circumference *C* equal to πd, or $C = 2\pi r$ and an area $A = \pi r^2$. If a circle is divided up by two radii, then the resulting divisions are termed major and minor *sectors*. The area of a circle (πr^2) can be shown by dividing a circle into very thin sectors and reassembling them to make an approximate rectangle.

circumference in geometry, the curved line that encloses a plane figure, for example, a circle or an ellipse. Its length varies according to the nature of the curve, and may be ascertained by the appropriate formula. Thus the circumference of a circle is $2\pi r$, where r is the radius and $\pi = 3.1415927 \dots$ or roughly $^{22}/_7$.

cone in geometry, a solid figure having a plane curve as its base and tapering to a point (the vertex). The line joining the vertex to the centre of the base is called the axis of the cone. A circular cone has a circle as its base; a cone that has its axis at right angles to the base is called a right cone. A circular cone of perpendicular height h and base of radius r has a volume $v = \frac{1}{3} \pi r^2 h$.

conic section curve obtained when a cone is intersected by a plane. Conic sections were first discovered by the ancient Greeks and have been of great importance in mathematics. If the intersecting plane cuts both extensions of the cone it yields a hyperbola; if it is parallel to the side of the cone it produces a parabola. Other intersecting planes produce a circle or an ellipse.

cosine in trigonomentry, a measure of an angle in a right-angled triangle found by dividing the length of the side adjacent to the angle by the length of the hypotenuse (the longest side). It is usually shortened to *cos*.

co-ordinate geometry a system of geometry, also called analytical geometry, in which points, lines, shapes, and surfaces and represented by algebraic expressions. In plane (two-dimensional) co-ordinate geometry, the plane is usually defined by two axes at right angles to each other, the horizontal *x*-axis and the vertical *y*-axis, meeting at O, the origin. A point on the plane can be represented by a pair of Cartesian co-ordinates, which define its position in terms of its distance along the *x*-axis and along the *y*-axis from O. These distances are

respectively the *x* and *y* co-ordinates of the point. Lines are represented as equations; for example, $y = 2x + 1$ gives a straight line, and $y = 3x^2 + 2x$ gives a parabola (a curve). Different lines and curves can be drawn by plotting the co-ordinates of points that satisfy their equations and joining up the points.

cube in geometry, a solid figure whose faces are all squares. It has six equal-area faces and 12 equal-length edges. If the length of one edge is l, the volume of the cube $V = l^3$ and its surface area $A = 6l^2$.

curve in geometry, the locus of a point moving according to specified conditions. The best-known of all curves is the circle, which is the locus of all points equidistant from a given point (the centre). Other common geometrical curves are the ellipse, parabola, and hyperbola, which are also produced when a cone is cut by a plane at different angles.

cycloid in geometry, a curve resembling a series of arches traced out by a point on the circumference of a circle that rolls along a straight line. It has such applications as studying the motion of wheeled vehicles along roads and tracks.

cylinder in geometry, a tubular solid figure with a circular base, ordinarily understood to be a right cyclinder, that is, having its curved surface at right angles to the base. The volume of a cylinder is given by: $V = \pi r^2 h$ where V is the volume, r is the radius, and h is the height. Its total surface area A has the formula: $A = 2\pi r (h + r)$ where A is the total area and $2 \pi r h$ is the curved surface area, and $2 \pi r^2$ is the area of both ends.

degree in mathematics, a unit of measurement of an angle. Written as°. One complete revolution is $360°$. A quarter-turn ($90°$) is a right angle; a half-turn ($180°$) is the angle on a straight line.

ellipse a curve joining all points (loci) around two fixed points (foci) so that the sum of the distances from those points is always constant. An ellipse is one of a series of curves known as conic sections; it can also be produced, for example, by imagining a slice taken from a solid cone with an oval base. The diameter passing through the foci is the major axis, and the diameter bisecting this at right angles is the minor axis.

envelope in geometry, a curve that touches all the members of a family of curves. For example, a family of three equal circles all touching each other and forming a triangle (like a clover leaf) has two envelopes: a small circle that fits in the triangular space in the middle, and a large circle that encompasses all three circles.

epicycloid in geometry, a curve resembling a series of arches traced out by a point on the circumference of a circle which rolls around another circle of a different diameter. If the two circles have the same diameter, the curve is a cardioid. Greek mathmaticians thought that planets moved in small circles (epicycles) while completing a large circle (the deferent) round the earth.

equilateral in geometry, of a figure having all sides of equal length. For example, a square and a rhombus are both equilateral four-sided figures. An equilateral triangle, to which the term is most often applied, has all three sides equal and all three angles equal (at 60°).

fractal name given by the French mathematician Benoit Mandelbrod to irregular shapes or surfaces outside the rules of conventional geometry (from Latin *fractus* meaning broken). Sets of curves with such discordant properties were developed by Georg Cantor and Karl Weierstrass. Generated on a computer screen, fractals are used in creating models for geographical or biological processes (for example, the creation of a coastline by erosion or accretion, or the growth of plants). They are also used for computer art, such as that used to illustrate science fiction films by George Lucas.

helix in mathematics, a curve resembling a screw thread. It is generated by a line that encircles a cylinder or cone at a constant angle.

hyperbola in geometry, a curve formed by cutting a right circular cone with a plane so that the angle between the plane and the base is greater than the angle between the base and the side of the cone. A member of the family of curves known as conic sections.

locus in mathematics, the path traced out by a moving point. For example, the locus of a point that moves so that it is always at the same distance from another fixed point is a circle; the locus of a point that is always at the same distance from two fixed points is a straight line that perpendicularly bisects the line joining them. From the Latin 'place'.

parabola

conic section

parabolic curve

parabola in mathematics, a curve formed by cutting a right circular cone with a plane parallel to the sloping side of the cone; one of the family of curves known as conic sections. It is a common shape for headlamp reflectors, dish-shaped microwave and radar aerials, and for radiotelescopes. A source of radiation placed at the focus of a paraboloidal reflector is propagated as a parallel beam.

parallelogram in mathematics, a quadrilateral (four-sided plane figure) with opposite pairs of sides equal in length and parallel. In the special cases when all four sides are equal in length, the parallelogram is known as a rhombus, and when the internal angles are right angles, it is a rectangle or square. The diagonals of a parallelogram bisect each other and angles diagonally opposite each other are equal. Its area is the product of the length and the height (the perpendicular distance between the longer pair of sides).

POLYGON

Polygon	number of sides	sum of interior angles (degrees)
triangle	3	180
quadrilateral	4	360
pentagon	5	540
hexagon	6	720
heptagon	7	900
octagon	8	1,080
decagon	10	1,440
duodecagon	12	1,800
icosagon	20	3,240

polygon in geometry, a plane (two-dimensional) figure with three or more sides. Common polygons have their own names, which define the number of sides (for example, triangle, quadrilateral, pentagon). These are all convex polygons, having no interior angle greater than 180°. In general, the more sides a polygon has, the larger the sum of its internal angles and, in the case of a convex polygon, the more closely it approximates to a circle.

polyhedron in geometry, a solid figure with four or more plane faces. Common polyhedra have their own names (for example, pyramid, tetrahedron, cube, cuboid, prism). There are only five types of regular polyhedra (with all faces the same size and shape), as was deduced by early Greek mathematicians; they are the tetrahedron (four equilateral triangular faces), cube (six square faces), octahedron (eight equilateral triangles), dodecahedron (12 regular pentagons) and icosahedron (20 equilateral triangles). The more faces there are on a polyhedron, the more closely it approximates to a sphere. Knowledge of the properties of polyhedra is important in crystallography and stereochemistry in determining the shapes of crystals and molecules.

prism in mathematics, a solid figure (polyhedron) with two equal polygonal faces (bases) in parallel planes; the other faces being parallelograms, of the same number as there are sides to one of the bases. If these faces are rectangles, it is a right prism. In optics triangular prisms (with triangular bases) are widely used in a variety of intruments including spectroscopes, binoculars, periscopes, and rangefinders, their properties depending on the refractive index of the material of which they are made and the angles at which they are cut.

pyramid

square pyramid

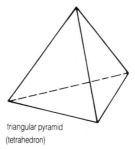

triangular pyramid
(tetrahedron)

pyramid in geometry, a solid figure with triangular side-faces meeting at a common vertex (point) and with a polygon as its base. A pyramid with a triangular base is called a tetrahedron; the Egyptian pyramids have square bases. The volume of a pyramid, no matter how many faces it has, is equal to the area of the base multiplied by one-third of the perpendicular height.

radian in mathematics, an alternative unit to the degree for measuring angles. It is defined as the angle subtended at the centre of a circle by an arc (length of circumference) equal in length to the radius of the circle. There are 2π (approximately 6.284) radians in a full circle or 360°; 1 radian is approximately 57°, and 1° is $\pi/180$ or approximately 0.0175 radians. Radians are commonly used to specify angles in polar co-ordinates.

rectangle a quadrilateral (four-sided figure) with opposite sides equal and parallel, and with right angles (90°) as the internal angles. A rectangle is a special case of a parallelogram. The diagonals of a rectangle bisect each other. Its area A is the product of the length l and breadth b; that is, $A = l \times b$. A rectangle with all four sides equal is a square.

rhombus a diamond-shaped plane figure, a parallelogram with four equal sides (opposite sides are equal in length and parallel) and no internal angle which is a right angle(otherwise it is a square). Its diagonals bisect each other at right angles. The area of a rhombus is equal to the length of a side multiplied by its height (the perpendicular distance between opposite sides).

right-angled triangle a triangle in which one of the angles is a right angle(90°). It is the basic form of triangle for defining trigonometrical ratios (for example, sine, cosine and tangent) and for which Pythagoras' theorem holds true. The longest side of a right-angled triangle is called the hypotenuse; its area is equal to half the product of the other two sides. A triangle constructed on the diameter of a circle with its opposite vertex (corner) on the circumference is a right-angled triangle, a fundamental theorem in geometry first credited to the Greek mathematician Thales (in the 580s BC).

sine in trigonometry, of an angle in a right-angled triangle, the ratio of the length of the side opposite the angle to the length of the

hypotenuse (the longest side). Various properties in physics vary sinsoidally, that is, they can be represented diagramatically by a sine wave (a graph obtained by plotting values of angles against the values of their sines). Examples include simple harmonic motion, such as the way alternating current (AC) electricity varies with time.

sphere in mathematics, a circular solid figure with all points on its surface the same distance from the centre. For a sphere of radius r, the volume $V = \frac{4}{3}\pi r^3$ and the surface area $A = 4\pi r^2$.

tangent in trigonometry, of an angle in a right-angled triangle, the ratio of the length of the side opposite an angle (not the right angle) to the length of the side adjacent to it; a way of expressing the slope of a line. In geometry, a tangent is a straight line that touches a curve and has the same slope as the curve at the point of contact. At a maximum or minimum, the tangent to a curve has zero slope.

tetrahedron

regular tetrahedron

tetrahedron in geometry, a solid figure (polyhedron) with four triangular faces; that is, a pyramid on a triangular base. Tetrahedra are important in chemistry and crystallography in describing the shapes of molecules and crystals; for example, the carbon atoms in a crystal of diamond are arranged in space as a set of interconnected regular tetrahedra.

trapezium in geometry, a four-sided plane figure quadrilateral with two of its sides parallel. If the parallel sides have lengths a and b and the perpendicular distance between them is h

(the height of the trapezium), its area $A = \frac{1}{2}((a + b) \times h)$.

triangle in geometry, a three-sided plane figure. A *scalene triangle* has no two sides equal; an *isosceles triangle* has two equal sides (and two equal angles); and *equilateral triangle* has three equal side (and three equal angles of 60°) A right-angled triangle has one angle of 90°. If the length of one side of a triangle is l and the perpendicular distance from that side to the opposite corner is h (the height or altitude of the triangle), its area $A = \frac{1}{2}l \times h$.

vector any physical quantity that has both magnitude and direction, such as velocity or acceleration of an object, as distinct from a scaler quantity which has magnitude but no direction, such as speed, density, or mass. A vector is often represented geometrically by an arrow on a line of equal length to its magnitude and in technical writing it is denoted by bold (Clarendon) type. Vectors can be added graphically by constructing a triangle of vectors (such as the triangle of forces commonly employed in physics and engineering).

volume in geometry, the space occupied by a three dimensional solid object. A cube, cubois, other prismatic figure or a cylinder has a volume equal to the area of the base multiplied by the perpendicular height. The volume of a sphere is equal to four-thirds of the cube of the radius multiplied by π.

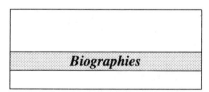

Biographies

al-Khwarizmi Muhammad ibn-Musa 780–c. 850 AD. Arab mathematician who lived and worked in Baghdad and is best known for introducing algorithms (a word based on his name and used for the step-by-step process needed to solve mathematical problems) and for introducing the word algebra (al-jabr) in an adaptation of an earlier Indian text. He com-

piled astronomical tables, put forward Arabic numerals, and pioneered calculation using decimal numbers.

Bernoulli Swiss family of mathematicians: *Jacques Bernoulli* 1654–1705, discovered Bernoullian numbers, a complex series of fractions used in higher mathematics; his brother *Jean Bernoulli* 1667–1748, discovered the exponential calculus; Jean's son *Daniel Bernoulli* 1700–82, made discoveries in hydrodynamics.

Briggs Henry 1561–1630. British mathematician. Savilian professor of geometry at Oxford from 1619, he is best known for his work in constructing the system of logarithms still in popular use.

Descartes René 1596–1650. French mathematician and philosopher. He aimed to express physical sciences in mathematical terms. He founded co-ordinate geometry as a way of defining and manipulating geometrical shapes by means of algebraic expressions. His method of representing points in this system is known as Cartesian co-ordinates in his honour. He was also influential in shaping contemporary theories of astronomy and animal behaviour.

Eratosthenes c. 276–c. 194 BC. Greek geographer and mathematician whose map of the ancient world was the first to contain lines of latitude and longitude. He calculated the earth's circumference, from the N–S distance between Aswan and Alexandria and their difference in latitude (obtained from the midday position of the sun), with an error of less than 320 km/200 mi.

Euclid c. 330–c. 260 BC. Greek mathematician from Alexandria who wrote the *Stoicheia/ Elements* in 13 books, of which nine deal with plane and solid geometry, and four with arithmetic. His main work lay in the systematic arrangement of previous discoveries, and his geometry formed the basis of standard textbooks for over 2,000 years and were still in regular use in English schools in the present century.

Euler Leonhard 1707–83. Swiss mathematician. He developed the theory of differential equations, the calculus of variations, and did important work in astronomy and optics.

Fermat Pierre de 1601–65. French mathematician who with Pascal founded the theory of probability and the modern theory of numbers. His *last theorem*, believed to be true, may have been proved by him, but no one else since has succeeded in doing so.

Fibonacci Leonardo c. 1170–c. 1230. Italian mathematician. He published his *Liber abaci* in Pisa in 1202, which led to the introduction of Arabic notation into Europe. From 1960 interest developed in his discovery of the *Fibonacci numbers*, in their simplest form a sequence of numbers in which each number is the sum of its two predecessors (1, 1, 2, 3, 5, 8, 13, and so on). They have unusual characteristics with possible applications in botany, psychology, astronomy. For example, the number of petals and sepals on flowers, the spirals in a spider's web, and the notes in certain scales in music, are all based on such sequences.

Gödel Kurt 1906–78. Austrian-born American mathematical philospher who proved that a mathematical system always contains statements that can be neither proved nor disproved within the system; in other words, as a science mathematics can never be totally consistent and totally complete. He was a friend of Einstein and worked on relativity, constructing a mathematical model of the Universe which made travel back through time theoretically possible.

Lagrange Joseph Louis 1736–1813. French mathematician who presided over the commission that introduced the metric system in 1793. His *Mécanique analytique* 1788 applied mathematical analysis, using principles established by Newton to such problems as the movements of planets when affected by each other's gravitational force.

Lobachevski Nikolai Ivanovich 1792–1856. Russian mathematician, who with the Hungarian Jănos Bulyai (1802–60), but independently of him, founded the non-Euclidean geometry in 1829. Lobachevski published the first account of the subject in 1829, but his work went unrecognized until Riemann's system was published.

Lorenz Luwig Valentine 1829–91. Danish

mathematician and physicist who developed mathematical formulae to describe various phenomena, such as the relationship between refraction of light and the density of a pure transparent substance, and the relationship between a metal's electrical and thermal conductivity and temperature.

Markov Andrei 1856–1922. Russian mathematician, formulator of the *Markov chain*. This concept holds that a chain of events is governed only by established probability and is uninfluenced by the past history of earlier links in the chain.

Napier John 1550–1617. Scottish mathematician who invented logarithms in 1614, and 'Napier's Bones', an early logarithmic calculating device for multiplication and division.

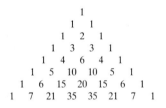

Pascal's Triangle

Pascal Blaise 1623–62. French mathematician physicist who is best known for his work on conic sections and (with Fermat) probability theory. Pascal's triangle is an array of numbers in which each is the sum of the pair of numbers above it. Plotted at equal distances along a horizontal axis, the numbers in the rows approximate to the normal (bell-shaped) probability distribution curve which describes the incidence of many natural phenomena; for example, a plot of IQs (intelligence quotient) against numbers of people with a particular IQ gives the bell-shaped graph. In physics, Pascal's chief work concerned fluid pressure and hydraulics. Pascal's principle states that the pressure everywhere in a fluid is the same, so that pressure applied at one point is transmitted equally to all parts of the container. This is the principle of the hydraulic press and jack.

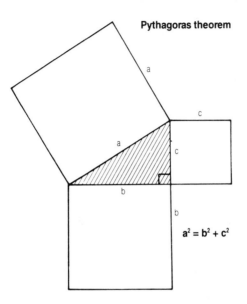

Pythagoras theorem

$$a^2 = b^2 + c^2$$

Pythagoras c. 580–c. 500 BC. Greek mathematician and philosopher who is best-known for the theorem that bears his name. Much of his work concerned numbers, to which he assigned mystical properties. For example, he classified numbers into triangular ones (1, 3, 6, 10,...) which can be represented as a triangular array, and square ones (1, 4, 9, 16,...) which form squares. He also observed that any two adjacent triangular numbers add to a square number (for example, 1 + 3 = 4, 3 + 6 = 9, 6 + 10 = 16,...). In geometry, Pythagoras' theorem states that in, a right-angled triangle, the square of the hypotenuse (the longest side) is equal to the sum of the square of the lengths of the other two sides. If the hypotenuse is h units long and the lengths of the other sides are a and b, then $h^2 = a^2 + b^2$. This provides a way of calculating the length of any side of such a triangle if the lengths of the other two sides are known.

Riemann Georg Friedrich Bernhard 1826–66. German mathematician whose system of non-Euclidean geometry, thought at the time to be a mere mathematical curiosity, was used by Einstein to develop his General Theory of Relativity.

Rubik Erno 1944– . Hungarian architect, who invented the *Rubik Cube*, a plastic multi-coloured puzzle which can be manipulated and rearranged in only one correct way, but around 43 trillion wrong. Intended to help his students understand three-dimensional design, it became a world craze.

Thales c. 624–c. 547 BC. First important Greek philosophic scientist who in the 6th century BC, at Miletus in Asia Minor, is believed to have made important advances in geometry, particularly regarding angles and triangles.

465

MATHEMATICAL SYMBOLS AND FORMULAE

Symbols

$a \rightarrow b$	a tending toward b
∞	infinity
lim	limiting value
$a \sim b$	a approximately equal to b
$a \approx b$	a very nearly equal to b
$a = b$	a equal to b
$a \equiv b$	a identical with b (for formulae only)
$a > b$	a greater than b
$a < b$	a smaller than b
$a \gg b$	a much greater than b
$a \ll b$	a much smaller than b
$a \neq b$	
$a \lessgtr b$	a not equal to b
$b < a < c$	*a greater than b and smaller than c*
$a \geqq b$	a equal to or greater than b, that is, a at least as great as b
$a \geq b$	
$a \leqq b$	a equal to or smaller than b, that is, a at most as great as b
$a \leq b$	
$b \leqq a \leqq c$	a lying between b and c
$\lvert a \rvert$	absolute value of a; this is always positive, for example $\lvert -5 \rvert = 5$
$+$	addition sign, plus, positive
$-$	subtraction sign, minus, negative
$\times$ or $\cdot$	multiplication sign, times
: or $\div$	division sign, divided by
$a+b=c$	$a+b$, read as 'a plus b', denotes the sum of a and b. The result of the addition, c, is also known as the sum.
$\int$	indefinite integral
$_a\int^b$	definite integral, or integral between $x = a$ and $x = b$
$a-b=c$	$a-b$, read as 'a minus b', denotes subtraction of b from a.
	$a-b$, or c, is the difference. Subtraction is the opposite of addition.
$a \times b = c$	
$ab = c$	$a \times b$, read as 'a times b', denotes multiplication of a by b. a and b are the multiplicands
$a \cdot b = c$	or factors; $a \times b$, or c, is the product.
$a:b=c$	$a{:}c$, read as 'a divided by b', denotes division. a is the dividend, b the divisor; $a{:}b$, or c, is the quotient. Division is the opposite of multiplication and can also be represented by the fraction
	$\frac{a}{b}$ or a/b
	In fractions, a, is the numerator ($=$ dividend), b the denominator ($=$ divisor)
$a^b=c$	a^b, read as 'a to the power b', a is the base, b the exponent
$^b\sqrt{a}=c$	$^b\sqrt{a}$, is the bth root of a, b being known as the root exponent. In the special case of $\sqrt[2]{a}=c$, $\sqrt[2]{a}$ or c is known as the square root of a, and the root exponent is usually omitted, that is, $\sqrt[2]{a} = \sqrt{a}$.
e	base of natural (napierian) logarithms $= 2.7182818284\ldots$
π	ratio of the circumference of a circle to its diameter $= 3.1415925535$

Numbers

Between any two real numbers a and b there can exist only one of the three relationships

$a = b$ or $a > b$ or $a < b$

$a + b = b + a$

$ab = ba$

$(a+b) + c = a + (b+c)$

$(ab)c = a(bc)$

$a(b+c) = ab+ac$

Factorials and Binomial Coefficients

For a positive integer r and any real number $n^{(r)}$ represents the products

$n^{(r)} = (n-1)(n-2)...(n-r+1)$

where

$n^{(O)} = 1$

by definition

The factorial of a positive integer n, symbol $n!$, is defined as

$n! = n(n-1)(n-2)...3 \times 2 \times 1$

where

$O! = 1$

by definition.

Technology

Technology is the practical application of science in industry and commerce. It encompasses not only the use but also the research, design, and development of equipment for such purposes as mining, construction, transport, and energy generation.

This section concentrates on four main areas of technology: *Construction* describes major types of purpose-built structures and their functions; *Telecommunications* looks primarily at the telephone, radio, and television as part of the new science of information technology; *Transport* reviews the main means of travel in the air and on sea, rail, and road; and *Energy* explains the science of the exploitation of renewable and non-renewable resources.

Construction

bridge a construction which provides a continuous path or road over water, valleys, ravines, or above other roads. Bridges may be classified into four main groups:

arch for example Sydney Harbour bridge (steel arch) with a span of 503 m/1,650 ft.

beam or girder as at Rio-Niteroi (1974), Guanabara Bay, Brazil, the world's longest continuous box and plate girder bridge: centre span 300 m/984 ft; length 13,900 m/8.7 mi.

cantilever for example Forth rail bridge which is 1,658 m/5,440 ft long and has two main spans, each consisting of two cantilevers.

suspension bridge such as the Humber bridge, the world's longest-span suspension bridge with a centre span of 1,410 m/4,626 ft.

canal an artificial waterway constructed for drainage, irrigation, or navigation.

irrigation canals carry water for irrigation from rivers, reservoirs, or wells, and are carefully designed to maintain an even flow of water over the whole length.

navigation and ship canals constructed at one level between locks, canals frequently link with other forms of waterway – natural rivers, modified river channels, and sea links – to form a waterway system. The world's two major international ship canals are the Suez canal and the Panama canal which provide invaluable short cuts for shipping respectively between Europe and the East and between the east and west coasts of the Americas.

The economy of energy for transporting in such a means of goods transport, where speed is not a prime factor, has encouraged a modern revival of canal transport.

dam a structure built to hold back water, so as to prevent flooding, provide water for irrigation and storage, and to provide hydro-electric power. The world's largest dam is the 10.8 km/6.7 mi long New Cornelia Tailings dam in Arizona, USA, which has a volume of 209 million cu m/274 million cu yds. Like all the biggest dams it is an *earth- and rock-fill dam*, also called an *embankment dam*. Such dams are generally built on broad valley sites. Deep, narrow gorges, however, dictate a concrete dam, the enormous strength of reinforced concrete being able to withstand the enormous water pressures involved. Many concrete dams are triangular in cross-section, with their vertical face pointing upstream. Their sheer weight holds them in position, and they are called *gravity dams*. Some concrete dams, however, are more slightly built in the shape of an arch, with the curve facing upstream. The *arch dam*

bridge

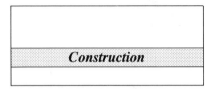

concrete arch

cantilever

suspension

steel arch

truss

derives its strength from the arch shape, just as an arch bridge does. A valuable development in arid regions, as in parts of Brazil, is the *underground dam*, where water is stored among sand and stones on a solid rock base, with a wall to ground level, so avoiding rapid evaporation.

tunnel an underground passageway. Tunnelling is an increasingly important branch of civil engineering in mining, transport, and other areas. In the 19th century there were two major advances: the use of compressed air within the tunnel to balance the external pressure of water and of the tunnel shield to support the face and assist excavation. In recent years there have been notable developments in linings, such as concrete segments and steel liner plates, and in the use of rotary diggers and cutters, and of explosives. Famous tunnels include: the world's longest road tunnel, the St Gotthard, Switzerland (1980) 16.3 km/10.1 mi; the world's longest rail tunnel, the Seikan, 1975, under Tsugaru Strait linking Honshu and Hokkaido, Japan, 53.85 km/33.5 mi. A Channel tunnel, or Chunnel, beneath the English Channel was planned as a military measure by Napoleon in 1802. In 1986 a scheme for twin rail tunnels was approved by the French and English governments.

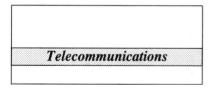

Telecommunications

telecommunications are communications over a distance. The first mechanical telecommunications systems were the *semaphore* and *heliograph* (which used flashes of sunlight). But the forerunner of the modern telecommunications age was the *electric telegraph*. The earliest practicable instrument was invented by Cooke and Wheatstone in Britain in 1837, and used by railway companies, the first public line being laid between Paddington and Slough in 1843. In the USA Morse invented a signalling code, Morse code, which is still used, and a recording telegraph, first used commercially between England and France in 1851. As a result of Hertz's discoveries using electromagnetic waves, Marconi pioneered a *'wireless' telegraph*, ancestor of the radio. He established wireless communication between England and France 1899 and across the Atlantic 1901. The modern telegraph uses teleprinters to send coded messages along telecommunications lines. They are keyboard-operated machines which transmit a five-unit baudot code. The receiving teleprinter automatically prints the received message.

Long-distance voice communication was pioneered in 1876 by Alexander Graham Bell, when he invented the *telephone* as a result of Faraday's discovery of electromagnetism. Today it is possible to communicate with most countries by telephone cable, several hundred simultaneous conversations being carried. However, the chief method of relaying long-distance calls on land is *microwave radio transmission*. The drawback to this is that the transmissions follow a straight line from tower to tower, so that over the sea the system becomes impracticable.

A solution was put forward in 1945 by Arthur C Clarke in *Wireless World*, when he proposed a system of *communications satellites* in an orbit 35,900 km/27,300 mi above the equator, where they would circle the earth in exactly 24 hours, and thus appear fixed in the sky. Such a system is now in operation internationally, operated by Intelsat. The satellites are called geostationary satellites, or synchronous satellites (syncoms). The first to be successfully launched, by *Delta* rocket from Cape Canaveral, was *Syncom 2* in Jul 1963. Numbers of such satellites are now in use, concentrated over heavy traffic areas such as the Atlantic, Indian and Pacific Oceans. Telegraphy, telephony, and television transmissions are carried simultaneously by high-frequency radio waves. They are beamed to the satellites from large dish antennæ or earth stations, which connect with international net-

radio

microphone

transmitting aerial

receiving aerial

modulator

radio frequency oscillator

tuned circuit

demodulator

amplifier

loudspeaker

earth

transmitter

receiver

audio frequency signal

voltage

time

carrier voltage

voltage

time

amplitude-modulated carrier

voltage

time

frequency-modulated carrier

voltage

time

tuned circuit   aerial

aerial coil   tuning coil   variable capacitor

signal from demodulator

voltage

time

amplified signal

voltage

time

works. The number of earth stations continues to increase.

In 1980 the Post Office opened its first System X (all electronic, digital) telephone exchange in London, a method already adopted in the USA. Other recent advances include the use of fibre-optic cables consisting of fine glass fibres for telephone lines instead of the usual copper cables. The telecommunications signals are transmitted along the fibres on pulses of laser light. Procedures, technical standards, frequencies, and so on, in telecommunications are controlled by the International Telecommunications Union (ITU).

Milestones in telecommunications

1794 Claude Chappe in France built a long-distance signalling system using semaphore.

1839 Charles Wheatstone and William Cooke devised an electric telegraph in England.

1843 Morse transmitted the first message along a telegraph line in the USA, using his Morse code of signals - short (dots) and long (dashes).

1858 The first transatlantic telegraph cable was laid.

1876 American Alexander Graham Bell invented the telephone.

1877 Edison invented the carbon transmitter for the telephone.

1894 Marconi pioneered wireless telegraphy in Italy, later moving to England.

1900 Fessenden in the USA first broadcast voice by radio.

1901 Marconi transmitted the first radio signals across the Atlantic.

1904 Fleming invented the thermionic valve.

1907 American Charles Krumm introduced the forerunner of the teleprinter.

1920 Stations in Detroit and Pittsburgh began regular radio broadcasts.

1922 The BBC began its first radio transmissions, for the London station 2LO.

1932 The Post Office introduced the Telex in Britain.

1956 The first transatlantic telephone cable was laid.

1962 Telstar pioneers transatlantic satellite communications, transmitting live TV pictures.

1966 Charles Kao in England advanced the idea of using optical fibres for telecommunications transmissions.

1969 Live TV pictures were sent from astronauts on the moon back to earth.

1975 The Post Office announced Prestel, the world's first viewdata system, using the telephone lines to link a computer data bank with the TV screen.

1977 The first optical fibre cable was installed in California.

1986 Voyager 2 transmitted images of the planet Uranus over a distance of some 3,000 million km/2,000 million mi, the signals taking 2 hours 45 minutes to make the journey back to earth.

1989 First transoceanic optical fibre cable, capable of carrying 40,000 simultaneous telephone conversations, laid between Europe and the USA.

radio the transmission and reception of radio waves. The theory of electromagnetic waves was first developed by James Clerk Maxwell 1864, given practical confirmation in the laboratory 1888 by Heinrich Hertz, and put to practical use by Marconi, who in 1901 achieved reception of a signal in Newfoundland transmitted from Poldhu in Cornwall.

radio transmission a microphone converts sound waves (pressure variations in the air) into an audio frequency electrical signal. The *oscillator* produces a carrier voltage of high frequency; different stations are allocated different transmitting carrier frequencies. A *modulator* superimposes the audio frequency signal on the carrier. There are two main ways of doing this: *amplitude modulation (AM)*, used for long and medium wave broadcasts in which the strength of the carrier is made to fluctuate in time with the audio signal; in *frequency modulation (FM)*, as used for VHF broadcasts, the frequency of the carrier is made to fluctuate. The transmitting aerial emits the modulated electromagnetic waves which travel outwards from it.

radio reception a receiving aerial produces voltages in response to the waves sent out by a transmitter. A *tuned circuit* selects a particular voltage frequency, usually by means of variable capacitor connected across a coil of wire. (The

473

television

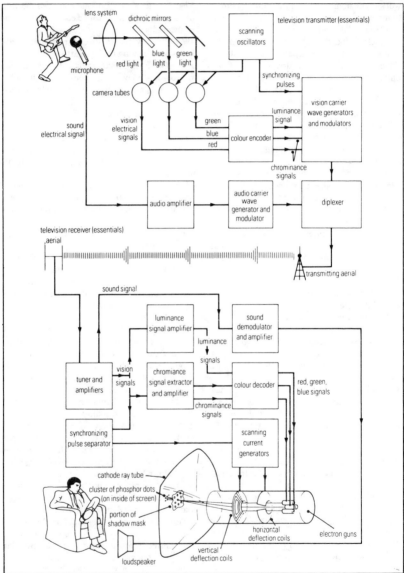

effect is similar to altering the tension in a piano wire, making it capable of vibrating at a different frequency.) The demodulator disentangles the audio signal from the carrier, which is now discarded, having served its purpose. The amplifier boosts the audio signal for feeding to the loudspeaker which produces sound waves.

television the reproduction at a distance by radio waves of visual images.

technology for transmission, a television camera converts the pattern of light it takes in into a pattern of electrical charges. This is scanned line-by-line by a beam of electrons from an electron gun, resulting in variable electrical signals that represent the visual picture. These vision signals are combined with a radio carrier wave and broadcast. The TV aerial picks up the wave and feeds it to the receiver (TV set). This separates out the vision signals, which pass to the picture tube, which is a cathode-ray tube. The broad end of the tube, upon which the scene is to appear, has its inside surface coated with a fluorescent material. The vision signals control the strength of a beam of electrons from an electron gun, aimed at the screen and making it glow more or less brightly. At the same time the beam is made to scan across the screen line-by-line, mirroring the action of the gun in the TV camera. The result is a re-creation spot-by-spot, line-by-line of the pattern of light that entered the camera. Twenty-five pictures are built up each second with interlaced scanning (30 in US), with a total of 625 lines (in Europe, but 525 lines in the US and Japan).

colour TV The method of colour reproduction in television is related to that used in colour photography and printing. It uses the principle that any colours can be made by mixing the primary colours red, green, and blue in appropriate proportions. In colour television the receiver reproduces only three basic colours: red, green and blue. It is thus possible to specify the colour which it is required to transmit by sending signals which indicate the amounts of red, green and blue light which are to be generated at the receiver.

The three signals are coded into one complex signal which is transmitted as a more or less normal black and white signal, and which produces a satisfactory – or compatible – picture on ordinary black and white receivers. A fraction of each primary red, green and blue signal is added together to produce the normal brightness, or luminance signal. The minimum of extra colouring information is then sent by a special subcarrier signal which is superimposed on the brightness signal. This extra colouring information corresponds to the hue and saturation (see Colour) of the transmitted colour, but without any of the fine detail of the picture. The impression of sharpness is conveyed only by the brightness signal, the colouring being added as a broad colour wash.

Milestones in television

1878 William Crookes in England invented the Crookes tube, which produced cathode rays.

1884 Paul Nipkow in Germany built a mechanical scanning device, the Nipkow disc, a rotating disc with a spiral pattern of holes in it.

1897 Karl Ferdinand Braun, also in Germany, modified the Crookes tube to produce the ancestor of the modern TV receiver picture tube.

1906 Boris Rosing in Russia began experimenting with the Nipkow disc and cathode-ray tube, eventually succeeding in transmitting some crude TV pictures.

1923 Zworykin in the USA invented the first electronic camera tube, the iconoscope.

1926 Baird demonstrated a workable TV system, using mechanical scanning by Nipkow disc.

1928 Baird demonstrated colour TV.

1929 The BBC began broadcasting experimental TV programmes using Baird's system.

1936 The BBC began regular broadcasting using Baird's system from Alexandra Palace, London.

1940 Experimental colour TV transmission began in the USA, using the modern system of colour reproduction.

1953 Successful colour TV transmissions began in the USA, using the modern system of colour reproduction.

1956 The first videotape recorder was produced in California by the Ampex Corporation.

1962 TV signals were transmitted across the

Atlantic via the Telstar satellite.

1970 The first videodisc system was announced by Decca in Britain and AEG-Telefunken in Germany, but it was not perfected until the 1980s, when laser scanning was used for playback.

1975 Sony introduced their videocassette tape recorder system, Betamax, for domestic viewers, six years after their professional U-Matic system; the British Post Office (now British Telecom) announced their Prestel viewdata system.

1973 The BBC and Independent Television introduced the world's first teletext systems, Ceefax and Oracle, respectively.

1979 Matsushita in Japan developed a pocket-sized flat-screen TV set, using a liquid-crystal display (LCD).

1989 Japanese begin broadcasting high-definition television.

Transport

air transport people first took to the air in balloons and began powered flight in airships. But the history of flying is dominated by the aeroplane. The aeroplane is a development of the model glider, first flown by Sir George Cayley (1773–1857) in 1804. But not until the invention of the petrol engine did powered flight become feasible. The Wright brothers in the USA first achieved success, when they flew their biplane *Flyer* on 17 Dec 1903. In Europe, inspired by the Wrights, France led in aeroplane design (Voisin brothers) and Louis Blériot brought aviation much publicity by crossing the Channel in 1909, as did the Reims air races of that year. The first powered flight in England was made by S F Cody in 1908. In 1912 Sopwith and Bristol both built small biplanes. The first big twin-engined aeroplane was the Handley Page bomber in 1917. The flight of the German Heinkel 178 (1939)

ushered in a new era in aviation. It was the first jet plane, propelled, not as all planes before it with a propeller, but by a jet of hot gases. The first British jet aircraft, the Gloster E.28/39 flew from Cranwell, Lincolnshire, on 15 May 1941, powered by a jet engine invented by Frank Whittle.

In the 1950s the first jet airliners, such as the Comet, were introduced into service. And today jet planes dominate both military and civilian aviation, although many light planes still use piston engines and propellers for propulsion. The late 1960s saw the introduction of the jumbo jet and the supersonic airliners, notably the Anglo-French *Concorde*.

aeroplane a heavier-than-air craft supported in flight by fixed wings (aerofoils): it may be unpowered (the glider) or powered, when it is propelled by the reaction from air accelerated rearwards by airscrew(s) (propellers) or jet(s) to overcome the air resistance (drag). Drag depends on frontal area (for example: large, airliner; small, fighter) and shape (drag coefficient); it equals thrust in straight level flight. Less drag (streamlining) means increased speed and lower fuel consumption from given power; less fuel need be carried for a given distance (range) and the aeroplane's weight is reduced.

Aerofoils are so shaped and cambered that air passing above them is speeded up, reducing pressure below atmospheric, while that above is slowed. This produces a vertical force (lift) to support the aircraft's weight. (Lift m4 weight in level flight.) Minimum weight is thus essential to an efficient aeroplane, requiring a smaller wing which has less drag. Very strong but light aluminium alloys (with copper, magnesium, and so on) are used, and also for the body (fuselage) and where possible for controls and in engines. For supersonic planes special stainless steel and titanium may be used. The thin skin (outer) panels, with ribs and stringers at intervals to prevent buckling, support all flight stresses with no separate structure (semi-monocoque construction). The payload (crew, passengers, bombs, and so on) may be up to one-third all-up weight.

Fastest aeroplane - the Lockheed SR-71, holder of the world air-speed record of 3,529 kph/2,193 mph (over Mach 3.3).

Fastest airliner - Concorde, which can cruise at up to Mach 2.2 (2,333 kph/1,450 mph).

Largest airliner - Boeing 747, with a wingspan of 59.6 m/195.7 ft and a length of 70.7 m/231.8 ft.

Largest volume aeroplane - the Guppy-201, with a usable volume of 1,104 cu m/39,000 cu ft.

airship essentially a power-driven balloon. All airships have streamlined envelopes or hulls, which contain the inflation gas, and are non-rigid, semi-rigid or rigid. Count Ferdinand von Zeppelin (1838–1917) was the pioneer of the rigid type, named after him, and used for bombing raids on Britain in World War I. The destruction by fire of the British R101 in 1930 led to a cessation of airship building in Britain. The Germans continued building airships, including the 248 m/812 ft long *Hindenburg*. In 1937, however, this airship exploded at Lakehurst, New Jersey, marking the effective end of airship travel. The early airships were vulnerable because they used hydrogen for inflation. It is the lightest gas, but highly flammable. Since World War II, now large supplies of non-flammable helium are available there has been renewed interest in airships which cause minimum noise pollution, can lift enormous loads, and are economical on fuel.

balloon bag or envelope of impermeable fabric which rises from the ground when filled with a gas lighter than air. The first successful human ascent was by Pilâtre de Rozier in Paris in Oct 1783 in a hot-air balloon of the type designed by the Montgolfier brothers. Balloons continue in use for sport, and as an economical means of making meteorological, infrared, gamma-ray, ultraviolet and other scientific observations . The first transalantic balloon crossing was made by three Americans (Presque Isle, Maine to Miserey, France) 11–17 Aug 1978.

helicopter an aircraft which achieves both lift and propulsion by means of a rotary wing, or rotor on top of the fuselage. It can take off and land vertically, move in any direction or remain stationary in the air. Igor Sikorsky in the USA built the first practical single rotor craft in 1939. The rotor of a helicopter has two or more blades, which are of aerofoil cross-section, like

an aeroplane's wings. Lift and propulsion are achieved by angling the blades as they rotate.

jet propulsion a method of propulsion in which an object is propelled in one direction by a jet, or stream of gases moving in the other. This follows from Newton's celebrated third law of motion 'to every action, there is an equal and opposite reaction'. The most widespread application of the jet principle is in the jet engine, the commonest kind of aero-engine.

The jet engine is a kind of gas turbine. Air, after passing through a forward-facing intake, is compressed by a compressor, or fan, and fed into a combustion chamber. Fuel (usually kerosene) is sprayed in and ignited. The hot gas produced expands rapidly rearwards, spinning a turbine that drives the compressor before being finally ejected from a rearward-facing tail pipe, or nozzle, at very high speed. Reaction to the jet of gases streaming backwards produces a propulsive thrust forwards which acts on the aircraft through its engine-mountings.

rocket a projectile driven through space by the reaction on the rocket of the fast-burning fuel within. Unlike the jet engine, which is also a reaction engine, the rocket engine carries its own oxygen supply to burn its fuel and is totally independent of any surrounding atmosphere. The only form of propulsion available which can function in a vacuum, rockets are essential to the exploration of outer space. Two kinds of rockets are used - one burns liquid propellants, the other solid propellants.

sea transport people have travelled on and across the seas throughout history. The Greeks and Phoenicians built wooden ships, propelled by oar or sail, to transport themselves and their goods across the sea. The Romans and Carthaginians fought in galleys equipped with rams and rowed by tiers of oarsmen. The wooden ships of the Norsemen were for rough seas, and the fleet of Richard Coeur de Lion was largely of sail. America and Britain made steam experiments as the 19th century opened. The *Comet* appeared in 1812, the Canadian *Royal William* crossed the Atlantic in 1833, and the English *Great Western* steamed from Bristol to New York in 1838. Pettit Smith applied the screw to the *Archimedes* in

1839, and after 1850 the paddle-wheel became obsolete. The introduction of the compound engine and turbine, the latter in 1902, completed the revolution in propulsion until the advent of nuclear-powered vessels after World War II, chiefly submarines.

hovercraft an air-cushion vehicle that rides on a cushion of high-pressure air, free from all contact with the surface beneath. Although hovercraft need a smooth terrain when operating overland, it need not be metalled, and snow and ice present no difficulties, but they are at present best adapted to use on lakes, sheltered coastal waters, river estuaries and swamps.

hydrofoil boat a boat whose hull rises out of the water when it travels at speed. The boat gets its 'lift' from a set of hydrofoils, underwater 'wings' that develop lift in the water in much the same way that an aeroplane wing develops lift in the air.

jetfoil an advanced kind of hydrofoil boat built by Boeing, which is propelled by water jets. It features horizontal fully submerged hydrofoils fore and aft, and has a sophisticated computerized control system to maintain its stability in all waters. Jetfoils have been in service worldwide since 1975.

submarine an underwater ship, especially a warship. An early venture was an underwater boat constructed for King James I by Dutchman Cornelius van Drebbel in 1620. A century and a half later, David Bushness in the USA designed a submarine called *Turtle* for attacking British ships. Robert Fulton designed a submarine called *Nautilus* for Napoleon, for the same purpose in 1800. The first naval submarine, or submersible torpedo boat, the *Gymnote*, was launched by France in 1888. John P Holland, an Irish emigrant to the USA, designed a submarine c. 1875, which was adopted by both the US and British navies at the turn of the century. In both World Wars submarines, from the ocean-going to the midget type, played a vital role. The conventional submarine of this period was driven by diesel engine on the surface and by battery-powered electric motors underwater. The diesel engine also drove a generator that produced electricity to charge the batteries.

In 1954 the USA launched the first nuclear-powered submarine, the *Nautilus*. The modern nuclear submarine *Ohio*, USA, in service from 1981, is 170 m/560 ft long, displacement about 18,700 tonnes, and carries 24 Trident missiles, each with a dozen independently targetable nuclear warheads with a range that is being extended to 11,000 km/6.750 mi. Operating depth is usually up to 300 m/1,000 ft, and nuclear power speeds of 30 knots (i.e. 55 kph/34 mph) are reached. As in all nuclear submarines, propulsion is by steam turbine driving a propellor. The steam is raised using the heat given off by the nuclear reactor.

Ship records

The first successful power-driven boat was the *Charlotte Dundas*, built in Scotland in 1801.

The first steam-assisted crossing of the Atlantic was by the US ship *Savannah* in 1819.

The *Great Britain* became the first propeller-driven ship to cross the Atlantic in 1845.

The first steam-turbine driven vessel was Sir Charles Parsons' *Turbinia*, built in 1894.

The largest liner ever was the *Queen Elizabeth*, 83,673 gross tonnes, 314 m/1,031 ft long with a beam of 36 m/118 ft. Launched in 1940, it was gutted by fire in 1972.

The fastest Atlantic crossing by ship was by the US *United States* in 1952, which took 3 days 20 hours 40 minutes to cross between the Ambrose light vessel and the Bishop Rock Light, Isles of Scilly.

The first nuclear-powered ship (as opposed to submarine) was the Russian icebreaker *Lenin*, launched in 1959.

The world's longest liner ever is the *Norway*, launched in 1961 as the *France*. Of 70,202 gross tonnage, it measures 316 m/1,035 ft long.

The world's largest ship is the 564,739 tonnes deadweight oil tanker *Seawise Giant*, which is 458 m/1,505 ft long, with a beam of 69 m/226 ft. It was launched in 1979.

Rail transport is by means of a system of parallel tracks laid upon the ground on which vehicles can travel. In the USA and Canada railways made the 19th-century exploitation of the central and western territories possible, and in the USA underpinned the victory of the north in the Civil War, the 'Railway War'. In countries with less developed road systems and large areas of difficult terrain, the railway is still important, as in India (where the British system survives), China, South America (system largely built by British engineers), and the USSR. Electrification, or the use of diesel electric engines, has superseded the steam engine in Britain and other developed countries.

monorail a railway that runs on a single (mono) rail. It was originally invented in 1882 to carry light loads, and when run by electricity was called a telpher. The most successful monorail, the Wuppertal Schwebebahn, has been running in Germany since 1901. It is a suspension monorail, the passenger cars hanging from an arm fixed to a trolley that runs along the rail. Most modern monorails are of the straddle type, the passenger cars running on top of the rail. Straddle-type monorails are often used to transport passengers between terminals at airports, as at Birmingham.

tramway a city transport system in which wheeled vehicles run along parallel rails, which originated in collieries in the 18th century. The earliest passenger system was in 1832, in New York, and by the 1860s horse-drawn trams plied in London and Liverpool. Trams are now powered either by electric conductor rails below ground or conductor arms connected to overhead wires, but their use on public roads is very limited because of their lack of manoeuvrability. Greater flexibility is achieved with the *trolleybus*, similarly powered by conductor arms overhead, but without tracks. In the 1980s these were in some areas being revived. Both vehicles have the advantage of being non-polluting.

Milestones on the railways

1500s Tramways – wooden tracks along which trolleys ran – were in use in mines.

1804 Richard Trevithick in England built the first steam locomotive and ran it on the track at the Pen-y-darren ironworks in South Wales.

1825 George Stephenson built the first public railway to carry steam trains – the Stockton and Darlington line.

1829 Stephenson designed his locomotive *Rocket*, which trounced its rivals at the Rainhill trials.

1830 Stephenson completed the Liverpool and Manchester Railway, the first steam passenger line; the first American-built locomotive, *Best Friend of Charleston*, went into service on the South Carolina Railroad.

1835 Germany pioneered steam railways in Europe, using *Der Adler*, a locomotive built by Stephenson.

1863 The Scotsman Robert Fairlie patented a locomotive with pivoting driving bogies, allowing tight curves in the track (this was later applied particularly in the Garratt locomotives); London opened the world's first underground railway.

1869 The first US transcontinental railway was completed at Promontory, Utah, when the Union Pacific and the Central Pacific Railroads met; George Westinghouse (USA) invented the compressed-air brake.

1879 Werner von Siemens demonstrated an electric train in Germany; Volk's Electric Railway along the Brighton seafront was the world's first public electric railway.

1883 Charles Lartique built the first monorail, in Ireland.

1885 The trans-Canada continental railway was completed, from Montreal in the east to Port Moody in British Columbia in the west.

1890 The first electric underground railway opened in London.

1901 The world's most successful monorail, the Wuppertal Schwebebahn, went into service.

1912 The first diesel locomotive took to the rails in Germany.

1926 The British steam locomotive *Mallard* set a steam rail speed record of 201 kph/125 mph.

1941 Swiss Federal Railways introduced a gas-turbine locomotive.

1964 Japan National Railways inaugurated the 512 km/320 mi New Tokaido line between Osaka and Tokyo, on which ran the 210 kph/130 mph 'bullet' trains.

1973 British Rail's High Speed Train (HST) set a diesel rail speed record of 229 kph/143 mph.

1979 Japan National Railways' maglev test vehicle ML-500 attained a speed of 517 kph/321 mph.

1981 France's TGV superfast trains began operation between Paris and Lyons, regularly

internal combustion engine: the four stroke cycle

attaining a peak speed of 270 kph/168 mph.

1987 British Rail set new speed record for diesel traction of 283 kph/176 mph on test run between Darlington and York.

1988 West German Intercity Experimental train reaches 405 kph/252 mph on test run between Würzburg amd Fulda.

Road transport

internal combustion engine a heat engine in which fuel is burned inside the engine, contrasting with an external combustion engine like the steam engine in which fuel is burned in a separate boiler. The petrol and diesel engine are both internal combustion engines. They are reciprocating piston engines in which pistons move up and down in cylinders to effect the engine operating cycle. This may be a four-stroke cycle or a two-stroke cycle. Gas turbines, jet and rocket engines are sometimes also considered to be internal combustion engines since they burn their fuel inside their combustion chambers.

motor car a self-propelled vehicle able to be run and be steered on normal roads. Although it is recorded that in 1479 one Gilles de Dom was paid 25 livres by the treasurer of Antwerp, for supplying such a vehicle, the 'father of the automobile' is generally agreed to be Nicolas-Joseph Cugnot's cumbrous steam carriage 1769, still preserved in Paris.

motor cycle a two-wheeled vehicle propelled by a petrol engine. Daimler created the first motor cycle, usually called motorbike, when he installed his lightweight petrol engine in a bicycle frame in 1885. The first really successful two-wheel design was devised by Michael and Eugene Werner in France 1901. They adopted the classic motor cycle layout with the engine low down between the wheels. Road races like the Isle of Man TT (Tourist Trophy), established in 1907, helped improve motor cycle design and it soon evolved into more or less its present form.

Milestones in motoring

1769 Nicholas-Joseph Cugnot in France built a steam tractor.

1801 Richard Trevithick built a steam coach.

1860 Jean Etienne Lenoir built a gas-fuelled internal combustion engine.

1831 The British government passed the 'Red Flag' Act, requiring a man to precede a 'horseless carriage' with a red flag.

1876 Nikolaus August Otto improved the gas engine, making it a practical power source.

1885 Gottlieb Daimler developed a successful lightweight petrol engine and fitted it to a bicycle to create the prototype of the modern motor-bike; Karl Benz fitted his lightweight petrol engine to a three-wheeled carriage to pioneer the motor car.

1886 Gottlieb Daimler fitted his engine to a four-wheeled carriage to produce a four-wheeled motor car.

1891 René Panhard and Emile Levassor established the modern design of cars by putting the engine in front.

1896 Frederick Lanchester introduced epicyclic gearing, which foreshadowed automatic transmission.

1901 The first Mercedes took to the roads. It was the direct ancestor of the modern car; Ransome Olds in the USA introduced mass production on an assembly line.

1906 Rolls-Royce introduced the legendary Silver Ghost, which established their reputation for superlatively engineered cars.

1908 Henry Ford also used assembly-line production to manufacture his famous Model T, nicknamed the Tin Lizzie because it used light-weight steel sheet for the body, which looked 'tinny'.

1911 Cadillac introduced the electric starter and dynamo lighting.

1913 Ford introduced the moving conveyor belt to the assembly line, further accelerating production of the Model T.

1920 Duesenberg began fitting four-wheel hydraulic brakes.

1922 The Lancia Lambda featured unitary (all-in-one) construction and independent front suspension.

1928 Cadillac introduced the synchromesh gearbox, greatly facilitating gear changing.

1934 Citroën pioneered front-wheel drive in their 7CV model.

1936 Fiat introduced their baby car, the Topolino, 500 cc.

1938 Germany produced their 'people's car', the Volkswagen 'beetle'.

1948 Jaguar launched the XK120 sports car; Michelin introduced the radial-ply tyre; Goodrich produced the tubeless tyre.

1950 Dunlop announced the disc brake.

1951 Buick and Chrysler introduced power steering.

1952 Rover's gas-turbine car set a speed record of 243 kph/152 mph.

1954 Bosch introduced fuel-injection for cars.

1955 Citroën produced the advanced DS-19 'shark-front' car with hydropneumatic suspension.

1957 Felix Wankel built his first rotary petrol engine.

1959 BMC (now Rover) introduced the Issigonis-designed Mini, with front-wheel drive, transverse engine and independent rubber suspension.

1966 California introduced legislation regarding air pollution by cars.

1972 Dunlop introduced safety tyres, which sealed themselves after a burst.

1980s Lean-burn engines were introduced to improve fuel consumption; electronic ignition and engine controls became widely available; on-board computers were introduced to monitor engine performance, speech synthesizers to issue audible warnings, and wind-tunnel testing to produce body shapes with low drag coefficients.

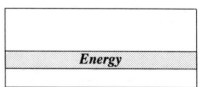

Energy

The chief direct sources of energy are oil, coal, wood, and gas, and indirectly, electricity produced by the use of such fuels or derived from water power or nuclear fission. Increasing costs and the prospect of exhaustion of coal, oil and gas resources, led in the 1970s to consideration of alternative sources. These included solar power, which provides completely 'clean' energy, wind power, tidal (sea) power, and geothermal power. The chief direct sources of energy are oil, coal, wood, and gas, and such animal products as chicken manure; photosynthetic power, produced by the use of simple, fast-reproducing plants as fuel; nuclear power, by fusion rather than fission.

Electricity is generated at power stations at a voltage of about 25,000 volts, which is not a suitable voltage for long-distance transmission. For minimal power loss transmission must take place at very high voltage – up to

electricity generation

coal-fired power station (highly simplified)

electricity generation and supply electricity is the most useful and most convenient form of energy there is. It can readily be converted into heat and light and used to power machines. Because electricity flows readily through wires, it can be made, or generated, in one place and distributed to anywhere it is needed. Electricity is generated at power stations, where a suitable energy source is made to drive turbines that spin the electricity generators. The generators produce alternating current (AC), and the producing units are generally called turboalternators.

400,000 volts or more. The generated voltage is therefore increased, or stepped-up, by a transformer. The resulting high voltage electricity is then fed into the main arteries of the grid system. This is an interconnected network of power stations and distribution centres covering a large area, sometimes (as in Britain) countrywide, even (as in Europe) from country to country. After transmission to a local sub-station, the line voltage is reduced by a step-down transformer and distributed by consumers.

geothermal energy either subterranean

hot water pumped to the surface and converted to steam or run through a heat exchanger, or dry steam, directed through turbines to produce electricity.

heat pump machine run by electricity, and so on, on a similar principle to a refrigerator, that is to cool the interior of a building or, conversely, by extracting energy from the atmosphere to give space heating. More than twice as much energy may be transferred as heat as is used to run it.

heat storage means of storing heat for release later. It is usually achieved by using materials which undergo phase changes, for example Glauber's salt, and sodium pyrophosphate, which melts at 7° C. The latter is used to store off-peak heat in the home, the salt being liquefied by cheap heat during the night, and then freezing – to give off heat during the day.

hydroelectric power electricity generated by water power. In a typical hydroelectric power (HEP) scheme water stored in a reservoir, often created by damming a river, is piped into water turbines, coupled to electricity generators. In pumped-storage plants water flowing through the turbines is recycled. A tidal power station is a HEP plant that exploits the rise and fall of the tides. Today about one-fifth of the world's electricity comes from hydroelectric power.

nuclear energy energy from the inner core or nucleus of atoms, as opposed to energy released in chemical processes, which is derived from the electrons surrounding the nucleus.

nuclear fission as in an atom bomb, is achieved by allowing a neutron to strike the nucleus of an atom of uranium-235, which then splits apart to release perhaps two to three other neutrons. If the material is pure uranium-235, a chain reaction is set up when these neutrons in turn strike other nuclei. This happens with great rapidity, resulting in the tremendous burst of energy we associate with the atom bomb. However, the process can be controlled by absorbing excess neutrons in 'control rods' (which may be made of steel alloyed with boron), and slowing down the speed of those neutrons allowed to act. This is what is done inside a nuclear power plant.

nuclear fusion the process (release of thermonuclear energy by the condensation of hydrogen nuclei to helium nuclei) which occurred in the hydrogen bomb and, as a continuing reaction, in the sun and other stars. It avoids the loss of much of the energy produced which occurs in the original atom bomb, so that it is correspondingly more powerful. Attempts to harness it for commercial power production have so far not succeeded.

reactors there are various types of (fission) reactor in commercial use. In a gas-cooled reactor, a circulating gas under pressure (such as carbon dioxide) removes heat from the core of the reactor, which usually contains natural uranium and has neutron-absorbing control rods made of boron. The Calder Hall reactor is of this type. An advanced gas-cooled reactor (AGR) generally has enriched uranium oxide as its fuel. A water-cooled reactor, such as the steam-generating heavy-water reactor at Winfrith, Dorset, has water circulating through the hot core. The water is converted to steam which drives turbo-alternators for generating electricity. In a pressurized water reactor (PWR) the coolant consists of a sealed system of pressurized heavy water (deuterium oxide), which heats ordinary water to form steam in heat exchangers. The spent fuel from either type of reactor contains some plutonium, which can be extracted and used as fuel for the so-called fast breeder reactor (such as the one at Dounreay, Scotland). This produces more plutonium than it consumes (hence its name) by converting uranium placed in a blanket round the main core. The usual coolant is liquid sodium, a substance that is difficult to handle. A major danger with any type of reactor is the possibility of meltdown, which can result in the release of radioactive material. Problems can also arise over the processing of nuclear fuel and disposal of nuclear waste.

nuclear accidents the most serious have been:
Apr 1986 at Chernobyl (USSR): a leak from a

advanced gas-cooled (AGR) reactor (highly simplified)

loader

reactor   hot carbon dioxide

concrete biological shield

high pressure steam   turbines   electrical output

reheater

electrical generator

boiler

water

condenser

heat shield   fuel rod   boron steel control rod

non-pressurized boiling-water reactor, one of the largest in the Soviet Union, caused by overheating. The resulting clouds of radioactive isotopes were traced as far away as Sweden. Vast tracts of land and hundreds of people were contaminated.

1979 at Three Mile Island, Harrisburg, USA: a PWR (*p*ressurized *w*ater *r*eactor) leaked radioactive matter, a leak caused by a combination of mechanical and electrical failure, as well as operator error. In this type of reactor the heat formed by the fission of the uranium is carried away in a sealed and pressurized loop of irradiated water (chiefly 'heavy' water) to steam generators.

1957 at Windscale (now Sellafield), England: fire destroyed the core of a reactor, releasing lethal radioactive fumes into the atmosphere.

solar energy energy derived from the sun's radiation. A solar furnace, such as that built in 1970 at Odeillo in the French Pyrenees, has thousands of mirrors to focus the sun's rays; it produces uncontaminated, intensive heat for industrial and scientific or experimental purposes. Other solar heaters produce less energy and may have industrial or domestic uses. They usually consist of a black (heat-absorbing) panel containing pipes through which air or water is circulated, either by thermal convection or by a pump. Solar energy may also be harnessed indirectly using solar cells, made up of panels of semiconductor material (usually silicon) which generate electricity when illuminated by sunlight. Because of their high cost and low-power output, solar cells have found few applications outside space probes and artificial satellites.

turbine an engine in which steam, water or gas is made to spin a rotating shaft. Turbines are among the most powerful machines. Steam turbines are used to drive generators in power stations and ships' propellers; water turbines spin the generators in hydroelectric power plants; and gas turbines, in the guise of jet engines, power most aircraft, and drive machines in industry. The high-temperature, high-pressure steam for steam turbines is raised in boilers heated by furnaces burning

coal, oil or gas, or by nuclear energy. A steam turbine consists of a shaft, or rotor, which rotates inside a fixed casing (stator). The rotor carries 'wheels' consisting of blades, or vanes. The stator has vanes set between the vanes of the rotor, which direct the steam through the rotor vanes at the optimum angle.

windmill a mill with sails or vanes which by the action of wind upon them drive machinery for grinding corn, pumping water, and so on. Windmills were used in the East in ancient times, and in Europe they were first used in Germany and the Netherlands in the 12th century. The main types of windmill are the *'post' mill*, which is turned round a post when the direction of the wind changes, and *'tower' mill* which has a revolving turret on top. It usually has a device (fantail) that keeps the sails pointing into the wind. The energy crisis has led to modern experiments with wind turbines, designed to use wind power on a major scale. Mostly they have a propeller-type rotor mounted on a tall shell tower. The turbine drives a generator for producing electricity. Some wind turbines in the USA have an output of 2 megawatts.

steam supply · emerging steam · blades · shaft · direction of rotation

Afghanistan
Republic of (De Afghanistan Jamhuriat)

area 652,090 sq km/251,707 sq mi
capital Kabul
towns Kandahár, Herát

physical mountainous, with rivers and desert areas
head of state and government Najibullah Ahmadzai from 1986
political system military emergency
exports dried fruit, rare minerals, natural gas (piped to USSR), karakul lamb skins, Afghan coats
currency afgháni (99.25=£1 Mar 1989)
population (1985) 18,400,000 (more than 3 million have become refugees since 1979); annual growth rate 0.6%
life expectancy men 37, women 37
language Pushtu
religion Muslim: 80% Sunni, 20% Shi'ite
literacy 39% male/8% female (1985 est)
GDP $3.5 bn (1982); $168 per head of population
chronology
1747 Afghanistan became an independent emirate.
1838–1919 Afghan Wars waged between Afghanistan and Britain to counter the threat to British India from expanding Russian influence in Afghanistan.
1919 Afghanistan recovered full independence following Third Afghan War.
1953 Lt-Gen Daud Khan became prime minister and introduced reform programme.
1963 Daud Khan forced to resign and constitutional monarchy established.
1973 Monarchy overthrown in coup by Daud Khan.
1978 Daud Khan ousted by Taraki and the People's Democratic Party (PDP) of Afghanistan.
1979 Soviet invasion installed Babrak Karmal in power.
1986 Replacement of Karmal as leader by Dr Najibullah Ahmadzai. Partial Soviet troop withdrawal.
1988 New non-Marxist constitution adopted.
1989 Withdrawal of Soviet troops; civil war.

Albania
Socialist People's Republic of (Republika Popullore Socialiste e Shqipërisë)

area 28,748 sq km/11,100 sq mi
capital Tirana
towns Shkodër, Vlorë, chief port Durrës

physical mainly mountainous, with rivers flowing E–W, and a small coastal plain
head of state Ramiz Alia from 1982
head of government Adil Carcani from 1982
political system communism
exports crude oil, bitumen, chrome, iron ore, nickel, coal, copper wire, tobacco, fruit

currency lek (10.14=£1 Mar 1989)
population (1985) 2,960,000; annual growth rate 2.2%
life expectancy men 69, women 73
language Albanian
religion Muslim 70%, although since 1967 Albania is officially a secular state
literacy 75% (1983)
GDP $2.3 bn (1981 est); $830 per head of population
chronology
1912 Albania achieved independence from Turkey.
1925 Republic proclaimed.
1928–39 Monarchy of King Zog.
1939–44 Under first Italian and then German rule.
1946 Communist republic proclaimed under the leadership of Enver Hoxha.
1949 Admitted into Comecon.
1961 Break with Khrushchev's USSR.
1978 Break with 'revisionist' China.
1985 Death of Hoxha.
1987 Normal diplomatic relations restored with Canada, Greece, and West Germany.

1954 War for independence from France led by the National Liberation Front (FLN).
1963 Independence achieved. Ben Bella elected president.
1965 Ben Bella deposed by military, led by Col Houari Boumédienne.
1976 New constitution approved.
1978 Death of Boumédienne.
1979 Bendjedid Chadli elected president. Ben Bella released from house arrest. FLN adopted new party structure.
1981 Algeria helped in securing release of US prisoners in Iran.
1983 Chadli re-elected.
1988 Riots in protest at government policies; 170 killed. Reform programme introduced. Diplomatic relations with Egypt restored.
1989 In a referendum, Algerians voted for an end to one-party rule.

Algeria

Democratic and Popular Republic of
(al-Jumhuriya al-Jazairiya ad-Dimuqratiya ash-Shabiya)

area 2,381,745 sq km/919,590 sq mi
capital al-Jazair/Algiers
towns Qacentina/Constantine; ports are Ouahran/Oran, Annaba
physical coastal plains, mountain plateau, desert
head of state Benjedid Chadli from 1979
political system nationalistic socialism
exports oil, natural gas, iron, wine, olive oil
currency dinar (11.87=£1 Mar 1989)
population (1985 est) 21,720,000 (75% Arab, 25% Berber); annual growth rate 3.0%
life expectancy men 59, women 62
language Arabic (official); Berber, French
religion Sunni Muslim
literacy 63% male/37% female (1985 est)
GDP $51.7 bn (1984); $2,085 per head of population
chronology

Andorra

Principality of (Principat d'Andorra)

area 465 sq km/180 sq mi
capital Andorra-la-Vella
physical mountainous, with narrow valleys
head of state Joan Marti y Alanis (bishop of Seo de Urgel, Spain) and François Mitterrand (president of France)
head of government Josef Pintat Solens from 1984
political system feudalism
exports main industries tourism and

smuggling
currency French franc (10.89=£1 Mar 1989)
and Spanish peseta (200.25=£1 Mar 1989)
population (1985) 43,000 (25% Andorrans,
75% immigrant Spanish workers)
language 30% Catalan (official), 58%
Spanish, 7% French
religion Roman Catholic
literacy 100% (1984)
chronology
1970 Extension of franchise to third-
generation women and second-generation
men.
1976 First political party formed.
1977 Franchise extended to first-generation
Andorrans.
1981 First prime minister appointed by
General Council.

Angola
People's Republic of *(República Popular de
Angola)*

area 1,246,700 sq km/481,226 sq mi
capital and chief port Luanda
towns Lobito and Benguela, also ports
physical elevated plateau, desert in the S
head of state and government José Eduardo
dos Santos from 1979
political system nationalistic socialism
exports oil, coffee, diamonds, palm oil, sisal,
iron ore, fish

currency kwanza (52.02=£1 Mar 1989)
population (1985 est) 8,750,000 (largest ethnic
group Ovimbundu); annual growth rate 2.5%
life expectancy men 40, women 44
language Portuguese (official); Umbundu,
Kimbundu
religion Roman Catholic 46%, Protestant
12%, animist 42%
literacy 59% (1985)
GDP $7.6 bn (1982); $500 per head of
population
chronology
1951 Angola became an overseas territory of
Portugal.
1956 First independence movement formed,
the People's Movement for the Liberation of
Angola (MPLA).
1961 Unsuccessful independence rebellion.
1962 Second nationalist movement formed,
the National Front for the Liberation of
Angola (FNLA).
1966 Third nationalist movement formed, the
National Union for the Total Independence
of Angola (UNITA).
1975 Transitional government of
independence formed from representatives
of MPLA, FNLA, UNITA, and Portuguese
government. MPLA supported by USSR
and Cuba, FNLA by 'non-left' power groups
of southern Africa, and UNITA by Western

powers. Angola declared independent.
MPLA proclaimed People's Republic under
the presidency of Dr Agostinho Neto. FNLA
and UNITA proclaimed People's Democratic
Republic of Angola.
1976 MPLA gained control of most of the
country. South African troops withdrawn but
Cuban units remained.
1977 MPLA restructured to become the
People's Movement for the Liberation of
Angola–Workers' Party (MPLA-PT).
1979 Death of Neto, succeeded by José
Eduardo dos Santos.
1980 Constitution amended to provide for an
elected people's assembly. UNITA guerrillas,
aided by South Africa, continued to operate
South African raids on the South West Africa
People's Organization's bases in Angola.
1984 The Lusaka agreement.
1985 South African forces officially
withdrawn.
1986 Further South African raids into
Angola. UNITA continuing to receive South
African support.
1988 Peace treaty, providing for the
withdrawal of all foreign troops, signed with
South Africa and Cuba.
1989 Ceasefire agreed with UNITA.

Antigua and Barbuda
State of

area Antigua 280 sq km/108 sq mi, Barbuda
160 sq km/62 sq mi, plus Redonda 1 sq
km/0.4 sq mi
capital and chief port St John's
physical tropical island country
head of state Elizabeth II from 1981
represented by Wilfred Ebenezer Jacobs
head of government Vere C Bird from 1981
political system liberal democracy
exports sea-island cotton, rum
currency East Caribbean dollar (4.66=£1 Mar
1989)
population (1986) 81,500; annual growth rate
1.3%
language English
religion Christian
literacy 90% (1985)
GDP $130 million (1983); $1,850 per head of

population
chronology
1967 Antigua and Barbuda became an
associated state within the Commonwealth,
with full internal independence.
1971 Progressive Labour Movement (PLM)
won the general election by defeating the
Antigua Labour Party (ALP).
1976 PLM called for early independence but
ALP urged caution. ALP won the general
election.
1981 Full independence.
1983 Assisted US invasion of Grenada.
1984 ALP won a decisive victory in the
general election.
1985 ALP re-elected.

Argentina
Republic of (República Argentina)

area 2,780,092 sq km/1,073,115 sq mi
capital Buenos Aires
towns Rosario, Córdoba, Tucumán,
Mendoza, Santa Fé; ports are La Plata and
Bahía Blanca
physical mountains in the W, forest in the N
and E, pampas (treeless plains) in the central
area; rivers Colorado, Paraná, Uruguay, Rio
de la Plata estuary
territories Tierra del Fuego; disputed claims
to S Atlantic islands; part of Antarctica
head of state and government Carlos Menem
from 1989

political system emergent democracy
exports beef, livestock, cereals, wool, tannin, groundnuts, linseed oil, minerals (coal, copper, molybdenum, gold, silver, lead, zinc, barium, uranium), and the country has huge resources of oil, natural gas, and hydroelectric power
currency austral (73.08=£1 Mar 1989)
population (1986) 31,060,000 (mainly of Spanish or Italian origin, only about 30,000 American Indians surviving); annual growth rate 1.6%
life expectancy men 66, women 73
language Spanish
religion Roman Catholic (state-supported)
literacy 96% male/95% female (1985 est)
GDP $58 bn (1983); $2,331 per head of population
chronology
1816 Achieved independence from Spain.
1946 Juan Perón elected president, supported by his wife 'Evita'.
1952 'Evita' Perón died.
1955 Perón overthrown and civilian administration restored.
1966 Coup brought back military rule.
1973 The Perónist party won the presidential and congressional elections. Perón returned from exile in Spain as president, with his

third wife, 'Isabelita', as vice-president.
1974 Perón died. Succeeded by 'Isabelita'.
1976 Coup resulted in rule by a military junta led by Lt-Gen Jorge Videla. Congress dissolved and hundreds of people, including 'Isabelita' Perón, detained.
1976–78 Ferocious campaign against left-wing elements. The start of the 'dirty war'.
1978 Videla retired. Succeeded by Gen Roberto Viola, who promised a return to democracy.
1981 Viola died suddenly. Replaced by Gen Leopoldo Galtieri.
1982 With a deteriorating economy, Galtieri sought popular support by ordering an invasion of the British-held Falkland Islands. After losing the short war, Galtieri was removed and replaced by Gen Reynaldo Bignone.
1983 Amnesty law passed and 1853 democratic constitution revived. General elections won by Dr Raúl Alfonsín and his party. Armed forces under scrutiny.
1984 Commission on the Disappearance of Persons (CONADEP) reported on over 8,000 people who had disappeared during the 'dirty war' of 1976–83.
1985 A deteriorating economy forced Alfonsín to seek help from the IMF and introduce a harsh austerity programme.
1986 Unsuccessful attempt on Alfonsín's life.
1988 Unsuccessful army coup attempt.
1989 30-day state of siege declared after rioting following price measures and dramatic inflation. Carlos Menem, a Perónist, elected president.

Australia
Commonwealth of

area 7,682,300 sq km/2,965,368 sq mi
capital Canberra
towns Adelaide, Alice Springs, Brisbane, Darwin, Melbourne, Perth, Sydney
physical the world's driest continent, arid in N and W, Great Dividing Range in the E; NE peninsula has rainforest; rivers N–S and Darling River and Murray system E–S; Lake Eyre basin and fertile Nullarbor Plain in S
territories Norfolk Island, Christmas Island,

Cocos Islands; part of Antarctica
head of state Elizabeth II from 1952
represented by Ninian Stephen
head of government Robert Hawke from 1983
political system liberal democracy
exports cereals, meat and dairy products;
wool (30% of world production); fruit, wine,
nuts, sugar, and honey; minerals include
bauxite (world's largest producer), coal,
iron, copper, lead, tin, zinc, opal, mineral
sands, and uranium; machinery and transport
equipment
currency Australian dollar (2.08=£1 Mar
1989)
population (1986) 15,970,000 (1.5%
Aborigines); annual growth rate 1.6%
life expectancy men 72, women 79
language English
religion Anglican 36%, other Protestant 25%,
Roman Catholic 33%
literacy 100% (1984)
GDP $170.2 bn (1984); $9,960 per head of
population
chronology
1901 Creation of Commonwealth of
Australia.
1911 Site for capital at Canberra acquired.
1944 Liberal Party founded by Robert
Menzies.
1966 Menzies resigned after being Liberal
prime minister for 17 years, and was
succeeded by Harold Holt.
1968 John Gorton became prime minister
after Holt's death.

1971 Gorton succeeded by William
McMahon, heading a Liberal–Country Party
coalition.
1972 Gough Whitlam became prime minister,
leading a Labour government.
1975 Senate blocked the government's
financial legislation; Whitlam declined to
resign but was dismissed by the governor
general, who invited Malcom Fraser to
form a Liberal–Country Party caretaker
government. The action of the governor
general, John Kerr, was widely criticized.
1977 Kerr resigned.
1983 Australian Labour Party, returned
to power under Bob Hawke, convened a
meeting of employers and unions to seek a
consensus on economic policy to deal with
growing unemployment.
1988 Labour foreign minister Bill Hayden
appointed governor general designate. Free
trade agreement with New Zealand signed.
1989 Leaders of both Opposition Liberal
and National parties ousted by votes of no
confidence.

Austria
Republic of (Republik Österreich)

area 83,855 sq km/32,368 sq mi
capital Vienna
towns Graz, Linz, Salzburg, Innsbruck
physical mountainous, with the Danube river

basin in the E
head of state Kurt Waldheim from 1986
head of government Franz Vranitzky from
1986
political system liberal democracy
exports minerals, manufactured goods
currency schilling (22.58=£1 Mar 1989)
population (1986) 7,570,000; annual growth
rate 0%
life expectancy men 70, women 77
language German
religion Roman Catholic 90%
literacy 98% (1983)
GDP $66.7 bn (1983); $8,280 per head of
population
chronology
1918 Hapsburg rule ended, republic
proclaimed.
1938 Incorporated into German Third Reich
by Hitler.
1945 1920 constitution reinstated and
coalition government formed by the Socialist
Party of Austria (SPÖ) and the Austrian
People's Party (ÖVP).
1955 Allied occupation ended and the
independence of Austria formally recognized.
1966 ÖVP in power with Josef Klaus as
chancellor.
1970 SPÖ formed a minority government,
with Dr Bruno Kreisky as chancellor.
1983 Kreisky resigned and was replaced by
Dr Fred Sinowatz, leading a coalition.
1986 Dr Kurt Waldheim elected president.
Sinowatz resigned and was succeeded
by Franz Vranitzky. In the Nov general
election no party won an overall majority
and Vranitzky formed a coalition of the
SPÖ and the ÖVP, with the ÖVP leader,
Dr Alois Mock, as vice-chancellor. Sinowatz
denounced the coalition as a betrayal of
socialist principles and resigned his SPÖ
chair.

Bahamas
Commonwealth of the

area 13,864 sq km/5,352 sq mi
capital Nassau on New Providence
physical comprises 700 tropical coral islands
and about 1,000 cays

head of state Elizabeth II from 1973
represented by Gerald C Cash from 1979
head of government Lynden Oscar Pindling
from 1967

political system liberal democracy
exports cement, pharmaceuticals, petroleum
products, crawfish, rum, pulpwood; over half
the islands' employment comes from tourism
currency Bahamian dollar (1.72=£1 Mar
1989)
population 235,000 (1986); annual growth rate
1.8%
language English
religion Christian
literacy 93% (1985)
GDP $780 million (1981); $5,756 per head of
population
chronology
1964 Internal self-government attained.
1967 First national assembly elections.
1972 Constitutional conference to discuss full
independence.
1973 Full independence achieved.
1983 Allegations of drug trafficking by
government ministers.
1984 Deputy prime minister and two cabinet
ministers resigned. Pindling denied any
personal involvement and was endorsed as
party leader.
1987 Pindling re-elected despite claims of
frauds.

493

Bahrain

area 687.75 sq km/265.5 sq mi
capital Manama on the largest island (also called Bahrain)
towns oil port Mina Sulman

physical 33 islands, flat and hot
head of state and government Sheikh Isa bin Sulman Al-Khalifa (1933–   ) from 1961
political system absolutism
exports oil and natural gas
currency Bahrain dinar (0.65=£1 Mar 1989)
population (1985) 400,000 (two thirds are nationals); annual growth rate 4.4%
life expectancy men 67, women 71
language Arabic, Farsi
religion Muslim (Shi'ite 60%, Sunni 40%)
literacy 79% male/64% female (1985 est)
GDP $4.1 bn (1984); $6,315 per head of population
chronology
1816 Under British protection.
1968 Britain announced its intention to withdraw its forces. Bahrain formed, with Qatar and the Trucial States, the Federation of Arab Emirates.
1971 Qatar and the Trucial States left the federation and Bahrain became an independent state.
1973 New constitution adopted, with an elected national assembly.
1975 Prime minister resigned and national assembly dissolved. Emir and his family assumed virtually absolute power.
1986 Gulf University established in Bahrain. A causeway (24 km/15 mi long) linking the island with Saudi Arabia was opened.

Bangladesh
People's Republic of

area 144,000 sq km/55,585 sq mi
capital Dhaka (formerly Dacca)
towns ports Chittagong, Khulna

physical flat delta of rivers Ganges and Brahmaputra; annual rainfall of 2,540 mm/100 in; some 75% of the land is less than 3 m/10 ft above sea level and vulnerable to flooding and cyclones
head of state and government Hussain Mohammad Ershad from 1983
political system emergent democracy
exports jute (50% of world production), tea
currency taka (55.00=£1 Mar 1989)
population (1985) 98,660,000; annual growth rate 2.7%
life expectancy men 48, women 47
language Bangla (Bengali)
religion Sunni Muslim 85%, Hindu 14%
literacy 43% male/22% female (1985 est)
GDP $11.2 bn (1983); $119 per head of population
chronology
1947 Formed into E province of Pakistan on

partition of British India.

1970 Half a million killed in flood.

1971 Independent Bangladesh emerged under leadership of Sheikh Mujib ur-Rahman after civil war.

1975 Assassination of Sheikh Mujib. Martial law imposed.

1976–77 Maj-Gen Zia ur-Rahman assumed power.

1978–79 Elections held and civilian rule restored.

1981 Assassination of Maj-Gen Zia.

1982 Lt-Gen Ershad assumed power in army coup. Martial law imposed.

1986 Elections held but disputed. Martial law ended.

1987 State of emergency declared in response to opposition demonstrations.

1988 Assembly elections boycotted by main opposition parties. State of emergency lifted. Islam made state religion. Monsoon floods and a cyclone left 35 million homeless and thousands dead.

Barbados

area 430 sq km/166 sq mi
capital Bridgetown

physical most easterly island of the West Indies; surrounded by coral reefs
head of state Elizabeth II from 1966 represented by Hugh Springer from 1984
head of government Erskine Lloyd Sandiford

from 1987
political system liberal democracy
exports sugar, rum, oil
currency Barbados dollar (3.47=£1 Mar 1989)
population (1985) 250,000; annual growth rate 0.3%
life expectancy men 70, women 75
language English
religion Christian
literacy 99% (1984)
GDP $1 bn (1984); $3,040 per head of population
chronology

1951 Universal adult suffrage introduced. The Barbados Labour Party (BLP) won the general election.

1954 Ministerial government established.

1961 Full internal self-government. Democratic Labour Party (DLP), led by Errol Barrow, in power.

1966 Barbados achieved full independence within the Commonwealth. Barrow became the new nation's first prime minister.

1972 Diplomatic relations with Cuba established.

1976 BLP, led by Tom Adams, returned to power.

1983 Barbados supported US invasion of Grenada.

1985 Adams died suddenly. Bernard St John became prime minister.

1986 DLP, led by Barrow, returned to power.

1987 Barrow died, succeeded by Erskine Lloyd Sandiford.

Belgium

Kingdom of (French *Royaume de Belgique*, Flemish *Koninkrijk België*)

area 30,513 sq km/11,779 sq mi
capital Brussels
towns Ghent, Liège, Charleroi, Bruges, Mons, Blankenburghe, Knokke; ports are Antwerp, Ostend, Zeebrugge
physical mostly flat, with hills and forest in SE
head of state King Baudouin from 1951
head of government Wilfried Martens from 1981
political system liberal democracy

exports iron and steel, textiles, manufactured goods, petrochemicals
currency Belgian franc (67.35=£1 Mar 1989)
population (1985 est) 9,900,000 (comprising Flemings and Walloons); annual growth rate 0.1%
life expectancy men 70, women 77
language in the N (Flanders) Flemish (a Dutch dialect, known as *Vlaams*) 55%, in the S (Wallonia) Walloon (a French dialect which is almost a separate language) 44%, with 11% bilingual, and German (E border); all are official
religion Roman Catholic
literacy 98% (1984)
GDP $77 bn (1984); $3,040 per head of population
chronology
1830 Belgium became an independent kingdom.
1914 Invaded by Germany.
1940 Again invaded by Germany.
1948 Belgium became founder member of Benelux Customs Union.
1949 Belgium became founder member of Council of Europe.
1951 Leopold III abdicated in favour of his son Baudouin.
1952 Belgium became founder member of European Coal and Steel Community (ECSC).

1957 Belgium became founder member of the European Community (EEC).
1971 Steps towards regional autonomy taken.
1972 German-speaking members of the cabinet included for the first time.
1973 Linguistic parity achieved in government appointments.
1974 Separate regional councils and ministerial committees established.
1978 Wilfried Martens succeeds Leo Tindemans as prime minister.
1980 Open violence over language divisions. Regional assemblies for Flanders and Wallonia and a three-member executive for Brussels created.
1981 Short-lived coalition led by Mark Eyskens was followed by the return of Martens.
1987 Martens head of caretaker government after breakup of coalition.
1988 Following a general election, Martens formed a new coalition.

Belize

area 22,963 sq km/8,864 sq mi
capital Belmopan
towns port Belize City

physical half the country is forested, much of it high rain forest
head of state Elizabeth II from 1981 represented by Elmira Minita Gordon
head of government Manuel Esquivel from 1984

political system liberal democracy
exports sugar, citrus, rice, lobster
currency Belize dollar (3.45=£1 Mar 1989)
population (1985) 170,000 (including Maya minority in the interior); annual growth rate 2.5%
language English (official), but Spanish is widely spoken
religion Roman Catholic 60%, Protestant 35%, Hindu and Muslim minorities
literacy 80% (1985)
GDP $176 million (1983); $1,000 per head of population
chronology
1862 Belize became a British colony.
1954 Constitution adopted, providing for limited internal self-government. General election won by George Price.
1964 Full internal self-government granted.
1965 Two-chamber national assembly introduced, with Price as prime minister.
1970 Capital moved from Belize City to Belmopan.
1975 British troops sent to defend the frontier with Guatemala.
1977 Negotiations undertaken with Guatemala but no agreeement reached.
1980 United Nations called for full independence.
1981 Full independence achieved. Price became prime minister.
1984 Price defeated in general election. Manuel Esquivel formed the government. Britain reaffirmed its undertaking to defend the frontier.

Benin
People's Republic of (République Populaire du Benin)

area 112,600 sq km/43,464 sq mi
capital Porto Novo
towns Abomey, Natitingou; chief port Cotonou
physical flat, humid, with dense vegetation
head of state and government Mathieu Kerekou from 1972
political system nationalistic socialism
exports cocoa, groundnuts, cotton, palm oil
currency CFA franc (544.87=£1 Mar 1989)

population (1985) 3,930,000; annual growth rate 3%
life expectancy men 42, women 46
language French (official); Fan 47%
religion animist 65%, Christian 17%, Muslim 13%
literacy 37% male/16% female (1985 est)
GDP $1.1 bn (1983); $290 per head of population
chronology
1851 Under French control.
1958 Became self-governing dominion within the French Community.
1960–72 Acute political instability, with switches from civilian to military rule.
1972 Military regime established by Gen Mathieu Kerekou.
1974 Kerekou announced that the country would follow a path of 'scientific socialism'.
1975 Name of country changed from Dahomey to Benin.
1977 Return to civilian rule under a new constitution.
1980 Kerekou formally elected president by the National Revolutionary Assembly.

Bhutan
Kingdom of (Druk-yul)

area 46,500 sq km/17,949 sq mi
capital Thimphu
physical occupies S slopes of the Himalayas, and is cut by valleys of tributaries of the Brahmaputra
head of state and government Jigme Singye

Wangchuk from 1972
political system absolutism
exports timber, minerals
currency ngultrum (27.00=£1 Mar 1989); also
Indian currency
population 1,300,000 (1986 est); annual
growth rate 2%
life expectancy men 47, women 45
language Dzongkha (a Tibetan dialect),
Nepáli, and English (all official)
religion Mahayana Buddhist
literacy 10%
GDP $150 million (1983); $120 per head of
population
chronology
1865 Trade treaty with Britain signed.
1907 First hereditary monarch installed.
1910 Anglo-Bhutanese Treaty signed.
1945 Indo-Bhutan Treaty of Friendship
signed.
1952 King Jigme Dorji Wangchuk installed.
1953 National assembly established.
1959 4,000 Tibetan refugees given asylum.
1968 King established first cabinet.
1972 King died and was succeeded by his son
Jigme Singye Wangchuk.
1979 Tibetan refugees told to take up
Bhutanese citizenship or leave. Most stayed.
1983 Bhutan became a founder member
of the South Asian Regional Cooperation
organization (SARC).

498

Bolivia
Republic of (República de Bolivia)

area 1,098,000 sq km/424,000 sq mi
capital La Paz (seat of government), Sucre
(legal capital and seat of judiciary)
towns Santa Cruz, Cochabamba

physical high plateau between mountain
ridges; forest and lowlands in the E
head of state and government Víctor Paz
Estenssoro from 1985
government emergent democracy
exports tin (second largest world producer),
other non-ferrous metals, oil, gas (piped to
Argentina), agricultural products
currency boliviano (4.35=£1 Mar 1989)
population (1985) 6,430,000; (Quechua 25%,
Aymara 17%, Mestizo 30%, European
14%); annual growth rate 2.7%
language Spanish (official); Aymara,
Quechua
religion Roman Catholic (state-recognized)
literacy 84% male/65% female (1985 est)
GDP $3 bn (1983); $570 per head of
population
chronology
1825 Independence achieved.
1952 Dr Víctor Paz Estenssoro elected
president.

1956 Dr Hernan Siles Zuazo became president.
1960 Estenssoro returned to power.
1964 Army coup led by vice-president.
1966 Gen René Barrientos became president.
1967 Uprising, led by 'Che' Guevara, put down with US help.
1969 Barrientos killed in air crash, replaced by vice-president Siles Salinas. Army coup deposed him.
1970 Army coup put Gen Juan Torres Gonzalez in power.
1971 Torres replaced by Col Hugo Banzer Suarez.
1973 Banzer promised a return to democratic government.
1974 An attempted coup prompted Banzer to postpone elections and ban political and trade-union activity.
1978 Elections declared invalid after allegations of fraud.
1980 More inconclusive elections followed by another coup, led by Gen Garcia. Allegations of corruption and drug trafficking led to cancellation of US and EEC aid.
1981 Garcia forced to resign. Replaced by Gen Celso Torrelio Villa.
1982 Torrelio resigned. Replaced by military junta led by Gen Vildoso. Because of worsening economy, Vildoso asked congress to install a civilian administration. Dr Siles Zuazo chosen as president.
1983 Economic aid from US and Europe resumed.
1984 New coalition government formed by Siles. Attempted abduction of president by right-wing officers. The president undertook a five-day hunger strike as an example to the nation.
1985 President Siles resigned. Election result inconclusive. Dr Paz Estenssoro, at the age of 77, chosen by congress.

Botswana

area 582,000 sq km/224,652 sq mi
capital Gaborone
physical desert in SW, plains in E, fertile lands and swamp in N
head of state and government Quett Ketamile

Joni Masire from 1980
political system liberal democracy
exports diamonds, copper-nickel, meat
currency pula (3.52=£1 Mar 1989)
population (1985) 1,090,000 (80% Bamangwato, 20% Bangwaketse); annual growth rate 3.8%
life expectancy men 53, women 56
language English (official); Setswana (national)
religion Christian (majority)
literacy 73% male/69% female (1985 est)
GDP $810 million (1984); $544 per head of population
chronology
1885 Became a British protectorate.
1960 New constitution created a legislative council.
1963 End of high-commission rule.
1965 Capital transferred fron Mafeking to Gaborone. Internal self-government granted. Seretse Khama elected head of government.
1966 Full independence achieved. New constitution came into effect. Name changed from Bechuanaland to Botswana. Seretse Khama elected president.
1980 Seretse Khama died and was succeeded by Vice-President Quett Masire.
1984 Masire re-elected.
1985 South African raid on Gaborone.

1987 Joint permanent commission with Mozambique established, to improve relations.

Brazil
Federative Republic of *(República Federativa do Brasil)*

area 8,512,000 sq km/3,286,000 sq mi
capital Brasília
towns Sao Paulo, Belo Horizonte, Curitiba, Fortaleza; ports are Rio de Janeiro, Recife, Porto Alegre, Salvador

physical the densely forested Amazon basin covers the N half of the country with a network of rivers; the S is fertile; enormous energy resources, both hydroelectric (Itaipú dam on the Paraná, and Tucurui on the Tocantins) and nuclear (uranium ores)
head of state and government José Sarney from 1985
political system emergent democracy
exports coffee, sugar, cotton, textiles, motor vehicles, iron, chrome, manganese, tungsten and other ores, as well as quartz crystals, industrial diamonds
currency cruzado (introduced 1986; value = 100 cruzeiros, the former unit) (1.72=£1 Mar 1989)
population (1985) 135,560,000 (including 200,000 Indians, survivors of 5 million, especially in Rondonia and Mato Grosso, mostly living on reserves); annual growth rate 2.2%
life expectancy men 61, women 66
language Portuguese; 120 Indian languages
religion Roman Catholic 89%, Indian faiths
literacy 79% male/76% female (1985 est)
GDP $218 bn (1984); $1,523 per head of population
chronology
1822 Brazil became an independent empire, ruled by Dom Pedro, son of the refugee King John VI of Portugal.
1889 Monarchy abolished and republic established.
1891 Constitution for a federal state adopted.
1930 Dr Getulio Vargas became president.
1945 Vargas deposed by the military.
1946 New constitution adopted.
1950 Vargas returned to office.
1954 Vargas committed suicide.
1956 Juscelino Kubitschek became president.
1960 Capital moved to Brasília.
1961 João Goulart became president.
1964 Bloodless coup made Gen Castelo Branco president. He assumed dictatorial powers, abolishing free political parties.
1967 New constitution adopted. Branco succeeded by Marshal da Costa e Silva.
1969 Da Costa e Silva resigned and a military junta took over.
1974 Gen Ernesto Geisel became president.
1978 Gen Baptista de Figueiredo became president.
1979 Political parties legalized again.
1984 Mass calls for a return to fully democratic government.
1985 Tancredo Neves became first civilian president for 21 years. Neves died and was succeeded by the vice-president, José Sarney.
1988 New constitution approved, transferring power from the president to the congress. Measures announced to halt large-scale burning of Amazonian rainforest.
1989 Forest Protection Service and Ministry for Land Reform abolished.

Brunei

area 5,765 sq km/2,225 sq mi
capital and chief port Bandar Seri Begawan

physical 75% of the area is forested; the
Limbang valley splits Brunei in two, and its
cession to Sarawak in 1890 is disputed by
Brunei
head of state and of government Muda
Hassanal Bolkiah Mu'izzaddin Waddaulah
from 1968
political system absolutism
exports liquefied natural gas (world's largest
producer) and oil, both expected to be
exhausted by 2000 AD
currency Brunei dollar (3.35=£1 Mar 1989)
population (1985) 220,000 (of Malaysian
origin); 50,000 Chinese (few granted
citizenship); annual growth rate 12%
language Malay (official), English
religion Muslim
literacy 75% male/50% female (1971)
GDP $3.8 bn (1983); $20,000 per head of
population
chronology
1888 Brunei became a British protectorate.
1941–45 Occupied by Japan.
1959 Written constitution made Britain
responsible for defence and external affairs.
1962 Sultan began rule by decree.

1963 Proposal to join Malaysia abandoned.
1967 Sultan abdicated in favour of his son
Hassanal Bolkiah.
1971 Brunei given internal self-government.
1975 UN resolution called for independence
for Brunei.
1984 Full independence achieved, with
Britain maintaining a small force to protect
the oil and gas fields.
1985 A 'loyal and reliable' political party
legalized.

Bulgaria
*People's Republic of (Narodna Republika
Bulgaria)*

area 110,912 sq km/42,812 sq mi
capital Sofia
towns Plovdiv, Rusé; Burgas and Varna are
Black Sea ports

physical Balkan and Rhodope mountains;
river Danube in the N
head of state Todor Zhivkov from 1971 (also
head of Politburo)
head of government Georgi Atanasov from
1986
political system communism
exports textiles, chemicals, non-ferrous
metals, timber, minerals, machinery
currency lev (1.49=£1 Mar 1989)
population (1985) 8,960,000 (including

501

800,000 ethnic Turks now subjected to compulsory assimilation); annual growth rate 0.5%
life expectancy men 69, women 74
language Bulgarian, Turkish
religion Eastern Orthodox Christian 90%, Sunni Muslim 10%, but the latter faith is discouraged
literacy 96% male/93% female (1980 est)
GNP $26 bn (1983); $2,625 per head of population
chronology
1908 Bulgaria became a kingdom independent of Turkish rule.
1944 Soviet invasion of German-occupied Bulgaria.
1946 Monarchy abolished and communist-dominated people's republic proclaimed.
1947 Soviet-style constitution adopted.
1949 Death of Georgi Dimitrov.
1954 Election of Todor Zhivkov as Communist Party general secretary.
1971 Constitution modified. Zhivkov elected president.
1985–86 Large-scale administrative and personnel changes made under Soviet stimulus.
1987 New electoral law introduced multi-candidate elections.

Burkina Faso
'Land of Upright Men'

area 274,000 sq km/106,000 sq mi
capital Ouagadougou
towns Bobo-Doiulasso
physical landlocked plateau, savannah country; headwaters of the river Volta
head of state and government Blaise Compaore from 1987
political system military authoritarianism
exports cotton, groundnuts, livestock, hides, skins
currency CFA franc (544.87=£1 Mar 1989)
population (1985) 6,640,000; annual growth rate 2.4%
life expectancy men 44, women 47
language French (official); about 50 native languages
religion animist 53%, Sunni Muslim 36%,

Roman Catholic 11%
literacy 21% male/6% female (1985 est)
GDP $1.2 bn (1983); $180 per head of population
chronology
1958 Became a self-governing republic within the French Community.
1960 Full independence achieved, with Maurice Yameogo as the first president.
1966 Military coup led by Col Lamizana. Constitution suspended, political activities banned, and a supreme council of the armed forces established.
1969 Ban on political activities lifted.
1970 Referendum approved a new constitution leading to a return to civilian rule.
1974 After experimenting with a mixture of military and civilian rule, Lamizana reassumed full power.
1977 Ban on political activities removed. Referendum approved a new constitution based on civilian rule.
1978 Lamizana elected president.
1980 Lamizana overthrown in a bloodless coup led by Col Zerbo.
1982 Zerbo ousted in a coup by junior officers. Maj Ouédraogo became president and Thomas Sankara prime minister.
1983 Sankara seized complete power.
1984 Upper Volta renamed Burkina Faso.
1987 Sankara killed in coup led by Blaise Compaore.

Burma
***Socialist Republic of the Union of** (Pyidaungsu Socialist Thammada Myanma Naingngandaw)*

area 678,000 sq km/261,789 sq mi
capital and chief port Rangoon
towns Mandalay, Karbe

physical over half is forested; rivers Irrawaddy and Chindwin; mountains in N, W, and E
head of state and government Saw Maung from 1989
political system nationalistic socialism
exports rice, rubber, jute, teak, jade, rubies, sapphires
currency kyat (11.41=£1 Mar 1989)
population (1985) 37,150,000; annual growth rate 1.9%
life expectancy men 56, women 59
language Burmese
religion Hinayana Buddhist; religious centre Pagan
literacy 76% male/66% female (1980 est)
GDP $6.5 bn (1983); $174 per head of population
chronology
1886 United as province of British India.
1937 Became crown colony in the British Commonwealth.
1942–45 Occupied by Japan.

1948 Granted independence from Britain. Left the Commonwealth.
1962 Gen Ne Win assumed power in army coup.
1973–74 Adoption of presidential-style 'civilian' constitution.
1975 Formation of opposition National Democratic Front.
1988 The government resigned after violent demonstrations. Two changes of regime later, Gen Saw Maung seized power in a military coup in Sept with over 1,000 killed. He announced the end of the one-party system and elections in May 1989.

Burundi
Republic of

area 27,834 sq km/10,747 sq mi
capital Bujumbura
towns Kitega

physical grassy highland
head of state and government Pierre Buyoya from 1987
political system military authoritarianism
exports coffee, cotton, tea, nickel, hides, livestock; there are also 500 million tonnes of peat reserves in the basin of the Akanyaru river
currency Burundi franc (264.38=£1 Mar 1989)
population (1985) 4,720,000 (of whom 15% are the Nilotic Tutsi, still holding most of the land and political power, and the remainder the Bantu Hutu); annual growth rate 2.8%

503

life expectancy men 45, women 48
language Kirundi (a Bantu language) and
French (official); Kiswahili
religion Roman Catholic over 50%, with a
Sunni Muslim minority
literacy 43% male/26% female (1985)
GDP $1 bn (1983); $273 per head of
population
chronology
1962 Separated from Ruanda-Urundi, as
Burundi, and given independence as a
monarchy under King Mwambutsa IV.
1966 King deposed by his son Charles, who
became Ntare V and was in turn deposed by
his prime minister, Capt Michel Micombero,
who declared Burundi a republic.
1972 Ntare V killed, allegedly by the Hutu
ethnic group. Massacres of 150,000 Hutus
by the rival Tutsi ethnic group, of which
Micombero was a member.
1973 Micombero made president and prime
minister.
1974 Union for National Progress
(UPRONA) declared the only legal political
party, with the president as its secretary
general.
1976 Army coup deposed Micombero. Col
Jean-Baptiste Bagaza appointed president by
Supreme Revolutionary Council.
1981 New constitution adopted, providing for
a national assembly.
1984 Bagaza elected president as sole
candidate.
1987 Bagaza deposed in coup in Sept. Maj
Pierre Buyoya headed new Military Council
for National Redemption.
1988 Some 24,000 majority Hutus killed by
Tutsis. First Hutu prime minister appointed.

Cameroon
United Republic of (République du Cameroun)

---

area 474,000 sq km/183,580 sq mi
capital Yaoundé
towns chief port Douala
physical desert in the far N in the Lake
Chad basin, dry savanna plateau in the
intermediate area, and in the S dense tropical
rainforest
head of state and of government Paul Biya

from 1982
political system authoritarian nationalism
exports cocoa, coffee, bananas, cotton,
timber, rubber, groundnuts, gold, aluminium
currency CFA franc (544.87=£1 Mar 1989)
population 10,190,000 (1985); annual growth
rate 2.7%
life expectancy men 49, women 53
language French and English in pidgin
variations (official), but there has been some
discontent with the emphasis on French;
there are 163 indigenous peoples with many
African languages
religion Roman Catholic 35%, animist 25%,
Muslim 22%, Protestant 18%
literacy 68% male/45% female (1985 est)
GDP $7.3 bn (1984); $802 per head of
population
chronology
1884 Under German rule.
1916 Captured by Allied forces in World War
I.
1922 Divided between Britain and France.
1946 French and British Cameroons made
UN trust territories.
1960 French Cameroon became the
independent Republic of Cameroon.
Ahmadou Ahidjo elected president.
1961 N part of British Cameroon merged with
Nigeria and S part joined the Republic of
Cameroon to become the Federal Republic of
Cameroon.
1966 A one-party regime was introduced.
1972 New constitution made Cameroon

a unitary state, the United Republic of Cameroon.

1973 New national assembly elected.

1982 Ahidjo resigned and was succeeded by Paul Biya.

1983 Biya began to remove his predecessor's supporters and was accused by Ahidjo of trying to create a police state. Ahidjo went into exile in France.

1984 Biya re-elected and defeated a plot to overthrow him. Country's name changed to Republic of Cameroon.

1988 Biya re-elected.

Canada
Dominion of

area 9,958,384 sq km/3,843,936 sq mi
capital Ottawa
towns Toronto, Montreal, Vancouver,

Winnipeg, Edmonton, Quebec, Hamilton, Calgary

physical St Lawrence Seaway, Mackenzie river; Great Lakes; Arctic Archipelago; Rocky Mountains; Great Plains or Prairies; Canadian Shield

territories Arctic sector N of mainland

head of state Elizabeth II from 1952 represented by Jeanne Sauvé

head of government Brian Mulroney from 1984

political system liberal democracy

exports wheat; timber, pulp and newsprint; fish, especially salmon; furs (ranched fox and mink exceed the value of wild furs); oil and natural gas; aluminium, asbestos, coal, copper, iron, nickel; motor vehicles and parts, industrial and agricultural machinery, fertilizers

currency Canadian dollar (2.05=£1 Mar 1989)

population (1986) 25,354,000 (including 300,000 American Indians, of whom 75% live on over 2,000 reserves in Ontario and the four W provinces; some 300,000 Métis (people of mixed race) and 19,000 Inuit (or Eskimo), of whom 75% live in the NW Territories). Over half Canada's population lives in Ontario and Quebec. Annual growth rate 1.1%

life expectancy men 72, women 79

language English, French (both official) (about 70% speak English, 20% French, and the rest are bilingual); there are also N American Indian languages and the Inuit Inuktitut

religion Roman Catholic 40%, Protestant 35%

literacy 99%

GDP $317 bn (1984); $13,000 per head of population

chronology

1957 Progressive Conservatives returned to power after 36 years in opposition.

1963 Liberals elected under Lester Pearson.

1968 Pearson suceeded by Pierre Trudeau.

1979 Joe Clark, leader of the Progressive Conservatives, formed a minority government.

1980 Clark defeated on budget proposals. Liberals under Trudeau returned with a large majority.

1982 Canada Act removed Britain's last legal control over Canadian affairs.

1983 Clark replaced as leader of the Progressive Conservatives by Brian Mulroney.

1984 Trudeau retired and was succeeded as Liberal leader and prime minister by John Turner. Progressive Conservatives won the general election and Brian Mulroney became

prime minister.
1988 Conservatives re-elected. Free trade agreement with USA signed.

Cape Verde
Republic of (*República de Cabo Verde*)

area 4,033 sq km/1,557 sq mi
capital Praia
physical archipelago of ten islands 565 km/218 mi W of Senegal

head of state and government Aristides Pereira from 1975
political system nationalistic socialism
exports bananas, coffee
currency Cape Verde escudo (131.61=£1 Mar 1989)
population (1985) 330,000 (including some 100,000 Angolan refugees); annual growth rate 1.9%
life expectancy men 57, women 61
language Creole dialect of Portuguese
religion Roman Catholic 80%
literacy 61% male/39% female (1985)
GDP $110 million (1983); $300 per head of population
chronology
1974 Moved towards independence through a transitional Portuguese-Cape Verde government.
1975 Full independence achieved. National people's assembly elected. Aristides Pereira became the first president.
1980 Constitution adopted providing for eventual union with Guinea-Bissau.

1981 Union with Guinea-Bissau abandoned and the constitution amended; became one-party state.

Central African Republic
(*République centrafricaine*)

area 625,000 sq km/240,000 sq mi
capital Bangui
physical most of the country is on a plateau, with rivers flowing N and S. The N is dry and there is rainforest in the SW

head of state and government André Kolingba from 1981
political system military authoritarianism
exports diamonds, uranium, coffee, cotton, timber
currency CFA franc (544.87=£1 Mar 1989)
population 2,610,000 (1985); annual growth rate 2.3%
life expectancy men 41, women 45
language Sangho, French (both official)
religion animist over 50%; Christian 35%, both Catholic and Protestant; Muslim 10%
literacy 53% male/29% female (1985 est)
GNP $690 million (1983); $310 per head of population
chronology
1960 Central African Republic achieved independence from France with David Dacko elected president.
1962 The republic made a one-party state.
1965 Dacko ousted in a military coup led by Col Bokassa.
1966 Constitution rescinded and national

assembly dissolved.

1972 Bokassa declared himself president for life.

1976 Bokassa made himself emperor of the Central African Empire.

1979 Bokassa deposed by Dacko following violent repressive measures by the self-styled emperor, who went into exile.

1981 Dacko deposed in a bloodless coup, led by Gen André Kolingba, and an all-military government established.

1983 Clandestine opposition movement formed.

1984 Amnesty for all political party leaders announced. President Mitterrand of France paid a state visit.

1985 New constitution, with some civilians in the government, promised.

1986 Formal trial of Bokassa started. Gen Kolingba re-elected.

Bokassa found guilty and received death sentence, later commuted to life imprisonment.

Chad
Republic of (République du Tchad)

---

area 1,284,000 sq km/495,600 sq mi
capital N'djamena
physical savanna and part of Sahara Desert in the N; rivers in the S flow N to Lake Chad in the marshy E

head of state and government Hissène Habré from 1982

political system authoritarian nationalism
exports cotton, meat, livestock, hides, skins, bauxite, uranium, gold, oil
currency CFA franc (544.87 = £1 Mar 1989)
population 5,241,000 (1987 est); annual growth rate 2.3%
life expectancy men 41, women 45
language French (official), Arabic
religion Muslim (north); Christian, animist (south)
literacy 40% male/11% female (1985 est)
GDP $360 million (1984); $88 per head of population
chronology
1960 Independence from France achieved, with François Tombalbaye as president.
1963 Violent opposition in the Muslim N, led by the Chadian National Liberation Front (Frolinat), backed by Libya.
1968 Revolt quelled with French help.
1975 Tombalbaye killed in military coup led by Felix Malloum. Frolinat continued its resistance.
1978 Malloum tried to find a political solution by bringing the former Frolinat leader Hissenè Habré into his government but they were unable to work together.
1979 Malloum forced to leave the country. An interim government was set up under Gen Goukouni. Habré continued his opposition with his Army of the North (FAN).
1981 Habré was now in control of half the country, forcing Goukouni to flee to Cameroon and then Algeria, where, with Libyan support, he set up a 'government in exile'.
1983 Habré's regime recognized by the Organization for African Unity (OAU) but in the north Goukouni's supporters, with Libyan help, fought on. Eventually a ceasefire was agreed, dividing the country into two halves either side of latitude 16° N.
1984 Libya and France agreed a withdrawal of forces.
1985 Fighting between Libyan-backed and French-backed forces intensified.
1987 Chad, France, and Libya agree on ceasefire proposed by OAU.
1988 Full diplomatic relations with Libya

restored.
1989 Libyan troop movements reported on border.

Chile
Republic of (República de Chile)

area 741,765 sq km/286,400 sq mi
capital Santiago
towns Concepción, Vina del Mar, Temuco;

ports are Valparaiso, Antofagasta, Arica, Iquique
physical Andes mountains along E border, Atacama Desert in N, arable land and forest in the S
territories Easter Island, Juan Fernandez Island, half of Tierra del Fuego, and part of Antarctica
head of state and government Augusto Pinochet from 1973
political system military authoritarianism
exports copper, iron, nitrate (Chile is the chief mining country of S America); paper and pulp
currency peso (437.20=£1 Mar 1989)
population (1985) 12,070,000 (the majority mestizo, of mixed American Indian and Spanish descent); annual growth rate 1.6%
life expectancy men 67, women 73
language Spanish

religion Roman Catholic
literacy 95.4% (1985)
GNP $21.8 bn (1983); $1,950 per head of population
chronology
1818 Achieved independence from Spain.
1964 Christian Democrats formed government under Eduardo Frei.
1970 Dr Salvador Allende became the first democratically elected Marxist president. He embarked on an extensive programme of nationalization and social reform.
1973 Government overthrown by the CIA-backed military, led by Gen Augusto Pinochet. Allende killed. Policy of repression began during which all opposition was put down and political activity banned.
1983 Growing opposition to the regime from all sides, with outbreaks of violence.
1988 Plebiscite asking whether Pinochet should serve a further term resulted in a clear 'No' vote.

China
People's Republic of (Zhonghua Renmin Gonghe Guo)

area 9,569,700 sq km/3,694,000 sq mi
capital Beijing (Peking)
towns Chongqing (Chungking), Shenyang

(Mukden), Wuhan, Nanjing (Nanking), Harbin; ports Tianjin (Tientsin), Shanghai,

Qingdao (Tsingtao), Lüda (Lü-ta), Guangzhou (Canton)
physical two-thirds of China is mountains (in the N and SW) or desert; the E is irrigated by rivers Huang He (Yellow River), Chang Jiang (Yangtze-Kiang), Xi Jiang (Si Kiang)
head of state Yang Shangkun from 1988
head of government Li Peng from 1987
political system communism
exports tea; livestock and animal products; textiles (silk and cotton); oil, minerals (China is the world's largest producer of tungsten), chemicals; light industrial goods
currency yuan (6.41=£1 Mar 1989)
population (1985 est) 1,059 million (of whom the majority are Han or ethnic Chinese; the 67 million of other ethnic groups, including Tibetan, Uigur, and Zhuang, live in border areas). The number of people of Chinese origin outside China, Taiwan, and Hong Kong is estimated at 15–24 million. Annual growth rate 1.2%
life expectancy men 67, women 69
language Chinese
religion officially atheist, but traditionally Taoist, Confucianist, and Buddhist; Muslim 13 million; Catholic 3–6 million (divided between the 'patriotic' church established 1958 and the 'loyal' church subject to Rome); Protestant 3 million
literacy 82% male/66% female (1985 est)
GDP $313 bn (1983); $566 per head of population
chronology
1949 People's Republic of China proclaimed by Mao Zedong.
1954 Soviet-style constitution adopted.
1956–57 Hundred Flowers Movement encouraged criticism of the government.
1958–60 Great Leap Forward commune experiment to achieve 'true communism'.
1960 Withdrawal of Soviet technical advisers.
1962 Sino-Indian border war.
1962–65 Economic recovery programme under Liu Shaoqi; Maoist 'socialist education movement' rectification campaign.
1966–68 Great Proletarian Cultural Revolution and overthrow of Liu Shaoqi.
1969 Ussuri river border clashes with USSR.

1970–76 Reconstruction under Mao and Zhou Enlai; purge of extreme left.
1971 Entry into United Nations.
1972 US president Nixon visited Beijing.
1975 New state constitution. Unveiling of Zhou's Four Modernizations programme.
1976 Death of Zhou Enlai and Mao Zedong; appointment of Hua Guofeng as prime minister and Communist Party chair. Deng in hiding. Gang of Four arrested.
1977 Rehabilitation of Deng Xiaoping.
1979 Economic reforms introduced. Diplomatic relations opened with USA. Punitive invasion of Vietnam.
1980 Zhao Ziyang appointed prime minister.
1981 Hu Yaobang succeeded Hua as party chair. Imprisonment of Gang of Four.
1982 New state constitution adopted.
1984 'Enterprise management' reforms for industrial sector.
1986 Student demonstrations for democracy.
1987 Hu was replaced as party leader by Zhao, with Li Peng as prime minister. Deng left the Politburo but remained influential.
1988 Yang Shankun became state president. Economic reforms encountered increasing problems; inflation rocketing.
1989 Largest-ever pro-democracy student demonstrations followed death of Hu Yaobang and introduction of austerity budget. Martial law declared in Beijing. Brutal repression of demonstrations in Tiananmen Square, Beijing. Over 1,000 workers and students arrested; an estimated 800 killed by soldiers.

Colombia
Republic of (República de Colombia)

area 1,141,748 sq km/440,715 sq mi
capital Bogotá
towns Medellin, Cali, Bucaramanga; ports Barranquilla, Cartagena
physical the Andes mountains run N–S; plains in the E; Magdalena River runs N to the Caribbean
head of state and government Virgilio Barco Vargas from 1986
political system emergent democracy
exports emeralds (world's largest producer),

coffee (second largest world producer),
bananas, cotton, meat, sugar, oil, skins, hides
currency peso (614.99=£1 Mar 1989)
population (1985) 29,481,852 (mainly of
mixed Spanish and American Indian
descent); annual growth rate 2.2%
life expectancy men 61, women 66
language Spanish
religion Roman Catholic
literacy 89% male/87% female (1985 est)
GNP $42.5 bn (1983); $1,112 per head of
population
chronology
1886 Full independence achieved.
Conservatives in power.
1930 Liberals in power.
1946 Conservatives in power.
1948 Left-wing mayor of Bogotá assassinated.
Widespread outcry.
1949 Start of near civil war, La Violencia,
during which 280,000 people died.
1957 Hoping to halt the violence,
Conservatives and Liberals agreed to form a
National Front, sharing the presidency.
1970 National Popular Alliance (ANAPO)
formed as a left-wing opposition to the
National Front.
1974 National Front accord temporarily
ended.
1975 Civil unrest because of disillusionment
with the government.
1978 Liberals, under Julio Turbay, revived
the accord and began an intensive fight

against drug dealers.
1982 Liberals maintained their control
of Congress but lost the presidency. The
Conservative president, Belisario Betancur,
attempted to end the violence by granting
left-wing guerrillas an amnesty, freeing
political prisoners, and embarking on a large
public works programme.
1984 Minister of justice assassinated by,
it was suspected, drug dealers. Campaign
against them was stepped up.
1986 Virgilio Barco Vargas, Liberal, elected
president by a record margin.

Comoros
*Federal Islamic Republic of (Republique
fédérale islamique des Comores)*

area 1,862 sq km/719 sq mi
capital Moroni
physical comprises the islands of Njazídja,
Nzwani, and Mwali (formerly Grand
Comoro, Anjouan, Maheli); poor soil

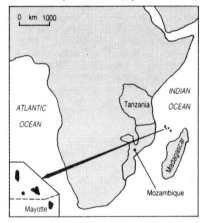

head of state and government Ahmed
Abdallah Abderemane from 1978
political system authoritarian nationalism
exports copra, vanilla, cocoa, sisal, coffee,
cloves, essential oils
currency CFA franc (544.87=£1 Mar 1989)
population 440,000 (1985 est); annual growth
rate 3.1%

life expectancy men 48, women 52
language French, Arabic (official); Comorian (Swahili and Arabic dialect)
religion Muslim (official)
literacy 15%
GNP $154 million (1982); $339 per head of population
chronology
1975 Independence achieved, but Mayotte remained part of France. Ahmed Abdallah elected president. The Comoros joined United Nations.
1976 Abdallah overthrown by Ali Soilih.
1978 Soilih killed by mercenaries working for Abdallah. Islamic republic proclaimed and Abdallah elected president.
1979 The Comoros became a one-party state. Powers of the federal government increased.
1985 Constitution amended to make Abdallah head of government as well as head of state.

Congo

People's Republic of the (République Populaire du Congo)

area 342,000 sq km/132,000 sq mi
capital Brazzaville
towns chief port Pointe Noire

ATLANTIC
OCEAN
Equ Guinea
Cameroon
C A Republic
Zaire
Gabon
Angola
0   km 1000

physical Zaïre (Congo) river on the border; half the country is rainforest
head of state and government Denis Sassau-Nguesso from 1979
political system nationalistic socialism
exports timber, potash, petroleum

currency CFA franc (544.87=£1 Mar 1989)
population (1985 est) 1,740,000 (chiefly Bantu); annual growth rate 2.6%
life expectancy men 45, women 48
language French (official)
religion animist 50%, Christian 48%
literacy 79% male/55% female (1985 est)
GDP $2.1 bn (1983); $500 per head of population
chronology
1960 Achieved full independence from France, with Abbe Youlou as the first president.
1963 Youlou forced to resign. New constitution approved, with Alphonse Massamba-Débat as president.
1964 The Congo became a one-party state.
1968 Military coup, led by Capt Marien Ngouabi, ousted Massamba-Débat.
1970 A Marxist state, the People's Republic of the Congo, was announced, with the Congolese Labour Party (PCT) as the only legal party.
1977 Ngouabi assassinated. Col Yhombi-Opango became president.
1979 Yhombi-Opango handed over the presidency to PCT, who chose Col Denis Sassou-Ngessou as his successor.
1984 Sassou-Ngessou elected for another five-year term.

Costa Rica
Republic of (República de Costa Rica)

area 51,100 sq km/19,725 sq mi
capital San José
towns ports Limón, Puntarenas
physical high central plateau and tropical coast
head of state and government Oscar Arias Sanchez from 1986
political system liberal democracy
exports coffee, bananas, cocoa, sugar
currency colón (138.51=£1 Mar 1989)
population (1985) 2,490,000 (including 1,200 Guaymi Indians); annual growth rate 2.6%
life expectancy men 71, women 76
language Spanish
religion Roman Catholic
literacy 94% male/93% female (1985 est)

GDP $2 bn (1982); $2,238 per head of population
chronology
1821 Independence achieved.
1949 New constitution adopted. National army abolished. José Figueres, co-founder of the National Liberation Party (PLN), was elected president. He embarked on an ambitious socialist programme.
1958–73 Mainly Conservative administrations returned.
1974 PLN regained the presidency and returned to socialist policies.
1978 Rodrigo Carazo, Conservative, elected president. Sharp deterioration in the state of the economy.
1982 Luis Alberto Monge of the PLN elected president. Harsh austerity programme introduced to rebuild the economy. Pressure from the USA to abandon neutral stance and condemn the Sandinista regime in Nicaragua.
1983 Policy of neutrality reaffirmed.
1985 Following border clashes with Sandinista forces, a US-trained anti-guerrilla guard was formed.
1986 Oscar Arias Sanchez won the presidency on a neutralist platform.
1987 Oscar Arias Sanchez won Nobel Peace Prize.

Cuba
Republic of (República de Cuba)

area 114,524 sq km/44,206 sq mi

512

capital Havana
physical comprises Cuba, the largest and westernmost of the West Indian islands, and smaller islands including Isle of Youth; low hills; Sierra Maestra mountains in E
head of state and government Fidel Castro Ruz from 1959
political system communism
exports sugar (largest producer after USSR), tobacco, coffee, iron, copper, nickel
currency Cuban peso (1.31=£1 Mar 1989, official rate)
population (1985) 10,090,000 (plus 125,000 refugees from the Cuban port of Mariel – *marielitos* – in USA); 66% are of Spanish descent, and a large number are of African origin; annual growth rate 0.6%
life expectancy men 72, women 75
language Spanish
religion Roman Catholic 45%
literacy 96% male/95% female (1979)
disposable national income $15.8 bn (1983); $1,590 per head of population
chronology
1901 Cuba achieved independence.
1933 Fulgencia Batista seized power.
1944 Batista retired.
1952 Batista seized power again to begin an oppressive regime.
1953 Fidel Castro led an unsuccessful coup against Batista.
1956 Castro led a second unsuccessful coup.
1959 Batista overthrown by Castro.

Constitution of 1940 replaced by a
'Fundamental Law', making Castro prime
minister, his brother Raul Castro his deputy,
and Che Guevara his number three.
1960 All US businesses in Cuba appropriated
without compensation. USA broke off
diplomatic relations.
1961 USA sponsored an unsuccessful
invasion, the Bay of Pigs episode. Castro
announced that Cuba had become a
communist state, with a Marxist-Leninist
programme of economic development.
1962 Cuba expelled from the Organization
of American States (OAS). Soviet nuclear
missiles removed from Cuba at US insistence.
1965 Cuba's sole political party renamed
Cuban Communist Party (PCC). With Soviet
help, Cuba began to make considerable
economic and social progress.
1972 Cuba became a full member of the
Moscow-based Council for Mutual Economic
Assistance (CMEA).
1976 New socialist constitution approved and
Castro elected president.
1976–81 Castro became involved in extensive
international commitments, assisting Third
World countries, particularly in Africa.
1982 Cuba joined other Latin American
countries in giving moral support to
Argentina in its dispute with Britain.
1984 Castro tried to improve US-Cuban
relations by discussing the exchange of US
prisoners in Cuba with Cuban 'undesirables'
in the USA.
1988 Peace accord with South Africa signed,
agreeing to withdrawal of Cuban troops from
Angola.

Cyprus
**Mediterranean island, divided between
the southern Republic of Cyprus (***Greek
Kypriaki Dimokratia***), and the Turkish
Republic of Northern Cyprus (***Turkish Kibris
Cumhuriyeti***)**

---

area 9,254 sq km/3,572 sq mi, 40% in
Turkish hands
capital Nicosia (divided between the Greeks
and Turks)
towns ports Paphos, Limassol, and Larnaca

(Greek); and Morphou, and ports Kyrenia
and Famagusta (Turkish)
physical central plain between two E–W
mountain ranges
heads of state and government Georgios
Vassilou (Greek) from 1988, Rauf Denktaş
(Turkish) from 1976
political system emergent democracy
exports citrus, grapes, Cyprus sherry,
potatoes, copper, pyrites
currency Cyprus pound (0.83=£1 Mar 1989)
population (1986) 673,000 (Greek Cypriot
81%, Turkish Cypriot 19%); annual growth
rate 1.2%
life expectancy men 72, women 76
language Greek and Turkish (official);
English
religion Greek Orthodox, Sunni Muslim
literacy 99% (1984)
GNP $2.11 bn (1983); $3,986 per head of
population
chronology
1955 Guerrilla campaign for enosis, or union
with Greece, started by Archbishop Makarios
and Gen Grivas.
1956 Makarios and enosis leaders deported.
1959 Compromise agreed and Makarios
returned to be elected president of an
independent Greek-Turkish Cyprus.
1960 Full independence achieved, with
Britain retaining its military bases.
1963 Turks set up their own government in N
Cyprus. Fighting broke out between the two

communities.
1964 UN peacekeeping force installed.
1971 Grivas returned to start a guerrilla war
against the Makarios government.
1974 Grivas died. A military coup deposed
Makarios, who fled to Britain. Nicos
Sampson appointed president. Turkish army
sent to N Cyprus to confirm the Turkish
Cypriots' control. The military regime in S
Cyprus collapsed and Makarios returned. N
Cyprus declared itself the Turkish
Federated State of Cyprus (TFSC), with Rauf
Denktaş as president.
1977 Makarios died and was succeeded by
Spyros Kyprianou.
1983 An independent Turkish Republic of
Northern Cyprus (TRNC) was proclaimed
but was recognized only by Turkey.
1984 UN peace proposals rejected.
1985 Summit meeting between Kyprianou
and Denktaş failed to reach agreement.
1988 Georgios Vassilou elected president.
Talks with Denktaş, under UN auspices,
began.

Czechoslovakia
*Socialist Republic of (Československá
Socialistická Republika)*

area 127,895 sq km/49,381 sq mi
capital Prague
towns Brno, Bratislava, Ostrava

physical Carpathian Mountains, rivers
Morava, Labe (Elbe), Vltava (Moldau); hills
and plateau; Danube plain in S
head of state Gustáv Husák from 1975
head of government Ladislav Adamec from
1988
political system communism
exports machinery, timber, ceramics, glass,
textiles
currency koruna (25.66 commercial rate,
16.63 tourist rate =£1 Mar 1989)
population (1985) 15,502,000 (60% Czech,
30% Slovak, with Hungarian, Polish,
German, Russian, and other minorities);
annual growth rate 0.4%
life expectancy men 68, women 75
language Czech and Slovak (official)
religion Roman Catholic with Protestant
minority
literacy 99% (1981)
GNP $85.8 bn (1982); $5,800 per head of
population
chronology
1945 Liberation of Czechoslovakia.
1948 Communists assumed power in coup and
new constitution framed.
1968 Prague Spring experiment with
liberalization ended by Soviet invasion.
1969 Czechoslovakia became a federal state.
Husák elected Communist Party leader.
1977 Emergence and suppression of Charter
77 human-rights movement.
1985–86 Criticism of Husák rule by new
Soviet leadership.
1987 Husák resigned as Communist leader;
replaced by Milos Jakes.
1988 Personnel overhaul of party and state
bodies, including replacement of Prime
Minister Štrougal by the technocrat Adamec.

Denmark
Kingdom of (Kongeriget Danmark)

area 43,075 sq km/16,627 sq mi
capital Copenhagen
towns Aarhus, Odense, Aalborg, Esbjerg, all
ports
physical the land is flat and cultivated; sand
dunes and lagoons on the W coast and long
inlets on the E

territories Faeroe Islands and Greenland
head of state Margrethe II from 1972
head of government Poul Schlüter from 1982
political system liberal democracy
exports bacon, dairy produce, eggs, fish,
mink pelts, car and aircraft parts, electrical
equipment, textiles
currency krone (12.55=£1 Mar 1989)
population 5,125,000 (1987); annual growth
rate 0%
life expectancy men 72, women 78
language Danish (official)
religion Lutheran
literacy 99% (1983)
GNP $50.4 bn (1983); $12,956 per head of
population
chronology
1940–45 Occupied by Germany.
1945 Iceland's independence recognized.
1947 Frederik IX succeeded Christian X.
1948 Home rule granted for Faeroe Islands.
1949 Became a founder member of NATO.
1960 Joined EFTA.
1972 Margrethe II became Denmark's first
queen for nearly 600 years.
1973 Left EFTA and joined EEC.
1979 Home rule granted for Greenland.
1985 Strong non-nuclear movement in
evidence.

Djibouti
Republic of (Jumhouriyya Djibouti)

area 23,000 sq km/8,880 sq mi
capital and chief port Djibouti

physical mountains divide an inland plateau
from a coastal plain; hot and arid
head of state and government Hassan Gouled
Aptidon from 1977
political system authoritarian nationalism
exports acts mainly as a transit port for
Ethiopia
currency Djibouti franc (299=£1 Mar 1989)
population (1985) 430,000 (Issa 40%, Afar
35%, Arab 25%); annual growth rate 3.4%
language Somali, Afar, French, Arabic
religion Sunni Muslim
literacy 17% (1985)
GNP $307 (1984); $400 per head of
population
chronology
1977 Full independence achieved. Hassan
Gouled elected president.
1979 All political parties combined to form
the People's Progress Assembly (RPP).
1981 New constitution made RPP the only
legal party. Gouled re-elected. Treaties of
friendship signed with Ethiopia, Somalia,
Kenya, and Sudan.
1984 Policy of neutrality reaffirmed.
1987 Gouled re-elected for a final term.

Dominica
Commonwealth of

area 750 sq km/290 sq mi
capital Roseau, with a deepwater port
physical largest of the Windward Islands,
mountainous, tropical
head of state Clarence Seignoret from 1983

515

head of government Mary Eugenia Charles from 1980
political system liberal democracy
exports bananas, coconuts, citrus, lime, bay oil
currency E Caribbean dollar (4.66=£1 Mar 1989), pound sterling, French franc
population (1985) 80,000 (mainly black African in origin, but with a small Carib reserve of some 500); annual growth rate 1.3%
language English (official), but the Dominican *patois* still reflects earlier periods of French rule
religion Roman Catholic 80%
literacy 80%
GNP $79 million (1983); $460 per head of population
chronology
1978 Dominica achieved full independence within the Commonwealth. Patrick John, leader of the Dominica Labour Party (DLP), elected prime minister.
1980 Dominica Freedom Party (FDP), led by Eugenia Charles, won a convincing victory in the general election.
1981 Patrick John was implicated in a plot to overthrow the government.
1982 John tried and acquitted.
1985 John retried and found guilty. Regrouping of left-of-centre parties resulted in the new Labour Party of Dominica (LPD). DFP, led by Eugenia Charles, re-elected.

Dominican Republic
(*República Dominicana*)

area 48,430 sq km/18,700 sq mi
capital Santo Domingo

physical comprises E part of island of Hispaniola; central mountain range; fertile valley in N
head of state and government Joaquín Balaguer from 1986
political system liberal democracy
exports sugar, gold, coffee, ferro-nickel
currency peso (10.96=£1 Mar 1989)
population (1985) 6,588,000; annual gröwth rate 2.3%
life expectancy men 61, women 65
language Spanish (official)
religion Roman Catholic
literacy 78% male/77% female (1985 est)
GNP $8.7 bn (1983); $1,221 per head of population
chronology
1930 Military coup established the dictatorship of Rafael Trujillo.
1961 Trujillo assassinated.
1962 First democratic elections resulted in Juan Bosch, founder of the Dominican Revolutionary Party (PRD) becoming president.
1963 Bosch overthrown in military coup.
1966 New constitution adopted. Joaquín Balaguer, leader of the Christian Social

Reform Party (PRSC), became president.
1978 PRD returned to power, with Silvestre
Antonio Guzmán as president.
1982 PRD re-elected, with Jorge Blanco as
president.
1985 Blanco forced by IMF to adopt austerity
measures to save the economy.
1986 PRSC returned to power, with Balaguer
re-elected president.

Ecuador
Republic of (República del Ecuador)

area 270,670 sq km/104,479 sq mi
capital Quito
towns Cuenca; chief port Guayaquil

physical Andes mountains, divided by a
central plateau, or Valley of the Volcanoes,
including Chimborazo and Cotopaxi, which
has a large share of the cultivable land and is
the site of the capital
head of state and government Rodrigo Borja
Cevallos from 1988
political system emergent democracy
exports bananas, cocoa, coffee, sugar, rice,
balsa wood, fish
currency sucre (759.07=£1 Mar 1989, official
rate)
population 9,380,000 (1985); annual growth
rate 2.9%

life expectancy men 62, women 66
language Spanish (official); Quechuan,
Jivaroan
religion Roman Catholic
literacy 85% male/80% female (1985 est)
GNP $11.6 bn (1983); $1,428 per head of
population
chronology
1830 Ecuador became an independent
republic.
1930–48 Great political instability.
1948–55 Liberals in power.
1956 First Conservative president for 60
years.
1960 Liberals returned, with José Velasco as
president.
1961 Velasco deposed and replaced by the
vice-president.
1963 Military junta installed.
1968 Velasco returned as president.
1972 A coup put the military back in power.
1978 New democratic constitution adopted.
1979 Liberals in power but opposed by
right- and left-wing parties.
1982 Deteriorating economy provoked
strikes, demonstrations and a state of
emergency.
1983 Austerity measures introduced.
1985 No party with a clear majority in the
national congress. Febres Cordero narrowly
won the presidency for the Conservatives.
1988 Roderigo Borja elected president for
moderate left-wing coalition.

Egypt
*Arab Republic of (Jumhuriyat Misr
al-Arabiya)*

area 1,002,000 sq km/386,772 sq mi
capital Cairo
towns Gîza; ports Alexandria, Port Said
physical mostly desert; hills in E; fertile land
along river Nile
head of state and government Hosni Mubarak
from 1981
political system emergent democracy
exports cotton and textiles
currency Egyptian pound (4.18=£1 Mar 1989)
population (1985) 46,694,000; annual growth
rate 2.4%

517

life expectancy men 57, women 60
language Arabic (ancient Egyptian survives to some extent in Coptic)
religion Sunni Muslim 95%, Coptic Christian 5%
literacy 59% male/30% female (1985 est)
GDP $32 bn (1983); $686 per head of population
chronology
1914 Egypt became a British protectorate.
1936 Independence recognized. King Fuad succeeded by his son Farouk.
1946 Withdrawal of British troops except from Suez Canal Zone.
1952 Farouk overthrown by the army in a bloodless coup.
1953 Egypt declared a republic, with Gen Neguib as president.
1956 Neguib replaced by Col Gamal Nasser. Nasser announced nationalization of Suez Canal; Egypt attacked by Britain, France and Israel. Ceasefire agreed because of US intervention.
1958 Short-lived merger of Egypt and Syria as United Arab Republic (UAR). Subsequent attempts to federate Egypt, Syria, and Iraq failed.
1967 Six-Day War with Israel ended in Egypt's defeat and Israeli occupation of Sinai and the Gaza strip.
1970 Nasser died suddenly and was succeeded by Anwar Sadat.
1973 Attempt to regain territory lost to Israel led to fighting. Ceasefire arranged by US secretary of state Henry Kissinger.

1977 Visit by Sadat to Israel to address the Israeli parliament was criticized by Egypt's Arab neighbours.
1978–79 Camp David talks in the USA resulted in a treaty between Egypt and Israel. Egypt expelled from the Arab League.
1981 Sadat assassinated and succeeded by Hosni Mubarak.
1983 Improved relations between Egypt and the Arab world; only Libya and Syria maintained a trade boycott.
1984 Mubarak's party victorious in the people's assembly elections.
1987 Mubarak re-elected. Egypt readmitted to Arab League.
1988 Full diplomatic relations with Algeria restored.

El Salvador
Republic of (República de El Salvador)

area 21,393 sq km/8,236 sq mi
capital San Salvador

physical flat in S, rising to mountains in N
head of state and government Alfredo Cristiani from 1989
political system emergent democracy
exports coffee, cotton
currency colón (8.63=£1 Mar 1989)
population (1985) 5,480,000 (mainly of Spanish-Indian extraction, including some 500,000 illegally in the USA); annual growth rate 2.9%

life expectancy men 63, women 67
language Spanish
religion Roman Catholic
literacy 75% male/69% female (1985 est)
GDP $4.3 bn (1984); $854 per head of population
chronology
1829 Achieved independence.
1961 Right-wing coup.
1972 Allegations of human-rights violations and growth of left-wing guerrilla activities. Gen Carlos Romero elected president.
1979 A coup replaced Romero with a military-civilian junta.
1980 Archbishop Oscar Romero assassinated. Country on verge of civil war. José Duarte became president.
1981 The Mexican and French governments recognized the guerrillas as a legitimate political force but the USA actively assisted the government in its battle against them.
1982 Assembly elections boycotted by left-wing parties and held amid considerable violence.
1985 Right-wing majority in the national assembly elections.
1986 Duarte sought a negotiated settlement with the guerrillas.
1988 Duarte resigned following diagnosis of terminal cancer.
1989 Right-wing Alfredo Cristiani elected president; allegations of rigging.

Equatorial Guinea
Republic of (República de Guinea Ecuatorial)

area 28,051 sq km/10,828 sq mi
capital Malabo
physical comprises mainland Rio Muni, plus the small islands of Corisco, Elobey Grande and Elobey Chico, and Bioko Island (formerly Fernando Po) together with Pagalu Island (formerly Annobon)
head of state and government Teodoro Obiang Nguema Mbasogo from 1979
political system military authoritarianism
exports cocoa, coffee, bananas, timber
currency ekuele; CFA franc (544.87=£1 Mar 1989)
population (1987) 384,000; annual growth rate

2.2%
life expectancy men 42, women 46
language Spanish (official); pidgin English is widely spoken, and on Pagalu (whose people were formerly slaves of the Portuguese) a Portuguese dialect
religion nominally Christian, mainly Catholic, but in 1978 Roman Catholicism was banned
literacy 55% (1984)
GDP $60 million (1983); $250 per head of population
chronology
1968 Achieved full independence from Spain. Francisco Macias Nguema became first president, soon assuming dictatorial powers.
1979 Macias overthrown and replaced by his nephew, Teodoro Obiang Nguema Mbasogo, who established a military regime. Macias tried and executed.
1982 Obiang elected president for another seven years. New constitution, promising a return to civilian government, adopted.

Ethiopia
People's Democratic Republic of (Hebrete hsebawit Ityopia, formerly also known as Abyssinia)

area 1,221,900 sq km/471,650 sq mi
capital Addis Ababa
towns Asmara (capital of Eritrea), Dire Dawa; ports are Massawa, Assab
physical a high plateau with mountains; plains in east; Blue Nile river
head of state and government Mengistu Haile

and Tigré, rebels claimed. Army accused of bombing civilian targets.

Fiji

area 18,337 sq km/7,078 sq mi
capital Suva on Viti Levu

Mariam from 1977
political system nationalistic socialism
exports coffee, pulses, oilseeds, hides, skins
currency birr (3.54=£1 Mar 1989)
population (1986) 46,000,000 (Oromo 40%, Amhara 25%, Tigré 12%, Sidama 9%); annual growth rate 2.5%
language Amharic (official); Tigré, Galla, Arabic
religion Christian (Ethiopian Orthodox church, which has had its own patriarch since 1976) 50%, Sunni Muslim 50%
literacy 18% (1985)
GNP $4.7 bn (1984); $141 per head of population
chronology
1974 Haile Selassie deposed and replaced by a military government led by Gen Teferi Benti. Ethiopia declared a socialist state.
1977 Teferi Benti killed and replaced by Col Mengistu Haile Mariam.
1984 The Workers' Party of Ethiopia (WPE) declared the only legal party.
1985 Worst famine for more than a decade. Western aid sent and internal resettlement programmes undertaken.
1987 New constitution adopted, Mengistu Mariam elected president. Provisional Military Administrative Council dissolved and elected National Assembly introduced. New famine; food aid hindered by guerrillas.
1988 Mariam agreed to adjust his economic policies in order to secure IMF assistance. Influx of refugees from Sudan.
1989 Government forces routed from Eritrea

physical comprises some 800 Melanesian islands (about 100 inhabited), the largest being Viti Levu (10,386 sq km/400 sq mi) and Vanua Levu (5,535 sq km/2,137 sq mi); mountainous, with tropical forest
head of state Ratu Sir Penaia Ganilau from 1987
head of government Ratu Sir Kamisese Mara from 1987
political system emergent democracy
exports sugar, coconut oil, ginger, timber, canned fish; tourism is important
currency Fiji dollar (2.47=£1 Mar 1989)
population (1986) 714,000 (46% Fijian, holding 80% of the land communally, and 49% Indians introduced in the 19th century to work the sugar crop); annual growth rate 1.9%
life expectancy men 67, women 71
language English (official); Fijian, Hindi
religion Hindu 50%, Methodist 44%
literacy 88% male/77% female (1980 est)
GDP $1.2 bn (1984); $1,086
chronology
1970 Full independence achieved. Ratu Sir Kamisese Mara elected as first prime minister.
1987 General election in Apr brought to

power an Indian-dominated coalition led by Dr Timoci Bavadra. Military coup in May by Col Sitiveni Rabuka removed new government at gunpoint. Governor General Ratu Sir Penaia Ganilau regained control within weeks. A second military coup by Rabuka in Sept proclaimed Fiji a republic and suspended the constitution. It was feared that ethnic rivalry would escalate and people of Indian extraction be forced to emigrate. In Oct Fiji ceased to be a member of the Commonwealth. In Dec a civilian government was restored with Rambuka retaining control of security as minister for home affairs.

Finland
Republic of (Suomen Tasavalta)

area 352,752 sq km/136,162 sq mi
capital Helsinki
towns Tampere, the port of Turku, Espoo, Vantaa

physical archipelago in south; most of the country is forest, with about 60,000 lakes; one third is within the Arctic Circle; mountains in the north
head of state Mauno Koivisto from 1982
head of government Harri Holkeri from 1987
political system liberal democracy
exports metal, chemical and engineering products (icebreakers and oil rigs), paper, timber, textiles, fine ceramics, glass, furniture

currency Finnish mark (7.27=£1 Mar 1989)
population 4,926,000 (1986); annual growth rate 0.5%
life expectancy men 70, women 78
language Finnish 94%, Swedish (official), Lapp
religion Lutheran 90%, Eastern Orthodox
literacy 99%
GNP $50.6 bn (1984); $10,477 per head of population
chronology
1917 Independence declared.
1939 Defeated by USSR in Winter War.
1941 Joined Hitler in invasion of USSR.
1944 Concluded separate armistice with Allies.
1948 Finno-Soviet Pact of Friendship, Co-operation, and Mutual Assistance signed.
1973 Trade treaty with EEC signed.
1977 Trade agreement with USSR signed.
1987 Social Democrats for coalition government with Conservatives.
1988 Koivisto re-elected president.

France
French Republic (République Française)

area (including Corsica) 543,965 sq km/209,970 sq mi
capital Paris
towns Lyon, Lille, Bordeaux, Toulouse, Nantes, Strasbourg; ports Marseille, Nice

physical rivers Seine, Loire, Garonne, Rhône, Rhine; mountain ranges Alps, Massif Central, Pyrenees, Jura, Vosges, Cévennes
territories Guadeloupe, French Guiana, Martinique, Réunion, St Pierre and Miquelon, Southern and Antarctic Territories, New Caledonia, French Polynesia, Wallis and Futuna
head of state François Mitterrand from 1981
head of government Michel Rocard from 1988
political system liberal democracy
exports fruit (especially apples), wine, cheese; cars, aircraft, chemicals, jewellery, silk, lace; tourism is very important
currency franc (10.90=£1 Mar 1989)
population (1985) 55,170,000 (including 4,500,000 immigrants, chiefly from Portugal, Algeria, Morocco, and Tunisia); annual growth rate 0.3%
life expectancy men 71, women 79
language French (regional languages include Breton)
religion mainly Roman Catholic; Muslim 3 million, Protestant 750,000
literacy 99% (1984)
GNP $568 bn (1983); $7,179 per head of population
chronology
1944–46 De Gaulle provisional government. Commencement of Fourth Republic.
1954 Independence granted to Indochina.
1956 Moroccan and Tunisian independence.
1957 Entry into EEC.
1958 Recall of de Gaulle following Algerian crisis. Commencement of Fifth Republic.
1959 De Gaulle became president.
1962 Algerian independence granted.
1966 France withdrew from NATO.
1968 'May events' crisis.
1969 De Gaulle resigned following referendum defeat. Pompidou became president.
1974 Giscard d'Estaing elected president.
1981 Mitterrand elected Fifth Republic's first socialist president.
1986 'Cohabitation' experiment, with the conservative Jacques Chirac as prime minister.
1988 Mitterrand re-elected. The moderate socialist Michel Rocard became prime minister and continued in this post despite the Socialist Party failing to obtain a secure majority in the National Assembly elections.

Gabon
Gabonese republic (République Gabonaise)

---

area 267,667 sq km/103,319 sq mi
capital Libreville

physical virtually the whole country is tropical rainforest; mountains alternate with lowlands; Ogooué River flows S–W
head of state and government Omar Bongo from 1967
political system authoritarian nationalism
exports petroleum, manganese, iron, uranium, timber
currency CFA franc (544.87=£1 Mar 1989)
population (1986) 1,336,000; annual growth rate 1.6%
life expectancy men 47, women 51
language French (official), Bantu
religion animist 60%, Roman Catholic 35%, small Muslim minority
literacy 70% male/53% female (1985 est)
GNP $3 bn (1983); $2,613 per head of population
chronology
1960 Independence from France achieved. Léon M'ba became the first president.
1967 Attempted coup by rival party foiled with French help. M'ba died and was succeeded by his protégé, Albert-Bernard Bongo.
1968 One-party state established.
1973 Bongo re-elected; converted to Islam,

he changed his first name to Omar.
1986 Bongo re-elected.

Gambia
Republic of The

area 10,689 sq km/4,126 sq mi
capital Banjul

physical banks of the river Gambia
head of state and government Dawda Kairaba
Jawara from 1970
political system liberal democracy
exports groundnuts, palm oil, fish
currency dalasi (11.22=£1 Mar 1989)
population 699,000 (1986); annual growth rate
1.9%
life expectancy men 34, women 37
language English (official)
religion Muslim 70%, with animist and
Christian minorities
literacy 36% male/15% female (1985 est)
GNP $200 million (1983); $330 per head of
population
chronology
1965 Achieved independence as a
constitutional monarchy within the
Commonwealth, with Dawda K Jawara as
prime minister.
1970 Declared itself a republic, with Jawara
as president.
1972 Jawara re-elected.
1981 Attempted coup foiled with the help of
Senegal.
1982 Formed with Senegal the Confederation
of Senegambia. Jawara re-elected.

1987 Jawara re-elected.

Germany, East
*German Democratic Republic (Deutsche
Demokratische Republik)*

area 108,333 sq km/41,817 sq mi
capital East Berlin
towns Leipzig, Dresden, Karl-Marx-Stadt,

Magdeburg; chief port Rostock
physical N flat, mountains in S; rivers Elbe,
Oder, and Neisse; many lakes, including
Müritz
head of state Erich Honecker from 1976
head of government Willi Stoph from 1976
political system communism
exports lignite, rare minerals (uranium,
cobalt, and others), coal, iron, steel,
fertilizers, plastics
currency GDR Mark, or Ostmark (2.99=£1
Sept 1987, not free rate)
population 16,640,000 (1985); annual growth
rate -0.1%
life expectancy men 70, women 75
language German
religion Protestant 80%, Catholic 11%
literacy 99% (1985)
GNP $86 bn (1983); $8,000 per head of
population
chronology
1949 The German Democratic Republic

established as an independent state.
1953 Riots in East Berlin suppressed by
Soviet troops.
1961 The Berlin Wall erected to stem flow of
refugees.
1964 Treaty of Friendship annd Mutual
Assistance signed with USSR.
1971 Erich Honecker elected Socialist Unity
Party (SED) leader.
1973 Basic Treaty ratified, normalizing
relations with Federal Republic.
1975 Friendship Treaty with USSR renewed
for 25 years.
1987 Official visit of Honecker to the Federal
Republic.

Germany, West
*Federal Republic of Germany (Bundesrepublik
Deutschland)*

area 248,706 sq km/96,001 sq mi
capital Bonn
towns West Berlin, Cologne, Munich,

Essen, Frankfurt-am-Main, Dortmund,
Düsseldorf; ports Hamburg, Kiel, Cuxhaven,
Bremerhaven
physical flat in N, mountainous in S with
Alps; rivers Rhine, Weser, Elbe flow N,
Danube flows SE
head of state Richard von Weizsacker from
1984

head of government Helmut Kohl from 1982
political system liberal democracy
exports machine tools (world's leading
exporter); cars and commercial vehicles,
electronics, industrial goods, textiles,
chemicals, iron and steel; wine
currency Deutschmark (2.99=£1 Sept 1987)
population (1985) 61,020,000 (including
4,400,000 guest workers, *Gastarbeiter*, of
whom 1,600,000 are Turks; the rest are
Yugoslavs, Italians, Greeks, Spanish, and
Portuguese); annual growth rate -0.2%
life expectancy men 70, women 77
language German
religion Protestant 49%, Roman Catholic
47%
literacy 99% (1985)
GNP $655 bn (1983); $9,450 per head of
population
chronology
1945 German surrender and division into
four (US, French, British, Soviet) occupation
zones.
1948 Berlin crisis.
1949 Establishment of Federal Republic
under the 'Basic Law' Constitution with
Adenauer as chancellor.
1954 Grant of full sovereignty.
1957 Entry into EEC. Recovery of Saarland.
1961 Construction of Berlin Wall.
1963 Retirement of Chancellor Adenauer.
1969 Willy Brandt became chancellor.
1972 Basic Treaty with East Germany.
1974 Resignation of Brandt. Helmut Schmidt
became chancellor.
1982 Kohl became chancellor.
1988 Death of Bavarian right-wing leader
Franz-Josef Strauss.
1989 Rising support for far-right in local
elections and declining support for Kohl.

Ghana
Republic of

area 238,305 sq km/91,986 sq mi
capital Accra
towns Kumasi, and ports Sekondi-Takoradi,
Tema
physical mostly plains; bisected by river Volta
head of state and government Jerry Rawlings

from 1981
political system military authoritarianism
exports cocoa, coffee, timber, gold,
diamonds, manganese, bauxite
currency cedi (448.88=£1 Mar 1989)
population 13,590,000 (1985 est); annual
growth rate 3.2%
life expectancy men 50, women 54
language English (official)
religion Christian 43%, animist 38%, Muslim
12%
literacy 64% male/43% female (1985 est)
GNP $3.9 bn (1983); $420 per head of
population
chronology
1957 Independence achieved, within the
Commonwealth, with Kwame Nkrumah as
president.
1960 Ghana became a republic and a
one-party state.
1966 Nkrumah deposed and replaced by Gen
Joseph Ankrah.
1969 Ankrah replaced by Gen Akwasi Afrifa,
who initiated a return to civilian government.
1970 Edward Akufo-Addo elected president.
1972 Another coup placed Col Acheampong
at the head of a military government.
1978 Acheampong deposed in a bloodless
coup led by Frederick Akuffo. Another coup
put Flight Lt Jerry Rawlings in power.
1979 Return to civilian rule under Hilla
Limann.
1982 Rawlings seized power again,
complaining about the incompetence of
previous governments.

Greece
Hellenic Republic (Elliniki Dimokratia)

area 131,957 sq km/50,935 sq mi
capital Athens
towns ports Thessaloniki, Patras, Larisa,
Iráklion

physical mountainous; a large number of
islands, notably Crete, Corfu, and Rhodes
head of state Christos Sartzetakis from 1985
head of government Tzannis Tzannetakis from
1989
political system emergent democracy
exports tobacco, fruit (including currants),
vegetables, olives, olive oil, textiles
currency drachma (271.20=£1 Mar 1989)
population 9,930,000 (1985); annual growth
rate 0.5%
life expectancy men 72, women 76
language Greek
religion Greek Orthodox Christian 97%
literacy 96% male/89% female (1985)
GNP $32.4 bn (1984); $3,260 per head of
population
chronology
1946 Civil war broke out between royalists
and communists. Communists defeated.
1949 Monarchy re-established with Paul as
king.
1964 King Paul succeeded by his son
Constantine.
1967 Army coup removed the king and

Col George Papadopoulos became prime minister. Martial law imposed and all political activity banned.

1973 Republic proclaimed, with Papadopoulos as president.

1974 Former premier Constantine Karamanlis recalled from exile to lead government. Martial law and ban on political parties lifted. Restoration of the monarchy rejected by a referendum.

1975 New constitution adopted, making Greece a republic.

1980 Karamanlis resigned as prime minister and was elected president.

1981 Greece became a full member of the EEC. Andreas Papandreou elected Greece's first socialist prime minister.

1983 Five-year defence and economic cooperation agreement signed with the USA. Ten-year economic cooperation agreement signed with USSR.

1985 Papandreou re-elected.

1988 Relations with Turkey improved. Major cabinet reshuffle following mounting criticism of Papandreou.

1989 Tzannis Tzannetakis, a Conservative backbencher, becomes prime minister, heading first all-party government for over 15 years.

Grenada

area (including the Grenadines, notably Carriacou) 344 sq km/133 sq mi

capital St George's
physical southernmost of the Windward Islands; mountainous
head of state Elizabeth II from 1974 represented by Paul Scoon
head of government Herbert A Blaize from 1984
political system emergent democracy
exports cocoa, nutmeg, bananas, mace
currency Eastern Caribbean dollar (4.66=£1 Mar 1989)
population (1985 est) 113,000; annual growth rate 1.2%
language English
religion Roman Catholic
literacy 85% (1985)

GDP $116 million (1983); $500 per head of population
chronology
1974 Full independence achieved, with Eric Gairy elected prime minister.

1979 Gairy was removed in a bloodless coup led by Maurice Bishop. Constitution suspended and a people's revolutionary government established.

1982 Relations with the USA and Britain deteriorated as ties with Cuba and USSR strengthened. Bishop feared impending US invasion.

1983 After Bishop's attempt to improve relations with the USA, he was overthrown by left-wing opponents. A coup established the Revolutionary Military Council (RMC) and Bishop and some of his colleagues were executed. The USA, accompanied by troops from some other E Caribbean countries, invaded Grenada, overthrowing the RMC. The 1974 constitution was reinstated.

1984 The newly formed New National Party (NNP) won 14 of the 15 seats in the house of representatives and its leader, Herbert Blaize, became prime minister.

1989 Blaize lost leadership of NNP.

Guatemala
Republic of (República de Guatemala)

area 108,889 sq km/42,031 sq mi
capital Guatemala City

towns Quezaltenango, Puerto Barrios (naval base)

physical mountainous, tropical
head of state and government Mario Vinicio Cerezo Arevalo from 1986
political system emergent democracy
exports coffee, bananas, cotton
currency quetzal (4.75=£1 Mar 1989)
population (1985) 8,403,000 (Mayaquiche Indians 54%, mestizos 42%); annual growth rate 2.8%
life expectancy men 57, women 61
language Spanish
religion Roman Catholic
literacy 63% male/47% female (1985 est)
GDP $9.9 bn (1984); $1,085 per head of population
chronology
1839 Independent republic.
1954 Col Carlos Castillo became president in a US-backed coup, halting land reform.
1963 Military coup made Col Enrique Peralta president.
1966 Cesar Méndez elected president.
1970 Carlos Araña elected president.
1974 Gen Kjell Laugerud became president. Widespread political violence.
1978 Gen Fernando Romeo became president.
1981 Growth of anti-government guerrilla movement.
1982 Gen Angel Anibal became president.

An army coup installed Gen Ríos Montt as head of a junta and then as president. Political violence continued.
1983 Montt removed in a coup led by Gen Mejía Victores, who declared amnesty for the guerrillas.
1985 New constitution adopted; Guatemalan Christian Democratic Party (PDCG) won congressional elections; Vincio Cerezo elected president.
1989 Over 100,000 people killed and 40,000 missing in past ten years.

Guinea
Republic of (République de Guinée)

area 245,857 sq km/94,901 sq mi
capital Conakry
towns Labe, N'Zerekore, KanKan

physical mainly mountainous; sources of rivers Niger, Gambia, and Senegal; forest in SE
head of state and government Lansana Conté from 1984
political system military authoritarianism
exports coffee, rice, palm kernels, alumina, bauxite, diamonds
currency syli or franc (517.80=£1 Mar 1989)
population (1986) 6,410,000 (chief peoples are Fulani 40%, Mandingo 25%); annual growth rate 2.3%
life expectancy men 39, women 42
language French (official)
religion Muslim 62%, Christian 15%, local 35%

527

literacy 40% male/17% female (1985 est)
GNP $1.6 bn (1983); $305 per head of
population
chronology
1958 Full independence from France
achieved. Sékou Touré elected president.
1977 Strong opposition to Touré's policies of
rigid Marxism forced him to accept the return
of a mixed economy.
1980 Touré returned unopposed for a fourth
seven-year term of office.
1984 Touré died. A bloodless coup
established a military committee for national
recovery, with Col Lansana Conté at its head.
1985 Attempted coup against Conté while
he was out of the country was foiled by loyal
troops.

Guinea-Bissau
(Republica da Guiné-Bissau)

area 36,125 sq km/13,949 sq mi
capital and chief port Bissau
physical flat lowlands

head of state and government JoaBernardo
Vieira from 1980
political system nationalistic socialism
exports rice, coconuts, peanuts, fish, salt
currency peso (1,121.90=£1 Mar 1989)
population (1985 est) 890,000; annual growth
rate 1.9%
life expectancy men 41, women 45
language Crioulo, Cape Verdean dialect of
Portuguese
religion Muslim 40%, Christian 4%

literacy 46% male/17% female (1985 est)
GDP $177 million (1982); $165 per head of
population
chronology
1956 African Party for the Independence
of Portuguese Guinea and Cape Verde
(PAIGC) formed to secure independence
from Portugal.
1973 Two-thirds of the country declared
independent, with Luiz Cabral as president of
a state council.
1974 Portugal recognized independence of
Guinea-Bissau.
1980 Cape Verde decided not to join a
unified state. Cabral deposed and JoaVieira
became chair of a council of revolution.
1981 PAIGC confirmed as the only legal
party, with Vieira as its secretary general.
1982 Normal relations with Cape Verde
restored.
1984 New constitution adopted, making
Vieira head of government as well as head of
state.

Guyana
Cooperative Republic of

area 215,000 sq km/83,000 sq mi
capital and port Georgetown
physical mostly tropical rainforest

head of state and government Desmond Hoyte
from 1985
political system emergent democracy

exports sugar, rice, rum, timber, diamonds
currency Guyana dollar (15.41=£1 Mar 1989)
population (1985 est) 790,000 (50% E Indians,
introduced to work the sugar plantations
after the abolition of slavery, 30% black, 5%
Amerindian); annual growth rate 2%
life expectancy men 66, women 71
language English (official), Hindi
religion Christian 57%, Hindu 33%, Sunni
Muslim 9%
literacy 97% male/95% female (1985 est)
GNP $419 million (1983); $457 per head of
population
chronology
1953 Assembly elections won by
left-wing party. Britain installed interim
administration, claiming fear of communist
takeover.
1961 Internal self-government granted.
1966 Full independence achieved.
1970 Guyana became a republic within the
Commonwealth.
1980 Forbes Burnham became the first
executive president under new constitution.
1985 Burnham died and was succeeded by
Desmond Hoyte.

Haiti
Republic of (République d'Haïti)

area 27,750 sq km/10,710 sq mi
capital Port-au-Prince
physical mainly mountainous

head of state and government Prosper Avril
from 1988
political system military authoritarianism
exports coffee, sugar, sisal, cotton, cocoa, rice
currency gourde (8.63=£1 Mar 1989)
population 5,272,000 (1985); annual growth
rate 2.5%
life expectancy men 51, women 54
language French (official, spoken by the
bourgeoisie), creole (spoken by 90% black
majority)
religion Roman Catholic (official, but
opposed to the regime)
literacy 40% male/35% female (1985 est)
GNP $1.6 bn (1983); $300 per head of
population
chronology
1804 Independence from France achieved.
1957 Dr François Duvalier (Papa Doc)
elected president.
1964 Duvalier pronounced himself president
for life.
1971 Constitution amended to allow the
president to nominate his successor. Duvalier
died and was succeeded by his son, Jean-
Claude (Baby Doc).
1986 Duvalier deposed and replaced by Lt-
Gen Henri Namphy, as head of a governing
council.
1988 Leslie Manigat became president in Feb
despite allegations of fraudulent elections.
Namphy staged a military coup in Jun, but
another coup in Sept replaced him with a
civilian government under military control.

Honduras
Republic of (República de Honduras)

area 112,088 sq km/43,266 sq mi
capital Tegucigalpa
towns San Pedro Sula; ports Henecan (on
Pacific), La Ceiba
physical mountainous; 45% forest
head of state and government José Simeon
Azeona del Hoyo from 1986
political system emergent democracy
exports coffee, bananas, timber (including
mahogany, rosewood)
currency lempira (3.45=£1 Mar 1989)
population (1985) 4,370,000 (90% mestizo,

10% Indians and Europeans); annual growth rate 3.4%
life expectancy men 58, women 62
language Spanish
religion Roman Catholic
literacy 61% male/58% female (1985 est)
GNP $2.8 bn (1983); $590 per head of population
chronology
1838 Honduras achieved independence.
1980 After more than a century of mostly military rule, a civilian government was elected, with Dr Roberto Suazo as president. The commander in chief of the army, Gen Gustavo Alvarez, retained considerable power.
1983 Close involvement with the USA in providing naval and air bases and allowing Nicaraguan counter-revolutionaries to operate from Honduras.
1984 Alvares ousted in a coup led by junior officers, resulting in a review of policy towards the USA and Nicaragua.
1985 José Azeona elected president after the electoral law was changed, making Suazo ineligible for presidency.

Hungary
Hungarian People's Republic (Magyar Népköztársaság)

area 93,032 sq km/35,910 sq mi
capital Budapest

towns Miskolc, Debrecen, Szeged, Pécs
physical Great Hungarian Plain covers E half of country; Bakony Forest; rivers Danube, Tisza; Lake Balaton
head of government Károly Grosz from 1988
political system communism
exports machinery, vehicles, chemicals, textiles
currency forint (93.28=£1 Mar 1989)
population (1985) 10,644,000 (Magyar 92%, Romany 3%, German 2.5%. A Hungarian minority in Romania is the cause of some friction between the two countries); annual growth rate 0%
life expectancy men 67, women 74
language Hungarian (or Magyar), one of the few languages of Europe with non-Indo-European origins. It is grouped with Finnish and Estonian in the Finno-Ugrian family
religion Roman Catholic 50%, other Christian denominations 25%
literacy 99.3% male/98.5% female (1980)
GNP $18.6 bn (1983); $4,180 per head of population
chronology
1946 Republic proclaimed.
1949 Soviet-style constitution adopted.
1956 Hungarian national rising: workers' demonstrations in Budapest, democratization reforms by Imre Nagy overturned by Soviet tanks, Kádár installed as party leader.

1968 Economic decentralization reforms.
1983 Competition introduced into elections.
1987 VAT and income tax introduced.
1988 Kádár replaced by Károly Grosz. First free trade union recognized. Rival political parties legalized.

Iceland
Republic of (Lýdveldd–idd– Ísland)

area 103,000 sq km/ 39,758 sq mi
capital Reykjavik

physical warmed by the Gulf Stream; glaciers and lava fields cover 75% of the country
head of state Vigdís Finnbogadóttir from 1980
head of government Thorsteinn Palsson from 1987
political system liberal democracy
exports cod and other fish products
currency krona (90.80=£1 Mar 1989)
population 241,000 (1985); annual growth rate 1.2%
life expectancy men 74, women 80
language Icelandic, the most archaic Scandinavian language, in which some of the finest sagas were written
religion Evangelical Lutheran
literacy 99.9% (1984)
GDP $2.1 bn (1983); $9,000 per head of population
chronology
1944 Independence from Denmark achieved.
1949 Joined NATO and the Council of Europe.

1953 Joined the Nordic Council.
1976 'Cod War' with the UK.
1979 Iceland announced a 200-mile exclusive fishing zone.
1983 Steingrímur Hermannsson appointed to lead a coalition government.
1985 Iceland declared a nuclear-free zone.
1987 New coalition government formed by Thorsteinn Palsson after general election.
1988 Vigdís Finnbogadóttir re-elected president for a third term.

India
(Hindi Bharat)

area 3,208,274 sq km/1,175,410 sq mi
capital New Delhi
towns Bangalore, Hyderabad, Ahmedabad;

ports Calcutta, Bombay, Madras, Kanpur, Pune, Nagpur
physical Himalaya mountains on the N border; plains around rivers Ganges, Indus, Brahmaputra; Deccan peninsula S of the Narmada River, a plateau between the W and E Ghats mountain ranges
territories Andaman and Nicobar Islands, Lakshadweep
head of state Ramaswami Iyer Venkataraman from 1987
head of government Rajiv Gandhi from 1984
political system liberal democracy

exports tea, coffee, fish, iron ore, leather, textiles, polished diamonds
currency rupee (27.00=£1 Mar 1989)
population 750,900,000 (1985 est); annual growth rate 1.9%
life expectancy men 56, women 55
language Hindi (official), English, and 14 other recognized languages: Assamese, Bengali, Gujarati, Kannada, Kashmiri, Malayalam, Marathi, Oriya, Punjabi, Sanskrit, Sindhi, Tamil, Telugu, Urdu
religion Hindu 80%, Sunni Muslim 10%, Christian 2.5%, Sikh 2%
literacy 57% male/29% female (1985 est)
GNP $190 bn (1983); $150 per head of population
chronology
1947 Independence achieved from Britain.
1950 Federal republic proclaimed.
1962 Border skirmishes with China.
1964 Death of Prime Minister Nehru. Border war with Pakistan over Kashmir.
1966 Indira Gandhi became prime minister.
1971 War with Pakistan leading to creation of Bangladesh.
1975–77 State of emergency proclaimed.
1977–79 Janata party government in power.
1980 Indira Gandhi returned in landslide victory.
1984 Assassination of Indira Gandhi. Rajiv Gandhi elected with record majority.
1987 Signing of 'Tamil' Colombo peace accord with Sri Lanka.
1988 New opposition party, Janata Dal, established by form er finance minister V P Singh.

Indonesia
Republic of (Republik Indonesia)

---

area 1,925,000 sq km/741,000 sq mi
capital Jakarta
towns ports Surabaya, Semarang
physical comprises 1,400 tropical islands, including the greater part of the Sunda Islands to the W of the Moluccas, both the Greater Sundas (including Java and Madura, part of Kalimantan/Borneo, Sumatra, Sulawesi and Belitung) and the Lesser Sundas/Nusa Tenggara (including

Bali, Lombok, Sumba, Timor), as well as Malaku/Moluccas and part of New Guinea (Irian Jaya)
head of state and government T N J Suharto from 1967
political system authoritarian nationalism
exports coffee, rubber, palm oil, coconuts, tin, tea, tobacco, oil, liquid natural gas
currency rupiah (3,034.82 £1 Mar 1989)
population (1985 est) 163,390,000 (including 300 ethnic groups); annual growth rate 2%
life expectancy men 52, women 55
language Indonesian, closely allied to Malay
religion Muslim 90%, Buddhist, Hindu, and Pancasila (a secular official ideology)
literacy 83% male/65% female (1985 est)
GNP $87 bn (1983); $560 per head of population
chronology
17th century Dutch rule established.
1942 Occupied by Japan. Nationalist government established.
1945 Japanese surrender. Nationalists declare independence under Sukarno.
1949 Formal transfer of Dutch sovereignty.
1950 Unitary constitution established.
1963 Western New Guinea (Irian Jaya) ceded by Holland.
1965–66 Attempted communist coup: Gen Suharto emergency administration.
1967 Sukarno replaced as president by Suharto.

1976 Annexation by force of the former Portuguese colony of East Timor.
1986 Institution of 'transmigration programme' to settle large numbers of Javanese on the sparsely populated outer islands, particularly Irian Jaya.
1988 Partial easing of travel restrictions to East Timor. Suharto re-elected for fifth term.

Iran
Islamic Republic of (Jomhori-e-Islami-e-Irân; until 1935 *Persia)*

area 1,648,000 sq km/634,724 sq mi
capital Tehran
towns Isfahan, Mashhad, Tabriz, Shiraz,

Ahwaz; chief port Abadan
physical plateau surrounded by mountains, including Elburz and Zagros; Lake Rezayeh; Dasht-Ekavir Desert
religious leader Sayed Ruholla Moussavi Khomeini from 1979
head of government Ali Akbar Rafsanjani from 1989 *political system* authoritarian Islamic nationalism
exports carpets, cotton textiles, metalwork, leather goods, oil, petrochemicals
currency rial (121.55=£1 Mar 1989)
population (1986) 49,857,384 (including minorities in Azerbaijan, Baluchistan, Khuzestan/Arabistan, and Kurdistan); annual growth rate 2.9%
life expectancy men 57, women 57

language Farsi, Kurdish, Turk, Arabic, English, French
religion Shi'ite Muslim (official)
literacy 62% male/39% female (1985 est)
GDP \$76.37 bn (1977); \$2,160 per head of population
chronology
1946 British, US, and Soviet forces left Iran.
1951 Oilfields nationalized by Prime Minister Mohammed Mossadeq.
1953 Mossadeq deposed and the shah took full control of the government.
1975 The shah introduced a single-party system.
1978 Opposition to the shah organized from France by Ayatollah Khomeini.
1979 Shah left the country and Khomeini returned to create an Islamic state. Students seized US hostages in Tehran.
1980 Start of Gulf War against Iraq.
1981 US hostages finally released.
1984 Egyptian peace proposals rejected.
1985 Gulf War fighting intensified. UN secretary general's peace moves were unsuccessful.
1988 Ceasefire in Gulf War, talks with Iraq began. Relations with Western powers improved.
1989 Khomeini's call for the murder of the British writer Salman Rushdie caused deterioration of relations with the West. Following the death of Khomeini, President Ali Khamenei named Leader of the Revolution by the Assembly of Experts.

Iraq
Republic of (Al Jumhouriya al 'Iraqia)

area 444,000 sq km/172,000 sq mi
capital Baghdad
towns Mosul and port of Basra
physical mountains in N, desert in W; wide valley of rivers Tigris and Euphrates NW–SE
head of state and government Saddam Hussein At-Takriti from 1979
political system nationalistic socialism
exports dates (80% of world supply), wool, oil
currency Iraqi dinar (0.54=£1 Mar 1989)
population 15,507,000 (1985); annual growth rate 3.6%

life expectancy men 62, women 63
language Arabic (official)
religion Shi'ite Muslim 60%, Sunni Muslim 30%, Christian 3%
literacy 68% male/32% female (1980 est)
GNP $31 bn (1981); $2,410 per head of population
chronology
1920 Iraq became a British League of Nations protectorate.
1921 Hashemite dynasty established, with Faisal I as king.
1932 Achieved full independence.
1958 Monarchy overthrown and Iraq became a republic.
1968 Military coup puts Gen al-Bakr in power.
1979 Al-Bakr replaced by Saddam Hussein.
1980 Gulf War between Iraq and Iran broke out.
1985 Gulf War fighting intensified. UN secretary general's peace moves were unsuccessful.
1988 Ceasefire in Gulf War, talks began with Iran. Iraq accused of using chemical weapons. Harsh repression of Kurdish rebels seeking greater autonomy.
1989 Unsuccessful coup against President Saddam.

Ireland, Republic of
(Irish Éire)

area 68,895 sq km/26,593 sq mi

capital Dublin
towns ports Cork, Dún Laoghaire, Limerick, Waterford
physical central plateau with hills; rivers Shannon, Liffey, Boyne
head of state Patrick J Hillery from 1976
head of government Charles Haughey from 1987
political system democracy
exports livestock, dairy products, Irish whiskey, microelectronic components and assemblies, mining and engineering products, chemicals, tobacco, clothing; tourism is important
currency punt (1.20=£1 Mar 1989)
population 3,537,000 (1986); annual growth rate 1.2%
life expectancy men 70, women 76
language Irish and English (both official)
religion Roman Catholic
literacy 99% (1984)
GNP $16.5 (1983); $4,750 per head of population
chronology
1739–41 Famine killed one-third of population of 1.5 million.
1845–46 Famine: 1.5 million emigrated, most to the USA.
1916 Easter Rising: nationalists seized the Dublin general post office and proclaimed a republic. The revolt was suppressed by the

British army and most of the leaders were executed.

1918–21 Guerrilla warfare (the 'Troubles') against British army led to split in rebel forces.

1921 Anglo-Irish Treaty resulted in creation of the Irish Free State (Southern Ireland).

1937 Eire established as an independent state.

1949 Eire left the Commonwealth and became the Republic of Ireland.

1973 Fianna Fáil defeated after 40 years in office. Liam Cosgrave formed a coalition government.

1977 Fianna Fáil returned to power, with Jack Lynch as prime minister.

1979 Lynch resigned and was succeeded by Charles Haughey.

1981 Garret FitzGerald formed a coalition.

1983 New Ireland Forum formed, but rejected by the British government.

1985 Anglo-Irish Agreement signed.

1986 Protests by Ulster Unionists against the agreement.

1987 General election won by Charles Haughey.

1988 Relations with UK at low ebb because of disagreement over extradition decisions.

1989 Haughey begins talks with Desmond O'Malley, leader Progressive Democrats after failing to win majority in Dail elections. Fianna Fáil formation of official coalition government.

Israel
State of (Medinat Israel)

area 20,770 sq km/8,017 sq mi (as at 1949 armistice)

capital Jerusalem (not recognized by the United Nations)

towns ports Tel Aviv/Jaffa, Haifa, Eilat; Bat-Yam, Holon, Ramat Gan, Petach Tikva, Beersheba

physical coastal plain of Sharon between Haifa and Tel Aviv noted since ancient times for fertility; high arid region in S and centre; river Jordan Rift Valley along the E is below sea level

head of state Chaim Herzog from 1983

head of government Itzhak Shamir from 1986

political system liberal democracy

exports citrus and other fruit, avocados, chinese leaves, fertilizers, plastics, petrochemicals, textiles, electronics (military, medical, scientific, industrial), electro-optics, precision instruments, aircraft and missiles

currency shekel (3.13=£1 Mar 1989)

population (1985) 4,230,000 (including some 750,000 Arabs as Israeli citizens and over 1 million Arabs in the occupied territories); under the Law of Return 1950, 'every Jew shall be entitled to come to Israel as an immigrant', those from the East and E Europe are *Ashkenazim*, and from Spain, Portugal, and Arab N Africa are *Sephardim* (over 50% of the population is now of Sephardic descent). An Israeli-born Jew is a *Sabra*; about 500,000 Israeli Jews are resident in the USA. Annual growth rate 1.8%

life expectancy men 73, women 76

language Hebrew and Arabic (official); Yiddish, European and W Asian languages

religion Israel is a secular state, but the predominant faith is Judaism; also Sunni Muslim, Christian, and Druse

literacy 97% male/93% female (1985 est)

GNP $23 bn (1983); $5,609 per head of population

chronology

1948 Independent state of Israel proclaimed with Ben Gurion as prime minister.

1963 Ben Gurion resigned and was succeeded by Levi Eshkol.
1964 Palestine Liberation Organization (PLO) founded with the aim of overthrowing the state of Israel.
1967 Israel victorious in the Six-Day War.
1968 Israel Labour Party formed, led by Golda Meir.
1969 Golda Meir became prime minister.
1974 Yom Kippur War. Golda Meir succeeded by Itzhak Rabin.
1977 Menachem Begin elected prime minister. Egyptian president addressed the Knesset.
1978 Camp David talks.
1979 Egyptian-Israeli agreement signed.
1982 Israel pursued PLO fighters into Lebanon.
1983 Agreement reached for withdrawal from Lebanon.
1985 Israeli prime minister Shimon Peres had secret talks with King Hussein of Jordan.
1986 Itzhak Shamir took over from Peres under power-sharing agreement.
1988 Criticism of Israel's handling of Palestinian uprising in occupied territories.
1989 New Likud-Labour coalition government formed under Sham ir. International calls for talks with PLO rejected.

Italy
Republic of (Repubblica Italiana)

area 301,245 sq km/116,300 sq mi
capital Rome
towns Milan, Turin; ports Naples, Genoa, Palermo, Bari, Catania
physical mountainous (Maritime Alps, Dolomites, Apennines); rivers Po, Adige, Arno, Tiber, Rubicon; islands of Sicily, Sardinia, Elba, Capri, Ischia
exports wine, fruit and vegetables, textiles (Europe's largest silk producer), leather goods, motor vehicles, electrical goods, chemicals, marble (Carrara), sulphur and mercury, iron and steel
head of state Francesco Cossiga from 1985
head of government Ciriaco de Mita from 1988
political system liberal democracy

currency lira (2366.00=£1 Mar 1989)
population (1985) 57,130,000; annual growth rate 0.1%
life expectancy men 71, women 78
language Italian, derived from Latin
religion Roman Catholic 90%
literacy 98% male/96% female (1985)
GNP $350 bn (1983); $6,914 per head of population
chronology
1946 Monarchy replaced by a republic.
1948 New constitution adopted.
1954 Trieste returned to Italy.
1976 Communists proposed the establishment of a broad-based, left-right government, the 'historic compromise'. Idea rejected by the Christian Democrats.
1978 Christian Democrat Aldo Moro, architect of the historic compromise, kidnapped and murdered by Red Brigade guerrillas.
1983 Bettino Craxi became the socialist leader of a broad coalition government.
1987 Craxi resigned, and the succeeding coalition fell within months.
1988 After several unsuccessful attempts to form a stable government, the leader of the Christian Democrats, Ciriaco de Mita, established a five-party coalition which included the socialists.
1989 De Mita replaced as Christian Democrat leader by Arnald o Foriani but continued as prime minister.

Ivory Coast
Republic of (République de la Côte d'Ivoire)

area 322,463 sq km/127,000 sq mi
capital Abidjan; capital designate
Yamoussouko
towns Bouaké

physical tropical rainforest (diminishing as
it is exploited) in the S; savanna and low
mountains in the N
head of state and government Félix
Houphouët-Boigny from 1960
political system authoritarian nationalism
exports coffee, cocoa, timber, petroleum
currency CFA franc (544.87=£1 Mar 1989)
population (1985 est) 9,810,000; annual
growth rate 3.7%
life expectancy men 49, women 52
language French (official)
religion animist 65%, Muslim 24%, Christian
11%
literacy 53% male/31% female (1985 est)
GNP $6.7 bn (1983); $1,100 per head of
population
chronology
1958 Achieved internal self-government.
1960 Achieved full independence, with
Félix Houphouët-Boigny as president of a
one-party state.

Jamaica

area 11,525 sq km/4,411 sq mi
capital Kingston
towns Montego bay, Spanish Town, St

Andrews
physical mountainous
head of state Elizabeth II from 1962
represented by Florizel Glasspole from 1973
head of government Michael Manley from
1989
political system liberal democracy
exports sugar, bananas, bauxite, rum, coffee,
coconuts, liqueurs, cigars
currency Jamaican dollar (9.28=£1 Mar 1989)
population (1985 est) 2,340,000 (a mixture of
several ethnic groups); annual growth rate
1.5%
life expectancy men 70, women 76
language English, Jamaican creole
religion Protestant 70%, Rastafarian
literacy 90% male/93% female (1980 est)
GNP $2.9 bn (1983); $1,340 per head of
population
chronology
1959 Granted internal self-government.
1962 Achieved full independence, with
Alexander Bustamente of the Jamaica
Labour Party (JLP) as prime minister.
1967 JLP re-elected under Hugh Shearer.
1972 Michael Manley of the People's
National Party (PNP) became prime minister.
1980 JLP elected, with Edward Seaga as
prime minister.
1983 JLP re-elected, winning all 60 seats.
1988 Island badly damaged by hurricane.
1989 PNP won a decisive victory with Michael
Manley returning as prime minister.

Japan
(Nippon)

area 370,000 sq km/142,680 sq mi
capital Tokyo
towns Fukuoka, Kitakyushu, Kyoto,

Sapporo; ports Osaka, Nagoya, Yokohama,
Kobe, Kawasaki
physical mountainous, volcanic; comprises
over 1,000 islands, of which the chief are
Hokkaido, Honshu, Shikoku, Kyushu
head of state (figurehead) Emperor Akihito
from 1989
political system liberal democracy
exports televisions, cassette and video
recorders, radios, cameras, computers,
robots, and other electronic and electrical
equipment, cars and other vehicles, ships,
iron and steel, chemicals, textiles
currency yen (225.75=£1 Mar 1989)
population 120,750,000 (1985); annual growth
rate 0.7%
life expectancy men 74, women 80
language Japanese
religion Shinto and Buddhist (often
combined), Christian (minority). 30% of the
population claim to have a personal religious
faith
literacy 99% (1985)
GNP $1,200 bn (1984); $10,266 per head of
population
chronology
1945 Japanese surrender. Allied control

commission in power.
1946 Framing of 'Peace Constitution'.
1952 Full sovereignty regained.
1958 Joined United Nations.
1972 Ryukyu Islands regained.
1974 Resignation of Prime Minister Tanaka
over Lockheed bribes scandal.
1982 Election of Yasuhiro Nakasone as prime
minister.
1987 Noboru Takeshita chosen to succeed
Nakasone.
1988 Recruit corporation insider-trading
scandal cast shadow over government and
opposition parties.
1989 Emperor Hirohito died and was
succeeded by his son Akihito. Takeshita
eventually resigned over Recruit and was
replaced by Sosuke Uno who resigned after
only a month over sex scandal.

Jordan
*Hashemite Kingdom of (Al Mamlaka al
Urduniya al Hashemiyah)*

area 98,000 sq km/38,000 sq mi
capital Amman
towns Aqaba, the only port

physical mostly desert
head of state and government King Hussein ibn
Talai from 1952
political system absolutism
exports potash, phosphates, citrus
currency Jordanian dinar (0.92=£1 Mar 1989)

population (1985 est) 3,510,000 (including Palestinian refugees); annual growth rate 3.7%
life expectancy men 62, women 66
language Arabic
religion Sunni Muslim
literacy 87% male/63% female (1985 est)
GDP \$4.2 bn (1984); \$552 per head of population
chronology
1946 Achieved full independence as Transjordan.
1949 New state of Jordan declared.
1953 Hussein ibn Talai became king of Jordan.
1958 Jordan and Iraq formed Arab Federation which ended when the Iraqi monarchy was deposed.
1982 Hussein tried to mediate in Arab-Israeli conflict.
1985 Hussein put forward a framework for a Middle East peace settlement. Secret meeting between Hussein and Israeli prime minister.
1988 Hussein announced a decision to cease administering the West Bank as part of Jordan, passing responsibility to Palestine Liberation Organization, and the suspension of parliament.
1989 Prime minister resigned and Hussein promised new parliamentary elections after rioting following criticism of economic policies.

Kampuchea
People's Republic of

area 181,000 sq km/71,000 sq mi
capital Phnom Penh
towns Battambang, and the seaport Kompong Som
physical mostly forested; flat, with mountains in S; Mekong River runs N–S
head of state Heng Samrin from 1979
head of government Hun Sen from 1985
political system communism
exports rubber, rice
currency Kampuchean riel (172.10=£1 Mar 1989)
population (1985 est) 7,280,000; annual growth rate 2.6%

life expectancy men 42, women 45
language Khmer (official), French
religion Theravada Buddhist
literacy 78% male/39% female (1980 est)
GDP \$100 per head of population (1984)
chronology
1863–1941 Vietnam became a French protectorate.
1941–45 Occupied by Japan.
1946 Recaptured by France.
1953 Granted full independence.
1970 Prince Sihanouk overthrown by US-backed Lon Nol.
1975 Lon Nol overthrown by Khmer Rouge.
1978–79 Vietnamese invasion and installation of Heng Samrin government.
1987 Partial withdrawal of Vietnamese troops.
1988 Vietnamese troop withdrawal continued.

Kenya
Republic of (Jamhuri ya Kenya)

area 583,000 sq km/224,960 sq mi
capital Nairobi
towns Kisumu, port Mombasa
physical mountains and highlands in the W and centre; coastal plain in S; the N is arid
head of state and government Daniel arap Moi from 1978

539

political system authoritarian nationalism
exports coffee, tea, sisal, pineapples
currency Kenya shilling (33.07=£1 Mar 1989)
population (1985) 20,330,000 (the dominant ethnic group is the Kikuyu); annual growth rate 4.1%
life expectancy men 51, women 55
language Swahili, but English is in general use
religion indigenous religions with Christian and Muslim minorities
literacy 70% male/49% female (1985 est)
GDP $5.6 bn (1983); $309 per head of population
chronology
1950 Mau Mau campaign began.
1953 Nationalist leader Jomo Kenyatta imprisoned.
1956 Mau Mau campaign defeated, Kenyatta released.
1963 Granted internal self-government, with Kenyatta as prime minister.
1964 Achieved full independence as a republic, within the Commonwealth, with Kenyatta as president.
1978 Death of Kenyatta. Succeeded by Daniel arap Moi.
1982 Attempted coup against Moi foiled.
1983 Moi re-elected.
1988 Moi re-elected.

Kiribati
Republic of

area 655 sq km/253 sq mi

capital and port Bairiki (on Tarawa Atoll)
physical comprises 33 Pacific islands: the Gilbert, Phoenix, and Line Islands, and Banaba (Ocean Island)
head of state and government Ieremia T Tabai from 1979
political system liberal democracy
exports copra
currency Australian dollar (2.08=£1 Sept 87)
population 61,000 (1985); annual growth rate 1.7%
language English and Gilbertese (official)
religion Christian, both Roman Catholic and Protestant
literacy 90% (1982)
GNP $30 million (1983)
chronology
1977 Gilbert Islands granted internal self-government.
1979 Achieved full independence, within the Commonwealth, as the Republic of Kiribati, with Ieremia Tabai as president.
1983 Tabai re-elected.
1985 Fishing agreement with Soviet state-owned company negotiated, prompting formation of Kiribati's first political party, the opposition Christian Democrats.
1987 Tabai re-elected.

Korea, North
Democratic People's Republic of (*Chosun Minchu-chui Inmin Konghwa-guk*)

area 121,250 sq km/46,815 sq mi
capital Pyongyang

physical mountainous
head of state Kim Il Sung from 1972 (also head of Communist Party)
head of government Yon Hyong Muk from 1988
political system communism
exports coal, iron, copper, textiles, chemicals
currency won (1.55=£1 Sept 1987)
population (1985 est) 20,380,000; annual growth rate 2.5%
life expectancy men 65, women 71
language Korean
religion traditionally Buddhist and Confucian
literacy 99% (1984)
GNP $18.1 bn (1982 est); $570 per head of population
chronology
1948 Democratic People's Republic of Korea declared.
1950 North Korea invaded South to begin Korean War.
1953 Armistice agreed to end Korean War.
1961 Friendship and mutual assistance treaty signed with China.
1972 New constitution, with executive president, was adopted.
1983 Four South Korean cabinet ministers assassinated in Rangoon, Burma, by North Korean army officers.

Korea, South
Republic of (Daehan Minguk)

---

area 99,999 sq km/38,450 sq mi

capital Seoul
towns Taegu, ports Pusan, Inchon
physical mountainous
head of state Roh Tae-Woo from 1988
head of government Kang Young Hoon from 1988
political system emergent democracy
exports steel, ships, chemicals, electronics, textiles, plastics
currency won (1,335=£1 Sept 1987)
population (1985) 41,210,000; annual growth rate 1.6%
life expectancy men 65, women 71
language Korean
religion traditionally Buddhist and Confucian
literacy 96% male/87% female (1980 est)
GNP $78.9 bn (1984); $1,187 per head of population
chronology
1948 Republic proclaimed.
1950–53 War with North Korea.
1960 President Syngman Rhee resigned amid unrest.
1961 Military coup by Gen Park Chung-Hee. Industrial growth programme.
1979 Assassination of President Park.
1980 Military coup by Gen Chun Doo-Hwan.
1987 Adoption of more democratic constitution following student unrest. Roh Tae-Woo elected president.
1988 Former president Chun, accused of corruption, publicly apologized for the misdeeds of his administration and agreed to hand over his financial assets to the state.

Kuwait
State of *(Dowlat al Kuwait)*

area 19,000 sq km/7,400 sq mi
capital Kuwait (also chief port)

physical hot desert
head of state and government Jaber al-Ahmad
al-Sabah from 1977
political system absolutism
exports oil
currency Kuwait dinar (0.49=£1 Mar 1989)
population (1985) 1,710,000 (40% Kuwaitis,
some 30% Palestinians); annual growth rate
5.5%
life expectancy men 70, women 74
language Arabic
religion Sunni Muslim, with Shi'ite minority
literacy 76% male/63% female (1985 est)
GNP $22 bn (1984); $11,431 per head of
population
chronology
1961 Achieved full independence, with
Sheikh Abdullah al-Salem al-Sabah as emir.
1965 Sheikh Abdullah died and was
succeeded by his brother, Sheikh Sabah.
1977 Sheikh Sabah died and was succeeded
by Crown Prince Jaber.

Laos
People's Democratic Republic of
*(Saathiaranagroat Prachhathippatay
Prachhachhon Lao)*

area 236,790 sq km/91,400 sq mi
capital Vientiane
towns Luang Prabang, the former royal
capital

physical high mountains in the E; Mekong
River in the W; jungle
head of state Prince Souphanouvong from
1975; Phoumi Vong Vichit acting president
from 1987
head of government Kaysone Phomvihane
from 1975
political system communism
exports tin, teak
currency new kip (742.18=£1 Mar 1989)
population (1985) 3,585,000; annual growth
rate 2.6%
life expectancy men 48, women 51
language Lao
religion traditionally Theravada Buddhist
literacy 76% male/63% female (1985 est)
GNP $601 million (1983); $85 per head of
population
chronology
1893–1945 Laos became a French
protectorate.
1945 Temporarily occupied by Japan.
1946 Retaken by France.
1950 Granted semi-autonomy in French
Union.
1954 Full independence achieved.

1960 Right-wing government seized power.
1962 Coalition government established; civil war continued.
1973 Vientiane ceasefire agreement.
1975 Communist-dominated republic proclaimed with Prince Souphanouvong as head of state.
1987 Phoumi Vong Vichit became acting president.
1988 Plans announced to withdraw 40% of the Vietnamese forces stationed in the country.
1989 First general election in 13 years.

Lebanon
Republic of (al-Jumhouria al-Lubnaniya)

area 10,400 sq km/3,400 sq mi
capital and port Beirut
towns ports Tripoli, Tyre, Sidon

physical valley N–S between mountain ranges
head of state presidency unfilled since 1988
heads of government Michel Aoun (military) from 1988, Selim El-Hoss (prime minister) from 1986
political system in state of crisis
exports citrus and other fruit; industrial products to Arab neighbours
currency Lebanese pound (832.38=£1 Sept 87)
population (1985 est) 2,670,000 (including 350,000 Palestinian refugees, many driven out, killed in fighting or massacred 1982–85); annual growth rate -0.1%
life expectancy men 63, women 67
language Arabic (official); French and English
religion Christian (Maronite and Orthodox) 40%, Muslim (Shi'ite 33%, Sunni 24%) 57%, Druse 3%
literacy 86% male/69% female (1985 est)
GNP $3 bn (1983); $1,150 per head of population
chronology
1944 Full independence achieved.
1964 Palestine Liberation Organization (PLO) founded in Beirut.
1975 Outbreak of civil war between Christians and Muslims.
1976 Ceasefire agreed.
1978 Israel invaded S Lebanon in search of PLO fighters. International peacekeeping force established. Fighting broke out again.
1979 Part of S Lebanon declared an 'independent free Lebanon'.
1982 Bachir Gemayel became president, but was assassinated before he could assume office. His brother Amin Gemayel became president.
1983 Agreement reached for the withdrawal of Syrian and Israeli troops, but not honoured.
1984 Most of international peacekeeping force withdrawn.
1985 Lebanon nearing chaos, with many foreigners being taken hostage.
1987 Syrian troops sent into Beirut.
1988 Attempts to agree a Christian successor to Gemayel failed. His last act in office was to establish a military government; Selim El-Hoss set up a rival government, and the threat of partition hung over the country.
1989 Civil war between Maronite Christians and Muslims.

Lesotho
Kingdom of

area 30,346 sq km/11,716 sq mi
capital Maseru
physical mountainous
head of state Moshoeshoe II from 1966

capital Monrovia
physical forested highlands; swampy coast where six rivers end

head of government Justin Lekhanya from 1986
political system military authoritarianism
exports wool, mohair, diamonds
currency maluti (4.38=£1 Mar 1989)
population (1985) 1,530,000; annual growth rate 2.5%
life expectancy men 46, women 52
language Sesotho and English (official)
religion Christian 70% (Roman Catholic 40%)
literacy 62% male/84% female (1985 est)
GNP $678.2 million (1981); $355 per head of population
chronology
1966 Basutoland achieved full independence, within the Commonwealth, as the Kingdom of Lesotho, with Chief Leabua Jonathan as prime minister.
1975 Members of the ruling party attacked by guerrillas backed by South Africa.
1986 South Africa imposed a border blockade, forcing the deportation of 60 African National Congress members.
1987 Gen Lekhanya ousted Chief Jonathan in a coup.

Liberia
Republic of

---

area 112,820 sq km/43,548 sq mi

head of state and government Samuel Kanyon Doe from 1980
political system emergent democracy
exports iron ore, rubber, diamonds, coffee, cocoa, palm oil
currency Liberian dollar (1.72=£1 Mar 1989)
population (1985) 1,190,000 (95% belonging to the indigenous peoples); annual growth rate 3.2%
life expectancy men 47, women 51
language English (official)
religion Muslim 20%, Christian 15%, traditional 65%
literacy 47% male/23% female (1985 est)
GNP $900 million (1983); $400 per head of population
chronology
1847 Founded as an independent republic.
1944 William Tubman elected president.
1971 Tubman died and was succeeded by William Tolbert.
1980 Tolbert assassinated in a coup led by Samuel Doe, who suspended the constitution and ruled through a People's Redemption Council (PRC).
1984 New constitution approved. National Democratic Party of Liberia (NDPL) founded by Doe.
1985 NDPL won decisive victory in general election. Unsuccessful coup against Doe.

Libya
Socialist People's Libyan Arab State of the Masses (Al-Jamahiriyah Al-Arabiya Al-Libya Al-Shabiya Al-Ishtirakiya)

area 1,780,000 sq km/680,000 sq mi
capital Tripoli
towns ports Benghazi, Misurata

physical desert; mountains in N and S
head of state and government Moamar Khaddhafi from 1969
political system nationalistic socialism
exports oil, natural gas
currency Libyan dinar (0.50=£1 Mar 1989)
population (1985) 3,752,000 (including 500,000 foreign workers); annual growth rate 3.9%
life expectancy men 57, women 60
language Arabic
religion Sunni Muslim
literacy 60% (1985)
GDP $25 bn (1984); $7,000 per head of population
chronology
1951 Achieved independence as the United Kingdom of Libya, under King Idris.
1969 King deposed in a coup led by Col Moamar Khaddhafi. Revolution Command Council set up and the Arab Socialist Union (ASU) proclaimed the only legal party.
1972 Proposed federation of Libya, Syria, and Egypt abandoned.
1980 Proposed merger with Syria abandoned. Libyan troops began fighting in Chad.
1981 Proposed merger with Chad abandoned.
1986 US bombing of Khaddhafi's headquarters, following allegations of his complicity in guerrilla activities.
1988 Diplomatic relations with Chad restored.
1989 USA accused Libya of building a chemical-weapons factory and shot down two Libyan planes.

Liechtenstein
Principality of

area 160 sq km/62 sq mi
capital Vaduz

physical Alpine; includes part of Rhine Valley
head of state Franz Josef II from 1938
head of government Hans Brunhart from 1978
government constitutional monarchy
exports microchips, precision engineering, processed foods, postage stamps; easy tax laws make it an international haven for foreign companies and banks
currency Swiss franc (2.79=£1 Mar 1989)
population (1985) 27,000 (33% foreign); annual growth rate 1.4%
life expectancy men 65, women 73
language German
religion Roman Catholic

545

literacy 100% (1986)
GDP 1 bn Swiss francs (1984); $16,440 per head of population
chronology
1938 Prince Franz Josef II came to power.
1984 Vote extended to women in national elections.

Luxembourg
Grand Duchy of (*Grand-Duché de Luxembourg*)

area 2,586 sq km/999 sq mi
capital Luxembourg

physical on the river Moselle; part of the Ardennes (Oesling) forest in the N
head of state Grand Duke Jean from 1964
head of government Jacques Santer from 1984
political system liberal democracy
exports iron and steel, chemicals, synthetic textiles; banking is very important; Luxembourg is economically linked with Belgium
currency Luxembourg franc (67.35=£1 Mar 1989)
population 366,000 (1985); annual growth rate -0%
life expectancy men 68, women 74
language French (official); local Letzeburgesch; German
religion Roman Catholic

546

literacy 100% (1983)
GDP $3.8 bn (1981); $10,444 per head of population
chronology
1948 With Belgium and the Netherlands, formed the Benelux customs union.
1958 Benelux became economic union.
1961 Prince Jean became acting head of state on behalf of his mother, Grand Duchess Charlotte.
1964 Grand Duchess Charlotte abdicated and Prince Jean became grand duke.

Madagascar
Democratic Republic of (*Repoblika Demokratika n'i Madagaskar*)

area 594,000 sq km/228,500 sq mi
capital Antananarivo
towns chief port Toamasina

physical central highlands; humid valleys and coastal plains
head of state and government Didier Ratsiraka from 1975
political system nationalistic socialism
exports coffee, sugar, spice, textiles
currency Malagasy franc (2,500=£1 Mar 1989)
population (1985) 9,980,000; annual growth rate 2.8%
life expectancy men 49, women 50

language Malagasy (of the Malayo-Polynesian family, official); French and English
religion animist 50%, Christian 40%, Muslim 10%
literacy 74% male/62% female (1985 est)
GNP $2.7 bn (1983); $279 per head of population
chronology
1960 Achieved full independence, with Philibert Tsiranana as president.
1972 Army took control of the government.
1975 Martial law imposed under a national military directorate. New constitution proclaimed the Democratic Republic of Madagascar, with Didier Ratsiraka as president.
1976 Front-Line Revolutionary Organisation (AREMA) formed.
1977 National Front for the Defence of the Malagasy Socialist Revolution (FNDR) became the sole legal political organization.
1983 Ratsiraka re-elected, despite strong opposition from radical socialist National Movement for the Independence of Madagascar (MONIMA) under Monja Jaona.

Malawi
Republic of (Malaŵi)

area 117,000 sq km/47,950 sq mi
capital Lilongwe
towns Blantyre-Limbe
physical occupies the mountainous W side of Lake Malawi
head of state and government Hastings Kamusu Banda from 1966
political system authoritarian nationalism
exports tea, tobacco, cotton, groundnuts, sugar
currency kwacha (4.58=£1 Mar 1989)
population 7,056,000 (1985); annual growth rate 3.1%
life expectancy men 44, women 46
language English (official); Chichewa
religion Christian 50%; Muslim 30%
literacy 52% male/31% female (1985 est)
GNP $1.1 bn (1984); $200 per head of population
chronology

1964 Nyasaland achieved independence, within the Commonwealth, as Malawi.
1966 Became a one-party republic, with Hastings Banda as president.
1971 Banda was made president for life.
1977 Banda started a programme of moderate liberalization, releasing some political detainees and allowing greater freedom of the press.
1986–89 Influx of over 650,000 refugees from Mozambique.

Malaysia

area 331,500 sq km/128,000 sq mi
capital Kuala Lumpur
towns Kuching in Sarawak and Kota Kinabalu in Sabah
physical comprises W Malaysia (the nine Malay states – Perlis, Kedah, Johore, Selangor, Perak, Negri Sembilan, Kelantan, Trengganu, Pahang – plus Penang and Malacca); and E Malaysia (Sarawak and Sabah); 75% of the area is covered in tropical jungle; there is a central mountain range; swamps in the E
head of state Rajah Azlan Shah (sultan of Perak) from 1989
head of government Mahathir bin Mohamad from 1981
political system liberal democracy

exports pineapples, palm oil, rubber, timber, petroleum (Sarawak), bauxite
currency ringgit (4.74=£1 Mar 1989)
population (1985 est) 15,560,000 (Malaysian 47%, Chinese 34%, Indians, Pakistanis 9%, and indigenous peoples – Dayaks, Ibans – of E Malaysia 10%); annual growth rate 2.5%
life expectancy men 65, women 69
language Malay (official, usually written in Arabic characters); in Sarawak English is also official
religion Muslim (official)
literacy 81% male/66% female (1985 est)
GNP $29.7 bn (1983); $714 per head of population
chronology
1963 Formation of federation of Malaysia.
1965 Secession of Singapore from federation.
1969 Anti-Chinese riots in Kuala Lumpur.
1971 Launch of Bumiputra 'new economic policy'.
1981 Election of Dr Mahathir bin Mohamad as prime minister.
1982 Mahathir bin Mohamad re-elected.
1986 Mahathir bin Mohamad re-elected.
1987 Mahathir responded to growing racial tension by arresting opposition leaders, lawyers, and journalists, and tightening press censorship.
1988 Split in ruling UMNO party
1989 Rajah Azlan Shah, sultan of Perak,

elected paramount ruler from Apr for a five-year term.

Maldives
Republic of (Divehi Jumhuriya)

area 298 sq km/115 sq mi
capital Malé

physical comprises some 1,000 coral islands, largely flat, none bigger than 13 sq km/5 sq mi
head of state and government Maumoon Abdul Gayoom from 1978
political system authoritarian nationalism
exports coconuts and copra, and bonito (fish related to tunny); tourism is important
currency Maldivian rupee (15.03=£1 Mar 1989)
population 182,000 (1985); annual growth rate 3.2%
language Divehi (related to Sinhalese)
religion Sunni Muslim
literacy 82% male/82% female (1977)
GNP $56 million (1983); $470 per head of population
chronology
1953 Originally a sultanate, the Maldive Islands became a republic within the Commonwealth.
1954 Sultanate restored.
1965 Achieved full independence outside the Commonwealth.

1968 Sultan deposed and a republic reinstated with Ibrahim Nasir as president.
1978 Nasir retired and was replaced by Maumoon Abdul Gayoom.
1982 Rejoined the Commonwealth.
1983 Gayoom re-elected.
1988 Gayoom re-elected. Unsuccessful coup attempt by mercenaries thought to have the backing of former president Nasir, was foiled by Indian troops.

Mali
Republic of (République du Mali)

area 1,204,000 sq km/465,000 sq mi
capital Bamako

physical river Niger in S; savanna; part of the Sahara in N
head of state and government Moussa Traoré from 1968
political system authoritarian nationalism
exports cotton, groundnuts, livestock
currency CFA franc (replacing Mali franc in 1984 (544.87=£1 Mar 1989)
population (1985) 8,210,000; annual growth rate 2.8%
life expectancy men 40, women 44
language French (official), Bambara
religion Sunni Muslim 65%, animist 35%
literacy 23% male/11% female (1985 est)
GNP $1.1 bn (1983); $140 per head of population
chronology
1959 With Senegal, formed the Federation of Mali.

1960 Became the independent Republic of Mali, with Mobido Keita as president.
1968 Keita replaced in an army coup by Moussa Traoré.
1974 New constitution made Mali a one-party state.
1976 New national party, the Malian People's Democratic Union, announced.
1983 Agreement between Mali and Guinea for eventual political and economic integration signed.

Malta
Republic of (Repubblika Ta'Malta)

area 316 sq km/122 sq mi
capital Valletta

physical includes the island of Gozo 67 sq km/26 sq mi and Comino 2.5 sq km/1 sq mi
head of state Paul Xuereb from 1987
head of government Eddie Fenech-Adami from 1987
political system liberal democracy
exports vegetables, knitwear, handmade lace, plastics, electronic equipment
currency Maltese pound (0.58=£1 Mar 1989)
population (1985 est) 380,000; annual growth rate 0.7%
life expectancy men 69, women 74
language Maltese (related to Arabic, with Phoenician survivals and influenced by Italian)
religion Roman Catholic

literacy 86% male/82% female (1985 est)
GNP $1.04 bn (1983); $2,036 per head of
population
chronology
1942 Awarded the George Cross.
1955 Dom Mintoff of the Malta Labour Party
(MLP) became prime minister.
1956 Referendum approved proposal for
integration with the UK. Proposal opposed
by the Nationalist Party.
1958 MLP rejected the integration proposal.
1962 Nationalists elected, with Borg Olivier
as prime minister.
1964 Achieved full independence, within
the Commonwealth. Ten-year defence and
economic aid treaty with Britain signed.
1971 Mintoff re-elected. The 1964 treaty
declared invalid and negotiations began for
the leasing of the NATO base in Malta.
1972 Seven-year NATO agreement signed.
1974 Became a republic.
1984 Mintoff retired and was replaced by
Mifsud Bonnici as prime minister and MLP
leader.
1987 Eddie Fenech-Adami (Nationalist)
became prime minister.

Mauritania
*Islamic Republic of (République Islamique de
Mauritanie)*

area 1,030,000 sq km/419,000 sq mi
capital Nouakchott

physical valley of river Senegal in S; the rest
is arid

head of state and government Moaouya Ould
Sidi Ahmed Taya from 1984
political system military authoritarianism
exports iron ore, fish
currency ouguiya (129.45=£1 Mar 1989)
population (1985 est) 1,890,000 (30% Arab
Berber, 30% black Africans, 30% Haratine
– descendants of black slaves, who remained
slaves till 1980); annual growth rate 2.9%
life expectancy men 42, women 46
language Arabic (official), French
religion Sunni Muslim
literacy 2.9%
GDP $614 million (1984); $466 per head of
population
chronology
1960 Achieved full independence, with
Moktar Ould Daddah, as president.
1975 Western Sahara ceded by Spain.
Mauritania occupied the southern part and
Morocco the rest. Polisario Front formed in
Sahara to resist the occupation by Mauritania
and Morocco.
1978 Daddah deposed in bloodless coup
and replaced by Mohamed Khouni Ould
Haidalla. Peace agreed with Polisario Front.
1981 Diplomatic relations with Morocco
broken.
1984 Haidalla overthrown by Moaouya Ould
Sidi Ahmed Taya. Polisario regime formally
recognized.
1985 Relations with Morocco restored.
1989 Violent clashes between Mauritanians
and Senegalese in Nouakchott and Dakar.

Mauritius
State of

area 1,865 sq km/720 sq mi; the island of
Rodrigues is part of Mauritius and there are
several small island dependencies
capital Port Louis
physical a mountainous, volcanic island
surrounded by coral reefs
head of state Elizabeth II represented by
Veerasamy Ringadoo from 1986
head of government Aneerood Jugnauth from
1982
political system liberal democracy
exports sugar, knitted goods; tourism is

increasingly important
currency Mauritius rupee (25.15=£1 Mar 1989)
population 1,024,900 (1985); annual growth rate 1.9%
life expectancy men 64, women 69
language English (official); creole French
religion Hindu 45%, Christian 30%, Muslim 15%
literacy 89% male/77% female (1985 est)
GNP $957 million (1984); $1,240 per head of population
chronology
1968 Achieved full independence within the Commonwealth, with Seewoosagur Ramgoolam as prime minister.
1982 Aneerood Jugnauth prime minister.
1983 Jugnauth formed a new party, the Mauritius Socialist Movement, pledged to make Mauritius a republic within the Commonwealth, but Assembly refused. Ramgoolam appointed governor general. Jugnauth formed a new coalition government.
1985 Ramgoolam died, succeeded by Ringadoo.
1987 Jugnauth's coalition re-elected.

Mexico
United States of (Estados Unidos Mexicanos)

area 1,979,650 sq km/763,944 sq mi
capital Mexico City
towns Guadalajara, Monterrey; port Veracruz

physical partly arid central highlands flanked by Sierra Madre mountain ranges E and W; tropical coastal plains
head of state and government Carlos Salinas de Gortari from 1988
political system liberal democracy
exports silver, gold, lead, uranium; oil and natural gas (to USA); traditional handicrafts; fish and shellfish
currency peso (free rate 4,109.63=£1 Mar 1989)
population (1985) 78,520,000 (a minority are *criollos* of Spanish descent, 12% are American Indian, and the majority are of mixed descent; 50% of the total are under 20 years of age); annual growth rate 2.6%
life expectancy men 64, women 68
language Spanish (official); Indian languages include Nahuatl, Maya, and Mixtec
religion Roman Catholic
literacy 92% male/88% female (1985)
GNP $168 bn (1983); $1,800 per head of population
chronology
1821 Mexico achieved independence from Spain.
1846–48 Mexico at war with USA.
1848 Maya Indian revolt suppressed.
1917 New constitution introduced, designed to establish permanent democracy.
1983–84 Financial crisis.
1985 Institutional Revolutionary Party (PRI) returned to power. Earthquake in Mexico

551

City.
1986 IMF loan agreement signed to keep the country solvent until at least 1988.
1988 The PRI candidate, Carlos Salinas, won the presidency amid allegations of election fraud.

Monaco
Principality of

area 1.5 sq km/0.575 sq mi
capital Monaco-Ville
town Monte Carlo, noted for its film festival,

motor races, and casino
physical steep slope
head of state Rainier III from 1949
head of government Jean Ausseil from 1986
government constitutional monarchy under French protectorate
exports some light industry, but economy depends on tourism and gambling
currency French franc (10.90=£1 Mar 1989)
population 28,000 (1985); annual growth rate -0.5%
language French
religion Roman Catholic
literacy 99% (1985)
chronology
1861 Became an independent state, under French protection.
1918 France given a veto over succession to the throne.
1949 Prince Rainier III ascended the throne.

Mongolia
Mongolian People's Republic (Bügd Nayramdakh Mongol Ard Uls)

area 1,560,000 sq km/600,000 sq mi
capital Ulaanbaatar (formerly Ulan Bator)
towns Darkhan, Choybalsan

physical a high plateau with steppe (grasslands)
head of state Jambyn Batmunkh from 1984
head of government Dumagiin Sodnom from 1984
political system communism
exports meat and butter; varied minerals; furs
currency tugrik (5.79=£1 Mar 1989)
population 1,893,000 (1985); annual growth rate 2.8%
life expectancy men 60, women 64
language Khalkha Mongolian (official), Chinese, Russian
religion formerly Tibetan Buddhist Lamaist, suppressed in the 1930s
literacy 93% male/85% female (1980 est)
GNP \$1.8 bn (1983); \$750 per head of population
chronology
1911 Outer Mongolia gained autonomy from China.
1924 People's Republic proclaimed.
1946 China recognized Outer Mongolia's independence.

1966 20-year friendship, cooperation, and mutual-assistance pact signed with USSR. Deterioration in relations with China.
1986 Soviet troop numbers reduced and Outer Mongolia's external contacts broadened.
1987 Further major Soviet troop reductions.

Morocco
Kingdom of (al-Mamlaka al-Maghrebia)

area 458,730 sq km/166,000 sq mi
capital Rabat
towns Marrakesh, Fez, Kenes; ports Casablanca, Tangier

physical mountain ranges NE–SW; plains in W
head of state Hassan II from 1961
head of government Mohamed Karim Lamrani from 1984
political system emergent democracy
exports dates, figs, cork, wood pulp, canned fish, phosphates; tourism is important
currency dirham (14.40=£1 Mar 1989)
population (1985 est) 21,940,000; annual growth rate 2.5%
life expectancy men 57, women 60
language Arabic (official); French, Spanish
religion Sunni Muslim
literacy 45% male/22% female (1985 est)
GNP $15.6 bn (1983); $800 per head of population
chronology

1956 Achieved independence from France as the Sultanate of Morocco.
1957 Sultan restyled king of Morocco.
1961 Hassan II came to the throne.
1972 Major revision of the constitution.
1975 Western Sahara ceded by Spain to Morocco and Mauritania.
1976 Guerrilla war in the Sahara by the Polisario Front. Sahrawi Arab Democratic Republic (SADR) established in Algiers. Diplomatic relations between Morocco and Algeria broken.
1979 Mauritania signed a peace treaty with Polisario.
1983 Peace formula for the Sahara proposed by the Organization of African Unity (OAU) but not accepted by Morocco.
1984 Hassan signed an agreement for cooperation and mutual defence with Libya.
1987 Ceasefire agreed with Polisario but fighting continued.
1988 Diplomatic relations with Algeria restored.
1989 Diplomatic relations with Syria restored.

Mozambique
People's Republic of (República Popular de Moçambique)

area 784,960 sq km/303,070 sq mi

capital and chief port Maputo
towns ports Beira, Nacala
physical mostly flat; mountains in W
head of state and government Joaquim
Chissano from 1986
political system nationalistic socialism
exports sugar, cashews, tea, cotton, copra,
sisal
currency metical (replaced escudo 1980)
(1188.90=£1 Sept 1987)
population (1985 est) 13,960,000 (mainly
indigenous Bantu peoples; Portuguese
50,000); annual growth rate 2.8%
life expectancy men 44, women 46
language Portuguese (official)
religion animist 69%, Roman Catholic 21%,
Muslim 10%
literacy 55% male/22% female (1985 est)
GDP $2.7 bn (1983); $220 per head of
population
chronology
1962 Frelimo (liberation front) established.
1975 Full independence achieved as a socialist
republic, with Samora Machel as president
and Frelimo as the sole legal party.
1983 Re-establishment of good relations with
Western powers.
1984 Nkomati Accord signed with South
Africa.
1986 Machel killed in air crash, and
succeeded by Joaquim Chissano.
1988 Tanzania announced complete
withdrawal of its troops.

Namibia

area 823,168 sq km/317,743 sq mi
capital Windhoek
physical mainly desert
head of state and government in transition
stage (currently governed by South Africa)
political system emergent democracy
exports diamonds and uranium
currency South African rand (4.39 = Mar
1989)
population (1985) 1.151m (85% black
African, 6% European)
language Afrikaans, German, and English
religion 51% Lutheran, 19% Roman
Catholic, 6% Dutch Reformed Church, 6%

Anglican
literacy 38%
GDP $1,247m (1985); $1,084 per head of
population

chronology
1884 German and British colonies
established.
1915 German colony seized by South Africa.
1920 Administered by South Africa, under
League of Nations mandate, as British South
Africa (SWA).
1946 Full incorporation in South Africa
refused by United Nations (UN).
1958 South West African People's
Organization (SWAPO) set up to seek racial
equality and full independence.
1966 South Africa's apartheid laws extended
to the country.
1968 Redesignated Nambia by UN.
1978 UN Security Council Resolution 435 for
the granting of full sovereignty accepted by
South Africa and then rescinded.
1988 Peace talks between South Africa,
Angola and Cuba led to agreement on full
independence for Namibia in 1989.
1989 Unexpected incursion by SWAPO
guerrillas from Angola into Namibia
threatened agreed timetable for
independence from South Africa.

Nauru
Republic of

area 21 sq km/8 sq mi
capital Yaren

physical island country in W Pacific
head of state and government Hammer
DeRoburt from 1987
political system liberal democracy
exports phosphates
currency Australian dollar (2.08=£1 Mar
1989)
population (1985 est) 8,000 (mainly
Polynesian; Chinese 8%, European 8%);
annual growth rate 3.1%
language Nauruan (official), English
religion Protestant 45%
literacy 99%
GDP $155 million (1981); $21,400 per head of
population
chronology
1888 Annexed by Germany.
1920 Administered by Australia, New
Zealand, and UK until independence, except
1942–45, when it was occupied by Japan.
1968 Full independence achieved, with
'special member' Commonwealth status.
Hammer DeRoburt elected president.
1976 Bernard Dowiyogo elected president.
1978 DeRoburt returned to power.
1986 DeRoburt resigned when his budget
plans were not approved, and the opposition
leader Kenneth Adeang took over.
1987 After fresh parliamentary elections

DeRoburt returned to power. Adeang, again
in opposition, established the country's first
official party, the Democratic Party of Nauru.

Nepál
(Sri Nepala Sarkar)

area 141,400 sq km/54,600 sq mi
capital Katmandu

physical descends from the Himalaya
mountain range in the N to the river Ganges
plain in the S
head of state King Birendra Bir Bikram Shah
Dev from 1972
head of government Marich Man Singh
Shrestha from 1986
political system absolutism
exports jute, rice, timber
currency Nepálese rupee (41.42=£1 Mar
1989)
population (1985) 16,630,000 (mainly known
by the name of the predominant clan,
the Gurkhas; the Sherpas are a Buddhist
minority of NE Nepál); annual growth rate
2.3%
life expectancy men 47, women 45
language Nepáli
religion Hindu, with Buddhist minority
literacy 39% male/12% female (1985 est)
GNP $2.6 bn (1983); $140 per head of
population

chronology
1768 Nepál emerged as unified kingdom.
1846–1951 Ruled by the Rana family.
1951 Monarchy restored.
1959 Constitution created elected legislature.
1960–61 Parliament dissolved by king and political parties banned.
1980 Constitutional referendum held following popular agitation.
1981 Direct elections held to national assembly.
1983 Overthrow of monarch-supported prime minister.
1986 New assembly elections returned a majority opposed to *panchayat* system.
1988 Strict curbs placed on opposition activity, with more than 100 supporters of banned opposition party arrested and tight censorship imposed.
1989 Border blockade imposed by India in treaty dispute.

Netherlands
Kingdom of the (*Koninkrijk der Nederlanden*), popularly referred to as *Holland*

area 34,000 sq km/13,020 sq mi
capital Amsterdam
towns The Hague (seat of government); chief port Rotterdam

physical almost completely flat; rivers Rhine,

Schelde (*Scheldt*), Maas; Frisian Islands
territories Aruba, Netherlands Antilles
head of state Beatrix Wilhelmina Armgard from 1980
head of government vacant until elections Sept 1989
political system liberal democracy
exports dairy products, flower bulbs, vegetables, petrochemicals, electronics
currency guilder (3.63=£1 Mar 1989)
population (1986) 14,529,000 (including 300,000 of Dutch-Indonesian origin absorbed 1949–64 from former colonial possessions); annual growth rate 0.5%
life expectancy men 73, women 80
language Dutch
religion Roman Catholic 35%, Protestant 28%
literacy 99% (1985)
GNP $122.4 bn (1984); $9,175 per head of population
chronology
1940–45 Occupied by Germany during World War II.
1947 Joined Benelux Union.
1948 Queen Juliana succeeded Queen Wilhelmina to the throne.
1949 Founder member of NATO.
1958 Joined European Community.
1980 Queen Juliana abdicated in favour of her daughter Beatrix.
1981 Opposition to cruise missiles averted their being sited on Dutch soil.
1989 Prime minister Lubbers resigned over environmental issue.

New Zealand

area 268,675 sq km/103,736 sq mi
capital Wellington
towns Hamilton, Palmerston North, Christchurch, Dunedin; ports Wellington, Auckland
physical comprises North and South islands, Stewart and Chatham islands; mainly mountainous
territories overseas comprise Tokelau Island (three atolls transferred 1926 from the former Gilbert and Ellice Islands colony) and Niue Island (one of the Cook Islands,

but separately administered from 1903: chief town Alafi). The Cook Islands are internally self-governing, but share common citizenship with New Zealand. The Ross Dependency is in the Antarctic
head of state Elizabeth II from 1952 represented by Paul Reeves from 1985
head of government David Lange from 1984
political system liberal democracy
exports lamb and beef, wool and leather, dairy products and other processed foods; kiwi fruit became a major export crop in the 1980s; seeds and breeding stock; timber, paper, pulp; light aircraft
currency New Zealand dollar (2.79=£1 Mar 1989)
population (1986) 3,302,000 (including 270,000 Maoris and 60,000 other Polynesians; the whites are chiefly of British descent); annual growth rate 0.9%
life expectancy men 71, women 77
language English (official); Maori (the Lange government pledged to give it official status)
religion Protestant 50%, Roman Catholic 15%
literacy 99% (1984)
GNP $21.4 bn (1984); $7,916 per head of population
chronology
1947 Full independence within the Commonwealth confirmed by the New Zealand parliament.
1972 National Party government replaced Labour Party, with Norman Kirk as prime minister.
1974 Kirk died and was replaced by Wallace Rowling.
1975 National Party returned, with Robert Muldoon as prime minister.
1984 Labour Party returned under David Lange.
1985 Non-nuclear defence policy created disagreements with France and the USA.
1987 National Party declared support for the Labour government's non-nuclear policy. Lange re-elected. New Zealand officially became a 'friendly' rather than 'allied' country in the eyes of the USA, because of its non-nuclear defence policy.
1988 Free-trade agreement with Australia signed.

Nicaragua
Republic of (República de Nicaragua)

area 148,000 sq km/57,150 sq mi
capital Managua
towns chief port Corinto

physical volcanic mountain ranges; lakes Nicaragua and Managua
head of state and government Daniel Ortega Saavedra from 1985
political system emergent democracy
exports coffee, cotton, sugar
currency cordoba (9493.00=£1 Mar 1989)
population (1986) 3,140,000 (70% mestizo, 15% Spanish descent, 10% Indian or black);

annual growth rate 3.3%
life expectancy men 59, women 61
language Spanish (official)
religion Roman Catholic
literacy 61% male/60% female (1980 est)
GDP $3.4 bn (1983); $804 per head of
population
chronology
1838 Achieved full independence.
1962 Sandinista National Liberation Front
(FSLN) formed to fight Somoza regime.
1979 Somoza government ousted by FSLN.
1982 Subversive activity against the
government promoted by the USA. State of
emergency declared.
1985 Denunciation of Sandinista government
by US president Reagan. FSLN won big
victory in assembly elections.
1987 Central American peace agreement
co-signed by Nicaraguan leaders.
1988 Peace agreement failed. Nicaragua held
talks with Contra rebel leaders. Hurricane
left 180,000 people homeless.
1989 Inflation reached 36,000% a year.
Political prisoners released and new elections
promised.

Niger
Republic of (République du Niger)

area 1,186,408 sq km/457,953 sq mi
capital Niamey
physical mountains in centre; arid except in S
(savanna) and SW (river Niger)

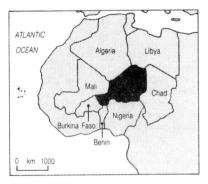

head of state and government Ali Seybou from
1987
political system military authoritarianism
exports groundnuts, livestock, gum arabic,
tin, uranium
currency CFA franc (544.87=£1 Mar 1989)
population (1986) 6,608,000; annual growth
rate 2.8%
life expectancy men 41, women 44
language French (official), Hausa, Djerma
religion Sunni Muslim 85%, animist 15%
literacy 19% male/9% female (1985 est)
GDP $2.3 bn (1982); $475 per head of
population
chronology
1960 Achieved full independence from
France with Hamani Diori elected president.
1974 Diori ousted in an army coup led by
Seyni Kountché.
1977 Cooperation agreement signed with
France.
1987 Kountché died and was replaced by the
army commander-in-chief Ali Seybou.

Nigeria
Federal Republic of

area 924,000 sq km/357,000 sq mi
capital and chief port Lagos
towns administrative headquarters Abuja;

Ibadan, Ogbomosho, Kano; ports Port
Harcourt, Warri, Calabar
physical the arid N becomes savanna and
farther S tropical rainforest, with mangrove

swamps along the coast; river Niger
head of state and government Ibrahim
Babangida from 1985
political system military authoritarianism
exports petroleum (richest African country in
oil resources), cocoa, groundnuts, palm oil,
cotton, rubber, tin
currency naira (12.68=£1 Mar 1989)
population (1986) 116,200,000 (of three main
ethnic groups, Yoruba in the W, Ibo in the E,
and Hausa-Fulani in the N); annual growth
rate 3.3%
life expectancy men 47, women 50
language English (official), Hausa, Ibo,
Yoruba
religion Sunni Muslim in the N, Christian in
the S
literacy 54% male/31% female (1985 est)
GDP $65 bn (1983); $750 per head of
population
chronology
1960 Achieved full independence within the
Commonwealth.
1963 Became a republic, with Nnamdi
Azikiwe as president.
1966 Military coup, followed by a counter-
coup led by Gen Yakubu Gowon. Slaughter
of many members of the Ibo tribe in the N.
1967 Conflict about oil revenues leads to
declaration of an independent state of Biafra
and outbreak of civil war.
1970 Surrender of Biafra and end of civil war.
1975 Gowon ousted in military coup; a
second coup puts Gen Obasanjo in power.
1979 Shehu Shagari becomes civilian
president.
1983 Shagari's government overthrown in
coup by Maj-Gen Buhari.
1985 Buhari replaced in a bloodless coup led
by Maj-Gen Ibrahim Babangida.
1989 Babangida promised a return to pluralist
politics.

Norway
Kingdom of (Kongeriket Norge)

area 323,878 sq km/125,017 sq mi
capital Oslo
towns Bergen, Trondheim
physical mountainous; forests cover 25%;

extends N of Arctic Circle
territories dependencies in the Arctic
(Svalbard and Jan Mayen) and in the
Antarctic (Bouvet and Peter I Island, and
Queen Maud Land)
head of state Olaf V from 1957
head of government Gro Harlem Brundtland
from 1986
political system liberal democracy
exports petrochemicals from North Sea oil
and gas, paper, wood pulp, furniture, iron
ore and other minerals, high-tech goods,
sports goods, fish
currency krone (11.68=£1 Mar 1989)
population (1986) 4,159,000; annual growth
rate 0.3%
life expectancy men 73, women 80
language Riksmal (formal Dano-Norwegian)
and Landsmal (based on the local dialects of
Norway)
religion Evangelical Lutheran (endowed by
state)
literacy 100% (1984)
GNP $56 bn (1982); $12,432 per head of
population
chronology
1814 Independent from Denmark.
1905 Links with Sweden ended.
1940–45 Occupied by Germany.
1949 Joined NATO.
1952 Joined Nordic Council.
1957 King Haakon VII succeeded by his son,
Olaf V.
1960 Joined EFTA.

1972 Accepted into membership of the European Community but application withdrawn after a referendum.

Oman
Sultanate of

area 272,000 sq km/105,000 sq mi
capital Muscat
towns Salalah

physical mountains and a high arid plateau; fertile coastal strip
head of state and government Qaboos bin Said from 1970
political system absolutism
exports oil, dates, silverware
currency Omani rial (0.66=£1 Mar 1989)
population (1985) 2 million; annual growth rate 4.7%
life expectancy men 51, women 54
language Arabic
religion Sunni Muslim
literacy 20% (1983)
GNP $7 bn (1983); $2,400 per head of population
chronology
1951 The Sultanate of Muscat and Oman achieved full independence. Treaty of friendship with Britain signed.
1970 After 38 years' rule, Sultan Said bin Taimur replaced in coup by his son Qaboos bin Said. Name changed to Sultanate of Oman.

1975 Left-wing rebels in the S defeated.
1982 Memorandum of Understanding with the UK signed, providing for consultation on international issues.

Pakistan
Islamic Republic of

area 796,095 sq km/307,293 sq mi; one-third of Kashmir is under Pakistani control
capital Islamabad
towns Karachi (largest city and port), Lahore

physical fertile plains; Indus river; Himalaya mountains in the N
head of state Ghulam Ishaq Khan from 1988
head of government Benazir Bhutto from 1988
political system emergent democracy
exports cotton textiles, rice, leather, carpets
currency Pakistan rupee (34.50=£1 Mar 1989)
population (1985) 99,199,000 (66% Punjabi, 13% Sindhi); annual growth rate 3.1%
life expectancy men 51, women 49
language Urdu and English (official); Punjabi
religion Sunni Muslim 75%, Shi'ite Muslim 20%, Hindu 4%
literacy 40% male/19% female (1985 est)
GDP $35 bn (1983); $280 per head of population
chronology
1947 Pakistan formed following partition of India.
1956 Proclaimed a republic.

1958 Military rule imposed by Gen Ayub Khan.

1969 Power transferred to Gen Yahya Khan.

1971 Secession of East Pakistan (Bangladesh). After civil war, power was transferred to Zulfiqar Ali Bhutto.

1977 Bhutto overthrown in military coup by Gen Zia ul-haq. Martial law imposed.

1979 Bhutto executed.

1981 Opposition Movement for Restoration of Democracy formed. Islamization process pushed forward.

1985 Non-party elections held, amended constitution adopted, martial law and ban on political parties lifted.

1986 Agitation for free elections launched by Benazir Bhutto.

1988 Zia introduced Islamic legal code, the *Shariah*. He was killed in a military air crash in Aug, and Benazir Bhutto was elected prime minister in Nov.

Panama
Republic of (República de Panamá)

area 78,046 sq km/30,126 sq mi
capital Panama City
towns Cristóbal, Balboa, Colón

physical mountain ranges; tropical rainforest
head of armed forces Manuel Antonio Noriega in power from 1981
head of state and government Manuel Solis Palma from 1988

political system military authoritarianism
exports bananas, petroleum products, copper from one of the world's largest deposits, shrimps
currency balboa (1.72=£1 Mar 1989)
population (1985) 2,180,000; annual growth rate 2.2%
life expectancy men 69, women 73
language Spanish
religion Roman Catholic
literacy 89% male/88% female (1985)
GDP $4.1 bn (1983); $1,116 per head of population
chronology
1903 Became independent from Colombia.
1974 Agreement to negotiate a full transfer of the Panama Canal from the USA to Panama.
1977 US-Panama treaties transfer the canal to Panama, with the USA guaranteeing its protection and an annual payment.
1984 Nicolas Ardito Barletta elected president.
1985 Barletta resigned to be replaced by Eric Arturo del Valle.
1987 Gen Noriega successfully resisted calls for his removal, despite the suspension of US military and economic aid.
1988 Trying to dismiss Noriega, del Valle was replaced by Manuel Solis Palma. Noriega, charged with drug smuggling by a US federal court, declared a state of emergency.
1989 Noriega defeated in fraudulent elections, declares result null and void. US sends 2,000 troops into Canal Zone US bases.

Papua New Guinea

area 462,840 sq km/178,656 sq mi
capital Port Moresby (on E New Guinea)
physical mountains in centre; thickly forested
head of state Elizabeth II, represented by Kingsford Dibela from 1983
head of government Rabbie Namaliu from 1988
political system liberal democracy
exports copra, coconut oil, palm oil, tea, copper
currency kina (1.43=£1 Mar 1989)
population (1986) 3,420,000 (including Papuans, Melanesians, Pygmies, and various

minorities); annual growth rate 2.6%
life expectancy men 51, women 53
language English (official); pidgin English
religion Protestant 33%, Roman Catholic
18%, local faiths
literacy 55% male/36% female (1985 est)
GNP $2.5 bn (1983); $480 per head of
population
chronology
1883 Annexed by Queensland, and soon
known became known as the Australian
Territory of Papua.
1884 NE New Guinea annexed by Germany;
SE claimed by Britain.
1914 NE New Guinea occupied by Australia.
1921–42 Held as a League of Nations
mandate.
1942–45 Occupied by Japan.
1975 Achieved full independence, within the
Commonwealth, with Michael Somare as
prime minister.
1980 Julius Chan became prime minister.
1982 Somare returned to power.
1985 Somare challenged by deputy prime
minister, Paias Wingti, who later formed a
five-party coalition government.
1988 Wingti defeated on no-confidence
vote and replaced by Rabbie Namaliu, who
established a six-party coalition government.

Paraguay
Republic of (República del Paraguay)

area 406,752 sq km/157,006 sq mi
capital Asunción

town port Concepción
physical mostly flat; divided by river
Paraguay; river Paraná in S
head of state and government Andrés
Rodriguez from 1989
political system military authoritarianism
exports cotton, soya beans, timber, tung oil,
maté
currency guaraní (690.40=£1 Mar 1989,
official rate)
population (1985) 3,680,000 (95% of mixed
Guaraní Indian-Spanish descent); annual
growth rate 3.0%
life expectancy men 63, women 68
language Spanish (official), spoken by 4%;
Guaraní 50%; remainder bilingual
religion Roman Catholic
literacy 91% male/85% female (1985 est)
GDP $5.6 bn (1983); $1,614 per head of
population
chronology
1811 Independent from Spain.
1865–70 At war with Argentina, Brazil and
Uruguay. Much territory lost.
1932–35 Much territory won from Bolivia
during the Chaco War.
1940–48 Gen Higino Morinigo president.
1948–54 Political instability with six different
presidents.

1954 Gen Alfredo Stroessner seized power. He was subsequently re-elected seven times, despite increasing opposition and accusations of human-rights violations.

1989 Stroessner ousted in coup led by Gen Andrés Rodríguez . Rodriguez elected president three months after seizing power.

Peru
Republic of (República del Perú)

area 1,332,000 sq km/514,060 sq mi
capital Lima, including port of Callao
towns Arequipa, Iquitos, Chiclayo

physical Andes mountains N–S cover 27%; Amazon river-basin jungle in NE
head of state and government Alan García Perez from 1985
political system emergent democracy
exports coffee, alpaca, llama and vicuna wool, fish meal, lead, copper, iron, oil
currency sol (free rate 2100.54=£1 Mar 1989)
population (1985) 19,700,000 (46% American Indian, mainly Quechua and Aymara; 43% of mixed Spanish-American Indian descent); annual growth rate 2.6%
life expectancy men 57, women 61
language Spanish, Quechua (both official)
religion Roman Catholic

literacy 91% male/78% female (1985 est)
GNP $18.6 bn (1983); $655 per head of population
chronology
1824 Achieved independence from Spain, the last South American country to do so.
1902 Boundary dispute with Bolivia settled.
1927 Boundary dispute with Colombia settled.
1942 Boundary dispute with Ecuador settled.
1948 Army coup, led by Gen Manuel Odria, installed a military government.
1963 Return to civilian rule, with Fernando Belaunde as president.
1968 Return of military government in a bloodless coup by Gen Juan Velasco.
1975 Velasco replaced, in a bloodless coup, by Gen Morales Bermudez.
1980 Return to civilian rule, with Fernando Belaunde as president.
1981 Boundary dispute with Ecuador renewed.
1985 Belaunde succeeded by Social Democrat Alan García Perez.
1987 President García delayed the nationalization of Peru's banks after a vigorous campaign against the proposal.
1988 García under pressure to seek help from the International Monetary Fund.
1989 Under terms of historic accord, Solidarity re-legalised and a new pluralist political structure adopted including an elected second chamber. Delay in debt repayments causes International Development Bank to suspend credit.

Philippines
Republic of the (Republika ng Pilipinas)

area 300,000 sq km/115,700 sq mi
capital Manila (on Luzon)
towns Quezon City
ports Cebu, Davao (on Mindanao) and Iloilu
physical comprises over 7,000 islands, with volcanic mountain ranges traversing the main chain N–S, and 50% of the area still forested. The largest islands are
Luzon 108,172 sq km/41,765 sq mi and
Mindanao 94,227 sq km/36,381 sq mi; others include Samar, Negros, Palawan, Panay,

wing coup suppressed. Communist guerrillas active. Government in rightward swing.
1988 Diluted land-reform act gave favourable compensation to large estateholders.

Poland
People's Republic of (Polska Rzeczpospolita Ludowa)

area 312,600 sq km/120,600 sq mi
capital Warsaw
towns Lódź, Kraków, Wroclaw, Poznań,

Katowice, Bydgoszcz, Lublin; ports Gdánsk, Szczecin, Gdynia

Mindoro, Leyte, Cebu and the Sulu group
head of state and government Corazón Aquino from 1986
political system emergent democracy
exports sugar, copra and coconut oil, timber, iron ore and copper concentrates
currency peso (36.50=£1 Mar 1989)
population (1985) 54,380,000 (93% Malaysian); annual growth rate 2.4%
life expectancy men 60, women 64
language Filipino (based on the Malay dialect Tagalog), but English and Spanish are in common use
religion Roman Catholic 84%, Protestant 9%, Muslim 5%
literacy 86% male/85% female (1985 est)
GNP $16 bn (1984); $772 per head of population
chronology
1542 Named the Philippines by Spanish explorers.
1565 Conquered by Spain.
1898 Ceded to the USA.
1935 Grant of internal self-government.
1942–45 Japanese occupation.
1946 Independence granted.
1965 Ferdinand Marcos elected president.
1983 Murder of Benigno Aquino.
1986 Overthrow of Marcos by Corazón Aquino's People's Power movement.
1987 New constitution approved in plebiscite; People's Power won majority in congressional elections. Attempted right-

physical comprises part of the great plain of Europe; Vistula, Oder, and Neisse rivers; Sudeten, Tatra, and Carpathian mountains
head of state Wojciech Jaruzelski from 1981
head of government Mieczyslaw Rakowski from 1988
political system communism
exports coal, softwood timber, chemicals, machinery, ships
currency zloty (979.06=£1 Mar 1989)
population (1985) 37,160,000; annual growth rate 0.9%
life expectancy men 67, women 75
language Polish, a member of the western branch of the Slavonic family
religion Roman Catholic 93%
literacy 99.3% male/98.3% female (1978)

GNP $110 bn (1984); $2,750 per head of population

chronology

1918 Poland revived as independent republic.

1939 German invasion and occupation.

1944 Germans driven out by Soviet force.

1945 Polish boundaries redrawn at Potsdam Conference.

1947 Communist people's republic proclaimed.

1956 Poznań riots. Gomulka installed as Polish United Workers' Party (PUWP) leader.

1970 Gomulka replaced by Gierek after Gdańsk riots.

1980 Emergence of Solidarity free trade union following Gdańsk disturbances.

1981 Imposition of martial law by General Jaruzelski.

1983 Ending of martial law.

1984 Amnesty for political prisoners.

1985 Zbigniew Messner became prime minister.

1987 Referendum on economic reform rejected.

1988 Solidarity strikes and demonstrations were called off after pay increases and government agreement to hold a church-state-union conference. Messner resigned and was replaced by the reformist Mieczyslaw Rakowski.

Portugal
Republic of (República Portuguesa)

area 91,631 sq km/34,861 sq mi (including Azores and Madeira)

capital Lisbon

towns Coimbra, ports Oporto, Setúbal

physical mountainous in the N, plains in the S

head of state Mario Alberto Nobre Lopes Soares from 1986

head of government Cavaco Silva from 1985

political system emergent democracy

exports port wine, olive oil, resin, cork, sardines, textiles, pottery, pulpwood

currency escudo (263.80=£1 Mar 1989)

population (1985) 10,230,000; annual growth rate 0.7%

life expectancy men 68, women 75

language Portuguese, one of the Romance languages, ultimately derived from Latin, but considerably influenced later by Arabic

religion Roman Catholic

literacy 89% male/80% female (1985)

GDP $19.4 bn (1984); $1,930 per head of population

chronology

1928–68 Military dictatorship under Antonio de Oliveira Salazar.

1968 Salazar succeeded by Marcello Caetano.

1974 Caetano removed in a military coup led by Gen Antonio Ribeiro de Spinola. Spinola was then replaced by Gen Fransisco da Costa Gomes.

1975 Independence granted to African colonies.

1976 New constitution, providing for a gradual return to civilian rule, adopted. Minority government appointed, led by the Socialist Party leader Mario Soares.

1978 Soares resigned.

1980 Francisco Balsemão formed a centre-party coalition after two and a half years of political instability.

1982 Draft of new constitution approved, reducing the powers of the presidency.

1983 Centre-left coalition government formed.

1985 Cavaco Silva became prime minister.

1986 Mario Soares elected first civilian president for 60 years. Portugal joined

European Community.
1987 Soares re-elected with large majority.
1988 Portugal joined the Western European Union.

Qatar
State of (Dawlat Qatar)

area 11,437 sq km/4,250 sq mi
capital and chief port Doha
towns Dukhan, centre of oil production

physical mostly flat desert
head of state and government Sheik Khalifa bin Hamad al-Thani from 1972
political system absolutism
exports oil and natural gas, petrochemicals, fertilizers, iron and steel
currency Qatar riyal (6.29=£1 Mar 1989)
population (1985) 320,000 (mainly in Doha); annual growth rate 6.8%
life expectancy men 65, women 70
language Arabic
religion Sunni Muslim
literacy 60% (1985)
GNP $5.9 bn (1983); $35,000 per head of population
chronology
1970 Constitution adopted, confirming the emirate as an absolute monarchy.
1971 Achieved full independence. New treaty of friendship with Britain signed.
1972 Emir Sheik Ahmad replaced in a bloodless coup, by his cousin, Crown Prince Sheik Khalifa.

Romania
Socialist Republic of (Republica Socialistă România)

area 237,500 sq km/91,699 sq mi
capital Bucharest
towns Brasov, Timisoara, Cluj, Iasi; ports

Galati, Constanta, Sulina
physical mountains surrounding a plateau, with river plains S and E
head of state Nicolae Ceauşescu from 1974
head of government Constantin Dascalescu from 1982
political system communism
exports petroleum products and oilfield equipment, electrical goods, cars (largely to communist countries)
currency leu (14.78=£1 Mar 1989)
population (1985 est) 23,020,000 (including 400,000 Germans); annual growth rate 0.7%
life expectancy men 68, women 73
language Romanian, a Romance language descended from that of Roman settlers, though later modified by Slav influences
religion Romanian Orthodox (linked with Greek Orthodox)
literacy 97% male/94% female (1980 est)
GNP $45 bn (1984); $5,250 per head of population
chronology
-1944 Pro-Nazi Antonescu government

overthrown.
1945 Communist-dominated government appointed.
1947 Boundaries redrawn. King Michael abdicated and People's Republic proclaimed.
1949 New constitution adopted. Joined Comecon.
1952 New Soviet-style constitution.
1955 Romania joined Warsaw Pact.
1958 Soviet occupation forces removed.
1965 New constitution adopted.
1974 Ceauşescu created president.
1985–86 Winters of austerity and power cuts.
1987 Workers demonstrations against austerity programme.

Rwanda
Republic of (Republika y'u Rwanda)

area 26,338 sq km/10,169 sq mi
capital Kigali

physical high savanna and hills, with volcanic mountains in NW
head of state and government Juvenal Habyarimana from 1973
political system military authoritarianism
exports coffee, tea, pyrethrum, tin, tungsten
currency Rwanda franc (132.69=£1 Mar 1989)
population (1985 est) 6,070,000 (Hutu 90%, Tutsi 9%); annual growth rate 3.3%
life expectancy men 45, women 48
language Kinyarwanda (a Bantu language), French

religion Christian (mainly Catholic) 54%, animist 45%, Muslim 1%
literacy 61% male/33% female (1985 est)
GNP $1.7 bn (1984); $270 per head of population
chronology
1962 Rwanda achieved full independence as the Republic of Rwanda, with Gregoire Kayibanda as president.
1962–65 Tribal warfare between the Hutu and the Tutsi.
1972 Renewal of tribal fighting.
1973 Kayibanda ousted in a military coup led by Maj-Gen Juvenal Habyarimana.
1978 New constitution approved but Rwanda remained a military-controlled state.

St Christopher (St Kitts)–Nevis

area 261 sq km/100 sq mi
capital Basseterre (on St Kitts)
towns Nevis (chief town of Nevis)

physical two islands in the Lesser Antilles
head of state Elizabeth II from 1983 represented by Clement Athelston Arrindell
head of government Kennedy Alphonse Simmonds from 1980
political system liberal democracy
exports sugar and molasses, cotton; tourism is important
currency East Caribbean dollar (4.66=£1 Mar 1989)

567

population (1985 est) 50,000; annual growth rate 2.3%
language English
religion Christian
literacy 90% (1984)
GNP $40 million (1983)
chronology
1967 St Christopher, Nevis and Anguilla were granted internal self-government, within the Commonwealth, with Robert Bradshaw, Labour Party leader, as prime minister.
1971 Anguilla left the federation.
1978 Bradshaw died and was succeeded by Paul Southwell.
1979 Southwell died and was succeeded by Lee L Moore.
1980 Coalition government led by Kennedy Simmonds.
1983 St Christopher–Nevis achieved full independence within the Commonwealth.
1984 Coalition government re-elected.
1989 Prime minister Simmonds won a third successive term.

St Lucia

area 616 sq km/238 sq mi
capital Castries

physical mountainous; mainly tropical forest
head of state Elizabeth II from 1979 represented by Vincent Floissac from 1987
head of government John G M Compton from 1982

political system liberal democracy
exports bananas, cocoa, copra; tourism is important
currency East Caribbean dollar (4.66=£1 Mar 1989)
population (1985 est) 130,000; annual growth rate 1.2%
language English
religion Roman Catholic 90%
literacy 78% (1984)
GNP $133 million (1982); $698 per head of population
chronology
1967 Granted internal self-government as a West Indies associated state.
1979 Achieved full independence within the Commonwealth, with John Compton, leader of the United Workers' Party (UWP), as prime minister. Allan Louisy, leader of the Saint Lucia Labour Party (SLP), replaced Compton as prime minister.
1981 Louisy resigned and was replaced by Winston Cenac.
1982 Compton returned to power at the head of a UWP government.
1987 Compton re-elected with reduced majority.

St Vincent and the Grenadines

area 389 sq km/150 sq mi, including N Grenadines 44 sq km/17 sq mi
capital Kingstown

physical volcanic mountains, thickly forested
head of state Elizabeth II from 1979
represented by Joseph Lambert Eustace from
1985
head of government James Mitchell from 1984
political system liberal democracy
exports bananas, tarros, sweet potatoes,
arrowroot, copra
currency Eastern Caribbean dollar (4.66=£1
Mar 1989)
population (1985 est) 138,000; annual growth
rate -4%
language English
religion Christian (47% Anglican, 28%
Methodist, 13% Roman Catholic)
literacy 85% (1981)
GNP $90 million (1983); $250 per head of
population
chronology
1969 Granted internal self-government.
1979 Achieved full independence within the
Commonwealth, with Milton Cato as prime
minister.
1984 James Mitchell replaced Cato as prime
minister.

Samoa, Western
Independent State of (Samoa i Sisifo)

area 2,842 sq km/1,097 sq mi
capital Apia on Upolu

physical comprises islands of Savai'i and
Upolu, with two smaller islands and islets;
mountain ranges on the main islands

head of state King Malietoa Tanumafili II
from 1962
head of government Tofilau Eti Alesana from
1988
political system liberal democracy
exports copra, bananas, cocoa; tourism is
important
currency taia (3.75=£1 Mar 1989)
population (1985 est) 160,000; annual growth
rate 1.1%
language English and Samoan (official)
religion Christian
literacy 90% (1983)
GDP $65 million (1978); $400 per head of
population
chronology
1959 Local government elected.
1961 Referendum favoured independence.
1962 Achieved full independence within
the Commonwealth, with Fiame Mata'afa
Mulinu'u as prime minister.
1975 Mata'afa died and was succeeded by
Tupuola Taisi Efi, the first non-royal prime
minister.
1982 Va'ai Kolone became prime minister,
but was replaced the same year by Tupuola
Efi. When the assembly failed to approve
his budget, Tupuola Efi resigned and was
replaced by Tofilau Eti Alesana.
1985 At the end of the year Tofilau Eti
resigned over his budget proposals and
the head of state refused to call a general
election, inviting Va'ai Kolombe to return to
lead the government.
1988 Elections produced a hung parliament,
with first Tupuola Efi as prime minister and
then Tofilau Eti.

San Marino
*Most Serene Republic of (Repubblica di San
Marino)*

area 58 sq km/22.5 sq mi
capital San Marino
physical on the slope of Mount Titano
head of state and government two captains-
regent, elected for a six-month period
political system direct democracy
exports wine, ceramics, paint
currency Italian lira (2,366=£1 Mar 1989)

population 22,300 (1985); annual growth rate 3%
language Italian
religion Roman Catholic
literacy 97% (1985)
chronology
1862 Treaty with Italy signed, recognizing its independence and providing for its protection.
1947–86 Governed by a series of left-wing and centre-left coalitions.
1986 Formation of Communist and Christian Democrat 'grand coalition'.

São Tomé e Principe
Democratic Republic of

area 964 sq km/372 sq mi
capital São Tomé

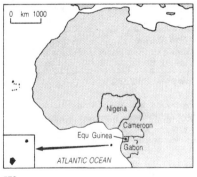

physical comprises the two main islands and several smaller ones, all of volcanic origin; thickly forested and fertile
head of state and government Manuel Pinto da Costa from 1975
political system nationalistic socialism
exports cocoa, copra
currency dobra (175.30=£1 Mar 1989)
population (1985) 110,000; annual growth rate 2.5%
language Portuguese
religion Roman Catholic
literacy 73% male/42% female (1981)
GNP $31 million (1983); $261 per head of population
chronology
1973 Granted internal self-government.
1975 Achieved full independence, with Manuel Pinto da Costa as president.
1984 Formally declared itself a nonaligned state.
1987 President now popularly elected.
1988 Unsuccessful coup attempt.

Saudi Arabia
Kingdom of (al-Mamlaka al-'Arabiya as-Sa'udiya)

area 2,400,000 sq km/927,000 sq mi
capital Riyadh
towns Mecca, Medina; ports Jidda, Dammam

physical desert, sloping to the Persian Gulf from a height of 2,750 m/9,000 ft in the W

head of state and government King Fahd Ibn Abdul Aziz from 1982
political system absolutism
exports oil
currency rial (6.47=£1 Mar 1989)
population (1985 est) 11,090,000; annual growth rate 4.2%
life expectancy men 59, women 63
language Arabic
religion Sunni Muslim, with a Shi'ite minority in the E under the influence of Ayatollah Khomeini
literacy 34% male/12% female (1980 est)
GDP $110.5 bn (1983); $11,500 per head of population
chronology
1926–32 Territories united and kingdom established.
1953 King ibn-Saud died and was succeeded by his eldest son, Saud.
1964 King Saud forced to abdicate and was succeeded by his brother Faisal.
1975 King Faisal assassinated by a nephew and succeeded by his half-brother Khalid.
1982 King Khalid died suddenly of a heart attack and was succeeded by his brother Crown Prince Fahd, who had effectively been ruling the country for some years because of King Khalid's ill health.

Senegal
Republic of (République du Sénégal)

area 197,000 sq km/76,000 sq mi
capital and chief port Dakar

towns Thies, Kaolack
physical plains; swamp and tropical forest in SW
head of state and government Abdou Diouf from 1981
political system nationalistic socialism
exports groundnuts, cotton, fish, phosphates
currency CFA franc (544.87=£1 Mar 1989)
population (1985 est) 6,440,000; annual growth rate 2.6%
life expectancy men 42, women 45
language French (official)
religion Muslim 80%, Christian 10% (chiefly Roman Catholic), animist 10%
literacy 37% male/19% female (1985 est)
GNP $2.7 bn (1983); $342 per head of population
chronology
1960 Achieved full independence, with Léopold Sedar Senghor, leader of the Sengalese Progressive Union (UPS), as president.
1966 UPS declared the only legal party.
1976 UPS reconstituted as the Sengalese Socialist Party (PS). Abdou Diouf nominated as Senghor's successor.
1980 Senghor retired and was succeeded by Diouf. Troops sent to defend The Gambia.
1981 Military help again sent to The Gambia.
1982 Confederation of Senegambia came into effect.
1983 Diouf re-elected. Post of prime minister abolished.
1988 Diouf decisively re-elected.
1989 Violent clashes between Senegalese and Mauritanians in Dakar and Nouakchott.

Seychelles

area 404 sq km/156 sq mi
capital Victoria on Mahé
physical comprises two distinct island groups, one concentrated, the other widely scattered, totalling over 100 islands and islets
head of state and government France-Albert René from 1977
political system nationalistic socialism
exports copra, cinnamon; tourism is important

currency Seychelles rupee (9.47=£1 Mar 1989)
population (1985 est) 70,000; annual growth rate 0.6%

language creole, spoken by 95%, English and French (all official)
religion Christian (Roman Catholic 90%)
literacy 60% (1983)
GDP $143 million (1982); $1,030 per head of population
chronology
1970 Constitutional conference in London on future status of Seychelles. James Mancham, leader of the Seychelles Democratic Party (SDP), argued for full independence, while France-Albert René, leader of the Seychelles People's United Party (SPUP), favoured full integration with the UK.
1975 Internal self-government granted.
1976 Full independence achieved as a republic within the Commonwealth, with Mancham as president.
1977 René ousted Mancham in an armed coup and took over the presidency.
1979 New constitution adopted, making the SPUP, restyled the Seychelles People's Progressive Front (SPPF), the only legal party.
1981 Attempted coup by South African mercenaries thwarted.
1984 René re-elected.
1989 René re-elected.

Sierra Leone
Republic of

area 73,325 sq km/27,925 sq mi
capital Freetown

towns Bo, Kenema, Makeni
physical mountains in E; hills and forest; coastal mangrove swamps
head of state and government Joseph Saidu Momoh from 1985
political system authoritarian nationalism
exports palm kernels, cocoa, coffee, ginger, diamonds, bauxite, rutile
currency leone (70.20=£1 Mar 1989)
population (1985 est) 3,600,000; annual growth rate 1.8%
life expectancy men 33, women 36
language English (official); local languages
religion Muslim 60%, animist 30%
literacy 38% male/21% female (1985 est)
GNP $1.2 bn (1983); $176 per head of population
chronology
1962 Achieved full independence as a constitutional monarchy within the Commonwealth, with Milton Margai, leader of the Sierra Leone People's Party (SLPP), as prime minister.
1964 Milton succeeded by his half-brother Albert Margai.
1967 General election results disputed by the army who set up a National Reformation Council and forced the governor general to leave.

1968 Another army revolt made Siaka
Stevens, leader of the All-People's Congress
(APC), prime minister.
1971 New constitution adopted, making
Sierra Leone a republic, with Stevens as
president.
1978 APC declared the only legal party.
Stevens sworn in for another seven-year
term.
1985 Stevens retired at the age of 80 and was
succeeded by Maj-Gen Joseph Momoh.

Singapore
Republic of

area 581.5 sq km/225.6 sq mi
capital Singapore City in the S of the island,
a major world port and financial centre,
founded by Stamford Raffles

physical comprises Singapore Island, which is
low and flat, and 54 small islands
head of state Wee Kim Wee from 1985
head of government Lee Kuan Yew from 1959
political system liberal democracy
exports electronics, petroleum products,
rubber, machinery, vehicles
currency Singapore dollar (3.35=£1 Mar
1989)
population (1985) 2,556,000 (Chinese 75%,
Malay 14%, Tamil 7%); annual growth rate
1.2%

life expectancy men 69, women 75
language Malay, Chinese, Tamil, and English
(all official)
religion Buddhist, Taoist, Muslim, Hindu,
Christian
literacy 93% male/79% female (1985 est)
GNP $17.9 bn (1984); $6,526 per head of
population
chronology
1819 Singapore leased to British East India
Company.
1858 Placed under crown rule.
1942 Invaded and occupied by Japan.
1945 Japanese removed by British forces.
1959 Independence granted from Britain: Lee
Kuan Yew became prime minister.
1963 Joined new Federation of Malaysia.
1965 Left federation to become independent
republic.
1984 Opposition made advances in
parliamentary elections.
1986 Opposition leader convicted of perjury,
debarred from standing for election.
1988 The ruling conservative party elected to
all but one of the available assembly seats.

Solomon Islands

area 27,556 sq km/10,637 sq mi
capital Honiara on Guadalcanal

physical comprises all but the northernmost
islands (which belong to Papua New Guinea)
of a Melanesian archipelago that stretches
nearly 1,500 km/900 mi. The largest is

Guadalcanal (area 6,475 sq km/2,500 sq mi); others are Malaita, San Cristobal, New Georgia, Santa Isabel, Choiseul; mainly mountainous and forested

head of state Elizabeth II, represented by Baddeley Devesi from 1978

head of government Solomon Mamaloni from 1989

political system liberal democracy

exports palm oil, copra, rice, timber

currency Solomon Island dollar (3.74=£1 Mar 1989)

population (1985) 267,000 (the majority Melanesian); annual growth rate 3.9%

language English (official)

religion Christian

literacy 13% (1980)

GDP \$160 million (1983); \$628 per head of population

chronology

1978 Achieved full independence, within the Commonwealth, with Peter Kenilorea as prime minister.

1981 Solomon Mamaloni replaced Kenilorea as prime minister.

1984 Kenilorea returned to power, heading a coalition government.

1986 Kenilorea resigned after allegations of corruption, and was replaced by his deputy, Ezekiel Alebua.

1988 Kenilorea back as deputy prime minister. The Solomon Islands joined Vanuatu and Papua New Guinea to form the Spearhead Group, aiming to preserve Melanesian cultural traditions and secure independence for the French territory of New Caledonia.

1989 Solomon Mamaloni (People's Action Party) returned as prime minister.

Somalia

***Democratic Republic of** (Jamhuriyadda Dimugradiga Somaliya)*

---

area 700,000 sq km/270,000 sq mi

capital Mogadishu

towns Hargeisa, Kismayu, port Berbera

physical mainly flat, with hills in the N

head of state and government Mohamed Siad Barre from 1969

political system nationalistic socialism

exports livestock, skins, hides, bananas

currency Somali shilling (410.78=£1 Mar 1989)

population (1985) 7,595,000 (including 1 million refugees from W Somalia); annual growth rate 4.1%

life expectancy men 39, women 43

language Somali (national language), Arabic (also official), Italian, English

religion Sunni Muslim

literacy 18% male/6% female (1985 est)

GNP \$1.2 bn (1983); less than \$500 per head of population

chronology

1960 Achieved full independence.

1963 Border dispute with Kenya, diplomatic relations with the UK broken.

1968 Diplomatic relations with the UK restored.

1969 Following the assassination of the president, the army seized power. Maj-Gen Mohamed Siad Barre suspended the constitution and set up a Supreme Revolutionary Council.

1978 Defeated in eight-month war with Ethiopia.

1979 New constitution for a socialist one-party state adopted.

1987 Barre re-elected.

1989 Civilian defence minister appointed.

South Africa
Republic of (Afrikaans Republiek van Suid-Afrika)

area 1,223,181 sq km/433,678 sq mi
capital Cape Town (legislative), Pretoria (administrative)
towns Johannesburg, Bloemfontein; ports

Cape Town, Durban, Port Elizabeth
physical a plateau
territories Prince Edward Island in the Antarctic
head of state Pieter W Botha from 1978
head of government F W de Clerk from 1989
government right-wing authoritarian and racist
exports maize, sugar, fruit; wool; gold, platinum (world's largest producer), diamonds
currency rand (commercial rate 4.39=£1 Mar 1989)
population (1985) 42,465,000 (68% black, of whom the largest nations are the Zulu, Xhosa, Sotho, and Tswana, 18% white, 10% of mixed ancestry, and 3% Asiatic); annual growth rate 2.5%
life expectancy men 55, women 55
language Afrikaans and English (both official); various Bantu languages
religion Christian; largest denomination is the Nederduits Gereformeerde Kerk/Dutch Reformed Church. Congregations are segregated
literacy 81% male/81% female (1980 est), ranging from 98% whites to 50% blacks
GNP $76.8 bn (1983); $1,296 per head
chronology
1910 Union of South Africa formed from two British colonies and two Boer republics.
1912 African National Congress (ANC) formed.
1948 Apartheid system of racial discrimination initiated by Daniel Malan.
1955 Freedom Charter adopted by African National Congress (ANC).
1958 Malan succeeded as prime minister by Hendrik Verwoerd.
1960 ANC banned.
1961 South Africa withdrew from the Commonwealth and became a republic.
1962 ANC leader Nelson Mandela jailed.
1964 Mandela, Walter Sisulu, Govan Mbeki, and five other ANC leaders sentenced to life imprisonment.
1966 Verwoerd assassinated and succeeded by B J Vorster.
1976 Soweto uprising.
1977 Death in custody of Pan African Congress activist Steve Biko.
1978 Vorster resigned and was replaced by Pieter W Botha.
1984 New constitution adopted, giving segregated representation to coloureds and Asians and making Botha president. Nonaggression pact with Mozambique signed but not observed.
1985 Growth of violence in black townships.
1986 Commonwealth agreed on limited sanctions. US Congress voted to impose sanctions. Some major multinational companies announced that they were closing down their South African operations.
1987 The government formally acknowledged the presence of its military forces in Angola.
1988 Botha announced 'limited constitutional reforms'. South Africa agreed to withdraw from Angola and recognize Namibia's independence.

1989 Botha resigned as party leader and was succeeded by F W de Clerk, whose five year action plan for 'constitutional reform', was met with scepticism from opposition parties. State president Botha met Nelson Mandela, amid speculation about Mandela's imminent release.

Spain
(España)

area 504,879 sq km/194,883 sq mi
capital Madrid
towns Bilbao, Valencia, Saragossa, Murcia;

0 km 1000
France
Andorra
Portugal
ATLANTIC OCEAN
Morocco
MEDITERRANEAN SEA

ports Barcelona, Seville, Málaga
physical a central plateau with mountain ranges; lowlands in the S
head of state Juan Carlos I from 1975
head of government Felipe González Marquez from 1982
political system emergent democracy
exports citrus, grapes, pomegranates, vegetables, wine (especially sherry), olive oil, tinned fruit and fish, iron ore, cork, cars and other vehicles, leather goods, ceramics
currency peseta (200.25=£1 Mar 1989)
population (1985) 38,600,000; annual growth rate 0.6%
life expectancy men 71, women 78
language Spanish (Castilian, official), but regional languages are recognized within their own boundaries (Basque, Catalan, Galician, Valencian, and Majorcan are the chief examples)
religion Roman Catholic (there are restrictions on the practice of Protestantism)
literacy 97% male/92% female (1985 est)
GDP $160.4 bn (1984); $5,500 per head of population
chronology
1947 Gen Franco announced a return to the monarchy after his death, with Prince Juan Carlos as his successor.
1975 Franco died and was succeeded by King Juan Carlos I as head of state.
1978 New constitution adopted with Adolfo Suárez, leader of the Democratic Centre Party, as prime minister.
1981 Suárez resigned and was succeeded by his deputy, Calvo-Sotelo. Attempted military coup thwarted.
1982 Socialist Workers' Party (PSOE), led by Felipe González, won a sweeping electoral victory. Basque separatist organization (ETA) stepped up its guerrilla campaign.
1985 ETA's campaign spread to holiday resorts.
1986 Referendum confirmed NATO membership. Spain joined the European Community.
1988 Spain joined the Western European Union.

Sri Lanka
Democratic Socialist Republic of (former name Ceylon)

area 65,000 sq km/25,332 sq mi
capital and chief port Colombo
towns Kandy; ports Jaffna, Galle, Negombo, Trincomalee
physical flat in the N and around the coast; hills and mountains in the S
head of state and government Dingiri Banda Wijetunge from 1989
political system liberal democracy
exports tea, rubber, coconut products; plumbago, sapphires, rubies, precious stones
currency Sri Lanka rupee (59.00=£1 Mar 1989)
population (1985) 15,840,000 (including 2,500,000 Tamils); annual growth rate 1.8%

life expectancy men 67, women 70
language Sinhalese (official, but English and Tamil are national languages)
religion Buddhist 67% (official), Hindu 18%
literacy 91% male/83% female (1985 est)
GNP $5.3 bn (1984); $340 per head of population
chronology
1948 Independence from Britain achieved (as Ceylon).
1956 Sinhalese established as official language.
1959 Assassination of Prime Minister Solomon Bandaranaike.
1972 Socialist Republic of Sri Lanka proclaimed.
1978 Presidential constitution adopted by new Jayawardene government.
1983 Tamil guerrilla violence escalated: state of emergency imposed.
1987 Violence continued despite ceasefire policed by Indian troops.
1988 Left-wing guerrilla campaign against the Indo-Sri Lankan peace pact. Prime Minister Premadasa elected president amid allegations of fraud.
1989 State of emergency lifted. Ruling UNP majority reduced in parliamentary elections marred by terrorist violence. India anounces withdrawal of troops by end 1989.

Sudan
Democratic Republic of (Jamhuryat es-Sudan)

area 2,500,000 sq km/967,500 sq mi
capital Khartoum
towns Omdurman, Juba; chief port Port Sudan

physical fertile valley of the river Nile separates Libyan Desert in W from high rocky Nubian Desert in E
head of state Ahmed Ali El-Mirghani from 1986
head of government Gen Omar Hasan Ahmed el Bashir from 1989
political system emergent democracy
exports cotton, gum arabic, sesame, groundnuts, durra
currency Sudanese pound (7.76=£1 Mar 1989)
population (1985 est) 21,550,000 (Arab-speaking and Muslim, 70%, in the N, and speakers of African languages in the S); annual growth rate 2.9%
life expectancy men 47, women 49
language Arabic (official), English
religion Sunni Muslim in the N, animist in the S, with a Christian minority
literacy 38% male/14% female (1981 est)
GNP $27.3 bn (1983); $361 per head of population
chronology
1955 Civil war between the Muslim N and non-Muslim S broke out.

1956 The Sudan achieved independence as a republic.

1958 Military coup replaced the civilian government with a Supreme Council of the Armed Forces.

1964 Civilian rule reinstated.

1969 Coup led by Col Gaafar Mohammed Nimeri established a Revolutionary Command Council (RCC) and the country's name was changed to the Democratic Republic of the Sudan.

1970 Agreement in principle on union with Egypt.

1971 New constitution adopted, Nimeri confirmed as president, and the Sudanese Socialist Union (SSU) declared to be the only legal party.

1972 Proposed Federation of Arab Republics, comprising Sudan, Egypt, and Syria, abandoned. Addis Ababa conference proposed autonomy for southern provinces.

1974 National assembly established.

1983 Nimeri re-elected amid growing opposition to his social, economic, and religious policies. *Sharia* (Islamic law) introduced.

1985 Nimeri deposed in a bloodless coup led by Gen Swar al-Dahab, who set up a transitional military council. State of emergency declared.

1986 More than 40 political parties fought the general election and a coalition government was formed.

1988 Al-Mahdi formed a new coalition. Another flare-up of civil war between N and S created tens of thousands of refugees. Floods made 1.5 million people homeless. Peace pact signed with Sudan People's Liberation Movement.

1989 Al-Mahdi overthrown in coup led by Gen Omar Hasan Ahmed el Bashir who, as head of National Salvation Revolutionary Council, announced unilteral ceasefire and sent delegation to meet rebels.

Suriname
Republic of

---

area 163,820 sq km/63,350 sq mi
capital Paramaribo

578

physical hilly and forested, with flat coast
head of state Ramsewak Shankar from 1988 (president), Desi Bouterse from 1982 (military ruler)
head of government Wym Udenhout from 1984
political system emergent democracy
exports bauxite, rice, citrus, timber
currency Suriname guilder (3.08 = £1 Mar 1989)
population (1985 est) 370,000 (Creole, Chinese, Hindu, and Indonesian peoples); annual growth rate 1.1%
life expectancy men 66, women 71
language Dutch, English (both official)
religion Christian 35%, Hindu 25%, Muslim 17%
literacy 90% male/90% female (1985)
GNP $1.2 bn (1983); $2,600 per head of population
chronology
1954 Granted internal self-government as Dutch Guiana.
1975 Achieved full independence with Dr Johan Ferrier as president and Henck Arron as prime minister. About 40% of the population, especially those of East Indian origin, emigrated to the Netherlands.
1980 Arron's government overthrown in an army coup but President Ferrier refused to recognize the military regime and appointed Dr Henk Chin A Sen to lead a civilian administration. Army replaced Ferrier with

Dr Chin A Sen.
1982 Army, led by Lt-Col Desi Bouterse, seized power, setting up a Revolutionary People's Front.
1985 Ban on political activities lifted.
1987 New constitution approved.
1988 Ramsewak Shankar elected president.

Swaziland
Kingdom of

area 17,400 sq km/6,716 sq mi
capital Mbabane

physical central valley; mountains in W
head of state and government King Mswati III from 1986
political system absolutism
exports sugar, citrus, timber, asbestos, iron ore
currency lilangeni (4.38 = £1 Mar 1989)
population (1986) 676,000; annual growth rate 3%
life expectancy men 47, women 50
language Swazi 90%, English (both official)
religion Christian, both Protestant and Catholic; animist
literacy 70% male/66% female (1985 est)
GNP $610 million (1983); $790 per head of population
chronology
1967 Achieved internal self-government.

1968 Achieved full independence from Britain, within the Commonwealth, as the Kingdom of Swaziland, with King Sobhuza II as head of state.
1973 The king suspended the constitution and assumed absolute powers.
1978 New constitution adopted.
1982 King Sobhuza died and his place was taken by one of his wives, Dzeliewe, until his son, Prince Makhosetive, reached the age of 21.
1983 Queen Dzeliewe ousted by another wife, Ntombi.
1984 After a royal power struggle, it was announced that the crown prince would become king at the age of 18.
1986 Crown prince formally invested as King Mswati III.
1987 A power struggle developed between the advisory council Liqoqo and Queen Ntombi over the accession of the king. Mswati dissolved parliament and a new government was elected with Sotsha Dlamini as prime minister.

Sweden
Kingdom of (Konungariket Sverige)

area 449,964 sq km/173,686 sq mi
capital Stockholm
towns Göteborg, Malmö, Uppsala,

Norrköping, Västera
physical mountains in the NW; plains in the S; much of the land is forested

head of state Carl XVI Gustav from 1973
head of government Ingvar Carlsson from 1986
political system liberal democracy
exports aircraft, cars, domestic equipment, ballbearings, drills, missiles, electronics, petrochemicals, textiles, furnishings, ornamental glass
currency krona (10.97 = £1 Mar 1989)
population (1985) 8,358,000 (including 1,200,000 postwar immigrants from Finland, Turkey, Yugoslavia, Greece); annual growth rate 0.1%
life expectancy men 73, women 79
language Swedish, one of the Scandinavian division of Germanic languages
religion Christian (Evangelical Lutheran)
literacy 99% (1984)
GNP $88 bn (1983); $14,821 per head of population
chronology
12th century United as an independent nation.
1397–1520 Under Danish rule.
1914–45 Neutral in both World Wars.
1951–76 Social Democratic Labour Party (SD) in power.
1969 Olof Palme became SD leader and prime minister.
1971 Constitution amended, creating a single-chamber parliament.
1975 Monarch's constitutional powers reduced.
1976 Thorbjörn Fälldin, leader of the Centre Party, became prime minister, heading centre-right coalition.
1982 SD, led by Palme, returned to power.
1985 SD won the largest number of seats in parliament and formed a minority government, with communist support.
1986 Olof Palme murdered in Stockholm. Ingvar Carlsson became prime minister and SD party leader.
1988 SD won reduced majority in general election; Green Party increased its vote dramatically.

Switzerland
Swiss Confederation (German *Schweiz*, French *Suisse*, Romansch *Suizzera*)

area 41,293 sq km/15,939 sq mi

580

capital Bern
towns Zürich, Geneva, Lausanne; river port Basel

physical most mountainous country in Europe (Alps and Jura Mountains)
head of state and government Jean-Pascal Delamuraz from 1989
political system liberal democracy
exports electrical goods, chemicals and pharmaceuticals, watches, precision instruments, confectionery, banking, insurance, and tourism are important
currency Swiss franc (2.49 = £1 Sept 1987)
population (1986) 6,485,000; annual growth rate 0.2%
life expectancy men 73, women 80
language German 65%, French 18%, Italian 10%; Romansch 1% (all official)
religion Roman Catholic 50%, Protestant 48%
literacy 99% (1985)
GNP $93.7 bn (1984); $14,408 per head of population
chronology
1648 Became independent of the Holy Roman Empire.
1798–1815 Helvetic Republic established by French Revolutionary armies.
1847 Civil war resulted in greater centralization.
1971 Women given the vote in federal elections.

1984 First female cabinet minister appointed.
1986 Referendum rejected a proposal for
membership of United Nations.

Syria
*Syrian Arab Republic (al-Jamhuriya al- Arabya
as-Suriya)*

area 186,000 sq km/72,000 sq mi
capital Damascus
towns Aleppo, Homs, Hama; chief port
Lattakia

physical mountains alternate with fertile
plains and desert areas; river Euphrates
head of state and government Hafez al-Assad
from 1971
political system nationalistic socialism
exports cotton, cereals, oil, phosphates
currency Syrian pound (official rate 36.25 =
£1 Mar 1989)
population (1985) 10,270,000; annual growth
rate 3.5%
life expectancy men 61, women 64
language Arabic (official)
religion Sunni Muslim, but the ruling minority
is Alawite, an Islamic sect; also Druse, again
an Islamic sect
literacy 76% male/43% female (1985 est)
GNP $16.5 bn (1983); $702 per head of
population
chronology
1946 Achieved full independence from
France.

1958 Merged with Egypt to form the United
Arab Republic (UAR).
1961 UAR disintegrated.
1967 Six-Day War resulted in the loss of
territory to Israel.
1970–71 Syria supported Palestinian guerrillas
against Jordanian troops.
1971 Following a bloodless coup, Hafez
al-Assad became president.
1973 Israel consolidated its control of the
Golan Heights after the Yom Kippur War.
1976 Substantial numbers of troops
committed to the civil war in Lebanon.
1981–82 Further military engagements in
Lebanon.
1982 Islamic militant uprising suppressed;
5,000 dead.
1984 Presidents Assad and Gemayel
approved a plan for government of national
unity in Lebanon.
1985 Assad secured the release of US
hostages held in an aircraft hijacked by an
extremist Shi'ite group.
1987 Improved relations with USA and
attempts to secure the release of western
hostages in Lebanon.
1989 Diplomatic relations with Morocco
restored.

Taiwan
Republic of China (Chung Hua Min Kuo)

area 36,000 sq km/14,000 sq mi
capital Taipei

towns ports Keelung, Kaohsiung
physical island (formerly Formosa) off the
coast of the People's Republic of China;
mountainous, with lowlands in the W
head of state Lee Teng-hui from 1988
head of government Yu Kuo-hua from 1984
political system emergent democracy
exports with US aid, Taiwan is highly
industrialized: textiles, petrochemicals, steel,
plastics, electronics
currency Taiwan dollar (47.23 = £1 Mar
1989)
population (1985) 19,117,322 (89%
Taiwanese, 11% mainlanders whose
dominance causes resentment); annual
growth rate 1.4%
language Mandarin Chinese
religion officially atheist, but traditional
religions are Taoist, Confucian, and Buddhist
literacy 89% (1983)
GNP $56.6 bn (1984); $3,000 per head of
population
chronology
1683 Taiwan (Formosa) annexed by China.
1895 Ceded to Japan.
1945 Recovered by China.
1949 Flight of Nationalist government to
Taiwan after Chinese revolution.
1954 US-Taiwanese mutual defence treaty.
1971 Expulsion from United Nations.
1972 Commencement of legislature elections.
1975 President Chiang Kai-shek died and was
succeeded by Yen Chia-kan.
1979 USA severed diplomatic relations and
annulled security pact.
1986 Formation of first opposition party to
the Nationalist Kuomintang.
1988 New president Lee Teng-hui accelerated
political liberalization. A number of old,
conservative Kuomintang members were
retired.

Tanzania
*United Republic of (Jamhuri ya Mwungano wa
Tanzania)*

area 945,050 sq km/364,789 sq mi
capital Dodoma
towns chief port Dar es Salaam
physical a central plateau with lakes in the W

and coastal plains
head of state and government Ali Hassan
Mwinyi from 1985
political system nationalistic socialism
exports coffee, cotton, sisal, cloves from
Zanzibar, tea, tobacco
currency Tanzanian shilling (226.50 = £1 Mar
1989)
population (1985) 21,730,000; annual growth
rate 3.5%
life expectancy men 49, women 53
language Kiswahili, English (both official)
religion Muslim 35%, Christian 35%,
traditional 30%
literacy 78% male/70% female (1978)
GNP 4.9 bn (1983); $225 per head of
population
chronology
1961 Tanganyika achieved full independence,
within the Commonwealth, with Julius
Nyerere as prime minister.
1962 Tanganyika became a republic with
Nyerere as president.
1964 Tanganyika and Zanzibar became the
United Republic of Tanzania with Nyerere as
president.
1967 East African Community (EAC)
formed. Arusha Declaration.
1977 Revolutionary Party of Tanzania
(CCM) proclaimed the only legal party. EAC
dissolved.

1979 Tanzanian troops sent to Uganda to help overthrow the president, Idi Amin.
1984 Nyerere announced his retirement but stayed on as CCM leader. Prime Minister Edward Sokoine killed in a road accident.
1985 Ali Hassan Mwinyi elected president.

Thailand
Kingdom of (Prathes Thai)

area 513,115 sq km/198,062 sq mi
capital and chief port Bangkok
towns Chiangmai

physical central valley flanked by highlands; tropical rainforest
head of state King Bhumibol Adulyadej from 1946
head of government Chatichai Choonhavan from 1988
political system emergent democracy
exports rice, sugar, rubber, teak, tin (fifth largest producer), rubies, sapphires
currency baht (45.50 = £1 Mar 1989)
population (1986) 52,800,000 (Thai 75%, Chinese 14%); annual growth rate 2%
life expectancy men 61, women 65
language Thai and Chinese (both official)
religion Buddhist
literacy 94% male/88% female (1985 est)
GNP $42 bn (1985); $828 per head of population

chronology
1782 Siam absolutist dynasty commenced.
1896 Anglo-French agreement recognized Siam as independent buffer state.
1932 Constitutional monarchy established.
1939 Name of Thailand adopted.
1941–44 Japanese occupation.
1947 Military seized power in coup.
1972 Withdrawal of Thai troops from S Vietnam.
1973 Military government overthrown.
1976 Military reassumed control.
1980 Gen Prem Tinsulanonda assumed power.
1983 Civilian government formed but martial law maintained.
1988 Prime Minister Prem resigned and was replaced by the conservative Chatichai Choonhavan.

Togo
Republic of (République Togolaise)

area 56,785 sq km/21,919 sq mi
capital Lomé

physical two savanna plains, divided by a range of hills NE–SW.
head of state and of government Etienne Gnassingbe Eyadema from 1967
political system authoritarian nationalism
exports cocoa, coffee, coconuts, copra, phosphate, bauxite
currency CFA franc (544.87 = £1 Mar 1989)
population (1986) 3,086,000; annual growth rate 3%

life expectancy men 49, women 52
language French (official), many local languages
religion traditional 60%, Muslim 20%, Christian 20%
literacy 53% male/28% female (1985 est)
GNP $790 million (1983); $348 per head of population
chronology
1960 Achieved full independence as the Republic of Togo with Sylvanus Olympio as head of state.
1963 Olympio killed in a military coup. Nicolas Grunitzky became president.
1967 Grunitzky replaced by Lt-Gen Etienne Gnassingbe Eyadema in a bloodless coup.
1973 The Assembly of Togolese People (RPT) formed as the only legal political party.
1979 Eyadema returned in election.
1986 Unsuccessful coup attempt.

Tonga
Kingdom of (Pule'anga Fakatu'i 'o Tonga) or *Friendly Islands*

area 748 sq km/289 sq mi
capital Nuku'alofa on Tongatapu

physical comprises three groups of islands in the SW Pacific, mostly coral formations, but the western are actively volcanic
head of state and of government King Taufa'ahau Tupou IV from 1965
political system absolutist
currency Tongan dollar or pa'anga (2.08 = £1

584

Mar 1989)
population (1986 est) 104,000; annual growth rate 2.4%
language Tongan and English
religion Wesleyan 47%, Roman Catholic 14%, Free Church of Tonga 14%, Mormon 9%, Church of Tonga 9%
literacy 93% (1985)
GNP $80 million (1983); $430 per head of population
chronology
1965 Death of Queen Salote. She was succeeded by her son, Prince Tupout'a, who took the title King Tupou IV.
1970 Achieved full independence within the Commonwealth.

Trinidad and Tobago
Republic of

area Trinidad 4,828 sq km/1,864 sq mi and Tobago 300 sq km/116 sq mi
capital Port of Spain
towns San Fernando

physical comprises the two main islands, and some smaller ones; Trinidad has coastal swamps, and hills E–W
head of state Noor Hassanali from 1987
head of government Arthur Robinson from 1986
political system liberal democracy
exports angostura bitters, asphalt, natural gas and oil

currency Trinidad and Tobago dollar (7.33 = £1 Mar 1989)

population (1986) 1,200,000 (equally divided between those of African and E Indian descent); annual growth rate 1.6%

life expectancy men 66, women 71

language English (official), Hindi, French, Spanish

religion Roman Catholic 33%, Protestant 14%, Hindu 25%, Muslim 6%

literacy 97% male/95% female (1985 est)

GNP $6.8 bn (1983); $6,800 per head of population

chronology

1956 The People's National Movement (PNM) founded.

1959 Granted internal self-government, with PNM leader Eric Williams as chief minister.

1967 Achieved full independence, within the Commonwealth, with Williams as prime minister.

1976 Became a republic, with Ellis Clarke as president and Williams as prime minister.

1981 Williams died and was succeeded by George Chambers, with Arthur Robinson as leader of the opposition.

1986 Arthur Robinson became prime minister.

1987 Noor Hassanali became president.

Tunisia
Republic of (al-Jumhuria at-Tunisiya)

---

area 154,530 sq km/59,649 sq mi

capital and chief port Tunis

towns ports Sfax, Sousse, Bizerta

physical arable and forested land in the N graduates towards desert in the S

head of state and of government Zine el Abdin Ben Ali from 1987

political system emergent democracy

exports oil, phosphates, iron ore

currency dinar (1.63 = £1 Mar 1989)

population (1986) 7,317,000; annual growth rate 2%

life expectancy men 60, women 61

language Arabic (official), French

religion Sunni Muslim, with a politically active fundamentalist opposition to the government; Jewish and Christian minorities

literacy 68% male/41% female (1985 est)

GNP $8.8 bn (1983); $844 per head of population

chronology

1955 Granted internal self-government.

1956 Achieved full independence as a monarchy, with Habib Bourguiba as prime minister.

1957 Became a republic with Bourguiba as president.

1975 Bourguiba made president for life.

1985 Diplomatic relations with Libya severed.

1987 In Oct Bourguiba removed Prime Minister Rashed Sfar and appointed Zine el Abdin Ben Ali. In Nov Ben Ali had Bourguiba declared incompetent and seized power.

1988 Constitutional changes towards democracy announced. Diplomatic relations with Libya restored.

Turkey
Republic of (Türkiye Cumhuriyeti)

---

area 779,452 sq km/300,868 sq mi

capital Ankara

towns ports Istanbul and Izmir

physical central plateau surrounded by mountains

head of state Kenan Evren from 1982

head of government Turgut Ozal from 1983

political system emergent democracy

exports cotton and yarn, hazelnuts, citrus, tobacco, dried fruit, chromium ores
currency Turkish lira (3,435 = £1 Mar 1989)
population (1985) 50,664,000 (85% Turkish, 12% Kurdish); annual growth rate 2.1%
life expectancy men 60, women 63
language Turkish (official; it is related to Mongolian, but is written in the Western Latin script), Kurdish Arabic
religion Sunni Muslim
literacy 86% male/62% female (1985)
GNP $58 bn (1983); $1,000 per head of population
chronology
1919–22 Turkish War of Independence provoked by Greek occupation of Izmir. Mustafa Kemal (Atatürk), leader of nationalist congress, defeated Italian, French, and Greek forces.
1923 Treaty of Lausanne established Turkey as independent republic under Kemal. Westernization began.
1950 First free elections; Adnan Menderes became prime minister.
1960 Menderes executed after military coup by Gen Cemal Gürsel.
1965 Suleyman Demirel became prime minister.
1971 Army forced Demirel to resign.
1973 Civilian rule returned under Bulent Ecevit.
1974 Turkish troops sent to protect the

Turkish community in Cyprus.
1975 Demirel returned at the head of a right-wing coalition.
1978 Ecevit returned, in the face of economic difficulties and factional violence.
1979 Demeril returned. Violence grew.
1980 Army took over and Bulent Ulusu became prime minister. Harsh repression of political activists attracted international criticism.
1982 New constitution adopted.
1983 Ban on political activity lifted. Turgut Ozal became prime minister.
1987 Ozal maintained his majority in general election.
1988 Improved relations and talks with Greece.

Tuvalu
South West Pacific State of

---

area 24.6 sq km/9.5 sq mi
capital Funafuti

physical low coral atolls in Polynesia
head of state Elizabeth II from 1978 represented by Tupua Leupena from 1986
head of government Tomasi Puapua from 1981
political system liberal democracy
exports phosphates, copra, handicrafts, stamps
currency Australian dollar (2.08 = £1 Mar 1989)
population (1985) 8,580 (mainly Polynesian); annual growth rate 3.4%
language Tuvaluan and English

religion Christian, chiefly Protestant
literacy 96% (1979)
GDP (1983) $711 per head of population
chronology
1978 Achieved full independence within the
Commonwealth with Toaripi Lauti as prime
minister.
1986 Islanders rejected proposal for
republican status.

Uganda
Republic of

area 236,860 sq km/91,428 sq mi
capital Kampala
towns Jingar, M'Bale, Entebbe

physical plateau with mountains in W; forest
and grassland; arid in N
head of state and government Yoweri
Museveni from 1986
political system emergent democracy
exports coffee, cotton, tea, copper
currency Uganda new shilling (344.89 = £1
Mar 1989)
population (1985 est) 15,480,000 (the largest
ethnic group is the Baganda, from whom the
name of the country comes; others include
the Langi and Acholi, and there are a few
surviving Pygmies); annual growth rate 3.3%
life expectancy men 47, women 51
language English (official); Swahili is a lingua
franca
religion Christian 50%, animist 45%, Muslim
5%
literacy 70% male/45% female (1985 est)

GNP $6.2 bn (1984); $40 per head of
population
chronology
1962 Achieved independence within the
Commonwealth with Milton Obote as prime
minister.
1963 Proclaimed a federal republic with King
Mutesa II as president.
1966 King Mutesa ousted in a coup led by
Obote, who ended the federal status and
became executive president.
1969 All opposition parties banned after an
assassination attempt on Obote.
1971 Obote overthrown in an army coup
led by Maj-Gen Idi Amin, who established
a ruthlessly dictatorial regime, expelling
nearly 49,000 Ugandan Asians. Up to 300,000
opponents of the regime are said to have
been killed.
1978 After heavy fighting, Amin was
forced to leave the country. A provisional
government was set up with Yusuf Lule as
president. Lule was replaced by Godfrey
Binaisa.
1978–79 Fighting with Tanzanian troops.
1980 Binaisa overthrown by the army.
Elections held and Milton Obote returned to
power.
1985 After years of opposition, mainly by
the National Resistance Army (NRA), and
uncontrolled indiscipline in the regular army,
Obote was ousted by Brig Basilio Okello,
who entered a power-sharing agreement with
the NRA leader, Yoweri Museveni.
1986 Agreement ended and Museveni
became president, heading a broad-based
coalition government.

Union of Soviet Socialist Republics
*(USSR; Soyuz Sovyetskikh Sotsialisticheskikh
Respublik)*

area 22,274,700 sq km/8,598,034 sq mi
capital Moscow
towns Kiev, Tashkent, Kharkov, Gorky,
Novosibirsk, Minsk, Sverdlovsk, Kuibyshev,
Chelyabinsk, Dnepropetrovsk, Tbilisi;
ports Leningrad, Odessa, Baku, Archangel,
Murmansk, Vladivostok, Vostochny, Rostov
physical the Ural Mountains separate the

European from the Asian plain; the Caucasus Mountains are in the S between the Black Sea and the Caspian Sea, and there are mountain ranges in the S and E of the Asiatic part; the USSR covers one-sixth of the earth's land mass and contains forest, tundra, marsh, steppe, and desert

head of state Mikhail Gorbachev from 1988

head of government Nikolai Ryzhkov from 1985 (premier); Mikhail Gorbachev from 1985 (head of Communist Party)

political system communism

exports cotton, timber, iron and steel, non-ferrous metals, electrical equipment, machinery, arms, oil and natural gas and their products, asbestos, gold, manganese. The USSR has 58% of world coal reserves, 59% of oil, 41% iron, 88% manganese, 54% potassium salts, 30% phosphates (55% of trade is with communist countries)

currency rouble (1.07 = £1 Mar 1989, but this is not a commercial rate)

population (1987) 281,700,000 (two-thirds living in towns, and of 125 different nationalities; 52% ethnic Russians, 17% Ukrainians); annual growth rate 1%

life expectancy men 67, women 75

language Slavic (Russian, Ukrainian, Byelorussian, Polish), Altaic (Turkish, Mongolian, and others), other Indo-European, Uralian, Caucasian

religion 'freedom of conscience' is guaranteed under the constitution, but religious belief is discouraged and considered incompatible with party membership (17,500,000 members); the largest Christian denomination is the Orthodox Church (30 million), but the largest religious sect is Sunni Muslim (40 million), making the USSR the fifth largest Muslim nation; Jews 2,500,000

literacy 99% (1985)

GNP $734 bn (1984); $2,600 per head of population

chronology

1917 Revolution: provisional democratic government established in Mar by Mensheviks. Communist takeover in Nov by Bolsheviks under Lenin.

1922 Soviet Union established.

1924 Death of Lenin.

1928 Stalin emerged as absolute ruler after ousting Trotsky.

1930s Purges of Stalin's opponents.

1939 Nonaggression pact signed with Germany.

1941–45 'Great Patriotic War'.

1949 Creation of Comecon.

1953 Death of Stalin. Removal of Beria. 'Collective leadership' in power.

1955 Creation of Warsaw Pact.

1956 Khrushchev's February 'secret speech'. Hungarian uprising.

1957–58 Ousting of 'anti-party' group and Bulganin.

1960 Sino-Soviet rift.
1962 Cuban missile crisis.
1964 Khrushchev ousted by new 'collective leadership'.
1968 Invasion of Czechoslovakia.
1969 Sino-Soviet border war.
1972 Salt I arms-limitation agreement with USA.
1977 Brezhnev elected president.
1979 Salt II. Soviet invasion of Afghanistan.
1980 Kosygin replaced as prime minister by Tikhonov.
1980–81 Polish crisis.
1982 Deaths of Suslov and Brezhnev. Yuri Andropov new Communist Party leader.
1984 Chernenko succeeded Andropov.
1985 Gorbachev succeeded Chernenko and introduced wide-ranging reforms. Gromyko appointed president.
1986 Gorbachev's power consolidated at 27th Party Congress. Chernobyl nuclear disaster.
1987 Border guards embarrassed by West German teenager Mathias Rust landing a private plane in Red Square, Moscow. USSR and USA agreed to scrap intermediate-range nuclear missiles. Boris Yeltsin, Moscow party chief, dismissed for criticizing the slow pace of reform.
1988 Serious nationalist challenges in Kazakhstan, Baltic republics, Armenia, and Azerbaijan. Earthquake killed 100,000 in Armenia.
1989 Troop withdrawal from Afghanistan completed. General election held, with candidate choice for new congress of People's Deputies. 20 killed in nationalist riots in Georgia. A third of the CPSU Central Committee removed in purge of the 'old guard'.

United Arab Emirates

(UAE) federation of the emirates of Abu Dhabi, Ajman, Dubai, Fujairah, Sharjah, Umm al Qaiwain, Ras al Khaimah

total area 83,657 sq km/32,292 sq mi
capital Abu Dhabi
towns chief port Dubai
physical mainly desert; mountains in E
head of state and of government Zayed Bin

Sultan al-Nahayan from 1971
political system absolutism
exports oil and natural gas
currency UAE dirham (6.34 = £1 Mar 1989)
population (1986 est) 1,770,000 (10% are nomadic); annual growth rate 6.1%
life expectancy men 65, women 70
language Arabic (official); Farsi, Hindi and Urdu are spoken by immigrant oilfield workers from Iran, India, and Pakistan
religion Muslim 90%, Christian, Hindu
literacy 56% (1985)
GNP $25 bn (1983); $23,000 per head of population
chronology
1952 Trucial Council established.
1971 Federation of Arab Emirates came into being but was later dissolved. Six of the Trucial States formed the United Arab Emirates, with the ruler of Abu Dhabi, Sheik Zayed, as president.
1972 The seventh state joined.
1976 Sheik Zayed threatened to relinquish presidency unless progress towards centralization became more rapid.
1985 Diplomatic and economic links with the USSR and with China established.
1987 Diplomatic relations with Egypt restored.

United Kingdom

of Great Britain and Northern Ireland (UK)

area 229,880 sq mi/88,734 sq km

capital London
towns Birmingham, Glasgow, Leeds,
Sheffield, Liverpool, Manchester,
Edinburgh, Bradford, Bristol, Belfast,
Newcastle-upon-Tyne, Cardiff

physical land mass became separated
from the European continent *c.* 6000 BC;
rolling landscape, becoming increasingly
mountainous towards the N, with the
Grampian Mountains in Scotland and
Snowdon in Wales. Rivers include Thames
and Severn
head of state Elizabeth II from 1952
head of government Margaret Thatcher from
1979
political system liberal democracy
exports agricultural (cereals, rape, sugar
beet, potatoes); meat and meat products,
poultry, dairy products; electronic and
telecommunications equipment; engineering
equipment and scientific instruments;
North Sea oil and gas, petrochemicals,
pharmaceuticals, fertilizers; film and
television programmes; tourism
currency pound sterling
population (1985) 56,620,000; annual growth
rate 0.1%
religion mainly Christian (Church of England
and other Protestant sects with Roman
Catholic minority); Jewish, Muslim, Hindu
minorities

language English, Welsh, Gaelic
literacy 99% (1984)
GNP $505 bn (1983); $7,216 per head of
population
territories Anguilla; Bermuda; British
Antarctic Territory; British Indian Ocean
Territory; British Virgin Islands; Cayman
Islands; Falkland Islands (disputed by
Argentina); Gibraltar; Hong Kong (until
1997); Montserrat; Pitcairn Islands; St
Helena and Dependencies (Ascension,
Tristan da Cunha); Turks and Caicos Islands
chronology
1707 Act of Union between England and
Scotland under Queen Anne.
1721 Walpole unofficially the first prime
minister under George I.
1783 Loss of the N American colonies.
1801 Act of Ireland united Britain and
Ireland.
1832 Great Reform Bill became law, shifting
political power from upper to middle class.
1848 Chartist working-class movement
formed.
1867 Second Reform Bill, extending the
franchise, introduced by Disraeli and passed.
1906 Liberal victory; programme of social
reform.
1911 Powers of House of Lords curbed.
1920 Home Rule Act incorporated the NE of
Ireland (Ulster) into the United Kingdom of
Great Britain and Northern Ireland.
1921 Ireland, except for Ulster, became a
dominion (Irish Free State, later Eire, 1937).
1924 First Labour government led by Ramsay
Macdonald.
1926 General Strike.
1931 National government; unemployment
reached 3 million.
1940 Churchill became head of coalition
government.
1945 Labour government under Attlee; birth
of welfare state.
1951 Conservatives defeated Labour.
1956 Suez crisis.
1964 Labour victory under Wilson.
1970 Conservatives under Heath defeated
Labour.
1972 Parliament prorogued in Northern

Ireland; direct rule from Westminster began.

1973 Britain joined EEC.

1974 Three-day week, coal strike; Wilson replaced Heath.

1979 Victory for Conservatives under Thatcher.

1981 Formation of Social Democratic Party (SDP). Riots in inner cities.

1982 Unemployment over 3 million. Falklands War.

1984–85 Coal strike, the longest in British history.

1986 Abolition of metropolitan counties.

1987 Thatcher re-elected for third term.

1988 Liberals and most of SDP merged into Democrats, leaving a splinter group. Inflation rose sharply.

United States of America
(USA)

area 9,169,142 sq km/3,539,289 sq mi

capital Washington DC

towns New York, Los Angeles, Chicago,

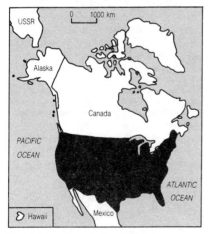

Philadelphia, Detroit, San Francisco, Washington, Dallas, San Diego, San Antonio, Houston, Boston, Baltimore, Phoenix, Indianopolis, Memphis, all metropolitan areas over 2 million population

physical mountain ranges parallel with E and W coasts, and the Rocky Mountains; separate rivers debouching in the Pacific from those flowing into the Gulf of Mexico; Great Lakes in N; rivers include Hudson, Mississippi, Missouri, Colorado, Columbia

territories commonwealths of Puerto Rico, and Northern Marianas; federated states of Micronesia; Guam, US Virgin Islands, American Samoa, Wake Island, Midway Islands, Marshall Islands, Belau, and Johnston and Sand Islands

head of state and of government George Bush from 1989

political system liberal democracy

currency US dollar (1.72 = £1 Mar 1989)

population (1985) 239,280,000 (ethnic minorities include 26,500,000 black, about 20,000,000 Hispanic, and 1,000,000 American Indians, of whom 50% concentrated in Arizona, California, New Mexico, North Carolina, Oklahoma); annual growth rate 0.9%

life expectancy men 71, women 78

language English; largest minority language Spanish

religion 73 million Protestant, 50 million Roman Catholic, 6 million Jewish, 4 million Eastern Orthodox

literacy 99% (1985)

GNP $3,855 bn (1983); $13,451 per head of population

chronology

1776 Declaration of Independence.

1787 US constitution drawn up.

1789 Washington elected as first president.

1803 Louisiana Purchase.

1812–14 War of 1812 with England, arising from commercial disputes caused by Britain's struggle with Napoleon.

1819 Florida purchased from Spain.

1836 The battle of the Alamo, Texas, won by Mexico.

1841 First wagon train left Missouri with emigrants for California.

1846–48 Mexican War resulted in cession to USA of Arizona, California, Colorado (part), Nevada, New Mexico, Texas, Utah.

1846 Mormons, under Brigham Young, founded Salt Lake City in Utah.

1848 California gold rush.
1860 Lincoln elected president.
1861–65 Civil War between North and South.
1865 Slavery abolished.
1867 Alaska bought from Russia.
1890 Battle of Wounded Knee, the last major battle between American Indians and US troops.
1898 War with Spain ended with the Spanish cession of Philippines, Puerto Rico, and Guam; it was agreed that Cuba be independent.
1898 Hawaii annexed.
1917–18 USA entered World War I.
1929 Wall Street stock-market crash.
1933 F D Roosevelt's New Deal to alleviate the Depression put into force.
1941–45 The Japanese attack on Pearl Harbor precipitated US entry into World War II.
1950–53 US involvement in Korean war. McCarthy anti-communist investigations.
1952 Gen Eisenhower elected president.
1960 J F Kennedy elected president.
1961 Bay of Pigs abortive CIA-backed invasion of Cuba.
1963 Assassination of Kennedy. Johnson assumed the presidency.
1964–68 'Great Society' civil-rights and welfare measures.
1964–73 US involvement in Vietnam War.
1968 Nixon elected president.
1973–74 Watergate scandal.
1974 Nixon resigned as president; replaced by Gerald Ford.
1975 Final US withdrawal from Vietnam.
1976 Carter elected president.
1979 US-Chinese diplomatic relations normalized.
1979–80 Iranian hostage crisis.
1980 Reagan elected president. Republicans gained Senate majority.
1983 US invasion of Grenada.
1986 Republicans lost Senate majority. Scandal over secret US arms sales to Iran and subsidies to anti-government Contra guerrillas in Nicaragua.
1987 INF treaty with USSR. Wall Street stock-market crash.
1988 Vice president Bush elected president.

Democrats retained control over both houses of Congress. Us reported world's largest debtor nation, owing $532 billion.
1989 Bush's nominee as defence secretary, John Tower, rejected by Senate.

Uruguay
Oriental Republic of (República Oriental del Uruguay)

area 196,945 sq km/72,180 sq mi
capital Montevideo

physical grassy plains (pampas)
head of state and of government Julio María Sanguinetti Cairolo from 1985
political system emergent democracy
exports meat and meat products, leather, wool, textiles
currency nuevo peso (863.00 = £1 Mar 1989)
population (1985 est) 3,010,000 (mainly of Spanish and Italian descent, also mestizo, mulatto, and black); annual growth rate 0.7%
life expectancy men 67, women 74
language Spanish
religion Roman Catholic 60%
literacy 95% male/95% female (1980 est)
GNP $7.3 bn (1983); $1,665 per head of population
chronology
1956 The Blanco party in power, with Jorge

Pacheco Areco as president.
1972 The Colorado Party returned, with Juan
Maria Bordaberry Arocena as president.
1976 Bordaberry deposed by the army and Dr
Méndez Manfredini became president.
1984 Violent anti-government protests after
ten years of repressive rule.
1985 Agreement reached between the
army and political leaders for a return to
constitutional government. Colorado Party
narrowly won the general election and Dr
Julio Maria Sanguinetti became president.
1986 A government of national accord
established under President Sanguinetti's
leadership.

Vanuatu
Republic of

area 14,750 sq km/5,700 sq mi
capital Vila on Efate

physical comprises about 70 islands, including
Espiritu Santo, Malekala, and Efate; densely
forested
head of state Fred Timakata from 1989
head of government Walter Lini from 1980
political system liberal democracy
exports copra, fish, coffee, tourism is
important
currency vatu (179.00 = £1 Mar 1989)
population (1985) 140,000 (90% Melanesian);
annual growth rate 23.6%
language Bislama (pidgin), English, French,
all official
religion Anglican 14%, Presbyterian 40%,

Roman Catholic 16%, animist 15%
chronology
1975 Representative assembly established.
1978 Government of national unity formed,
with Father Gerard Leymang as chief
minister.
1980 Revolt on the island of Espiritu Santo
delayed independence but it was achieved,
within the Commonwealth, with George
Sokomanu as president and Father Walter
Lini as prime minister.
1988 An attempt by Sokomanu to unseat Lini
led to Sokomanou's arrest for treason.
1989 Sokomanu succeeded as president by
Fred Timakata.

Vatican City State
(Stato della Città del Vaticano)

area 0.4 sq km/109 acres
physical forms an enclave in the heart of
Rome, Italy

head of state and government John Paul II
from 1978
government absolute Catholic
currency issues its own coinage, which
circulates together with that of Italy
population (1985) 1,000
language Italian
religion Roman Catholic
chronology
1947 New Italian constitution confirmed the
sovereignty of the Vatican City State.

1978 John Paul II became the first non-Italian pope for more than 400 years.
1985 New concordat signed under which Roman Catholicism ceas ed to be the state religion.

Venezuela
Republic of (República de Venezuela)

area 912,068 sq km/352,150 sq mi
capital Caracas
towns Barquisimeto, Valencia; port Maracaibo

physical valleys and delta of river Orinoco flanked by mountains
head of state and of government Carlos Andrés Pérez from 1988
political system liberal democracy
exports coffee, cocoa, timber, oil, aluminium, iron ore, petrochemicals
currency bolívar (61.29 = £1 Mar 1989)
population (1985) 17,317,000 (70% mestizos, 32,000 American Indians); annual growth rate 2.8%
life expectancy men 66, women 72
religion Roman Catholic
language Spanish (official), Indian languages 2%
literacy 84% male/78% female (1980 est)
GNP $70.8 bn (1983); $4,716 per head of population
chronology
1961 New constitution adopted, with Rómulo

Betancourt as president.
1964 Dr Raúl Leoni became president.
1969 Dr Rafael Caldera became president.
1974 Carlos Andrés Pérez Rodríguez became president.
1979 Dr Luis Herrera became president.
1984 Dr Jaime Lusinchi became president. He tried to solve the nation's economic problems through a social pact between the government, trade unions, and business, and by rescheduling the national debt.
1987 Widespread social unrest triggered by inflation; student demonstrators shot by police.
1988 Andrés Pérez elected president. Payment of foreign debts suspended.
1989 Economic austerity programme enforced by $4.3 billion loan from International Monetary Fund triggered riots in which 300 people were killed. Martial law declared.

Vietnam
Socialist Republic of (Công Hòa Xã Hôi Chu Nghĩa Viêt Nam)

area 336,000 sq km/129,000 sq mi
capital Hanoi
towns ports Ho Chi Minh City (formerly

Saigon), Da Nang, and Haiphong
physical Red River and Mekong deltas, where

cultivation and population are concentrated; some tropical rainforest; the rest is barren and mountainous
head of state Vo Chi Cong from 1987
head of government Do Muoi from 1988
political system communism
exports rice, rubber, coal, iron, apatite
currency dong (7767.00 = £1 Mar 1989)
population (1985 est) 59,710,000 (some 750,000 refugees, the majority ethnic Chinese, left the country 1975–79, some settling in SW China, others fleeing by sea – the 'boat people' – to Hong Kong and elsewhere); annual growth rate 2%
life expectancy men 57, women 61
language Vietnamese, of uncertain origin but tonal like Chinese and Thai
religion traditionally Buddhist and Taoist
literacy 78% (1978)
GNP $9.8 bn (1983); $189 per head of population
chronology
1945 Japanese removed from Vietnam.
1946 Commencement of Vietminh war against French.
1954 France defeated at Dien Bien Phu. Vietnam divided along 17th parallel.
1964 USA entered Vietnam War.
1973 Paris ceasefire agreement.
1975 Saigon captured by North.
1976 Socialist Republic of Vietnam proclaimed.
1978 Admission into Comecon. Invasion of Kampuchea.
1979 Sino-Vietnamese border war.
1986 Retirement of old-guard leaders.
1987–88 Over 10,000 political prisoners released.
1988–89 Troop withdrawals from Kampuchea continued.

Yemen, North

Yemen Arab Republic (al Jamhuriya al Arabiya al Yamaniya)

area 195,000 sq km/75,000 sq mi
capital San'a
towns Ta'iz, and chief port Hodeida
physical hot moist coastal plain, rising to plateau

head of state and of government Ali Abdullah Saleh from 1978
political system authoritarian nationalism
exports cotton, coffee, grapes
currency riyal (16.82 = £1 Mar 1989)
population (1985) 6,850,000; annual growth rate 2.7%
life expectancy men 47, women 50
language Arabic
religion Sunni Muslim 50%, Shi'ite Muslim 50%
literacy 27% male/3% female (1985 est)
GNP $3.9 bn (1983); $475 per head of population
chronology
1962 North Yemen declared the Arab Republic of Yemen (YAR), with Abdullah al-Sallal as president. Civil war broke out between royalists and republicans.
1967 Civil war ended with the republicans victorious. Sallal deposed and replaced by a Republican Council.
1971–72 War betwen South Yemen and YAR. Both sides finally agreed to a union but the agreement was not kept.
1974 Ibrahim al-Hamadi seized power and a Military Command Council was set up.
1977 Hamadi assassinated and replaced by Ahmed ibn Hussein al-Ghashmi.
1978 Constituent People's Assembly appointed and the Military Command Council dissolved. Ghashmi killed by an envoy from South Yemen and succeeded by

Ali Abdullah Saleh. War broke out again between the two Yemens.
1979 Ceasefire agreed with, again, a commitment to a future union.
1983 Saleh elected president for a further five-year term.
1984 Joint committee on foreign policy for the two Yemens met in Aden.
1988 President Saleh re-elected.

Yemen, South
People's Democratic Republic of Yemen
(Jumhurijah al-Yemen al Dimuqratiyah al Sha'abijah)

area 160,000 sq km/62,000 sq mi
capital Aden

physical desert and mountains; very hot and dry
head of state and government Haydar Abu Bakr Al-Attas from 1986
political system nationalistic socialism
exports cotton goods, coffee
currency Yemeni dinar (0.59 = £1 Mar 1989)
population (1985) 2,290,000; annual growth rate 2.8%
life expectancy men 47, women 50
language Arabic
religion Sunni Muslim 91%
literacy 39% (1980)
GNP $1 bn (1983); $310 per head of population
chronology
1967 People's Republic of Southern Yemen

founded.
1970 Country renamed the People's Democratic Republic of Yemen (PDRY), led by the Marxist National Front Party (NF).
1971–72 War with North Yemen.
1978 North Yemen president killed by a bomb carried by a PDRY envoy. Yemen Socialist Party (YSP) formed as a 'Marxist-Leninist vanguard party'. War between North and South Yemen.
1979 Ceasefire agreed and the two Yemens agreed to move towards eventual union.
1983 Joint Yemen council established.
1985 Ali Nasser Muhammad elected president but was deposed after his personal guards had killed three of his party opponents.
1986 Hayder Abu Bakr al-Attas became president and secretary general of the YPS Politburo.
1987 Discussions with North Yemen about possible merger.

Yugoslavia
Socialist Federal Republic of (Socijalistička Federativna Republika Jugoslavija)

area 255,874 sq km/98,740 sq mi
capital Belgrade
towns Zagreb, Skopje, Ljubljana; ports Split, Rijeka

physical mountainous; river Danube plains in N and E
head of state Raif Dizdarevic from 1988
head of government Ante Markovic from 1989
political system communism
exports machinery, electrical goods, chemicals
currency dinar (13,658.80 = £1 Mar 1989)
population (1985) 23,124,000 (Serbs 36%, Croats 20%, Muslims 9%, Slovenes 8%, Albanians 7%, Macedonians 6%); annual growth rate 0.8%
life expectancy men 68, women 74
language individual national languages have equality, but Serbo-Croat is the most widespread
religion Orthodox (Serbs), Roman Catholic (Croats), Muslim (50% in Bosnia)
literacy 97% male/86% female (1985 est)
GNP $46.3 bn (1984); $3,109 per head of population
chronology
1917–18 Creation of Kingdom of the Serbs, Croats, and Slovenes.
1929 Name of Yugoslavia adopted.
1941 Invasion by Germany.
1945 Communist federal republic formed under leadership of Tito.
1948 Split with USSR.
1953 Self-management principle enshrined in constitution.
1961 Formation of Nonaligned Movement under Yugolavia's leadership.
1974 New constitution adopted.
1980 Death of Tito. Collective leadership assumed power.
1987 Threat to use the army to curb unrest.
1988 Economic difficulties and regional tensions forced party reshuffles and the resignation of the government.
1989 A reformist Croatian, Ante Markovic, became prime minister. 29 die in ethnic riots in Kosovo province.

Zaïre
Republic of (République du Zaïre)

area 2,345,000 sq km/895,000 sq mi
capital Kinshasa
towns Kananga, Lubumbashi, Kisangani; ports Matadi, Boma

physical Zaïre river basin has tropical rainforest and savanna; mountains in E and W
head of state and of government Mobuto Sésé Séko Kuku Ngbendu wa Zabanga from 1965
political system authoritarian nationalism
exports palm oil, coffee, tea, rubber, timber; copper, cobalt (80% of world output), zinc, cadmium, industrial diamonds
currency zaïre (540.25 = £1 Mar 1989)
population (1985) 30,360,000; annual growth rate 2.9%
life expectancy men 48, women 52
language French (official), Swahili, Lingala
religion 70% Christian, 10% Muslim
literacy 79% male/45% female (1985 est)
GNP $5 bn (1983); $127 per head of population
chronology
1960 Achieved full independence as the Republic of the Congo. Civil war broke out between the central government and Katanga province.
1963 Katanga war ended.
1967 New constitution adopted.
1970 Col Mobutu elected president.
1972 Country became the Republic of Zaïre, with the Popular Movement of the Revolution (MPR) the only legal political party.

1974 Foreign-owned businesses and plantations seized by Mobutu and given in political patronage.
1977 Original owners of confiscated properties invited back.

Zambia
Republic of

area 752,620 sq km/290,586 sq mi
capital Lusaka
towns Kitwe, Ndola, Kabwe, Chipata, Livingstone

physical a forested plateau cut through by rivers
head of state and government Kenneth Kaunda from 1964
political system nationalistic socialism
exports copper, emeralds, tobacco
currency kwacha (17.40 = £1 Mar 1989)
population (1985 est) 6,670,000; annual growth rate 3.3%
life expectancy men 50, women 53
language English (official); the majority speak Bantu languages
religion mainly animist, 21% Roman Catholic, also Protestant, Hindu, and Muslim minorities
literacy 84% male/67% female (1985 est)
GNP $2.6 bn (1984); $570 per head of population

chronology
1964 Achieved full independence, within the Commonwealth, as the Republic of Zambia with Kenneth Kaunda as president.
1972 United Independence Party (UNIP) declared the only legal party.
1976 Support for the Patriotic Front in Rhodesia declared.
1980 Unsuccessful coup against President Kaunda.
1985 Kaunda elected chair of the Front Line States.
1987 Kaunda elected chair of the Organization of African Unity (OAU).
1988 Kaunda re-elected unopposed for sixth term.

Zimbabwe
Republic of

area 390,600 sq km/150,820 sq mi
capital Harare
towns Bulawayo, Gweru, Kwekwe, Mutare, Hwange

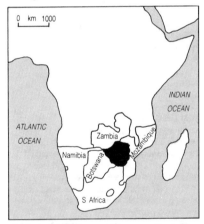

physical a high plateau with mountains in the E
head of state and government Robert Mugabe from 1987
political system nationalistic socialism
exports tobacco, citrus, tea, coffee; gold and silver

currency Zimbabwe dollar (3.43 = £1 Mar 1989)

population (1985) 8,300,000 (Shona 80%, Ndbele, of Zulu descent, 20%; before independence there were some 275,000 whites, in 1985 about 100,000); annual growth rate 3.5%

life expectancy men 54, women 58

language English (official); Shona, Ndbele, Nyanja

religion Christian

literacy 81% male/67% female (1985 est)

GDP $5 bn (1983); $640 per head of population

chronology

1961 Zimbabwe African People's Union (ZAPU) formed, with Joshua Nkomo as leader.

1962 ZAPU declared illegal.

1963 Zimbabawe African National Union (ZANU) formed, with Robert Mugabe as secretary general.

1964 Ian Smith became prime minister. Nkomo and Mugabe imprisoned.

1965 ZANU banned. Smith declared unilateral independence.

1966–68 Abortive talks between Smith and UK prime minister Harold Wilson.

1974 Nkomo and Mugabe released.

1975 Geneva conference agreed a date for constitutional independence.

1979 Smith produced a new constitution and established a government with Bishop Abel Muzorewa as prime minister. New government denounced by Nkomo and Mugabe. Conference in London agreed independence arrangements (Lancaster House Agreement).

1980 Full independence achieved, with Robert Mugabe as prime minister.

1981 Rift between Mugabe and Nkomo.

1982 Nkomo dismissed from the cabinet and left the country temporarily.

1984 ZANU–People's Front (PF) Party Congress agreed to create a one-party state at some time in the future.

1985 Relations between Mugabe and Nkomo improved.

1986 Joint ZANU-PF rally held amid plans for merger.

1987 White-roll seats in the assembly were abolished. President Banana retired and Mugabe combined the posts of head of state and prime minister with the title executive president.

1988 Nkomo returned to the cabinet.

Index

607